Deception

Deception

Russiagate and the New Cold War

Richard Sakwa

LEXINGTON BOOKS
Lanham • Boulder • New York • London

Published by Lexington Books
An imprint of The Rowman & Littlefield Publishing Group, Inc.
4501 Forbes Boulevard, Suite 200, Lanham, Maryland 20706
www.rowman.com

86-90 Paul Street, London EC2A 4NE

Copyright © 2022 by The Rowman & Littlefield Publishing Group, Inc.

All rights reserved. No part of this book may be reproduced in any form or by any electronic or mechanical means, including information storage and retrieval systems, without written permission from the publisher, except by a reviewer who may quote passages in a review.

British Library Cataloguing in Publication Information Available

Library of Congress Cataloging-in-Publication Data

Names: Sakwa, Richard, author.
Title: Deception : Russiagate and the new cold war / Richard Sakwa.
Description: Lanham, Maryland : Lexington Books, 2021. | Includes bibliographical references and index.
Identifiers: LCCN 2021043255 (print) | LCCN 2021043256 (ebook) |
  ISBN 9781793644954 (cloth) | ISBN 9781793644978 (paperback) |
  ISBN 9781793644961 (ebook)
Subjects: LCSH: Presidents—United States—Election—2016. | Elections—Corrupt practices—United States. | Propaganda, Russian—United States. | Hacking—Russia (Federation) | United States—Foreign relations—Russia (Federation) | Russia (Federation)—Foreign relations—United States.
Classification: LCC E911 .S25 2021 (print) | LCC E911 (ebook) |
  DDC 324.973/0932—dc23
LC record available at https://lccn.loc.gov/2021043255
LC ebook record available at https://lccn.loc.gov/2021043256

Contents

Introduction	1
1 The Russians Are Coming	5
2 Trump Ascends	23
3 Trump and Russia	47
4 Russiagate and the New Cold War	67
5 Hacking the Election	89
6 Social Media Meddling	111
7 Conspiracy, Collusion and Crossfire Hurricane	129
8 The Steele Dossier	149
9 Spinning Russiagate	173
10 Flynn and the Russian Concussion	199
11 Suspicious Activity	225
12 Mueller Investigates	251
13 Russiagate Questioned	271
14 Fruit of a Poisoned Tree	289
15 Worse than Watergate	307
16 Deception and the New Cold War	329
Bibliography	347
Index	361
About the Author	375

Introduction

Donald J. Trump's extraordinary rise to the presidency of the United States evoked astonishment and wonder, but also concern. Was Trump some sort of Russian agent? Had Moscow propelled Trump into the White House, and in the process sowed discord in society while undermining American democracy? Russia was presented as some sort of all-seeing and all-powerful malevolent force. According to this version, Moscow with extraordinary foresight had long cultivated Trump, and had enough *kompromat* (compromising material) to render him a faithful tool of Russian interests. The two colluded to get Trump elected on 8 November 2016, and that explains why he refused to accept the evidence presented by his intelligence agencies that Russia had 'meddled' in the election, and why he was so complimentary about the Russian president Vladimir Putin. To critics, this version lacks factual basis, and while Russia may have been involved in 2016, its 'active measures' (*aktivnye meropriyatiya*) were at the most marginal and certainly did not determine the outcome. As some of the more extreme versions of the Russiagate allegations unravelled, opinions converged on the view that the response to the claims of Russian interference may have been more damaging than the meddling itself.

Four powerful narratives collide with explosive effect. First, Trump's rise to the presidency was so extraordinary that people looked for some sort of external force that helped him win the most powerful office in the Western hemisphere. Second, U.S. domestic politics, social discontents, insurgent social movements, discordant political ideologies, and institutional and policy paralysis were clearly aligned in such a way as to allow this maverick figure to win an election that even he expected to lose. Third, by 2016, the crisis of the post-cold war international order had precipitated wars in Georgia and Ukraine and the remilitarisation of European security signalled the onset of a new cold war. Finally, the contradictions and achievements of Russia's domestic transformation gave rise to the Putin phenomenon, a mixture of tough-minded re-assertion of perceived Russian national interests accompanied by a thorough disenchantment with the West. Thus, if anyone was going to be blamed for Trump's ascent, then it would be Russia.

This has been a difficult book to write. First, there is the fundamental methodological problem that we still do not know what really happened. Much of the relevant material remains classified, although in the late Trump years much important material came into the public domain. Amid the swirling tide of conspiracy theories and endless allegations and counter-claims, it is hard to maintain balance and judgement. This work has drawn on major official documentation, Congressional records, a rich seam of first-hand memoirs and reams of secondary analysis, as well as interviews with some Russian and American policy analysts and participants. Second, the logic and dynamic of Russian actions remain the source of considerable controversy. Some Russian actions were misguided, some outright malevolent, and some largely innocent, but in this story always interpreted in the worst possible light by those responsible for America's security. To err on the side of caution is understandable, even commendable, but the projection of domestic political polarisation and conflicts into international affairs, especially when dealing with a nuclear-armed power, is dangerous to the point of foolhardiness. One of Trump's few stable policy preferences was improved relations with Russia, which itself induced suspicion, and Moscow was ready to reciprocate. The Russiagate allegations not only put an end to hopes of rapprochement but also damaged relations to make them worse than for most of the original cold war. Third, and this is the essence of the Russiagate tragedy, many people acting out of the best of motives – U.S. security and the defence of American democracy – helped provoke the further polarisation of American society, the deepening of distrust in the electoral process, the corruption of the media, the politicisation of the security services and, above all, the sowing of mistrust between two great powers that will poison relations for years to come.

The problem, then, is how to cover all four issues, without the book becoming monstrous in size and confused in presentation. In what follows coverage of the four themes will be unequal, with the focus on the first: the core Russiagate charge that Russia 'meddled' in the U.S. presidential election in a variety of ways to shape the outcome, accompanied by the fundamental allegation that Trump in some way 'colluded' with Russia to win the White House. The overall methodology is an interpretive analysis accompanied by process-tracing and detailed analysis. In trying to make sense of it all, the question then arises: Sense from whose perspective? In the polarised politics of today, and in conditions of the intense passions provoked by the new cold war, truth itself has become a victim, just as it did in the original cold war from the late 1940s to 1989. In the cold war, foundational perspectives themselves became the basis of the confrontation, with varieties of socialism (mostly in conflict with each other) ranged against defenders of liberal capitalist modernity, with an important strand of democratic socialism in between, accompanied by various peace movements and the Non-Aligned Movement. Such foundational narratives are now mostly a thing of the past, but instead of heralding a new era of peace, reconciliation and enlightenment (as so many anticipated at the end of the cold war in 1989), the institutional and ideational structures of the cold war were perpetuated in the West, while in the East, the democratic norms of tolerance, political pluralism, transparency and accountability remain far from consolidated.

It soon became clear that official narratives and accounts were no more truthful, and often quite considerably less so, than a range of alternative sources. The traditional print media and their associated websites lined up on one side or another as the Russiagate story unfolded, and very few remained objective as the traditional values of impartiality and truth-seeking became victim to partisanship. Trump freely denounced anything he did not like as 'fake news' and his relationship with the fact-based world was notoriously tenuous, but his opponents, some of whom called themselves 'the resistance', often created a no less misleading 'alternative reality' that undermined their own credibility. Commentary on Russia became a free-fire zone, in which respectable journalists and commentators presented distortions and misrepresentations as fact. Standard methods of causality, intentionality and rationality appear to have gone out of the window. In coverage of Russiagate, old-fashioned mainstream standards of 'bourgeois objectivity' appear to have dissolved. There is little of use in the voluminous output of the various think tanks on both sides of the Atlantic, and some is as propagandistic as it was during the cold war. This explains why alternative sources of information have become so important. The web-based information sphere is certainly full of cranky views and conspiracy theories, but some sites offered consistently fine and critical analysis, and despite the intense polarisation some journalists have emerged with credit.

Russiagate is a combination of many things. Ultimately, it throws a profound light on the major political dilemmas of our times, ranging from the rise of a new type of societal and state-centred populism, the breakdown of the post-cold war international order, the erosion of traditional patterns of civility and due process, the consolidation of the power of a cross-national security apparatus that became the driver of a whole set of political actions and the legitimate scope for resistance to a properly elected president who threatened the foundations of the system that allowed him to be elected. Russia was used as the stick by Trump's opponents with which to beat him, but thereby only exacerbated the domestic and international crises which gave rise to him in the first place. With so many plots, sub-plots and red herrings, it is hard to make sense of it all, but if at the end the reader understands at least the main issues and facts of the case, then this book will have succeeded in its purpose.

Canterbury, June 2021

Chapter 1

The Russians Are Coming

It was not supposed to be like this. The world was surprised in 2016 when Donald J. Trump became the Republican Party candidate for the American presidency, and amazed when he went on to win the presidential election on 8 November. The Democratic Party nominee, Hillary Rodham Clinton, was an experienced politician with a long record of public service, whereas Trump had never held public office. Polls throughout the campaign had shown Clinton with a strong lead, and although the gap narrowed in the final days, her victory appeared assured. How, then, did she manage to lose a race that was hers to win? The answer had been lurking in the background throughout the campaign, but now emerged with full force: Russian interference. This explained the inexplicable. A malevolent entity with extraordinary foresight had cultivated Trump and gathered compromising material to turn him into a faithful servant of Russian interests. As a result, so the story goes, the Russian president Vladimir Putin colluded with Trump to get the latter elected as the 'Manchurian candidate', a man whose identity had been reshaped to serve his masters in the Kremlin.[1] It appeared to fulfil Philip Roth's *Plot against America*, in which an outsider with weak democratic credentials takes the presidency with the help of a foreign power.[2] For his critics, this explains why Trump refused to accept the evidence presented by intelligence agencies that Russia had interfered in the election, and why he was so complimentary about Vladimir Putin. However, for Trump and his supporters, the Russia accusations were not only absurd but also tainted his victory and deprived him of room for manoeuvre in relations with Russia. The idea that he was little more than a Russian stooge who collaborated with Moscow for political and economic benefit undermined the legitimacy of his victory and paralysed his ability to govern. By any standards, this is an extraordinary story, and its various elements come together as 'Russiagate'.

RUSSIAN MISDEEDS

Russiagate is one of the most mystifying yet consequential events of our time. It stymied Trump's declared foreign policy ambitions while damaging the quality of American democracy. Two issues collided with explosive effect. The first was the crisis in American domestic institutions and political processes. American domestic conflicts, social discontents, working-class job insecurity, stagnant middle-class incomes, insurgent social movements, polarised political ideologies and institutional paralysis combined with business, defence and intelligence groups to allow a maverick figure to win an election that even he expected to lose. The country was clearly looking for change, but instead of offering a fresh candidate Clinton was the epitome of establishment thinking, who effectively stood as the continuity candidate of the Barack Obama two-term presidency (2009–2017). These domestic tensions intersected with the crisis of the post-cold war international order. By 2016, the conflict in Ukraine was in its third year, accompanied by the increased militarisation of European security and the deprecation of Russia. This signalled the onset of a new cold war, in which the ideological confrontation and great power contestation of the original cold war from the late 1940s to 1989 were resurrected. The roots of the second conflict lie in the way that issues remained unresolved at the end of the first. In the twenty-five years, between the end of the original cold war in 1989 and the onset of the second in 2014, none of the fundamental problems of European security had been resolved. The expansion of North Atlantic Treaty Organisation (NATO) and Russia's increasing resistance to the enlargement of the Atlantic power system gave way to renewed cold war.[3] Russia became a challenger state apparently seeking revenge by supporting Trump, who had signalled that he would improve relations with Moscow.

The basic allegation is that in one way or another, the Russian state or affiliated agencies colluded with Trump's campaign team to enhance his prospects while reducing those of Clinton. Collusion is defined as 'secret or illegal cooperation, especially between countries or organisations', which suggests that such activity may be either good or bad, although the illegal character of the activity means that there is a presumption of something nefarious going on. In our case, this is certainly the relevant interpretation. The collusion between Trump and the Russian authorities was allegedly prompted by a long-term strategy to cultivate him as a Russian 'asset', including by supporting his schemes, some of which faced perilous finances (it was not for nothing that Trump was known as 'the king of debt'), as well as holding compromising material (*kompromat*) on him. The collusion is alleged to have taken the form of various meetings between campaign staffers and the Russian authorities, including with the veteran Russian ambassador to the

United States, Sergei Kislyak. The various contacts between Trump associates and the Russian regime are alleged to have been the result of some sort of malfeasance or collusion, turning Trump into the 'Siberian candidate', a mutation of the earlier cold war Manchurian variant.

To achieve their goal, Russian military intelligence (the GRU) 'hacked' into the server of the Democratic National Committee (DNC) and the Democratic Campaign Congressional Committee (DCCC) and released embarrassing materials to WikiLeaks, the web-based investigative site founded by Julian Assange in 2006. The publication of 44,053 emails and 17,761 attachments from senior DNC officials provoked speculation that their release was coordinated with the Trump team. The messages revealed that the DNC was not impartial but sought to facilitate the nomination of Clinton and acted to the detriment of the independent left-leaning senator from Vermont, Bernie Sanders. The aim was to mine political intelligence, but whether it was intended specifically to help Trump win the election is more questionable. As we shall see, there is a question whether the DNC was *hacked*, with WikiLeaks insisting that the material was *leaked* from an identified source.

The hackers also gained access to the emails of Clinton's campaign director, John Podesta, following a successful spearphishing email sent on 19 March 2016. The Podesta emails exposed Clinton's close relationship with Wall Street bankers, high speaking fees for secret speeches and apparent hypocrisy in condemning privilege while enjoying its benefits. There was also information about the Clinton Foundation and unflattering personal material about Clinton. The genuine revelations spawned a sub-industry of conspiracy theories, including the fabricated claim that the emails contained coded messages that connected leading Democrats with some restaurants and an alleged human trafficking and child sex ring (the Pizzagate conspiracy theory). Overall, WikiLeaks published 64,000 Podesta emails, releasing them gradually (unlike the massive 22 July DNC release), which kept the email issue in the news all the way through to the November election. There was a ceaseless drip of embarrassing revelations, above all about the relentless pursuit of funds by Clinton and her team. The Podesta emails reinforced the image of Clinton as unprincipled and greedy.

At the same time, Russia is alleged to have waged a social media campaign to support Trump but above all to 'sow discord' in American politics, and thus to undermine American democracy. The Internet Research Agency (IRA) based in St Petersburg deployed sock-puppet (trolls) accounts (humans who pretend to be what they are not) and their automated versions (bots) to influence public debate by sharing sites and voicing divisive opinions. These allegedly shaped voter preferences and depressed turnout among some key constituencies, above all people of colour. In what turned out to be a tight election, Russian social media interference may have switched the vote in crucial swing states, notably Michigan, Pennsylvania and Wisconsin. A swing of just 77,744 votes would have tipped these states into Clinton's camp.[4] There is much debate over the effect of these Russian social media interventions, which were tiny in comparison with the total vast output. The IRA did pump out material that was derogatory about Clinton, but much of this output had nothing to do with the election (it was clickbait designed to increase traffic), and a large proportion came after voting day. However, even small pressure could have tilted the scales in certain strategic locations, especially when amplified by mass media reporting of the issue.

During the campaign, John Bolton, who was to serve as Trump's third national security adviser between April 2018 and September 2019, called Russian electoral interference an 'act of war'.[5] The seriousness of the allegations provoked numerous investigations by U.S. security agencies and Congressional committees, complemented from May 2017 by a special counsel investigation headed by Robert S. Mueller III. Mueller was tasked to investigate 'any links and/or coordination between the Russian government and individuals associated with the campaign of President Donald Trump'. During his term as director of the FBI from 2001 to 2013, Mueller shifted the focus of the agency's work from combating U.S. crime to fighting global terror. A graduate of Princeton, Mueller was one of the last of the old-school Ivy League Republicans whose sense of public duty eschewed personal vanity and entitlement. The contrast could hardly be greater with Trump, who dismissed the investigation as a 'witch-hunt' and brusquely rejected the charge of collusion.

The Mueller Report was completed in March and a redacted version was published on 28 April 2019. The Introduction boldly asserted that 'The Russian government interfered in the 2016 election in sweeping and systematic fashion'.[6] Those who looked to Mueller to provide some startling new evidence that would torpedo the Trump presidency were disappointed. The report examined the two known operations by Russian agencies, the GRU hacking and the St Petersburg trolling operation, and analysed the activities of the Russiagate cast and its major incidents: Trump's foreign policy adviser Carter Page's relations with Russia, the 9 June 2016 Trump Tower meeting between some Russians and Donald Trump Jr, the Paul Manafort case, the alleged offences of George Papadopoulos (another of Trump's short-lasting foreign policy advisers), the meetings with Kislyak and other *arcana* associated with the saga. Mueller's equivocal formulation – that Russia interfered in a 'systematic' manner yet had not colluded with Trump, and the various incidents demonstrated not 'sweeping' but surprisingly insubstantial interference – opened a floodgate of commentary. The outcome came as no surprise for those who had long questioned the fundamental premise of the investigation, while for others Mueller was the God that failed to destroy the Trump presidency.

The material on the IRA summarised the February 2018 indictment of thirteen Russian nationals and Yevgeny Prigozhin ('Putin's cook') who bankrolled the operation. The report asserted that the IRA's aim was to 'sow social discord', but this was imputed rather than proved. The report concluded that 'these operations constituted "active measures"', a reference to Soviet disinformation activities. The report detailed Prigozhin's publicly known ties to Putin, but the precise relationship between the IRA and the Kremlin was not analysed. The report cited the $100,000 that the IRA spent on Facebook ads as evidence of its influence on American society yet failed to place this in context. It implied that this paltry sum could have a greater effect than the $1.2 billion spent by the Clinton campaign, the Democratic Party and associated Political Action Committees (PACs), twice as much as the $600 million spent by the Trump campaign. The original indictment named a company that did not exist at the time, but this was later dropped from Mueller's report.[7]

The report then detailed the specific GRU cyber-warfare units which hacked the Clinton campaign and the DNC and then released the emails through Russian-sponsored cut-outs, Guccifer 2.0 and DCLeaks, as well as WikiLeaks. These were 'designed and timed to interfere with the 2016 US presidential election and undermine the Clinton Campaign'. Large parts were redacted, but as with the July 2018 indictment, the report suggested detailed knowledge of the inner workings of the GRU, to the point that 'evidence was sufficient to support computer-intrusion (and other) charges against GRU officers'. The report claims that the GRU hacked into 30 DNC and 29 DCCC computers and downloaded data using the 'X-Tunnel' software. The GRU gained access to Clinton campaign co-chair Podesta's email account when he clicked on a spearphishing message on 19 March and gained access to the DCCC's account when a staffer clicked on a similar email on 6 April 2016. As for the main hack of the DNC servers, the FBI or Mueller never conducted forensic examinations of their own. Instead, they relied on CrowdStrike, a private contractor hired by the Democrats to examine the servers. The material was then published, according to the report, through DCLeaks and Guccifer 2.0, 'fictitious online personas' created by the GRU, and later through WikiLeaks. Mueller argues that Guccifer 2.0 was the source of the emails and that he was a persona managed by Russian operators.

Surprisingly, Mueller provided no proof of this, and neither did he give specific evidence of the transfer of the DNC emails from Guccifer 2.0 to WikiLeaks. Mueller admits that the 'first known contact' between Guccifer 2.0 and WikiLeaks was on 15 September 2016, months after the documents were published. Instead, the report speculates on the use of 'intermediaries' in summer 2016.[8] As we shall see, the degree to which WikiLeaks coordinated with the Kremlin in the publication of the emails is a matter of considerable controversy. Assange strongly rejects the charge that he worked for or conspired with Russian agencies and states unequivocally that the Russian government was not the source of the emails. This supports the view of those who argue that the DNC download took place via a local thumb drive (USB memory stick) and not remote exfiltration. Mueller devoted 199 pages to conspiracy (he rejected the term 'collusion' as having no legal weight), but the evidence to support conspiratorial behaviour was remarkably thin. The second part of the report was devoted to obstruction, detailing eleven instances in which Trump and his team impeded or subverted the investigation.

As the Mueller investigation ground on, the Trump administration tried to govern. It managed to push through a massive tax cut, intended to unleash hitherto suppressed entrepreneurial energies, but its immediate effect was to deepen inequality. Funds to build Trump's vaunted anti-immigrant wall with Mexico were not forthcoming, and in foreign policy, Trump was unable to fulfil his campaign pledge to improve relations with Russia. The promise itself became the object of suspicion and fuelled the Russiagate investigations. Senior agent Peter Strzok, the head of the FBI's counter-espionage section and lead Russiagate investigator, argues that 'many of Trump's actions, large and small, public and secret, were so inexplicably aligned with those of Russia that the coincidence – if it was a coincidence – had become impossible to ignore'.[9] Trump's challenge to the bipartisan new cold war consensus was considered less a rational policy option than some sort of intrigue. The FBI was convinced that Moscow held *kompromat* on Trump, forcing him to kowtow to Moscow.[10] Trump then was forced to prove otherwise, encouraging the administration to adopt harsh measures including ramping up sanctions, expelling diplomats, closing consular offices and pursuing uncompromising policies in Ukraine and elsewhere.

This was exacerbated by Trump's appointment of hard-line security veterans to key positions, the so-called 'adults in the room'. National security adviser General H. R. McMaster, chief of staff John Kelly and defence secretary Jim 'mad dog' Mattis were conventional cold war defenders of American primacy and exceptionalism. Bolton, who replaced McMaster in April 2018, was even more a forceful neoconservative interventionist, while Rex Tillerson's replacement as secretary of state in the same month, Mike Pompeo, was hardly less militant. As the former head of ExxonMobil, Tillerson at least had the advantage of a close relationship with Putin, whom he visited regularly and from whom he received the Order of Friendship medal in 2013. Tillerson recounts how in 2014 in Sochi Putin told him that 'I've given up on your President Obama. He doesn't do anything he says he's going to do. I can't deal with someone who does not follow through on his promises. I'll wait for your next president'.[11] Putin also felt that the

U.S. treated Russia 'like a banana republic', and a year earlier warned that 'You Americans think you won the cold war. You did not win the cold war. We never fought that war. We could have, but we didn't', and he reminded Tillerson that Russia was a nuclear power 'As powerful as you'.[12] Tillerson told Mattis that the new president would have 'an opening with Putin and could perhaps even develop a constructive relationship'.[13] Mattis was sceptical, and in the end, the Russiagate scandal put paid to whatever chance there may have been for that.

Trump was undoubtedly the most disruptive post-war American president. His disdain for the multilateral institutions of the post-war international system and his open contempt for many of America's traditional allies and the country's alliance system as a whole did as much to weaken the country's status and prestige as any other event in the modern era. To the degree that Moscow's intervention helped get Trump elected, Russia was responsible for the deleterious consequences. This explains the intense bipartisan pressure to hold Russia to account. Congress was fired up by the charges of Russian interference to adopt draconian new sanctions, greatly extending those adopted by executive order by Obama. In July 2017, the House of Representatives voted 419–3 and on 28 July the U.S. Senate voted 98–2 in support of what is officially called 'HR 3364 Countering America's Adversaries through Sanctions Act', or CAATSA. The measure limited the president's ability to ease or lift sanctions. Given the overwhelming vote in Congress, Trump on 2 August 2017 (regretfully) signed the legislation into law. Concessions, and even engagement, with Russia were interpreted as proof that Trump was in some way beholden to Moscow. Relations with Russia deteriorated to a level below anything seen during the original cold war. With few substantive channels of communication between the two major nuclear powers and with no rules of engagement, the danger of conflict was probably higher than at any point since World War II.

RUSSIAGATE AND NEW COLD WAR

The suffix 'gate', since the Watergate break-in and subsequent cover-up by President Richard Nixon in the early 1970s, denotes some sort of scandal and is today used to cover a multitude of sins. The roots of the Watergate scandal lie in Nixon's attempt to spy on the campaign of his Democratic opponents in 1972, and since then the term has been cheapened by its profligate use, yet in this case its application is appropriate.[14] The Russiagate scandal is if anything of greater consequence than the original Watergate scandal. In the earlier case, the dogged investigation by two *Washington Post* reporters, Carl Bernstein and Robert Woodward, in the end provoked Nixon's resignation on 9 August 1974.[15] Their investigation still has the power to enthral and remains a testimony to the values of independent journalism of a more innocent era. Truth could still be distinguished from falsehood and so-called 'fake news' had still not appeared, although 'disinformation' – the presentation of material intended to deceive – was certainly present. In Russiagate, the main media organisations and commentators lined up on one side or the other and accused the other of disinformation. Russiagate is a symptom of the polarised political culture of our times and the decline of what were once described as the Enlightenment values of impartiality and truth-seeking. This creates 'neo-journalism', in which the story is tailored to an existing set of beliefs.

This was exacerbated by the pressures of post-war international confrontation. Michael Glennon advances a sophisticated version of the idea of a 'deep state', based not on some conspiracy of the left or right to undermine democratic institutions but the structural development of the American state after 1945. Drawing on the distinction drawn in the late nineteenth century by the British journalist Walter Bagehot between the 'dignified' institutions, such as the monarchy and the House of Lords, and the 'efficient' institutions, such as the cabinet and House of Commons, that actually do the governing, Glennon applies this dual state model to the United States. The 'dignified' institutions in his view are Madisonian: the courts, Congress and the presidency that draw their authority from the constitution. However, in foreign and security policy, the country is governed by 'Trumanite' entities: the ramified national security structures and associated corporations spawned by the cold war that survived and proliferated afterwards.[16] The close ties between business, the state and the public sphere are well documented.[17] The Trumanite bodies endure because of the legitimacy they gain by being embedded in the Madisonian matrix; but the effectiveness of constitutional control has withered because of the inherent complexity of national security issues, as well as the enduring bipartisan ideological consensus on America's 'leadership' (reformulated in the Trump era as 'greatness') in world affairs. Obama-era White House staffer Ben Rhodes termed the foreign policy establishment 'the blob'.[18] This group, mostly located in Washington and its environs, is preoccupied by the apparent decline of American hegemony: 'It has been distinguished by its unwillingness, or inability, to reconsider or reprioritize national interests that were first defined after World War II, and then continued, by and large, on auto-pilot after the end of the cold war'.[19] Trump challenged what he considered to be the ossified and anachronistic 'Trumanite' multilateral formats of the national security state abroad, notably NATO, which confirmed the concerns of the military-intelligence community, who then naturally ramped up the Russiagate allegations.

The Democrats argue that Trump conspired with the Russians to win the election, but Michael Wolff (the author of one of the earliest exposés of the

Trump administration) notes that 'the Trumpers believed that the Obama administration had conspired with the intelligence community to make it *seem* [italics in original] as if Trump and his people had conspired with the Russians to fix the election. It was not Trump and the Russians who had successfully stolen the election; it was Obama and his cohorts who had tried and failed to steal it'.[20] According to Andrew McCarthy, a trenchant critic of the Russiagate allegations, the 'real collusion scheme' was not with Russia. Instead, the Obama administration 'put the awesome powers' of the U.S. security apparatus in the service of getting Clinton elected and, failing that, to set in motion an 'insurance policy' in the unlikely event that Trump won. This took the form of an investigation that Trump 'would be powerless to shut down', which would 'simultaneously monitor and taint him', and that would internalise 'Clinton campaign-generated opposition research, limning Trump and his campaign as complicit in Russian espionage'. The investigation would 'hunt for a crime under the guise of counterintelligence'.[21] In short, Trump's opponents used the collusion narrative to defeat him, 'and if they could not defeat him, to undermine his presidency – in hopes of defeating him next time'.[22] Gregg Jarrett describes how the FBI and Obama's administration improperly worked to get Clinton elected, and when that failed, they went on the offensive against Trump to undo the election and to remove him as president. He argues that there was never any real evidence of 'collusion' between Trump and the Russians.[23] If these accounts are accurate, then the real deception was perpetrated by elements within the Obama administration and intelligence community.[24]

While Trump and his supporters became convinced that the deep state was out to get him, many liberals, who had previously been sceptical if not outright critical of the surveillance state, now believed that the security services were protecting democracy from ruin.[25] In the original cold war, particularly on the right, democracies were considered to be at a disadvantage against non-democracies because of the proclivity of publics to appease dangerous adversaries.[26] Paradoxically, as Russiagate developed, it was the right-wing public that was less enthusiastic about 'confronting' Russia than the liberal-progressive internationalists, with the Clintonian Democrats in the lead. Threat inflation by interested parties tap into a deep well-spring of 'militarized patriotism' left over from the cold war to distort public debate.[27] In the case of Russiagate, cold war legacies clearly predisposed leaders and the public to accept an exaggerated discourse of Russian malevolence.

Democratic Party supporters were particularly inclined to take this view. The 'reset' policy launched by Obama in 2009 ran into the sands because of the West's intervention in Libya in 2011 and Russia's turn to social conservatism and repression in the wake of the demonstrations against electoral fraud in the December 2011 State Duma election. The Putin who was elected for a third presidential term in March 2012 was alienated from the West and embittered by what he perceived to be the ingratitude of the Russian middle classes. The 'anti-gay propaganda' law of June 2013 particularly alienated Western liberals and prompted Obama to boycott the Sochi Winter Olympics in February 2014. The outbreak of open conflict over Ukraine in 2014 represented a further sharp deterioration in relations. This is what gave traction to the Russiagate allegations, and why during the campaign Clinton tried to link Trump to her pet enemy, Putin, and why afterwards this was transformed into an explanation for her defeat. This did not have the power to reverse the outcome, 'but it did have enough influence to draw the nation into a prolonged period of hysterical denial of reality . . . for the Clinton fanatics it was self-evident – only some malevolent outside power could account for the triumph of the most repugnant monster who ever emerged from our television screens'.[28] The Clintonian Democrats needed a scapegoat, and Russia proved more than fitting. The Kremlin explicitly challenged American hegemony, and in Russiagate, this challenge was redefined as a threat to American democracy.

The relentless Russiagate investigation enraged Trump, but more importantly, it stymied his declared intention of normalising relations with Russia. As Isikoff and Corn note, 'Russia had become a rallying cry for his [Trump's] tormentors – the original sin of his presidency, a scandal that raised questions about both his legitimacy and the nation's vulnerability to covert information warfare'.[29] Trump insisted that the whole business was 'fake news', whereas his opponents simply could not understand why he refused to accept the apparent unanimous findings of the intelligence community that Russia had 'hacked' the election.[30] It was, after all, as the *Washington Post* put it, 'the 'crime of the century'.[31] Former CIA director Michael Hayden described it as the 'most successful covert operation in the history of intelligence'.[32] Since Trump so wilfully appeared to ignore the information provided by his intelligence services and the consensus view of Russian malevolence shared by members of Congress and the media, he must have something to hide. The default explanation was that Trump was in some way beholden to Putin, either because of financial dependency or because the Kremlin held power over him: 'With Trump unable or unwilling to come to terms with Putin's war on American democracy, it fell to government investigators and reporters to piece together the complete story.'[33]

Russiagate once again demonstrates the power of narrative. American innocence and democracy were portrayed as under attack from a uniquely and historically malevolent force. Instead of focusing on the social and political discontents exposed by the campaign and Trump's election, attention shifted to the Russian attack on American democracy. The outcome was presented as an historical aberration that could be remedied not at the ballot box but by some sort of judicial procedure.³⁴ This prompted the impeachment attempt from mid-2019, which served only to reinforce the elements of crisis in American democracy. Politics could not be revived by non-political means. It was no longer just generals and elites who fostered the confrontation, but the hatred of Russia's alleged misdeeds and misbehaviour became a social project of information warfare and ultimately media manipulation. Sceptics were hesitant to speak out, given the powerful combination of forces arrayed against them. This Trump-era pathology of 'resistance journalism' relieved commentators of traditional standards of integrity as long as their target was sufficiently disliked by mainstream liberal media venues.³⁵ This reckless form of neo-journalism 'caused US politics to be drowned for three years in little other than salacious and fact-free conspiracy theories about Trump and his family members and closest associates', notably that 'Putin had infiltrated and taken over the US government through sexual and financial blackmail leverage over Trump and used it to dictate US policy'.³⁶ Matt Taibbi describes Russiagate as this generation's 'WMD', comparable to the falsehoods over weapons of mass destruction that justified the Iraq War in 2003.³⁷ The *New York Times* published over 3,000 stories on Russiagate, with several published a day at the peak, most peddling the same line. In sum, 'Future media historians may hold the Trump-Russia story to be a laboratory-perfect specimen of discourse concentration. For nearly two years, it towered over the information landscape and devoured the attention of the media and the public.'³⁸

This is the context for Russiagate. Trump, of course, dismissed not only the collusion narrative but the whole intelligence community view of Russian interference. He did this for obvious reasons since the alleged Russian interference not only constrained his policy choices but above all derailed his presidency and undermined the legitimacy of his election. Alleged Russian interference became bound up with virulently partisan considerations in which deception and self-deception operated in equal measure. Sanctions and the sharp fall in the oil price from late 2014 weakened Russia, and hence it was both a convenient and easy target. It had a long track record of opposing the West, something that irked the Democrats even more than the Republicans. Russia challenged not only U.S. military hegemony but also America's role as the champion of the 'democratic peace'. The Russiagate scandal intersected with major challenges in domestic and international politics and amplified both. The election of a nonconformist outsider challenged the given order. Trump's style was combative and extreme, and his business dealings had long shown disrespect for the rule of law and propriety and a propensity to gamble with the money of others. Yet Trump's election reflected deep-rooted dissatisfaction in American society to which he gave voice and expression. This book is not about the Trump presidency, but it will inevitably have to consider the way that his policies and behaviour, as well as that of his opponents, contributed to the crisis. In international politics, Trump challenged many of the accustomed patterns of behaviour, and his 'America first' strategy discounted traditional alliances and multilateral organisations in favour of a raucous display of American power. Yet Trump in foreign policy, as at home, raised important questions about the character of the post-cold war international system. These issues came together in the Russiagate scandal.

DECEPTION AND WAR

What if Russian actions during the 2016 election were minimal and defensive, and there was no grand plot to 'sow discord' and undermine American democracy? What if Trump was right (and he was uniquely positioned to know) and there had been no collusion with Russia, and that Russian meddling was at the most marginal and exerted no influence on the outcome? In that case, the endless years of the Russiagate scandal, in which every scrap of evidence was portrayed as the 'smoking gun' before being discredited, only for another issue to be played up for its few hours as the *scandal du jour*. If this is the case, it was not the actual events associated with Russiagate that harmed the country, but the ensuing exaggerated response. The portrayal of what may well have been a set of random actions as equivalent to an attack on the country recalls other incidents in American history. In February 1898, the USS *Maine* blew up in Havana harbour, and the vast outpouring of patriotic anger attributed the loss to an act of Spanish perfidy, whereas it appears that a spark from ship's furnace blew up the ammunition magazine. The explosion set the United States on the path of imperial expansion, with the seizure of Cuba and a savage war in the Philippines. Equally, the Gulf of Tonkin incident in August 1964 propelled the United States into full-scale war in Vietnam.

Deception is defined as 'the deliberate attempt on the part of leaders to mislead the public about the thrust of official thinking'.[39] By this definition, deception must be deliberate. Based on three case studies – Franklin Roosevelt preparing the American public for war in 1941 (a case of strategic deception, considered to be in the national interest); the disinformation that accompanied America's full-scale entry into the Vietnam War in 1964; and the outright falsehoods that provoked the United States and its allies to attack Saddam Hussein's government in Iraq in 2003 – John Schuessler argues that deceit can in certain circumstances be justified if the goal is something that is in the national interest. The deceptive strategies employed by the British to get the United States to enter the war against Hitler are an example of this.[40]

All the leaders were 'economical with the truth', but by the time we get to the Iraq War, the U.S. government and its allies peddled outright falsehoods. This also applies to the Afghanistan War launched in autumn 2001. In a report with disturbing echoes of the Pentagon Papers, documentation on U.S. military involvement in Vietnam since 1945 exposed by Daniel Ellsberg in 1971, the American public was consistently misled about the scale of military failure in Afghanistan.[41] The invasion of Iraq in March 2003 was presented as 'a necessary war, not a war of choice, and the intelligence services and politicians provided an exaggerated and uniformly menacing view of the potential threat. Anyone who doubted that claim was almost certain to be labelled an appeaser or a fool, or even accused of being unpatriotic'.[42] The 'marketplace of ideas' did not function very well in the run-up to this war.[43]

Sun Tzu in *The Art of War* declared that 'all warfare is based on deception', but in our case, this applies not only to the normal disinformation and propaganda campaigns waged by hostile states, but a situation in which 'the art of war' characterises domestic political conflict. In recent years, American politics has become intensely polarised, and parties have come to see each other as the enemy. Strategies of deception and misinformation are routinely deployed. In conditions of an emerging new cold war, a foreign power was implicated in these struggles, forging new chains of deception, and at the same time, domestic political struggles were projected into the international arena. John Mearsheimer notes that 'if lying is pervasive in a democracy, it might alienate the public to the point where it loses faith in democratic government and is willing to countenance some form of authoritarian rule'.[44] Deception has profoundly deleterious foreign policy consequences, but self-deception has harmful domestic effects. Russiagate turned Russia from an adversary into an enemy and changed a confrontation into a new cold war.[45] It also further polarised American domestic politics, with each side in the Russiagate conflict mobilising and distorting the evidence to buttress their case, with those loudest in condemning disinformation often the most egregious in distorting the facts.

Two major narratives contend. In the first, a 'soft on Russia' fifth column had emerged, which then merged with the Trump campaign. Michael Flynn was the leading exemplar of this tendency. He headed the Defence Intelligence Agency (DIA) from July 2012 to August 2014 and argued that the main problem was not Russia but Iran and allied terrorist groups. He warned Obama against arming the resistance to Bashar Al-Assad in Syria, predicting that it would only empower Islamic extremists. Concern was intensified in intelligence circles when Trump repeatedly spoke of the need to improve relations with Russia and refused to criticise Putin. This shaped the mainstream Russiagate narrative: that Trump in some way actively colluded with the Russian authorities to swing the election his way; that the various hacks of Democrat emails and their publication by WikiLeaks was coordinated with Moscow to damage the Clinton campaign; and that Russian social media activism substantively changed the outcome of the ballot. Entwined with all of these is the larger picture that Russia was an aggressive and dangerous foe determined to destroy Clinton's campaign and above all to subvert American democracy. These are serious charges, and hence it was the duty of patriotic Americans and their allies to defeat these attacks, which bordered on war. Russia's dupes, including Trump, were to be constrained, while exposing Trump's unsuitability for office and opening avenues for impeachment.

The second narrative is generated by the central paradox of Trump's leadership. He was so manifestly unsuited for high office that 'defenders of this established order were of course compelled to protect it from him'. However, once he unexpectedly won the election, Trump became the representative of the established order, and attempts to undermine him thereafter verged on the unconstitutional.[46] Trump was the legal president, but his legitimacy was questioned. When Flynn joined the Trump campaign in 2016 and spoke of improved relations with Moscow, the Russia-worried hands in the intelligence community went into over-drive. This prompted the alleged entrapment campaign against the Trump staffers Carter Page (who had long been involved with Russia) and George Papadopoulos (who had never had anything to do with Russia, but through contact with the mysterious professor Joseph Mifsud had apparently gained access to emails incriminating Clinton held by Russia). Above all, Flynn became a victim of the deep state's attempt to hold the line against Russia, with the added benefit for them of weakening Trump's presidency. In other words, this second narrative regards the ensemble of Russiagate allegations as largely manufactured, but they then became self-sustaining. The acts of alleged deception by security agency officials later themselves became the subject of investigation by several Congressional committees and the Department of Justice (DoJ) once Wiliam Barr was confirmed as attorney general in February 2019.

The first narrative carried over into the attempt to impeach Trump following his 25 July 2019 call with the new Ukrainian president, Volodymyr Zelensky, which brought to the fore a whole new set of contending narratives that soon acquired the 'Ukrainegate' moniker. Whatever slight chance there may have been for rapprochement with Russia, which Trump saw as a potential ally in the looming struggle with China, were dashed. Domestically, the clash of Russiagate narratives exacerbated political polarisation and damaged the quality of political discourse. Commentators exploited 'information and propaganda advantages to frame issues in misleading ways, cherry-pick supporting evidence, suppress damaging revelations, and otherwise skew the public debate in advantageous directions'.[47] Russiagate became a symbol of renewed confrontation marked by the hysteria characteristic of times when vital interests are threatened. In the Joseph McCarthy period in the 1950s, there was acute social paranoia and the disciplining of alternative views, and elements of this were now reproduced.[48] Liberal democracy in condition of new cold war was not immune from deception. The result is always the same, involving some sort of blowback that undermines the original goal.[49]

NOTES

1. The image draws on the spy-fiction novel by Richard Condon, *The Manchurian Candidate* (New York, McGraw Hill, 1959), which was twice filmed (1962 and 2004), in which the Kremlin places an agent in the White House. For an analysis of the cold war anxieties explored by the book and the 1962 film, see Matthew Frye Jacobson and Gaspar Gonzalez, *What Have they Built You To Do? The Manchurian Candidate and Cold War America* (Minneapolis, University of Minnesota Press, 2006).

2. In Roth's case, the outsider was Charles Lindbergh, and the outside power in the 1940 election was Nazi Germany, Philip Roth, *The Plot against America* (New York, Vintage, 2005).

3. Richard Sakwa, *Russia against the Rest: The Post-Cold War Crisis of World Order* (Cambridge, Cambridge University Press, 2017); Robert Legvold, *Return to Cold War* (Cambridge, Polity, 2016).

4. Larry J. Sabato, Kyle Kondik and Geoffrey Skelley (eds), *Trumped: The 2016 Election that Broke all the Rules* (New York, Rowman &Littlefield, 2017), p. 5.

5. John Bolton, *The Room Where It Happened* (New York, Simon & Schuster, 2020), p. 174.

6. Robert S. Mueller III, *Report on the Investigation into Russian Interference in the 2016 Presidential Election*, March 2019, Vol. 1, p. 1, https://www.justice.gov/storage/report.pdf.

7. Helen Buyniski, 'FBI Chief Drops Indictments against Russia Intel Ops', *Global Research*, 15 July 2018, https://www.globalresearch.ca/fbi-chief-mueller-drops-indictments-against-russia-intel-ops-as-deep-state-panics-over-trump-putin-summit/5647560.

8. Mueller, *Report*, Vol. 1, p. 47.

9. Peter Strzok, *Compromised: Counterintelligence and the Threat of Donald J. Trump* (Boston, Houghton Mifflin Harcourt, 2020), p. xvii.

10. This is why Strzok titled his book *Compromised*, p. xxx.

11. Bob Woodward, *Rage* (London and New York, Simon & Schuster, 2020), p. 8.

12. Woodward, *Rage*, p. 9.

13. Woodward, *Rage*, p. 18.

14. Cf. Robert Parry, 'Russia-gate is no Watergate or Iran-Contra', *Consortium News*, 28 June 2017, https://consortiumnews.com/2017/06/28/russia-gate-is-no-watergate-or-iran-contra/.

15. Described in Bob Woodward and Carl Bernstein, *All the President's Men* (London, Simon & Schuster, 2012) and the 1976 docudrama film of that name.

16. Michael J. Glennon, *National Security and Double Government* (Oxford, Oxford University Press, 2015).

17. For a detailed study of the 'revolving doors connecting government, conservative think tanks, lobbying firms, law firms and the defense industry', see Richard Cummings, 'Lockheed Stock and Two Smoking Barrels', *Corpwatch*, 16 January 2007, https://corpwatch.org/article/us-lockheed-stock-and-two-smoking-barrels.

18. For his account of working with the 'blob', see Ben Rhodes, *The World As It Is: Inside the Obama White House* (New York, Vintage, 2019). Stephen M. Walt, *The Hell of Good Intentions: America's Foreign Policy Elite and the Decline of US Primacy* (New York, Farrar, Straus, and Giroux, 2019) devotes an instructive chapter to 'defining the "blob"', pp. 91–136.

19. Hunter DeRensis, 'The Blob Strikes Back', *The National Interest*, 23 October 2019, https://nationalinterest.org/feature/blob-strikes-back-90476.

20. Michael Wolff, *Siege: Trump under Fire* (Boston, Little, Brown, 2019), p. 105.

21. Andrew C. McCarthy, *Ball of Collusion: The Plot to Rig an Election and Destroy a Presidency* (New York, Encounter Books, 2019), pp. vii-viii.

22. McCarthy, *Ball of Collusion*, p. xxii.

23. Gregg Jarrett, *The Russia Hoax: The Illicit Scheme to Clear Hillary Clinton and Frame Donald Trump* (Northampton, MA, Broadside Books, 2018).

24. Many make this argument, notably Dan Bongino with D.C. McAllister and Matt Palumbo, '*Spygate: The Attempted Sabotage of Donald J. Trump* (Nashville, TN, Post Hill Press, 2018), and Dan Bongino, *Exonerated: The Failed Takedown of President Donald Trump by the Swamp* (New York, Post Hill Press, 2019).

25. Wolff, *Siege*, p. 43.

26. John J. Mearsheimer, *Why Leaders Lie: The Truth about Lying in International Politics* (London, Duckworth Overlook, 2012), p. 63.

27. Jane Kellett Cramer, 'Militarized Patriotism: Why the U.S. Marketplace of Ideas Failed before the Iraq War', *Security Studies*, Vol. 16, No. 3, 2007, pp. 489–524.

28. Diana Johnstone, *Circle in the Darkness: Memoir of a World Watcher* (Atlanta, GA, Clarity Press, 2020), p. 395.

29. Michael Isikoff and David Corn, *Russian Roulette: The Inside Story of Putin's War on America and the Election of Donald Trump* (New York, Twelve, 2018), p. x. Earlier the two had analysed the attempt to sell the 'war of choice' by manipulating information flows, Michael Isikoff and David Corn, *Hubris: The Inside Story of Spin, Scandal, and the Selling of the Iraq War* (New York, Crown Publishers, 2006). The sceptical duo of 2003 had become the credulous couple of 2016.

30. Outlined by Michael V. Hayden, *The Assault on Intelligence: American National Security in an Age of Lies* (London, Penguin, 2018).

31. Greg Miller, Ellen Nakashima and Adam Entous, 'Obama's Secret Struggle to Punish Russia for Putin's Election Assault', *Washington Post*, 23 June 2017, https://www.washingtonpost.com/graphics/2017/.../national.../obama-putin-election-hack.

32. Wanda Carruthers, 'Hayden: Russia's Meddling "Most Successful Covert Operation in History"', *Newsmax*, 21 July 2017, https://www.newsmax.com/politics/michael-hayden-russia-election-meddling/2017/07/21/id/803152/.

33. Isikoff and Corn, *Russian Roulette*, p. xi.

34. The point is made by Matt Taibbi, 'On Russiagate and Our Refusal to Face Why Trump Won', *Rolling Stone*, 29 March 2019, https://www.rollingstone.com/politics/politics-features/taibbi-trump-russia-mueller-investigation-815060/.

35. Ben Smith, 'Is Ronan Farrow too Good to be True?', *New York Times*, 17 May 2020, https://www.nytimes.com/2020/05/17/business/media/ronan-farrow.html?smid=tw-share.

36. Glenn Greenwald, 'Ben Smith's NYT Critique of Ronan Farrow Describes a Toxic, Corrosive, and Still-Vibrant Trump-Era Pathology: "Resistance Journalism"', *The Intercept*, 18 May 2020, https://theintercept.com/2020/05/18/ben-smiths-nyt-critique-of-ronan-farrow-describes-a-toxic-corrosive-and-still-vibrant-trump-era-pathology-resistance-journalism/.

37. Matt Taibbi, 'It's Official: Russiagate is this Generation's WMD: The Iraq War Faceplant Damaged the Reputation of the Press. Russiagate Just Destroyed It', *Rolling Stone*, 23 March 2019, https://taibbi.substack.com/p/russiagate-is-wmd-times-a-million.

38. Martin Gurri, 'Slouching Toward Post-Journalism', *City Journal*, Winter 2021, https://www.city-journal.org/journalism-advocacy-over-reporting.

39. John M. Schuessler, *Deceit on the Road to War: Presidents, Politics and American Democracy* (Ithaca and London, Cornell University Press, 2015), p. 8.

40. Thomas E. Mahl, *Desperate Deception* (Lincoln, NE, Brassey's US, 2000).

41. The confidential interviews come from the Special Inspector General for Afghanistan Reconstruction (SIGAR), Lessons Learned programme, published by *The Washington Post* and reported by Peter Beaumont, 'Afghanistan Files Reveal US Public was Misled about Unwinnable War', *Guardian*, 10 December 2019, pp. 22–23.

42. Mearsheimer, *Why Leaders Lie*, p. 3.

43. Schuessler, *Deceit on the Road to War*, p. 6.

44. Mearsheimer, *Why Leaders Lie*, p. 89.

45. Stephen F. Cohen, *War With Russia: From Putin and Ukraine to Trump and Russiagate* (New York, Hot Books, 2018).

46. Wolff, *Siege*, p. 107.

47. Schuessler, *Deceit on the Road to War*, p. 3.

48. Richard J. Hofstadter, 'The Paranoid Style in American Politics', *Harper's Magazine*, November 1964, pp. 77–86.

49. For the U.S. case, see Eric Alterman, *When Presidents Lie: A History of Official Deception and Its Consequences* (New York, Viking, 2004).

Chapter 2

Trump Ascends

On 16 June 2015, Trump 'magisterially, like some kind of lord from on high' descended the escalator in Trump Tower to announce that he would run for the presidency.[1] He argued that only someone 'really rich' could 'take the brand of the United States and make it great again'. The announcement was accompanied by racist comments about Mexican immigrants: 'When Mexico sends its people, they're not sending their best. . . . They're bringing drugs. They're bringing crime. They're rapists'[2] – prompting NBC to fire him from the reality show *The Apprentice* (and *Celebrity Apprentice*) that he had hosted for fourteen seasons. By then, Trump's public image had changed from a 'skeezy hustler' into 'a plutocrat with impeccable business instincts and unparalleled wealth'.[3] An extraordinary combination of events in the end propelled Trump to the White House: the flaws of the other sixteen Republican contenders handed Trump the Republican nomination on 21 July 2016; the weakness of his Democratic opponent, Hillary Clinton, who conducted a wooden, entitled and uninspired campaign; the blunder of James Comey, the director of the FBI, in reopening the Clinton email enquiry on the eve of the election; and Russian interference in the form of a social media campaign and theft of Democrat campaign files that tarnished their campaign. Trump's opponents portrayed him as little more than a Kremlin stooge, enraging Trump, who hated being beholden to anyone, and ensured that the subsequent investigations would poison his presidency.

Chapter 2

THE GREATEST POLITICAL UPSET
IN AMERICAN HISTORY

On 8 November 2016, Trump pulled off 'the greatest political upset in American history'.[4] Trump won 62.98 million votes, 2.86 million fewer than Clinton's 65.84 million. However, this translated into 304 Electoral College votes, compared to Clinton's 227, making Trump the fifth U.S. president to win office without a popular majority. However, he did win 2,649 counties (mostly rural) compared to Clinton's 503 (largely concentrated in the big coastal cities). The huge majorities won by Clinton in California (4.1 million votes more than Trump) and New York (winning by a margin of 1.7 million) were too concentrated and only accentuated her flagging support in the American heartland. Trump's achievement was all the greater since Clinton had a billion-dollar campaign war chest, the largest in American history. This was the biggest upset since Harry Truman defeated Thomas Dewey in 1948, yet Trump's 'victory was decades in the making, and the signs of a victory like his were there for years'.[5] Michael Cohen, Trump's long-time personal lawyer and general fixer, describes how Trump channelled the resentment of people labelled as racist in the Obama years, 'who were sick of political correctness and tolerating illegal immigration and having to pretend that they believed things they simply didn't believe'.[6] KT McFarland, who served as deputy national security adviser until May 2017, notes that 'By the 2016 election, it was clear that America was ready for change.'[7] However, there was no consensus on the character of the necessary changes.

Since the 1970s, the two major parties 'have increased their ideological uniformity', particularly among Republicans, who increasingly self-identified as conservatives.[8] Clinton in effect ran as 'the candidate of Barack Obama's third term', and anger against the establishment status quo was directed against her. Trump was already closing the ratings gap by the time Comey reopened the investigation into her use of a private email server on 28 October, just eleven days before the election.[9] Trump's long-time associate and an original contestant on *The Apprentice*, Omarosa Manigault Newman (or Omarosa as she styles herself), argues that the widespread assumption that Clinton would win 'demotivated her base' and led to the lower turnout of her supporters.[10] Above all, Trump's election was part of the great 'populist' uprising against established elites, of which the Brexit vote for the UK to leave the European Union was the harbinger in June of that year.[11] Trump's election is interpreted as a 'whitelash' against the liberal order.[12] In this context, we should not over-personalise the victory. Trump used traditional Republican campaign techniques and applied them particularly effectively in the big (post)industrial states, where he won narrowly. With the nomination in the bag, some traditional Republican leaders rallied behind him, although they knew that Trump was far from being a traditional Republican.[13] His success was prepared by nearly a decade of Tea Party populist anti-elitist agitation and a generation of stagnating blue-collar and middle-class incomes. Even then, income and unemployment rates were a weak predictor of voting intentions, and exit polls revealed that those most concerned with economic problems voted disproportionally for Clinton, while those most concerned about immigration voted for Trump.[14]

McFarland defends sophisticated 'populist' and 'nationalist' positions and argues not only that 'The Washington Establishment was unaware of the growing anger of the working and middle classes' but also that it had 'failed to pursue an effective national security policy for much of the last twenty years'. Bogged down in various 'forever wars' in the Middle East, in her view 'the real strategic threats posed by a revanchist Russia and an expansionist China' had been neglected.[15] Her approach is analysed by Pippa Norris and Ronald Inglehart, who argue that Trump used 'populist rhetoric to legitimize his style of governance, while promoting authoritarian values that threaten the liberal norms underpinning American democracy'.[16] They define populism as political style focused on the first-order question of who should rule, invoking 'the people' against corrupt elites; while second-order questions of what precisely should be done and policy decisions are left vague, endowing the rhetoric with a 'chameleon-like quality'.[17] This certainly applies to Trump, but as they point out, his rise was an element in a broader phenomenon, part of what they call the 'cultural backlash' against the 'silent revolution' of post-material and socially liberal values of the previous four decades. Together with concerns over immigration, this rather than the economic insecurity of the 'losers' of globalisation tilted older white working-class voters towards Trump.[18] He also took advantage of the changes in the Republican Party, starting with Newt Gingrich's irreconcilable congressional partisanship following their midterm success in winning both houses in 1994, through to Sarah Palin's denunciation of the 'Washington establishment' as John McCain's running mate in 2008 and to the Tea Party insurgency launched the following year.[19] The Trump phenomenon represented the culmination of a 'silent counter-revolution' against liberal social and political liberalism.[20]

Trump's campaign was haphazard and chaotic yet sparked a powerful response among alienated constituencies. One of Trump's associates who would figure largely in the Russiagate scandal was Paul Manafort. He had long known Trump, and on 29 March 2016 he joined the staff and on 19 May became campaign chairman, and on 20 June replaced Corey Lewandowski as campaign manager.[21] Manafort had been a business partner of one of Trump's close advisers, Roger Stone, in the political consulting firm of Black, Manafort, Stone and Kelly, established in 1980. Manafort was part of Nixon's re-election campaign in 1972 and later worked for presidents Gerald Ford, Ronald Reagan and George H. W. Bush, and also Senator Robert Dole. He also acted as consultant to unsavoury authoritarian leaders, including Ferdinand Marcos in the Philippines and Angolan war leader Jonas Savimbi. However, his work in Ukraine from 2004 proved his downfall. He advised the Russophone Party of Regions on how to improve its image and helped its leader, Viktor Yanukovych, to win the presidency in 2010. They were 'pro-Russian' to the degree that they offered a more 'multivector' and politically plural alternative to that of the more neo-nationalistic pro-Western groups, but mostly they saw politics as a means of enhancing their power and privileges.[22] Yanukovych's greedy corruption alienated other oligarchs and ultimately provoked the 'revolution of dignity' that ousted him in February 2014. As for Manafort, he processed some $75 million through dozens of U.S. and foreign banks and corporations.[23] With Yanukoych in exile in Russia, Manafort's involvement with the Trump campaign was dogged by scandal, and he became the subject of an FBI investigation. Following the exposure of secret payments from the Party of Regions, on 14 August 2016 Manafort was sacked. Republican operative Kellyanne Conway became campaign manager, with the ideologue Steve Bannon as chief strategist.

The Trump campaign at that stage was no more than 'a few people in a room', and thereafter it worked with the Republican National Committee (RNC), chaired by Reince Priebus, to provide organisational muscle.[24] In fact, Lewandowski and Bossie argue that Manafort was a disaster as manager, and the campaign was only saved after Bannon and Conway took over.[25] They stress that Trump's rapturous welcome at rallies across the country showed that the electorate was looking for something different: 'we were no longer just a campaign, but a movement'.[26] In their view, Trump 'rekindled a dream for millions of Americans – and that's why they elected him president'.[27] They dismiss the 'absurd conspiracy about collusion with Russia, which we can both tell you firsthand is ridiculous'.[28] As for the RNC, learning from Obama, it poured over $175 million into analytics and big data, and was even able to track individual primary voters.[29] Trump's son-in-law Jared Kushner and Brad Parscale from June 2016 ran the digital media and data analytics side of things, while Priebus built 'the most comprehensive voter file that the country had ever seen, and it [the RNC] would fold it all into a complex digital operation'.[30] In 2016, Parscale placed 5.9 million ads on Facebook based on only thirty-five root narratives.[31] This technological and informational sophistication is important, because it puts any putative Russian interference in the shade. Compared to the massive investment in big data by the major campaigns, outside interference pales into insignificance. Despite the support of the Republican machine, 'Trump was an insurgent candidate with no clear link to the Republican Party'.[32] He behaved like a third-party outsider both as candidate and as president. In the end, Trump won thirty-eight Republican primaries, a record in a contested season.

Three points stand out amid the vast literature on Trump's victory. First, as the conservative commentator and speechwriter (author of the 'axis of evil' concept in 2002) David Frum notes, 'Trump gained the presidency thanks in part to voters disgusted by a status quo that was ceasing to work for more and more of them'.[33] The median Trump voter was not especially ideologically militant or religious, but what 'set them apart from other Republicans was their economic insecurity and their cultural anxiety'.[34] With the end of the cold war and the decline of national security concerns, domestic politics had been conducted with 'intensifying ferocity'.[35] In one of the many paradoxes of the election, Trump, a three-time married adulterer with hitherto socially liberal views, captured four in five white evangelical voters, more than any of the more traditional Republicans like Mitt Romney, John McCain or George W. Bush. Reasons given are fear over the decline of Christian values, the failure of previous Republican presidents to deliver on their promises, and Trump's ruthless commitment, in the event fulfilled, of packing federal courts with conservative judges.[36]

The crisis of conservatism was recognised and analysed by commentators such as Frum, but there was also a crisis of liberalism, which its partisans refused to acknowledge.[37] Peter Thiel, the founder of PayPal and one of Trump's few early supporters at the top of corporate America, argued that

> Just as much as it's about making America great, Trump's agenda is about making America a normal country. A normal country doesn't have a half-trillion dollar trade deficit. A normal country doesn't fight five simultaneous undeclared wars. In a normal country, the government actually does its job. And today it's important to recognise that the government has a job to do.[38]

Steven Rosefielde argues that Trump's victory reflected a desire for an elected government that was responsive to the concerns of common people. The grievances of ordinary middle- and working-class Americans focused on the domestic and international consequences of America becoming a 'Global Nation', to which the established order appeared to be increasingly deaf. Instead, Trump put himself at the head of a movement seeking to build a Jeffersonian populist America, a programme that if successful would transform the position of the middle and working classes. Paradoxically, in Rosefielde's interpretation, it was the new populists who defended pluralism and open societies against the cloying and stifling orthodoxies of the post-war globalist consensus.[39]

The second point is that Trump offered a rethink of foreign-policy priorities. Again, this did not come out of nowhere, and Republican interventionism and neo-conservative foreign-policy hawkishness were already encountering increasing resistance before Trump's advocacy of Kissinger-style realism.[40] Trump was the only Republican candidate who tempered the militant cold war talk. In comparison to Clinton's foreign-policy hawkishness, Trump appeared the voice of reason and moderation. As he put it in October 2015, 'If we're going to have World War III, it's not going to be over Syria'. In contrast to politicians, like Clinton, who were calling for a no-fly zone over Syria, which would have meant shooting down Russian jets, Trump commented: 'I won't even call them hawks. I call them fools'.[41] From this perspective, Trump's call for a transformation of American foreign policy was the logical counterpart of his domestic programme. Trump argued that U.S. foreign engagements in recent decades had not benefited the mass of Americans. Instead of the traditional globalism, he advanced a 'democratic nationalism' that prioritised the needs of Americans over those abroad.[42] As the legal scholar and diplomat Rein Müllerson puts it,

> Hillary Clinton, epitomising the corrupt politics of the Democrats, lost the 2016 presidential election not because of some foreign interference but because the rift between the political elite and the American people had become all too obvious. Externally, she has been a perfect example of those 'liberal interventionists' who differ too little from the 'neocons' who were running the show under the Republican presidency of George W. Bush.[43]

The circle now closed, and 'being anti-Trump has become synonymous with being anti-Russian', with the 'Washington ruling class' unable to accept Clinton's defeat and hence 'floated dozens of theories of how the only reason Trump won was because the Russians intervened'.[44]

The third point focuses on the flaws of Clinton's campaign and the weakness of her candidacy. Interim DNC chair Donna Brazile considered Clinton such an 'anaemic' candidate, both politically and at times physically, that she contemplated replacing her with her running mate, Senator Tim Kaine of Virginia, with Obama's vice president Joe Biden as his deputy.[45] There had long been various questions about the funding of the Clinton Foundation. The Uranium One case, involving both Russian and Kazakh entities, combined donations to the Foundation and support for the company.[46] A book sponsored by the hedge-fund billionaire Robert Mercer and his daughter Rebekah describes the case, and other money-making ventures, in exhaustive but not always convincing detail.[47] Clinton's inappropriate use of a private email account for government business, her intimacy with Wall Street, her embrace of the identity politics of race and gender but not class, the use of administrative resources against the left-wing candidate Bernie Sanders, her status as long-time insider, and the burden of coming over as Obama's 'third-term' continuity candidate, all alienated potential voters. Her campaign strategy was also flawed, taking some crucial swing states (in particular, Michigan, Pennsylvania and Wisconsin) for granted, whereas Trump conducted a barnstorming campaign that motivated his base. As a result, Trump was gaining on Clinton even before Comey's bombshell about reopening the FBI investigation into a new batch of Clinton's emails on the eve of the election. Non-college educated voters turned out to vote for Trump in great numbers, some 10 per cent of whom were former Obama supporters but shifted allegiance because of their economic plight, while 60 per cent of military veterans voted for Trump.[48]

RUSSIA AND CLINTON'S DOWNFALL

The election was Clinton's to lose. As Benjamin Free notes in a famous polemic, 'Donald Trump's win over Hillary Clinton is considered to be the most controversial win in modern United States history'. He asks the fundamental question: 'Why would over half of an entire nation elect a man with no political career over a woman whose entire career was political?' Clinton was 'the most qualified person to ever run for president'.[49] She lost the Democratic Party nomination in 2008 to Obama, but then served as his secretary of state, in which capacity she advocated military intervention in Libya in 2011, sanctions on Iran, and endorsed (although reluctantly) Obama's 'reset' policy with Russia. When Libya became yet another failed state, her record as a militant interventionist (she supported the war on Iraq in 2003) shadowed her presidential bid. In the congressional investigation into the attack on the U.S. diplomatic mission in Benghazi on 11 September 2012, in which the U.S. ambassador (Christopher Stevens) and three others were killed, Clinton accepted formal responsibility, but her defence 'that she simply didn't know' the detailed security arrangements, despite repeated requests for security upgrades, 'outraged the public'.[50] In the next four years, there were eight separate congressional investigations into the attack. Much of this was partisan, but there were some genuine questions to be answered.

Russia became an obsessive theme of Clinton's campaign. Clinton was a classic liberal interventionist, and thus her foreign-policy activism crossed the aisle to meet the neo-conservative advocates of American primacy. When it came to Russia, the country was judged by the degree to which it adapted to Western models of democracy and integrated into the Western power system. Clinton had long criticised Putin and was dismissive of his policies.[51] President George W. Bush had famously been 'able to get a sense of his soul' when he met Putin in Slovenia in June 2001, but in 2008, the putative Democrat candidate Clinton declared that she would have told Bush that Putin did not have a soul because he 'was a KGB [Soviet Committee for State Security] agent'.[52] Obama's reset stressed the relationship with President Dmitry Medvedev, who had taken over from Putin at the end of the latter's constitutionally limited two terms in 2008. This made sense, but the accompanying denigration of Putin did not, and neither did Vice President Joe Biden's warning during his visit to Moscow in March 2011 against Putin returning to the presidency. This, together with the Libyan fiasco, destroyed Medvedev's chances for a second term.

On 24 September 2011, a presidential transition back from Medvedev to Putin was declared. The announcement was heavy-handed and insulting, as if the presidency was the property of the Kremlin elite, and provoked widespread discontent.[53] Following the deeply flawed parliamentary election of 4 December, discontent exploded into the largest political protests of the Putin era. Clinton added fuel to the fire by calling for a full investigation of electoral fraud. She observed:

> Russian voters deserve the right to have their voices heard and their votes counted, and that means they deserve free, fair, transparent elections and leaders who are accountable to them.[54]

This is a fair comment, but in conditions where the West had engaged repeatedly in regime change operations under the guise of human rights and democracy, the alarm bells rang in the Kremlin. Clinton was associated with democracy promotion as a mode of regime change, hence Putin appeared to believe that she had in some way sponsored, if not provoked, the protests. He argued:

> From the outset the secretary of state said that [the elections] were not honest and not fair, but she had not yet even received the material from the observers. She set the tone for some actors in our country and gave them a signal. They heard the signal and with the support of the US State Department set to work.

He went on to stress that 'We are the largest nuclear power, and our partners have certain concerns and shake us so that we don't forget who is the master of this planet, so that we remain obedient and feel that they have leverage to influence us within our own country'.[55]

He warned that those who 'dance to the tune of a foreign state' would be held to account. His denunciation set the tone for an anti-American campaign that targeted NGOs funded by Western agencies. The 'foreign agents law' of November 2012, broadly modelled on America's 1938 Foreign Agents Registration Act (FARA), imposed harsh conditions on Russian NGOs engaged in loosely defined political activities drawing on foreign grants. It also provoked the inappropriate harassment of the newly appointed American ambassador, Michael McFaul. One of his first acts in January 2012 was to meet with civil society activists as part of his commitment to engage with Russian society, but this was interpreted as part of the regime change strategy.[56] Clinton thus had a history of sharp antagonism to Putin and his government, and this would shape her response to alleged Russian meddling in the U.S. election. It also suggested a motive for Russian actions, as a way of punishing Clinton. McFaul puts it succinctly: 'For Putin, the 2016 US presidential election was an opportunity for payback. Putin, his intelligence officers, and his surrogates went on the offensive against candidate Clinton and against the US democratic system more generally'.[57] McFaul argues that Putin is motivated not by material or security interests but ideological factors that fail to reckon with the costs of various interventions, in Ukraine and Syria, as well as the United States. However, this view is itself part of the new cold war narrative about Russia. It far too readily discounts more structural approaches to Russian foreign policymaking, which see the country as facing genuine challenges from the expansive and radicalised post-cold war Atlantic power system, which was approaching its borders from several directions.

Clinton also had domestic problems to deal with. On appointment as secretary of state in 2009 she established a private email system in her home in Chappaqua, New York. The State Department set up a classified email account on a secure government server, but for some reason she only used the private server to handle personal and classified emails despite explicit State Department instructions not to do so. The Benghazi congressional investigation discovered its use, and in summer 2014, the investigators demanded access to her emails. After various negotiations, on 5 December she handed over 30,490 emails that she considered work-related, but withheld 31,839, insisting that they were personal and private.[58] The matter became public on 2 March 2015 and dogged her campaign.[59] Matters were exacerbated by the destruction of the emails that she had held back on 25 March, despite congressional instructions to preserve them. The inspector general of the intelligence community referred the matter to the FBI in July to investigate whether 'Clinton had mishandled classified information while using her personal email system'.[60]

The question was not so much whether she had mishandled classified information – she had palpably done so – but 'What was she thinking when she had done this?'[61] In May 2016, the State Department's inspector general concluded that she had violated the Department's policies and protocols. Despite her denials, on 5 July 2016, Comey announced that classified information had in fact been found in 110 emails and 52 chain emails, and over 2,000 additional emails had later been classified as confidential. He judged Clinton's behaviour 'extremely careless' – the term 'gross negligence' was taken out because it carried a specific legal meaning.⁶² One of the Mueller special counsel investigators, Andrew Weissmann, describes Clinton's email use as 'indefensible imperiousness', and harshly condemns Comey's behaviour.⁶³ Nevertheless, assuming the DoJ's prerogatives, Comey terminated the case (we will return to this later).⁶⁴ The FBI officials who exonerated Clinton, notably Andrew McCabe (appointed deputy FBI director on 29 January 2016) and Strzok, became leading exponents of the Russiagate narrative.⁶⁵

The Clinton email issue then intersected with the Russia story. On 12 June, WikiLeaks editor Assange announced in an interview with ITV's Robert Peston that 'We have upcoming leaks in relation to Hillary Clinton . . . we have emails pending publication'.⁶⁶ By then WikiLeaks had published a searchable index of the 30,000 known Clinton emails, so the assumption was that somehow Assange had got hold of copies of the 32,000 deleted emails. However, two days later came the news (in the *Washington Post*, citing two CrowdStrike executives) that DNC computers had been hacked by Russians. Instead of calling in the FBI, the DNC hired CrowdStrike, a computer security company affiliated with the hawkish Atlantic Council. CrowdStrike announced that malware inserted by Russians had been found on the DNC servers. On the same day, Ellen Nakashima, who had been briefed by the DNC,⁶⁷ was the first to report that

> Russian government hackers penetrated the computer network of the Democratic National Committee and gained access to the entire database of opposition research on GOP presidential candidate Donald Trump. . . . The intruders so thoroughly compromised the DNC's system that they were also able to read all email and chat traffic.

Nevertheless, the report argued that 'the breach was traditional espionage' and categorised it as

> an example of Russia's interest in the US political system and its desire to understand the policies, strengths, and weaknesses of a potential future president – much as American spies gather similar information on foreign candidates and leaders.⁶⁸

This may well have been the case, but what was new, according to McCabe, was the weaponisation of information from the DNC 'in a way that we've never seen before'.⁶⁹

CrowdStrike asserted that not one but two groups of hackers, believed to be based in Russia, had undertaken the hack. One was dubbed Cozy Bear (APT29), also known as The Dukes, affiliated with the foreign intelligence service (SVR).⁷⁰ The other was Fancy Bear (APT28), linked to Russian military intelligence (GRU). The two teams had apparently enjoyed a two-year spree in 2014 and 2015 roaming the unclassified email systems at the White House, the State Department and the joint chiefs of Staffs, and it had taken years to repair the damage. Obama at the time decided not to name Russia as the perpetrator, a decision that in the light of Russiagate was later considered a mistake.[71] In 2016, the two teams not only worked independently but were unaware of each other's existence, and even competed for dominance as they scoured the highways and byways of the DNC systems. The SVR team at some point withdrew, and it was the GRU team (Fancy Bear) that apparently made public the hacked DNC emails. CrowdStrike's attribution of Russian government responsibility was not independently verified by the FBI or other federal law enforcement or security agency.[72] The DNC's IT director, Yared Tamene Wolde Yohannes, testified to the House Permanent Select Committee on Intelligence (HPSCI), then under the leadership of the Republican, Devin Nunes, that the FBI never requested access to the physical servers, while Michael Sussmann, the DNC's outside counsel, told the same committee that the FBI refused a DNC offer for full access to its servers.[73] This directly contradicts Comey when he told the Senate Intelligence Committee in January 2017 that there had been 'multiple requests at different levels' for access to the DNC servers, and he agreed with the question posed by the committee chairman Richard Burr that direct access to the servers and devices would have helped the FBI investigation: 'Our forensics folks would always prefer to get access to the original device or server that's involved, so it's the best evidence'.[74] Yohannes stated that the DNC gave images of its servers to CrowdStrike, who in turn passed them on to the FBI in May and June 2016, and these were then used by Mueller, along with grand jury materials (redacted in his report) to demonstrate that Russian hackers stole the DNC emails. Quite why no federal agency subjected the DNC servers (apparently, there were 140 of them) to forensic analysis remains one of the great mysteries of Russiagate.[75] Even stranger, it later emerged that CrowdStrike never produced a full final report for the government, because the FBI never asked for one – something that Comey was hard put to explain.[76]

This was the context in which Clinton's struggle for the Democratic nomination encountered serious competition from Sanders. He won an astonishing twenty-three primaries and put up a spirited fight to the end. American voters were clearly looking for an alternative, and even socialism appeared to be back on the agenda.[77] On 22 July 2016, WikiLeaks published 19,252 DNC emails with 8,000 attachments of communications between key actors, covering the period from January 2015 to May 2016. The DNC material showed how top Democratic Party officials 'were attempting to undermine Sanders' entire campaign in order to secure the party's nomination even before 'she [Clinton] began to pull ahead of Bernie in the primary votes'. Free notes,

'This issue alone cemented her untrustworthiness as president, but it spawned many others to vote for her volatile counterpart to prove a point'. The slanted light it shed on the Democrats 'caused the entire party to buckle in on itself and uproar. And it is this buckling that would give the Republican Party the fuel it needed to win'.[78]

In the days before the Democratic National Convention in Philadelphia, 25–28 July, the Clinton campaign and its press allies 'saw Russia as a potentially valuable weapon for attacking Trump'.[79] Paul Krugman in *The New York Times* talked of 'Donald Trump, The Siberian Candidate', and asked 'If elected, would Donald Trump be Vladimir Putin's man in the White House?'[80] Two days after the WikiLeaks release, on 24 July Clinton campaign manager Robby Mook went on the major television news stations to claim not only that Russia was behind the hack but also that the Trump campaign was in league with Russia, citing various unnamed 'experts', who were later proved wrong.[81] On CNN he stated, 'What's disturbing to us is that experts are telling us Russian state actors broke into the DNC, stole these emails, and other experts are now saying that the Russians are releasing these emails for the purpose of actually helping Donald Trump'.[82] The next day, the *New York Times* noted that 'the Russian intervention narrative fits with Mrs. Clinton efforts to establish the idea that President Vladimir V. Putin of Russia wants to see Mr. Trump elected to weaken America and hurt its closest NATO allies'.[83] Mook also claimed that 'Donald Trump changed the Republican platform to become what some experts would regard as pro-Russian', which was also false.[84] Clinton's formal nomination as the party's candidate on 26 July did not put an end to the matter, and some Sanders' supporters felt betrayed by the Democratic Party machine and only reluctantly supported Clinton's campaign. Free details the DNC's apparent malfeasance and suggests that once Trump became the Republican nominee, 'Sanders was the only one set up to beat Donald Trump, and that Hillary Clinton didn't stand a chance'. Free is obviously a Sanders supporter, but insists that Clinton's defeat was not a 'gender situation' but reflected the deeper currents in American political life. Trump's invocation of the 'silent majority' appealed to real constituencies and concerns, 'and this is what the Democratic Party overlooked'.[85]

The larger context did not help. His cautious approach to the deployment of American power in Syria 'lowered Obama's standing within the hawkish Washington establishment'. It was infuriated when, despite his red line against the use of chemical weapons, he refused to order air strikes against Syria following a chemical attack in Ghouta, in the suburbs of Damascus, in the early hours of 21 August 2013. 'Simmering frustration at Obama's inaction and America's seeming impotence while Putin acted decisively and effectively was like dry kindling waiting for a match'. The spark was the publication of the DNC material showing bias against Sanders. Instead of contrition, the Democrat establishment went on the offensive: 'Journalists who backed Clinton quickly tried to turn attention from the embarrassing emails to the idea of "a Kremlin conspiracy to aid Donald J. Trump"'.[86] WikiLeaks was vilified as an instrument of the Kremlin, although the connection is at best circumstantial. WikiLeaks was created by Assange as an outlet for leaked documents, and it published classified intelligence material and diplomatic cables.[87] Bradley (later Chelsea) Manning, an intelligence analyst stationed in Iraq, downloaded 750,000 classified diplomatic and military files onto a thumb drive and handed them over. From November 2010, WikiLeaks published some 250,000 U.S. diplomatic cables taken from Clinton's State Department, which if nothing else turned her against the platform. In 2013, Edward Snowden, a contract worker in an outsourced facility, exposed the inner workings of the National Security Agency (NSA) and how it bulk-collected metadata about the phone calls and emails of millions of Americans – what he calls 'surveillance capitalism'.[88] Russia had nothing to do with any of this, yet the official American view is that WikiLeaks is a 'non-state hostile intelligence service'.[89] Assange defended his position: 'If it's true information, we don't care where it comes from. Let people fight with the truth, and when the bodies are cleared there will be bullets of truth everywhere'.[90]

Assange in 2012 hosted twelve episodes of 'The World Tomorrow' on RT (formerly Russia Today, the TV channel established in 2005 to advance Russian perspectives internationally), airing from the Ecuadorian embassy in London. It was produced separately, but RT was the only channel willing to broadcast the show. In the eyes of his critics, this turned Assange into little more than a 'useful idiot' for Moscow, and later justified assertions of collusion between RT and WikiLeaks.[91] Assange took refuge in the embassy in 2012 to avoid facing rape charges in Sweden, which he believed were politically motivated to ensure his extradition to the United States. WikiLeaks was condemned by governments because of its exposures, 'including of the US-UK "special relationship" in running a joint foreign policy of deception and violence that serves London and Washington's elite interests'. For example, files released by WikiLeaks in 2016 from the Clinton archive show William Burns, the U.S. deputy secretary of state (and later Joseph Biden's director of the CIA), talking with the British foreign secretary, William Hague, about a 'post-Qaddafi' Libya, three weeks before military operations began. There was clear intent to overthrow Colonel Muammar Qaddafi, with the 17 March 2011 UN Resolution 1973 on protecting civilians used as cover.[92] Although WikiLeaks is routinely accused of working with Russia, no evidence has emerged of any active collusion with Russian agents. As for RT, it was designated a 'foreign agent' in November 2017, leading the network to be banned from press events and its delisting from social media.

Assange certainly distrusted Clinton. He warned in February 2016 that

> 'A vote for Hillary Clinton is a vote for endless, stupid war', and he blamed her for the mess in Libya: 'Hillary's problem is not just that she's a war hawk. She's a war hawk with bad judgment who gets an unseemly emotional rush out of killing people. She shouldn't be let near a gun shop, let alone an army. And she certainly should not become president of the United States'.[93]

The feeling was mutual, and Clinton supporters claimed that WikiLeaks and Assange were little more than Russian stooges. Once WikiLeaks started publishing the DNC material, Assange denied that Russia was involved and warned that

> the natural instincts of Hillary Clinton and the people round her, that when confronted with a serious domestic political scandal, that she tries to blame the Russians, blame the Chinese, et cetera, because if she does that when she's in government, that's a political, managerial style that can lead to conflict.[94]

Assange repeatedly asserted that Russia had nothing to do with the emails, telling Fox News on 3 January 2017 that 'our source is not the Russian government or any state party'.[95] WikiLeaks has not been noticeably soft on Moscow, publishing tens of thousands of documents critical of the Russian government while defending opposition activists. In 2017, it published Spy Files Russia, exposing Moscow's surveillance practices.

As the campaign entered its final stages, on 26 September, thousands of Clinton's emails were discovered on a laptop owned by Anthony Weiner, the estranged husband of Huma Abedin, Clinton's close assistant. We have seen that in 2014 Clinton turned over the emails on her private server to the FBI but deleted another 30,000 (the possible resurrection of which fuelled much speculation), but now thousands of new emails from her personal domain were found. The investigation was mismanaged, falling between the FBI's Washington and New York offices, and Comey was only informed about them on 27 October.[96] The next day, he sent a letter to Congress (which was promptly leaked) announcing that he was reopening the Clinton investigation. He believed that he either had to 'speak or conceal'.[97] In his characteristically sententious manner, Comey felt that 'the credibility of the institutions of justice was at stake'.[98] This went against the fundamental FBI principle of no public action before an election that could affect its outcome. In any case, there were more options than the binary choice he suggested.[99]

Having publicly judged the case on 5 July, he felt that he was locked on the path that led to the 28 October announcement. This may well have cost Clinton the presidency.[100] At the time Clinton was 5.9 points ahead of Trump, but a week later her lead had shrunk to just 2.9 per cent as the email issue dominated the news. On 6 November, the FBI announced that its investigation was complete, and Clinton was once again exonerated. By then, it was too late. Pollsters suggest that it was this, rather than the dark arts of Russian persuasion, that swung the vote in Michigan, Pennsylvania, Wisconsin and Florida, and possibly also North Carolina and Arizona. Comey believes that he acted honourably, but his judgement is suspect. His motivation is also open to question. He took it for granted that Clinton's victory was in the bag so acted to get the revived email issue out of the way before she assumed office. This spectacular miscalculation opened the door to Trump.

System Shock

It is hard to exaggerate the shock that Trump's election delivered to the post-war world order. With little experience in politics, Trump brought to the conduct of domestic and international affairs the brutality and disregard for standard procedures and norms that characterised his work as a businessman. As he put it in his *The Art of the Deal*, 'You can't be imaginative or entrepreneurial if you've got too much structure. I prefer to come to work each day and just see what develops'.[101] What may have served him well in business (and there are doubts about that) was not an approach conducive to good governance. Equally, what had made Trump such a success in *The Apprentice* was his 'impulse to transgress', but his presidency evoked 'a painful feeling of dispossession, as cherished norms and national institutions are eviscerated'.[102] Trump 'loved conflicts, chaos, and confusion; he loved seeing people argue or fight'.[103] Omarosa notes that Trump had 'more power than one man should have, and definitely not a man who has the soul of an anarchist'.[104] His presidency became the greatest show on earth as the society of the spectacle waited for the next sensation.[105]

With Trump's inauguration on 20 January 2017 'the United States entered the eye of the most extraordinary political storm since at least Watergate'.[106] Levitsky and Ziblatt argue that 'Democracies may die at the hands not of generals but of elected leaders – presidents or prime ministers who subvert the very process that brought them to power'.[107] Frum eloquently describes the threat:

> The thing to fear from the Trump presidency is not the bold overthrow of the Constitution, but the stealthy paralysis of governance; not the open defiance of law, but an accumulating subversion of norms; not the deployment of state power to intimidate dissidents, but the incitement of private violence to radicalize supporters.[108]

The election of a man who could barely complete a coherent sentence, and even then overloaded his syntax with adjectives and adverbs – 'great', 'huge', 'horrible', 'beautiful', 'bigly' – was so shocking that it prompted the search for some external cause. There had to be a villain commensurate with the gravity of the crisis. Nothing else but Russia, the historic cold war enemy, would do. Parts of the American elite went into overdrive: 'What could arguably be called the greatest intelligence operation in the history of the world had been executed and the result was that the candidate Moscow had supported had won'. Putin's political mission 'had successfully influenced the American public's mindset so deeply that they were in total denial that it had been done at all' – the best trick of the devil is to convince you he doesn't exist.[109] Trump's election was an event so unlikely, 'so utterly extreme' as Joshua Green puts it in his study of Steve Bannon, only some sort of Hollywood-like revelation could explain the mystery; but 'the revelation never arrived. Even now, there's a sense that some vital piece of the puzzle is missing'.[110] In the end, it was the Russian interference narrative that filled the revelation gap and completed the puzzle.

In fact, the key to Clinton's defeat lay much closer to home. 'By the time she launched her 2016 campaign, Bannon was sitting at the nexus of a far-flung group of conspirators whose scope and reach Clinton and her campaign didn't fathom until far too late'.[111] In 1998, Clinton condemned the machinations of a 'vast right-wing conspiracy', but when confronted by precisely such a conspiracy, she placed the blame elsewhere, exacerbating the 'paranoid style' and McCarthyite practices in American politics. To do otherwise would have risked tearing at the foundations of the American polity as it had developed in the neoliberal years, for which the Clintons were so deeply responsible. Similarly, the 'remain' campaign in the Brexit vote only realised far too late that they were trying to reverse in weeks what had in effect been decades of unchallenged anti-EU propaganda. They were ranged against sophisticated U.S.-financed electoral analytics, but they too chased after the chimera of 'Russian meddling'. In both the United Kingdom and the United States, the events of 2016 put an end to the long post-war consensus and opened up a new world of chaos and conspiracy. In both countries, rational policy analysis gave way to the search for some deeper purpose. A large part of the electorate did not believe that Clinton would deliver on her promises, while Trump proposed a re-affirmation of elements of national identity that were perceived to have been denigrated by coastal elites and establishment interests. Clinton proposed policies, but Trump offered meaning.

Trump assumed office in remarkably benign times, although his 'American carnage' inaugural address (drafted by Bannon) cast matters in a dark light. The American economy had recovered from the sub-prime financial crisis of 2008 and thereafter registered impressive growth, the stock market was booming, inflation and unemployment were low, and although America was still engaged in Afghanistan, its longest war ever, and in conflicts in Iraq and Syria, none immediately threatened the United States itself. The election gave Trump a united party government, with Republican majorities in both the House of Representatives (241 to 194) and the Senate (52 to 48).[112] Despite the fortunate circumstances, Trump's early period was beset by permanent crisis. The Russiagate allegation hung like an incubus over all that he did, and he would later claim that his first two years in office were stolen because of the allegations.

Trump's rampage through the institutions of American democracy and the customs of international affairs was by any standard awesome. In international affairs, Trump led the putative defection of the United States from the liberal international order that it created after 1945. Many of the ideas advanced by Trump had been raised in one way or another by American leaders before him, including the need for greater 'burden-sharing' in NATO, but none fundamentally challenged the network of multilateral institutions and bilateral relations that are foundational for U.S. foreign policy. A traditional view of internationalism defeated Woodrow Wilson's attempts to create a multilateral world order in the wake of World War I and kept the United States out of the League of Nations. After 1945, a new breed of internationalists understood that American power would be enhanced by embedding it in institutions representing universal values of law and development.[113] After 1989, this system took the form of intensified globalisation, allowing China and some other countries to achieve a spectacular rise in prosperity and power. Trump now sought to disassociate American great power globalism from economic globalisation through the policy of 'America first'.

Bannon was the only Trump insider able 'to offer a coherent vision of Trump's populism – aka Trumpism'.[114] At the Conservative Political Action Conference (CPAC) in February 2017, Bannon announced the three strands of Trump's policy: national security and sovereignty; economic nationalism; and, for the first time, 'the deconstruction of the administrative state'.[115] However, a few months later, the two had fallen out – in part because of Wolff's book, which portrayed Bannon as an intriguer of the worst sort, promiscuously leaking against Kushner and Trump's daughter Ivanka – whom he dubbed 'Jarvanka' – and Bannon was cut loose on 19 August 2017. Trump was particularly annoyed by Bannon's claim that he was 'Trump's brain'.[116] Green's book quotes freely from Bannon and basically credits him for winning the election, which did not go down well with the proud and jealous Trump.[117] After the initial shock of victory, Trump lacked any 'larger sense of sober reflection', and 'he immediately seemed to rewrite himself as the inevitable president'.[118] This was rather less than a personal relationship with history or even a sense of destiny, but the presumption of a man whose narcissism overwhelmed the most responsible office on the planet. As for Russia, it looks for allies where it can find them. If that meant taking Trump at his word that it 'made sense' to 'get on with Russia', then of course Moscow would not reject the opportunity. Against the background of collusion allegations, this proved provocative, verging on the seditious.

NOTES

1. Michael Cohen, *Disloyal—A Memoir: The True Story of the Former Personal Attorney to President Donald J. Trump* (New York, Skyhorse Publishing, 2020), p. 219.
2. Cohen, *Disloyal*, pp. 220–1.
3. Patrick Radden Keefe, 'How Mark Burnett Resurrected Donald Trump as an Icon of American Success', *New Yorker*, 7 January 2019, https://www.newyorker.com/magazine/2019/01/07/how-mark-burnett-resurrected-donald-trump-as-an-icon-of-american-success.
4. Joshua Green, *Devil's Bargain: Steve Bannon, Donald Trump, and the Storming of the Presidency* (Melbourne/London, Scribe, 2017), p. 236. The element of surprise is reflected in many other works, notably in the powerful insider account by KT McFarland, *Revolution: Trump, Washington and 'We the People'* (New York, Post Hill Press, 2020), pp. 3, 137 and *passim*.
5. Steven E. Schier and Todd E. Eberly, *The Trump Presidency: Outsider in the Oval Office* (Lanham, MD, Rowman & Littlefield, 2017), pp. 2, 3.
6. Cohen, *Disloyal*, p. 223.
7. McFarland, *Revolution*, p. 5.
8. Steven E. Schier and Todd E. Eberly, *Polarized: The Rise of Ideology in American Politics* (Lanham, MD, Rowman & Littlefield, 2016), p. 6; but see p. 61 for a challenge to the 'sorting' argument, the view that America is dividing along ideological lines.
9. Schier and Eberly, *The Trump Presidency*, pp. 4, 6.
10. Omarosa Manigault Newman, *Unhinged: An Insider's Account of the Trump White House* (London, Simon & Schuster, 2018), p. 160.
11. For analysis of this view, see Jan-Werner Müller, 'Capitalism in One Family', *London Review of Books*, 1 December 2016, pp. 10–14, and for a full study see his *What is Populism?* (London, Penguin, 2017).
12. For analysis, see Eric Kaufmann, *Whiteshift: Populism, Immigration and the Future of White Majorities* (London, Allen Lane, 2018).
13. Jon Herbert, Trevor McCrisken and Andrew Wroe, *The Ordinary Presidency of Donald J. Trump* (London, Palgrave Macmillan, 2019).
14. Ronald F. Inglehart, *Cultural Evolution: People's Motivations are Changing, and Reshaping the World* (Cambridge, Cambridge University Press, 2018), p. 181.
15. McFarland, *Revolution*, pp. 15, 20.

16. Pippa Norris and Ronald Inglehart, *Cultural Backlash: Trump, Brexit, and Authoritarian Populism* (Cambridge, Cambridge University Press, 2019), p. 3.
17. Norris and Inglehart, *Cultural Backlash*, p. 4.
18. Norris and Inglehart, *Cultural Backlash*, pp. 139, 362–3 and *passim*.
19. Analysed by Norris and Inglehart, *Cultural Backlash*, pp. 331–67.
20. Norris and Inglehart, *Cultural Backlash*, p. 341.
21. For his loyalist account of the campaign, see Corey R. Lewandowski and David N. Bossie, *Let Trump be Trump: The Inside Story of his Rise to the Presidency* (New York and Nashville, Center Street, 2017). For an unflattering portrait of Lewandowski, see Cohen, *Disloyal*, pp. 214–15 and *passim*.
22. Richard Sakwa, *Frontline Ukraine: Crisis in the Borderlands* (London and New York, I. B. Tauris, 2016).
23. Craig Unger, *House of Trump, House of Putin: The Untold Story of Trump and the Russian Mafia* (London, Bantam Press, 2018), p. 186.
24. The quotation comes from Bob Woodward, *Fear: Trump in the White House* (London & New York, Simon & Schuster, 2018), p. 9.
25. Lewandowski and Bossie, *Let Trump be Trump*, pp. 120, 140–4.
26. Lewandowski and Bossie, *Let Trump be Trump*, p. 100; p. 95 on the demand for change.
27. Lewandowski and Bossie, *Let Trump be Trump*, p. 104.
28. Lewandowski and Bossie, *Let Trump be Trump*, p. 154.
29. Woodward, *Fear*, p. 23.
30. Lewandowski and Bossie, *Let Trump be Trump*, p. 175.
31. Woodward, *Rage*, p. 269.
32. Schier and Eberly, *The Trump Presidency*, p. 94.
33. David Frum, *Trumpocracy: The Corruption of the American Republic* (New York, Harper, 2018), p. xv.
34. Frum, *Trumpocracy*, p. 38.
35. Frum, *Trumpocracy*, p. 2.
36. David Smith, 'Unholy Alliance: President Delivers for Religious Right', *Guardian*, 14 May 2019, p. 31.
37. For an introduction to the main issues, see Adrian Pabst, *Liberal World Order and its Critics: Civilisational States and Cultural Commonwealths* (London, Routledge, 2018).
38. Peter Thiel, Speech at the National Press Club, Washington, DC, 31 October 2016, https://www.realclearpolitics.com/video/2016/10/31/peter_thiel_what_trump_represents_isnt_crazy_and_its_not_going_away.html.
39. Steven Rosefielde, *Trump's Populist America* (London, World Scientific Publishing, 2017).
40. For a good analysis of the various foreign trends in the party, see Colin Dueck, *Hard Line: The Republican Party and US Foreign Policy since World War II* (Princeton, NJ, Princeton University Press, 2010).
41. Robert Costa, Philip Rucker and Dan Balz, 'Donald Trump Plots his Second Act', *Washington Post*, 7 October 2015, https://washngtonpost.com/politics/donal

d-trump-plots-his-second-act/2015/10/06/305790c2-6c68-11e5-9bfe-e59f5e244f92_story.html.

42. Daniel Quinn Mills and Steven Rosefielde, *The Trump Phenomenon and the Future of US Foreign Policy* (London, World Scientific Publishing, 2017).

43. Rein Müllerson, 'Donald Trump – Not an American Deng Xiaoping, Maybe its Gorbachev?', *Valdai Club*, 9 August 2018, http://valdaiclub.com/a/highlights/not-an-american-deng-xiaoping/.

44. McFarland, *Revolution*, p. 129.

45. Michael Nelson, *Trump's First Year* (Charlottesville, University of Virginia Press, 2018), p. 16.

46. McCarthy, *Ball of Collusion*, pp. 10–16 gives details.

47. Peter Schweizer, *Clinton Cash: The Untold Story of How and Why Foreign Governments and Businesses Helped Make Bill and Hillary Rich* (New York, Harper Paperbacks, 2014/2016). Steve Bannon appears to have been involved in the book's production.

48. Nelson, *Trump's First Year*, p. 19.

49. Benjamin Free, *Hillary Clinton Shattered: How Donald Trump Shattered Hillary Clinton and the Democratic Party* (Google Books, June 2017), no page numbers.

50. Free, *Hillary Clinton Shattered*.

51. A persistent, if not obsessive, theme in Hillary Rodham Clinton, *Hard Choices: a Memoir* (New York, Simon & Schuster, 2014).

52. David S. Foglesong, 'Putin: From Soulmate to Archenemy', *Raritan*, Vol. 38, No. 1, Summer 2018, p. 18.

53. See Richard Sakwa, *Putin* Redux*: Power and Contradiction in Contemporary Russia* (London & New York, Routledge, 2014), pp. 111–33.

54. Reuters, 'US Voices "Serious Concerns" about Russia Vote', 5 December 2011, https://www.reuters.com/article/us-usa-russia-whitehouse/u-s-voices-serious-concerns-about-russia-vote-idUSTRE7B42GK20111205.

55. Ellen Barry, 'Rally Defying Putin's Party Draws Tens of Thousands', *New York Times*, 10 December 2011, https://www.nytimes.com/2011/12/11/world/europe/thousands-protest-in-moscow-russia-in-defiance-of-putin.html. See also 'Russia PM Vladimir Putin Accuses US over Poll Protests', BBC News, 8 December 2011.

56. Putin later defended this, arguing 'I can hardly imagine the Ambassador of the Russian Federation to the US actively working with members of the "Occupy Wall Street Movement"', 'Interview to Channel One and Associated Press News Agency', Kremlin.ru, 4 September 2013, http://eng.kremlin.ru/news/5935.

57. Michael McFaul, 'Putin, Putinism, and the Domestic Determinants of Russian Foreign Policy', *International Security*, Vol. 45, No. 2, Fall 2020, p. 134.

58. Jarrett, *The Russia Hoax*, p. 5.

59. Michael S. Schmidt, 'Hillary Clinton Used Personal Email Account on State Dept., Possibly Breaking Rules', *New York Times*, 2 March 2015.

60. James Comey, *A Higher Loyalty: Truth, Lies, and Leadership* (London, Macmillan, 2018), p. 161.

61. Comey, *Higher Loyalty*, p. 163.

62. Strzok, *Compromised*, p. 90. Greg Miller, *The Apprentice: Trump, Russia and the Subversion of American Democracy* (New York, William Collins, 2018), p. 142. Andrew McCabe, *The Threat: How the FBI Protects America in the Age of Terror and Trump* (New York, St Martin's Press, 2019), p. 187 notes that the statement was written by Comey and after editing was entered on Strzok's computer. The conspiratorial allegations in this case are mistaken.

63. Andrew Weissmann, *Where Law Ends: Inside the Mueller Investigation* (New York, Random House, 2020), pp. 41, 51–55 and *passim*.

64. For full details, see Jarrett, *The Russia Hoax*, pp. 21–46.

65. Jarrett, *The Russia Hoax*, p. 46.

66. Mark Tran, 'WikiLeaks to Publish More Hillary Clinton Emails – Julian Assange', *Guardian*, 12 June 2016, https://www.theguardian.com/media/2016/jun/12/wikileaks-to-publish-more-hillary-clinton-emails-julian-assange.

67. Senate Committee on Intelligence, *Report on Russian Active Measures Campaigns and Interference in the 2016 US Election*, Vol. 3, *Government Response to Russian Activities* (Washington, DC, US Senate, 6 February 2020), p. 5.

68. Ellen Nakashima, 'Russian Government Hackers Penetrated DNC', *Washington Post*, 14 June 2016.

69. Senate Committee on Intelligence, *Report*, Vol. 3, p. 10.

70. APT29 is sometimes mistakenly linked with the domestic security service, the FSB. In 2014 Dutch intelligence identified nearly a dozen FSB hackers working out of an anonymous building near Moscow University, but this appears to be a separate operation.

71. David E. Sanger, 'Russian Hackers Broke into Federal Agencies, US Officials Suspect', *New York Times*, 13 December 2020, https://www.nytimes.com/2020/12/13/us/politics/russian-hackers-us-government-treasury-commerce.html.

72. In his Congressional testimony on 8 June 2017, Comey admitted that the FBI 'did not have access to the devices themselves. We got relevant forensic information from a private party, a high class entity, that had done the work but we didn't get direct access', 'Full Text: James Comey Testimony Transcript on Trump and Russia', *Politico*, 8 June 2017, https://www.politico.com/story/2017/06/08/full-text-james-comey-trump-russia-testimony-239295.

73. House Permanent Select Committee on Intelligence (HPSCI), *Russia Investigation Transcripts and Documents*, 'Interview of Yared Tamene Wolde-Yohannes', 30 August 2017, https://intelligence.house.gov/uploadedfiles/ty54.pdf; 'Interview of Michael Sussmann', 18 December 2017, https://intelligence.house.gov/uploadedfiles/ms53.pdf.

74. Emily Schultheis, 'FBI Director Comey: Agency Requested Access to DNC Servers', *CBS News*, 10 January 2017, https://www.cbsnews.com/news/fbi-director-comey-agency-requested-access-to-dnc-servers/.

75. Thomas Rid (who gives the 140 figure) argues that access to a physical server is not required for a forensic examination, 'What Mueller Knows about the DNC Hack—And Trump Doesn't', *Politico*, 17 July 2018, https://www.politico.com/magazine/story/2018/07/17/dnc-server-hack-russia-trump-2016-219017.

76. Ray McGovern, 'FBI Never Saw CrowdStrike Unredacted or Final Report on Alleged Russian Hacking Because None was Produced', *Consortium News*, 17 June 2019, https://consortiumnews.com/2019/06/17/fbi-never-saw-crowdstrike-unredacted-or-final-report-on-alleged-russian-hacking-because-none-was-produced/.

77. John Nichols, 'Socialism is More Popular than you Think, Mr President', *The Nation*, 6 February 2019, https://www.thenation.com/article/socialism-sotu-donald-trump-bernie-sanders/.

78. Free, *Hillary Clinton Shattered*.

79. Byron York, 'Retrospective: Mueller and the Fatal Flaw of the Trump-Russia Affair', *Washington Examiner*, 29 May 2019, https://www.washingtonexaminer.com/opinion/columnists/byron-york-retrospective-mueller-and-the-fatal-flaw-of-the-trump-russia-affair.

80. Paul Krugman, 'Donald Trump, The Siberian Candidate', *New York Times*, 22 July 2016, https://www.nytimes.com/2016/07/22/opinion/donald-trump-the-siberian-candidate.html.

81. Patrick Lawrence, 'Shades of the Cold War: How the DNC Fabricated a Russian Hacker Conspiracy to Deflect Blame for its Email Scandal', *Salon*, 25 July 2016, http://patricklawrence.us/shades-cold-war-dnc-fabricated-russian-hacker-conspiracy-deflect-blame-email-scandal/.

82. Eric Bradner, 'Clinton's Campaign Manager: Russia Helping Trump', *CNN*, 24 July 2016, https://edition.cnn.com/2016/07/24/politics/robby-mook-russia-dnc-emails-trump/index.html.

83. Todd Heisler, 'Democrats Allege DNC Hack is Part of Russian Effort to Elect Donald Trump', *New York Times*, 25 July 2016, https://www.nytimes.com/2016/07/26/us/politics/democrats-allege-dnc-hack-is-part-of-russian-effort-to-elect-donald-trump.html.

84. York, 'Retrospective'.

85. Free, *Hillary Clinton Shattered*.

86. Foglesong, 'Putin', p. 36.

87. For a detailed portrait, see Raffi Khatchadourian, 'Julian Assange, a Man Without a Country', *New Yorker*, 21 August 2017, https://www.newyorker.com/magazine/2017/08/21/julian-assange-a-man-without-a-country.

88. Edward Snowden, *Permanent Record* (London, Macmillan, 2019), p. 5. See pp. 267ff. for how the Five Eyes moved into the era of mass surveillance.

89. Brian Bennett, 'CIA Chief calls WikiLeaks "Non-State Hostile Intelligence Service"', *Los Angeles Times*, 13 April 2018, https://www.latimes.com/politics/washington/la-na-essential-washington-updates-pompeo-are-you-sure-trump-1492114120-htmlstory.html.

90. Khatchadourian, 'Julian Assange'.

91. Strzok, *Compromised*, p. 51.

92. Mark Curtis, 'WikiLeaks' Legacy of Exposing US-UK Complicity', *Consortium News*, Vol. 24, No. 302, 29 October 2018, https://consortiumnews.com/2018/10/27/wikileaks-legacy-of-exposing-us-uk-complicity/.

93. Malcolm Nance, *The Plot to Hack America: How Putin's Cyberspies and WikiLeaks Tried to Steal the 2016 Election*, 2nd edn (New York, Skyhorse Publishing, 2016), p. 119; Isikoff, and Corn, *Russian Roulette*, p. 132.

94. Matthew Chance, 'Julian Assange: "A Lot More Material" Coming on US Elections', CNN, 26 July 2016, https://edition.cnn.com/2016/07/26/politics/julian-assange-dnc-email-leak-hack/index.html.

95. Sean Hannity, 'Julian Assange: Our Source is Not the Russian Government', *Fox News*, 3 January 2017, https://www.realclearpolitics.com/video/2017/01/02/assange_to_hannity_our_source_was_not_the_russian_government.html.

96. Jeffrey Toobin, *True Crimes and Misdemeanors: The Investigation of Donald Trump* (London, Bodley Head, 2020), p. 25.

97. This is the title of his chapter on the subject, Comey, *Higher Loyalty*, pp. 188–210. McCabe disagreed with Comey's decision to go public on the eve of the election, *The Threat*, pp. 194–6.

98. Comey, *Higher Loyalty*, p. 195.

99. Weissmann, *Where Law Ends*, p. 54.

100. Strzok, *Compromised*, p. 172; Toobin, *True Crimes*, p. 28.

101. Donald J. Trump with Tony Schwartz, *Trump: The Art of the Deal* (London, Arrow, 2016), p. 1. Schwarz wrote the book and later argued that it should have been called *The Sociopath*, Martin Pengelly, 'Trump "Writing the Book of all Books" – But it May Never Get Printed', *Guardian*, 16 June 2021, p. 2.

102. Keefe, 'How Mark Burnett Resurrected Donald Trump'.

103. Omarosa, *Unhinged*, p. 29.

104. Omarosa, *Unhinged*, p. 259. McFarland also notes that Trump 'thrives on taking risks', *Revolution*, p. 38.

105. See Guy Debord, *Society of the Spectacle* (London, Rebel Press, 1994), originally published in 1967.

106. Michael Wolff, *Fire and Fury: Inside the Trump White House* (London, Little, Brown, 2018), p. ix.

107. Steven Levitsky and Daniel Ziblatt, *How Democracies Die* (New York, Viking, 2018), p. 3.

108. Frum, *Trumpocracy*, p. xi.

109. Malcolm Nance, *The Plot to Destroy Democracy: How Putin and his Spies are Undermining America and Dismantling the West* (New York, Hachette Books, 2018), p. 7.

110. Green, *Devil's Bargain*, p. 20.

111. Green, *Devil's Bargain*, p. 21.

112. Nelson, *Trump's First Year*, p. 7.

113. Stephen Wertheim, *Tomorrow, the World: The Birth of US Global Supremacy* (Cambridge, Belknap Press, 2020).

114. Wolff, *Fire and Fury*, p. 31.

115. Wolff, *Fire and Fury*, p. 133.

116. Wolff, *Fire and Fury*, p. 143.

117. Wolff, *Fire and Fury*, p. 289.

118. Wolff, *Fire and Fury*, p. 34.

Chapter 3

Trump and Russia

Trump's presidency was the greatest deception of all. It was always rather ridiculous but also very serious.[1] It was unable to deliver much of its domestic agenda, and in foreign policy it failed to achieve the rethinking of grand strategy that it promised. The new cold war intensified and relations with Russia plummeted to new depths. However, personal relations between Trump and Putin remained cordial, which only deepened the suspicions of his critics. Russia cast a shadow over his entire presidency. Roger Ailes, the former head of Fox News and onetime political mentor to Bannon, warned Trump shortly after the election, 'You've got to get right on Russia', warning him of potentially damaging material on its way. Wolff comments as follows:

> The charge that Trump colluded with the Russians to win the election, which he scoffed at, was, in the estimation of some of his friends, a perfect example of his inability to connect the dots. Even if he hadn't personally conspired with the Russians to fix the election, his efforts to curry favour with, of all people, Vladimir Putin had no doubt left a trail of alarming words and deeds likely to have enormous political costs.[2]

No one in the Trump White House was prepared to deal with the collusion charge. Trump 'regarded the Russia story as senseless and inexplicable and having no basis in reality'.[3] Bannon himself dismissed it as 'just a conspiracy theory', adding for good measure that the Trump team was not up to conspiring about anything.[4]

Chapter 3

TRUMP GOES TO MOSCOW

Craig Unger provides the most detailed analysis of the possible *kompromat* held by Russia on Trump. He tells the story of

> one of the greatest intelligence operations in history, an undertaking decades in the making, through which Russian Mafia and Russian intelligence operatives successfully targeted, compromised, and implanted either a wilfully ignorant or an inexplicably unaware Russian asset in the White House as the most powerful man on earth.[5]

In a later work unsparingly called *American Kompromat,* he recounts the charge by ex-KGB colonel Yuri Shvets, who was posted to Washington in the 1980s, that in fact Trump had been a KGB asset for forty years.[6] Is this really the case?

The story begins with Trump's marriage to a Czechoslovak citizen when the country was part of the Soviet bloc. Trump met Ivana Zelníčková at the Montreal Olympic Games in August 1976, and they were married on 7 April 1977. Ivana, an only child, was a talented athlete, a member of the Czechoslovak ski team at the Sapporo Winter Olympics in 1972, and then a top model. The couple visited the bride's homeland in 1978. Not surprisingly, this prompted the interests of the Czechoslovak Ministry of State Security, the StB, and a file was opened on her, as well as her father Miloš, an electrical engineer. The StB would naturally share information with the KGB, but it is not known when a Soviet file was opened on Trump.[7] One can assume that between his business ventures, politics was discussed at home, and Ivana provided an insight into life in the communist world. This was the grim period of 'normalisation' in Czechoslovakia, still suffering the effects of the Soviet-bloc invasion of August 1968, which had snuffed out the few months of 'socialism with a human face'. Nevertheless, his marriage helped 'normalise' Trump's perception of Eastern Europe. His third wife, Melania Knauss (Knavs), also comes from the region, from Slovenia.

Gorbachev came to power in March 1985, and soon after launched a radical programme of *perestroika* (restructuring), *glasnost'* (openness) and then *demokratizatsiya* (democratisation), and Trump showed a renewed interest in politics. Hitherto Trump had focused on getting politicians to bend to his will, a task entrusted to his pugnacious lawyer Roy Cohn, who Trump admits 'was no Boy Scout'. Cohn spent 'more than two-thirds of his adult life under indictment on one charge or another'.[8] Cohn was the hatchet man for Senator Joseph McCarthy in an earlier version of Russiagate, leading the hunt against communists in the 1950s. With reform under way in the Soviet Union, in March 1986 Trump met the Soviet ambassador to the UN, Yuri Dubinin, and his daughter Natalia Dubinina, who was already a member of the Soviet UN delegation. This was Yuri's first visit to New York, so Natalia took him on a tour of the city. He was so impressed by Trump Tower on Fifth Avenue at 57th Street that he asked to see the owner. The building occupied the site of the former Bonwit Teller luxury department store. Construction began in June 1980, and two-and-a-half years later, the 58-storey (although Trump insists it has 68 floors) skyscraper was complete, with a spectacular atrium and waterfall, trimmed in bronze and gold, six floors of shopping, thousands of square feet of office space and 263 residential apartments (many of them bought by wealthy Russians, some with dubious backgrounds). Ignoring diplomatic protocol, they took the lift and saw Trump in his pomp on the top floor. A few months later, Trump and Dubinin were seated together at a lunch hosted by the cosmetics mogul Leonard Lauder, and according to Trump, 'One thing led to another, and now I'm talking about building a large luxury hotel, across the street from the Kremlin, in partnership with the Soviet government'.[9] Dubinin, who in late 1986 became ambassador to the United States, appears to have massaged Trump's ego, which worked wonders. Natalia recalled that 'He [Trump] is an emotional person, somewhat impulsive. He needs recognition. And, of course, when he gets it he likes it. My father's visit worked on him like honey to a bee'.[10]

In January 1987, Dubinin invited Trump to visit Moscow, adding that Intourist, the Soviet tourist agency, 'had expressed interest in pursuing a joint venture to construct and manage a hotel in Moscow'.[11] Vitaly Churkin, who between 2006 and his death in February 2017 served as Russia's permanent representative to the UN, helped arrange the visit. On 4 July 1987 for the first time, Trump flew to Moscow with Ivana and two assistants and stayed 'in the Lenin suite at the National Hotel' overlooking the entrance to Red Square. He inspected some possible sites for a hotel, including several near Red Square, and was 'impressed with the ambition of the Soviet officials to make a deal'.[12] The Soviet Union was opening to foreign business, but instead of a regulated market, a buccaneering carpet-bagging capitalism soon poured through the widening doors of the liberalising economy. Trump was thus good company for the emerging Russian oligarchs, many of whom were former *apparatchiks* or members of the Soviet mafia underworld. There was talk 'about building a large luxury hotel, across the street from Kremlin, in partnership with the Soviet government'.[13] Not for the first time in Trump's dealings with Moscow, he returned empty-handed, and none of the grandiose schemes were achieved.

Back in America, Trump declared himself an expert on strategic security, warning of the dangers of nuclear proliferation and claiming that he was 'dealing at a very high level' with people in the Reagan White House. With his typical bombast, he declared that he had the expertise to solve the world's nuclear problems, and that it would 'take an hour-and-a-half to learn everything there is to know about missiles'.[14] By now, Trump had wider horizons than real estate and harboured the modest ambition to save the world.[15] His calls for nuclear disarmament were undoubtedly noted in Moscow.[16] Speaking with Trump on the issue in 1987, journalist Ron Rosenbaum came to the conclusion that many voters reached later. He describes some of the more outlandish theories of the time, such as secretary of defence Caspar Weinberger's 'dense pack' notion that incoming Soviet missiles would collide and blow themselves up mid-air if MX intercontinental ballistic missiles (ICBMs) were concentrated in a small area in the American Midwest. As he notes, 'If Congress could listen to Weinberger propose spending billions of dollars for this mad-as-hatter scheme without having him medicated, I could certainly listen to Trump's plan to halt nuclear weapons spread, and take it seriously'.[17] The complacent establishment line had become so out of kilter with the lived experience of millions of Americans, crumbling infrastructure and incompetent over-reach in foreign policy, that in November 2016 they were ready to give the outsider a chance – he could (it seemed at the time) hardly be worse.

Although Trump's vision is partial and distorted, he appears to have been genuinely worried by the peculiar kind of rationality associated with the official doctrine of Mutually Assured Destruction (MAD). Trump's uncle, Dr John Trump, was a professor at MIT working on cancer research and radiation therapy, and this apparently got Trump interested in the subject and awareness 'of just how much danger nukes put the world in'.[18] This was no mere passing interest, and later he asked for more information from Bernard Lown, the inventor of the defibrillator, who shared the Nobel Peace Prize with Yevgeny Chazov, Gorbachev's personal physician. On Lown's return from meeting Gorbachev, Trump asked him for 'everything you know about Gorbachev', and claimed that within an hour of meeting Gorbachev, he would end the cold war. Lown commented 'The arrogance of the man, and his ignorance about the complexities of one of the complicating issues confronting mankind! The idea that he could solve it in one hour!'.[19]

Having mastered strategic nuclear issues, Trump turned his attention to mundane trade and security matters. On 2 September 1987, Trump paid nearly $100,000 for full page advertisements in the *Boston Globe*, the *Washington Post* and the *New York Times*, running under the headline 'There's nothing wrong with America's foreign defence policy that a little backbone can't cure', calling on the United States to end the expensive commitment to defend Japan and the Gulf States. He argued that Japan was dependent on the Persian Gulf for its oil supplies, whereas for the United States, the region was of marginal significance: 'It's time for us to end our vast deficits by making Japan and others who can afford it pay. Our protection is worth hundreds of billions of dollars to these countries and their stake in their protection is far greater than ours'. He made the same point in *The Art of the Deal*, published in November 1987, where he argued 'What's unfortunate is that for decades now they [Japan] have become wealthier in large measure by screwing the United States with a self-serving trade policy that our political leaders have never been able to fully understand or counteract'.[20] This was an early indication of the 'America first' mercantilist approach to foreign affairs, in which the U.S. post-war alliance system appeared to have no value unless it paid for itself and served American commercial interests. The hostility that in the 1980s was directed towards Japan was later focused on China. Trump's disruptive nationalism, dismissal of the traditional alliance system and contempt for multilateral institutions are long-standing positions. While they may coincide with Russian preferences, they were generated long before Trump entered the 2016 presidential campaign.[21] It is unlikely that in the late 1980s Moscow had some sort of *kompromat* that shaped Trump's policies, and even Unger admits that we do not know when the KGB opened a file on him.[22] However, it was already clear that Trump had 'an uncanny knack for channelling the fears and resentments of the age'.[23]

The publication of *The Art of the Deal* transformed Trump from an eccentric businessman into a public, if controversial, figure. Trump was impressed by the openness sweeping the Soviet Union and the intensifying ambition to put an end to the cold war. In the end, the Soviet Union reformed itself out of existence in 1991. By contrast, the West consolidated and then enlarged its post-war security institutions (above all NATO) and radicalised its ideological and territorial ambitions. There was 'no place for Russia', and an escalating series of crises ultimately set the stage for the new cold war.[24] As for Trump, he made his mark as a budding politician. In 1980, he had toyed with the idea of standing for the presidency on behalf of the marginal Reform Party. Now, on 2 September 1987, the *New York Times* suggested that Trump could enter the 1988 Republican presidential primaries against George H. W. Bush, the incumbent vice president. Trump dismissed the notion, but his presidential ambitions were no secret. Trump took a keen interest in Soviet and Russian developments. On 2 December 1988, Gorbachev delivered his landmark speech to the United Nations, which in effect declared the cold war over. Donald and Ivana were due to have dinner with Gorbachev and his wife Raisa in New York, but the idea was scotched, and instead Trump shook hands with a Gorbachev impersonator outside Trump Tower.[25] The following year, the Berlin Wall came down, and soon after the Soviet bloc fell apart, the Soviet system dissolved, and the USSR itself disintegrated. In his interview with *Playboy* in 1990, Trump was sceptical about Gorbachev at a time when he was being lauded in the West:

I predict he will be overthrown, because he has shown extraordinary weakness. Suddenly, for the first time ever, there are coal-miner strikes and brush fires everywhere – which will ultimately lead to a violent revolution. Yet Gorbachev is getting credit for being a wonderful leader – and we should continue giving him credit, because he's destroying the Soviet Union.[26]

This cynical if realistic approach chimes with later Russian views of Gorbachev.

In November 1996, Trump once again visited Moscow for three days, when he discussed a Trump Tower residential complex. Following a series of bankruptcies,[27] Trump had to fly on a commercial airline to get there, which according to his girlfriend of the time, Marla Maples, he took as a grievous affront.[28] There was also talk of Trump renovating the iconic Moskva hotel, and even the giant Rossiya hotel complex, but by 1998, these plans had been abandoned.[29] In autumn 2002 Trump once again visited, staying in the Baltschug Hotel, but this time the plan was not to build in Moscow but to sell apartments in his North American properties to rich Russian investors.[30] By 2005, Trump had handed responsibility for Moscow projects to the Bayrock development company founded by Tevfik Arif, an émigré from Kazakhstan, with the convicted felon Felix Sater taking the lead on various plans. Sater was a Russian-born New York real estate developer with alleged links to the mafia and who in December 1998 became an FBI 'cooperating witness' after he was caught in a stock-fraud scheme.[31] As usual, none of these plans came to fruition.[32] In November 2007, Trump attended the Millionaire's Fair in Crocus City, a vast luxury shopping mall and concert hall built by Aras Agalarov on the western outskirts of Moscow. The aim was to launch Trump's branded '24K Super Premium Vodka', presented in a bottle braided with 24-carat gold.[33] Even in a country still impressed by Western bling, the venture was not a success. Trump's elder son, Donald Jr, visited Moscow in 2008 with plans to expand the Trump empire into new territories. By then, Trump was less a developer than a licenser of his brand, usually for a hefty fee. Once again, there were ambitious but fruitless discussions of Trump reconstructing the Moskva and Rossiya hotels.[34] Trump was as much an outsider to Russian business circles as he was to its political elite.

By the early years of the new century, the Trump brand was fading and his business model failing.[35] In *The Art of the Deal* Trump described his casinos in Atlantic City as cash machines, but by 1990, the Taj Mahal became the first of his six corporate (but never personal) bankruptcies.[36] With the collapse of the Soviet Union, Russian mobsters moved to the United States and squeezed out some of the more established mafia groups.[37] Not surprisingly, when Trump launched his campaign in 2015 his alleged mafia ties were explored.[38] By then, Trump had reinvented himself as a celebrity and even as some sort of cultural icon. This was overseen by Mark Burnett, the British-born TV reality show entrepreneur (and veteran of the 1982 Falklands War), who hit on the idea of Trump hosting *The Apprentice*. The first episode was aired in January 2004, and in various formats, NBC filmed fourteen seasons. Burnett's 'chief legacy is to have cast a serially bankrupt carnival barker in the role of a man who might plausibly become the leader of the free world'.[39] The TV show acted as a bridge to the White House.[40]

Trump's fame as the host of *The Apprentice* brought him into contact with the Agalarov family. Aras Agalarov was one of the first developers of luxury housing in post-Soviet Moscow. His extensive property empire, including the Crocus Group, soon turned him into a billionaire. His son Emin was an aspiring Russian pop star and businessman, and married to Leila Aliyeva, the daughter of President Ilham Aliyev of Azerbaijan. Emin persuaded Trump to figure in one of his pop videos, which ended with Trump 'firing' him. Trump acquired the rights to the Miss Universe beauty contest in October 1996, and Aras's company now bought the rights to stage the November 2013 pageant in his Crocus City Hall, a 7,500-seat concert venue built four years earlier. Trump visited Moscow again for the competition. This was when the former British spy Christopher Steele alleges in his first memo that Trump hired a couple of prostitutes to urinate on each other on the same hotel bed in the Ritz-Carlton hotel where the Obamas had slept during their one and only visit to Moscow on 6–7 July 2009.[41] Trump was obsessed with meeting Putin, tweeting: 'Do you think Putin will be going to the Miss Universe Pageant in November in Moscow – if so, will he become my new best friend?'.[42] In the event, Putin did not attend the event, and there was no meeting. Putin did not become his 'new best friend'.

Nevertheless, the short visit was packed with events. On its eve, on 7 November Trump attended Billy Graham's 95th birthday party, needing the support of the evangelical right to make a credible bid for the presidency.[43] He landed in Moscow on Friday morning 8 November, and headed to the Ritz-Carlton, where he stayed in the same presidential suite as the Obamas. He had a long lunch that day with Russian businesspeople and sponsors of the gala, and that evening attended Aras Agalarov's 58th birthday party at Crocus City. Exhausted, he got back to the hotel at about 1.30 am and was up early to shoot a music video with Emin. This was his only night in the hotel, and while it does not preclude the 'golden showers' incident recorded in the Steele dossier, it seems unlikely.[44] The 9th was as hectic as the previous day, including a press conference in which Trump was asked about his relationship with Putin, which at that point was non-existent. Trump still hoped that Putin would attend the contest that evening and praised the Russian president:

Look, he's done a very brilliant job in terms of what he represents and who he's representing. If you look at what he's done with Syria, if you look at so many of the different things, he has really eaten our president's lunch. Let's not kid ourselves. He's done an amazing job. . . . He's put himself at the forefront of the world as a leader in a short period of time.[45]

The two did not meet because Putin was delayed waiting for the Dutch monarch, Willem-Alexander, who was stuck in traffic. Following the party after the Miss Universe pageant, Trump very late at night headed to the airport.[46]

The music promoter Rob Goldstone made the arrangements for the Miss Universe contest, for which Trump received a fee of $12.2 million from Aras Agalarov. In a later interview, Goldstone noted that Trump invited Putin to the pageant and scrawled at the bottom 'lots of beautiful women'. Putin's reaction to the invitation is not known. Goldstone says that if the events described by Steele had occurred, he would have heard of it. He stresses 'on the night in question, Trump should have been getting five or six hours of much-needed sleep in order to be ready for our video shoot early that morning, which would then be followed by an extremely long day'.[47] Whether Moscow gathered *kompromat* on Trump during this visit, rendering him 'the Muscovian candidate', is the crux of the Russiagate allegation. Alex Sapir, a Soviet émigré who arrived in New York in 1975, was with Trump in Moscow, and the idea of building a Moscow Trump Tower was discussed. By the time Sapir became acquainted with Trump in 2001, he had already been working for U.S. intelligence agencies for three years.[48] Between 2006 and 2010, Sapir and his associates in the Bayrock Group built the Trump SoHo hotel and condominium complex in Manhattan. The troubled project was the subject of a lawsuit in 2011, with potential buyers claiming that they had been defrauded by the Trump team exaggerating early sales figures by claiming that 'more than half' of the units had been sold.[49] Now a letter of intent was signed with Agalarov's company, and it looked as if Trump's ambitions in Moscow were finally going to be realised. Soon after the pageant, Agalarov's daughter presented Trump with a black lacquer box, which contained a letter from Putin – whose contents have not been revealed, prompting much speculation.[50] Following the imposition of Ukraine-related sanctions in 2014, Trump's daughter Ivanka visited various potential sites in Moscow with Emin, but in the end decided to kill the deal for business reasons.[51] In short, despite repeated attempts to do business in Russia, the story is one of failure, like the U.S.–Russian relationship as a whole.

FOLLOW THE MONEY

In the Watergate scandal, the Deep Throat insider source famously advised Woodward and Bernstein to 'follow the money', and this became the catchphrase of the film *All the President's Men*. The trail ultimately led to the White House. Trump's persistent refusal to condemn Putin and Russia is explained by the Kremlin's financial hold over him. According to the recent account by Catherine Belton, Russia backed Trump's commercial interests as far back as the 1990s, exploiting his vanity and financial vulnerability long before he assumed the presidency, and then exploited these long-term connections when he entered the White House.[52] The trail is long and tangled, but the main outlines are clear.

Trump's business model is convoluted at the best of times, but when it converges with what the *Financial Times* calls the 'shadowy post-Soviet world where politics and personal enrichment merge', things become even more complex. Trump's early business dealings may have rendered him vulnerable to 'undue influence now that he is in the White House'.[53] The case in question here is the building of Trump Tower in Toronto, a project that was launched in 2007. This is a 65-storey tower containing 261 luxury hotel rooms and condominiums, and its financing was as complex as any of Trump's schemes.[54] Still unfinished by the original completion date of 2010, a further $40m was required. It was provided by Alex Shnaider, an early partner in the project, who in 2010 is alleged to have approved a $100m 'commission' to fixers representing the Kremlin's interests. The payment was designed to facilitate the sale of the enormous Zaporozhe steel mill (Zaporishstal) in Eastern Ukraine and represented 10 per cent of the $850 million sale price. The deal apparently was financed by Vnesheconombank (VEB), the Russian state investment bank, whose chairman at the time was Putin (he had been appointed in 2008). With the $100 million facilitation payment made, the steel mill sale went ahead, and part of the profit was invested in Trump Toronto. In a subsequent dispute between Shnaider and his business partners, it was alleged that some of the money may have ended up in the pocket of Russian government officials. If that was the case, then the steel mill sale would fall foul of Canadian anti-bribery laws.[55]

Although Trump proudly proclaimed himself the 'king of debt', boasting of 'doing things with other people's money', Trump was perceived by lenders as a high risk because of his serial business bankruptcies and comparatively few successful ventures. The global financial crisis from 2008 hit Trump hard. His casino business in Atlantic City had long become defunct, but now Trump Mortgage collapsed and Trump companies defaulted on a $334 million debt repayment to Deutsche Bank due on the loan to build Trump Tower Chicago, the last of Trump's personally directed projects. By now, Trump had reinvented himself as a TV star in *The Apprentice*, and his business strategy was to license his brand globally.[56] Cohen notes that by 2006, 'the Trump name was basically all that the Trump Organization had left to sell'.[57] In 2008, Don Jr. informed a real estate conference that 'Russians make up a pretty disproportionate cross-section of a lot of our assets. We don't rely on American banks. We have all the funding we need out of Russia'.[58] It is not clear what Trump Jr. had in mind, but the comment has been endlessly repeated as proof of Russian influence on Trump.

Because of a repeated cycle of bankruptcies in which creditors lost their investments, 'virtually all the banks in the United States refused to do business with him'.[59] Deutsche Bank was the only mainstream financial organisation willing to lend to Trump after 1998, but as with all of his partners, the relationship was long and difficult. In 2010, Trump was granted a major loan by the private wealth division of Deutsche Bank at a time when it was handling a considerable quantity of Russian money.[60] Even Deutsche was wary of dealing with Trump because of the way he 'used incredibly inflated valuations of his real estate holdings to justify his company's loans'.[61] The details are unclear, and this has given rise to a mass of speculation. Deutsche Bank has a long history of working in Russia and is alleged to have helped launder funds for wealthy Russians. It now faces charges of helping launder some $20bn in Russian assets through what is known as the 'Global Laundromat' case.[62] The question is why the bank in total lent some $2.5bn to Trump at a time when the risk were known, although no evidence has emerged that any lending 'was connected to the Russian government, companies or individuals'.[63] Two congressional committees in April 2019 subpoenaed the materials, including tax returns from 2010, and in August the bank revealed that it had tax returns relating to Trump's family and businesses. This provoked yet another round of speculation, including what transactions Trump may have engaged in with Russian or other foreign nationals.

There have been enduring questions over whether Trump is a billionaire, despite his boastful claims.[64] Trump was forced to change his business model, licensing others to brand skyscraper developments with the Trump Organisation, which then managed the development under contract.[65] Real estate developers paid Trump a large fee to use his name, but assumed all the risk themselves; that is, apart from people who put a down payment on units, who often lost their deposits.[66] Financial problems forced Trump to work with the Bayrock Group, which had been involved in the plans to build a hotel in Moscow in 2005, with Sater working as the intermediary. Bayrock was chaired by Tevfik Arif, who introduced Trump to various Russian investors, although in the end, the actual development took place in Manhattan. Trump worked with Bayrock and Tamir Sapir, an émigré from Georgia who made millions in New York real estate, to develop the scandal-ridden Trump SoHo hotel and condominium complex in lower Manhattan.

Trump was never too choosy about his clients, noting that when he was selling apartments in the original Trump Tower 'Many wealthy foreigners didn't have the proper social references for these cooperatives [where there were stringent checks], or didn't want to put themselves through the scrutiny of a bunch of prying strangers. Instead, they came to us'.[67] Unger puts this rather more harshly, noting that Trump Tower was one of only two buildings in New York that allowed shell companies to buy condos, thus allowing dirty money to be laundered.[68] In 2016, Trump was the first presidential candidate to refuse access to his tax records, and the Trump Organisation has had a chequered history with the tax authorities. There are suggestions that in the early 1990s Trump took an enormous tax loss of $900 million to reduce his tax liability in subsequent years, and that he paid no income tax at all in 1978, 1979, 1992 and 1994. Accordingly, Trump 'is a shameless flim-flam man with practically no regard for the truth or the quaint notion that wealthy people like him have a civic duty to pay their fair share of taxes'.[69]

The purchase by a Russian oligarch, Dmitry Rybolovlev, of Trump's Palm Beach (Florida) mansion called Maison de l'Amitié for $96m in 2008 has provoked much discussion. The price was over double the $41 million that Trump paid only four years earlier.[70] As so often in these cases, on closer examination, there is less to the affair than suspected. There is nothing to suggest that the transaction was part of a Russian bail-out to help Trump.[71] Rybolovlev is known as an extravagant spender, having bought the world's most expensive picture, Leonardo da Vinci's 'Salvator Mundi', for $127.5 million in 2013 (sold at a later auction for $450 million). In 2010, Rybolovlev sold his Russian potash and fertiliser business, Uralkali, for $7.5 billion, and by the following year had pulled out of Russia entirely and relocated to Monaco.[72] His net worth is estimated at $10.5 billion, including some $2.7 billion held in art and real estate. In other words, Rybolovlev had no enduring ties with the Russian government; hence, his dealings with Trump are unlikely to have been part of a covert operation. For Rybolovlev, $95 million is no more than small change, and even in 2008 had no known links with the Kremlin.

The transition to market economies in the post-Soviet states created a peculiar type of buccaneering capitalism, entwined with the remnants of the Soviet bureaucratic state. Capital and power are closely linked in Western states, but mechanisms have been devised to ensure some sort of separation at the functional level, but in many of the post-Soviet states, it is precisely at the functional level that the authorities and business work together. The model changed in Russia when Putin came to power in 2000, and the free-wheeling oligarchic relations of the 1990s gave way to a more ordered system, although the functional relationship continued in new forms. The state stymied the development of an independent entrepreneurial class, an aspiration identified in particular with Yukos oil company head Mikhail Khodorkovsky.[73] In the new dispensation, business people could keep their wealth as long as they aligned themselves with the regime's goals. A new class of 'state oligarchs' ('stoligarchs') emerged. Given the enormous wealth generated by rising energy prices in the 2000s, much of this money coursed through the Western financial system. Already in the 'wild East' days of the 1990s, the newly enriched class learnt the value of offshore tax havens and shell companies, where layer upon layer of legal entities (typically with similar names) is created to disguise the ultimate beneficial owner.

The real estate sector is particularly prone to such activity, with a U.S. Treasury investigation in 2017 suggesting that a third of top-end property cash purchases were suspicious.[74] Russians were eager purchasers of apartments in Trump-branded properties, some of which may have been used to launder ill-gotten assets. A Kazakh network is alleged to have been at work in Trump SoHo. In this context, it is hardly surprising that a group of sixty-three Russians spent $100 million to buy property at seven Trump-branded luxury towers in Florida. For the new rich in the former Soviet Union, real estate investment is the primary vehicle to launder money. The problem is 'especially egregious in the United Kingdom, where some have called the UK luxury real-estate industry "a money laundering machine"'. This possibly applies to Trump's purchase in 2014 of a loss-making golf course in Scotland, renamed Trump Turnberry, although Trump is an enthusiastic golfer. Trump's finances continue to raise questions, provoking 'realistic fears about past business partners using their knowledge to unduly influence the President and his policies'.[75]

It is hardly surprising that Trump and Russian money intersected. Trump's failure to divest himself of his interests in the many companies that comprise the Trump Organisation and his refusal to release his tax returns means that his presidency was torn by conflicts of interest. The fundamental question remains: were Trump's policies in general, and specifically vis-à-vis Russia, 'shaped by the alignment of his interests with those who brought him the money that sustained his career'.[76] Trump enterprises are not known for the rigour of due diligence, and his business conduct is akin to some dubious post-Soviet practices. Business and politics converge at the functional level, and money is applied liberally and directly to achieve political goals. Trump's business activities and Russian money did intersect at various points, but there is no evidence that his views, let alone his policies, have been shaped by these interests. Trump is notoriously negligent of the concerns of partners and investors, and there is nothing to suggest that Russia is any different. Nevertheless, Russiagate made talking with Russian leaders and officials suspicious, and contacts were reduced to a minimum.

Discussions for a development in Moscow were revived on the eve of the 2016 presidential election, with fateful consequences for those involved. The facilitator once again was Sater. Ivanka Trump had earlier pulled the plug on Moscow projects, but when Trump announced his presidential bid, Sater reappeared – perhaps coincidentally, but the timing raises questions. Trump appeared keen to seal a lucrative Moscow contract, as an insurance policy if his presidential bid failed. In October 2015, Sater revived the idea with Cohen, whom he had known since his teenage years in Brighton Beach, of building a luxury hotel, office and residential complex that would be called Trump Tower Moscow.[77] Cohen is dismissive of Sater's abilities and connections, and stresses that he certainly was not 'some criminal genius conspiring with Russian oligarchs to launder vast sums of money through the Trump Organization'.[78] Trump signed a letter of intent with the little-known Russian developer I.C. Expert that month.[79] The project soon stalled, with no site found or serious partner chosen, at which point Sater suggested that Cohen get help from the Kremlin. There then followed a farcical attempt to find the relevant email address, and as we shall see, a speculative email was sent in mid-January 2016 to Dmitry Peskov, Putin's press secretary. A fortnight later Cohen, without consulting Trump, for 'business reasons' once again abandoned the project (or so it appeared).[80] In his press conference of 11 January 2017, Trump insisted 'I have no deals in Russia, I have no deal that could happen in Russia because we've stayed away, and I have no loans with Russia'.[81] As we shall see, Mueller discovered that the project continued well into 2016.[82]

ALL THINGS BRIGHT AND COLOURFUL

Trump's four visits to Moscow, his laudatory comments about Putin and his murky finances produced endless speculation about his relationship with the Kremlin. One of the more extreme versions is advanced by Jonathan Chait. On the eve of the July 2018 Helsinki summit he outlined what he called a 'plausible theory of mind-boggling collusion':

> As Trump arranges to meet face-to-face and privately with Vladimir Putin later this month, the collusion between the two men metastasizing from a dark accusation into an open alliance, it would be dangerous not to consider the possibility that the summit is less a negotiation between two heads of state than a meeting between a Russian-intelligence asset and his handler.[83]

He runs through the Russiagate allegations in a classic neo-journalistic manner, shaping the evidence to prove an already decided case. Chait's allegations drew lines between dots that in fact may have no necessary connection. The Russiagate controversy moved conspiracy theories to the centre of American life, even while that centre was destabilised by the allegations. This was a double movement undermining traditional institutions, ethical standards and norms of governance.

For those looking to taint him with the Russian brush, Trump did his cause no good. Trump provocatively lauded Putin as a strong and decisive leader, compared to Obama's 'weakness'. In the presidential debate of 19 October 2016, Clinton called Trump Putin's 'puppet', painting him as a Kremlin stooge who would sacrifice American interests to Russia if elected. This further polarised American politics. Republican voters were more likely to approve of the Russian leader (which rose to 37 per cent during the campaign), whereas Democratic voters went the other way, a split that endures to this day. Trump's questioning of traditional U.S. foreign policy commitments, which began long before his presidential campaign, and his vexing behaviour intersected with Russia's assertiveness with explosive effect.

Putin's comments only stoked the flames. In his annual press conference on 17 December 2015, he stressed:

> We're never closed to this [working with the US], no matter who the American people elect as their president. It's them who are constantly trying to tell us what we should do in our county, who should get elected and who shouldn't, and what procedures to follow. We never meddle in other people's affairs. They say it's dangerous to do so in America. They say that if foreign observers get closer than five metres to a line of voters, they could end up in prison. We aren't doing even that, right? We are open and will work with any president voted in by the American people.[84]

As he was leaving he was asked about Trump:

> Well, he is a colourful person. Talented, without a doubt. But it's none of our business, it's up to the voters in the United States. But he is the absolute leader of the presidential race. He says he wants to shift to a different mode of relations, a deeper level of relations with Russia. How could we not welcome that? Of course we welcome it. As for the domestic politics of it, the turns of phrase he uses to increase his popularity, I'll repeat, it's not our business to evaluate his work.[85]

The Russian word Putin used for colourful is *yarkii*, which can be described as bright, vivid or talented. Trump of course put the best slant on the comment and asserted that Putin called him 'brilliant', which is a misreading of the word. In his interview with MSNBC's 'Morning Joe' on 18 December, Trump said he welcomed Putin's compliment: 'When people call you brilliant, it's always good, especially when the person heads up Russia'. Trump asserted that 'It is always a great honor to be so nicely complimented by a man so highly respected within his own country and beyond'. He went on to argue 'I have always felt that Russia and the United States should be able to work well with each other towards defeating terrorism and restoring world peace, not to mention trade and all of the other benefits derived from mutual respect'. Asked by Joe Scarborough what he thought of the high number of Russian journalists murdered on Putin's watch, Trump responded, 'He's running his country, and at least he's a leader, you know unlike what we have in this country'. Pushed further, Trump compared Russia to the United States: 'Well I think our country does plenty of killing also, Joe', he said. 'So, you know. There's a lot of stupidity going on in the world right now, Joe. A lot of killing going on, a lot of stupidity'. He noted Putin's high standing in the polls, a sign of his high leadership qualities: 'I've always felt fine about Putin. I think he's a strong leader'.[86]

Later, at the St Petersburg International Economic Forum (SPIEF) in June 2016, the American journalist Fareed Zakaria, who was moderating a panel, asked Putin what had prompted him to describe Trump as 'brilliant, outstanding, talented'. In fact, of the epithets, Putin had only used the word 'talented', without specifying what talent he had in mind. Putin pushed back and accused Zakaria of exaggerating:

> I made an off-hand remark about Trump being a colourful person. Are you saying he is not colourful? I did not characterise him in any other way. But what I did note, and what I certainly welcome, and I see nothing wrong with this – Mr. Trump has stated that he is ready for the renewal of a full-fledged relationship between Russia and the United States. What is wrong with that? We all welcome it. Don't you?[87]

Omarosa warned Trump against pro-Putin rhetoric, and noted that he understood very little about the cold war and international affairs: 'Donald was not a student of history. He wasn't a student of anything . . . I just don't think that he had the attention span to even watch a documentary about Russia', but he 'fixated on Vladimir Putin as a feared, respected and admired leader'. She notes that Trump may have been envious of the control Putin allegedly exerts over Russia, but 'Trump went with his gut, and his gut told him, "I like Putin, and I want him to be my friend". Nothing else mattered'.[88] Cohen argues that it was Putin's alleged wealth that was attractive, with Trump portraying Putin as 'the richest man in the world'.[89] Bob Woodward suggests that Trump's apparent obeisance was not because Putin had some *kompromat* on him, but that Trump had an affinity for strongmen. He believed that his skills in the art of the deal worked best through personal diplomacy, with people who could deliver like North Korea's leader Kim Jong-un and Turkey's president Recep Tayyip Erdoğan: 'The tougher and meaner they are, the better I get along with them'.[90]

NOTES

1. David Cay Johnston, *It's Even Worse than You Think: What the Trump Administration Is Doing to America* (New York, Simon & Schuster, 2018).
2. Wolff, *Fire and Fury*, p. 24.
3. Wolff, *Fire and Fury*, p. 96.
4. Wolff, *Fire and Fury*, p. 97.
5. Unger, *House of Trump*, pp. 1–2.
6. Craig Unger, *American Kompromat: How the KGB Cultivated Donald Trump and Related Tales of Sex, Greed, Power, and Treachery* (London, Scribe, 2021).
7. Craig Unger, 'When a Young Trump went to Russia', *The New Republic*, 15 August 2018, https://newrepublic.com/article/150646/young-trump-went-russia.
8. Trump, *The Art of the Deal*, pp. 99–100.
9. Trump, *The Art of the Deal*, p. 27.
10. Michael Weiss, 'What Russia Understands about Trump', *New York Review of Books*, 2 August 2018, https://www.nybooks.com/daily/2018/08/02/what-russia-understands-about-trump/.
11. Trump, *The Art of the Deal*, p.364.
12. Trump, *The Art of the Deal*, p. 364; Unger, *The House of Trump*, pp. 49–50. Unger stresses that Lenin and his wife stayed in the hotel in 1917 and how it then became a place for 'honey traps' set by the KGB, but he does not explain how Trump could have taken advantage of 'good parties with nice girls' if he was accompanied by his wife and her assistant Lisa Calandra, and his executive assistant Norma Foerderer. But perhaps I am missing something.
13. Weiss, 'What Russia Understands about Trump'.
14. Unger, *House of Trump*, p. 44.
15. Ron Rosenbaum, 'Trump's Nuclear Experience: In 1987 he Set out to Solve the World's Biggest Problem', *Slate*, 1 March 2016, http://www.slate.com/articles/news_and_politics/the_spectator/2016/03/trump_s_nuclear_experience_advice_for_reagan_in_1987.html?via=gdpr-consent. The article reprints the original interview between Trump and Rosenbaum in the November 1987 issue of the journal *Manhattan, Inc.*
16. Seth Hettena, *Trump/Russia: A Definitive History* (Brooklyn, Melville House, 2018), p. 15.
17. Rosenbaum, 'Trump's Nuclear Experience'.
18. Rosenbaum, 'Trump's Nuclear Experience'.
19. Unger, *House of Trump*, p. 45.
20. Trump, *The Art of the Deal*, p. 186.
21. Lewandowski and Bossie, *Let Trump be Trump*, p. 73 confirm this point.
22. Unger, 'When a Young Trump went to Russia'; Unger, *House of Trump*, p. 43.
23. Cohen, *Disloyal*, p. 103.
24. William H. Hill, *No Place for Russia: European Security Institutions since 1989* (New York, Columbia University Press, 2018).
25. Hettena, *Trump/Russia*, p. 16.

26. Glenn Plaskin, 'The 1990 Interview with Donald Trump', *Playboy*, 1 March 1990, https://www.playboy.com/read/playboy-interview-donald-trump-1990.

27. For an analysis of the early days (the book was first published in 1992), see Wayne Barrett, *Trump: The Greatest Show on Earth – The Deals, the Downfall, and the Reinvention* (New York, Regan Arts, 2016).

28. Hettena, *Trump/Russia*, p. 43.

29. Hettena, *Trump/Russia*, p. 47.

30. Hettena, *Trump/Russia*, p. 76.

31. Michael Rothfeld, 'Ex-Trump Affiliate Secretly Worked with Prosecutors, FBI and CIA for Years', *Wall Street Journal*, 24 August 2019, https://www.wsj.com/articles/ex-trump-affiliate-secretly-worked-with-prosecutors-fbi-and-cia-for-years-11566582029. There are useful details in Unger, *House of Trump*, p. 136; Glenn Simpson and Peter Fritsch, *Crime in Progress: The Secret History of the Trump-Russia Investigation* (London, Allen Lane, 2019), p. 38, and Sater's role is confirmed by Weissmann, *Where Law Ends*, p. 40.

32. Hettena, *Trump/Russia*, pp. 98–100.

33. Catherine Belton, *Putin's People: How the KGB Took Back Russia and then Took on the West* (New York, Farrar, Straus and Giroux, 2020), p. 473.

34. Nance, *The Plot to Hack America*, p. 38.

35. David Cay Johnston, *The Making of Donald Trump* (London, Melville House Publishing, 2017).

36. Unger, *The House of Trump*, pp. 66, 91–92.

37. Analysed by Robert Friedman, *Red Mafiya: How the Russian Mob has Invaded America* (Boston, Little, Brown and Company, 2000).

38. Robert O'Harrow, 'Trump Swam in Mob-Infested Waters in Early Years as NYC Developer', *Washington Post*, 16 October 2015.

39. Keefe, 'How Mark Burnett Resurrected Donald Trump as an Icon of American Success'.

40. Green, *Devil's Bargain*, p. 97.

41. Hettena, *Trump/Russia*, pp. 118–25 provides one of the most detailed accounts.

42. Nance, *The Plot to Hack America*, p. 39; Isikoff, and Corn, *Russian Roulette*, pp. 2, 9; Unger, *House of Trump*, p. 204.

43. Hettena, *Trump/Russia*, p. 122.

44. Wolff, *Siege*, p. 76 gives credence to the incident, but Cohen argues that it never occurred, and his view is corroborated by Trump's long-term bodyguard, Keith Schiller, *Disloyal*, p. 179 and even more adamantly ('it never happened'), p. 323.

45. Isikoff, and Corn, *Russian Roulette*, p. 14.

46. There are conflicting versions of Trump's time in Moscow but even Unger confirms Trump's account, stating that he flew out at 3.58am on Sunday 10 November, Unger, *House of Trump*, p. 210.

47. Kim Sengupta, 'Trump Tried to Tempt Putin with "Lots of Beautiful Women", Says UK Music Promoter at Centre of Russia Probe', *The Independent*, 24 September 2018, https://www.independent.co.uk/news/world/americas/us-politics/trump-russia-mueller-rob-goldstone-investigation-donald-jr-manafort-meeting-email-a8551771.html.

48. Belton, *Putin's People*, p. 462.
49. Belton, *Putin's People*, p. 471; Cohen, *Disloyal*, p. 252.
50. Isikoff and Corn, *Russian Roulette*, p. 18.
51. Isikoff and Corn, *Russian Roulette*, p. 55.
52. Belton, *Putin's People*, pp. 448–88.
53. Tom Burgis, 'Trump's Tower of Secrets', *FT.com/magazine*, 14/15 July 2018, p. 14.
54. Hettena, *Trump/Russia*, pp. 101–2.
55. Burgis, 'Trump's Tower of Secrets', p. 20. For more information, see Belton, *Putin's People*, p. 468.
56. Frum, *Trumpocracy*, p. 61.
57. Cohen, *Disloyal*, p. 28.
58. Burgis, 'Trump's Tower of Secrets', p. 14; Jonathan Chait, 'Will Trump be Meeting with his Counterpart—Or His Handler?', *New York Magazine*, 9 July 2018, http://nymag.com/daily/intelligencer/2018/07/trump-putin-russia-collusion.html.
59. Cohen, *Disloyal*, p. 47.
60. Chait, 'Will Trump be Meeting with his Counterpart'.
61. Cohen, *Disloyal*, p. 202.
62. Luke Harding, 'Deutsche Bank Faces Action over $20bn Russian Money-Laundering Scheme', *Guardian*, 17 April 2019, https://www.theguardian.com/business/2019/apr/17/deutsche-bank-faces-action-over-20bn-russian-money-laundering-scheme.
63. David Enrich, 'Deutsche Bank Has a Lot of Detailed Information', *New York Times*, 28 August 2019, https://www.nytimes.com/2019/08/28/business/deutsche-bank-trump.html.
64. Timothy L. O'Brien, *TrumpNation: The Art of Being the Donald* (New York, Grand Central Publishing, reprinted 2016).
65. Unger, *House of Trump*, p. 125.
66. Adam Davidson, 'Is Fraud Part of the Trump Organization's Business Model?', *New Yorker*, 17 October 2018, https://www.newyorker.com/news/swamp-chronicles/is-fraud-part-of-the-trump-organizations-business-model.
67. Trump, *Art of the Deal*, p. 182.
68. Unger, *House of Trump*, pp. 12–13.
69. John Cassidy, 'The Trump Family's Tax Dodging is Symptomatic of a Larger Problem', *New Yorker*, 3 October 2018, https://www.newyorker.com/news/our-columnists/the-trump-familys-tax-dodging-is-symptomatic-of-a-larger-problem.
70. Wolff, *Siege*, pp. 14–15.
71. Confirmed by Cohen, *Disloyal*, pp. 248–50, although he does suggest (p. 250) that Trump believed that the buyer ultimately was Putin.
72. Leonid Bershidsky, 'There's No escape for Russian Billionaires', *Bloomberg*, 8 November 2018, https://www.bloomberg.com/opinion/articles/2018-11-08/there-s-no-escape-for-russian-billionaires.
73. Richard Sakwa, *Putin and the Oligarch: The Khodorkovsky—Yukos Affair* (London, I. B. Tauris; New York, Palgrave Macmillan, 2014).
74. Burgis, 'Trump's Tower of Secrets', p. 14.

75. Adam Davidson, 'Where did Donald Trump get Two Hundred Million Dollars to buy his Money-Losing Scottish Golf Club?', *New Yorker*, 13 July 2018, https://www.newyorker.com/news/swamp-chronicles/where-did-donald-trump-get-200-million-dollars-to-buy-his-money-losing-scottish-golf-club.

76. Burgis, 'Trump's Tower of Secrets', p. 16.

77. Isikoff and Corn, *Russian Roulette*, p. 79; Belton, *Putin's People*, pp. 474–5.

78. Cohen, *Disloyal*, p. 244.

79. Weissmann, *Where Law Ends*, p. 265.

80. Isikoff, and Corn, *Russian Roulette*, p. 82; Hettena, *Trump/Russia*, p. 104.

81. 'Donald Trump's News Conference: Full Transcript and Video', *New York Times*, 11 January 2017, https://www.nytimes.com/2017/01/11/us/politics/trump-press-conference-transcript.html.

82. Admitted by Cohen, *Disloyal*, in which he notes that he kept Trump and his children closely informed, p. 15.

83. Chait, 'Will Trump be Meeting with his Counterpart'.

84. 'Vladimir Putin's Annual News Conference', Kremlin.ru, 17 December 2015, http://en.kremlin.ru/events/president/news/50971.

85. 'Vladimir Putin Calls Donald Trump a "Very Colourful and Talented Man"', *Guardian*, 17 December 2015, https://www.theguardian.com/world/2015/dec/17/vladimir-putin-donald-trump-very-bright-talented-man-russia-us-presidential-race.

86. Tyler Pager, 'Putin Repeats Praise of Trump: He's a "Bright" Person', *Politico*, 17 June 2016, http://www.politico.com/story/2016/06/putin-praises-trump-224485.

87. Masha Gessen, 'Russia, Trump & Flawed Intelligence', *New York Review of Books*, 9 January 2017, https://www.nybooks.com/daily/2017/01/09/russia-trump-election-flawed-intelligence/.

88. Omarosa, *Unhinged*, p.136.

89. Cohen, *Disloyal*, p. 245.

90. Woodward, *Rage*, p. 224.

Chapter 4

Russiagate and the New Cold War

In the most important foreign policy speech of his campaign, delivered at the Mayflower Hotel in Washington on 27 April 2016, Trump argued that

> I believe an easing of tensions and improved relations with Russia – from a position of strength – is possible. . . . Common sense says this cycle of hostility must end. Some say the Russians won't be reasonable. I intend to find out.

The speech outlined his 'America first' strategy, and excoriated Obama's alleged foreign policy failings: overextending military resources which he then under-funded; of failing to get allies to pay their fair share for defence; causing allies to doubt their ability to rely on the United States; causing adversaries no longer to respect the United States; and continuing the unclear U.S. foreign policy that had predominated since the end of the cold war. America would get 'out of the nation-building business and instead [focus] on creating stability in the world'.[1] Amid the welter of Trumpian venality and excess, one big idea emerged – the need to rethink the strategic priorities of U.S. foreign policy and at the heart of that was rapprochement with Russia. Many of the themes had sounded before, but together they questioned the foundations of the post-cold war international order. Trump challenged some of the most sacred shibboleths of U.S. foreign policy, above all the venerable principle of 'liberal hegemony'. His victory 'revealed considerable public dissatisfaction with the foreign policy of the past three US presidents'.[2] His challenge to the grand strategy that had long guided American foreign policy was incoherent and ill-informed, but the evident and expensive failures of so many U.S. foreign policy initiatives (such as wars in Afghanistan and Iraq) gave credence to Trump's 'America First' rhetoric. It also suited Russia since the expansive Atlantic system was increasingly perceived as a threat. This geopolitical coincidence of interests intersected with domestic U.S. political conflicts to devastating effect.

INTERNATIONAL POLITICS AND RUSSIAGATE

Trump viewed post-communist Russia as just another country, like France and Germany, with whom it made sense to 'get along'. However, for his critics France and Germany are not just other countries but close allies at the heart of the Atlantic alliance, whereas Russia was perceived as an adversary.[3] When Mitt Romney during the 2012 presidential election identified Russia 'without question our No. 1 geopolitical foe' he was reprimanded by Obama, but by the time of the 2016 election, the dissenting position had become the new orthodoxy. If in 2012 only 2 per cent of Americans considered Russia their greatest enemy, by 2015 this had risen to 18 per cent and topped the list of adversaries, overtaking North Korea, China and Iran.[4] Trump viewed Russia as a business opportunity and a potential ally in the life-and-death struggle with China. He was one of the few American leaders who had repeatedly visited the country, which itself provoked suspicion. Trump's desire to 'normalise' perceptions of Russia and to establish pragmatic relations encountered resistance, and Russia was used as the stick with which to drive Trump back into the new cold war fold.

But why Russia? The cold war ended in 1989 amid much celebration that a new era of peace and reconciliation was at hand. However, no inclusive and universal peace order was established. On the one side, the U.S.-led liberal international order expanded and became the dominant model for global order. This was accompanied by the institutional enlargement of its main organisations, NATO and the European Union. In the early years, Russia sought to adapt to the expanding 'historical West', and indeed to become part of it. However, from the very first, Gorbachev in the late Soviet years, President Boris Yeltsin in the 1990s and then Putin from 2000 argued that Russia deserved a special status in the new order. This was because of Russia's long history as a great power, its role in putting an end to the cold war, its status as one of the two nuclear superpowers, its role as the continuer state of the Soviet Union, and its assumption of a permanent seat on the UN Security Council. Russia anticipated not just the enlargement of an existing system but a transformation that would recognise Russia's status as a co-founder of a new security system. The clash between these contending visions of post-cold war international order – the expansive version pushed by the West and the transformative one desired by Moscow – set the scene for the twenty-five years of the cold peace from 1989, and thereafter the new era of confrontation from 2014.[5]

The pattern of Russia's relations with the West since the end of the cold war has been a downward spiral, with rare moments of cooperation alternating with intensifying conflicts. Neither side wanted conflict but the general trend was negative, culminating in the return to open confrontation in 2014.[6] Whether this should be called a new cold war has been dismissed as both anachronistic and misleading. Anachronistic, because it suggests a return to the previous conflict, whereas many of the earlier features – relatively stable bipolarity, confrontation between the two ideologies of capitalism and revolutionary socialism, and the focus on a divided Europe –are either not present or greatly changed. It is misleading because this new confrontation is truly global and involves a new set of actors and encompasses a different range of issues.[7] Nevertheless, elements of a new cold war have undoubtedly been revived, and for this reason it will be used as shorthand for the current confrontation. There is intense ideological and increasingly militarised conflict, although taking far more diffuse forms than earlier, with the main dividing line between democracies and authoritarian systems. There has also been intense informational mobilisation, with accusations traded between Moscow and Washington and other capitals of electoral interference, regime change operations, hacking, cyber warfare and disinformation campaigns. In short, as George Beebe puts it, 'The United States and Russia are fighting an undeclared virtual war'.[8]

Why did relations between Russia and the Atlantic system deteriorate to the point that we now talk of new cold war? Is Russia solely to blame, or are there larger structural forces to blame? Certainly, long-term factors apply, including the way that Russia historically has been 'a screen on which Americans [project] their hopes and fears'.[9] The diplomat and historian George F. Kennan observed that 'A large segment of the American population has the need to cultivate the idea of American innocence and virtue – which requires an opposite pole of evil'.[10] Russia over the generations has served in this capacity, although at crucial moments the two have been on the same side. Russia supported American independence, the Union forces in the Civil War, and the two were allies in the two great wars of the twentieth century. At the same time, Soviet Russia prompted the Red Scare of 1919 and was the antagonist of the cold war after 1945. The failure to secure an enduring peace drove the two apart after 1945 and again after 1989. In Russiagate the view of Russia as a revisionist power, determined to avenge its alleged humiliation and loss of status since the end of the cold war, predominated. Russia was aggrieved about what it perceived to have been the bad faith of the Western powers, when repeated promises that NATO would not enlarge were not only repudiated but even the fact that such commitments were given is denied.

Russiagate grew out of the way that the cold war ended, and the failure in the subsequent twenty-five years of the cold peace to establish an equitable and stable security order in Europe and globally. In the 1990s, Yeltsin had been the West's willing ally, but even he found working with the United States difficult and humiliating, notably when NATO launched the seventy-eight-day bombing campaign against its traditional ally, Serbia, in 1999 without UN authorisation.[11] In 1996, the United States sent numerous election experts and public relations consultants to Moscow to help Yeltsin win re-election (accompanied by a timely $10.2bn IMF loan). After a dirty campaign in which Yeltsin's adversaries were portrayed as an existential threat to democracy and even to Russia's existence as a normal state, and in which the spending limits were greatly exceeded, Yeltsin was returned to the Kremlin. The U.S. provision of money and advisors contravened Russian laws against foreigners working directly in campaigns. Nevertheless, *Time* magazine wrote gleefully about 'Yanks to the Rescue'.[12] What the United States did in 1996 is sometimes used to justify Russia's intervention in the 2016 U.S. election.

Putin pursues a 'Russia first' agenda, although in his early years, he tried to find a formula whereby this could be achieved in partnership with the West. This was the phase of the 'new realism', which encompassed the Medvedev interregnum of 2008–2012 and the reset. The realism was new to the extent that Putin sought to defend perceived Russian interests and its status as a great power while integrating into the liberal world order. In the end, the combination proved impossible. In his infamous speech at the Munich Security Conference in February 2007, Putin rudely punctured the West's belief that the 'unipolar world' would remain unchallenged.[13] The reset launched by Obama in 2009, when Medvedev was president, represented one of the peaks of cooperation, but it too ended in 2011 in renewed confrontation because of conflict over Libya and the Arab Spring. By 2012, Putin believed that he had failed to establish what he considered a more equitable relationship between Russia and the Atlantic system and to temper what he considered to be the ill-advised and catastrophic actions of the Atlantic power system. Foreign policy entered a 'neo-revisionist' phase in which Russia's perceived interests and status in world affairs were asserted more forcefully, with or without Western approval. The aim was not to destroy the existing international system but to revise its hierarchy to allow 'rising powers' greater scope to pursue their interests.

Putin's image in the West turned from reformer to foe, and by 2016, this had become the new orthodoxy. Russia challenged American global dominance (hegemony), but not in the way usually portrayed. Russian neo-revisionism challenged the practices of the Atlantic powers while still committed to the norms of international system as reflected in the rules of international society, above all represented by the UN and other institutions of global governance. Putin's critics are right to stress that he represented a challenge to the hegemony of the U.S.-led liberal international order but are wrong to argue that he sought to undermine the international system and destroy the order represented by the leading capitalist democracies. The goal was more complex: to change the balance of power in the system rather than to destroy the system itself.[14]

RUSSIA AND TRUMP'S ELECTION

Putin returned to the Russian presidency in May 2012 aggrieved and suspicious of the West. He also had a particular animus against Clinton, whom he perceived as having encouraged the protesters in 2011. But does this mean that Putin sought revenge? Russia certainly is an aggrieved power and Putin resented perceived and genuine grievances. Moscow sought recognition of its status as a great power, and thus cooperation on an equal basis in tackling global and regional problems. This does not translate into a model of vengeance. Equally, the view that Russia's domestic problems and contradictions impel it to assume an aggressive stance abroad is misleading; the relationship between domestic and foreign policy is more complicated. The liberal view is that domestic politics and regime type determines foreign policy, whereas realists argue that structural factors shape foreign policy decision-making.[15] Putin is an arch-pragmatist, and his actions draw on the Russian consensus view of the country's national interests. Trump's and Putin's views of international politics did not coincide, yet they were both pragmatists, and it was on this basis that there was potential for cooperation. Rather than being hell-bent on damaging American democracy and working to advance Trump, Russia's concerns were rather different. Some politicians were certainly keen on Trump, seeing him as a necessary alternative to Clinton's militarism and interventionism, but Moscow had seen too many American presidents come and go for any great hopes to be vested in any individual.[16] However, some security and other actors in Russia exploited cyber and social media technologies to fish in muddy waters.

At the Helsinki summit on 16 July 2018, Putin admitted that he had hoped that Trump would win, because of his expressed view that he sought better relations with Russia. The Russian elite feared a Clinton victory because of her known antagonism. In the aftermath of the return of Crimea to Russia in March 2014 she likened Putin to Hitler, and she sought to ramp up military support for Ukraine.[17] Above all, Moscow condemned her aggressive interventionist foreign policy. She promised to provide Ukraine with lethal weapons and to impose a no-fly zone in Syria, policies that threatened direct confrontation between the two powers. Not surprisingly, from Moscow's perspective Trump appeared the more reasonable potential interlocutor. He was the first major presidential candidate since 1945 to question the U.S. commitment to European security. As he put it in a major interview in the heat of the campaign, 'Congratulations, you will be defending yourself'. Despite their 'massive wealth', NATO members were not 'paying their bills', and unless that changed, the alliance would have to be rethought.[18]

This was undoubtedly music to the ears of the Russian ambassador, Kislyak, who ended up taking a rather more prominent part in American political life than he would have wished. He assumed the post in 2008 and his sociability soon turned him into a Washington insider. McFaul describes Kislyak as 'old-school, more Soviet than post-Soviet'.[19] Kislyak is a classic Russian *intelligent*: erudite, well-educated and with a deep understanding of international politics. Later, he was bemused and perplexed by the enormity of the scandal in which he was engulfed.[20] He was a realist in both senses of the word: in international affairs, sceptical about the interests driving the promotion of democracy and human rights; but a practical realist as well, looking to exploit opportunities to advance Russia's interests, but willing to engage with the United States and other countries to pursue common interests. He was thus a quintessential member of the contemporary Russian elite, sharing classic Putinite views about the country and its place in the world.

This perspective is sharply at odds with that of Clintonite internationalists. As McFaul puts it, 'The United States emerged from the cold war as the world's only superpower. Yet this super-superpower proved unable, inept, or unwilling to influence domestic change in Russia'.[21] Like Clinton (and he probably influenced her view), McFaul is deeply critical of Putin, which made him a problematic ambassadorial choice. He condemned Bush's attempts to connect with Putin at a personal level, arguing at the time of the Slovenian summit in June 2001 that 'I think there is plenty of good reason not to trust President Putin. This is a man who was trained to lie'.[22] Later, in Obama's first term, McFaul worked tirelessly to promote the reset in relations, correctly arguing that 'a more benign international environment for the Russian government would create better conditions for democratic change internally'.[23] But such a reset had to respect Russian security and sovereignty concerns accompanied by diplomatic finesse, something that was lacking. It certainly did not help when both McFaul and Clinton argued that their strategy was to engage with the Russian people over the heads of the Russian government. No administration would take kindly to such a potentially disruptive strategy, least of all the traumatised Russian leadership. The Soviet system had disintegrated barely two decades earlier, and the collapse of the Russian Empire in 1917 and the Time of Troubles (*Smuta*) in the early seventeenth century are part of everyday history and cultural reference points.[24]

Putin equally made little attempt to hide his dislike of McFaul, considering him partly responsible for the deterioration in U.S.–Russian relations.[25]

McFaul holds to the idea of Russia as an 'autocracy', and believes 'A new ideological struggle has emerged between Russia and the West, not between communism and capitalism but between democracy and autocracy'.[26] This is why, with Putin back in the Kremlin, Clinton in June 2012 urged Obama to take a harder line, arguing that Putin was 'deeply resentful of the US and suspicious of our actions', and sought to reclaim lost influence in the neighbourhood. She argued that although the project to create a Eurasian Union was called 'regional integration', it was in fact 'code for rebuilding a lost empire'.[27] In her final memo about Russia in January 2013, Clinton noted that the reset had in the end turned into a setback, and she urged Obama to set a 'new course' by taking a harder line. She argued that the relationship between Washington and Moscow would 'likely get worse before it got better', and Obama had to be 'realistic' about 'the danger that Putin posed to his neighbours and the world order'.[28] She argued 'We should hit the pause button on new efforts. Don't appear too eager to work together. Don't flatter Putin with high-level attention'. Russian intransigence would not prevent the United States pursuing its goals in Syria and elsewhere: 'Strength and resolve were the only language Putin would understand'.[29] As mentioned, she later compared Russian actions in Ukraine to those of Hitler in 1938.[30] These were the basic principles of her campaign in 2016, which McFaul helped draft. He summed it up as follows: defend the results of the reset, support Obama's coercive response to 'Putin's invasion of Ukraine', and 'pledge to do more'; in other words, 'Obama plus' meant an enhanced NATO presence in the Baltic, more military and economic support for Ukraine, new sanctions on Russia, the creation of no-fly zones in Syria, stronger support for democracy and human rights, and a stronger pushback against 'Russian propaganda' worldwide.[31] This programme was a recipe for intensified confrontation, if not war.

There could be no meeting of minds, and irenic ambitions on all sides were frustrated. McFaul frames the events of 2016 in the context of what happened in 2011: 'Five years later, Putin seized his moment for revenge when he intervened in the 2016 US presidential election to help Trump and hurt Clinton'.[32] McFaul's relentless defence of the Russiagate allegations flowed naturally from his model of Russian politics, in which 'Putin needs an enemy' and the domestic legitimacy of the Putin administration is questioned. The Russiagate narrative rests on the questionable assumption that Putin took revenge on Clinton by making mischief in the 2016 election.

Subverting the West

Election interference is nothing new. According to one study, the United States and the USSR intervened 117 times in foreign elections during the cold war, with the United States using dirty tricks and other methods 81 times. It appears that in 2016, 'the United States was about to get a taste of its own medicine'.[33] The concept of 'interference' became stretched and unclear, with generalised assertions of 'meddling' and 'collusion'. Trump did not help his case by confusing the character of collusion. In a tweet of 30 July 2018, he reiterated a point made by his lawyer Rudy Giuliani the day before: what's wrong with collusion? In his tweet Trump wrote, 'Collusion is not a crime, but that doesn't matter because there was No Collusion'.[34] Collusion takes place all the time between countries that are allied, but it is Russia's specific status as a competitor that made contacts problematic, prompting charges of interference. Plenty of countries, moreover, seek to influence U.S. politics, but the legacy of cold war conflict and renewed hostility made communication with Russia suspect.

The Communist International (Comintern) was established in March 1919 to spread the revolution globally and prompted the Palmer raids in November of that year as part of the Red Scare. During the cold war, there were plenty of times when Moscow tried to influence U.S. politics.[35] In 1948, the Soviet Union backed the Progressive Party's Henry Wallace, who had been Roosevelt's vice president but split with the Democratic Party over President Harry Truman's hawkish cold war stance. In 1964, Soviet and Czechoslovak agencies smeared the Republican candidate, Barry Goldwater, as a racist and Ku Klux Klan supporter. In 1968, the Soviet Union offered an unprecedented level of support for the Democratic candidate, Hubert Humphrey, including financial aid (which naturally was refused). In 1976, the KGB adopted 'active measures' against Democratic Senator Henry 'Scoop' Jackson, a virulent anti-Soviet hawk.[36] In 1983, KGB agents were instructed to help defeat Reagan in his bid for re-election. The overall goal was to undermine 'support in the United States and overseas for policies viewed as threatening to Moscow, discrediting US intelligence and law enforcement agencies, weakening US alliances and US relations with partners, and increasing Soviet power and influence across the globe'.[37] This is part of the larger pattern of mutual election interference. The CIA intervention in the Italian election of 1948 became the template for later actions, although after the cold war covert U.S. election interference allegedly became 'a tool of last resort', whereas Russia apparently gained a taste for it along with new skills.[38]

These are now conventionally described as 'active measures', but the term has been used indiscriminately. It is not the same as disinformation, of the sort which was used against Goldwater. Neither is it confined to cyber-enhanced informational warfare and cyberattacks, of the sort launched against Estonia, Georgia and Ukraine.[39] Active measures are now considered central to Russia's 'hybrid warfare', part of a sustained strategy undertaken by the Russian security services to undermine the enemy. However, the

Russian theory of hydrid warfare (*gibridnaya voina*) differs from the Western version, with more emphasis on psychological factors and the use of the media to demoralise the protagonist. A recent study argues that excessive Western politicisation of the concept represents 'an unhelpful and alarmist perception of an almost existential threat to the Western world', whereas a 'calm, pragmatic and detailed understanding of Russian actions' could temper the exaggerated view that Russia was trying 'to undermine the US-led liberal democratic order'.[40] The idea of informational battles fought through trolls, hacking teams and other proxies to gain advantage in the 'fifth domain' (cyberspace) gained notoriety following the publication of a famous article by Valerii Gerasimov, the chief of the Russian General Staff, in which he analysed the lessons of the Arab spring. He stressed that the 'very rules of war have changed', arguing that non-military means such as the 'use of political, economic and informational, humanitarian, and other non-military measures – applied in coordination with the protest potential of the population', can exceed 'the power of force of weapons in their effectiveness'.[41] The article was a response to what was perceived to be new forms of Western 'hybrid warfare', but it was taken as a statement of a new Russian doctrine.

In conditions of renewed cold war, the Soviet goals outlined above were revived, and that is why terms such as 'active measures' and 'disinformation' have been applied to the Russiagate affair.[42] Most Soviet actions were inept and remarkably ineffective.[43] Nevertheless, they provoked a neuralgic (and understandable) fear about foreign subversion that once again erupted as allegations of Russian meddling gained traction. Putin stands accused of trying to subvert Western democracy. Russian agencies have supported right-wing populists and other opponents of the liberal order. Such contacts began in the 1990s, but after 2012 intensified as Russia pivoted towards a more radical politics of resistance. Links have also been established with left-wing critics of the Atlantic consensus. These ties are intended to justify Russian policies and perspectives internationally, which is a legitimate goal; but more questionable is the alleged attempt to gain leverage over Western politics while undermining the liberal consensus – to 'sow discord', as the mantra became. The methods include information warfare, funding for radical right and pro-Moscow organisations and electoral interventions.[44] Stories about the latter made the U.S. public and elites receptive not only to claims that Russia substantively 'interfered' in 2016 but that it also sought to undermine American democracy. There is also an intriguing twist to the narrative, with claims that classic cold war double-bluff is at play. In keeping with the long tradition of deception, Russia's adversarial campaign 'although poorly executed [was] designed to be overestimated'.[45] In other words, however cack-handed and minimal Russian meddling in 2016 may have been, the goal was to provoke a reaction that would sow the desired discord.

The extent of Russian support for right-wing groups and electoral interventions has been exaggerated. In 2014, a Russian bank did provide a €9 million loan to Marine Le Pen's *Front National* (now *Rassemblement National*), but later the loan was recalled, and the bank closed as part of the Central Bank of Russia's attempt to clean up the Russian financial system. This does not look like a concerted plan to subvert French democracy. The same applies to the feared Russian attack on the German parliamentary elections in 2017, where Moscow was strangely quiet. The far-right Alliance for Germany (AfD) tripled its share of the vote from 4.7 to 12.6 per cent to become the third largest party, but this had nothing to do with Russia. Fear of Russian interference played its part in the French presidential election in 2017. Two days before the second round on 7 May, 20,000 campaign emails from the Emmanuel Macron campaign were uploaded to Pastebin, a file-sharing site, and then posted on 4chan, an anonymous message board. Most of the emails dealt with quotidian matters and none were scandalous. They were published by WikiLeaks in July and then publicised on various social media accounts, some of them with right-wing or Russian connections. In the end, no evidence emerged to prove that Russia was responsible. In sum, the endlessly repeated accusation that Russia 'hacked' the French presidential election in 2017 is questionable.

Russia was categorised as a cold war-style adversary, and its history of electoral interference was projected onto the new situation. Russia has become an adversary, but this is far from pre-ordained.[46] Unlike the Communist regime established in 1917, Russia does not seek to promote a revolution to destroy Western capitalist democracy. In keeping with its neo-revisionist stance, Russia seeks not to undermine the existing international system but to make it work in a more equitable manner. This may well be a quixotic endeavour, given the enormous discrepancy in power between the U.S.-led Atlantic system and Russia. Nevertheless, the Russian attempt to 'democratise' international politics is supported by China and other countries in the global South, but in the short-term Russia faced the enlarging Atlantic system on its own. Russia opposes NATO expansion and is critical of Western interventionism and punitive policies. This does not necessarily make Russia an adversary, as Trump seemed to understand, hence his attempts to engage. However, the traditional 'Trumanite' security state recognised a challenge when they saw one and mobilised against Moscow. Lacking an institutional political base of his own, Trump drew overwhelmingly from the traditional national security establishment to staff his administration. This provoked a striking contradiction between his expressed wishes and his actions.

The 'West' as a political concept only took shape during the cold war. It represented more than a geographical power system but a set of values that claimed to be universal, and these shaped the network of global governance institutions that regulate global affairs today.⁴⁷ The collapse of the Soviet Union and its associated Communist bloc in 1989–1991 reaffirmed the power and validity of the West's governance and economic institutions, as well as its purported values. Russia after 1991 also claimed to be committed to these values as it embarked on the rocky road of democratisation and economic transformation. However, the failure to transcend the institutional and political logic of the cold war, through the creation of a set of mutually acceptable security arrangements and practices that would include Russia as part of an extended 'greater West' in the end led to alienation, renewed confrontation, and ultimately a new cold war.⁴⁸ Russia is assumed to be leading a campaign to subvert the West. In this endeavour, Trump's apparent hostility to democratic institutions and his undoubted contempt for enshrined standards of public discourse made him, in the eyes of his critics, Putin's accomplice.

FORWARD TO THE PAST

Trump came to power with very few consistent positions, but one of them was that it made sense 'to get on with Russia'. If Trump had stopped there, then that claim would be a controversial yet legitimate policy position. However, he went on to observe that Putin was a strong leader, 'far more than our president [Obama] has been', at which point Trump alienated all but his core supporters.⁴⁹ Trump's attempt to normalise relations were stymied by claims of electoral collusion, hacking and the use of social media to sow discord and undermine American democracy. Trump praised his personal relationship with Putin, as he did with the Chinese President Xi Jinping, but his policies towards both countries were confrontational. It was Trump who took the lead in destroying the whole structure of arms control that had been so painstakingly built up during the cold war, and who sought to push Russia out of its traditional European energy market. Trump did not ultimately challenge the view of Russia as an adversary alongside China, Iran and North Korea. He did entertain the idea that Russia could be peeled away from its alignment with China, although he offered no serious incentives for Russia to do so.

Many of the themes sounded by Trump had been advanced earlier in one form or another by American leaders, but none with such intensity or generated by ideas that were so fundamentally at odds with the multilateral normative Atlanticism that took shape after 1945. Trump insisted that allies contribute more to their own defence, a long-term stance of U.S. leaders but now couched in terms of a transactional relationship rather than the traditional commitment to multilateral cooperation. It is in this light that Trump in 2016 argued that NATO was 'obsolete', and in power he made little effort to hide his distaste for the EU. He appeared to make NATO's Article 5 security guarantee dependent on whether a state met the 2 per cent defence spending target set by the NATO summit in Wales in September 2014. This represents a shift from collective to transactional defence, where security guarantees apply only if the appropriate contribution has been made.

There is a 'deep Trump', and on some important matters he held views that endured for decades. Trump's detestation of free trade, collective defence and multilateral institutions were unmoveable. According to one of his senior aides, 'There's some things where he's already reached the conclusion and it doesn't matter what you say. It doesn't matter what arguments you offer. He's not listening'.[50] Trump was the consummate opportunist, having little respect for international institutions or multilateral processes if they stood in the way of perceived American interests. International affairs were understood by Trump in the same way as domestic matters: a struggle for dominance in which there could be no enduring cooperation or alliances. Bob Woodward's book *Fear* shows a man out of his depth on most major international issues, yet repeatedly asking the right questions, such as why the United States after nearly two decades was still at war in Afghanistan.[51] By 2010, the United States had spent an astonishing $444bn on the war, twelve times the amount given in non-military aid to Afghanistan.[52] Trump's talk of spending more on America's decayed infrastructure made a lot of sense, although in the end not much was delivered.

Trump pursued a distinctive policy towards Russia. As candidate and then as president, he insisted on keeping channels of communication open. Trump refused to condemn Russia's alleged malfeasance, despite enormous pressure to do so, not so much out of respect for Russia, but because it tainted his victory. This stance entailed considerable costs, intensifying suspicion of some sort of clandestine links during his time as a businessman, of collusion as presidential candidate and then as some sort of Russian hostage in the White House. Russiagate reinforced a structural shift in American politics, with the Democrat's globalist agenda making them the party of militarism, while the Republicans questioned the cost and effectiveness of foreign engagements. Neoconservatives focused on the potential threat from China, whereas cosmopolitan liberals were more concerned by Russia's alleged threat to the liberal international order. Democrats aligned with the Trumanite national security establishment against Trump.

Russia rejected post-cold war U.S. expansive hegemony, which for some has become the national liberation struggle of our times accompanied by 'the need to combat official deception'.[53] With Trump in the White House, Russia sought to end its diplomatic isolation. To that end in March 2017, it sent an ambitious proposal to Washington to normalise relations across the board, but the offer was rejected. Russia in July then offered a more modest non-interference agreement to regulate behaviour in each other's elections, but it was also rejected by the State Department.⁵⁴ Instead, relations took a sharp turn for the worse, and from July 2017, Congress adopted increasingly severe sanctions while providing Ukraine with offensive weapons. Moscow's calls for talks about some sort of agreed cyber-security regime were also rejected. Defenders of the 'rules-based order' threatened regulatory restrictions, financial pressure and restrictions on political and media pluralism to counter the Russian threat.

Trump's approach to Russia is in line with his hard-nosed pragmatic view of international relations. He pressed for engagement but this did not prevent him taking numerous measures against Russia, including the sale of lethal arms to Ukraine, ramping up funding for the European Reassurance Initiative and reinforcing the U.S. troop presence in Europe, trying to stop the construction of the Nord Stream 2 natural gas pipeline across the Baltic from Ust-Luga to Germany, imposing harsh sanctions, expelling Russian diplomats and closing down Russian diplomatic facilities in the United States, and much more. Some derived from Trump being forced to act tough to prove that he was not in hock to Putin, but most came from his deep-seated beliefs in a competitive commercial world. Hence, Nord Stream 2 was viewed an impediment to increased U.S. LNG deliveries to Europe, reinforced by the long-term U.S. argument that this rendered Germany dependent on Moscow. Russiagate was one of the drivers of Trump's foreign policy, but *The Art of the Deal* was another.

Russian actions in 2016 were compared to Japan's sneak attack on Pearl Harbour in December 1941, and in various ways called an act of war. Even relative moderates stressed the need to 'stand up to the Kremlin' and argued that more forceful measures needed to be taken against Russia's 'malign activities' across the world. Joe Biden and his co-author lamented that the White House was likely to ignore their recommendations: 'Too many times, President Donald Trump has equivocated on whether Russia interfered in the 2016 election, even after he received briefings from top intelligence officials on precisely how Moscow did it'.⁵⁵ Trump's overall strategy was in the Henry Kissinger mode (and early on was advised by him), namely to try to recruit Russia to align with the United States against what was perceived as the greatest long-term threat, China. In practice, the sum of U.S. actions only reinforced the Russo-Chinese alignment, and there was zero chance of Russia defecting. The two countries considered the United States an unreliable partner. Instead of Trump's more realist foreign policy instincts, he presided over an increasingly ideologically charged confrontation with both Moscow and Beijing. As Timothy Phillips notes in his study of the intelligence service and Russia in the 1920s, the British authorities scared themselves with spectres of their own making, provoking a war scare and the rupturing of diplomatic relations.⁵⁶ The new cold war recreated this past.

The 16 July 2018 Helsinki Summit

By the time he sat down with Trump for their first summit, Putin had met with U.S. leaders some forty times since taking office, including twice with Trump – at the G20 meeting in Hamburg on 7 July and the Asia-Pacific Economic Cooperation (APEC) meeting in Da Nang, Vietnam, on 10 November 2017. There was also the meeting between the Russian foreign minister, Sergei Lavrov, and Trump in the Oval Office on 10 May 2017, with Kislyak in attendance. Distrusting the media, Trump allowed only Russian news agencies in to cover the meeting, which not surprisingly rather alienated Western reporters. Trump informed his bewildered visitors that he had just sacked Comey and believed that 'pressure because of Russia' had been taken off, although in that regard (as we shall see) he could not have been more mistaken. The goal from the Russian side was to normalise relations, above all through the lifting of sanctions and the return of diplomatic compounds, and this apparently was also Trump's intention. In the end, his lack of diplomatic experience only made matters worse. Trump is charged with revealing a crucial counter-terrorism secret about a planned ISIS operation.[57] In fact, Trump did not reveal Israel as the source of the intelligence or the specific intelligence-gathering method, but this was done by White House leakers.[58] Obama-era officials, the State Department and intelligence agencies united to thwart Trump's attempt to improve relations, which in the context was perceived as selling out to Russia.[59] As Frum notes, 'In order to stop him from betraying his office and the country, the professionals around him [Trump] have also effectively prevented him from fulfilling his office and serving his country, supposing he were ever minded to do that'.[60]

The auguries were not good when Trump and Putin met in Helsinki. Just three days earlier, Mueller indicted a dozen Russian intelligence officers for hacking the DNC, placing Russiagate at the centre of press attention.[61] Comparable to the 4 June 1961 Kennedy-Khrushchev summit in Vienna, when cold war pressures (and Kennedy's apparent unpreparedness) torpedoed the intention of both leaders to normalise relations, this one also had devastating consequences. It inflicted 'a psychological trauma on the US establishment and public opinion more broadly'. Trump, like Gorbachev after his summit with Reagan in Reykjavik in 1986, was accused of 'selling out the country'.[62] Trump tried to keep the issue of Russian electoral interference and global politics separate, whereas his opponents ensured that the former shaped the latter. Mueller's indictment acted as 'a warning to the US president and a calculated affront to the Russian president'.[63] Bolton advised that the Mueller indictments were 'better announced before the summit, for Putin to contemplate'.[64]

The two-hour talk between Putin and Trump, with only interpreters present, covered arms control and prohibiting weapons in space, regional security issues including security for Israel, Syria, Russia's annexation of Crimea and support for separatists in Eastern Ukraine, and the Nord Stream 2 gas pipeline to Germany. The Russian side called for 'strategic stability' consultations to discuss the difficult issues, including how to include destabilising new types of weapons into the arms control process. Moscow also called for an extension of the New START Treaty by five years after its expiry in February 2021.[65] However, the positive discussions were scuppered by the disastrous press conference. Putin took control, outlining the broad outlines of the discussion and the burning issues of the day, while Trump's statement was anodyne and awkward. Putin stressed the complex international situation:

> It's quite to clear to everyone that the bilateral relationship is going through a complicated stage, and yet those impediments, the current tension, the tense atmosphere, essentially have no solid reason behind it. The cold war is a thing of the past, the era of acute ideological confrontation of the two countries is a thing of the remote past, is a vestige of the past. . . . Today, both Russia and the United States face a whole new set of challenges [above all] a dangerous maladjustment of mechanisms for maintaining international security and stability.

When it came to the burning topic of the day, he noted,

> Once again, President Trump mentioned the issue of the so-called interference of Russia with the American elections, and I had to reiterate things I said several times, including during our personal contacts, that the Russian state has never interfered and is not going to interfere into American internal affairs, including the election process.[66]

Trump stressed the potential for cooperation: 'We're getting together and we have a chance to do some great things, whether it's nuclear proliferation in terms of stopping, we have to do it – ultimately, that's probably the most important thing that we can be working on'. He noted that 'Our relationship has never been worse than it is now. However, that changed as of about four hours ago. I really believe that'.

His optimism was misplaced. In response to a question on Russian electoral interference, Trump's response was equivocal. He did not actually deny that interference took place, arguing that it was under Obama that there was inaction on the matter, while asserting that there was no 'collusion', and that he had won fairly, after a 'brilliant campaign'. In response to a question on the Mueller investigation, Trump agreed that 'the probe is a disaster for our country. I think it's kept us apart, it's kept us separated. There was no collusion at all'. Putin chipped in to argue 'Isn't is natural to be sympathetic towards a person who is willing to restore the relationship with our country, who wants to work with us?'. After some more points, he brought up the Bill Browder case (discussed below), who he claimed earned over $1.5 billion in Russia but 'never paid any taxes' and 'they sent huge amount of money, 400 million to the campaign of Hillary Clinton'. The final question proved fatal, with a reporter asserting that 'Every US intelligence agency has concluded that Russia did [interfere in the 2016 election]'. The first question was 'who do you believe?' and the second could not be more provocative: 'would you now, with the whole world watching, tell President Putin, would you denounce what happened in 2016 and would you warn him to never do it again?'. Rather than some anodyne answer, Trump mentioned the DNC's refusal to let the FBI examine their server, then after some confused phraseology he said,

> I have President Putin: he just said it's not Russia. I will say this: 'I don't see any reason why it would be, but I really do want to see the server. . . . I have great confidence in my intelligence people, but I will tell you that President Putin was extremely strong and powerful in his denial today'.[67]

Trump's refusal to accept the conclusions of his intelligence agencies provoked a firestorm of criticism. He was forced to backtrack the following day, when he asserted rather more forcefully that Russia did in fact interfere in the election. Trump never denied that some sort of cyber-hacking had taken place, but Trump naturally preferred to stress that he had won fairly and because of his own efforts. Even as he acknowledged interference, he emphasised that it had not affected the outcome of the election. Trump's strategy of separating the conduct of foreign policy from the election interference issue failed catastrophically, as did his attempt to establish a constructive dialogue with Russia. His stumbling performance at Helsinki added to the charge sheet against him. Bannon described his demeanour at the press conference 'like a beaten dog' after Trump had endured a two-hour tirade by Putin.[68] Trump was not only out of his depth but shown to the world to be so, and this represented a national humiliation for America.

Trump appeared awkward and ill-prepared when standing next to a man who had been president for eighteen years and who was famous for his mastery of detail. The normal hierarchies were inverted, and instead of the United States assuming the lead, as Obama and his predecessors would naturally do, it was Russia which looked like the dominant power. The perception was reinforced by the body language, which appeared to show the smaller man in charge, an observation that enraged Trump's critics. Further, the Russian offer to allow Mueller to question the indicted Russians only inflamed matters. Collaboration with Russia on the investigation was viewed as a new type of 'collusion', and hence summarily rejected. This was even more the case when Putin suggested that Russia should be allowed to question Browder, long a Russian *bête noire*. The request was logical, although provocative, but what was certainly irrational was the addition of McFaul's name to the list of suspects Russia sought to question. Whatever one thinks of McFaul's understanding of international politics, no can doubt his sincere attempt to improve relations through the early Obama-era reset and, in his own way, as ambassador.

Bolton notes that 'Trump believed that acknowledging Russia's meddling in US politics, or in that of many other countries in Europe and elsewhere, would implicitly acknowledge that he had colluded with Russia in his 2016 campaign'.[69] American domestic politics certainly exacerbated the situation: 'The post-Helsinki hysteria reveals not merely the mindset of the president's enemies, but the depth of their determination to destroy him'. Trump himself sailed on imperturbably, and on 19 July commented: 'The Fake News Media want so badly to see a major confrontation with Russia, even a confrontation that could lead to war. They are pushing so recklessly and hate the fact that I'll probably have a good relationship with Putin'.[70] Kissinger commented that 'It was a meeting that had to take place. I have advocated it for several years. It has been submerged by American domestic issues. It is certainly a missed opportunity'. As for the broader context, Kissinger was judicious: 'I think Trump may be one of those figures in history who appears from time to time to mark the end of an era and to force it to give up its old pretences. It doesn't necessarily mean that he knows this, or that he is considering any great alternative. It could just be an accident'.[71] As the master of geopolitics, Kissinger encouraged Trump in his ambition to 'get on' with Putin, to temper Russia's drive to create an anti-hegemonic alignment with China, India and other like-minded countries, tired of what they perceived to be Western double standards, in which desirable universal norms were subordinated to the power system in which they were embedded. Kissinger encouraged Trump to have closer relations with Russia to contain a rising China.[72] Such larger considerations were lost in the Russiagate maelstrom.

NOTES

1. 'Transcript: Donald Trump's Foreign Policy Speech', *New York Times*, 27 April 2016, https://www.nytimes.com/2016/04/28/us/politics/transcript-trump-foreign-policy.html.

2. Walt, *Hell of Good Intentions*, pp. 5, 260.

3. For analysis, see Angela Stent, *Putin's World: Russia against The West and With the Rest* (New York, Twelve, 2019).

4. Jeffrey M. Jones, 'Americans Increasingly see Russia as Threat, Top US Enemy', 16 February 2015, https://news.gallup.com/poll/181568/americans-increasingly-russia-threat-top-enemy.aspx.

5. Examined by Sakwa, *Russia against the Rest*.

6. Legvold, *Return to Cold War*.

7. Cf. Andrew Monaghan, *A 'New Cold War'? Abusing History, Misunderstanding Russia* (London, Chatham House Research Paper, May 2015).

8. George S. Beebe, *The Russia Trap: How Our Shadow War With Russia Could Spiral Into Nuclear Catastrophe* (New York, Thomas Dunne Books, 2019), p. 3. He provides one of the best accounts of the slide into renewed confrontation, with empathetic understanding of the perspectives of both sides.

9. David S. Foglesong, *The American Mission and the "Evil Empire": The Crusade for a "Free Russia" since 1881* (Cambridge, Cambridge University Press, 2007), p. 62.

10. Cited by Foglesong, *The American Mission*, p. 193.

11. For a perceptive analysis of the growing estrangement, see Strobe Talbott, *The Russia Hand: A Memoir of Presidential Diplomacy* (New York, Random House, 2003).

12. 'Yanks to the Rescue: The Secret Story of How American Advisors Helped Yeltsin Win', *Time*, 15 July 1996, cover and inside story by Michael Kramer, 'Rescuing Boris', http://content.time.com/time/magazine/article/0,9171,984833,00.html.

13. Vladimir Putin, 'Speech and the Following Discussion at the Munich Conference on Security Policy', *Kremlin.ru*, 10 February 2007, http://eng.kremlin.ru/transcripts/8498.

14. Richard Sakwa, *The Lost Peace: How We Failed to Prevent a New Cold War* (London, Yale University Press, forthcoming 2022).

15. For a recent enunciation of this view, see John J. Mearsheimer, *The Great Delusion: Liberal Dreams and International Realities* (New Haven and London, Yale University Press, 2018).

16. The Liberal Democratic Party of Russia (LDPR) and its leader Vladimir Zhirinovsky believed that Trump's election would be a game changer, and that is why they cracked open the champagne when news of his election reached the State Duma.

17. Nance, *The Plot to Hack America*, pp. 69, 76.

18. David E. Sanger and Maggie Haberman, 'Transcript: Donald Trump on NATO, Turkey's Coup Attempt and the World', *New York Times*, 21 July 2016, https://www.nytimes.com/2016/07/22/us/politics/donald-trump-foreign-policy-interview.html.

19. Michael McFaul, *From Cold War to Hot Peace: The Inside Story of Russia and America* (London, Allen Lane, 2018), p. 100.

20. Personal talk, Sochi, 19 October 2017.

21. McFaul, *Cold War to Hot Peace*, p. 55.

22. McFaul, *Cold War to Hot Peace*, p. 64.

23. McFaul, *Cold War to Hot Peace*, p. 93.

24. For a powerful expression of this argument, see Patrick Lawrence, 'Discerning Vladimir Putin', *Raritan*, Vol. 38, No. 1, Summer 2018, pp. 1–15.
25. McFaul, *Cold War to Hot Peace*, p. ix.
26. McFaul, *Cold War to Hot Peace*, p. x.
27. Clinton, *Hard Choices*, p. 236.
28. Clinton, *Hard Choices*, p. 244.
29. Joby Warrick and Karen De Young, 'From "Reset" to "Pause": The Real Story behind Hillary Clinton's Feud with Vladimir Putin', *Washington Post*, 3 November 2016.
30. 'Hillary Clinton Says Vladimir Putin's Crimea Occupation Echoes Hitler', *Guardian*, 6 March 2014, https://www.theguardian.com/world/2014/mar/06/hillary-clinton-says-vladimir-putins-crimea-occupation-echoes-hitler.
31. McFaul, *Cold War to Hot Peace*, p. 430.
32. McFaul, *Cold War to Hot Peace*, p. 244.
33. Hettena, *Trump/Russia*, p. 199.
34. Alex Ward, 'Trump Says "Collusion is Not a Crime". Not Quite', *Vox*, 31 July 2018, https://www.vox.com/world/2018/7/31/17634146/trump-collusion-crime-russia-mueller.
35. For the context and activities, see Jonathan Haslam, *Russia's Cold War: From the October Revolution to the Fall of the Wall* (New Haven, CT, Yale University Press, 2012).
36. Paul Kengor, *Dupes: How America's Adversaries Have Manipulated Progressives for a Century* (Wilmington, DE, ISI Books, reprint 2018).
37. Seth Jones, *Russian Meddling in the United States: The Historical Context of the Mueller Report* (Washington, DC, CSIS, 2019), p. 2, https://csis-prod.s3.amazonaws.com/s3fs-public/publication/190328_RussianMeddlingintheUS_WEB_V.2.pdf.
38. David Shimer, *Rigged: America, Russia, and One Hundred Years of Covert Electoral Interference* (London, William Collins, 2020).
39. Piret Pernik, 'The Early Days of Cyberattacks: the Cases of Estonia, Georgia and Ukraine', in Nicu Popescu and Stanislav Secrieru (eds), *Hacks, Leaks and Disruptions: Russian Cyber Strategies*, Chaillot Papers No. 148 (Paris, European Union Institute for Security Studies, October 2018), pp. 53–64.
40. Ofer Fridman, *Russian Hybrid Warfare: Resurgence and Politicisation* (London, Hurst, 2018), pp. 168, 125.
41. Valerii Gerasimov, 'Tsennost' nauki i predvidenii', *Voenno-promyshlennyi kur'er*, No. 8, 27 February 2013, http://vpk-news.ru/articles/14632.
42. For an excellent historical analysis, see Thomas Rid, *Active Measures: The Secret History of Disinformation and Political Warfare* (London, Profile Books, 2020).
43. A point made by Paul Robinson, 'Corrupting Democracy', Irrussianality, 22 April 2019, https://irrussianality.wordpress.com/2019/04/22/corrupting-democracy/.
44. Anton Shekhovtsov, *Russia and the Western Far Right: Tango Noir* (London, Routledge, 2017).
45. Rid, *Active Measures*, p. 8.

46. Gary Leupp, 'Is Russia an Adversary?', Counterpunch.org, 9 August 2018, https://www.counterpunch.org/2018/08/09/is-russia-an-adversary/.

47. Michael Kimmage, *The Abandonment of the West: The History of an Idea in American Foreign Policy* (New York, Basic Books, 2020).

48. Cohen, *War with Russia*. See also Sakwa, *Russia against the Rest*.

49. For a scathing critique, see Thomas L. Friedman, 'Donald Trump's Putin Crush', *New York Times*, 14 September 2016, https://www.nytimes.com/2016/09/14/opinion/donald-trumps-putin-crush.html.

50. Woodward, *Fear*, p. 232.

51. Woodward, *Fear*, p. 124. Wolff argues that Woodward's main source was McMaster, so not surprisingly his book reflected the latter's concerns, *Siege*, p. 225. McFarland also notes Trump's 'surprisingly accurate grasp on the big issues', *Revolution*, p. 34.

52. John Gittings, *The Glorious Art of Peace: Paths to Peace in the New Age of War* (Oxford, Oxford University Press, 2018).

53. Johnstone, *Circle in the Darkness*, p. 424.

54. John Hudson, 'No Deal: How Secret Talks with Russia to Prevent Election Meddling Collapsed', *BuzzFeed*, 8 December 2017, https://www.buzzfeednews.com/article/johnhudson/no-deal-how-secret-talks-with-russia-to-prevent-election.

55. Joseph R. Biden Jr. and Michael Carpenter', 'How to Stand up to the Kremlin', *Foreign Affairs*, 2018, Vol. 97, No. 1, January-February 2018, p. 56.

56. Timothy Phillips, *The Secret Twenties: British Intelligence, the Russians and the Jazz Age* (Cambridge, Granta Books, 2017).

57. Greg Miller and Greg Jaffe, 'Trump Revealed Highly Classified Information to Russian Foreign Minister and Ambassador', *Washington Post*, 15 May 2017, https://www.washingtonpost.com/world/national-security/trump-revealed-highly-classified-information-to-Russian-foreign-minister-and ambassador/2017/05/15/530c172a-3960-11e7-9e48-c4f199710b69_story.html.

58. Marc Thiessen, 'Trump is Surrounded by Leakers: Why Should he Trust them with his Putin Notes?', *Washington Post*, 16 January 2019.

59. Frum, *Trumpocracy*, p. 171.

60. Frum, *Trumpocracy*, p. 174.

61. Apparently, Mueller offered Trump the choice of whether the indictment should be delivered before or after the summit, and his 'choice surprised the prosecutors. He wanted the announcement of the indictment to take place prior to the Helsinki summit', Philip Rucker and Carol Leonnig, *A Very Stable Genius* (London, Bloomsbury, 2020), p. 273.

62. Maxim Suchkov, 'Beyond the Horizon: Who Won in Helsinki?', *Valdai Discussion Club*, 19 July 2018, http://valdaiclub.com/a/highlights/beyond-the-horizon-who-won-in-helsinki/.

63. Wolff, *Siege*, p. 168.

64. Bolton, *The Room Where It Happened*, p. 149.

65. Bryan Bender, 'Leaked Document: Putin Lobbied Trump on Arms Control', 7 August 2018, https://www.politico.com/story/2018/08/07/putin-trump-arms-control-russia-724718.

66. 'News Conference Following Talks between the Presidents of Russia and the United States', Kremlin.ru, 16 July 2018, http://en.kremlin.ru/events/president/news/58017.
67. 'News Conference', 16 July 2018.
68. Wolff, *Siege*, pp. 174–5.
69. Bolton, *Room Where It Happened*, p. 63.
70. Patrick J. Buchanan, 'Trump Stands his Ground on Putin', 19 July 2018, Official Website, https://buchanan.org/blog/trump-stands-his-ground-on-putin-129692.
71. Edward Luce, 'Henry Kissinger: "We are in a Very, Very Grave Period"', *Financial Times*, 20 July 2018, https://www.ft.com/content/926a66b0-8b49-11e8-bf9e-8771d5404543.
72. Asawin Suebsaeng, Andrew Desiderio, Sam Sein and Bethany-Allen-Ebrahimian, 'Henry Kissinger Pushed Trump to Work with Russia to Box in China', *Daily Beast*, 25 July 2018, https://www.thedailybeast.com/henry-kissinger-pushed-trump-to-work-with-russia-to-box-in-china.

Chapter 5

Hacking the Election

The core of the Russiagate affair is the claim that two teams from Russian intelligence, unbeknown to each other, gained access to the DNC's computer network from July 2015, and maintained it until at least June 2016. They then allegedly transferred the material through two 'cut-outs' (false personas) Guccifer 2 and DCLeaks to WikiLeaks. The initial leak of 19,952 emails clearly benefitted the Republican Party and Trump personally, hence the claim that the material was published in coordination with the Trump campaign to cause maximum damage to Clinton, a goal that Assange pursued, because he was being used (knowingly or not) by Moscow to advance its aims. Later another 20,000 emails were published.[1] However, the forensic evidence for these three charges – that Russia was responsible for accessing the emails, that they were published in coordination with the Trump campaign and that the whole operation was conducted at Moscow's behest – is disputed. Instead of a hacking operation, some sort of leak may be involved. Equally, the claimed attacks on state election infrastructure turned out to be exaggerated.

THE DEMOCRATIC PARTY EMAILS

The Foreign Intelligence Service (SVR, the former First Department of the KGB) team had been identified since 2008 as Advanced Persistent Threat 29 (APT29), also known by a range of monikers, the best-known of which is Cozy Bear although The Dukes is also commonly used. Fancy Bear (APT28) is identified as a unit within the Main (Intelligence) Administration of the General Staff of the Defence Ministry. The body was established in its present form in 1953 and until 2010 was known as the Main Intelligence

Administration, GRU, and the latter name has stuck although GU today would be more accurate since the word 'Intelligence' has been dropped. In the United States, the CIA and Defence Intelligence Agency (DIA) have broadly similar functions. The GRU shares foreign intelligence concerns with the civilian SVR and the FSB's counter-intelligence divisions. Of them all, it is the GRU that in recent years has gained a reputation for recklessness, including the hack of the DNC and the attempted killing of Sergei and Yulia Skripal in Salisbury, England, on 4 March 2018 and the attempted assassination of the oppositionist Alexei Navalny in Tomsk on 20 August 2020. The GRU team (APT28) was given the cryptonym Fancy Bear (although it goes by many other names, depending on who discovers it), and appears to have been active since 2007. There are estimated to be about a hundred APTs worldwide. These are not actual groups of people but a description of the malware kits used by hackers working in cyberspace.[2] There is a long list of alleged targets hit by the Bear bestiary and their associates, beginning with Estonia in 2007 all the way through to the American election, with Fancy Bear apparently attacking the German Bundestag in May 2015.[3]

Cozy Bear was present in the DNC computer systems from July 2015 and was relatively 'quiet'; but in early 2016, it was joined by the GRU's far more aggressive Fancy Bear. It appears that they worked independently and were not aware of the others' presence. FBI agent Adrian Hawkins was the first to spot the activity, and on 6 August 2015 contacted the DNC. However, through a series of miscommunications, the responsible people were not alerted until much later.[4] In March 2016, the email account of John Podesta, the Clinton campaign chair, was accessed through a phishing attack by Cozy Bear. When the DNC acted, it turned to an outside company, CrowdStrike, to investigate. Established in 2011 and based in Sunnyvale, California, CrowdStrike is a major military and cyber intelligence contractor to the Pentagon. One of its founders and CTO, Dmitry Alperovitch, is a non-resident senior fellow, Cyber Statecraft Initiative, of the Atlantic Council, which receives funding from outspoken critics of Russia and leading defence contractors. It is dedicated to maintaining 'liberal hegemony and US global leadership'.[5] Employing CrowdStrike for such a sensitive operation clearly triggered multiple conflicts of interest. Equally, at no point was the FBI allowed to conduct a forensic examination of the DNC servers. The outsourcing of state capacity may well be the trend of our days, but the absence of an independent FBI investigation inevitably casts doubt on the findings. CrowdStrike is just one element in the vast military–intelligence–cyber (MIC) complex, where Google and the other tech giants set the pace for innovation and para-statal activity. Corporate diplomacy is substituting for public engagement as the MIC complex reshapes society and citizenship.[6]

CrowdStrike began its investigation in April 2016, and soon discovered the two entities in the system. Cozy Bear had long been rooting about the emails and stealing files, whereas Fancy Bear only gained access in April 2016. Surprisingly, there was no evidence of collaboration between the two groups.[7] Fancy Bear targeted the vital opposition research files held on the seventeen Republican hopefuls, and above all the material on Trump.[8] The Trump opposition research dossier was compiled by DNC staffer Alexandra Chalupa, a Ukrainian American who would later figure as part of investigations into 'Ukrainegate' interference in the election. CrowdStrike asked DNC managers to keep quiet about the intrusion, arguing that it needed time to identify the Russian hackers and their tools, and only then block their access. It appears (according to the Mueller indictment) that the GRU hackers detected that they were being monitored and on 31 May, two weeks before the public disclosure of the hack, began to resist CrowdStrike. After that, the contest escalated into the virtual equivalent of hand-to-hand combat.[9] CrowdStrike decided that the software on every machine had to be changed, and until then secrecy was considered essential. On Friday 10 June, employees were asked to leave their laptops and vacate the premises, and for the next two days, CrowdStrike replaced the software and applied new log-in passwords. In June, Alperovich, published the report *Bears in the Midst*, the first public accusation of Russian responsibility for the DNC hacking.[10] We know from testimony provided by Trump associate Roger Stone that CrowdStrike provided three reports to the FBI in redacted and draft form, but according to federal prosecutors, the administration never obtained CrowdStrike's full and unedited report, and there is no evidence that Mueller received any additional information beyond that provided by CrowdStrike.[11]

The DNC is considered a valid intelligence target, and it appears (rather worryingly) that such scanning goes on all the time. However, the usual procedure is to hoard the information, as may have happened with material gleaned from the RNC. Placing the material on the internet during an election campaign is something new.[12] This sustains the charge that Russia 'hacked' American democracy by waging a cyber-enabled information warfare (CEIW) campaign to damage Clinton's campaign and to boost Trump's. By the time the DNC network had been cleansed, a trove of data had been extruded. This material was then made public through a Wordpress blog, beginning from 15 June under the auspices of a persona by the name of Guccifer 2.0. The original Guccifer (Marcel Lazar Lehel) was by then in jail, and by all accounts, he was a Romanian hacker who accessed high-profile U.S. government accounts, including Clinton's private email system.[13] WikiLeaks and DCLeaks (a site established in June 2016 and considered a cut-out for Fancy Bear) were later also used to make the material public. The 15 June document posted by Guccifer 2.0 was tainted with 'Russian fingerprints', including Cyrillic language metadata and the author's designation as 'Feliks Edmundovich', the given name and patronymic of Dzerzhinsky, the founder of the Soviet secret police, the Cheka, in December 2017. Forensic analysis indicates that the material may have been synthetically adulterated with Russian characteristics (more on this below).[14]

The DNC material was incendiary. It showed the Democrats' political machine to be 'petty, vindictive, and determined to anoint Hillary Clinton as the Democratic nominee despite grassroots enthusiasm for challenger Bernie Sanders'.[15] The timing here is crucial. On 12 June, Assange announced that he would be publishing 'emails related to Hillary Clinton'; on 14 June, CrowdStrike announced that malware had been found on the DNC server and claimed to have evidence it was inserted by Russians; and on 15 June, Guccifer 2.0 claimed responsibility for the hack and WikiLeaks' source; and posted documents that appear synthetically tainted with Russian attributes. This is where we move into intensely contested terrain. The mainstream version advanced by Mueller argues that the various personas, Guccifer 2.0 and DCLeaks, were simply Russian cut-outs transmitting the material to WikiLeaks, which in turn coordinated its actions with its masters in Moscow. The main alternative argument is that there is no evidence to prove that the material got to WikiLeaks in this way, and that it may have been leaked through a thumb-drive. As for the view that WikiLeaks coordinated its actions with Moscow, the evidence is at the most circumstantial and is forcefully denied by Assange. Clintonian Democrats certainly argue that this was part of a 'pre-emptive move to associate Russia with anything WikiLeaks might have been about to publish and to "show" that it came from a Russian hack'.[16]

Again, the timing is crucial. Over 98 per cent of the 44,000 emails published by WikiLeaks were sent or received by senior DNC officials between 18 April and 25 May 2016, and for over half that time CrowdStrike had already installed its software and was monitoring the network. On 12 June, Assange announced that he had emails related to Clinton, and the first public report of the hack was published by Nakashima on 14 June. She stated that malware has been found on the DNC, which CrowdStrike affirmed had been placed by the Russians. The next day, Guccifer 2.0, emerging from nowhere but described by Mueller as a GRU creation, confirmed the previous day's allegations and claimed responsibility for hacking the DNC, as well as being the source for WikiLeaks. He released a 237-page document called *Donald Trump Report*, dated 19 December 2015, summarising Chalupa's opposition research on the Republican candidate with sections, such as 'Trump is a Liar' and 'Bad Businessman', followed by a section detailing his multiple bankruptcies.[17] Guccifer 2.0 also published an Excel spreadsheet called 'Big Donors', listing twenty-one people who had contributed over $500,000 to the DNC and claimed to have many other documents in his possession.[18] Guccifer 2.0 denied that he was Russian: 'I don't like Russians and their foreign policy. I hate being attributed to Russia', and insisted that he was from Romania, 'just like the first Guccifer'. He then gave details, saying that he hacked into the DNC system in summer 2015 by exploiting an unknown vulnerability in NGP VAN, software provided for the DNC that used a Windows system, and then installed Trojans on several PCs. He insisted that he had left Russian metadata in the leaked documents as his personal 'watermark'. He admitted that he had been expelled on 12 June when CrowdStrike rebooted the system.[19]

The mainstream line is that Guccifer 2.0 was a Russian front: 'considering a long trail of breadcrumbs pointing back to Russia left by the hacker, as well as other circumstantial evidence, it appears more likely that Guccifer 2.0 is nothing but a disinformation or deception campaign by Russian state-sponsored hackers to cover up their own hack – and a hasty and sloppy one at that'.[20] Sceptical points have been raised, including the view that the Russian metadata could easily have been inserted to achieve false attribution.[21] The 'Russian fingerprints' corroborated the claims made by CrowdStrike the day before. Another sign of fakery is that Guccifer 2 operated mostly in U.S. time zones and with local settings specific to a device configured for use within the United States.[22] Guccifer 2.0 released more documents from the DNC on 30 June on the WordPress blog, and once again denied Russian links and spoke warmly of Assange. Others note that WikiLeaks did not use any of the emails sent to it by Guccifer 2, although it published similar emails, implying that whoever created Guccifer 2 knew what WikiLeaks had and sent duplicates with Russian fingerprints. This suggests that 'Guccifer 2.0 had malicious intent towards WikiLeaks from the outset'.[23]

WikiLeaks in the end published the most consequential and embarrassing emails. Assange as we have seen first went public on 12 June to announce that his website would soon be publishing a raft of emails related to the Clinton campaign, stressing that 'WikiLeaks has a very big year ahead'. Assange at the time had been holed up in the Ecuadorian embassy in London since 19 June 2012, when he asked for political asylum after he had lost his legal fight against extradition to Sweden. On 22 July, Assange tweeted 'Are you ready for Hillary?' and that day WikiLeaks posted the first tranche of stolen documents, 19,252 DNC emails and 8,000 attachments covering the period from January 2015 to 25 May 2016. The timing of publication was certainly devastating, just three days before the Democratic convention in Philadelphia, 25–28 July. The campaign plans of the Clinton campaign were disrupted, and the revelation that the DNC was biased against Sanders forced DNC chair Debbie Wasserman Schultz to resign. She co-chaired Clinton's 2008 campaign against Obama, which raises questions about her ability to manage the campaign impartially. The atmosphere at the convention was fractious, with Sanders' supporters embittered and alienated. One email chain showed how DNC officials planned a line of attack on Sanders' religious beliefs, while another sought to portray his campaign as a mess. In response – and this is the crucial beginning of the Russiagate narrative – all senior Clinton campaign staff agreed that they would 'get the word out that this was a Russian hit job', while others (some of whom had been briefed on the early Steele memos) argued that 'the Russians were using WikiLeaks as part of a plot to elect Trump'.[24] The stock reaction of the Clintonites was 'to keep the Russian intervention in the spotlight', arguing that 'the Russians were covertly attacking the election'.[25]

Trump fanned the flames of the collusion narrative in his 27 July press conference in Florida. In response to a reporter's provocative question if he would call on Putin to 'stay out' of the election, he insisted that he had 'nothing to do with Putin' and cast doubt on whether Russia had hacked the Democrats. He insisted, 'Nobody knows who it is', but if the Russians were responsible, he had a message for them. He called on 'Russia, if you're listening, I hope you're able to find the 30,000 emails that are missing [referring to the emails that Clinton had deleted from her server]. I think that you'll probably be rewarded mightily by our press'.[26] Trump of course was being ironic, but his comment was taken as evidence of collusion, if not treason. In fact, the provenance of the DNC material remains contested, as does the issue of coordination between Assange and the alleged Russian cut-outs. When asked about this, by Sean Hannity on Fox News, Assange insisted, 'Our source is not the Russian government and it is not a state party', and he accused the Obama administration of trying to delegitimise Trump's election.[27] Assange repeatedly insisted that Russia had nothing to do with the emails, but how WikiLeaks got the emails remains a mystery – Assange insists that he has to protect his sources, and acted only as publisher. They could have come through the route suggested by Mueller, but the flash drive version (or uploading on to an encrypted remote server) is also credible.

Assange added more fuel to the fire when on Twitter on 9 August 2016 he offered a $20,000 reward for information about the murder in Washington of Seth Rich. Shortly afterwards, he suggested that Rich may have been a 'source' for the hacked material, thus suggesting a motive for the killing. Rich was a twenty-seven-year-old DNC staffer shot to death in an unsolved murder case in the early hours of 10 July in what appears to have been a bungled street burglary. Since 2014 Rich had worked for the DNC as a voter expansion director. He was shot several times in the back, but nothing was stolen. When WikiLeaks published the DNC emails on 22 July, the case went viral. Trump-supporting conspiracy theorists argue that Rich leaked the DNC emails, and had then been killed either in retaliation (by Clintonians) or to keep him quiet (by the CIA). On the other side, there are reports that the whole Rich conspiracy theory originated with the SVR and was amplified by the IRA.[28] Either way, Russiagate sceptics make much of the Rich case. Fox News in May 2017 asserted that Rich had leaked the DNC emails to WikiLeaks. The article suggested that Rich downloaded the documents, then uploaded them in a Drop Box account for Assange.[29] Rich's family reacted with fury and sued Fox, a suit that was dismissed in August 2018.

No less incendiary was the activity of Roger Stone, the veteran political campaigner associated with the Trump campaign. On 21 August, he indicated fore-knowledge about the WikLeaks releases of John Podesta's emails, infamously tweeting 'Podesta's time in the barrel will come'.[30] Later, Mueller would use this as evidence that he had advance information, proving coordination between the Trump campaign and publication of the emails. In mid-September, DCLeaks started publishing email chains from Podesta, including messages to Clinton. Once again, 'The Clintonites devised a strategy for shaping the story. This was not about the documents coming out, they told reporters. This was about Russia interfering in US democracy'.[31] Nothing spectacular was revealed, but for a few crucial months, news coverage focused on Democratic Party emails. The Clinton team was naturally concerned about internal communications being made public, especially if they had been stolen by a country that they considered an adversary. Stone was later accused of having coordinated the publication of Podesta emails with WikiLeaks to divert attention from the *Access Hollywood* revelations on 7 October.

Guccifer 2.0 published another seven blog posts with DNC materials between 18 June and 14 July, but after WikiLeaks released the DNC emails on 22 July restricted himself to generalised blog posts. On 31 July, Comey took the momentous decision to launch a counter-intelligence investigation into possible links between the Trump campaign and the Kremlin. The key issue was ultimately the 'weaponisation' of the stolen material. It is not unusual for foreign powers to penetrate American computers, and the Chinese had accessed the networks of the Obama and McCain campaigns in 2008. However, in 2016, the material was published by a site (WikiLeaks) that did not exist in 2008, and Assange was virulently critical of Clinton, a position that was assumed to coincide with that of the Russian leadership. Given the track record of mutual hostility between Putin and Clinton, this is a reasonable assumption, and there were certainly many politicians in Moscow who preferred Trump over his opponent. A political preference, however, is not proof of conspiracy.

The Indictment of the Twelve

Just three days before the first summit between Putin and Trump, on 13 July 2018, the DoJ indicted twelve individuals from Russian military intelligence (the GRU) for their involvement in hacking the DNC servers and the publication of Clinton campaign materials. The twenty-nine-page special counsel indictment asserted that the hackers 'conducted large-scale cyber operations to interfere with the 2016 US presidential election'.[32] Beginning in March 2016, GRU officers of Unit 26165 under the direction of Commander Viktor Netyshko spearphished Clinton campaign officials and broke into the DCCC and DNC networks that April, installing copies of the X-Tunnel malware and used it to transfer files to GRU-leased servers in Illinois and Arizona, with intermediary servers used to mask the GRU's presence. They tunnelled into over thirty computers on the DNC network, its mail server and shared file server. The stolen log-in credentials from DCCC officials were used to access the DNC network. A Unit 26165 hacker by the name of Ivan Yermakov is alleged to have stolen 50,000 emails from Clinton's campaign chairman, John Podesta, as early as March 2016. Unit 26165 is considered an elite team of computer scientists formed in the cold war as a signals decrypting office for the Soviet military, and was described on a Russian website as 'able to decipher any code within three minutes and re-encrypt it without breaking away from writing a doctoral dissertation on quantum physics'.[33] A parallel GRU unit under Alexander Osadchuk, Unit 74455, created an information operation using fake online personas to manage the release of the documents, including Guccifer 2.0 and DCLeaks. They also contacted other organisations, including WikiLeaks, to which they sent thousands of documents. Private direct messages between one of the cut-outs and WikiLeaks noted that the latter would have a 'much higher impact' on the election. At the same time, in summer 2016, another officer under Osadchuk's direction, Anatoly Kovalev, also hacked into the website of a state electoral board and stole voter data for 500,000 U.S. citizens and targeted state officials responsible for administering elections.[34]

According to the indictment, by May 2016, Netyshko's team stole thousands of emails from DNC employees and exfiltrated these and other documents to servers leased by the GRU in the United States, paid for with Bitcoin. One of Netyshko's team used the same email account as for the spearphishing operation to register the 'DCLeaks.com' website. The stolen emails from the DNC and the Clinton campaign received over a million page views within a year. DCLeaks also had a Twitter account, which it used to release material. Guccifer 2.0 also released numerous documents. With questions raised about the credibility of Guccifer 2.0, in June 2016, the hackers allegedly passed over 50,000 documents to WikiLeaks, with nearly all the documents released in stages by the election. According to the indictment, Guccifer 2.0 passed the entire archive of the DNC emails to WikiLeaks, and as we have seen on 22 July, the website published all 19,252 of them, just three days before the DNC convention.[35] The emails exposed the DNC's bias towards Clinton to the detriment of her main challenger, Sanders. Wasserman Schulz resigned and the convention was bitterly divided. Later, the indictment of Roger Stone (see below) suggests that he acted as some sort of go-between. This is why WikiLeaks is considered a 'Russian front'.[36]

This is a powerful list of charges based on a wealth of detail. It is not clear how the information was gained but the underlying assumption appears to be that the U.S. intelligence community knew what the Russian were doing since they were probably doing much the same to the Russians. Only the exceptional circumstances of the special counsel investigation forced them to reveal what they knew. American (and possibly Dutch) intelligence services shared information, thus revealing their ability to monitor Russian security agency computers. A rather more prosaic explanation is provided by Scott Ritter, the former UN weapons inspector at the time of the Iraq war, who suggests that Mueller compiled his list from a classified organisational chart of a Russian military intelligence unit obtained by the NSA.[37] The Mueller report largely incorporated the Netyshko indictment, but provided some more sourcing, but it was still unclear how the investigation came to its conclusions. Much of the material appears to be based not on intelligence collection but 'analytical supposition – i.e. guesswork'.[38]

There is also the fundamental question of intent. The timing of the DNC releases does not convincingly suggest that the goal was to help Trump, since he declared his candidacy in June 2015, but he was only taken seriously from around June 2016. It would have taken enormous prescience for the Russians to have taken Trump's candidacy seriously before anyone else did.[39] The director of national intelligence (DNI), Dan Coats, argued that 'the digital infrastructure that serves the country is literally under attack' and that 'the warning lights are blinking red again', just as before 9/11. Obama was more measured and admitted that the phishing attack was standard and 'not particularly sophisticated'. The charges outlined in the indictment do not in themselves contravene international law, although are a domestic criminal offence.[40] The timing of the indictment damaged the prospect of rapprochement with Russia. As Trump tweeted on its release, 'Our relationship with Russia has NEVER been worse thanks to many years of US foolishness and stupidity and now, the Rigged Witch Hunt!'.[41]

HACK OR LEAK?

Did Russia 'hack' the DNC and then pass on the materials to various cut-outs and then WikiLeaks? The presence of Russian intelligence is more than likely, but some questions remain: Was there a direct order to target the DNC, or was this part of a normal scanning operation, and if the former, at what level was the order given? Did the Kremlin really set out to undermine American democratic institutions, or was it simply trying to demonstrate its cyber capabilities to deter hostile American activities? There are plenty more questions. Instead of deploying its cyber action team, the FBI outsourced the investigation to a partisan body, CrowdStrike.[42] A serious investigation would have immediately demanded access to the DNC and associated servers, interviews with all DNC staff, Podesta and Nakashima (the author of the first public report of the hack on 14 June). It would also have entailed a thorough analysis of the metadata of all relevant published material. Instead, the U.S. security agencies and Mueller appear to have been remarkably incurious, attributing not only the hack but also publication to Russian agencies. This assertion has roiled American society since 2016, and while it may be correct, the evidentiary basis for such far-reaching claims, with major political implications, is remarkably thin.

As with so much in the Russiagate case, the official narrative is neither coherent nor consistent. Larry Johnson, a former CIA analyst and State Department official, identifies at least eleven 'contradictions, inconsistencies or oddities' in the public narrative about CrowdStrike and its findings: (1) two different dates – 20 April (Nakashima) or 6 May (Ward) – are given about the date that Crowdstrike was hired; (2) there are two accounts of who hired CrowdStrike – Nakashima reports that the DNC called Michael Sussmann of the law firm Perkins Coie, who in turn contacted CrowdStrike's CSO and president, Shawn Henry, but Alperovich told Nakashima that the DNC called direct; (3) CrowdStrike improbably claims to have discovered within twenty-four hours that the 'Russians' were responsible for the DNC 'intrusion'; (4) CrowdStrike's installation of its proprietary anti-hack Falcon software on DNC IT systems on 1 or 6 May would have alerted the intruders that they had been detected; (5) CrowdStrike told Nakashima that they were 'not sure how the hackers got in' and did not 'have hard evidence'; (6) in a blogpost of 14 June (the same day as Nakashima's *Washington Post* article) Alperovich wrote that the DNC was intruded by two Russian entities using malware identified as Fancy Bear (APT28) and Cozy Bear (APT29); (7) but Alperovich reports that there was no evidence that the two coordinated their attack or even knew of the presence of the other; (8) there is confusion over what actually was obtained, with DNC officials claiming that the hackers took the entire database of opposition research on Trump and 'all email and chat traffic', although they insisted that 'no financial, donor or personal information appears to have been accessed or taken', while CrowdStrike claims that 'The hackers stole two files'; (9) Alperovich does not make it clear whether Cozy Bear or Fancy Bear took the files; (10) when WikiLeaks published the emails on 22 July the files show that the last message taken from the DNC was dated 25 May, and the bulk was far more than 'two files'; and (11) far from least, why did CrowdStrike wait five weeks before disconnecting the DNC computers from the network and sanitising them.[43]

Not surprisingly, Mueller's conclusions have been challenged.[44] The Veteran Intelligence Professionals for Sanity (VIPS) group argues that the DNC emails were physically downloaded and then transferred (by unknown persons) to WikiLeaks rather than being extruded via an electronic download. They argue that if there had been any external electronic download, both the sender and the receiver would have been registered by the NSA – whose impressive capabilities had been revealed by Snowden. They conclude that the DNC emails 'were leaked by an insider'.[45] Their memorandum of 24 July 2017 argued that 'We do not think that the June 12, 14 & 15 timing was pure coincidence. Rather, it suggests the start of a pre-emptive move to associate Russia with anything WikiLeaks might have been ready to publish and to "show" that it came from a Russian hack'.[46] It asserted that the sheer volume of material could not have been obtained via a computer hack. They argue that on 5 July (i.e., after CrowdStrike had cleansed the DNC) a computer directly connected to the DNC server or DNC Local Area Network (LAN) copied 1,976 megabytes of data in 87 seconds onto an external storage device. They examined the 35,813 emails posted by WikiLeaks, in three batches, downloaded according to last modified times on 23, 25 and 26 May 2016. The transfer rate of 22.7 megabytes per second was far more than can be achieved through a remote download. In other words, 'an insider copied DNC data onto an external storage device'. Later remote internet transfer speed tests, by an investigator called Forensicator, found that 11.8 megabytes of data per second was the maximum possible with the technology of the time.[47] No less important, the investigation revealed that the copying took place on the East coast of the United States.[48] All the files had a last modified time rounded to an even second, which is consistent not with a remote hack but with a batch transfer to an external storage device, using the standard FAT (File Allocation Table) formatting.[49] VIPS concluded, 'This finding alone is enough to raise reasonable doubts, for example, about Mueller's indictment of 12 Russian intelligence officers for hacking the DNC emails given to WikiLeaks'. The group, moreover, was dismayed that the NSA did not do a forensic analysis of its own, and instead relied on 'assessments'.[50] Any hack over the internet would almost certainly have been discovered by the dragnet coverage by the NSA or allied foreign intelligence services.[51]

This challenges the 'Russian hack' narrative and not surprisingly attracts intense criticism.[52] The argument is advanced not by some marginal crackpots or conspiracy mongers but by people who had served with distinction at the highest levels of the U.S. security agencies and business. William Binney worked successfully as the technical director at the NSA, while Skip Folden for twenty-five years was IBM program manager for information technology.

Their work is analysed and publicised by Ray McGovern, one of the co-founders of VIPS in 2003 who worked as a CIA analyst from 1963 to 1990. In the 1980s, he chaired the National Intelligence Estimates and prepared the Presidential Daily Brief for Reagan. They filled the gap left by the FBI's failure to conduct independent forensic analysis of the original 'Guccifer 2.0' material. A joint article by Binney and McGovern in January 2017 argued that the DNC emails were stolen at the DNC headquarters and concluded:

> Because NSA can trace exactly where and how any 'hacked' emails from the Democratic National Committee or other servers were routed through the network, it is puzzling why NSA cannot produce hard evidence implicating the Russian government and WikiLeaks. Unless we are dealing with a leak from an insider, not a hack, as other reporting suggests. From a technical perspective alone, we are convinced that this is what happened.[53]

In later papers, they demonstrated that the same copy/leak process took place at two different times for different purposes. First, an inside leak to WikiLeaks before Assange announced on 12 June 2016 that he had DNC documents and planned to publish them, which he did on 22 July; and second, a separate leak on 5 July 2016 'to pre-emptively taint anything WikiLeaks might later publish by "showing" it came from a "Russian hack"'.[54] The Guccifer 2.0 files were tampered with to make it look as if WikiLeaks had ties to Russia. VIPS looked at five files that Guccifer 2.0 posted on 15 June with Russian signatures but then found that the same five files posted by WikiLeaks from the Podesta emails did not have the Russian signatures. The bottom line was that 'No one "hacked" the Democratic party's mail in the summer of 2016. It was leaked locally'. The motive appears to have been 'to expose the party leadership's corrupt efforts to sink Bernie Sanders' campaign to win the Democratic nomination'.[55]

In other words, as they put it in a memo to Trump, their research challenged the Intelligence Community Assessment (ICA) of 6 January 2017 and 'cast serious doubt on the underpinnings of the extraordinarily successful campaign to blame the Russian government for hacking'. This appears to have been a 'desperate effort' to blame the Russians for publishing the highly embarrassing DNC emails just before the Democratic convention in July 2016. They note how Clinton's press officer Jennifer Palmieri made the rounds at the convention in a golf cart, in her words, 'to get the press to focus on something even we found difficult to process: the prospect that Russia had not only hacked and stolen emails from the DNC, but that it had done so to help Donald Trump and hurt Hillary Clinton'. The VIPS50 report not surprisingly aroused a storm of criticism. In a later correction, the authors reaffirmed that the 15 June 2016 Guccifer 2.0 document 'was synthetically tainted with

"Russian fingerprints"', but they admit that they were mistaken to suggest that 'such tainting was *also* found in the "Guccifer 2.0" metadata from the copying event on July 5'. There was even criticism from within VIPS focusing not so much on the weakness of the claim that Russia was responsible for the hack, but for excessive confidence in alternative explanations. The dissenters argued that data transfer speeds could have reached those required for a hack, depending on the capacity of the network and access method. The data transfer, moreover, could have taken place on a server separate from the DNC's, with data previously derived from the DNC.[56] In response, the VIPS team argued that the download speeds available in 2016 were much lower than those effective later, and the data downloaded on 5 July was transferred at a speed not available to East Coast ISPs, while being entirely consistent with the use of a memory stick. Further study, this time with Duncan Campbell, a British journalist specialising in security matters, found that Guccifer 2.0 had separated two sets of data, one dated 5 July 2016 (which was known) and the other 1 September (new information), and when merged, they fitted together perfectly. Guccifer 2.0 then used various algorithms to modify 'range change' dates, in addition to the suspected insertion of Russian 'fingerprints'. In other words, Guccifer 2.0 was a fabricator and a fabrication.[57]

Later, Trump ordered CIA director Mike Pompeo to invite Bill Binney to CIA Headquarters to brief him on the VIPS findings.[58] In his presentation on 24 October 2017, Binney gave a typically no-holds-barred explanation of their findings and of how Pompeo's subordinates were being 'less than candid'.[59] In the face of persistent criticism, McGovern issued a rebuttal:

> We stand by our main conclusion that the data from the intrusion of July 5, 2016, into the Democratic National Committee's computers, an intrusion blamed on "Russian hacking", was not a hack but rather a download/copy onto an external storage device by someone with physical access to the DNC. That principal finding relied heavily on the speed with which the copy took place – a speed much faster than a hack over the Internet could have achieved at the time – or, it seems clear, even now. Challenged on that conclusion – often by those conducting experiments within the confines of a laboratory – we have conducted and documented additional tests to determine the speeds that can be achieved now, more than a year later.[60]

Former British ambassador to Uzbekistan between August 2002 and October 2004, Craig Murray, has much to say on the issue, yet he was never interviewed by the FBI or Mueller. Murray states 'I know who leaked them [the DNC emails]. I've met the person who leaked them, and they are certainly not Russian and it's an insider. It's a leak, not a hack: the two are different things'.[61]

The VIPS group argued that the Russia hack allegation was reminiscent of the evidence-free dogma that Iraq had weapons of mass destruction before the United States attacked the country. Some who had earlier promoted the Iraq WMD disinformation campaign were prominent architects of the new one. The former DNI, James Clapper, before 2003 was responsible for the analysis of satellite imagery, and he admitted in his memoir that 'intelligence officers, including me, were so eager to help [spread the Cheney/Bush claim that Iraq had a "rogue WMD program"] that we found what wasn't really there'.[62] If they could do it once, so VIPS argued, they could do it again. In a memo to Obama, delivered just three days before he left office in January 2017, VIPS questioned the findings of the IC Assessment, reminding the president of the trail of deception that led to the Iraq invasion. The assessment by 'hand-picked analysts' from the FBI, CIA and NSA seemed to fall into the same 'agenda-driven' category. In their view, the NSA was the competent body to determine conclusively what had happened. One of the enduring anomalies of the Russian hack narrative is that no federal law enforcement or intelligence agency was granted access to the DNC computer servers and files, even though a foreign government was accused of perpetrating the crime.

No less worrying was the point made by VIPS50 about the publication from 7 March 2017 of a trove of original CIA documents dubbed by WikiLeaks 'Vault 7'.[63] WikiLeaks stated that it received the material from a current or former CIA contractor, and argued that it was comparable in scale and significance to Snowden's material in 2013. Vault 7 exposed a vast array of cyber warfare tools developed, in conjunction with the NSA, by the CIA's Engineering Development Group, part of the CIA's enormous Directorate of Digital Information, established by CIA director Brennan in 2015. The material revealed astonishing digital tools, including the ability to spy through a TV. The third Vault 7 release on 31 March exposed the 'Marble Framework' program designed for 'obfuscation', as well as source code for a 'deobfuscator' tool to reverse CIA text obfuscation. The obfuscation program could be used to conduct a 'forensic attribution double game' or false-flag operation, and included test samples in Chinese, Russian, Korean, Arabic and Farsi. The documents show that the Marble tool had been used in 2016.[64] The Vault 7 material shows how easy it is to camouflage hacking to ensure false attribution and to mask the real source. In response to this revelation, CIA director Pompeo called Assange and his associates 'demons' and argued: 'It's time to call out WikiLeaks for what it really is, a non-state hostile intelligence service, often abetted by state actors like Russia'.[65]

The lack of independent verification is a matter of concern. CrowdStrike's credibility was undermined when forced to retract the contention of December 2016 that Fancy Bear had used identical tools (the 'X-Agent' malware) and methods to hack into the Ukrainian military. Kiev rejected the claim that this led to the loss of 80 per cent of Ukraine's howitzers in the battle with rebel Donbas forces.[66] Attribution is notoriously difficult and complex software can lay false trails and plant false flags. The use of the Cyrillic setting by the user named Feliks Edmundovich is beyond sloppy, and some sort of double bluff may have been at work. Software is available that can pin the blame for a 'hack' on another intelligence service.[67] The Vault 7 releases revealed the CIA's ability to hack computers and leave the signature of others. The Guccifer 2.0 data had been clearly tampered with and manipulated, suggesting that this persona is a deceptive fabrication.

In sum, three types of evidence suggest that the 2016 email compromises may have been an inside job: download speeds, Russian 'fingerprints' planted on manipulated files, and the numerical codes on the stolen files. If this evidence is correct, a remote hack via the internet is unlikely. The January 2016 ICA and the Mueller report made questionable and unproven assertions about how the DNC material reached WikiLeaks, and potential underlying evidence has been redacted. The ICA, importantly, concluded that 'Disclosures through WikiLeaks did not contain any evident forgeries'. In other words, the revelations about the way the Clinton campaign traduced Sanders and in general behaved in a high-handed manner were true. Any putative Russian involvement did not 'degrade' American democracy but exposed how it was being degraded.

Interference in State Voting Systems and Infrastructure

The first sign of Russia's alleged digital intrusions or 'reconnoitring' had been picked up by the NSA and FBI in local and state electoral boards' computerised voter registration rolls, lists of voters' names and addresses, in summer 2015. Clapper immediately informed Obama, preparing the ground for later allegations.[68] The Department of Homeland Security (DHS) preliminary assessment came out on 29 September 2016, a few weeks after the hacking of election websites in Illinois and Arizona. The headline asserted that Russian hackers had targeted twenty voter registration systems, and successfully infiltrated four. Later, a senior DHS official testified to Congress that twenty-one states had potentially been targeted by Russian state cyber actors, but that was not based on specific individual activity. A number of states subsequently repudiated the suggestion that they had been targeted, and another senior DHS official described 'the majority of the activity' as 'simple scanning . . . a regular activity across the Web. I would not characterize that as an attack'.[69] The DHS assessment of 28 October 2016 suggested that Russian hackers breached systems in Illinois, a county database in Arizona, a Tennessee state website and an information technology vendor in Florida, but even this modest list was later modified.[70] The only substantial evidence adduced to support the claim of Russian ballot interference is a leaked NSA document dated 5 May 2017 that accused the GRU of impersonating a software company and sending spearphishing emails loaded with malware to over 100 state and local jurisdictions involved with voter registration.

Even the NSA document was cautious in its assessment of the results of the attack and about attributing responsibility to Russian state actors.[71] Voter registration data was hacked in only one state, Illinois, and even then it was not clear by whom. Expert studies concur that 'there's no evidence that the Russians breached any election systems or interfered in the actual vote'.[72] The DHS compiled an intelligence report suggesting that Russian hackers targeted voter-related websites in several states, and then leaked sensational accounts that turned out to be false and sometimes risible. Mueller took up the issue to suggest that Russian military intelligence was behind election infrastructure hacking. Mueller's 13 July 2018 indictment of 12 GRU officers does not cite any violations of U.S. election laws, even though the central charge was that Russia had interfered in the 2016 election. The DHS competed with other security agencies to get state and local voter registration systems designated 'critical infrastructure', which would release substantial funds. The Russia threat became part of the inter-agency and federal competition for resources. Several states objected to the power grab, but Jeh Johnson, the head of the DHS, on 6 January 2017 – the day of the ICA – went ahead anyway.[73]

As for the alleged Russian interference, analysis of the July 2016 hack of the Illinois voter registration system showed that the personal information of as many as 200,000 (for some reason, Mueller in July 2018 gave the figure of 500,000) registered voters was stolen – although the hackers only copied the information and left it unchanged in the database. It appears that the Arizona hack, like the one in Illinois, was 'possibly for the purpose of selling personal information'. State voter registration systems have long been under attack by criminal groups seeking information to be sold for profit. In other words, criminal hacking was conflated with Russian government intervention. The Russian hacking version offers no explanation about what the perpetrators sought to do with the information, hence the rapid shift in the narrative to Russia 'sought to undermine public confidence in electoral processes and potentially the outcome'. Later it was revealed that in fourteen of the twenty-one states on the list, there had been no more than routine scanning, and only six involved attempts at site penetration. The July 2018 Mueller indictment appears to offer more information, but this too disintegrates on examination. Paragraph 71 talks about the way that Alexander Kovalev and his co-conspirators scanned the relevant electoral websites, and when the FBI was alerted, he deleted his search history but not of his alleged collaborators, suggesting the absence of a conspiracy.[74]

On 25 July 2019, the Senate Intelligence Committee released a heavily redacted report on supposed interference in the 2016 at state and local level, arguing that the Russian government 'directed extensive activity' against U.S. election infrastructure, beginning in 2014 and continuing into 2017.[75] The report 'found no evidence that vote tallies were altered or that voter registry files were deleted or modified', so reverted to the default claim that the Russian government 'was developing and implementing capabilities to interfere in the 2016 election, including undermining confidence in US democratic institutions and voting processes'.[76] The report discerned no pattern to the scanning activity, but in the end claimed that 'all 50 states probably' were targeted.[77]

In late 2016, the *Washington Post* ran a story arguing that Russian hackers had penetrated the U.S. electricity grid through a utility in Vermont.[78] It appears that a computer at Burlington Electric had triggered a malware alert (after discovering a Russian IP address on a list released by the DHS and FBI in December 2016). The story apparently started with anonymous DHS officials who leaked the information, apparently only too ready to advance the Russiagate narrative. Basic checks would have discounted the story, but in yet another example of neo-journalism, a false account was aired and is still circulating (even though the *Washington Post* retracted the story two days later). The DHS is still fighting to increase its stake in cyber-protection, and thus has played up the Russian threat to America's critical infrastructure, including energy, nuclear water, aviation and critical manufacturing sectors.[79]

The Russian scare, nevertheless, did have salutary effects, and cyber-security procedures have been greatly improved. By 2018, it was claimed that 'voters will be casting ballots in what experts say will be the most secure US election since the birth of the internet, thanks to steps taken since 2016'. The DHS took the lead in protecting voting machines, while state election officials hired technology experts and purchased new voting equipment with paper-ballot back-ups that allowed the results to be checked in case of problems with electronic systems. These were sensible and probably overdue measures, and as the 2018 midterms approached, 'There [was] no evidence that election infrastructure, including voter registration systems or voting machines, has been targeted by Russia'. Nevertheless, 'Officials are worried that Russia or others could deploy new, unpredictable tactics on election day, and are unnerved by how quiet Russian hackers have been compared with 2016.'[80] The absence of activity had now become suspicious.

NOTES

1. See WikiLeaks: DNC Email Database, https://wikileaks.org/dnc-emails/.

2. Nance, *Plot to Hack America*, pp. 83, 85.

3. Described in detail by Nance, *Plot to Hack America*, pp. 96–107.

4. For details, see Isikoff and Corn, *Russian Roulette*, pp. 62–76; Miller, *The Apprentice*, pp. 21–24.

5. Walt, *The Hell of Good Intentions*, p. 116.

6. Yasha Levine, *Surveillance Valley: The Secret Military History of the Internet* (London, Icon, 2019).

7. Isikoff and Corn, *Russian Roulette*, p. 76.

8. Nance, *The Plot to Hack America*, pp. 2 and 6.

9. Vividly portrayed by Scott Shane and Mark Mazzetti, 'The Plot to Subvert an Election: Unraveling the Russia Story So Far', *New York Times*, 20 September 2018, https://www.nytimes.com/interactive/2018/09/20/us/politics/russia-interference-election-trump-clinton.html.

10. Dmitri Alperovich, *Bears in the Midst: Intrusion into the Democratic National Committee*, CrowdStrike Blog, 14 June 2016, https://web.archive.org/web/20160615025759/https://www.crowdstrike.com/blog/bears-midst-intrusion-democratic-national-committee/

11. Aaron Maté, 'Hidden over 2 Years: Dem Cyber-Firm's Sworn Testimony it had no Proof of Russian Hack of DNC', *Real Clear Investigations*, 13 May 2020, https://www.realclearinvestigations.com/articles/2020/05/13/hidden_over_2_years_dem_cyber-firms_sworn_testimony_it_had_no_proof_of_russian_hack_of_dnc_123596.html.

12. Spencer Ackerman, 'Foreword', to Nance, *The Plot to Hack America*, p. x.

13. Strzok, *Compromised*, p 57.

14. For analysis of the Guccifer 2.0 persona, see Tim Leonard, 'Guccifer 2.0's Hidden Agenda', *Consortium News*, 26 May 2020, https://consortiumnews.com/2020/05/21/guccifer-2-0s-hidden-agenda/. The reliability of this source, who also used the alias Adam Carter, has been questioned.

15. Ackerman, 'Foreword', p. ix.

16. McGovern, 'FBI Never Saw CrowdStrike Unredacted or Final Report'.

17. Democratic National Committee, *Donald Trump Report*, Submitted 19 December 2015.

18. Jason Koebler, '"Guccifer 2.0" Claims Responsibility for DNC Hack, Releases Docs to Prove It', *Motherboard*, 15 June 2016, https://motherboard.vice.com/en_us/article/3davvy/guccifer-20-claims-responsibility-for-dnc-hack-releases-documents.

19. Lorenzo Franceschi-Bichierai, 'We Spoke to DNC Hacker "Guccifer 2.0"', *Motherboard*, 21 June 2016, https://motherboard.vice.com/en_us/article/aek7ea/dnc-hacker-guccifer-20-interview.

20. Lorenzo Franceschi-Bichierai, '"Guccifer 2.0" is Likely a Russian Government Attempt to Cover up its own Hack', *Motherboard*, 16 June 2016, https://motherboard.vice.com/en_us/article/wnxgwq/guccifer-20-is-likely-a-russian-government-attempt-to-cover-up-their-own-hack.

21. For the contrary case, see Isikoff, and Corn, *Russian Roulette*, p. 134.

22. Ray McGovern, 'How an Internet "Persona" Helped Birth Russiagate', *Consortium News*, 15 June 2020, https://consortiumnews.com/2020/06/15/ray-mcgovern-how-an-internet-persona-helped-birth-russiagate/.

23. Leonard, 'Guccifer 2.0's Hidden Agenda'.
24. Isikoff and Corn, *Russian Roulette*, p. 171.
25. Isikoff and Corn, *Russian Roulette*, p. 175.
26. David Lawler, 'Donald Trump Calls on Vladimir Putin and Russia to Find Hillary Clinton's Missing 30,000 Emails', *Daily Telegraph*, 27 July 2016, https://www.telegraph.co.uk/news/2016/07/27/donald-trump-calls-on-vladimir-putin-and-russia-to-find-hillary/. For commentary, see Woodward, *Fear*, p. 173; Isikoff and Corn, *Russian Roulette*, p. 180.
27. Alex Shephard, 'Julian Assange and Sean Hannity Are Giving Donald Trump the Cover he Needs on Russia', *New Republic*, 3 January 2017, https://newrepublic.com/minutes/139582/julian-assange-sean-hannity-giving-donald-trump-cover-needs-russia.
28. Zack Budryk, 'Russian Intel Planted Seth Rich Conspiracy Theory: Report', *The Hill*, 9 July 2019, https://thehill.com/homenews/media/452157-russias-foreign-intelligence-service-secretly-planted-fake-report-that-seth.
29. Malia Zimmerman, 'Slain DNC Staffer Had Contact with WikiLeaks', *Fox News*, 16 May 2017. The article was later retracted and is currently unavailable.
30. AP, 'Clinton Advisor Connects Trump's Long-Time Aide to WikiLeaks', *Fortune*, 12 October 2016, http://fortune.com/2016/10/11/clinton-john-podesta-roger-stone-wikileaks-russia/. The adviser was none other than Podesta himself.
31. Isikoff and Corn, *Russian Roulette*, p. 136.
32. *United States v. Netyshko et al., No. 1:18-cr-00215-ABJ*, criminal indictment filed 13 July 2018, US District Court for the District of Columbia, https://www.justice.gov/file/1080281/download, para. 1.
33. Rucker and Leonnig, *Very Stable Genius*, p. 159.
34. More details are provided by Rid, *Active Measures*, pp. 377–88.
35. Rid, *Active Measures*, pp. 387–96 on Guccifer 2.0.
36. David A. Graham, 'Is WikiLeaks a Russian Front', *The Atlantic*, 29 November 2018, https://www.theatlantic.com/politics/archive/2018/11/wikileaks-trump-mueller-roger-stone-jerome-corsi/576940/.
37. For context, see Scott Ritter, 'Leaked NSA Report Short on Facts, Proves Little in "Russiagate" Case', Popular Resistance.org, 8 June 2017, https://popularresistance.org/leaked-nsa-report-short-on-facts-proves-little-in-russiagate-case/. The document was titled 'Spear-Phishing Campaign TTPs used against US and Foreign Government Political Entities', and was published by Matthew Cole et al, 'Top-Secret NSA Report Details Russian Hacking Effort Days Before 2016 Election', *The Intercept*, 5 June 2017, https://theintercept.com/2017/06/05/top-secret-nsa-report-details-russian-hacking-effort-days-before-2016-election/.
38. Scott Ritter, 'US Plans to Conduct Cyberwar against Russia in Retaliation for Unproven Election Meddling', RT.com, 28 December 2019, https://www.rt.com/op-ed/477005-cyberwar-dod-russia-elections-meddling/.
39. George Beebe, 'Russia's Role in the US Elections: The Case for Caution', *The National Interest*, 16 December 2016, https://nationalinterest.org/feature/russias-role-the-us-elections-the-case-caution-18756.
40. Jack Goldsmith, 'Uncomfortable Questions in the Wake of Russia Indictment 2.0 and Trump's Press Conference with Putin', *Lawfare*, 16 July 2018, https://www

.lawfareblog.com/uncomfortable-questions-wake-russia-indictment-20-and-trumps-press-conference-putin.

41. Shane and Mazzetti, 'Plot to Subvert an Election'.

42. For a detailed analysis of CrowdStrike and its DNC investigation, see Vicky Ward, 'The Russian Expat Leading the Fight to Protect America', *Esquire*, 24 October 2016, https://www.esquire.com/news-politics/a49902/the-russian-emigre-leading-the-fight-to-protect-america/.

43. The list is provided because it summarises some of the key questions. Larry C. Johnson, 'Why Is CrowdStrike Confused on Eleven Key Details about the DNC Hack?, *Sic Semper Tyrannis*, 17 March 2020, https://turcopolier.typepad.com/sic_semper_tyrannis/2020/03/why-is-crowdstrike-confused-on-eleven-key-details-about-the-dnc-hack-by-larry-c-johnson.html.

44. For a forensic critique of Mueller's findings, see Aaron Maté, 'CrowdStrike Out: Mueller's Own Report Undercuts its Core Russia-Meddling Claims', *Realclearinvestigations*, 5 July 2019, https://www.realclearinvestigations.com/articles/2019/07/05/crowdstrikeout_muellers_own_report_undercuts_its_core_russia-meddling_claims.html.

45. 'US Intel Vets Dispute Russia Hacking Claims', *Consortium News*, 12 December 2016, https://consortiumnews.com/2016/12/12/us-intel-vets-dispute-russia-hacking-claims/.

46. 'Intel Vets Challenge "Russia Hack" Evidence', *Consortium News*, 24 July 2017, https://consortiumnews.com/2017/07/24/intel-vets-challenge-russia-hack-evidence/.

47. Patrick Lawrence, 'A New Report Raises Big Questions about Last Year's DNC Hack', *The Nation*, 9 August 2017, https://www.thenation.com/article/a-new-report-raises-big-questions-about-last-years-dnc-hack/.

48. 'Intel Vets Challenge "Russian Hack" Evidence'.

49. William Binney and Larry Johnson, 'Why the DNC was not Hacked by the Russians', *Sic Semper Tyrannis*, 13 February 2019, https://turcopolier.typepad.com/sic_semper_tyrannis/2019/02/why-the-dnc-was-not-hacked-by-the-russians.html.

50. 'VIPS: Mueller's Forensics-Free Findings', memorandum for the Attorney General from VIPS', *Consortium News*, 13 March 2019, https://consortiumnews.com/2019/03/13/vips-muellers-forensics-free-findings/

51. Ray McGovern, 'New House Documents Sow Further Doubt that Russia Hacked the DNC', *Consortium News*, 9 May 2020, https://consortiumnews.com/2020/05/09/ray-mcgovern-new-house-documents-sow-further-doubt-that-russia-hacked-the-dnc/.

52. One of the best-researched critiques is by the veteran investigative journalist Duncan Campbell. Among other points, he describes how the British programmer Tim Leonard (assuming the alias Adam Carter) worked with mostly right-wing Americans to advance the claim that Democratic 'insiders' and non-Russian agents were responsible for hacking the DNC. Duncan Campbell, 'Briton Ran Pro-Kremlin Disinformation Campaign that Helped Trump Deny Russian Links', 31 July 2018, https://www.computerweekly.com/news/252445769/Briton-ran-pro-Kremlin-disinformation-campaign-that-helped-Trump-deny-Russian-links.

53. William Binney and Ray McGovern, 'Emails Were Leaked, Not Hacked', *Baltimore Sun*, 5 January 2017.
54. 'Intel Vets Challenge "Russian Hack" Evidence'.
55. Patrick Lawrence, '"Too Big to Fail": Russia-gate One Year after VIPS Showed a Leak, Not a Hack', *Consortium News*, 13 August 2018, https://consortiumnews.com/2018/08/13/too-big-to-fail-russia-gate-one-year-after-vips-showed-a-leak-not-a-hack/.
56. Patrick Lawrence, 'A New Report Raises Big Questions about Last Year's DNC Hack', *The Nation*, 9 August 2017, https://www.thenation.com/article/archive/a-new-report-raises-big-questions-about-last-years-dnc-hack/; Various authors, 'A Leak or a Hack? A Forum on the VIPS Memo', *The Nation*, 1 September 2017, https://www.thenation.com/article/archive/a-leak-or-a-hack-a-forum-on-the-vips-memo/. For another detailed assessment, see Sam Biddle, 'Here's the Public Evidence Russia Hacked the DNC – It's Not Enough', *The Intercept*, 13 December 2016, https://theintercept.com/2016/12/14/heres-the-public-evidence-russia-hacked-the-dnc-its-not-enough/.
57. Lawrence, '"Too Big to Fail"'. This is questioned by Campbell, 'Briton Ran Pro-Kremlin Disinformation Campaign'.
58. Duncan Campbell and James Risen, 'CIA Director Met Advocate of Disputed DNC Hack Theory at Trump's Request', *The Intercept*, 7 November 2017, https://theintercept.com/2017/11/07/dnc-hack-trump-cia-director-william-binney-nsa/.
59. Personal communication with Ray McGovern.
60. William Binney and Ray McGovern, 'More Holes in Russia-Gate Narrative', *Consortium News*, 20 September 2017, https://consortiumnews.com/2017/09/20/more-holes-in-russia-gate-narrative/.
61. Randy Credico and Dennis J. Bernstein, 'The Russia-Did-It Certitude Challenged', *Consortium News*, 10 August 2017, https://consortiumnews.com/2017/08/10/the-russia-did-it-certitude-challenged/.
62. Ray McGovern, 'Orwellian Cloud Hovers over Russia-Gate', *Consortium News*, 3 May 2019, https://consortiumnews.com/2019/05/03/orwellian-cloud-hovers-over-russia-gate/.
63. For the outcome of the internal CIA investigation into the leak, the largest unauthorised disclosure of classified information in the CIA's history, see Ellen Nakashima and Shane Harris, 'Elite CIA Unit that Developed Hacking Tools Failed to Secure its own Systems, Allowing Massive Leak, an Internal Report Found', *Washington Post*, 16 June 2020, https://www.washingtonpost.com/national-security/elite-cia-unit-that-developed-hacking-tools-failed-to-secure-its-own-systems-allowing-massive-leak-an-internal-report-found/2020/06/15/502e3456-ae9d-11ea-8f56-63f38c990077_story.html
64. Ellen Nakashima, 'WikiLeaks Latest Release of CIA Cyber-Tools Could Blow the Cover on Agency Hacking Operations', *Washington Post*, 31 March 2017.
65. 'Intel Vets Challenge "Russian Hack" Evidence'.
66. CrowdStrike used data from the International Institute for Strategic Studies to make the case, but IISS disavowed the report.
67. Robert Parry, Fresh Doubts about Russian "Hacking"', *Consortium News*, 8 March 2017, https://consortiumnews.com/2017/03/08/fresh-doubts-about-russian-hacking/.

68. Woodward, *Fear*, p. 27.

69. Aaron Maté, 'With Just Days to go to the Midterms, Russiagate is MIA', *The Nation*, 29 October 2018, https://www.thenation.com/article/russiagate-2018-midterms-interference/.

70. Reuters, 'Arizona Election Database Targeted in 2016 by Criminals, Not Russia: Source', 8 April 2018, https://uk.reuters.com/article/uk-usa-cyber-election/arizona-election-database-targeted-in-2016-by-criminals-not-russia-source-idUKKBN1HF12G.

71. Matthew Cole, Richard Esposito, Sam Biddle and Ryan Grim, 'Top-Secret NSA Report Details Russian Hacking Effort Days Before 2016 Election', *The Intercept*, 5 June 2017, https://theintercept.com/2017/06/05/top-secret-nsa-report-details-russian-hacking-effort-days-before-2016-election/.

72. Schier and Eberly, *The Trump Presidency*, p. 5.

73. Gareth Porter, 'How the Department of Homeland Security Created a Deceptive Tale of Russia Hacking US Voter Sites', *Consortium News*, 28 August 2018, https://consortiumnews.com/2018/08/28/how-the-department-of-homeland-security-created-a-deceptive-tale-of-russia-hacking-u-s-voter-sites/.

74. Porter, 'How the Department of Homeland Security Created a Deceptive Tale'.

75. Senate Committee on Intelligence, *Report on Russian Active Measures Campaigns and Interference in the 2016 US Election*, Vol. 1, *Russian Efforts against Election Infrastructure* (Washington, DC, US Senate, 25 July 2019), p. 3.

76. Senate Committee on Intelligence, *Report*, Vol. 1, p. 5.

77. Senate Committee on Intelligence, *Report*, Vol. 1, p. 20.

78. Adam Entous, 'Russian Hackers Penetrated US Electricity Grid Through a Utility in Vermont, US Officials Say', *Washington Post*, 31 December 2016. The story was retracted on 1 January 2017, but it would have been more professional to check the facts first.

79. Porter, 'How the Department of Homeland Security Created a Deceptive Tale'.

80. Dustin Volz, 'US Girds for Possible Russian Meddling on Election Day', *Wall Street Journal*, 5 November 2018, https://www.wsj.com/articles/u-s-girds-for-possible-russian-meddling-on-election-day-1541421000.

Chapter 6

Social Media Meddling

A study of the 'electronic warfare' waged by Russian trolls and hackers calls this activity 'epistemic violence' committed by 'discourse saboteurs'. A tiny investment in copy-cat ads allegedly amplified existing divisions and shifted the terms of the debate. Drawing on academic study of the kinds of persuasion that can influence voters and under what circumstances, Kathleen Hall Jamieson argues that the targeted cyberattacks by hackers and trolls in the 2016 election were decisive. She focuses on the 78,000 votes in Michigan, Pennsylvania and Wisconsin, which delivered a majority in the Electoral College to Trump. Applying studies of communication effects in the 2000 and 2008 presidential elections, she argues that in the 2016 election the efforts of Russian hackers, trolls and bots were amplified by the media, social media platforms, the candidates, party leaders and a polarised public. She concludes that Russia delivered Trump victory: without Russian meddling, there would have been no Trump presidency. Russian 'discourse saboteurs' persuaded just enough people to either vote a certain way or not to vote at all.[1] The Russians pulled off an electoral coup by alienating voters from Clinton, inadvertently aided and abetted by the American media.[2] The anti-Russian popular author Timothy Snyder amplifies the argument, asserting that Russia has long been practising successful information and influence operations against the West.[3] This chapter will assess the validity of these arguments.

THE INTERNET RESEARCH AGENCY (IRA) AND MUELLER INDICTMENT

The main Russian social media intervention came from the IRA, established in July 2013 at 55 Savushkina Street in St Petersburg's Olgino district. It was primarily a commercial operation whose initial focus was on working the Russian internet on behalf of clients, for example, governors whose popularity was falling by adding 'likes' to their social media presence. In other words, the agency was originally created 'to mess not with American voters but with Russia's domestic opposition, among other subjects, by increasing traffic to certain regime-friendly outlets'.[4] The agency was staffed not by intelligence officials but by college students and the like attracted by the pay. The IRA first came to public attention when it spread online propaganda in support of the Russophone insurgents in the Donbass in 2014, and by 2016, it apparently had a staff of hundreds working in twelve-hour shifts churning out online material, first for the post-Soviet market and then the American public. The business model was to profit by attracting clicks to the relevant page, which is why ads were planted covering every side of issues as well as having puppy dog and other human-interest pages.

The IRA is a privately owned company run by the entrepreneur Yevgeny Prigozhin, whose various catering contracts and high-end restaurant in St Petersburg earned him the moniker of 'Putin's chef'. Prigozhin is a billionaire with close links to the presidential administration, from which it gained some major contracts. In return, Prigozhin allegedly fulfilled undercover tasks for the Kremlin. Prigozhin is the financier behind the Wagner Group that reportedly sent private military contractors to Ukraine, Syria, Libya and sub-Saharan Africa.[5] Three journalists investigating Wagner's activities in the Central African Republic were killed in July 2018.[6] Sanctions were imposed on Prigozhin in December 2016 and soon afterwards also on his two acknowledged companies, Concord Management and Consulting, and Concord Catering.[7] The purported 'private' status of these various organisations allowed the regime to disavow responsibility for their activities. Plausible deniability is certainly one explanation, but there is no conclusive evidence that the whole operation was conducted on behalf of the Kremlin, let alone Putin personally. If there was a decision to interfere in U.S. politics, at what level was the decision made? Prigozhin undertakes a range of freelance tasks, sometimes on behalf of the Russian state and sometimes to pursue his own interests, and when the two diverge, the consequences can be catastrophic (as in the February 2018 battle near Deir Ezzor in Syria). Although Russia today is considered a hyper-centralised state, the 'vertikal' of power is challenged by powerful corporate and regional actors at the horizontal level. Kremlin oversight over this complex and contradictory system can at times be minimal if not altogether absent.[8]

The IRA disseminated internet hoaxes ranging from an alleged explosion in a Louisiana chemical plant in September, an Ebola outbreak, and in December 2014 the police shooting of an unarmed black woman. None of these events took place, and following the source led the reporter Adrian

Chen to the IRA in Olgino. In his revealing study published in June 2015, he noted how the IRA had 'industrialized the art of trolling', with the management 'obsessed by statistics, page views and the number of posts', yet after speaking with the operatives, he found that 'the exact point of their work was left unclear to them'. Chen was right to warn that the operation threatened 'the utility of the Internet as a democratic space'.[9] The IRA itself became the target of the hacktivist group Anonymous International, releasing hundreds of its emails. This indicated a point stressed by Chen in a later article published following Mueller's indictment of IRA operatives. Chen argued that 'the whole issue had been blown out of proportion', stressing that rather than being some 'kind of giant machine, in which talking points generated by the Kremlin are "amplified" through a network of bots, fake Facebook pages, and sympathetic human influencers', he highlighted 'just how inept and haphazard these attempts were'.[10]

On 16 February 2018, Prigozhin was indicted with others by a federal grand jury for interfering in the American election.[11] The Mueller indictment accused thirteen Russian citizens and three Russian organisations, one of which was the IRA, of trying to influence the 2016 election using social media. The indictment revealed that two IRA employees (Anna Bogacheva and Aleksandra Krylova) spent three weeks in the United States in June 2014, visiting nine states to gauge the country's political atmosphere.[12] Prigozhin owns the IRA through his Concord Management company, and according to the indictment, Concord was the IRA's 'primary source of funding', paying over $1.25 million a month.[13] The small group of 'professional trolls' in St Petersburg manipulated social media platforms to fan the flames of partisanship and to exacerbate American political divisions. The indictment talked of a multi-year campaign of 'information warfare against the United States of America'.[14] The IRA initiative 'Project Lakhta' from 'around' May 2014 to several months after the presidential election targeted audiences in Russia and across the world, and only later the United States. Lakhta focused on posting advertisements and comments on the internet. The 'Translator [*Perevodchik*] Project' from April 2014 focused on U.S. social media outlets like YouTube, Facebook, Instagram and Twitter and continued until February 2018.[15] Some eighty people worked in twelve-hour shifts to push out messages directed to the U.S. public.[16]

The indictment asserted that the IRA 'had a strategic goal to sow discord in the US political system, including the 2016 US presidential election'.[17] Social media outlets were 'weaponised' by creating pages that posed as genuine U.S. political groups such as 'Secured Borders', 'Blacktivist' and 'Army of Jesus' on Facebook and other social media platforms. The IRA operatives faked American identities by using virtual private networks (VPNs) and the stolen identities of real American citizens. They posted messages about divisive social issues like abortion, gun rights and immigration. They also issued misinformation, such as voter fraud by the Democratic Party, to suppress turnout.[18] The operatives also used false identities to get genuine Americans to organise political rallies, such as a 'March for Trump' in June 2016. There were also rallies in Florida, New York and Pennsylvania. The IRA apparently focused its activities on 'purple' states (those without a clear alignment with the major parties) such as Colorado, Virginia and Florida.[19] In short, Mueller found that the IRA used a network of shell companies, with names such as MediaSintez LLC, MixInfo LLC and many others, to hide its activities and funding. Investigators found internal documentation that described IRA activities as 'information warfare against the United States of America', which one compared to Japan's attack on Pearl Harbour in December 1941.[20]

The Mueller indictment, according to Chen, failed to 'shed light on the extent to which the Kremlin and, specifically, the Russian President, Vladimir Putin, were involved in the Agency's work. Nor does the indictment move us any closer to a conclusion regarding whether anyone in the Trump campaign colluded with the Russian operation'.[21] The relationship between the IRA and the Russian government is unclear, and Putin denied any links. He argued that even if the individuals and organisations had really meddled in the 2016 election, it was of no interest to him: 'I'm absolutely indifferent to this, because they do not represent the interests of the Russian state'. Only if they had violated Russian laws, 'then we will bring them to justice. If they did not violate Russian laws, then there is no reason for indicting them'.[22] By contrast, the Senate Intelligence Committee report on the issue in October 2019 argued that 'Russia's targeting of the 2016 U.S. presidential election was part of a broader, sophisticated, and on-going information warfare campaign designed to sow discord in American politics and society'.[23] The report argued that paid advertisements were just a small part of the campaign. Instead, 'the IRA co-opted unwitting Americans to engage in offline activities in furtherance of their objectives', including the mobilisation of African-Americans through social media 'to sign petitions, share personal information, and teach self-defense training courses'.[24]

In a revealing interview with the independent Russian newspaper *Novaya Gazeta* in November 2018, Andrei Mikhailov, who helped Prigozhin create his media empire, spilled some of the beans after falling out with him. Mikhailov was recruited by Prigozhin in 2012 to oversee a media campaign against one of his competitors. Mikhailov asserts that Prigozhin is no stranger to dirty tricks, such as staging a food poisoning incident against a rival catering company, as well as defaming news outlets by tricking them into publishing 'fake news'. One such media campaign targeted the poet Dmitry Bykov and another *Forbes* magazine. In 2013, an attack of this sort was launched against the relatively independent RIA Novosti news agency, and in December of that year, its highly professional and courageous head, Svetlana Mironyuk, was summarily dismissed and the agency folded into the new militantly loyal *Rossiya Segodnya (Russia Today)* media conglomerate headed by Dmitry Kisilëv. In Mikhailov's view, the IRA's 2016 U.S. election social media campaign was Prigozhin's personal idea: 'I am convinced that he received no orders from anyone and did not ask for any permission. There were never any orders from any of the [Kremlin] towers – it all came directly from Prigozhin'. Mikhailov argued that Prigozhin had chosen Olgino as the site for the troll factory since it was 'on the way to his dacha' in the nearby Lakhta district.[25] Mikhailov described other nasty campaigns launched by Prigozhin, exposing the dark underside of Putinite stability as well as the degree of latitude allowed a 'stoligarch' like Prigozhin.

The Mueller accusations appear to have had no effect on the IRA 'troll factory'. On the contrary, the enterprise moved into bigger offices a couple of kilometres across town and continued to target U.S. audiences. As always with Russia, the response to threats and accusations is to dig in deeper. One of Concord's new projects is an English-language web news site called USAReally, covering American affairs for American readers. In an interview with the Associated Press, its chief editor, Alexander Malkevich (an avowed Trump fan), admitted, 'Yes, we are a Russian site. We talk to Americans about America. But is that forbidden? . . . Influence readers? Every media wants to do that. . . . and so what?' Some of the Russians indicted by Mueller moved on to other jobs, went underground, or shut down their social media presence. One of them, Sergei Polozov, announced on the Russian social media site VKontakte (VK) that he was 'using his notoriety for a good cause', and had persuaded Russian censors to block four Ukrainian sites. He vowed to continue fighting those who 'try to drag Russia through the mud', and thanked 'those who want to join me in the fight against informational enemies'.[26] The renewed cold war has now sunk deep social roots and is set to endure and intensify as both sides consider themselves under siege.

THE IRA IN CONTEXT

The IRA pumped out a stream of social media posts, and its employees even assumed various false U.S. personas to encourage people to attend rallies and engage in other political activities. Nevertheless, the IRA appears to be more of a commercial than a political organisation. The Mueller indictment charged several of its officers with minor commercial infractions but left out the political aspects of its activities. The indictment overall confirmed the commercial intent behind IRA's work. Point 95 of the indictment makes this clear:

Defendants and their co-conspirators also used the accounts to receive money from real US persons in exchange for posting promotions and advertisements on the organization-controlled social media pages. Defendants and their co-conspirators typically charged certain US merchants and US social media sites between 25 and 50 US dollars per post for promotional content on their popular false US persona accounts, including Being Patriotic, Defend the 2nd, and Blacktivist.

Little of the IRA's output was concerned with the election, and instead it used sock-puppets on Facebook and Twitter to attract views by posting pictures of puppies and the like, with the aim of selling advertisements and promotions on these sites. This confirms the questionable ability of $100,000 spent by the IRA on clickbait pages through Facebook ads to move people to vote for Trump. Some 56 per cent of the 3,517 ads ran after the election, and 25 per cent were not seen by anyone. Only about 100 of the ads mentioned support for Trump or opposition to Clinton, a few dozen mentioned the election and a handful of the other candidates. Most of the posts were not targeted on a constituency smaller than the whole United States, and some of the targets were irrelevant in electoral terms, such as Maryland and Missouri. In February 2018, Facebook executive Rob Goldman tweeted that 'I have seen all the Russian ads and I can say very definitely that swaying the election was *not* the man goal' [italics in original].[27] Thomas Rid confirms this view, arguing that it is unlikely that the trolls convinced many American voters to change their minds, with only 8.4 per cent of its activity election-related.[28] In short, the IRA was a politicised commercial clickbait business.

A very different reality is portrayed by Scott Shane and Mark Mazzetti in their landmark 10,000-word article in the *New York Times* in September 2018 describing 'The Plot to Subvert an Election'. They argue that 'Acting on the personal animus of Mr. Putin, public and private instruments of Russian power moved with daring and skill to harness the currents of American politics' and launched a 'surprise attack' that they characterise as a 'stealth cyberage Pearl Harbor'. This 'succeeded in delivering the presidency to his admirer, Mr. Trump'. They admit 'Mr Trump's frustration with the Russian investigation is not surprising. He is right that no public evidence has emerged showing that his campaign conspired with Russia in the election interference or accepted Russian money'. Despite claiming at the beginning that there was a 'mountain of evidence', by the end they concede that the charges 'cannot be proved or disproved', but they spend thousands of words suggesting otherwise.[29]

Shane and Mazzetti stress the scale of the IRA's work on Facebook, with 2,700 fake Facebook accounts, 80,000 posts and 'an eventual audience of 126 million Americans on Facebook alone', which they stress 'was not far short of the 137 million people who would vote in the 2016 presidential elections'. For their data, they draw on Facebook's presentation to the Senate Judiciary Committee in November 2017 in which Colin Stretch, the company's general counsel, stated that 'Our best estimate is that approximately 126 million may have been served one of these [IRA-generated] stories as some time during the two year period'.[30] Stretch's figure is the number of people who could hypothetically have come into contact with an IRA-generated story not in the ten weeks of the election campaign but over the full 194 weeks from 2015 to 2017, when some 29 million could have received an IRA story in their feed. A number of assumptions are built into that figure, including that over the two-year period the 29 million people may have received at least one story in their Facebook feed and that they shared it with others at a specified rate. Facebook did not claim that most of the 80,000 IRA posts were election related. Stretch testified that IRA content over the two-year period represented just four ten-thousandths (.0004) of the total content of Facebook newsfeeds. Gareth Porter calculates that this means that each piece of IRA content was submerged in 23,000 of non-IRA content.

Some 44 per cent were displayed before 8 November, and 56 per cent after the election. About 25 per cent of the ads were never shown to anyone, because of the auction system based on relevance. Less than $3 was spent on 50 per cent of the ads, and less than $1,000 was spent on 99 per cent of them. Some 5 per cent of the 3,000 ads appeared on Instagram.[31] This means that the headline figure that 'Russian propaganda reached 126 million Americans' is deeply misleading.[32] The 80,000 Russia-linked posts on Facebook between 2015 and 2017 were just a drop in the ocean of 33 trillion posts viewed by Americans in the two-year period before and after the 2016 vote. The same applies to the $4,700 Russia spent on Google ads.[33] In any case, Adam Moseri, Facebook's vice president for news, admitted in 2016 that subscribers read only about ten per cent of stories that enters their daily News Feed. As an informed critic of the Shane and Mazzetti article notes, 'The *Times*' touting of the bogus 126 million out of 137 million voters, while not reporting the 33 trillion figure, should vie in the annals of journalism as one of the most spectacularly misleading uses of statistics of all time'.[34] It was yet another example of neo-journalism.

As for Twitter, the IRA sponsored 3,814 accounts, which supposedly 'interacted with 1.4 million Americans', as Shane and Mazzetti put it. However, over 90 per cent of the tweets had nothing to do with the election, and those that did were a tiny stream in the flood of Twitter messaging related to the election. Twitter stated that the IRA-linked accounts posted 175,993 tweets during the ten weeks of the election campaign, but only 8.4 per cent were election-related. Those 15,000 tweets represented just .00008 (eight one hundred thousandth) of the estimated 189 million tweets identified as election-related in those ten weeks. A study by Darren Linvill and Patrick Warren of the 2.97 million tweets on 2,848 Twitter handles issued by the IRA accounts over a two-year period focused on various strategies for 'agenda-building', with five handle categories: right troll, left troll, news feed, hashtag gamer and fearmonger. Elements were interchangeable, thus they conclude that the IRA engaged in 'industrialized political warfare'. Their data show that nearly a third had normal commercial content or were not in English; another third were straight local newsfeeds from U.S. localities or largely non-political 'hashtag games'; and the final third dealt with right or left populist themes in U.S. politics. There were more political IRA tweets in 2017 than in the election year.[35]

There is another category identified by Twitter comprising 50,258 automated election-related Twitter accounts connected to Russia, generating a total of 2.1 million tweets, about 1 per cent of election-related tweets in that period. The media made much of these figures, but Twitter's Sean Edgett told the Senate Intelligence Committee in November 2017 that the company had used an 'expansive approach to defining what qualifies as a Russian-linked account'. Twitter considered the account to be 'Russian' if any of the following characteristics were found: it was created in Russia or if the user registered the account with a Russian phone user or a Russian email; the user's display name included Cyrillic characters; the user regularly tweets in Russian; or the user has logged in from a Russian IP address. This is such a broad definition as to be virtually meaningless. Many countries use Cyrillic, and geographical origin is often masked by VPN, accompanied by the frequent sale of automated accounts. Thus, as Porter stresses, the idea that 'the Russian government seriously threatened to determine the winner of the election does not hold up when the larger social media context is examined more closely . . . the Russian private sector effort accounted for a minuscule proportion of the election-related output of social media'.[36] In the universe of information, the Russian input was negligible.

Decisive or Not

In an extremely tight race, the election was decided by fewer than 80,000 votes in three states, Michigan, Pennsylvania and Wisconsin, where Trump's winning margin was less than one per cent in each. In his book *Messing with the Enemy*, the former FBI agent Clint Watts is adamant that Russia influenced the outcome.[37] This was the view of two reports issued in December 2018, which argued that Russian operatives used social media to 'confuse, distract, and ultimately discourage' black people to vote for Clinton. Black turnout in 2016 declined for the first time in 20 years, falling to 58 per cent from the record high of 66.6 per cent in 2012. The Senate Intelligence

Committee on 17 December 2018 reviewed the two reports, one from a group of academics from Oxford University, the Computational Propaganda Project, and the other by New Knowledge, an American cyber-security firm. Both suggested that the major social media companies – Facebook, Google and Twitter – failed to provide the U.S. authorities with exhaustive data. They argue that Russian trolls flooded social media with right-wing pro-Trump material, to get black voters to boycott the election or to vote for third-party candidates. New Knowledge claimed to have identified an 'immersive influence ecosystem', in which posts on various platforms reinforced each other.[38] The Oxford team argued that the IRA's activities sought to polarise the U.S. public and interfere in the elections by campaigning for African American voters to boycott the election or to follow the wrong voting procedures.[39]

Two-thirds of eligible black voters cast their ballot in the 2012 election, with the overwhelming majority going to Obama and just 6 per cent for Romney. Without a popular black leader to vote for, it is hardly surprising that black turnout in 2016 fell, with Trump receiving 8 per cent. However, some of the decline is explained by the voter suppression procedures put in place following Republican victories at the state and local level in the Obama years. The election was 'the first presidential contest in 50 years without the full protections' of the 1965 Voting Rights Act.[40] With 4.6 million 'likes', the bogus Russian Facebook Blacktivist account highlighted the disproportionate poverty rates and the endemic use of police violence against people of colour to divert political energy away from established parties.[41] A detailed study of the 'influence operation' targeted on Black Lives Matter discourse found that the IRA participated on both sides of the argument, with left- and right-leaning false personas, but the two converged to critique the 'mainstream media'.[42] The Soviet Union had a long record of using 'information operations' to 'disrupt the information streams and information systems of a geopolitical adversary', with disinformation of a specific type of information operation.[43] The IRA used fictitious identities to 'reflect and shape social divisions', while undermining 'trust in information intermediaries like "the mainstream media"'. There is a fundamental problem of identifying 'authenticity' in social media environments.[44] The Oxford report argued that ultimately this effort was dwarfed by competing armies of 'cyber troops' mobilised by government or political party actors seeking to manipulate public opinion online.[45]

In December 2018, it was discovered that New Knowledge had run its own disinformation campaign, using fake Russian bots to discredit Republican candidate Roy Moore when he was running for the U.S. Senate seat vacated by Jeff Sessions in Alabama in 2017. The far-right Moore, who faced sexual misconduct charges, was presented as the Russia-preferred candidate in a 'false flag' operation and thus discredited, and he lost by just 1.5 per cent in a tight race. Russia's alleged tactics were imitated in what New Knowledge claimed was an experiment, dubbed 'Project Birmingham', arguing that it had almost no effect on the outcome.[46] There is an obvious 'disconnect' between what was described as the enormous power of Russian tweets and botnets in the presidential election in 2016, and the claimed lack of impact in the Alabama senatorial race that cost $51 million: 'If it was impossible for a $100,000 New Knowledge operation to affect a 2017 state election, then how could a comparable – perhaps even less expensive – Russian operation possibly impact [affect] a $2.4 billion US presidential election in 2016?'. As for the 2016 election, 'Rather than ruminating over whether they were duped by Russian clickbait, reporters who have actually spoken to black Midwest voters have found that political disillusionment led many to stay at home.' This is the key reason incumbent elites have been so concerned about the purported threat of Russian meddling: 'It deflects attention from their own failures, and the failings of the system that grants them status as elites.'[47]

The IRA engaged in a covert influence operation, which is morally reprehensible, but in terms of the effect on electoral outcomes, there are strong grounds to be sceptical. The posts did not possess magical properties that acted like a hypodermic syringe to send messages directly into the minds of voters. It is unlikely that a small number of Russian media posts tilted the election in Trump's favour, but Jamieson shifts the focus to the hacked Democratic campaign emails. She assumes that Russia was responsible and argues that their effect was amplified by the U.S. media, particularly around the time of the three presidential debates, and thus was able to tip the scales in a tight race.[48] As we have seen, the first tranche of stolen DNC material was published on 22 July, disrupting the Clinton campaign and sharpening divisions between supporters. The slow release of the Podesta documents began on 7 October, immediately after the *Access Hollywood* video. The third release of emails on 11 October revealed that a Democrat operative, Donna Brazile, while working at CNN, had provided debate questions to Clinton, and that senior Catholic Democratic campaign officials had disparaged Republicans as allegedly cherry-picking their faith for political gain. All this allowed Trump to argue that the election was 'rigged', and repeatedly referred to the WikiLeaks material, no fewer than 164 times in the last month of the campaign alone.

The Russian intervention allegedly pushed undecided voters to vote in a certain way, but Jamieson concedes that numerous factors were involved. The WikiLeaks revelations, for example, are questionably counted as Russian interference, but the last-minute Comey intervention was enough to shift enough undecided voters, especially 'Hillary defectors' in the three key swing states. Clinton did not need Russian help to alienate voters, notably because of her long career littered with scandals, her 'basket of deplorables' *faux pas* (used to describe Trump supporters in a campaign speech on 9 September), and her perceived sense of entitlement (an impression which she worked hard to dispel). Above all, as the book *Identity Crisis* argues, Trump's brutal exploitation of divisive race, gender, religious, migration and ethnicity issues propelled him to the White House. The state of the economy, the Obama presidency and the changing demographics of the political parties indicated that the election would be tight, and although for long periods this was obscured by Trump's various gaffes, on election night the predictions proved justified.[49] Nevertheless, although it is unlikely that the IRA had any serious effect on voting patterns, its existence was 'a major historical novelty', and its impact was achieved by the mainstream press coverage that '*generated* [italic in original] the actual effect of a disinformation operation'.[50]

Mark Zuckerberg, the head of Facebook, initially dismissed the idea that fake news on his platform could have helped elect Trump as president. The $100,000-worth of ads placed with the company by the IRA was a minuscule sum by any standard – the National Rifle Association alone spent $30 million to help get Trump elected. Three days after the election, Zuckerberg argued that it was a 'pretty crazy idea' to think fake Russian messages influenced the outcome. He asserted that voters 'make decisions based on their lived experience', but he soon changed his tune.[51] When pressed about how much 'inauthentic' Russian content there was on Facebook, Sheryl Sandberg, Facebook's chief operating officer, argued that 'any amount is too much', but she ultimately gave the 0.004 estimate, a negligible amount on any scale. The larger question is that the business model of Facebook, Twitter and YouTube is based on generating engagement, and for this, 'inflammatory and hateful' posts are best. Two weeks before the vote, a senior official with the Trump campaign admitted that they had 'three major voter suppression operations underway', aimed at young women, African-Americans and white idealistic liberals. Facebook was so useful to the Trump campaign that it spent the bulk of its $94 million budget on the platform, and Facebook even had staff embedded in the Trump campaign (a common practice with major advertisers, and they offered identical support to the Clinton campaign) to advise on how to spend the money most effectively, including presumably on how to get voters out – or to stay at home.[52]

On the Internet, Nobody Knows You're a Dog

As the various congressional hearings and other investigations gathered pace, Zuckerberg was forced not only to recant but also to increase monitoring. By September 2018 Facebook, Google and Twitter had announced some 125 initiatives to combat 'fake news'. Despite the minuscule amounts involved, the Russiagate scandal took its toll on the mighty Facebook empire. In March

2018, its shares took a battering when reports emerged that Cambridge Analytica, an American data analysis firm largely owned by Robert Mercer, mined the data of 50 million users to create profiles to target them in elections.[53] In 2014 and 2015, Facebook allowed an app developed by Alexander Kogan, at the time a research associate at Cambridge University, to harvest 87 million profiles of users around the world. This was then used by Cambridge Analytica to target voters in the 2016 U.S. election. The company overall boasted of having access to 230 million Americans' voter-registration data, as well as other personal information. The company broke Facebook rules by using data collected for research purposes.[54] The case provoked regulators to clamp down on the big technology companies to defend citizen privacy rights. Facebook in 2018 agreed with the Federal Trade Commission that it would inform users when their data was being shared with anyone other than their friends.[55]

Trump's digital campaign was based in San Antonio, Texas, and twelve Cambridge Analytica people worked there in 2016.[56] The company gleaned the personality profiles of the 230 million Americans and matched them to the Republican Party's exhaustive Voter Vault data base. The persuaders homed in on the 13 million fence-sitters, who could potentially be nudged one way or another, and this was further refined by focusing on voters in the crucial swing states of Michigan, Pennsylvania and Wisconsin. In the end, their votes made all the difference and Trump won in these states by tiny margins. As a senior Facebook executive, Andrew Bosworth, put it, Trump 'didn't get elected because of Russia or misinformation or Cambridge Analytica. He got elected because he ran the single best digital ad campaign I've ever seen'.[57] The Russian interference issue diverted attention from tackling the problem of big data and democracy.[58]

The veteran pollster, Nate Silver, doubted whether the Russian troll farms, memes and tweets had any effect, arguing, 'If you wrote out a list of the most important factors in the 2016 election, I'm not sure that Russian social media memes would be among the top 100. The scale was quite small and there's not much evidence that they were effective.' Russia's 5,000 post-election tweets hardly compared to the 500 million posted each day.[59] The report admitted that only a small proportion of Russian social media activity, 11 per cent, was related to the election, and that far from 'the scale of the operation being unprecedented' Stretch demonstrated that approximately 1 out of 23,000 pieces of content had anything to do with the IRA. The expenditure was also minuscule, with Facebook spending according to the Oxford report coming in at just $73,711 between 2015 and 2017. Aaron Maté, one of the most incisive analysts of the Russiagate affair, sums up Russian social media activity as follows: 'It was mostly unrelated to the 2016 election; microscopic in reach, engagement, and spending; and juvenile or absurd in its content'.[60]

Parscale, who was appointed Trump's campaign manager for 2020, compared Russia's impact to 'three pieces of salt inside a giant salad bowl the size of Madison Square Garden and you're never going to taste it'. The Russians spent less than $10,000 over the same period that the Trump campaign spent $100 million.[61]

The Trump campaign in total ran 5.9 million Facebook ads and the Clinton campaign only 66,000.[62] The scale of Russian social media intervention in the 2016 election was minuscule in comparison with the activities of the candidates and other interested parties, yet it has been endowed with supernatural powers to influence American voters and to shape public discourse. Why would a relatively minor investment by Russia outweigh the enormous funds expended by the Clinton and Trump campaigns? Mere contact with a Russian-inspired message in the popular imagination and the minds of Russiagate proponents was apparently enough to change people's convictions. What was 'the black magic, the propaganda alchemy, the special sauce that makes Russian copycat ads into weaponized tools of democracy-destruction, while those others are just normal discourse?'.[63] The great majority of the messages were not directly about the election, and can be categorised as 'clickbait' – items designed to attract interest, and thus enhance viewing figures and attract advertisers.[64] Even the New Knowledge report admitted that 'Merchandise perhaps provided the IRA with a source of revenue'.[65] Equally, some two-thirds of the relevant items were posted after the election. The political items, moreover, were broadly equally split between the Trump and Clinton campaigns.

This explains the emphasis on Russia's attempts to exacerbate divisions in U.S. society, which is an indirect admission that the ads and posts were mostly abstract and not always partisan. This takes us on to the other fundamental question: is the American polity so fragile and divided that a few Facebooks ads and tweets could alter the balance. This does not deny the other big question: should Russian agencies have been tweeting and Facebooking during the election at all? This understandably fed the Russiagate narrative, which Boyd-Barrett ultimately argues itself functioned as a disinformation or distraction campaign. While meddling of any kind is to be deplored, the substantive charge about Russian interference is weak, and pales into relative insignificance in the context of the hidden persuasion environment during election campaigns, reinforced by social media campaigns. According to Boyd-Barrett, many factors weaken the integrity of the American democratic process, and Russia in 2016 was but a minor one. The problem with the whole Russiagate narrative, in his view, 'was its narrow understanding of "election meddling" . . . Examining only Russia, without reference to other sources [of non-transparent interference in elections] was deceptive'.[66] The whole Russiagate affair in his view can only be understood in the context of the great power rivalry for the domination of Eurasia, which is another way of saying that the larger international context explains the extraordinary power of the Russiagate narrative.

Russiagate was used to discipline the upstart social media companies. Despite attempts to scapegoat Facebook, 'What drove the election decision was not Russian trolls or fake news on social media but a *pas de deux* of the mainstream centre-left media and conservative upstarts like Fox and Breitbart'.[67] This is the argument of Harvard's Berkman Klein Centre for Internet & Society, which in a comprehensive analysis of the media from 2015 and through the election argues that political cultural changes since the 1970s interacted with the development of social media and new forms of political communication to marginalise the traditional centre right media and politicians while radicalising 'the right wing ecosystem', notably Fox News, rendering the public vulnerable to foreign and domestic propaganda efforts.[68] The mainstream media unwittingly followed the agenda of the right-wing media and Trump with their focus on immigration, jobs and trade. The fact that Russian trolls favoured Trump was no big news, since 'The internet is a welter of dubious information and fake claims by people pretending to be somebody they aren't. On the internet, nobody knows you're a dog'. But as the book notes,

> Critically, if the biggest win for Russian information operations is to disorient American political communications, then overstating the impact of those efforts actually helps consolidate their success. . . . It is important not to confuse the high degree to which Russian operations are observable with the extent to which they actually make a difference to politically active beliefs, attitudes, and behaviours on America.[69]

Jack Matlock, the penultimate U.S. ambassador to the Soviet Union from 1987 to 1991, wisely noted that 'It had never occurred to me that our admittedly dysfunctional political system is so weak, undeveloped, or diseased that inept Internet trolls could damage it. It that is the case, we better look at a lot of other countries as well, not just Russia!'[70]

NOTES

1. Kathleen Hall Jamieson, *Cyberwar: How Russian Hackers and Trolls Helped Elect a President—What we Don't, Can't and do Know* (Oxford, Oxford University Press, 2018).

2. The argument is analysed by Jane Mayer, 'How Russia Helped Swing the Election for Trump', *New Yorker*, 1 October 2018, https://www.newyorker.com/magazine/2018/10/01/how-russia-helped-to-swing-the-election-for-trump.

3. Timothy Snyder, *The Road to Unfreedom: Russia, Europe, America* (London, Bodley Head, 2018).

4. Anna Arutunyan, 'There is No Russian Plot against America: The Kremlin's Electoral Interference is all Madness and No Method', *Foreign Affairs*, 5 August 2020, https://www.foreignaffairs.com/articles/united-states/2020-08-05/there-no-russian-plot-against-america.

5. Kimberly Marten, 'Russia's Use of Semi-State Security Forces: The Case of the Wagner Group', *Post-Soviet Affairs*, Vol. 35, No. 3, 2019, pp. 181–204.

6. Kimberly Marten, *Into Africa: Prigozhin, Wagner, and the Russian Military*, PONARS Eurasia Policy Memo No. 561, January 2019.

7. Neil MacFarquhar, 'Yevgeny Prigozhin, Russian Oligarch Indicted by US, is Known as "Putin's Cook"', *New York Times*, 16 February 2018, https://www.nytimes.com/2018/02/16/world/europe/prigozhin-russia-indictment-mueller.html.

8. Richard Sakwa, 'Heterarchy: Russian Politics between Chaos and Control', *Post-Soviet Affairs*, Vol. 37, No. 3, 2021, pp. 222–41.

9. Adrian Chen, 'The Agency', *The New York Times Magazine*, 2 June 2015, https://www.nytimes.com/2015/06/07/magazine/the-agency.html.

10. Adrian Chen, 'A So-Called Expert's Uneasy Dive into the Trump-Russia Frenzy', *New Yorker*, 22 February 2018, https://www.newyorker.com/tech/annals-of-technology/a-so-called-experts-uneasy-dive-into-the-trump-russia-frenzy.

11. *United States v. Internet Research Agency et al., No.-1:18-cr-00032-DLF* (Washington, DC, filed 16 February 2018), https://www.justice.gov/file/1035477/download.

12. Strzok, *Compromised*, p. 57.

13. *US v. IRA*, para. 11.

14. *US v. IRA*, para. 10c.

15. *US v. IRA*, para. 10d.

16. Hettena, *Trump/Russia*, p. 199.

17. *US v. IRA*, para. 6.

18. *US v. IRA*, para. 46c.

19. *US v. IRA*, paras. 69–71.

20. Weissmann, *Where Law Ends*, p. 135.

21. Adrian Chen, 'What Mueller's Indictment Reveals about Russia's Internet Research Agency', *New Yorker*, 16 February 2018, https://www.newyorker.com/news/news-desk/what-muellers-indictment-reveals-about-russias-internet-research-agency. Weissmann also concedes the latter point, *Where Law Ends*, pp. 139 and 224.

22. 'Putin Notes Russians Charged with Influencing US Election "May be Brought to Justice"', *TASS*, 6 March 2018, http://tass.com/politics/993021.

23. Senate Committee on Intelligence, *Report on Russian Active Measures Campaigns and Interference in the 2016 US Election*, Vol. 2, *Russia's Use of Social Media* (Washington, DC, US Senate, October 2019), p. 5.

24. Senate Committee on Intelligence, *Report*, Vol. 2, p. 7.

25. Denis Korotkov, 'Povar so svoimi tarakanami', *Novaya Gazeta*, 8 November 2018, https://www.novayagazeta.ru/articles/2018/11/08/78496-provokatsii-prigozhin

a. For an English summary, see 'An Accomplice to the Founder of Russia's "Troll Factory" Comes Forward and Says US Election Interference Wasn't a Kremlin Initiative', *Meduza*, 8 November 2018, https://meduza.io/en/feature/2018/11/09/an-accomplice-to-the-founder-of-the-troll-factory-comes-forward-and-says-russia-s-u-s-election-interference-wasn-t-a-kremlin-initiative.

26. Associated Press, 'Why It's Still in Russia's Interest to Mess with US Politics', 4 November 2018, https://leaderpost.com/pmn/news-pmn/why-its-still-in-russias-interest-to-mess-with-us-politics/wcm/fddcc208-5e7f-41bd-a813-f9608b53d2e9. For portraits of self-anointed 'Putin trolls', see Phil Butler, *Putin's Praetorians: Confessions of the Top Kremlin Trolls* (Heraklion, Pamil Visions, 2017).

27. The tweet was reposted by Trump – with the comment 'Absolutely pal' – and provoked a Twitterstorm. For a discussion, see Sheera Frenkel, 'Fact-Checking a Facebook Executive's Comments on Russian Interference', *New York Times*, 19 February 2018, https://www.nytimes.com/2018/02/19/technology/facebook-executive-russia-tweets-fact-check.html.

28. Rid, *Active Measures*, p. 406.

29. Shane and Mazzetti, 'The Plot to Subvert an Election'.

30. Testimony of Colin Stretch, 'Social Media Influence in the 2016 US Election', Hearing before the Senate Select Committee on Intelligence, 115th Congress, 13, 1 November 2017.

31. Elliot Schrage, Vice President of Policy and Communications, 'Hard Questions: Russian Ads Delivered to Congress', *Facebook press release*, 2 October 2017, https://newsroom.fb.com/news/2017/10/hard-questions-russian-ads-delivered-to-congress/.

32. Gareth Porter, 'The Shaky Case that Russia Manipulated Social Media to Tip the 2016 Election', *Consortium News*, 6 October 2018, https://consortiumnews.com/2018/10/10/the-shaky-case-that-russia-manipulated-social-media-to-tip-the-2016-election/.

33. Data from Sundar Pichai, Google's CEO, 'Google's Pichai Reveals the Extent of Google Ads', Scott.net, 13 December 2018, https://www.sott.net/article/402781-Googles-Pichai-reveals-the-extent-of-Russian-meddling-4700-on-Google-ads.

34. Gareth Porter, '33 Trillion More Reasons Why the *New York Times* Gets it Wrong on Russia-gate', *Consortium News*, 2 November 2018, https://consortiumnews.com/2018/11/02/33-trillion-more-reasons-why-the-new-york-times-gets-it-wrong-on-russia-gate/.

35. Darren L. Linvill and Patrick Warren, 'Troll Factories: The Internet Research Agency and State-Sponsored Agenda Building', unpublished paper, The Social Media Listen Centre, Clemson University, http://pwarren.people.clemson.edu/Linvill_Warren_TrollFactory.pdf; Oliver Roeder, 'Why We're Sharing 3 Million Russian Troll Tweets', FiveThirtyEight, 31 July 2018, https://fivethirtyeight.com/features/why-were-sharing-3-million-russian-troll-tweets/. The data are available here: https://github.com/fivethirtyeight/russian-troll-tweets/.

36. Porter, 'The Shaky Case that Russia Manipulated Social Media to Tip the 2016 Election'.

37. Clint Watts, *Messing with the Enemy: Surviving in a Social Media World of Hackers, Terrorists, Russians, and Fake News* (New York, Harper, 2018).

38. New Knowledge, *The Tactics and Tropes of the Internet Research Agency*, 18 December 2018, https://www.hsdl.org/c/tactics-and-tropes-of-the-internet-research-agency/, pp. 16, 43–44, 53 *and passim*; Jon Swaine, 'Black Americans "Targeted by Russian Troll Factories"', *Guardian*, 18 December 2018, p. 2.

39. Philip N. Howard, Bharath Ganesh, Dimitra Liotsiou, John Kelly and Camille François, *The IRA, Social Media and Political Polarization in the United States, 2012-2018* (Oxford, Project on Computational Propaganda, Working Paper 2018), pp. 3, 7, 9, 17–19, 23 and *passim*.

40. Frum, *Trumpocracy*, pp. 125–8.

41. Howard et al., *The IRA*, pp. 33–35.

42. Ahmer Arif, Leo G. Stewart and Kate Starbird, 'Acting the Part: Examining Information Operations Within #BlackLivesMatter Discourse', *Proceedings of the ACM on Human-Computer Interaction*, Vol. 2, CSCW, Article 20, November 2018, pp. 2, 18–19.

43. Arif et al., 'Acting the Part', p. 3.

44. Arif et al., 'Acting the Part', p. 23.

45. Howard et al., *The IRA*, pp. 39–40.

46. Danielle Ryan, 'Irony Alert: Firm that Warned Americans of Russian Bots . . . Was Running an Army of Fake Russian Bots', RT.com, 29 December 2018, https://www.rt.com/op-ed/447630-russian-bots-new-knowledge/.

47. Aaron Maté, 'New Studies Suggest Pundits are Wrong About Russian Social-Media Involvement in US Politics', *The Nation*, 28 December 2018, https://www.thenation.com/article/russiagate-elections-interference/.

48. Jamieson, *Cyberwar*.

49. John Sides, Michel Tesler and Lynn Vavreck, *Identity Crisis: The 2016 Presidential Campaign and the Battle for the Meaning of America* (Princeton, NJ, Princeton University Press, 2018). See also Norris and Inglehart, *Cultural Backlash*.

50. Rid, *Active Measures*, p. 408.

51. Hettena, *Trump/Russia*, p. 201; Sam Levin, 'Zuckerberg Regret at Ridiculing Fears over Facebook's Effect on US Vote', *Guardian*, 29 September 2017, p. 28.

52. Zeynep Tufekci, 'Russian Meddling is a Symptom, Not the Disease', *New York Times*, 3 October 2018, https://www.nytimes.com/2018/10/03/opinion/midterms-facebook-foreign-meddling.html.

53. For details and context, see Peter Geoghegan, *Democracy for Sale: Dark Money and Dirty Politics* (London, Apollo, 2020).

54. Brittany Kaiser, *Targeted: My Inside Story of Cambridge Analytica and how Trump, Brexit and Facebook Broke Democracy* (London, HarperCollins, 2019); Christopher Wylie, *Mindf*ck: Inside Cambridge Analytica's Plot to Break the World* (London, Profile Books, 2019).

55. Hannah Kuchler, Aliya Ram and Federica Cocco, 'Facebook Takes $35bn Battering as Backlash Rises over Data Harvest Claims', *Financial Times*, 20 March 2018, p. 1.

56. One of the Parscale team in San Antonio argues that 'Cambridge Analytica brought [nothing] to the table beyond what was standard campaign practice', Andrew Marantz, 'The Man Behind Trump's Facebook Juggernaut: Brad Parscale used Social

Media to Sway the 2016 Election. He's Poised to do it Again', *New Yorker*, 2 March 2020, https://www.newyorker.com/magazine/2020/03/09/the-man-behind-trumps-facebook-juggernaut.

57. Marantz, 'The Man Behind Trump's Facebook Juggernaut'.

58. Jamie Bartlett, *The People vs. Tech: How the Internet is Killing Democracy (and How We Can Save it)* (London, Ebury Press, 2018), and personal discussion 7 November 2018; Kris Shaffer, *Data versus Democracy: How Big Data Algorithms Shape Opinions and Alter the Course of History* (New York, Apress, 2019).

59. https://twitter.com/NateSilver538/status/1074833714931224582; Brian Flood, 'Nate Silver Dismisses Russian Trolls' Influence on 2016 Election', *Fox News*, 18 December 2018, https://www.foxnews.com/politics/nate-silver-dismisses-russian-trolls-influence-on-2016-election.

60. Maté, 'New Studies Suggest Pundits are Wrong about Russian Social-Media Involvement'.

61. Ian Schwartz, 'Trump Strategist Brad Parscale vs. PBS "Frontline" on Campaign Use of Facebook: "A Gift"', *RealClearPolitics*, 3 December 2018, https://www.realclearpolitics.com/video/2018/12/03/trump_strategist_brad_parscale_vs_pbs_frontline_on_campaigns_use_of_facebook.html.

62. Marantz, 'The Man Behind Trump's Facebook Juggernaut'.

63. The question is posed by Fred Weir, of the *Christian Science Monitor*, in a Facebook post, 4 September 2018, in Johnson's Russia List 2018/161/31, responding to the question raised by the *New York Times*, https://www.nytimes.com/interactive/2018/09/04/technology/facebook-influence-campaigns-quiz.html.

64. Moon of Alabama, 'Senate Reports on "Russian Influence Campaign" Fail to Discuss its Only Known Motive', 18 December 2018, https://www.moonofalabama.org/2018/12/senate-reports-on-russian-influence-campaign-fail-to-discuss-its-only-known-motive.html#more.

65. New Knowledge, *Tactics and Tropes of the Internet Research Agency*, p. 31.

66. Oliver Boyd-Barrett, *RussiaGate and Propaganda: Disinformation in the Age of Social Media* (London, Routledge, 2020), p. 4.

67. Holman W. Jenkins Jr., 'The Scapegoating of Facebook', *Wall Street Journal*, 21 November 2018, https://www.wsj.com/articles/the-scapegoating-of-facebook-1542757846.

68. Yochai Benkler, Rob Faris and Hal Roberts, *Network Propaganda: Manipulation, Disinformation, and Radicalization in American Politics* (New York, Oxford University Press, 2018).

69. Quoted in Jenkins, 'The Scapegoating of Facebook'.

70. Jack F. Matlock, 'Amid "Russiagate" Hysteria, What are the Facts?', *The Nation*, 1 June 2018, https://www.thenation.com/article/amid-russiagate-hysteria-what-are-the-facts/, as well as personal discussion, North Carolina, 13 February 2020.

Chapter 7

Conspiracy, Collusion and Crossfire Hurricane

In a tangled story, the George Papadopoulos affair is more knotted than most. He had the ill-fortune to fall down a rabbit hole in which nothing was as it appeared, and he became the victim of multiple intrigues. Who is Professor Mifsud, and what part did he play in Russiagate? Many questions are also raised by the notorious 9 June 2016 Trump Tower meeting between members of Trump's team and a Russian lawyer. In both cases, nothing is as it seems, and it is not clear who was deceiving whom. In the end, on 31 July 2016, the FBI opened the Crossfire Hurricane counterintelligence investigation into the Trump campaign's alleged Russia ties that dominated the Trump presidency and embroiled America in a cycle of claims and counterclaims.

THE BRITISH LINK

The first suggested allegation of collusion between Trump and Russia came not from the U.S. security agencies but Britain's Government Communications Headquarters (GCHQ). In late 2015 GCHQ forwarded 'leads' to Washington, informing CIA director Brennan that it was tracking communications between Trump associates and Russia. Brennan headed the CIA from March 2013 to January 2017 and had earlier been 'one of the leading architects of the war on terror' and managed the 'kill list' of people deemed eligible for lethal 'signature strikes'.[1] He had a chequered history as director. In one controversial incident, in 2014 he admitted that the agency spied on Senate staffers investigating CIA use of torture.[2] As in Russiagate, this was a case of 'political spying under the guise of legitimate national security monitoring'.[3] Brennan went on to become a leading advocate of Russiagate claims. It appears that he created a secret interagency 'Trump Task Force' in early 2016 to investigate

Trump's links with the Kremlin, and vigorously promoted the narrative that Russia interfered in the 2016 election.[4] Brennan fed British leads into the mix, since 'US and UK intelligence sources acknowledge that GCHQ played an early, prominent role in kick-starting the FBI's Trump-Russia investigation'.[5] The content of these communications has never been revealed, but they were allegedly 'extensive'. As Boyd-Barrett notes, 'British involvement in the 2016 US presidential election would not only have constituted illegal support to the Clinton campaign but would likely have far exceeded in magnitude and subterfuge the efforts attributed to Russia in behalf of Trump.'[6] The information set the hare running, with fateful consequences for American democracy and society.

In summer 2016 the head of GCHQ, Robert Hannigan, secretly travelled to Washington to brief Brennan on British findings about a 'stream of illicit communications' between Trump campaign officials and Russians, although the nature of these contacts remains secret.[7] Brennan admitted later that this is what prompted an FBI probe, and in August he referred the matter to the interagency task force to investigate.[8] The group included the FBI, the Treasury Department, the DoJ, the CIA, the Office of the DNI, headed since August 2010 by James Clapper, and the NSA. In late August and early September Brennan briefed the 'Gang of Eight', the top-ranking Democratic and Republican leaders in the House and Senate, when he told them individually that the agency had evidence that Russia was trying to help Trump win the presidency.[9] On 17 August Trump and two of his leading campaigners, Michael Flynn and New Jersey governor Chris Christie, were also briefed by three top FBI officials at their New York offices by Joe Pientka, Kevin Clinesmith and Peter Strzok, all of whom would take the lead in investigating and promoting Russiagate. They had been investigating Trump as a witness in his own case rather than as a possible president, as became evident when a redacted note of the meeting finally appeared in August 2020.[10] As for the gang of eight briefings, there are no notes, but later most participants vocally condemned Russian activities. For example, Senator Diane Feinstein, the ranking Democrat on the Senate Intelligence Committee, and Adam Schiff, vice-chair of the HPSCI, on 22 September warned 'that Russian intelligence agencies are making serious and concerted effort to influence the US election'.[11] Schiff would lead the Russiagate campaign as well as the impeachment efforts in 2019. Above all, in August the CIA reportedly told Obama that Putin not only ordered an election interference campaign but did so specifically 'to help elect ... Donald Trump'. The information was so sensitive that it was delivered by special courier and Brennan kept it out of the Presidential Daily Brief on intelligence matters.[12]

A British intelligence tip-off lit the fuse, but Hannigan's behaviour is puzzling. According to the protocols of Five Eyes (the intelligence-sharing agreement between the United States, UK, Australia, New Zealand and Canada), Hannigan should have contacted the NSA director Mike Rogers, the U.S. counterpart to GCHQ. Rogers was a known Russiagate sceptic, unlike Brennan who, in the words of one critical commentator, 'peddled the conspiracy theories of his like-minded European counterparts'.[13] Rogers was an Obama outsider with poor relations with both Brennan and Clapper, and he later criticised their behaviour. Rogers discovered that at least since November 2015 Foreign Intelligence Surveillance Act (FISA) applications had been used inappropriately. Congress enacted FISA in 1978 to regulate domestic surveillance for national-security investigations, creating the Foreign Intelligence Surveillance Court (FISC) to grant individual warrants in domestic intelligence operations. In October 2016 Clapper tried, unsuccessfully, to get Rogers fired.[14] The NSA was the most sceptical – it turned out correctly – about the Russian collusion narrative. Clapper, on the other hand, had already distinguished himself in 2003, at the head of the Department of Defence's National Imagery and Mapping Agency, in his dogged insistence that WMD had been found in Iraq, asserting that they existed but had 'unquestionably' been moved into Syria.[15] In March 2013 Clapper testified under oath to the Senate Intelligence Committee that the NSA did not engage in the bulk collection of the communications of U.S. citizens, a statement that he later admitted was false when Snowden's files revealed that the NSA had been doing just that.[16] In his memoirs Clapper asserts that Putin's interference in the 2016 election was 'staggering' and decisively tilted the result in Trump's favour.[17]

PAPADOPOULOS GETS CAUGHT

In early March 2016 the twenty-eight-year-old Papadopoulos was taken on by the Trump campaign as a foreign affairs adviser.[18] He was interviewed for the post by Sam Clovis, the Trump campaign's national co-chair and chief policy advisor, who declared that improved Russian-U.S. relations were a top priority for the Trump team.[19] Papadopoulos was one of five advisors on foreign affairs (another was Carter Page), although he had modest credentials for such a role.[20] While working as a researcher at the Hudson Institute he called for an Israeli-Cyprus-Greece energy alliance to exploit Eastern Mediterranean resources. He also recommended good relations with Egypt, despite the return of authoritarian governance, and a turn away from Turkey, even though it was a NATO member.[21]

From the beginning Papadopoulos was one of the targets of the Mueller investigation, with his case handled by the indefatigable Jeannie Rhee. Papadopoulos advanced several theories about the ultimate source of his travails. When appointed to the Trump team he was working at the London Centre for International Law Practice (LCILP); although he observes there was not much law going on there.[22] On joining the campaign, Naga Khalid Idris, the founder of LCILP, was at first hostile to the idea of Papadopoulos working for Trump. According to Papadopoulos, he later reversed his position and insisted that Papadopoulos go to a conference at the Link Campus in Rome, an institution that is reputed to be the venue for non-classified CIA events and 'a training ground for spies'.[23] Arriving in Rome on 12 March, Papadopoulos met Professor Joseph Mifsud, a former Maltese diplomat and director of the London Academy of Diplomacy (LAD) who also had ties with LCILP. Idris introduced Mifsud as a man with vital connections, and this is indeed the case. From personal experience I can confirm that Papadopoulos's characterisation is accurate: 'Mifsud spins himself as a worldly insider, a guy with an I-have-connections-everywhere arrogance', offset by 'flashing warmth'.[24]

Mifsud has been accused at various times of working for the Russian, British or American intelligence services, and he certainly was a cosmopolitan denizen of a transnational world of politics, diplomacy and intelligence. His friend Stephan Roh claims that Mifsud was linked to British and American intelligence.[25] The DoJ's inspector general Michael Horowitz conducted two major reviews into Russiagate (see below), and footnotes to the second one declassified in April 2020 state that the FBI could find no record of Mifsud as a confidential human source (CHS) and neither could the requested searches from other U.S. security agencies.[26] However, there are attested links with British intelligence, in particular through Claire Smith of the Joint Intelligence Committee and Britain's Security Vetting panel, with whom he had worked at the Link University in Rome.[27] Soon after the story became public Mifsud disappeared. A *Times* profile suggested that he was a Potemkin village comprised of honorary professorships, loss-making 'diplomatic academies', and the name-dropping of prominent political figures with whom he claimed to have worked.[28] In fact, Mifsud is a complex individual driven by an abiding concern for a united and peaceful Europe from Lisbon to Vladivostok, and thus sought to overcome the new cold war.

That evening Mifsud turned the conversation to Russia, although Papadopoulos had no expertise or even interest in the country. Papadopoulos would soon learn that while he may not have been interested in Russia, others certainly were, and he became a pawn in a web of intrigue intended to tar the Trump campaign with the brush of collusion. Mifsud promised to facilitate a meeting between Trump and Putin, and on 14 March Papadopoulos sent a triumphant email to Clovis about his networking success.[29] Back in London Mifsud emailed Papadopoulos to set up a meeting with 'somebody very important'. Strangely, Idris already knew the identity of the 'important' person – none other than Putin's 'niece'. On 24 March they had lunch at the Grange Holborn Hotel, where he was introduced to an 'attractive, fashionably dressed young woman with dirty blonde hair' by the name of Olga Vinogradova (earlier reports name her as Olga Polonskaya). She barely spoke English, and Papadopoulos noticed 'a big, burly, bald guy in a leather jacket and jeans keeping a casual gaze on Olga'. The occasion was 'another opportunity for Mifsud to spin dreams of deal-making with Russia'.[30] In the following weeks Papadopoulos exchanged emails with Vinogradova about a possible summit, although by now her English had become fluent. Even Papadopoulos suspected that she was not all that she made herself out to be, doubts reinforced by the fact that Putin has no niece by this or any other name.

On 31 March Papadopoulos attended the first meeting of Trump's foreign policy team at the Trump International Hotel (the Old Post Office) in Washington. He told Trump that he had met people in Europe 'who are eager to set up a meeting for you with Russia'. Trump asked Sessions for his opinion and he responded: 'It's a good idea. We should look into this'.[31] Papadopoulos then worked to set up a top-level summit, despite a prescient warning from Page (who had not attended the 31 March meeting) to 'Be very careful about talking about Russia'.[32] Perhaps Page had an intimation of his own fate when he was identified by Steele as the intermediary between the campaign and Russian officials keen to see Trump in the White House. On 18 April Mifsud introduced Papadopoulos by email to Ivan Timofeev, programme director at the Russian International Affairs Council (RIAC). On 25 April Timofeev told Papadopoulos in an email that he had discussed the plan for a meeting with Igor Ivanov, RIAC's president and Russia's foreign minister between 1998 and 2004, but they agreed that protocols needed to be observed. While Trump had an open invitation by Putin to meet when he was ready, they would make no moves until a more senior figure went through the appropriate channels.[33] Timofeev acted with professionalism and integrity, unlike many others for whom Russia was the foil against which a conspiracy was woven.[34]

On 26 April Papadopoulos enjoyed a breakfast meeting with Mifsud at the Andaz Hotel near Liverpool Street station. Mifsud had recently returned from a meeting of the Valdai International Discussion Club, and apparently made the epochal statement that is at the core of the Russiagate investigation. He is alleged to have told Papadopoulos that he had met top officials in Moscow and that they had obtained 'dirt' on Clinton: the Russians 'had emails of Clinton. They have thousands of emails'.[35] It was never clear what emails were in question – Clinton's deleted emails, or less likely those (not yet) taken from the DNC and Clinton staffers. The Mueller report describes the Valdai Club as 'close to Russia's foreign policy establishment', which is true, but it is unlikely that at an event of this kind anyone would have offered 'dirt' on Clinton.[36] In an interview with Jake Tapper on CNN on 7 September 2018, Papadopoulos argued that Mifsud simply stated that he had access to emails, but did not ask whether he (Papadopoulos) or the Trump campaign wanted them. Mifsud has since disappeared, but before doing so he denied ever making such a statement.[37] The Mueller investigators are scathing about Papadopoulos's reliability as a witness and accuse him of repeatedly lying (above all about the timing of his meetings with Mifsud), and although he was their first successful prosecution they were frustrated: 'Papadopoulos represented a promising door that just couldn't be nudged open'.[38]

Papadopoulos first came to public attention through an interview with the London *Times* on 4 May, in which he castigated the British prime minister, David Cameron, for calling Trump's policies 'divisive, stupid and wrong' and allegedly called on him to apologise, otherwise the 'special relationship' would be damaged.[39] At this point matters become even more intriguing. On 3 May Papadopoulos met his friend Christian Cantor, the chief of the political department at the Israeli embassy in London, who introduced him to his girlfriend, Erika Thompson. She happened to work as a senior adviser to Alexander Downer, Australia's High Commissioner to the UK between 2014 and 2018. Downer had been Australia's longest-serving foreign minister (1996–2007) and in that capacity was responsible for the Australian Secret Intelligence Service (ASIS) and cooperated closely with the Five Eyes group. After leaving politics in 2008 he joined Hakluyt & Co., a secretive private intelligence agency run by former MI6 operatives. He resigned from the agency when he was appointed High Commissioner, but apparently continued to attend agency functions. Like Steele's Orbis Business Intelligence, these companies do business that formal state agencies prefer to outsource to ensure what the CIA calls 'plausible deniability'.

Downer professed interest in the work that Papadopoulos was doing on Mediterranean oil and gas reserves, and on that basis Cantor arranged for the three to meet in the Kensington Wine Rooms on 10 May (there is now a plaque to mark the occasion). Papadopoulos later wrote: 'In the space of less than an hour, a promising, well-intentioned adventure will turn into a long-running nightmare that will destroy my career, my finances, and strain relations with the people I care about the most'.[40] According to Papadopoulos, Downer was 'oozing aggression', condemning his comments about Cameron, his policy recommendations about Cyprus energy policy and Turkey, and admitted that he was a 'big fan' of Hillary Clinton. Then Downer claimed that Papadopoulos told him that 'the Russians have a surprise or some damaging material related to Hillary Clinton'. Papadopoulos claims that 'I have no memory of this. None, Zero. Nada'.[41] Other versions have it that Papadopoulos told Downer that the Russians had hacked Clinton's computers and would use the information against her. According to Downer, Papadopoulos claimed that Mifsud had told him that Russia had acquired 'thousands' of emails hacked from the personal server used by Clinton when she was secretary of state, the publication of which would damage her presidential campaign. Papadopoulos insists that he never said anything of the sort and made no mention of hacking in the short meeting. He did mention that he had met Mifsud on a business trip to Rome, who asserted that he had 'dirt' on Clinton, but there was no mention of hacking in his conversation with Downer and Thompson. Papadopoulos insists that he was being circumspect since he suspected that the conversation was being recorded on Downer's mobile phone, a suspicion that he later relayed to the FBI. Downer reported the conversation to the Australian foreign ministry, which after a two-month delay forwarded the information to Washington.

The brief encounter between Papadopoulos and Downer ostensibly served as the basis for the FBI on 31 July 2016 to launch the counterintelligence investigation into Russia's interference in the U.S. election and the FISA warrants against Carter Page. Information about Papadopoulos relayed by the Australian and British authorities 'so alarmed American officials to provoke the FBI to open a counterintelligence investigation into the Trump campaign months before the presidential election'.[42] The point is crucial, because it allows federal prosecutors and Mueller to argue that it was not the Steele dossier, now largely discredited, that was the initial source of the Russia investigation but the Papadopoulos information. However, the Papadopoulos information is no more substantial than the Steele dossier, and in some ways more troubling. Downer did not initially think much of what Papadopoulos allegedly told him at their meeting on 10 May, but it was only when the DNC emails were published by WikiLeaks on 22 July that he went to the U.S. embassy in London and reported the two-month-old conversation to Elizabeth Dibble, the chargé d'affaires (the ambassador, Matthew Barzun, was on holiday at the time). State Department official Dibble immediately reported the information to the FBI, and the Russiagate machine was set in motion. It is not clear why Downer waited so long, especially since the theft of the DNC emails had become public knowledge by 15 June, yet he held back another five weeks.

The matter did not end there. On 15 July Papadopoulos was contacted by Sergei Millian (real name Siarhei Kukuts), a native of Belarus who at the time was the 38-year-old head of the obscure New York-based Russian-American Chamber of Commerce. Millian has been identified as both Source D and E in the Steele dossier, although logically he cannot be both, as well as being the source of the pee tape story.[43] Millian claimed a close relationship with Trump, although the two were barely acquainted. Above all, Millian appears to have been the source of Steele's fundamental claim that there 'was a well-developed conspiracy of cooperation between [Trump] and the Russian leadership' involving Manafort and Page.[44] Meeting a few days later at the Andaz Hotel in New York, Millian steered the conversation towards Russia, but by now Papadopoulos was cautious, especially since the Trump campaign had made it clear that it was 'lukewarm about connecting with Russia'.[45] Millian may well have been some sort of 'state intelligence asset', but it is not clear on whose side he was on.[46] According to Strzok, he was definitely not 'directed by the FBI'.[47]

On 2 September 2016 Papadopoulos was contacted by Stefan Halper, born an American but who had long been domiciled in the UK. Halper worked as an adviser to Nixon and Reagan and was the former son-in-law of Ray Cline, one of the CIA's lead analysts during the Cuban Missile crisis in October 1962. Halper now worked as a Cambridge University professor and by all accounts was still associated with American security agencies as well as being active in the Cambridge Security Initiative run by Sir Richard Dearlove, the head of MI6 from 1999 to 2004.[48] Apparently, Halper was known to MI6 as 'The Walrus', because of his portly gait. After a dinner hosted by the Initiative in February 2014 attended by Flynn, then head of the DIA, concerns were raised (and reported to American intelligence) about his contact at the event with Svetlana Lokhova, a Russian-born specialist in Soviet intelligence and espionage at Cambridge University. The false allegation was circulated that Flynn had an affair with Lokhova on the orders of Russian intelligence. Not surprisingly, Lokhova later sued. At an event hosted by Dearlove on 11 July 2016 Halper had his first contact with Carter Page, just three days after the latter's return from Moscow.[49] The conference was organised by Stephen Schrage, a former State Department official who was then Halper's PhD student.[50] He notes that in the last session on 12 July Dearlove 'went far off the script' and lambasted Trump as a national security threat in front of the Trump advisor, and that after a discussion with Dearlove Halper suddenly became very interested in Page.[51] Lokhova claims that Halper (whom she dubs 'The Spider') from September 2015 was at the centre of a dark web of intrigue against Trump and one of the main instigators of the Russiagate conspiracy. Flynn was one of the first targets, and Papadopoulos another.[52] Amidst allegations that there was a Russian conspiracy in Cambridge, Halper and Dearlove quit the seminar that hosted Flynn because of 'unacceptable Russian influences'.[53] Like the Cambridge spy ring of the 1930s, it may take decades before the full story is revealed.

By now Papadopoulos was short of funds, so he accepted Halper's invitation to return to the UK to discuss a research paper on Mediterranean oil, with an honorarium of $3,000. The much ill-used Papadopoulos believes that he was the subject of an FBI sting operation to extract information from Trump campaign officials. In September an investigator working for the

U.S. intelligence community going by the name of Azra Turk (the pseudonym can hardly be bettered, especially when dealing with a Turkophobe like Papadopoulos) posed as a Halper's research assistant and met him for a drink on Papadopoulos' arrival in London on 15 September. In his account, she was 'a vision right out of central casting for a spy flick. She's a sexy bottle blonde in her thirties, and she isn't shy about showing her curves – as if anyone could miss them'. Within five minutes, she directly asked him 'are we working for Russia?'[54] He saw Turk three times: in the bar, over dinner and then once with Halper. Papadopoulos felt that something was amiss, and thus refused her blandishments. He suspected that she tried to 'seduce' him to 'make me slip up and say something that they knew I had no info on'.[55] At their meeting, Halper pressed Papadopoulos on Trump campaign links with Russia, asking leading questions such as 'It's great that Russia is helping you and the campaign, right, George?'[56] Hardly subtle, but possibly effective. Papadopoulos believes that Halper contacted him as part of the already-started FBI Russia-Trump investigation. Halper also arranged a meeting, using a similar pretext, with Page, and grilled him on alleged Trump-Russia links. The investigation led by Horowitz later examined the role of informants in Russiagate.

By then Papadopoulos's political career was over. He was dismissed from the Trump team in early October 2016 following the adverse criticism generated by an interview he gave to the Russian news agency Interfax in which he called for an end to sanctions, which in his view had only turned Russia towards China. He adopted the Kissinger line that 'It is not in the interests of the West to align China and Russia in a geopolitical alliance that can have unpredictable consequences for US interests'.[57] By now Papadopoulos was angry and identified the source of his woes:

> The deep state is the movement of anti-Trump operatives in America's three branches of government who have been working against Donald Trump, his campaign, and his administration to strip it of authority. These operatives are government employees loyal to Hillary Clinton and Barack Obama. They are hellbent on playing politics and using the tools of the state – politically driven investigations, rubber-stamped FISA warrants, leaked memos and legal documents – as well as planted stories in the press and social media to wage war on Trump, his team, and the Republican Party.[58]

Papadopoulos' travails were not over. In October he once again met up with Millian, who Papadopoulos suspects was wearing a bugging device while asking provocative questions.[59] On 24 January 2017 the *Wall Street Journal* reported that Millian was the source behind the Steele dossier, including the compromising Moscow hotel sex tape.

On 27 January the FBI finally appeared in person, pounding on the door of his mother's home in Chicago. Papadopoulos was questioned by agents who like Turk, Halper and others asked, 'Now, let's talk about Russian interference. Who in the campaign knew about interference?' As in the previous encounters, Papadopoulos claims that he had no idea what they were talking about.⁶⁰ They repeatedly asked about the precise timeline of meetings with Mifsud, Downer, Millian, Turk and Halper, and without his computer or calendar to hand, discrepancies in dates were enough for the FBI to claim that he deceived them. According to Strzok, Papdopoulos lied about the timeline, extent and character of relations with Mifsud and the other Russians associated with him.⁶¹ In a second interview a few weeks later Papdopoulos declared that he was willing to cooperate, but soon after he deactivated a Facebook account that Strzok claims 'he had used to communicate directly with the Russians'.⁶² Mueller later indicted him for lying – in particular over when he met Mifsud, which Papadopolous stated took place a fortnight earlier than in reality. As Papadopoulos notes, there is 'a difference between having a faulty memory and actively lying', but not 'when you are dealing with the FBI'.⁶³ The story does not end there. In March 2017 Papadopoulos was contacted by the U.S.-Israeli dual citizen Charles Tawil with alleged links to U.S. intelligence and invited to Israel and given $10,000 for research on energy issues. Papadopoulos was suspicious about the money and deposited it with his lawyer in Greece before returning to the United States, whereupon he was arrested as his flight from Munich landed in Dulles (Washington DC) on 27 July. Papadopoulos feared that the FBI planned to catch him with $10,000 in undeclared cash, and when he appeared before House committees he asked whether the money consisted of marked bills originating with the FBI.

Papadopoulos was arraigned on 28 July, and charged with lying to the FBI about the timing of certain events (the meeting with Mifsud), an issue of no consequence in itself but which, according to Mueller, 'hindered investigators' ability to effectively question Mifsud' when he was interviewed in the lobby of a Washington hotel on 10 February 2017.⁶⁴ In the interview and a follow-up email from Mifsud sent a few hours later he denied any advance knowledge of Russian hacking, and the FBI did not press the issue. Mifsud insisted that his contacts with Papadopoulos were entirely innocuous and academic in character, dealing mostly with geopolitical issues and how a new cold war could be averted.⁶⁵ The next day Mifsud left the United States and disappeared. The Mueller indictment nevertheless asserted that Papadopoulos had obtained advance information about the alleged Russian hacking of the DNC and Clinton campaign computers. Papadopoulos was the first of the Trump team to plead guilty in Mueller's investigation, confessing to making a 'material false statement' to the FBI about his contacts in the 27 January FBI interview. Prosecutors argued that Papadopoulos had caused irreparable damage to the investigation after allegedly repeatedly lying, causing the FBI to fail to interview a key witness. He reached a plea deal with Mueller on 5 October 2017 and after a year of cooperation, on 7 September 2018, Papadopoulos confessed to a crime that he insists he did not commit.[66] He was sentenced to 14 days in jail, 200 hours of community service, and a $9,000 fine, but was pardoned by Trump in December 2020. Papadopoulos played only a small and brief part in the Trump campaign, yet the case is pivotal to the Russiagate allegations.[67]

A Theory of Conspiracy

In an interview with Martha MacCallum of Fox News on 19 September 2018, Papadopoulos argued that the meddling was not so much by the Russians as by the Australian and British authorities.[68] He accused the FBI and British intelligence of persecuting him as part of a plan to derail the Trump campaign and presidency. Papadopoulos believes that he was the victim of an entrapment campaign, since all three – Cantor, Downer and Thompson – had made clear their anti-Trump views, and Downer's request to met him was particularly suspicious. Papadopoulos believes that 'these people were looking for a way to find evidence of collusion by planting a false flag story – that the Russians had dirt on Clinton – and then tracking the campaign to see who pursued the phony story'.[69] Papadopoulos considered that he was 'the lynchpin of their conspiracy case'.[70] He certainly came under pressure from the FBI, realising that 'I'm facing five years in prison for lies I don't remember making, and twenty years for obstruction because I followed my lawyer's advice and deleted my Facebook account'.[71] Papadopoulos had not told campaign members about Mifsud's claim, no 'matter how much Robert Mueller and his team of FBI agents and prosecutors wished I had'.[72] In his view, 'The Mueller Investigation needs convictions, not just for public relations purposes but as a scare tactic for future suspects and people of interest'.[73] He was right at least in that respect, since the Mueller team made no secret of their ambition of getting Papadopoulos to 'flip' and testify against others.

Downer played a critical role in launching what was to become the FBI's Crossfire Hurricane investigation.[74] However, when McCabe was asked by the HPSCI why the FISA warrant in October 2016 was requested only for Carter Page and not for the man on which the Trump investigation was predicated, he answered 'Papadopoulos's comment didn't particularly indicate that he was the person that had had – that was interacting with the Russians'.[75] In other words, even the FBI did not think that he had serious contact with Russians. Papadopoulos appeared to be the trump card in Mueller's prosecution of the collusion case, but in fact it demonstrates the opposite. Mueller's sentencing memo claimed that Papadopoulos 'did not provide "substantial assistance"' during his interviews in August and September 2017, but Papadopoulos insisted that 'I did my best . . . and offered what I knew'. This is hardly surprising, since Papadopoulos had not achieved much during his brief tenure as a campaign adviser, with the Trump campaign rebuffing his attempts to set up meetings with Russian officials. Papadopoulos insists that 'I never met with a single Russian official in my life'. Papadopoulos was blamed by Mueller for having impeded the FBI's investigation into Mifsud, although Papadopoulos had voluntarily provided information about his contact with the professor – in other words, Papadopoulos refused to accept that he had lied about Mifsud, only conceding that he had made misleading statements about being a member of the Trump campaign when he first met Mifsud.[76]

As for contacts with Russia, in response to a misleading article in the *Washington Post* on 15 August 2017, which tried to prove 'Russian meddling', Timofeev issued a detailed rebuttal. He admitted that Papadopoulos contacted RIAC in spring 2016 in the form of unofficial emails suggesting a possible visit to Russia by Trump. Following normal protocols RIAC requested an official 'enquiry' (the technical term for such a visit) to test the seriousness of the initiative. No response was received, and that was the end of the matter.[77] RIAC was doing what it was set up to do – to foster dialogue and analysis. The attempt to turn this into some sort of conspiracy demonstrates the pervasive lack of knowledge about Russian institutions and the insubstantiality of many Russiagate allegations.

Papadopoulos certainly believes that he was the subject of an extended entrapment scheme, beginning in March 2016 when he announced that he was joining the Trump team to his colleagues at the LCILP. He calls it a 'strange operation' since there appeared to be no law going on, and suspects that it was an intelligence front.[78] The initial response to Papadopoulos joining the Trump campaign was hostile, but soon after he was invited by the director to a three-day conference at the Link campus in Rome, where he was introduced to Mifsud, and the byzantine story develops from there. Out of the blue he was contacted by the Cambridge academic Stefan Halper, an old CIA hand, and questioned about Russia. A mysterious Belarusian-American Sergei Millian offers him a secret $30,000 per month PR job but only if he continues working for Trump. The Israeli-American businessman Charles Tawil buys him lunch in Illinois, and they go clubbing together in Mykonos, and then Tawil flies Papadopoulos to Israel where he gives him $10,000 in cash, money that the suspicious Papadopoulos leaves with a lawyer in Thessaloniki. Flying back to the United States in July 2017, he is surrounded by a squad of FBI agents when changing planes, and as they go through his bags it dawns on him that they are looking for the money. In a dishevelled state, he is hauled before a judge and warned that he faces twenty-five years in prison on charges of obstruction and lying to the FBI. Papadopoulos was 'caught up in the biggest scandal to rock American politics since Watergate' in his view because 'the deep state of former Obama and Clinton-loving lawmen' aimed to kill three birds with one stone: to protect the U.S.-Turkish power relationship; to 'cripple the Trump campaign and administration to prevent any warming of relations between the United States and Russia'; and to send a message to the Trump team, thus 'sowing chaos and distrust inside and outside of the administration'.[79] The purpose of the whole exercise was to stop Trump, and it is 'a story of abuse of power and prosecutorial overreach'.[80]

The murky details of the Papadopoulos affair may one day be exposed, but for now we have to make sense of what we have. One of the main interpretations is that Brennan's CIA was the main driver working with Clapper's DNI while using the hapless Comey and colluding with foreign intelligence services.[81] The motive was high-minded – to prevent the election of someone they believed represented a danger to the republic and its allies. If this version is correct, then Russia was collateral damage. Rather than demonstrating 'a Russian operation that was more aggressive and widespread than previously known',[82] the Papadopoulos case reveals how Russia was mobilised by contending domestic groups. Already in late July 2018 Nunes, the HPSCI chair, expressed confidence 'that once the American people see these 20 pages [the classified part of the FISA application to bug Carter Page] . . . they will be shocked by what's in that FISA application'.[83] To get to the bottom of the matter, on 17 September 2018 Trump called for the immediate declassification of all Russiagate documents. However, those called upon to do the declassifying were precisely those whose activities would be revealed. Pressure from the DoJ and the intelligence community, home and abroad, forced Trump on 21 September to retract his order. Trump revealed that 'key allies' had asked for the documents not to be released. In a tweet, Papadopoulos asserted that these 'allies' were the Australian and British governments. The *Wall Street Journal* on 24 September 2018 admitted as much when it wrote 'As for the allies, sometimes US democratic accountability has to take precedence over the potential embarrassment of British intelligence'. This implies that three of the Five Eyes states may have been part of a potentially criminal intelligence operation to sabotage the campaign of an American presidential candidate. They believed they were acting for the public good, but deception always demands its own price.

CROSSFIRE HURRICANE

Shortly after dropping the investigation into Clinton's emails, on 31 July 2016 Comey started an investigation into the Trump campaign's links with

Russia, codenamed Crossfire Hurricane. It was an investigation in its own right as well as a portmanteau for four related sub-investigations into Carter Page, Paul Manafort, George Papadopoulos and, above all, Michael Flynn. The matter was opened as a counterintelligence investigation, but it was also potentially a criminal investigation.[84] Above all, it appears that Trump himself was the object of the investigation, and not just his campaign or later his administration. The decision ranks as one of the most important in American intelligence history. Seldom if ever has the FBI investigated a presidential campaign while the battle was in full flood, but the stakes could not have been higher: 'whether a major political campaign had conspired with a foreign enemy to throw the outcome of a presidential election'.[85]

Although the probe was kept secret, the charge of political bias inevitably arises.[86] When the document opening the enquiry was finally published in May 2020, suspicions were reinforced by the flimsy predicate for the case and the unprofessional construction of the FBI Electronic Communication (EC) itself.[87] Instead of complete 'from' and 'to' lines in the EC, only the 'from' line was filled: from the FBI's counterintelligence division with Strzok listed as the contact. The EC was also drafted by Strzok, and then approved by Strzok, an absurdity that violated normal FBI procedures. The names in the 'cc' line were redacted, but Strzok's was listed at the end (for some reason he sent the message to himself), with more senior people listed first if normal protocols were observed. These people are likely to have been FBI director Comey, his deputy McCabe and counterintelligence assistant director Bill Priestap.[88] The intensity of concern over Russia as the new cold war intensified fed back into American domestic politics to create an atmosphere where unsubstantiated intelligence leads were magnified by domestic political polarisation.

An investigation was launched by an incumbent administration into the legal opposition, and it did so with the aid of obscure and rarely used statutes. Crossfire Hurricane was opened as a FARA investigation, which involves a criminal violation of the 1938 law requiring registration with the U.S. government for work or services on behalf of a foreign country. The law had been amended in 1966 to tighten disclosure requirements about lobbying on behalf of foreign governments. Before Russiagate FARA suits had been extremely rare, with only seven criminal prosecutions and three convictions in the half century from 1965 to 2015. Aware of civil liberties issues, the DoJ encouraged 'people doing work for covered foreign powers or entities to comply with the law, not to indict them for failure to do so'.[89] The EC does not explain why the FBI believed that individuals associated with the Trump presidential campaign had been engaged by a foreign government to work on its behalf. As we shall see, Flynn (who became Trump's short-lived national security adviser) had been hired by the Turkish government, and a separate counterintelligence case was opened against him on 9 August. However, this was not mentioned in this EC. Instead, it quoted verbatim from the email received on 29 July from the U.S. embassy in London about the information provided two days earlier by Downer, in which he reported on his conversation in the London bar with Papadopoulos. Downer 'suggested the Trump team had received some kind of suggestion from Russia that it could assist this process with the anonymous release of information that would be damaging to Mrs Clinton (and President Obama)'. This was all rather nebulous, but Strzok jumped to the conclusion that Papadopoulos and possibly others had been engaged by Russia to act as foreign agents on its behalf. Downer himself was cautious, warning in his report that it was 'unclear whether he or the Russians were referring to material acquired publicly of [sic] through other means'. It was also 'unclear' how the Trump campaign had reacted to the Russian offer, and irrespective of the Trump team's reaction the Russians would probably do whatever they planned to do with the information 'with or without Mr Trump's cooperation'.

In his conclusion Strzok does not mention Papadopoulos and instead writes that Crossfire Hurricane was opened to examine whether 'individual(s) associated with the Trump campaign are witting of and/or coordinating activities with the Government of Russia'. This was all very vague and based on a prejudice that Russia may have been up to something and that the Trump campaign may have been complicit. As a former FBI assistant director of intelligence notes, 'No reasonable FBI counterintelligence squad supervisor in the field would have approved and opened that Strzok EC. They know the rules too well'. He goes on to argue:

> Instead, the nation was left with an investigation of a presidential campaign that had no legitimate predication; that spawned a Foreign Intelligence Surveillance Act intercept of a US citizen that had no legitimate predication; that resulted in a confrontation with a new administration's national security adviser that had no legitimate predication; and, finally, that led to an expansive special counsel investigation that had no legitimate predication. No pattern-recognition software needed here.[90]

The fundamental question remains: Why did the FBI open the investigation? Was this an investigation in search of a crime? We now know that the Papadopoulos information from Downer was crucial, and according to Strzok 'provided the sole basis. Period'. He insists that when the investigation was opened Steele 'was completely unknown to me'.[91] There is no formal mention in the EC of the Steele dossier, but we know that the first memo was already available to the FBI (although not necessarily to the investigators dealing with the case). The security services were inclined to believe that the Trump campaign would be susceptible to Russian influence, and that was because of the revival of cold war contestation.

NOTES

1. Walt, *Hell of Good Intentions*, pp. 50, 197.
2. 'CIA Admits To Spying On Senate Staffers', *Guardian*, 31 July 2014, https://www.theguardian.com/world/2014/jul/31/cia-admits-spying-senate-staffers.
3. Mccarthy, *Ball of Collusion*, p. 73.
4. Larry C. Johnson, 'Growing Indicators of Brennan's CIA Trump Task Force', *Sic Semper Tyrannis*, 2 November 2019, https://turcopolier.typepad.com/sic_semper_tyrannis/2019/11/growing-indicators-of-brennans-cia-trump-task-force-by-larry-c-johnson.html.
5. Luke Harding, Stephanie Kirchgaessner and Nick Hopkins, 'British Spies Were First To Spot Trump Team's Links With Russia', *Guardian*, 13 April 2017, https://www.theguardian.com/uk-news/2017/apr/13/british-spies-first-to-spot-trump-team-links-russia.
6. Boyd-Barrett, *Russiagate and Propaganda*, p. 10.
7. Jane Mayer, 'Christopher Steele: The Man Behind the Steele Dossier', *New Yorker*, 12 March 2018, https://www.newyorker.com/magazine/2018/03/12/christopher-steele-the-man-behind-the-trump-dossier.
8. For an analysis of the british connection, See Tyler Durden, 'All Russiagate Roads Lead to London: Evidence Emerges of Mifsud's Links to UK Intelligence', *Defend Democracy Press*, 4 May 2018, http://www.defenddemocracy.press/all-russiagate-roads-lead-to-london-evidence-emerges-of-mifsuds-links-to-uk-intelligence/.
9. Senate Committee on Intelligence, *Report*, Vol. 3, pp. 12–13.
10. Andrew Mccarthy, 'New Disclosures Confirm: Trump Himself Was the Target of Obama Administration's Russia Probe', *National Review*, 1 August 2020, https://www.nationalreview.com/2020/08/new-disclosures-confirm-trump-was-the-target-of-obama-administrations-russia-probe/.
11. Senate Committee on Intelligence, *Report*, Vol. 3, p. 33.
12. Miller et al, 'Obama's Secret Struggle to Punish Russia', *Washington Post*, 23 June 2017; Matt Taibbi, 'The Intelligence Community Needs A House-Cleaning', 30 May 2019, https://taibbi.substack.com/p/the-intelligence-community-needs.
13. Mccarthy, *Ball of Collusion*, p. 99, And On Rogers, p. 146.
14. Mccarthy, *Ball of Collusion*, P. 98.
15. Douglas Jehl, 'The Struggle for Iraq: Weapons Search', *New York Times*, 29 October 2003.
16. Snowden, *Permanent Record*, p. 231; Walt, *The Hell of Good Intentions*, p. 196.
17. James R. Clapper with Trey Brown, *Facts and Fears: Hard Truths From A Life In Intelligence* (New York, Viking, 2018).
18. Unger, *The House of Trump*, p. 228.

19. Strzok, *Compromised*, p. 83. Clovis later denied making such a statement. George Papadopoulos, *Deep State Target: How I Got Caught in the Crosshairs of The Plot To Bring Down President Trump* (New York, Diversion Books, 2019), p. 35.

20. Papadopoulos, *Deep State Target*, pp. 9, 29–35 contests that view, noting that he has a degree in political science from Depaul University, an MA in security studies from University College London, consulting experience with The Hudson Institute, and campaign experience with republican candidate Ben Carson.

21. Papadopoulos, *Deep State Target*, p. 17.

22. Papadopoulos, *Deep State Target*, p. 27.

23. Papadopoulos, *Deep State Target*, p. 37.

24. Papadopoulos, *Deep State Target*, p. 39.

25. Stephan C. Roh and Thierry Pastor, *The Faking of Russia-Gate: The Papadopoulos Case* (Zurich, ILS Publishing, 2018).

26. Office of the director of national intelligence, letter from Richard Grennell To Senator Charles E, Grassley and Ron Jonson, DHS, 15 April 2020, https://www.grassley.senate.gov/sites/default/files/2020-04-15%20odni%20to%20ceg%20rhj%20%28fisa%20footnote%20declassification%29.pdf, Note 205 (Henceforth Cited As Horowitz, *Review*, Notes), pp. 164 And 484.

27. Elizabeth Lee Vos, 'All Russiagate Roads Lead to London as Evidence Emerges of Joseph Mifsud's Links to UK Intelligence', *Disobedient Media*, 4 April 2018, http://www.defenddemocracy.press/all-russiagate-roads-lead-to-london-evidence-emerges-of-mifsuds-links-to-uk-intelligence/.

28. Sean O'Neill, 'University of Stirling Link to Hillary Clinton "Dirt"', *The Times*, 4 November 2017, https://www.thetimes.co.uk/edition/scotland/university-of-stirling-link-to-hillary-clinton-dirt-dxqgdt873.

29. Papadopoulos, *Deep State Target*, p. 41.

30. Papadopoulos, *Deep State Target*, p. 42.

31. Papadopoulos, *Deep State Target*, p. 49. By Contrast, Isikoff and Corn, *Russian Roulette*, p. 107, state that sessions shot down the idea based on his later testimony as attorney general to the house judiciary committee On 14 November 2017 when he stated that he 'pushed back' against the idea of 'reaching out' to Russia.

32. Papadopoulos, *Deep State Target*, p. 52.

33. Mueller report and personal discussion with Timofeev, October 2018.

34. I have long known timofeev and have discussed the case with him. He, like Kislyak, is bemused and repelled by being drawn into the complex web of deceit.

35. Isikoff and Corn, *Russian Roulette*, p. 107; Papadopoulos, *Deep State Target*, p. 60.

36. In any case, On 18 April 2016 The Valdai Club was meeting in Rome to discuss EU-Russian relations, so it is not clear what event mifsud may have attended.

37. This Is often reported, but there is no definitive source (mueller does not shed light on the matter). See, For Example, Barnini Chakraborty, 'Devin Nunes: FBI has

"Something To Hide" On Joseph Mifsud, A Key Player in Russia Probe', *Fox News*, 21 May 2019, https://www.foxnews.com/politics/devin-nunes-fbi-has-something-to-hide-on-joseph-mifsud-russia-probe.

38. Weissmann, *Where Law Ends*, P. 88.

39. George Papadopoulos, 'Say Sorry to Trump or Risk Special Relationship', *The Times*, 4 May 2016, https://www.thetimes.co.uk/article/say-sorry-to-trump-or-risk-special-relationship-cameron-told-h6ng0r7xj. Papadopoulos, *Deep State Target*, pp. 64–66 argues that he was deliberately misquoted.

40. Papadopoulos, *Deep State Target*, p. 73.

41. Papadopoulos, *Deep State Target*, p. 76.

42. Sharon Lafraniere, Mark Mazzetti and Matt Apuzzo, 'How the Russia Inquiry Began: A Campaign Aide, Drinks and Talk of Political Dirt', *New York Times*, 30 December 2017, https://www.nytimes.com/2017/12/30/us/politics/how-fbi-russia-investigation-began-george-papadopoulos.html.

43. Mccarthy, *Ball of Collusion*, p. 165.

44. Mccarthy, 'Steele's Shoddy Dossier'.

45. Papadopoulos, *Deep State Target*, p. 94.

46. Simpson and Fritsch, *Crime in Progress*, p. 82.

47. Strzok, *Compromised*, p. 150.

48. Glenn Greenwald, 'The FBI Informant Who Monitored the Trump Campaign', *The Intercept*, 19 May 2018, https://theintercept.com/2018/05/19/the-fbi-informant-who-monitored-the-trump-campaign-stefan-halper-oversaw-a-cia-spying-operation-in-the-1980-presidential-election/.

49. David Runciman provides a first-hand account of the conference, The Subject of Various Conspiracy Theories: 'How to Get Screwed', *London Review Of Books*, 6 June 2019, pp. 15–17. Runciman was not impressed by page's abilities: 'Frankly, He Didn't Seem Capable of Advising Anyone of the Best Way Out of a Paper Bag', p. 15.

50. For a discussion of his role and larger significance, See Scott Horton, 'Matt Taibbi on the Origins of the Russiagate Hoax', Antiwar.Com, 20 August 2020, https://original.antiwar.com/scott/2020/08/19/matt-taibbi-on-the-origins-of-the-russiagate-hoax/.

51. Steven P. Schrage, Who Knew Halper and Others Who Comprise What He Calls the 'Cambridge Four' Who Pushed the Russiagate Narrative, 'The Spies Who Hijacked America', 9 August 2020, https://taibbi.substack.com/p/the-spies-who-hijacked-america.

52. Svetlana Lokhova, *The Spider: Stefan A. Halper And The Dark Web of a Coup* (Nashville, TN, Post Hill Press, 2020).

53. Stefan Halper, 'Intelligence Experts Accuse Cambridge Forum of Russian Links', *Financial Times*, 16 December 2016.

54. Papadopoulos, *Deep State Target*, p. 101.

55. Brooke Singman, 'US Attorney John Durham Has Been Reviewing Origins of Russia Probe "For Weeks": Source', Foxnews.Com, 14 May 2019, https://www.foxnews.com/politics/us-attorney-john-durham-has-been-reviewing-origins-of-russia-probe-for-weeks-source.

56. Papadopoulos, *Deep State Target*, p. 106.
57. George Papadopoulos, 'Sanctions Have Done Little More Than To Turn Russia Towards China', Interfax, 30 September 2016, http://www.interfax.com/interview.asp?id=704556.
58. Papadopoulos, *Deep State Target*, p. 112.
59. Papadopoulos, *Deep State Target*, pp. 112–14.
60. Papadopoulos, *Deep State Target*, p. 133.
61. Strzok, *Compromised*, p. 218.
62. Strzok, *Compromised*, p. Xv.
63. Papadopoulos, *Deep State Target*, p. 135.
64. Mueller, *Report*, Vol. 1, p. 193.
65. The FBI's interview notes (302s) were released in August 2020. Margot Cleveland, 'Mifsud Notes Provide More Proof Crossfire Hurricane Was An Excuse To Spy On Trump', *The Federalist*, 4 September 2020, https://thefederalist.com/2020/09/04/mifsud-notes-provide-more-proof-crossfire-hurricane-was-an-excuse-to-spy-on-trump/.
66. Papadopoulos, *Deep State Target*, pp. 201–2 For his confessional speech, and for his regret, p. 206.
67. For A Good Analysis, See Mccarthy, *Ball of Collusion*, pp. 125–40.
68. For The Video, See https://twitter.com/foxnews/status/1042199672759218177?lang=en.
69. Papadopoulos, *Deep State Target*, p. 176.
70. Papadopoulos, *Deep State Target*, p. 177.
71. Papadopoulos, *Deep State Target*, p. 178.
72. Papadopoulos, *Deep State Target*, p. 180.
73. Papadopoulos, *Deep State Target*, p. 190.
74. Lafraniere et al., 'How The Russia Inquiry Began'.
75. HPSCI, 'Interview of Andrew Mccabe', 19 December 2017, p. 13, https://intelligence.house.gov/uploadedfiles/am33.pdf.
76. Aaron Maté, 'The Mueller Investigation is Sending People to Jail – But Not For Collusion', *The Nation*, 13 September 2018, https://www.thenation.com/article/the-mueller-investigation-is-sending-people-to-jail-but-not-for-collusion/.
77. Ivan Timofeev, 'In Search of Russian Meddling', *RIAC*, 15 August 2017, http://russiancouncil.ru/en/news/in-search-of-russian-meddling/ And Personal Discussions.
78. Papadopoulos, *Deep State Target*, p. 33.
79. Papadopoulos, *Deep State Target*, pp. 209–10.
80. Papadopoulos, *Deep State Target*, p. 218.
81. This is the version presented to me by a former senior CIA officer in October 2019.
82. Lafraniere et al., 'How The Russia Inquiry Began'.
83. Ray Mcgovern, 'Justice Dept Likely To Slow-Walk Declassification', *Consortium News*, 18 September 2018, http://raymcgovern.com/2018/09/18/justice-dept-likely-to-slow-walk-declassification/.

84. This is confirmed by the investigation conducted by John Durham, Who describes the FBI's Trump-Russia investigation as a criminal one from the start, although this is not technically accurate. For details and links to relevant documents, See Mccarthy, 'New Disclosures Confirm'.

85. For Strzok's Account, See *Compromised*, pp. 106–24.

86. Denied By Strzok, *Compromised*, p. 113.

87. Federal Bureau of Investigation Electronic Communication, Crossfire Hurricane, 31 July 2016, https://www.judicialwatch.org/documents/jw-v-doj-reply-02743/.

88. Strzok, *Compromised*, p. 107.

89. Andrew C. Mccarthy, 'Connecting Dots in Clinesmith's Russiagate Guilty Plea', *National Review*, 14 August 2020, https://www.nationalreview.com/corner/connecting-the-dots-in-clinesmiths-russiagate-guilty-plea/.

90. Kevin R. Brock, 'New FBI Document Confirms The Trump Campaign Was Investigated Without Justification', *The Hill*, 27 May 2020, https://thehill.com/opinion/white-house/499586-new-fbi-document-confirms-the-trump-campaign-was-investigated-without.

91. Strzok, *Compromised*, pp. 110, 143.

Chapter 8

The Steele Dossier

Hillary Clinton's defeat at the hands of someone with no political or military experience aggravated an already deeply polarised American public. Some sort of external factor was sought to explain Trump's election, an endeavour aggravated because of Trump's obdurate insistence, at the rhetorical level at least, that it made sense to have good relations with Russia. Clinton herself labelled purported Russian actions as 'unprecedented'.[1] She argues, 'We can't understand what happened in 2016 without confronting the audacious information warfare waged from the Kremlin'. She also noted Comey's intervention, the hostile media and the 'deep currents of anger and resentment flowing through our culture'.[2] She quotes, evidently with approbation, that Trump's presidency 'was not legitimate because of the mounting evidence of Russian interference in the election'.[3] At the heart of this was the Steele dossier.

THE STEELE DOSSIER

The dossier prepared by the former British intelligence agent Christopher Steele is one of the foundation stones of the Russian collusion narrative.[4] Steele joined MI6 in 1986 and was posted to Moscow in 1990 before being expelled in 1993. He returned to London, and following various postings headed the Russia desk from 2006. In that capacity, he was former FSB agent Alexander Litvinenko's handler in London and was then in charge of the MI6 investigation into his poisoning in November of that year. Steele retired in 2009, apparently believing that further promotion within the service would be blocked.[5] Then, with another former MI6 officer Chris Burrows, he established the investigative research firm Orbis Business Intelligence. Following

Russia's successful bid to host the 2018 FIFA World Cup (and England's miserable failure, winning only one other country's support), the British, who had hitherto supported the head of FIFA, Sepp Blatter, now demanded his head.[6] Steele took the lead in investigating alleged FIFA corruption. The United States was also miffed at having lost out to Qatar in its bid to host the 2022 event. It was during joint work on this sports corruption scandal that Steele forged close links with the FBI.[7] In February 2016, when he was in contact with the deputy attorney general (the No. 4 man at the DoJ), Bruce Ohr, Steele emailed a private client a Russian Leadership Report making the provocative claim that 'Russian leader Vladimir Putin might be losing his grip on power'. This flew in the face of the evidence and drew on the same sort of dubious sources that he would use later.[8]

The private intelligence dossier compiled by Steele consists of seventeen separate memos comprising thirty-five pages in total, with the first dated 20 June and the last published on 13 December 2016. Technically, it is not a dossier at all, but a compendium of individual intelligence memos. Claimed sources included people inside Russia, as well as 'field operatives' outside the country.[9] The version published online by *BuzzFeed* on 10 January 2017 is mostly in chronological order and takes the form of photocopied pages, including sections highlighted in yellow, reflecting the fact that this was a personal copy.[10] Various agencies and people had some but not all copies, and therefore 'the dissemination of Steele's information was a confusing mess'.[11] The tone is that of an official intelligence report, with surnames in capital letters, and each memo containing a summary followed by detail. The informants are given as letters of the alphabet, and often described as a 'source close to the Kremlin', in other words, unidentified Russian originators. As the journalist Luke Harding, who has written a book on the subject, admits, 'normally an intelligence officer would debrief sources directly, but since Steele could no longer visit Russia, this had to be done by others, or in third countries'.[12] Or, we might add, not at all.

The Steele material is inflammatory and propounds 'a conspiracy of vast proportions'.[13] The first memo begins with the startling assertion that the 'Russian regime has been cultivating, supporting and assisting Trump for at least five years', and that Trump accepted 'a regular flow of intelligence from the Kremlin'. The aim 'endorsed by Putin, has been to encourage splits and divisions in western alliance'. In words that have been repeated *ad nauseam*, the goal was 'to sow discord and disunity both within the US itself, but more especially within the Transatlantic alliance which was viewed as inimical to Russian interests'. Trump was allegedly offered 'various sweetener real estate deals', although he declined them, but 'his inner circle have accepted a regular flow of intelligence from the Kremlin, including on his Democratic and other political rivals'. The FSB had allegedly 'compromised Trump sufficiently to be able to blackmail him', including through 'perverted sexual acts'. These were detailed as 'hiring the presidential suite of the Ritz-Carlton Hotel, where he knew President and Mrs Obama (whom he hated) had stayed on one of their official visits to Moscow, and defiling the bed where they had slept by employing a number of prostitutes to perform a "golden showers" (urination) show in front of him'. The Russian intelligence services had also allegedly collated a dossier of compromising material on Clinton, controlled personally by the Kremlin spokesman Dmitry Peskov.[14]

The memos continue in this vein. The second report warned that 'Russia has an extensive programme of state-sponsored offensive cyber operations', with the FSB often using 'coercion and blackmail to recruit most capable cyber operatives in Russia'.[15] The third report was the most explicit in alleging collusion, noting 'Further evidence of extensive conspiracy between Trump's campaign team and Kremlin, sanctioned at highest levels and involving Russian diplomatic staff based in the US'. The 'well-developed conspiracy of co-operation' was allegedly managed on the Trump side by the Republican candidate's campaign manager Paul Manafort, using foreign policy adviser Carter Page and others as intermediaries'. A Trump associate allegedly admitted that the 'Kremlin [was] behind recent appearance of DNC e-mails on WikiLeaks, as means of maintaining plausible deniability'. The collaboration had been conducted 'with the full knowledge and support of Trump and senior members of his campaign team'. In return, Trump allegedly 'agreed to sideline Russian intervention in Ukraine as a campaign issue', as well as diverting attention away from 'Trump's business dealings in China'. The issue was repeated several times, although the alleged Chinese connection was never pursued by the media or investigators.[16]

Other allegations will be examined later, but a few points already stand out. First, the text is at the root of everything that followed, and its language was used to press the master-charges of collusion and hacking. Second, there is no definite evidence for the charges, which cite 'high-ranking' Russian officials as the source, with no opportunity for cross-checking. Nigel West (the pen name of former MP Rupert Allason), an espionage expert, already in January 2017 noted that 'there is . . . a strong possibility that all Steele's material has been fabricated'. He identified some major errors. Eleven people are cited in the dossier as unnamed sources, with seven assigned an alphabetic code, but one source ('E') was treated as an expert in three entirely different fields, beginning as a middle manager at the Ritz-Carlton in Moscow, then described as an expert on cyber warfare, and later as an expert on money laundering. In addition, a non-existent Russian consulate in Miami was mentioned.[17] Third, despite allegedly having sources in the Kremlin, it was only after WikiLeaks published the DNC materials that Steele first mentioned them. In other words, in this case and others information was drawn from press reports and social media chatter rather than from highly placed sources, Fourth, the credulity with which the material was received by leading officials, politicians and journalists is disturbing. The unverified material was eagerly used to reinforce prejudices and to serve political purposes, a deception whose shamelessness in an earlier age would have discredited the perpetrators.[18] Fifth, the provenance of the reports and the uses to which they were put is crucial. In essence, beginning life as opposition analysis on various potential presidential candidates, from June 2016 the research was commissioned by Fusion GPS and was paid for by the Clinton campaign (which must by any standard cast doubt on its impartiality), especially when it was used by the FBI in its Trump investigations.

The written account by deputy assistant secretary of state Kathleen Kavalec of her meeting with Steele on 11 October 2016 describes how he admitted that his research was political and faced an election-day deadline. Her account reveals an attempt to 'frame' the future president by tarring him with the brush of collusion with Russia.[19] Kavalec was sceptical from the start, noting that there is no Russian consulate in Miami. Even less credibly, Steele told Kavalec that two of his insider Kremlin sources were Vladislav Surkov and Vyacheslav Trubnikov. Surkov was known as the Kremlin's 'grey cardinal' and had been deputy head of the presidential administration responsible for domestic politics up to December 2011, but mistakenly staked on a second term for Medvedev and by 2016 had been relegated to an advisory position on the Donbass and other regional conflicts. Trubnikov was SVR director from 1996 to 2000 and thereafter held several senior diplomatic posts. It is unlikely that either would have access to the Kremlin's secrets, and if they did, they would not have told Steele's informants. This is where we enter the world of double-bluff: were they feeding information 'to have the West believe what the Kremlin wants the West to believe'?[20] Even more cunningly, perhaps they were feeding garbled nonsense to Steele to provoke a counterintelligence investigation that would incapacitate the Trump presidency and set the Democrats on a wild goose chase. If the latter, the operation was a brilliant success.

Steele was fired as a paid FBI informant when it was revealed that he had been double-dipping with the Democrats and leaking confidential anti-Trump information to the media. Steele nevertheless prepared a final memorandum dated 13 December which made the extraordinary claim that Trump's lawyer Michael Cohen (accompanied by three unnamed colleagues) held a secret meeting in Prague in August (or September) 2016 with Kremlin operatives. They allegedly met with Oleg Solodukhin, an associate of the Kremlin's then chief of staff, Sergei Ivanov, to discuss how deniable cash payments were to be made to hackers working in Europe under the Kremlin's direction against the Clinton campaign and to pay for covering up the campaign and suppressing information about Moscow's secret connections with the Trump team. In Prague, Cohen agreed to various plans to protect the operation and discussed what was to be done if Clinton won the election. Solodukhin apparently admitted that payments to the hackers had been made by both the Trump team and the Kremlin. Cohen contemptuously dismisses the account but notes how it elevated him from relative obscurity into an international object of vilification 'because of the horseshit report of some washed-up former MI-6 intelligence operative in England who I knew for a fact didn't have his facts straight'.[21] Cohen also notes that if his denial was accepted, 'then the entire logic of the Russia-Trump conspiracy theory fell apart. The Russia connection had to be true because it had to be true, circular thinking that in its way provided the perfect counter-point to the idol worship of Trump'.[22]

FORGING THE DOSSIER

Although the Steele dossier played a central part in the Russiagate narrative, its assertions have never been independently verified and some of its points have been repudiated. It has undated and misdated reports and other mistakes. For example, it spells Alfa Bank (a major Russian financial institution) as Alpha Bank, variously ascribes the pee tape to Source D and then Source E, states that Trump made a 'recent trip' to Moscow when he made no such trip. It talked of the exchange of anti-Clinton intelligence and money at the Russian consulate in Miami, although (as Kavalec noted) no such consulate exists. The material is not predictive (as it would be if the sources were genuine) and instead is reactive, incorporating events as they unfolded (such as the WikiLeaks emails and Carter Page's visit to Moscow) into the designated narrative of Trump–Russia collusion. The style is rambling and imprecise, in the manner of someone trying to impersonate someone writing a professional intelligence document. When Steele was sued for libel in a British court and answered questions under oath, he admitted that his memos contained 'unverified' items of 'raw intelligence' that he had reported, because they 'warranted further investigation', and not because they were true.[23] Steele was concerned that there may have been a national security threat, not that there was one.[24]

The genealogy of the dossier is as convoluted as its contents. In September 2015, the *Washington Free Beacon Foundation*, a conservative website funded by the hedge-fund billionaire Paul Singer, a 'never Trump' Republican, hired Fusion GPS, an analytics firm headed by Glenn Simpson, to investigate Trump.[25] The aim was to support the candidacy of Marco Rubio and to stop the outsider from winning the Republican nomination. When this failed, the investigation was taken up by others. The HPSCI chaired by Nunes later took the lead in investigating the origins of the dossier. Their landmark report of February 2018 revealed that in April 2016, the law firm Perkins Coie hired Fusion GPS on behalf of the Clinton campaign and the DNC to examine alleged collusion between Trump and Russia. Fusion GPS in turn contracted Steele's firm Orbis to undertake the work. The DNC paid more than $1 million for the dossier.[26] The commission was managed by Marc Elias, a Democrat lawyer working for both the DNC and the Clinton campaign, with the funds going through his law firm, Perkins Coie. The payments to Fusion GPS were stated as legal fees to the law firm, and it is alleged that only later did senior officials in the Clinton campaign became aware of the arrangement.[27] However, it could be that 'the Clinton machine knew that what is was doing was controversial. That's why it did backflips to disguise the operation from Congress and the public, and in its Federal Election Commission (FEC) reports'.[28] As for Simpson, he appeared to take pride in selling himself and the work of his company as 'journalism for rent', an obvious oxymoron since the very act of selling information corrupts the process.[29] This did not prevent the dossier becoming a 'media obsession' and allowed Fusion GPS go on to tap into the lucrative funds available for the shadowy 'Integrity Initiative', a cold war-style self-defined counter-disinformation exercise. As Barry Meier aptly argues, 'Today, private spying has boomed into a renegade, billion-dollar industry, one that is increasingly invading our privacy, profiting from deception and manipulating the news'.[30]

Steele was hired by Fusion GPS in May 2016, and from the first the FBI received and reviewed his reports.[31] In June 2016, Steele contacted Michael Gaeta, with whom he had worked on the FIFA corruption case and who was now an assistant legal attaché at the U.S. embassy in Rome. Victoria Nuland, the State Department's head of European and Eurasian Affairs, approved the FBI's request to meet Steele.[32] A later declassified State Department 126-page document revealed that Steele had in fact been in contact with Nuland since 2014, through the auspices of the State Department official Jonathan Winer. He convinced her of the authenticity of Steele's material on Russia, although the reports delivered between May and November 2014 are the same disorganised tissue of fact and invention as his later dossier. For example, on 21 August, Steele reported that an increasingly isolated Putin, influenced by the defeatist mood in the Kremlin and advisors unhappy with his Ukraine policy, the imposition of Western sanctions and the subsequent turn to China, was ready to capitulate under U.S. and NATO pressure. Soon after Steele told Nuland that within a year, the Russian regime could be 'on its knees'. The reports had not been requested by the State Department but were sent by Steele 'unilaterally', and to her credit, Nuland asked Winer about Steele's sources. In stark contrast, the material from Winer, an expert on the Middle East and North Africa, was substantive, well-organised and analytical.[33]

On 5 July, FBI agent Gaeta met with Steele in his London offices.[34] There Gaeta read the first of the memos that would become the dossier, and shocked by what he read he is reported to have told Steele 'I have to report this to headquarters'.[35] In his HPSCI testimony, FBI deputy director McCabe confirms that Gaeta received the material, but argues that he could find no one at the FBI interested in pursuing the matter until the file arrived at FBI headquarters in September.[36] However, the 2019 Horowitz report suggests that the delay was caused by the sensitive nature of the material in an election year, with the FBI agents already aware of Steele's connection (via Simpson and Perkins Coie) to the Clinton campaign. This is why advice was sought on 13 July from a senior FBI agent in New York, who was already investigating Page (the case was later transferred to the Washington office).[37] Bruce Ohr also passed on information received from Steele and Fusion GPS to senior FBI officials McCabe, senior FBI lawyer Lisa Page and Strzok in July.[38] However, although officials were aware of the Steele material, as we have seen, it was the information from Downer that formally triggered the Russia probe.

Steele became a paid FBI confidential human source (CHS) from at least February 2016, and possibly from 2013.[39] According to a footnote to the Horowitz review declassified in April 2020, he received $95,000 in payment for his services in 2016.[40] However, his contract was terminated in October because he revealed his relationship to a reporter from *Mother Jones*.[41] Strzok notes that Steele was 'closed' not because his information was bad, but because 'he was a control problem'.[42] Steele began supplying his reports to the FBI on 5 July, the same day that Comey dismissed the Clinton email server case.[43] Steele repeatedly urged the press to publish his incendiary information, but most outlets were cautious. Michael Isikoff on 23 September was the first to publicise the work after meeting with Steele.[44] He now argues that Steele's sensational Russia collusion charges lack evidence and are 'likely false'. Nevertheless, Steele's report was used by the FBI to justify four FISA warrants on Page. *Mother Jones* magazine's David Corn wrote the second major story on 31 October.[45] Corn also met with Steele, who admitted that he was desperate to stop the Trump campaign and to intensify the FBI investigation.[46] Steele was dismissed the following day, with the FBI concluding that 'Steele seemed more interested in getting the story out rather than quietly working with them on the investigation'.[47]

Nine separate U.S. media organisations refused to publish any of the dossier's claims in the latter part of 2016, despite determined efforts by Fusion GPS to make it public. In his book on the subject, Glenn Simpson tells us how keen he was to have Steele's material in the public domain, even though the FBI was sceptical about some of the assertions. The final memo took a circuitous route, including via the Republican Senator John McCain, the chair of the Senate Armed Services Committee, before getting to the FBI.[48] It is not known whether McCain provided a copy to CIA director Brennan, but the CIA head attached a two-page summary when he delivered the ICA on Russian collusion to outgoing president Obama on 5 January 2017. David Kramer, a long-time McCain associate, in March 2019 admitted that he contacted at least fourteen journalists about the Steele dossier. Kramer travelled to London and met with Steele on 28 November, when they discussed all the memos, but was only given a physical copy of the dossier (then consisting of sixteen memos) by Simpson on 29 November on his return to Washington.[49] In addition to press briefings, he gave a copy to the then-senior director for Russian affairs at the NSC, Celeste Wallander and in early December briefed her and Nuland. On 29 December, he allowed a *Buzzfeed* reporter, Ken Bensinger, to photograph the dossier at the McCain Institute, hence the published version had his highlights marked in yellow.

This was the version published on 10 January 2017, after it was mentioned by the FBI and journalists started asking about Trump's ties to Russia. McCain on 18 October 2017 famously denied providing a copy of the dossier to *BuzzFeed*, insisting that he had given it only to the director of the FBI, but we now know that it was provided by his associate.[50] An email from FBI officer Peter Strzok to FBI attorney Lisa Page dated 10 January confirms that the FBI knew that the version published by *BuzzFeed* was 'identical' to the version given to the FBI by McCain.[51]

THE STEELE STORM

James Baker, the FBI's general counsel between 2014 and 2017, met with Sussmann, the lawyer from Perkins Coie who handled the DNC account, some weeks before the 2016 election. The meeting discussed Russian interference, including hacking and supposed ties to Trump. As a report of the meeting notes, it suggests 'FBI investigatory malpractice'. The mere fact that the FBI's general counsel was meeting with a top lawyer working for the Clinton campaign shortly before the election 'is proof that the bureau strayed beyond obvious guardrails':

> It's alarming enough that the FBI felt free to open a counterintelligence investigation into an active presidential campaign. That it also felt free to gather information for that probe from the opposing campaign is mind-boggling. Team Clinton had the most powerful position on earth to gain from Mr. Trump's downfall. No conflict there, right?[52]

The HPSCI memo of February 2018 revealed that 'senior DoJ and FBI officials' by this time knew that the Clinton campaign was behind the Steele

Dossier, and the Baker-Sussmann meeting 'raises the likelihood that those "senior officials" extended into Mr. Comey's inner circle and that quite a few people understood the bureau was moving against a campaign based on the rival campaign's opposition research'.

FBI documents released in August 2018 confirm that the FBI stopped formal contact with Steele a week before the election. In December 2018, the House Oversight Committee released the 235-page transcript of Comey's questioning before the House Judiciary Committee and Oversight Committee on 11 August 2018. Comey's memory appeared to be failing, since his responses contained 166 'don't knows', 71 'I don't remember', and eight 'I don't recall'. Nevertheless, Comey admitted that the FBI did not verify the dossier, even though it was used to spy on a senior politician in the Trump camp (Page). Work on checking the dossier, Comey admitted, was still not complete by the time he left office in May 2017. He once again asserted that it was not the dossier but the Papadopoulos case that kick-started the investigation.[53] This does not let the FBI off the hook, since the Papadopoulos affair is hardly more substantive than the Steele dossier.

This is typical of the way in which the Russiagate allegations shift shape and mutate into unrelated charges to reinforce the central allegation. In the Mueller investigation, secondary issues gain prominence in proportion to the weakness of the central charge. This was the case with the accusations against Cohen, which replaced Russian collusion for a time as the reason to investigate Trump. We will deal with his prosecution later, but here note that he continued to deny ever having visited Prague, something that was once again asserted by his lawyer, Lanny Davis, in August 2018. Davis insisted that all the charges in the dossier were false, and Cohen certainly did not travel to Prague to discuss 'cash payments' to hackers of the Clinton campaign. Cohen repeatedly offered his passport as proof that he did not travel to the city. This did not stop at least 'two sources' claiming that Mueller had evidence that Cohen travelled through Germany to the Czech Republic.[54] A further sub-plot about the genesis of the Steele dossier involves Cody Shearer, who provided opposition research for the Clintons and apparently passed on information about the 'golden showers' incident to Winer.[55] Winer in turn passed the story on to Steele.[56]

The DoJ's inspector general Michael Horowitz and several Congressional committees investigated whether the FBI properly handled the Trump–Russia collusion allegations. In particular, the FBI failed to complete due diligence procedures to ensure that Steele's alleged expertise could be trusted. The FBI was still verifying the Steele dossier when it was submitted as evidence for the FISA warrant. Comey himself testified in June 2017 that the dossier was considered 'unverified and salacious'.[57] Notwithstanding these doubts, the dossier was deployed to investigate the campaign of the nominated

Republican candidate, even though the document was developed as opposition research paid for by the Democrats.

In his first report on the issue in June 2018, Horowitz exposed a pattern of anti-Trump bias in communications between FBI officials as they pursued the Russia enquiry.[58] The report focused on the handling of the FBI's investigation (called Midyear Exam) into Clinton's emails, but noted that the same FBI team which investigated the Clinton emails deployed at least one informant among Trump advisors, and obtained FISA wiretap warrants on Carter Page, issued national security letters to obtain records, and unmasked the identities of surveilled campaign officials. The report revealed that 'FBI officials displayed not merely an appearance of bias against Donald Trump, but animus bordering on hatred'.[59] This stricture has been applied to the team leading the FBI investigation of Trump. Strzok's virulent anti-trump texts to Lisa Page (with whom he was having a relationship) later became evidence of anti-Trump collusion.[60] Strzok investigated Clinton's use of a private email server and then took the lead in the Trump–Russia probe.[61]

Horowitz revealed the inflammatory text messages on FBI-issued devices between Strzok and Page.[62] On 3 March 2016, Page noted that 'God Trump is a loathsome human', to which Strzok responded 'God Hillary should win'. On the opening of Crossfire Hurricane, Strzok on 31 July texted Page to say 'And damn this feels momentous. Because this matters', and clearly to him it mattered more than the Midyear investigation.[63] Discussing Trump's presidential bid on 8 August, Strzok infamously stated 'we'll stop it', although later argued that the reference was to the American people at large. A week later on 15 August, Strzok texted Page to say: 'I want to believe the path you threw out for consideration in [McCabe's] office, that there's no way he [Trump] gets elected, but I'm afraid that we can't take that risk. It's like an insurance policy in the unlikely event you die before you're 40'.[64] Strzok argues that this was 'a risk assessment like any other', evaluating the potential harm of a hypothetical event.[65] Page a few weeks earlier had made no secret of her prejudices: 'I do always hate the Russians'.[66] She stressed 'there is very little I find redeeming' about Russia, although she generously conceded a 'couple of good writers and artists I guess'. Strzok was less indulgent: 'F*cking, conniving cheating savages'.[67] Russiagate combined their two pet hates, Trump and Russia.[68]

Horowitz criticised Strzok for his slow reaction to the discovery in September 2016 of thousands of Clinton's emails on Weiner's laptop. Strzok prioritised the Trump–Russia investigation over the email investigation.[69] The day after Mueller was appointed, on 18 May 2017, Strzok texted Page about whether he should join the special counsel team, arguing that 'For me, and this case, I personally have a sense of unfinished business. I unleashed it with MYE [Midyear]. Now I need to fix and finish it'. Later in the same exchange he talked about working on an 'investigation leading to impeachment'. Strzok denied that this meant he contributed to Clinton's defeat by investigating her emails and would now fix it by destroying Trump.[70] Horowitz argued that Strzok's messages 'potentially indicated or created the appearance that investigative decisions were impacted [affected] by bias or improper considerations'.[71] The culture of leaking by DoJ and FBI officials about on-going investigations was criticised. When his email exchanges with Page were revealed, Mueller promptly removed Strzok from the Russiagate enquiry in late July 2017.

A declassified footnote to the Horowitz review reveals that Steele stressed that his 'source network did not involve sources from his time as a former government employee and was developed entirely in the period after he retired from governmental service'.[72] Other footnotes states that 'sensitive source reporting' from June 2017 indicated that a person affiliated with an unnamed Russian oligarch was aware of Steele's investigation possibly as early as July 2016.[73] This gave rise, as we shall see, to speculation that this conduit may have fed Kremlin disinformation to Steele. Ohr records, moreover, that in a meeting in December 2016 Simpson told him that Steele's primary source was not in Moscow but a former Russian intelligence officer living in the United States.[74] In other words, the information came not from the ground in Russia but a continent away in America. Horowitz's report reveals that when interviewed by the FBI, one of Steele's sources disavowed all the information in the dossier and claimed that it misrepresented several things he had said. Not surprisingly, with sources such as these, the dossier is as reliable as Steele's prediction in early 2016 that Putin was about to fall. Above all, if Steele (and by implication the CIA) really did have access to information from highly placed moles in the Kremlin, this would be an extraordinary coup, not to be lightly wasted on a 'salacious and unverified' document. To expose their existence in such an off-hand manner would run against the fundamental tradecraft of spying and would have precipitated a ferocious investigation in the Kremlin, but there was no hint of that.

On 12 July 2018, Strzok testified to the House Judiciary and Oversight committees that he was not biased against a president that he still described as 'horrible' and 'disgusting'.[75] Strzok, bizarrely, described the hearing as a win for Putin.[76] Strzok was dismissed from the FBI on 13 August 2018 because of his anti-Trump texts. The information passed on to the FBI from Steele and other sources adopted an undifferentiated view of Russia, in which every passing oligarch (in fact, every mentioned Russian) was 'close to Putin', and every shady character (and we have already met a few) was engaged in some nefarious business on behalf of the Kremlin. McCabe's extreme view of Russia – that 'the Russian government itself' was 'the ultimate Russian criminal organization'[77] – is rooted in a distinctively parochial American type of Russophobia. Fired by what they believed was the righteousness of their cause, namely to stop what they believed was a 'crime in progress' and the ascent to the presidency of the Kremlin-supported Trump, Russiagaters accepted threads of unsubstantiated allegations and disinformation, joining dots that were in no way connected, to ensnare the presidency and the country in 'a web of deception'.[78]

On 28 August 2018, Justice Department lawyer Bruce Ohr testified to a Congressional committee about his part in the FBI launching the Trump investigation. It had earlier been revealed that his wife, Nellie, worked for Fusion GPS, the research firm that sponsored the Clinton-funded Steele dossier. It was then discovered that Ohr, one of the most senior officials in the Justice Department, also had various interactions with the head of Fusion GPS, Simpson and Steele, and he passed information about these talks to the FBI. In other words, multiple sources were informing the FBI about the dossier. It had earlier been known that notes taken by Ohr of a meeting with Steele in September 2016 stated that the dossier's author 'was desperate that Donald Trump not get elected and was passionate about him not being president'. Now the 28 August meeting revealed that 'he verbally warned the FBI that its source had a credibility problem, alerting the bureau to Mr. Steele's leanings and motives'. He also told the FBI that Nellie was working for Fusion and the dossier project. This information was given to the FBI before the first FISA application for a warrant against Carter Page in October 2016. This was not mentioned in the FISA application, and they instead asserted that Steele was a 'reliable' source. Neither did the application mention that the spouse of a senior Justice Department official was working on the dossier, and thus benefitting financially from a document that the FBI was using in an investigation. The FBI thus failed to flag the potential conflict of interest and the provenance of Steele's dossier.[79] By then, at least five sources had informed the FBI about the political origins of Steele's work. Congressional investigations later tried 'to determine whether that omission was part of a larger, intentional campaign to mislead the FISA court and Congress in order to keep the Russia investigation going despite a lack of evidence supporting the collusion theory'.[80]

DEBUNKING STEELE

More questions should have been asked about how a former British spy who was banned from travelling to Russia was able to access highly placed sources in the Kremlin and Russian intelligence over unsecured email and telephone lines to gain information that well-resourced intelligence agencies were unable to do:

After all, a foreign citizen [Steele] produces a catalogue of unverifiable, scandalous accusations against a US presidential candidate, attributed to unnamed Russian officials. Paying for this 'opposition research' is the candidate of the party in power. Her confederates, including elected Democrats, conspire to use the FBI's possession of this document to get US media outlets to report allegations from sources who won't identify themselves, who offer no support for their claims, passed along by an operator whose political motives are manifest.[81]

As noted, at no point does Steele foretell events but instead casts them in a collusive light in hindsight, such as the publication of the DNC emails by WikiLeaks. 'Steele's project was not intelligence-gathering. It was the crafting of a campaign narrative about a traitorous Trump–Russia espionage conspiracy, into which new developments were melded as they occurred', and this is why Steele fed the information to the media at the same time as passing it to the FBI and DoJ.[82] Too many actors were ready to lend credence to unverified assertions because they reinforced existing beliefs or suited instrumental purposes.[83] The conspiracy theory about Trump as a Russian asset, or as someone so hopelessly comprised by some sort of *kompromat* held against him, was always implausible but it seized the imagination of a large part of the American elite and by mere dint of repetition was taken as fact. For the intelligence services and the media, this was 'an epic disaster'.[84]

It did not go unchallenged. In May 2017, Alfa Bank owners, Mikhail Fridman, Petr Aven and German Khan, filed a defamation lawsuit against *BuzzFeed* for publishing the Trump–Russia dossier that alleged financial ties and collusion between Putin, Trump, and the three bank owners. Alfa Bank was established by Fridman in the late Soviet years, and with his associate Aven, a former Russian minister for foreign economic relations, it became one of Russia's most successful financial institutions and its largest commercial bank with a presence in several Western countries. In October 2017 Aven, Fridman, and Khan also filed a libel suit against Fusion GPS and its founder Simpson, for circulating the dossier among journalists and allowing it to be published. Following a meeting between the Kremlin, Aven and Fridman in May 2018, the Kremlin released a statement asserting that they did not represent the interests of Putin or the Russian government. In April 2018, Aven, Fridman, and Khan filed a libel suit against Steele in the Superior Court of the District of Columbia, but the suit was dismissed in August 2018. In a sealed deposition of 2 August 2018 in response to the defamation suit, Steele admitted that the law firm Perkins Coie wanted to be in a position to contest the results of the election, on the grounds that Trump had conspired with Moscow. His American lawyers filed his answers in December in the libel lawsuit in Washington, and it was at that point that his comments became public. In a previous filing in a separate case in April–May

2017, Steele stated that his task was to find links between Trump associates and Moscow. In the new libel suit, Fusion GPS, typically, sought to depict the three bankers as corrupt Putin cronies. The three lost the libel suit in the United States on the grounds that the dossier served the public interest by examining possible Russian influence in the 2016 election.

In a parallel libel suit in London, the three insisted that they were not 'creatures of the Kremlin', and Steele's claim that in the 1990s they delivered 'large amounts of illicit cash' to Putin when he was deputy mayor of St Petersburg was demonstrably false.[85] On 8 July 2020, the High Court of England and Wales ruled that Steele had used 'hearsay, some of it opinion, and much of it based on unverifiable information from unidentified sources'.[86] The court ruled that Steele violated the 1998 Data Protection Act, by failing to check the accuracy of information in his dossier, and ordered Orbis Business Intelligence to pay damages to two Alfa Bank principals for making comments about them that were not only a fabrication but also unlawful.[87] The summing up by High Court judge Sir Mark Warby applies to much of the commentary on Russiagate: 'To treat hearsay reports as established fact . . . is an unsatisfactory approach'. He found that the dossier's allegations about the bank's executives were 'inaccurate or misleading', and reasonable steps to verify the claims had not been undertaken. He noted that Steele frequently offered 'very different versions' of key events, which were 'mutually inconsistent in a number of respects'.[88] The fines plus court costs threatened to bankrupt Orbis.

In the second defamation suit in London, Russian tech entrepreneur Alexei Gubarev, owner of XBT Holdings that provided computer servers, challenged Steele's assertion in the final memo that his Webzilla service provider was used by the Russian security services to hack the Clinton campaign.[89] Gubarev strongly denied the charge, and separately in Florida sued *BuzzFeed*.[90] In his July 2018 deposition in the *BuzzFeed* defamation case, Steele admitted that while writing the dossier, he relied upon a 'random' not fact-checked article posted to CNN's old iReports website, among other sources.[91] He also admitted being separately paid by the FBI for his research, and that he leaked information about his investigation to *Mother Jones* and had off-the-record meetings with the *New York Times*, the *Washington Post*, *Yahoo! News*, the *New Yorker* and CNN in September and October 2016, which led to the FBI terminating his contract.[92] In a written statement to the High Court in July 2020, Steele insisted that he had never wanted the dossier to be made public, and would have done 'whatever I could do to prevent *BuzzFeed* from publishing the document', previously arguing that his report had been commissioned to provide Clinton with a legal basis to challenge the 2016 election.[93] The *in camera* court proceedings in London, in which Gubarev sued Steele, from 20–24 July 2020 also revealed the far more prominent role played by David

Kramer, McCain's associate, than had previously been known. We saw earlier that it was Kramer who provided the dossier to *BuzzFeed*, but court records now revealed that he acted as a key conduit between journalists and Steele, offering to 'feed' stories about Trump associates, and in particular Flynn, to *Washington Post* columnist David Ignatius.[94] In late 2020, Gubarev lost the case, with the judge ruling that even if the material about him and his company in the dossier was defamatory, he had failed to prove financial damages as a result of the disclosure.[95]

In August 2020, DNI John Ratcliffe revealed a declassified footnote of the January 2017 ICA. It noted that Steele had only 'limited corroboration' and that he used 'identified and unidentified sub-sources' that offered 'highly politically sensitive information from the summer to the fall of 2016 on Russian influence efforts aimed at the presidential election'. As part of Trump's order to declassify documents related to the Trump–Russia investigation, on 8 October the FBI disclosed the ninety-four-page spreadsheet that it had used to try to corroborate Steele's explosive assertions and came to the same conclusion as the earlier ICA footnote: there was at best 'limited corroboration'.[96] This was confirmed by FBI supervisory analyst Brian Auten, who oversaw work on the spreadsheet. He admitted under oath to staff investigators of the Senate Judiciary Committee in October 2020 (declassified months later) that 'the actual allegations and actions described in those reports could not be corroborated'. Auten and the Crossfire Hurricane team knew that the dossier was junk yet failed to inform the FISA court and used the material in all four warrant applications to spy on Carter Page. Former acting FBI head McCabe, who approved and signed the final application, testified that without the dossier, the warrants would not have been issued.[97]

The Senate Judiciary Committee continued its release of Russiagate materials. On 17 July 2020, it declassified the FBI's interviews over three days in January 2017 with the primary source of the Steele dossier.[98] The fifty-seven pages of notes reveal in vivid terms what the FBI knew about the dossier, yet it continued to use it in presentations to the FISA court. This had already been revealed by the Horowitz report in December 2019, but the interview transcripts provide a shocking view into how the dossier was compiled.[99] It now became clear that Steele had based his dossier on a single main source, someone who had earlier provided Steele with business intelligence. The source was 'uncomfortable' when in March 2016 Steele asked him to investigate the Trump campaign, and in particular Paul Manafort and later Donald Trump. He warned Steele that his friends and contacts were 'too far removed' from these matters, yet he felt obliged to provide him with material. Later Steele asked him to investigate five people associated with the Trump campaign, but he only remembered three names – Manafort, Page and Cohen. He drew not so much on a network but on his 'social circle', and since Steele warned him that it was a security risk to take notes, he forgot what information came from whom. At one point, he even reported information from an anonymous 'Russian male' who 'never identified himself' (later alleged to be Sergei Millian, although he denies providing any information).[100] Regarding Trump's alleged 'unorthodox sexual behaviour' in Moscow, the main subsource simple reported the 'well known story' about Trump's involvement in 'water sports' at the Ritz-Carlton. The source warned Steele that his information was 'rumour and speculation' and was unable to corroborate his reporting.[101]

Although the report redacted the name and other identifying information, two days later, the primary subsource was exposed on the internet and his name was then published by RT.[102] The source was revealed to be Igor Danchenko, who was tasked by Steele in March 2016 to start digging up dirt on Manafort, a brief that in June was broadened to include Trump, Page, Cohen, Flynn and some others whose names he could not remember. Danchenko worked as a senior research analyst at the Brookings Institution from 2005 to 2010 and then, among other things, as a freelancer for Steele's Orbis company. Danchenko was born in Ukraine and is a Russian-trained lawyer who subsequently took degrees at the University of Louisville and Georgetown University. Together with another researcher at Brookings, Clifford Gaddy, he obtained Putin's doctoral (*kandidatskaya*) dissertation and found evidence of plagiarism.[103] Greg Jarrett, whom we have quoted earlier, noted that he had come across Danchenko's name several times before, but in media comments stressed, 'I could never piece it together. Because frankly . . . it is so wild and stupid that Steele's source was not from Russia but – it's a guy in Washington DC working for the liberal Brookings Institution'. He went on to state, 'Now, it sort of makes sense because the president of Brookings at the time was Strobe Talbott: [a] long-time Hillary Clinton ally who was hoping to fuel the collusion narrative and had his own contacts with Christopher Steele'. He notes that Talbott's brother-in-law was the 'Clinton sycophant' Cody Shearer.[104] Early in the collusion investigation, Talbott asked Steele to send him a copy of the dossier as it was being compiled to share with Obama administration officials and Brookings staff, according to Steele's testimony in the British lawsuit.[105]

In his book *Witch Hunt,* Jarret describes how Shearer compiled a second dossier with some of the same allegations and which became public in September 2016, some of which was used in Steele's dossier. Jarret now highlighted the awful symmetry of the case: 'So, I mean, the machinations of this – and it's all Hillary Clinton. Her campaign is paying for the dossier. And, it turns out some of her allies are feeding the dossier information, all fabricated'. Equally disturbing, the main source turned out not even to be a Russian but a Ukrainian. The FBI knew all of this when they interviewed

Danchenko in January 2017 yet allowed the Steele version to run rampant for three years. Reports note that Danchenko was shocked that his speculations and random materials, gleaned from acquaintances and chance encounters to earn his fee from Steele, became the foundation for years of accusations and recriminations.[106] However, an official letter from Attorney General Barr to Senator Lindsey Graham in September 2020 revealed that the FBI had investigated Danchenko in 2009–2011 over the claim by a Brookings colleague that in 2008 Danchenko had offered classified information for sale, met a known Russian intelligence agent and had meetings at the Russian embassy.[107] This is why the Steele dossier was considered Russian disinformation.

NOTES

1. Hillary Rodham Clinton, *What Happened* (London, Simon & Schuster, 2017), p. 356.
2. Clinton, *What* Happened, p. xii.
3. Clinton, *What* Happened, p. 3.
4. Taken as authoritative by Luke Harding, *Collusion: How Russia Helped Trump Win the White House* (London, Guardian Faber Publishing, 2017).
5. Miller, *The Apprentice*, p. 78.
6. Reported on BBC News, 29 May 2015.
7. Isikoff and Corn, *Russian Roulette*, p. 142.
8. John Solomon, 'Questions Grow about FBI Vetting of Christopher Steele's Russia Expertise', *The Hill*, 19 November 2018, https://www.realclearpolitics.com/2018/11/22/questions_grow_on_fbi_vetting_of_steele039s_russia_expertise_459519.html.
9. Simpson and Fritsch, *Crime in Progress*, p. 5.
10. Ken Bensinger, Miriam Elder and Mark Schoofs, 'These Reports Allege Trump has Deep Ties to Russia', *BuzzFeed*, 10 January 2017, https://www.buzzfeednews.com/article/kenbensinger/these-reports-allege-trump-has-deep-ties-to-russia. The above article links to the actual dossier: https://www.documentcloud.org/documents/3259984-Trump-Intelligence-Allegations.html. The copy came from David Kramer, discussed earlier.
11. Strzok, *Compromised*, p. 144.
12. Luke Harding, 'How Putin Walked into Putin's Web', *Guardian*, 15 November 2017, https://www.theguardian.com/news/2017/nov/15/how-trump-walked-into-putins-web-luke.
13. Wolff, *Fire and Fury*, p. 37.
14. 'Company Intelligence Report 2016/080', 20 June 2016. For stylistic reasons, I have not capitalised the surnames, but the grammar is unchanged.
15. 'Company Intelligence Report 2016/086', 20 June 2016.
16. 'Company Intelligence Report 2016/095', no date.

17. The report was originally published in *The Sunday Times* in January 2017, but reprised by Tim Shipman, 'Ex-MI6 Spy "Fabricated Dossier on Trump and Prostitutes"', *The Sunday Times*, 26 January 2020, https://www.thetimes.co.uk/art icle/ex-mi6-spy-fabricated-dossier-on-trump-and-prostitutes-wz2hr8zz7.

18. For a list of the worst offenders see Aaron Maté, 'The Rise and Fall of the "Steele Dossier"', *The Nation*, 11 January 2021, https://www.thenation.com/article/p olitics/trump-russiagate-steele-dossier/.

19. The document was only exposed through a Freedom of Information request by Citizens United and was presented in a heavily redacted form accompanied by attempts to classify it. John Solomon, 'Steele's Stunning pre-FISA Confession: Informant Needed to Air Trump Dirt before Election', *The Hill*, 7 May 2019, https://thehill.com/opinion/white-house/442592-steeles-stunning-pre-fisa-confession-inform ant-needed-to-air-trump-dirt.

20. McCarthy, *Ball of Collusion*, p. 166.

21. Cohen, *Disloyal*, p. 325.

22. Cohen, *Disloyal*, p. 327.

23. Andrew McCarthy, 'Steele's Shoddy Dossier', *National Review*, 6 June 2019, https://www.nationalreview.com/magazine/2019/06/24/steeles-shoddy -dossier/.

24. Gubarev et al v. Orbis Business Intelligence Ltd, and Christopher Steel, High Court of Justice, Queens Bench Division, Claim No. HQ17D00413, Defendant's Response to Claimants' Request for Further Information, 18 May 2017, https://www .scribd.com/document/368706403/Steele-Additional-Filing-in-London-Action.

25. Simpson and Fritsch, *Crime in Progress*, p. 18.

26. Sonam Sheth and Pat Ralph, 'The House Intel Committee Report on its Controversial Russian Investigation is out – Here are the Big Points', *Business Insider UK*, 27 April 2018, http://uk.businessinsider.com/house-intel-committee-rep ort-russia-investigation-2018-4. The full (redacted) report is House Permanent Select Committee on Intelligence, *Report on Russian Active Measures*, 22 March 2018, https://docs.house.gov/meetings/IG/IG00/20180322/108023/HRPT-115-1_1-p1-U3. pdf. The date given is June, whereas in fact Perkins Coie hired Fusion GPS in May, Simpson and Fritsch, *Crime in Progress*, p. 56.

27. Isikoff and Corn, *Russian Roulette*, p. 144, a position confirmed by Simpson and Fritsch, *Crime in Progress*, p. 57.

28. John Solomon, 'Hillary Clinton's Russia Collusion IOU: The Answers She Owes America', *The Hill*, 3 June 2019, https://thehill.com/opinion/white-house/ 446736-hillary-clintons-russia-collusion-iou-the-answers-she-owes-america.

29. Barry Meier, *Spooked: The Trump Dossier, Black Cube, and the Rise of Private Spies* (New York, HarperCollins, 2021), pp. 30, 128 and *passim*.

30. Barry Meier, 'Secret Sharers: The Hidden Ties between Private Spies and Journalists', *New York Times*, 15 May 2021, https://www.nytimes.com/2021/05/15/ business/media/spooked-private-spies-news-media.html.

31. Isikoff and Corn, *Russian Roulette*, p. 223; Simpson and Fritsch, *Crime in Progress*, pp. 79–81.

32. Simpson and Fritsch, *Crime in Progress*, p. 84.

33. Department of State, *State Combined: Produced to HSGAC*, with the injunction 'Not for Public Release', 13 October 2020, https://www.hsgac.senate.gov/imo/media/doc/STATE_combined.pdf.
34. McCarthy, *Ball of Collusion*, p. 205.
35. McCarthy, 'The FBI's Trump-Russia Investigation'.
36. HPSCI, 'Interview of Andrew McCabe', 19 December 2017, p. 16, https://intelligence.house.gov/uploadedfiles/am33.pdf.
37. John Solomon, 'FBI Knew Steele's Research Connected to Clinton, Dems from Earliest Interactions', *Just the News*, 10 June 2020, https://justthenews.com/accountability/russia-and-ukraine-scandals/fbi-knew-steeles-russia-research-connected-clinton-dems.
38. Simpson and Fritsch, *Crime in Progress*, p. 96.
39. Meier, *Spooked*, p. 139.
40. Horowitz, *Review*, note.
41. Department of Justice, Office of the Inspector General, *Review of Four FISA Applications and Other Aspects of the FBI's Crossfire Hurricane Investigation*, December 2019 (henceforth Horowitz *Review*), https://www.justice.gov/storage/120919-examination.pdf, pp. i, 87–89, 91, 172, 173, 198, 270, 386.
42. Strzok, *Compromised*, p. 152.
43. McCarthy, *Ball of Collusion*, p. 26.
44. Michael Isikoff, 'US Intel Officials Probe Ties Between Trump Adviser and Kremlin', Yahoo!, 23 September 2016, https://uk.news.yahoo.com/u-s-intel-officials-probe-ties-between-trump-adviser-and-kremlin-175046002.html
45. Steele spoke with Corn by Skype on 31 October 2016, and that day Corn published online the story 'A Veteran Spy has Given the FBI Information Alleging a Russian Operation to Cultivate Donald Trump'; Simpson and Fritsch, *Crime in Progress*, p. 118.
46. Rowan Scarborough, 'Dossier Fails the Test of Time', *Washington Times*, 30 December 2018, https://www.washingtontimes.com/news/2018/dec/30/michael-steeles-russia-dossier-donald-trump-fails-/
47. Isikoff and Corn, *Russian Roulette*, p. 267.
48. McCain gave a copy of the dossier to Comey on 9 December 2016. Judicial Watch, 'FBI Records Show Dossier Author Deemed "Not Suitable for Use" as Source, Show Several FBI payments in 2016', 3 August 2018, https://www.judicialwatch.org/press-room/press-releases/judicial-watch-fbi-records-show-dossier-author-deemed-not-suitable-for-use-as-source-show-several-fbi-payments-in-2016/. More details available in discussion of the Judicial Watch documents by Sic Semper Tyrannis, ''Christopher Steele, FBI's Confidential Human Source', 7 August 2018, https://turcopolier.typepad.com/sic_semper_tyrannis/2018/08/christopher-steele-fbis-confidential-human-source-by-publius-tacitus.html.
49. For details of the Kramer/McCain involvement, see Simpson and Fritsch, *Crime in Progress*, pp. 126–31.
50. Later confirmed by Kramer. He also admitted that he was approached about the Steele dossier on 19 November 2016 by Sir Andrew Wood, the former British ambassador to Russia, during a meeting of the Halifax International Security Forum

in Nova Scotia, Canada. Wood was listed as an associate of Steele's company, Orbis. Later that day Wood told McCain and Kramer that 'he was aware of this information that had been gathered that raised the possibility of collusion and compromising material in the president-elect. And he explained that he knew the person who gathered the information and felt that the person was of the utmost credibility'. Kramer ascribed the word 'collusion' three times to Wood in his deposition. Wood also gave credence to the existence of the sex tape of Trump in Moscow. Jeff Carlson, 'Deposition Reveals Late Sen. McCain's Role in Spygate Scandal', *The Epoch Times*, 15 (updated 18) March 2019, https://www.theepochtimes.com/deposition-reveals-late-senator-mccains-role-in-spygate-scandal_2840198.html.

51. 'Judicial Watch: Emails Suggest Obama FBI Knew McCain Leaked Trump Dossier', 21 April 2020, https://www.judicialwatch.org/press-releases/judicial-watch-emails-suggest-obama-fbi-knew-mccain-leaked-trump-dossier/.

52. Kimberley A. Strassel, 'Who Is Michael Sussmann?', *Wall Street Journal*, 12 October 2018, p. A13.

53. House Judiciary Committee and House Oversight Committee, 'Full Transcript and Video of James Comey's Capitol Hill Testimony', 11 August 2018, https://www.zerohedge.com/news/2018-12-08/full-transcript-and-video-james-comeys-capitol-hill-testimony.

54. Editorial, 'A Dossier Debunking', *Wall Street Journal*, 28 August 2018, https://www.wsj.com/articles/a-dossier-debunking-1535413060.

55. Hettena, *Trump/Russia*, pp. 170, 176.

56. The story appeared in the *Washington Post* on 6 February 2018. For a detailed analysis, see Diana Johnstone, 'The Real Russian Interference in US Politics', *Consortium News*, 29 August 2018, https://consortiumnews.com/2018/08/27/the-real-russian-interference-in-us-politics/. See also Simpson and Fritsch, *Crime in Progress*, p. 113.

57. 'Full Text: James Comey Testimony', 8 June 2017.

58. Department of Justice, Office of the Inspector General, *Review of Various Actions by the Federal Bureau of Investigation and Department of Justice in Advance of the 2016 Election*, June 2018, https://www.justice.gov/file/1071991/download.

59. David B. Rivkin Jr. and Elizabeth Price Foley, 'Mueller's Fruit of the Poisonous Tree', *Wall Street Journal*, 23 June 2018, https://www.wsj.com/articles/muellers-fruit-of-the-poisonous-tree-1529707087.

60. The case is made at length by Jarrett, *The Russia Hoax*, notably pp. 94–5 and *passim*.

61. Strzok repeatedly insists on his impartiality in the Midyear Exam and other investigations, see *Compromised*, pp. 61–81, 113 and *passim*.

62. DoJ, OIG, *Review of Various Actions*, pp. 395–430. For investigation of the gap in text message collection from the devices of Strzok and Page between 15 December 2016 and 17 May 2017 by the DoJ's OIG, see Department of Justice, *Report of Investigation: Recovery of Text Message from Certain FBI Mobile Devices*, December 2018, https://oig.justice.gov/reports/2018/i-2018-003523.pdf.

63. DoJ, OIG, *Review of Various Actions*, p. 403.

64. DoJ, OIG, *Review of Various Actions*, p. 404.

65. Strzok, *Compromised*, p. 140.
66. Jeff Carlson, 'Transcripts of Lisa page's Closed-Door Testimonies Provide New Revelations in Spygate Scandal, *Epoch Times*, 11 January 2019, https://www.theepochtimes.com/transcripts-of-lisa-pages-closed-door-testimonies-provide-new-revelations_2763452.html.
67. Miller, *The Apprentice*, p. 146.
68. Freedom of Information requests by Judicial Watch of their email exchanges show their favourable treatment of lawyers acting on behalf of Hillary Clinton in the FBI investigation of her emails. For example, Judicial Watch, 'New Strzok-Page Emails Reveal DoJ Special Treatment to Clinton Lawyers', 9 January 2020.
69. John Cassidy, 'The FBI Needs to Explain its Reasons for Firing Peter Strzok', *New Yorker*, 13 August 2018, https://www.newyorker.com/news/our-columnists/the-fbi-needs-to-explain-its-reasons-for-firing-peter-strzok.
70. DoJ, OIG, *Review of Various Actions*, p. 405.
71. DoJ, OIG, *Review of Various Actions*, p. iii.
72. Horowitz, *Review*, note 214.
73. Horowitz, *Review*, notes 211 and 342.
74. Solomon, 'Questions Grow about FBI Vetting'.
75. Kimberley A. Strassel, 'Brennan and the 2016 Spy Scandal: Obama's CIA Director Acknowledged Egging on the FBI's Probe of Trump and Russia', *Wall Street Journal*, 20 July 2018, https://www.wsj.com/articles/brennan-and-the-2016-spy-scandal-1532039346.
76. '"Circus" at US Congress'.
77. McCabe, *The Threat*, p. 262.
78. The term is used in Simpson and Fritsch, *Crime in Progress*, p. 109.
79. Kimberley A. Strassel, 'What Bruce Ohr Told Congress', *Wall Street Journal*, 31 August 2018, https://www.wsj.com/articles/what-bruce-ohr-told-congress-1535668660.
80. Solomon, 'FBI Knew Steele's Research Connected to Clinton'
81. Holman W. Jenkins, 'The Press Abets a Coverup', *Wall Street Journal*, 18 August 2018, https://www.wsj.com/articles/the-press-abets-a-coverup-1534544446.
82. Andrew C. McCarthy, 'The Steele Dossier's "Corroborated" Claims were Old News', *National Review*, 4 March 2019, https://www.nationalreview.com/2019/03/trump-russia-steele-dossier-claims-old-news/.
83. The point is made by George Beebe, 'Making Sense of our Russiagate Failure', *The National Interest*, 4 April 2019, https://nationalinterest.org/feature/making-sense-our-russiagate-failure-50712.
84. The term is from 'Did the Media Botch the Russia Story? A Conversation with Matt Taibbi', *Vox.com*, 1 April 2019, https://www.vox.com/2019/3/31/18286902/trump-mueller-report-russia-matt-taibbi. For his larger argument, see Matt Taibbi, *Hate Inc.: Why Today's Media Makes Us Despise One Another* (OR Books, 2019).
85. Jonathan Browning, 'Russian Oligarchs Dismiss Kremlin Links in Trump Dossier Case', Bloomberg, 16 March 2020, https://www.bloomberg.com/news/articles/2020-03-16/russian-oligarchs-dismiss-kremlin-links-in-trump-dossier-case.

86. In the High Court of Justice, Queen's Bench Division, Media and Communications List, before Mr Justice Warby, between Petr Aven, Mikhail Fridman and German Khan vs. Orbis Business Intelligence Limited, Approved Judgment, 8 July 2020, para. 155, http://www.bailii.org/ew/cases/EWHC/QB/2020/1812.html.

87. John Solomon, 'British Court Rules against Christopher Steele', *Just the News*, 8 July 2020, https://justthenews.com/accountability/russia-and-ukraine-scandals/british-court-rules-against-christopher-steele-orders.

88. In the High Court of Justice, para. 200.

89. Simpson and Fritsch, *Crime in Progress*, p. 138.

90. Rowan Scarborough, 'Anti-Trump Dossier Author was Hired to Help Hillary Challenge 2016 Election Results', *Washington Times*, 12 December 2018, https://www.washingtontimes.com/news/2018/dec/12/christopher-steele-hillary-clinton-was-preparing-t/.

91. Jerry Dunleavy, 'Christopher Steele Admitted using Posts by "Random Individuals" on CNN Website to Back Up Trump Dossier', *Washington Examiner*, 15 March 2019, https://www.washingtonexaminer.com/news/steele-admitted-in-court-he-used-unverified-website-to-support-the-trump-dossier.

92. 'Observers on "Political Hack Job" & Who Really "Meddled" in US 2016 Elections', Sputnik, 6 May 2019, https://www.arabnews24.ca/en/World_news/2037.html.

93. 'Pangs of Conscience or Howl of an Empty Wallet?', RT.com, 22 July 2020, https://www.rt.com/usa/495561-steele-dossier-public-lawsuit-webzilla/.

94. The transcript of the proceedings is available on Scribe, 'Gubarev and others v Orbis Business Intelligence Ltd and another', Day 4, 23 July 2020, p. 81, https://www.opus2.com. Ignatius, as we shall see, in his column of 12 January 2017 revealed that Flynn had spoken by telephone with Russian ambassador Kislyak, thus 'The Flynn calls story is picking up legs' (p. 88), setting in train Flynn's downfall.

95. Meier, *Spooked*, p. 257.

96. Mike Emanuel and Brooke Singman, 'FBI Declassifies Spreadsheet Used to Try to Corroborate Steele Dossier', Fox News, 14 October 2020, https://www.foxnews.com/politics/fbi-declassifies-steele-dossier-spreadsheet.

97. Paul Sperry, 'Meet the Russiagate Prober Who Couldn't Verify Anything in the Steele Dossier yet Said Nothing for Years', *RealClearInvestigations*, 30 March 2021, https://www.realclearinvestigations.com/articles/2021/03/30/meet_the_russiagate_prober_who_couldnt_verify_anything_in_the_steele_dossier_yet_said_nothing_for_years_769667.html.

98. 'Judiciary Committee Releases Declassified Documents that Substantially Undercut Steele Dossier, Page FISA Warrants', 17 July 2020, https://www.judiciary.senate.gov/press/rep/releases/judiciary-committee-releases-declassified-documents-that-substantially-undercut-steele-dossier-page-fisa-warrants.

99. Federal Bureau of Investigation, *Interview of Primary Subsource*, Electronic Communication, 9 February 2017, https://www.judiciary.senate.gov/imo/media/doc/February%209,%202017%20Electronic%20Communication.pdf.

100. Paul Sperry, 'Meet the Steele Dossier's "Primary Subsource": Fabulist Russian From Democrat Think Tank Whose Boozy Past the FBI Ignored', *RealClearInvestigations*, 24 July 2020, https://www.realclearinvestigations.com/articles/2020/07/24/meet_steele_dossiers_primary_subsource_fabulist_russian_at_us_think_tank_whose_boozy_past_the_fbi_ignored_124601.html/.

101. For full analysis, see Eric Felten, 'The "Primary Subsources's" Guide to Russiagate, as Told to the FBI', *RealClearInvestigations*, 20 July 2020, https://www.realclearinvestigations.com/articles/2020/07/20/the_primary_subsources_guide_to_russiagate_as_told_to_the_fbi_124516.html.

102. The blog post is 'I Found the Primary Sub-source', 18 July 2020, https://ifoundthepss.blogspot.com/2020/07/tracking-primary-sub-source.html; '"Russian agent" or Steele Patsy? "Revealed" Identity of Steele Sub-Source for Russiagate Dossier Sparks Fresh Speculation', RT.com, 20 July 2020, https://www.rt.com/usa/495342-russiagate-steele-dossier-source/.

103. A lawyer for Danchenko confirmed that his client was Steele's main source, Adam Goldman and Charlie Savage, 'The FBI Pledged to Keep a Source Anonymous: Trump Allies Aided his Unmasking', *New York Times*, 25 July 2020, https://www.nytimes.com/2020/07/25/us/politics/igor-danchenko-steele-dossier.html.

104. Julia Musto, 'Greg Jarrett: Why Steele's Secret Source Working at the Brookings Institution "Makes Sense"', *Fox News*, 28 July 2020, https://www.foxnews.com/media/gregg-jarrett-investigation-christopher-steele-dossier-igor-danchenko.

105. Sperry, 'Meet the Steele Dossier's "Primary Subsource"; John Solomon, 'Revelation of Steele's Primary Source Triggers Focus on Think Tank Tied to Clinton, Biden', *Just the News*, 27 July 2020, https://justthenews.com/accountability/russia-and-ukraine-scandals/revelation-steeles-primary-source-triggers-focus-think.

106. One of these was alleged to be Danchenko's classmate Olga Galkina, who was named as a source on Alexei Gubarev by the *Wall Street Journal* in October 2020, but she denied having anything to do with the Steele dossier. Jonny Tickle, 'Russian PR Executive Outed as "Source" of "Russiagate" Steele Dossier Claims it was Made up by British Spy's Employee', RT.com, 3 November 2020, https://www.rt.com/russia/505341-steele-dossier-trump-madeup/.

107. Holman W. Jenkins, 'Fake and Real Russian News', *Wall Street Journal*, 25 September 2020, https://www.wsj.com/articles/fake-and-real-russia-news-11601073192.

Chapter 9

Spinning Russiagate

Stories of Russian hacking circulated in Washington for some time. Franklin Foer was one of the first to make the case for a trump–Putin conspiracy in *Slate* on 4 July 2016, seeking to explain the contradiction between Trump's supposed embrace of Putin and his goal of making America great again. Trump was either drawn to authoritarian strongmen or he was reliant on dirty money coming from Russia. According to Foer, there may well have been collusion between Trump and Putin to hack the DNC and release the material to cause maximum damage to the Democrats, or Putin did indeed hold *kompromat* on Trump.[1] The article was a classic mix of fact and supposition, all neatly folded into a neo-journalistic story to confirm an existing narrative. On 6 January 2017, the Intelligence Community Assessment (ICA) asserted that Russia had 'hacked' the presidential election. Along with the Steele dossier, the ICA is one of the cornerstones of the Russiagate affair, but how accurate is it?

AUTUMNAL BLUES

As late as July 2016 DNI Clapper refused publicly to state who was responsible for the alleged hack or to assign motivation. The FBI at this point believed that the cyber-attack sought to disrupt the American political system rather than specifically help Trump. CIA director Brennan could not run the risk of being seen to interfere directly in U.S. domestic politics but encouraged the FBI to start a counterintelligence operation (the absence of evidence meant that there was no basis for a criminal investigation).[2] Comey launched operation Crossfire Hurricane on 31 July, and shortly afterwards Brennan and Comey briefed Congress. Although the investigation remained secret, the Trump–Russia collusion narrative entered the public domain.

The Obama administration was uncertain about whether to go public, with Brennan allegedly calling for restraint to protect CIA informants. The CIA apparently had information from two separate sources in the Kremlin that Putin had personally authorised a covert operation to destabilise the American presidential election.[3] On 4 August, Brennan told Alexander Bortnikov, the head of the FSB, 'You're meddling in our election. We know it. We have it cold', a charge that Bortnikov flatly denied.[4] Brennan later told the HPSCI that he warned Bortnikov that the United States was aware of Russian operations and that it would damage relations between the two countries.[5] The Obama administration as a whole was 'concerned that any statement it made about Russia's actions might be cast as trying to help Clinton and hurt Trump'.[6] Trump was sceptical, for which he was roundly admonished. Trump was accused by Mike Morell, the deputy head of the CIA from 2010 to 2013 and twice acting director, of being 'an unwitting agent of the Russian Federation'. He warned that Trump was 'not only unqualified for the job, but he may well pose a threat to our national security'.[7]

It was at this point that Steele made his memos known, turning them into an open secret in Washington. Brennan contacted Senate minority leader Harry Reid and told him that Russia was trying to help Trump win the election, and that 'Trump advisers might be colluding with Russia'.[8] It was assumed that this would soon be made public, and two days later, Reid's letter to Comey was published in the *New York Times* on 29 August. Reid announced that he had learned of 'evidence of a direct connection between the Russian government and Donald Trump's presidential campaign', which had 'employed a number of individuals with significant and disturbing ties to Russia and the Kremlin'. In short, Reid asserted that 'The evidence of a direct connection between the Russian government and Donald Trump's presidential campaign continues to mount', repeating the Clinton's team's supposition that the Russians were helping Trump while referring to at least one of Steele's claims. Reid's letter was the first formal airing of the collusion narrative. In their book, Isikoff and Corn note that Reid believed that Brennan had an 'ulterior motive' with the briefing, but 'concluded the CIA chief believed the public needed to know about the Russia operation, including the information about the possible links to the Trump campaign'.[9]

The following day, the ranking Democratic members of four House committees issued a public letter to Comey requesting 'that the FBI assess whether connections between Trump campaign officials and Russian interests' may have contributed to the DNC hack so as 'to interfere with the US presidential election'.[10] Soon after, Fusion GPS briefed its media allies about the dossier, including a meeting with some leading journalists at the Tabard

Inn in Washington on 22 September.[11] As Hettena notes, 'It's a safe bet that the Clinton campaign was in some way behind these efforts'.[12] Steele briefed the media about his findings, but they declined to use this 'unverified information, with its unclear provenance'.[13]

In an interview with *Bloomberg* on 1 September 2016 at the Eastern Economic Forum, in response to a question about the hack of the Democratic Party, Putin insisted:

> I know nothing. There are a lot of hackers today, you know, and they perform their work in such a filigreed and delicate manner and they can show their 'tracks' anywhere and anytime. It may not even be a track; they can cover their activity so that it looks like hackers operating from other territories, from other countries. It is hard to check this activity, maybe not even possible. Anyway, we do not do that at the national level. Besides, does it really matter who hacked Mrs. Clinton's election campaign team database? Does it? What really matters is the content shown to the community. This is what the discussion should be held about. There is no need to distract the attention of the community from the essence of the subject substituting it with secondary questions dealing with the search of those who did it. I would like to repeat: I know absolutely nothing about it, and Russia has never done anything like this at the State level.[14]

Putin even went so far as to suggest that that the hackers had provided a public service.[15] Obama was having none of it, and at the Hangzhou G20 summit on 4–5 September he met Putin on the sidelines for over an hour. In addition to discussing Syria and Ukraine, Obama delivered a warning about Russia's cyber intrusions: 'We know what you're doing; if you don't cut it out, we will impose onerous and unprecedented penalties'.[16] Obama was pressured by some leading Democrats to go further and publicly denounce Russian interference, but he was sensibly circumspect. He came under enormous pressure from the Democratic establishment, such as Diane Feinstein, the ranking Democrat on the Senate Intelligence Committee, to denounce Russia.

Putin sought to shift attention from the provenance of the leaked emails to their content, while the Clinton camp naturally concentrated on the source to objuscate the content. The DNC emails exposed the bias of the Democrat leadership against Sanders, while Podesta's emails showed that he hoped that the media would advance Trump (who was considered unwinnable) and thus allow Clinton to pillory him and boost her own position. The views of Sanders were surprisingly popular in this campaign, and he gave Clinton a good run for her money and may well have been a more credible candidate against Trump. A socialist as president of the United States would have represented as big a shock to the American polity as Trump, but the election of the latter demonstrates that the system was ripe for change. As for the treatment of Jill Stein, the Green Party candidate in the 2012 and 2016 elections, the Democratic establishment came close to suggesting that an independent run was somehow illegitimate. Third-party independent candidates have historically, like Ross Perot in 1992, siphoned enough votes to force unexpected outcomes. In 2016, 3 per cent of the vote was cast for libertarian candidate Gary Johnson and 1 per cent (1.4 million votes) for Stein. The total of some five million people who voted for third-party candidates could have made a significant difference in swing states, although it is unclear how many of the second preference votes would have gone to Clinton.

This phase of the Russiagate scandal culminated on 23 September, when Michael Isikoff of Yahoo News reported on the Steele dossier's allegations regarding Carter Page. He was a minor character in the Trump campaign yet figures largely in the Russiagate affair. As noted, according to the Steele dossier, Page met with Rosneft head Sechin and discussed a possible deal. Hettena notes that officials were 'seeking to determine' if Page had private communications about the possible lifting of economic sanctions if Trump became president.[17] This brought the collusion narrative into the open. On 30 October, Reid once again publicly wrote to Comey 'In my communications with you and other top officials in the national security community, it has become clear that you possess explosive information about close ties between Donald Trump, his top advisors, and the Russian government'.[18] Mueller found no such 'explosive information' and none has yet come to light.

A team of computer scientists at this time combed the Domain Name System (DNS), a global network that acts as the phonebook for the internet, for potential anomalous patterns involving Russian contacts with American entities. Every DNS query (look-up) is logged, leaving records. Examining Trump's domain, the scientists found frequent and repeated DNS lookups from servers owned by Alfa Bank. Between May and September 2016, Alfa looked up the Trump Organisation's domain over 2,000 times. Only one other organisation contacted the Trump Organisation with a comparable frequency, Spectrum Health of Grand Rapids, Michigan. Spectrum Health is linked to the DeVos family, and Betsy DeVos was appointed secretary of education in Trump's first cabinet. Her brother, Erik Prince, is a Trump associate who was investigated by Mueller, in particular his meeting following the election with a Russian official in the Seychelles, where they apparently discussed establishing a back channel between Trump and Putin, a meeting that Prince insists was 'incidental' (see below). The scientists decided that the Trump server was being used as a covert channel for communication and was proof of an illicit link between Russia and the Trump campaign. The subject was aired in the press, notably following Reid's 30 October letter to Comey charging that the FBI was withholding information. Franklin Foer added a new wrinkle to the story in late October 2016, when he suggested that the Trump server may well have been communicating with Russia.[19] However, the mainstream media was more cautious, and rightly so.[20] Most likely an automated marketing email system (spam) triggered the repeated communications. The story was kept alive not only by Congressional interventions but also by activists, notably Daniel Jones at the head of the Democracy Integrity Project, working closely with Glenn Simpson at Fusion GPS.[21] Ostensibly established to keep elections free from foreign interference, the Democracy Integrity Project exploited new cold war fears to generate funds. In the same spirit, Cambridge Analytica now stood accused of transferring its illicitly gained information to help Russia target American voters – one of the more far-fetched claims.[22]

In September, Obama commented that in allegedly supporting Trump, Putin had 'backed the wrong horse', and thus there seemed little point to do much in response.[23] Obama has been much criticised for his alleged weak reaction to Russian malfeasance. David Shimer examines two possible reasons: the probability that Clinton would be elected and the fear that a defeated Trump would claim that he had been cheated. He goes on to claim that the White House under-estimated the scale of Russia's intervention, and therefore failed to launch a covert cyber-attack or some other kinetic response.[24] As a reviewer notes, 'The Obama team worried less about what Putin had done than what he could do, and, as a result, they missed the fact that Russia's interference represented the greatest degree of Kremlin risk-taking aimed at the United States since the Cuban missile crisis'.[25] In the event, history proved Obama right – to a point.

Clinton continued to push the Russian interference theme. In the first of the three presidential debates, this one at Hofstra University on Long Island on 26 September, she was asked by NBC anchor Lester Holt what could be done to thwart the Russian assault. Clinton responded: 'There is no doubt now that Russia has used cyberattacks against all kinds of organizations in our country. And I am deeply concerned about this. I know Donald's very praiseworthy [*sic*] of Vladimir Putin, but Putin is playing a really tough, long game here'. She condemned Trump's (ironic) invitation to hack her deleted emails: 'I was so shocked when Donald publicly invited Putin to hack into Americans. That is just unacceptable'.[26] Trump was dismissive: 'She is saying Russia, Russia, Russia. But I don't – maybe it was. I mean, it could be Russia, but it could also be China, it could also be lots of other people. It could also be somebody sitting on their bed who weighs four hundred pounds, OK?'[27]

The Trump team considered the whole Russia business something invented by opponents that was failing to register with the public. He 'believed the idea that they were colluding with the Russians ludicrous'.[28] To counter this view, Clapper and DHS head Jeh Johnson were keen to go public about Russia's alleged interference, while the FBI's Comey was more cautious since he knew that a counterintelligence investigation was under way. Finally, a joint statement on 7 October 2016 officially accused Russia of interfering in the election:

> The US intelligence community (USIC) is confident the Russian government directed the recent compromise of emails from US persons and institutions, including from US political organisations. The recent disclosures of alleged hacked emails on sites like DCLeaks.com and WikiLeaks and by the Guccifer 2.0 online persona are consistent with the methods and motivations of Russian-directed efforts. These thefts and disclosures are intended to interfere with the US election process. Such activity is not new to Moscow – the Russians have used similar tactics and techniques across Europe and Eurasia, for example, to influence public opinion there. We believe, based on the scope and sensitivity of these efforts, that only Russia's senior-most officials could have authorised these activities.[29]

The document made the bold claim that Russia's leadership had directly ordered the attack, although Clapper and Johnson were careful not to attribute any election site hack to the Russians. The sensational revelation was expected to dominate the news cycle. Instead, an hour after the announcement, the *Washington Post* released a conversation caught on a hot-mike in 2005 between Trump and Billy Bush, then host of an NBC show called *Access Hollywood*. Trump 'bragged in vulgar terms about kissing, groping and trying to have sex with women', and talked of how he could get away with groping women: 'When you're a star, they let you do it', Trump said. 'You can do anything. Grab them by the pussy'.[30] The Russia story was eclipsed.

The eventful day was not yet over. Conspiracy theories were further stimulated by WikiLeaks dumping some 2,000 emails just an hour after the *Access Hollywood* tape aired, taken from Podesta's personal Gmail account. Part of a declared trove of some 50,000 emails, this tranche revealed Clinton's paid speeches to Wall Street executives, including Goldman Sachs. She noted the difference between 'a public and a private position', implying that they need not take her reforming rhetoric too seriously. The emails also exposed collusion between the Clinton campaign and DNC campaign chair Donna Brazile about the questions and topics to be raised in the presidential debates and campaign meetings. Once again, the Clinton team focused on the provenance of the emails rather than their damaging content, arguing that 'This is a Russia-orchestrated October Surprise, and our campaign is being attacked by Putin'.[31] This was also the view of the FBI, regarding it as extremely unlikely that the release was not timed to limit the damage of the *Access Hollywood* audiotape.[32]

The second presidential debate was held at Washington University in St Louis, Missouri, on 10 October, and the dramatic events of three days earlier dominated. In addition, on 8 October, Bill Pruitt, a producer on the early *Apprentice* seasons, tweeted that there were far worse recordings of Trump than the *Access Hollywood* material, implying that outtakes of the show exposed Trump using the N-word.[33] For the debate, Bannon devised the bizarre plan of inviting four women – Juanita Broaddrick, Kathleen Willey, Paula Jones and Kathy Shelton – three of whom had earlier accused Bill Clinton of sexual misconduct or assault, and Shelton had been traduced by Hillary during the trial of her rapist, for whom she was acting as attorney. When Clinton was asked about the hypocrisy revealed by the Podesta emails, she deflected the charge to suggest that Russian intelligence provided the material to WikiLeaks and was now shaping the discussion in a presidential debate: 'We have never in the history of our country been in a situation where an adversary, a foreign power, is working so hard to influence the outcome of the election. And believe me, they're not doing it to get me elected. They're doing it to try to influence the election for Donald Trump'. Trump questioned why 'they always blame Russia', and answered his own question: 'And the reason they blame Russia because they think they're trying to tarnish me with Russia'. He went on to assert: 'I don't deal there. I have no businesses there'.[34] Trump's various business projects in Moscow had repeatedly failed to get off the ground, but it was later revealed that he continued to pursue the Trump Tower Moscow project until well into 2016.

In the third presidential debate, held on 19 October in Las Vegas, Clinton declared 'We have 17, 17 intelligence agencies, civilian and military, who have all concluded that these espionage attacks, these cyberattacks, come from the highest levels of the Kremlin, and they are designed to influence our election. I find that deeply disturbing'.[35] The 7 October statement had been issued in the name of only two agencies (DHS and ODNI) and it was misleading to suggest that all seventeen agencies carried out their separate investigations, and all had come to the same conclusion. It relied on the circular logic of assumed Russian behavioural norms to explain the country's actions, all without concrete evidence of any specific Kremlin policy to support Trump. Nevertheless, on 31 October, the Obama administration used the 'red phone' to issue a warning to the Kremlin, including a hint that cyber activities were covered by the 'law for armed conflict' (in other words, the laws of war) and stressed that meddling in the election 'would represent serious interference in the fundamentals of US society'.[36] Overall, as mentioned, Obama was reticent about making a public fuss, fearing that it could be construed as interfering in the election. Ben Rhodes describes the internal debate about how to respond, and while claiming more could have been done publicly, the scope for action was limited.[37] The 'Russia problem', clearly, was one that it was anticipated would be dealt with once Clinton was elected.

This was not to be, and within 24 hours of her defeat Mook, Clinton's campaign manager, and Podesta assembled her communications team at campaign headquarters in Brooklyn to outline the strategy that would be pursued for the next few years – that Russia was responsible for the defeat and for an egregious attack on American democracy. This story was amplified by the media and the 'intelligence assessments' of the security agencies.[38] The strategy shifted attention from the mistakes of the Clinton campaign and her inadequacies as a potential leader and avoided analysing the way that the Sanders Democrats had been marginalised. It also helped manage dissent and set the terms of debate, which in the end enforced conformity through restrictions on social media. New cold war hostility escalated informational warfare.[39]

CARTER PAGE AND THE FISA WARRANTS

On 21 March 2016, Page, along with Papadopoulos, was part of the eclectic group invited to become Trump's foreign policy advisers. There were good reasons to be suspicious about Page. He was a consultant and businessman specialising in energy matters and Central Asian affairs who had lived and worked in Russia between 2003 and 2007 as deputy manager of Merrill Lynch's Moscow's office, and then established an energy investment company in New York. Page twice failed to gain a PhD degree from SOAS, University of London, with the examiners scathing about his work, until he finally passed in 2011 at the third attempt with an unknown examiner.[40] In 2013, an SVR agent, Viktor Podobny, posing as an attaché at the UN, contacted him in New York and gave him some energy-related documents and held out the prospect of profitable deals in Moscow. The FBI had been tracking the agent but believed that Page had no idea that he was not dealing with a bona fide commercial prospect. According to an FBI transcript of a conversation between Podobny and another Russian intelligence officer, the former stated, 'I promised him a lot . . . How else to work with foreigners? You promise a favour for a favour'.[41] In the FBI's intercept, Podobny was recorded as calling Page an 'idiot' who 'wants to earn lots of money' and did not consider him worth recruiting.[42] By 2015, the Podobny group was broken up and the FBI dropped the Page investigation.

In his capacity as a Trump adviser, Page was invited to speak at the New Economic School in Moscow, where Obama had delivered a lecture during his visit in 2009. The institution is private and defends its independence, although it naturally has links with senior government ministers. In 2016, the liberal deputy prime minister Arkady Dvorkovich was chair of its board. On 7 July, Page delivered what is universally agreed to have been a boring speech. He reprised his long-standing view that Washington's policy should focus on the mutual interests between Russia and the United States rather than on values such as democracy. According to the Steele dossier dated 19 July, Page met earlier that month with Igor Sechin, the head of Rosneft, Russia's top oil company. According to Steele, Sechin was so keen to have sanctions lifted that he offered Page the opportunity to broker the sale of 19 per cent of Rosneft stock.[43] This would have been worth billions, and it is simply not credible to believe that Moscow would be willing to pay such vast sums for such dubious benefits or use such a political lightweight as the intermediary. In the same visit, Steele alleges that Page met with a senior figure in the presidential administration, Igor Diveykin, who told him that the Kremlin possessed not only a file of *kompromat* on Clinton but also on Trump, 'which the latter should bear in mind in his dealings with them'.

In March 2016, Page was interviewed by the FBI, and later in the year, a FISA warrant was taken out against him.[44] Page was removed from any involvement in the Trump campaign on 24 September, so the point of the FISA surveillance is not clear. Strzok admits that the Steele dossier 'ended debate as to whether we had probable cause for a FISA application'.[45] The first 90-day FISA warrant against Page was issued on 21 October, followed by three more on 12 January, 7 April and 29 June 2017. The warrants covered not only Page but also anyone with whom he was in contact under the so-called two-hop surveillance procedure – that is, anyone Page talked to, and anyone they in turn talked to.[46] The repeated warrants have become the centrepiece of investigations into Russiagate malfeasance and FBI overreach. Comey was intent on renewing the FISA applications to use Page surveillance as a window into the Trump camp, although by then Page was an outsider. To do so, he relied excessively on the uncorroborated Steele dossier, a matter later investigated by the DoJ's inspector general Michael Horowitz.[47]

Four major issues stand out. First, the FISA court was not adequately informed that the information justifying the requests came from a dossier created by Fusion GPS, which was funded by the Clinton campaign. In the requests, Steele is referred to as 'Source#1'. There is a page-long footnote about Steele's background, but it is ambiguous about the credibility of Steele's material. Even after the dubious source of the information became known, Comey signed off two more FISA warrants and even included information from the final, 13 December memorandum. In other words, the FBI continued to use information from Steele even after his credentials and integrity had been questioned. As Judicial Watch president Tom Fitton notes, 'The anti-Trump Russia "investigation" had Christopher Steele at its centre and his misconduct was no impediment to using information from his Russia intelligence collaborators to spy on the Trump team. The corruption and abuse is astonishing'.[48] Later, the FBI argued that the dossier was secondary in its investigation (and thus in the FISA warrants), by asserting that in fact it was the Papadopoulos material that prompted the investigation into alleged Russian election interference and the Trump campaign's knowledge of Russian actions. That may be the case, but there no doubt that the FBI relied in large part on the dossier to obtain the surveillance warrants against Page.

Second, the December 2019 Horowitz report found that an FBI lawyer doctored a CIA email to portray Page falsely to the FISA court as a Kremlin agent when he was really a CIA informant. On 17 August 2016, the CIA sent a note to the FBI stating that Page (described as 'Individual #1') had been approved as an 'operational contact' for the CIA from 2008 to 2013, and that he had provided information about his earlier contacts with Russian intelligence officers.[49] Why, then, did the FBI application for the first FISA warrant not include information about Page's work with the CIA? Even more pertinently, why did the FBI seek repeated warrants on the basis that Page was a secret Russian agent when they knew that he had worked as a CIA informant against Russia? Part of the answer emerged during the criminal investigation into the actions of Kevin Clinesmith, the FBI assistant general counsel working on Crossfire Hurricane, which emerged at the time when the fourth FISA warrant was being sought. An unidentified FBI supervisory special agent (SSA) wanted to know whether Page had ever been a 'source' and insisted on receiving a copy of the 17 August 2016 CIA message. Clinesmith forwarded it but doctored the text to add the words 'and not a source'.[50] Clinesmith was dismissed from the FBI in late 2019.[51] He later pleaded guilty to the felony of falsifying evidence to support the FISA warrant against Page. Before sentencing in December 2020, he agreed to a plea deal whereby he cooperated with the John Durham investigation into Russiagate, which we shall discuss later. Later, in an extremely unusual move, the FISA court retrospectively retracted two of the four warrants and barred any of the agents involved in the original warrants from submitting future applications.[52]

Third, it was only in late October 2017 that the public and Congress first learned that the law firm Perkins Coie, on behalf of the DNC and Clinton's campaign, hired the research form Fusion GPS, who in turn hired Steele, to investigate Trump's Russia connections. This was confirmed in the four-page Nunes memo of 18 January, released by the Republican-controlled HPSCI on 2 February 2018. It revealed that Strzok opened the investigation into Trump–Russia collusion based on 'information' about Papadopoulos and not on the Steele dossier. Steele, the memo noted, was dropped as an FBI source because of contacts with the media. The memo went on to assert that the dossier 'formed an essential part' of the case for the first FISA warrant, but none of the warrants disclosed the source of funding, and that Steele was dropped by the FBI because he 'lied' about his media and other disclosures, although he remained in contact with Bruce Ohr. The devastating conclusion of the Nunes memo is that the FBI and DoJ knew that the Steele dossier was unverified and paid for by Clinton and the Democrats and compiled by someone who despised Trump, yet it was used to spy on a Trump associate.[53] Nunes claimed that the FBI failed to alert the court to Steele's anti-Trump agenda. As noted, a footnote in the first FISA warrant outlines Steele's ties to the DNC and problematic political motivations but obscured more than it revealed. A Democratic-led minority memo of 29 January 2018, prepared by ranking member Adam Schiff, sought to refute the charges. It insisted that the Steele dossier had nothing to do with opening Crossfire Hurricane and that the justification for monitoring Page was 'multi-pronged'. It stressed information that was independent of the dossier, including 'Page's past relationships with Russian spies', and noted that Page was interviewed by the FBI in March 2016 'about his contact with Russian intelligence, the very month Donald Trump named him a foreign-policy adviser'.[54] The Schiff memo failed to mention that Page had been reporting to the CIA about his contacts with Russian intelligence, and instead the FBI used these contacts as the basis of the allegation that Trump was colluding with the Russians. The December 2019 Horowitz report confirms the Nunes version and noted seventeen mistakes, omissions, and acts of misconduct in applying for the original FISA warrant against Page in October 2017 (more on this below).

Fourth, the pertinent question is the degree to which the FBI tried to corroborate the charges, and above all to verify the Steele dossier's provenance and contents.[55] This itself became the subject of partisan struggles. Congressional Democrats insisted that the agencies submit any such documents to them before publicising them, fearing that possible collusion with intelligence and law enforcement agencies would be revealed. As Trump's lawyer John Dowd argued, 'The entire enquiry appears to be the product of a conspiracy by the DNC, Fusion GPS – which sponsored the Steele dossier – and senior FBI intelligence officials to undermine the Trump presidency'.[56] Others stress the 'complicity of our allies, particularly Britain', to explain why Trump 'has refrained from unsealing and publicizing most memoranda, files, and court documents pertaining to the Trump-Russia investigation's origins'.[57] The bottom line is that the warrant applications obscured the Clinton campaign provenance of the Steele dossier and its credibility problems and were 'unabashed about using counterintelligence authorities to conduct a criminal investigation in the absence of a predicate crime'.[58]

THE ICA

On 29 November 2016, a letter from eight Democrats on the Senate Intelligence Committee asked Obama to declassify documents about 'Russian active measures', the evidence that underlay the 7 October statement. Obama did not declassify the material but instead asked Clapper to respond.⁵⁹ On 6 December, Obama ordered Brennan to prepare a detailed ICA on Russian interference, to be delivered within a month. The timescale was very tight for such a complex investigation but ensured that it would be delivered while Obama was still president. Clapper took a leading role, supported by the CIA and NSA, and only 'a small number of people within the three agencies would compile the study or even know about it'.⁶⁰

On 6 January 2017, the intelligence community published the twenty-five-page document (with ten blank pages) *Assessing Russian Activities and Intentions in Recent US Elections*, issued in the name of seventeen intelligence agencies.⁶¹ It described itself as 'a declassified version of a highly classified assessment', and devoted the first two pages to the 'tradecraft' involved in producing such a document. The analytic assessment covered the 'motivation and scope of Moscow's intentions regarding US elections and Moscow's use of cyber tools and media campaigns to influence US public opinion'.⁶² The document was prepared by DNI Clapper with the CIA and the NSA, but surprisingly, not the State Department's Bureau of Intelligence and Research (INR), the body which had objected (it later turned out correctly) to aspects of the October 2002 Estimate on Iraq. Similarly, it was surprising that the DIA did not take the lead since it had the greatest expertise on Russia. Contrary to Clinton's repeated assertions, the report was not prepared by 'all 17 intelligence agencies'. In fact, Clapper confessed on 8 May 2017 in testimony to the Senate that the authors were some two dozen 'hand-picked seasoned experts from each of the [three] contributing agencies' [the CIA, FBI and NSA].⁶³ The outcome was determined by the choice of analysts.⁶⁴

Clapper's views are clear. On 28 May 2017 in an NBC interview, Clapper argued that Russians 'are almost genetically driven to co-opt, penetrate, gain favour, whatever, which is a typical Russian technique'.⁶⁵ During a visit to Australia on 7 June, Clapper criticised Trump for thinking that there could ever be substantive cooperation between Russia and the United States. He condemned what he claimed to have been Russia's attempt to interfere with the U.S. presidential election. The objective, in his view, was 'to sow doubt, discontent, and discord about our political system. They achieved, I am sure, beyond their wildest expectations'. He insisted that 'The Russians are not our friends; they (Putin specifically) are avowedly opposed to our democracy and values, and see us as the cause of all their frustrations'. He claimed that 'It is in their genes to be opposed, diametrically opposed to the United States and to Western democracies', and assumedly to work for their downfall.⁶⁶

The paucity of hard evidence in the ICA is striking, and this is perhaps why the NSA endorsed the report with only 'moderate' confidence, compared to the FBI's and CIA's 'high confidence'.⁶⁷ The document argued that Putin 'sought to use disclosures to discredit the image of the United States and cast it as hypocritical' and asserted:

> Russian efforts to influence the 2016 US presidential election represent the most recent expression of Moscow's longstanding desire to undermine the US-led liberal democratic order, but these activities demonstrated a significant escalation in directness, level of activity, and scope of effort compared to previous operations.

Crucially, the report went on to state that

> We assess Russian President Vladimir Putin ordered an influence campaign in 2016 aimed at the US presidential election. Russia's goals were to undermine public faith in the US democratic process, denigrate Secretary Clinton, and harm her electability and potential presidency. We further assess Putin and the Russian Government developed a clear preference for President-elect Trump. We have high confidence in these judgments.

Putin was held personally responsible, since he was angry that the United States had used the Panama Papers and the Olympic doping scandal against him. The circularity of the argument is striking: the activity accorded with what the U.S. intelligence community believed to be Russian motivations, and therefore the Russians must have been responsible, and the order must have come from the top. The report argued that

> Moscow's influence campaign followed a Russian messaging strategy that blends covert intelligence operations – such as cyber activity – with overt efforts by Russian Government agencies, state-funded media, third-party intermediaries, and paid social media users or 'trolls'.[68]

Moscow used fake social media personas ('trolls') and automated accounts ('bots') to influence the election. The report concluded that 'Moscow will apply lessons learned from its Putin-ordered campaign aimed at the US presidential election to influence future efforts worldwide, including against US allies and their election processes'.[69]

The report noted that Russian intelligence had gained access to DNC networks in July 2015 and 'maintained that access until at least June 2016', while the GRU 'probably began cyber operations aimed at the US election by March 2016'.[70] With 'high confidence', the ICA argued that the GRU 'used the Guccifer 2.0 persona, DCLeaks.com, and WikiLeaks to release US victim data obtained in cyber operations publicly and in exclusives to media outlets'.[71] A large part of the report was devoted to 'Russian propaganda efforts' through 'Russia's state-run propaganda machine', targeting global audiences through RT and Sputnik and a network of quasi-government trolls. From March 2016, they allegedly 'began openly supporting President-elect Trump's candidacy'.[72] The report noted that 'The likely financier of the so-called Internet Research Agency of professional trolls located in Saint Petersburg is a close Putin ally with ties to Russian intelligence'.[73] The election operation was described as the 'new normal' in Russian influence efforts, and that Russia 'has sought to influence elections across Europe'.[74]

Seven of the ICA's twenty-two substantive pages were taken up by Annex A, describing how 'Kremlin's TV Seeks to Influence Politics, Fuel Discontent in US'. The annex was originally published in 2012 and described RT as a 'Kremlin-financed channel operating within the United States' and condemned its coverage of 'US election' fraud and the Occupy Wall Street movement. RT was not the only Western media channel to suggest that the American political system was 'corrupt' and dominated by corporations, or that America was a 'surveillance state' afflicted by police brutality.[75] Annex B was devoted to the methodology of 'estimative language', noting that a 'high confidence' assessment is based on 'high quality information from multiple sources', although it 'does not imply that the assessment is a fact or a certainty'.[76]

On 9 June 2020, DNI John Ratcliffe declassified the two-page so-called Annex A of the ICA (not to be confused with the other addendum on Russian media interference), revealing that the FBI was wary about the Steele dossier.[77] Nevertheless, the FBI had been keen for everything, vetted and unvetted, to be included but the CIA disagreed, as did Michael Rogers of the NSA. The secret Annex was a compromise, with none of the ICA's analytical conclusions to be drawn from the dossier or even refer to it, and the Annex would note the 'limited corroboration'. The Annex begins by noting: 'An FBI source, using both identified and unidentified subsources, volunteered highly politically sensitive information from the summer to the fall of 2016 on Russian influence efforts aimed at the US presidential election. We have only limited corroboration of the source reporting in this case and did not use it to reach the analytic conclusions of the CIA/FBI/NSA assessment'. The Annex noted the leaking of the material into the public domain: 'The source's reporting appears to have been acquired by multiple Western press organizations starting in October'. Referring to Steele, the Annex states

> The most politically sensitive claims by the FBI source alleged a close relationship between the President-elect and the Kremlin. The source claimed that the President-elect and his top campaign advisers knowingly worked with Russian officials to bolster his chances of beating Secretary Clinton; were fully knowledgeable of Russia's direction of leaked Democratic emails; and were offered financial compensation from Moscow.

Another point notes that 'The FBI source claimed that the Kremlin had cultivated the President-elect for at least five years; had fed him and his team intelligence about Secretary Clinton and other opponents for years, and agreed to use WikiLeaks in return for policy concessions by the President-elect – assuming he won the election – on NATO and Ukraine'. The FBI was right to have been wary, and given the extravagant nature of the dossier's claims, it is hardly surprising that it was relegated to a secret Annex.

THE LONG SHADOW

A further matter of concern is the 'oversized impact that private spies were suddenly having on politics, business and our personal lives'.[78] Private agencies and political entrepreneurs, with unclear funding routes, were able to shape the political agenda with the connivance of those whose job it was precisely to protect against such interference in the relationship between the citizen and the state. Private spying has become big business, and Steele was at home in this twilight world whose currency is information. Unfortunately, much of it is counterfeit. In withering criticism, the journalist Masha Gessen (who is no friend of Putin) demonstrated with forensic skill that the headline conclusion that Putin ordered an 'influence campaign' to help Trump win the presidency was not supported by the evidence. She notes what strikes any reader: although the report is only twenty-five pages long, there is not much to read, after the various blank pages and extraneous materials are subtracted, and neither did it present anything new. The three 'key judgments' were that: (1) 'We assess Russian President Vladimir Putin ordered an influence campaign in 2016 aimed at the U.S. presidential election'; (2) 'Moscow's influence campaign followed a Russian messaging strategy that blends covert intelligence operations – such as cyber activity – with overt efforts by Russian Government agencies, state-funded media, third-party intermediaries, and paid social media users or "trolls"'; and (3) 'We assess Moscow will apply lessons learned from its Putin-ordered campaign aimed at the US presidential election to future influence efforts worldwide, including against US allies and their elections processes'.[79]

The first charge was based on the view that Moscow sought to discredit Clinton since Putin disliked her, accompanied by the broader goal of undermining 'the US-led liberal democratic order'. This explains why after June 2016 Putin avoided praising Trump, since the Kremlin apparently feared that this would be counter-productive and undermine Trump's pledge to work with Russia, especially over Ukraine and Syria. Thus, perversely, the *absence* of support for Trump is taken as proof of Russian collusion in his election. Equally, as Gessen notes, Putin earlier had not been exactly effusive in his praise of Trump, having mentioned him only twice before: after his press conference in December 2015 when he described Trump as 'colourful', and then in the follow-up conversation with Zakaria at SPIEF in June the following year. This exchange can hardly be used to demonstrate Russian 'meddling' in the U.S. election, as the ICA suggested. The various other arguments purporting to show that Putin had a preference were even weaker, including the view that Putin hoped to create with Trump an international anti-ISIS (Islamic State, Daesh) coalition (which in fact already existed, although not in the form proposed by Putin in his UN General Assembly speech of 28 September 2015); and that Putin liked to work with political leaders 'whose business interests made them more disposed to deal with Russia', such as former Italian prime minister Silvio Berlusconi or former German chancellor Gerhard Schroeder. In fact, Schroeder only moved into business (becoming chair of the shareholder's committee of the Nord Stream 1 consortium) after he left the German chancellor's office in November 2005. The report also suggested that Russian officials stopped criticising the U.S. election system after Trump's election and cancelled the #DemocracyRIP campaign, planned to lament Clinton's victory. In other words, Moscow had anticipated a Clinton victory and was as surprised by the outcome as everyone else. As Gessen notes, 'The logic of these arguments is as sound as saying, "You were so happy to see it rain yesterday that you must have caused the rain yourself"'. The conclusion is devastating: 'That is the entirety of the evidence the report offers to support its estimation of Putin's motives for allegedly working to elect Trump: conjecture based on other politicians in other periods, on other continents – and also on misreported or mistranslated public statements'.[80]

The rest of the ICA dealt with technical aspects of alleged Russian interference, including the hack of the DNC and its scanning of local electoral boards, although not of vote counting procedures, and the extensive and rather bizarre section dealing with Russia's 'state-run propaganda machine', covering RT and Sputnik. Vladimir Zhirinovsky, the long-time head of the populist Liberal Democratic Party of Russia (LDPR), was also considered part of the campaign. While aligned with the Kremlin on most major policy issues, the LDPR can hardly be considered representative of the Putin leadership. Zhirinovsky toasted Trump's victory, but there is no evidence that the Kremlin celebrated. The ICA claimed that the Russian media 'hailed President-elect Trump's victory as a vindication of Putin's advocacy of global populist movements – the theme of Putin's annual conference for Western academics in October 2016'. Having participated in that session, I can attest that the statement is fundamentally misleading. The theme of the annual Valdai Club Conference was 'The Future Begins Today: Outlines of the World Tomorrow' and examined challenges to global order. The debate was broad-ranging and diverse, focusing on changes in the international system and the implications of global shifts in power.[81] It certainly was not an endorsement of any state-directed populist subversion of liberal democracy.

The reception of the ICA is as important as its contents. The media overwhelmingly accepted the various assessments as proof that Putin had intervened in the election, whereas the report failed to demonstrate that this was the case. It was even less convincing when it came to demonstrating that the social media campaign had any discernible effect. Instead, it was endlessly trumpeted that it would be hard to counter the assessment of seventeen intelligence agencies, when as we have seen only three were involved, and then only select individuals drafted the report. Nevertheless, the report has been accepted as the canonical statement that the November 2016 election was distorted, reinforcing the view of those who argue that Trump's election was illegitimate. Gessen concludes that

> the intelligence report does nothing to clarify the abnormalities of Trump's campaign and election. Instead, it risks perpetuating the fallacy that Trump is some sort of foreign agent rather than a home-grown demagogue, while doing further damage to our faith in the electoral system. It also suggests that US intelligence agencies' Russia expertise is weak and throws into question their ability to process and present information.[82]

The ICA was rejected by the HPSCI in March 2018, arguing that any influence exercised by Russia did not specifically favour Trump.[83] The methodological point is taken up by Matlock. Although billed as an 'intelligence community assessment', in his view 'A report of the intelligence community in my day would include the input of all the relevant intelligence agencies and reveal whether all agreed with the conclusions. Individual agencies did not hesitate to "take a footnote" or explain their position if they disagreed with a particular assessment. A report would not claim to be that of the "intelligence community" if any relevant agency was omitted'. Referring to Clapper's selection of analysts, he noted that 'if you can hand-pick the analysts, you can hand-pick the conclusions', the same procedure that was applied in 2003 to report falsely that Saddam Hussein had stocks of WMD. Above all, he questions why the specialist expertise of the DIA, the DNI's National Intelligence Council or that of the State Department's INR was not used, and instead the FBI was drawn in. Worse, he was even informed by a senior official that the INR 'did, in fact, have a different opinion but was not allowed to express it'. The ICA notes that the WikiLeaks DNC emails 'did not contain any evident forgeries', so 'what was disclosed was the truth'. Russians were accused of 'degrading our democracy' by 'revealing that the DNC was trying to fix the nomination of a particular candidate rather than allowing the primaries and state caucuses to run their course. I had always thought that transparency is consistent with democratic values'. He concludes that 'Prominent American journalists and politicians seized upon this shabby, politically motivated, report as proof of "Russian interference" in the US election without even the pretence of due diligence'.[84]

TELLING TRUMP

On 5 January, the day before the report was released, Obama was briefed by Clapper and the heads of the CIA, FBI and NSA on its contents, with Joe Biden and other senior officials in attendance. Although the Clapper team insisted that Russian interference was extensive, Obama clearly still had doubts. These were reinforced by a succession of VIPS memos questioning the hack theory, with another one published on 17 January demanding proof that Russia was responsible for the DNC intrusion.[85] In his final press conference on 18 January Obama stated: 'The conclusions of the intelligence community with respect to the Russian hacking were not conclusive as to whether WikiLeaks was witting or not in being the conduit through which we heard about the DNC emails that were leaked'.[86] In other words, he accepted that there was reasonable doubt about how the material got to WikiLeaks. As for Trump, he sought to take advantage of the situation, and during the 2016 campaign repeatedly referred to WikiLeaks. From the FBI's perspective, it was 'problematic that a presidential candidate would use material stolen from a hostile foreign adversary for his own political gain'.[87]

On 6 January, the intelligence heads came to Trump Tower to see Trump. DNI head Clapper, CIA director Brennan, FBI director Comey and NSA director Mike Rogers met to discuss the main talking points, and Clapper was designated to take the lead, in full awareness that the report would challenge the legitimacy of Trump's win. Comey volunteered to stay behind and present the Steele dossier. As for the CIA, Brennan was haunted by the failures of his organisation in the Iraq War, accepting the account of a source codenamed Curveball that Iraq had WMD. In the words of the CIA director at the time, George Tenet in his presentation to President Bush, it was a 'slam dunk'.[88] Although such extravagant language was avoided on this occasion, Clapper argued that Russia had a long-standing desire 'to undermine the US-led liberal democratic order', that Putin had 'ordered an influence campaign in 2016 aimed at the US presidential election' and 'to undermine public faith in the US democratic process', and had 'developed a clear preference for President-elect Trump'. When it appeared that Clinton would win, 'the Russian influence campaign began to focus more on undermining her future presidency'.[89]

Trump responded with his disturbing mix of shrewdness and belligerence. Trump evinced scepticism about the lack of sources for such a bold assessment, and it was clear to Clapper that 'Trump was obsessed with anything that might challenge the legitimacy of his election victory'.[90] Three days later, Trump argued that the same people now warning against Russia were the same as those who had asserted that Saddam Hussein had WMD, and later that day told Fox News: 'They have no idea if it's Russia or China or somebody sitting in a bed some place', and he tweeted 'Unless you catch "hackers" in the act, it is very hard to determine who was doing the hacking. Why wasn't this brought up before the election?.[91] This was the start of a pattern in which Trump disparaged the 'intelligence community' and condemned the Russia investigation as a 'witch-hunt'. The intelligence community fought back. Already on 5 January Clapper told the Senate Armed Services Committee that 'There's a difference between scepticism and disparagement. Public trust and confidence in the intelligence community is crucial'.[92] Trump's questioning of what could legitimately be considered dubious intelligence community information was condemned as undermining confidence in the intelligence community. This tautological noose around Trump affected not only his domestic agenda but above all his ability to conduct an independent Russia foreign policy. This exasperating logic culminated at the July 2018 Helsinki summit, when Trump was excoriated for failing to endorse intelligence assessments and the Mueller indictments (an indictment of course is not the same as a conviction).

After the others had left, Comey provided Trump with a two-page summary of the Steele dossier.[93] Comey gives a vivid account of the meeting, telling Trump that 'the Russians allegedly had tapes involving him and prostitutes at the presidential suite at the Ritz-Carlton in Moscow from about 2013'. Trump interjected 'there were no prostitutes; there were never prostitutes' and argued that he was 'the type of guy who didn't need to "go there"'. In any case, Trump 'said he always assumed that hotel rooms he stayed in when he travels are wired in some way'.[94] Comey stated that 'We are not investigating you, sir'. 'That seemed to quiet him'.[95] Trump later stated that he felt that he had been 'shaken down' by Comey.[96] The briefing gave the dossier a legitimacy that was unwarranted. It licensed CNN to reveal its existence on 8 January, which in turn provoked *Buzzfeed* to publish the report two days later.[97] Clapper appears personally to have leaked Comey's meeting with Trump to CNN.[98]

The day after publication, in his 11 January 2017 press conference, Trump asked 'Does anybody really believe that story? I'm also very much of a germaphobe, by the way. Believe me', and he excoriated CNN for having reported on the Steele dossier.[99] The episode intensified the war between Trump and the intelligence community.[100] Trump was livid, and the day after the Steele dossier was published, he issued the intemperate tweet: 'Intelligence agencies should never have allowed this fake news to "leak" into the public. One last shot at me. Are we living in Nazi Germany?'.[101] In turn, the intelligence community was incensed by the comparison with the Nazis. Soon after the Senate Intelligence Committee, headed by Republican Richard Burr of North Carolina and Democratic vice chair Mark Warner of Virginia, announced the launch of a wide-ranging investigation into the alleged Russian attack on the American election, and the HPSCI soon followed suit. In the wake of the Church Committee's inquiry into CIA abuses, standing intelligence committees had been set up in both the Senate and the House in 1976 to hold the intelligence services to account, but Russiagate proved a severe test.

Woodward makes his view clear: 'I was surprised, not at the allegations, which might be true, but that the intelligence chiefs, particularly the FBI director, would present any of this to Trump'.[102] Clapper in his book *Facts and Fears* describes the ICA as 'a landmark product – among the most important ever produced by US intelligence', yet, Woodward notes, 'almost as an afterthought, Comey had introduced the dossier as if to say, by the way, here is this scurrilous, unverified, unsupported footnote with some of the ugliest allegations against you. They wanted the formal assessment to be believed by the president-elect. Why pollute it with the dossier summary?' Woodward argues that the Steele dossier is 'a garbage document. It should never have been presented as part of an intelligence briefing'.[103] Wolff puts the point well: 'The implicit conclusion: a compromised Trump had conspired with the Russians to steal the election and to install him in the White House as Putin's dupe'. Wolff nicely lays out the options: 'If this was true, then the nation stood at one of the most extraordinary moments in the history of democracy, international relations, and journalism'.[104] Commentators took this as the unvarnished truth and sustained the Russiagate story for several years. But Wolff goes on: 'If it was not true – and it was hard to fathom a middle ground – then it would seem to support the Trump view (and the Bannon view) that the media, in also quite a dramatic development in the history of democracy, was so blinded by an abhorrence and revulsion, both ideological and personal, for the democratically elected leader that it would pursue any avenue to take him down'.[105]

NOTES

1. Franklin Foer, 'Putin's Puppet', *Slate*, 4 July 2016, http://www.slate.com/articles/news_and_politics/cover_story/2016/07/vladimir_putin_has_a_plan_for_destroying_the_west_and_it_looks_a_lot_like.html?via=gdpr-consent.

2. Kimberley A. Strassel, 'Brennan and the 2016 Spy Scandal: Obama's CIA Director Acknowledged Egging on the FBI's Probe of Trump and Russia', *Wall Street Journal*, 20 July 2018, https://www.wsj.com/articles/brennan-and-the-2016-spy-scandal-1532039346.
3. Miller, *The Apprentice*, pp. 150, 153.
4. Woodward, *Fear*, p. 28.
5. Nance, *Plot to Destroy Democracy*, p. 21.
6. Strzok, *Compromised*, p. 136.
7. Mike Morell, 'I Ran the CIA: Now I'm Endorsing Hillary Clinton, *New York Times*, 5 August 2016, https://www.nytimes.com/2016/08/05/opinion/campaign-stops/i-ran-the-cia-now-im-endorsing-hillary-clinton.html.
8. Strassel, 'Brennan and the 2016 Spy Scandal'.
9. Strassel, 'Brennan and the 2016 Spy Scandal'.
10. Rivkin and Foley, 'Mueller's Fruit of the Poisonous Tree'.
11. The reporters included Jane Meyer of the *New Yorker*, Michael Isikoff of Yahoo News, and David E. Sanger of the *New York Times*. For wry commentary, see Meier, *Spooked*, pp. 148–51.
12. Hettena, *Trump/Russia*, p. 182.
13. Wolff, *Fire and Fury*, p. 37.
14. Vladimir Putin, 'Interview to Bloomberg', Kremlin.ru, 5 September 2016, http://en.kremlin.ru/events/president/news/52830.
15. Jake Rudnitsky, John Micklethwait and Michael Riley, 'Putin Says DNC Hack Was a Public Service, Russia Didn't do It', Bloomberg, 2 September 2016, https://www.bloomberg.com/news/articles/2016-09-02/putin-says-dnc-hack-was-a-public-good-but-russia-didn-t-do-it.
16. Isikoff and Corn, *Russian Roulette*, p. 212.
17. Isikoff, 'US Intel Officials Probe Ties'.
18. Rivkin and Foley, 'Mueller's Fruit of the Poisonous Tree'.
19. Franklin Foer, 'Was a Trump Server Communicating with Russia?', *Slate*, 31 October 2016, http://www.slate.com/articles/news_and_politics/cover_story/2016/10/was_a_server_registered_to_the_trump_organization_communicating_with_russia.html.
20. Eric Lichtblau and Steven Lee Myers, 'Investigating Donald Trump, FBI Sees no Clear Link to Russia', *New York Times*, 1 November 2016, https://www.nytimes.com/2016/11/01/us/politics/fbi-russia-election-donald-trump.html.
21. Meier, *Spooked*, pp. 208–11.
22. Dexter Filkins, 'Was There a Connection between a Russian Bank and the Trump Campaign?', *New Yorker*, 15 October 2018, https://www.newyorker.com/magazine/2018/10/15/was-there-a-connection-between-a-russian-bank-and-the-trump-campaign.
23. Comey, *Higher Loyalty*, p. 190.
24. Shimer, *Rigged*.
25. Timothy Naftali, 'How Generations of Russians Have Tried to Influence American Elections', *New York Times*, 5 July 2020, https://www.nytimes.com/2020/06/30/books/review/david-shimer-rigged.html.

26. Isikoff, and Corn, *Russian Roulette*, p. 230.
27. Isikoff, and Corn, *Russian Roulette*, p. 231.
28. Isikoff, and Corn, *Russian Roulette*, p. 255.
29. US Department of Homeland Security, 'Joint Statement from the Department of Homeland Security and Office of the Director of National Intelligence on Election Security', 7 October 2016, https://www.dhs.gov/news/2016/10/07/joint-statement-department-homeland-security-and-office-director-national; Woodward, *Fear*, p. 29, and other sources.
30. David A. Fahrenthold, 'Trump Recorded Having Extremely Lewd Conversation about Women in 2005', *Washington Post*, 7 October 2016, https://www.washingtonpost.com/politics/trump-recorded-having-extremely-lewd-conversation-about-women-in-2005/2016/10/07/3b9ce776-8cb4-11e6-bf8a-3d26847eeed4_story.html.
31. Isikoff and Corn, *Russian Roulette*, p. 245.
32. Strzok, *Compromised*, p. 165.
33. Omarosa, *Unhinged*, pp. 145, 305–6 and *passim*. While Omarosa did not personally hear him use the word, she believes that such tapes do exist.
34. 'Transcript of the Second Debate', *New York Times*, 10 October 2016, https://www.nytimes.com/2016/10/10/us/politics/transcript-second-debate.html.
35. 'Full Transcript: Third 2016 Presidential Debate', *Politico*, 20 October 2016, https://www.politico.com/story/2016/10/full-transcript-third-2016-presidential-debate-230063.
36. Miller, *The Apprentice*, p. 199.
37. Rhodes, *The World As It Is*.
38. Jonathan Allen and Amie Parnes, *Shattered: Inside Hillary Clinton's Doomed Campaign* (New York, Broadway Books, 2017).
39. For more detail, see Kevin Gosztola, 'It's Time to Reckon with Clinton Democrats who Pushed Russiagate', Medium.com, 26 March 2019, https://medium.com/@kevin_33184/its-time-to-reckon-with-clinton-democrats-who-pushed-russiagate-9ecb67cb60ae.
40. Personal discussion with Professor Greg Andrusz and Dr Peter Duncan, the two original examiners. See also Luke Harding and Stephanie Kirchgaessner, 'Ex-Trump Adviser Carter Page Accused Academics Who Twice Failed His PhD of Bias', *The Guardian*, 22 December 2017, https://www.theguardian.com/world/2017/dec/22/trump-carter-page-phd-thesis-trump.
41. Shane and Mazzetti, 'The Plot to Subvert an Election'.
42. Isikoff, and Corn, *Russian Roulette*, p. 181.
43. Hettena, *Trump/Russia*, p. 180. In the event, the 'privatisation' of 19% of Rosneft turned out to be a loan from Qatar.
44. Hettena, *Trump/Russia*, p. 179.
45. Strzok, *Compromised*, p. 148.
46. Ray McGovern, 'Comey's Amnesia Makes Senate Session an Unforgettable Hop, Skip & Jump to Fraud', *Consortium News*, 5 October 2020, https://consortiumnews.com/2020/10/05/ray-mcgovern-comeys-amnesia-makes-senate-session-an-unforgettable-hop-skip-jump-to-fraud/.

47. For details, see Ray McGovern, 'Will Comey's Words Come Back to Haunt Him?', Antiwar.com, 19 February 2021, https://original.antiwar.com/mcgovern/2021/02/18/will-comeys-words-come-back-to-haunt-him/.

48. Judicial Watch, 'FBI Records Show Dossier Author Deemed "Not Suitable for Use"'.

49. McCarthy, 'Connecting Dots in Clinesmith's Russiagate Guilty Plea'.

50. Horowitz does not name the lawyer, but it was later identified to be Kevin Clinesmith, Rowan Scarborough, 'FBI Deliberately Hid Carter Page's Patriotic Role as CIA Asset, IG Report Shows', *Washington Times*, 11 December 2019, https://www.washingtontimes.com/news/2019/dec/11/kevin-clinesmith-fbi-attorney-hid-carter-page-cia-/.

51. McCarthy, 'Connecting Dots in Clinesmith's Russiagate Guilty Plea'.

52. Ted Galen carpenter, 'How the Media has Whitewashed FBI Abuses in the Russia Probe', *The National Interest*, 14 October 2020, https://www.cato.org/publications/commentary/how-media-has-whitewashed-fbi-abuses-russia-probe.

53. HPSCI, 'Memorandum', 18 January 2018, https://intelligence.house.gov/uploadedfiles/memo_and_white_house_letter.pdf. For a summary, see Jarrett, *The Russia Hoax*, pp. 150–1.

54. HPSCI Minority, 'Correcting the Record: The Russia Investigation', 29 January 2018, https://cryptome.org/2018/02/democrat-page.pdf.

55. Editorial, 'A Dossier Debunking'.

56. Woodward, *Fear*, p. 327.

57. McCarthy, *Ball of Collusion*, p. 24.

58. McCarthy, *Ball of Collusion*, p. 273.

59. The official DNI response to the senators came on 27 January and reiterated the material in the 6 January ICA. Jason Leopold, 'Here's the Classified Letter about Russia that Senate Democrats Sent to Obama after Trump was Elected', *BuzzFeed*, 9 November 2018, https://www.buzzfeednews.com/article/jasonleopold/heres-the-classified-letter-about-russia-senate-democrats.

60. Strzok, *Compromised*, p. 182.

61. Office of the Director of National Intelligence, *"Assessing Russian Activities and Intentions in Recent US Elections", Intelligence Community Assessment, ICA 2017-01D*, 6 January 2017, https://www.dni.gov/files/documents/ICA_2017_01.pdf. (henceforth *ICA*).

62. *ICA*, p. i.

63. 'Full Transcript: Sally Yates and James Clapper Testify on Russian Interference', *Washington Post*, 8 May 2017; also in Senate transcripts, 8 May 2017, http://transcripts.cnn.com/TRANSCRIPTS/1705/08/cnr.06.html.

64. Ray McGovern, 'A Look Back at Clapper's Jan. 2017 "Assessment" on Russia-gate', *Consortium News*, 7 January 2019, https://consortiumnews.com/2019/01/07/a-look-back-at-clappers-jan-2017-assessment-on-russia-gate/.

65. Kailani Koenig, 'James Clapper on Trump-Russia Ties: "My Dashboard Warning Light was Clearly On"', *NBC News*, 28 May 2017, https://www.nbcnews.com/politics/politics-news/james-clapper-trump-russia-ties-my-dashboard-warning-light-was-n765601.

66. James Clapper, speech to the National Press Club, Canberra, 8 June 2017, http://www.anu.edu.au/news/all-news/speech-professor-james-clapper-ao-address-to-the-national-press-club.

67. For an uncritical assessment of the assessment, see Senate Committee on Intelligence, *Report on Russian Active Measures Campaigns and Interference in the 2016 US Election*, Vol. 4, *Review of the Intelligence Community Assessment with Additional Views* (Washington, DC, US Senate, 20 April 2020), https://www.intelligence.senate.gov/sites/default/files/documents/Report_Volume4.pdf.

68. *ICA*, p. ii and p. 1.

69. *ICA*, p. iii.

70. *ICA*, p. 2.

71. *ICA*, pp. 2–3.

72. *ICA*, p. 3.

73. *ICA*, p. 4.

74. *ICA*, p. 5.

75. *ICA*, pp. 6–12.

76. *ICA*, p. 13.

77. https://www.scribd.com/document/465248379/Declass-Document-503-20200610174821.

78. Meier, *Spooked*, p. 3.

79. Gessen, 'Russia, Trump & Flawed Intelligence'.

80. Gessen, 'Russia, Trump & Flawed Intelligence'.

81. See *Global Revolt and Global Order*, materials for discussion at the 13th annual meeting of the Valdai Discussion Club, October 2016, http://valdaiclub.com/files/13306/.

82. Gessen, 'Russia, Trump & Flawed Intelligence'.

83. Boyd-Barrett, *Russiagate and Propaganda*, p. 15.

84. Jack Matlock, 'Former US Envoy to Moscow Calls Intelligence Report on Alleged Russian Interfreence "Politically Motivated"', *Consortium News*, 3 July 2018, https://consortiumnews.com/2018/07/03/former-us-envoy-to-moscow-calls-intelligence-report-on-alleged-russian-interference-politically-motivated/.

85. 'A Demand for Russian Hacking Proof', *Consortium News*, 17 January 2017, https://consortiumnews.com/2017/01/17/a-demand-for-russian-hacking-proof/.

86. 'Obama's Last News Conference: Full Transcript and Video', *New York Times*, 18 January 2017, https://www.nytimes.com/2017/01/18/us/politics/obama-final-press-conference.html.

87. Strzok, *Compromised*, p. 157.

88. Woodward, *Fear*, p. 64.

89. Woodward, *Fear*, p. 67.

90. Isikoff and Corn, *Russian Roulette*, p. 291.

91. Woodward, *Fear*, p. 65.

92. Woodward, *Fear*, p. 65.

93. Strzok, *Compromised*, pp. 192–3 gives a good account of the meeting.

94. James Comey, 'Ex-FBI Director James Comey's Memos', https://assets.documentcloud.org/documents/4442900/Ex-FBI-Director-James-Comey-s-memos.pdf.

95. Comey, *Higher Loyalty*, p. 225; Comey, 'Ex-FBI Director James Comey's Memos'.

96. Woodward, *Fear*, p. 69.

97. Evan Perez, Jim Sciutto, Jake Tapper and Carl Bernstein, 'Intel Chiefs Presented Trump with Claims of Russian Efforts to Compromise Him', CNN 10 January (later updated to 12 January) 2017, https://edition.cnn.com/2017/01/10/politics/donald-trump-intelligence-report-russia/index.html. Following his resignation as CIA chief effective from 20 January 2017, Clapper was hired as CNN's national security analyst.

98. Jeff Carlson, 'Spygate: The True Story Collusion (Infographic)', *The Epoch Times*, 12 October 2018, updated 25 March 2019, https://www.theepochtimes.com/spygate-the-true-story-of-collusion_2684629.html.

99. 'Trump's News Conference', 11 January 2017.

100. Woodward, *Fear*, p. 71.

101. Isikoff, and Corn, *Russian Roulette*, p. 292.

102. Woodward, *Fear*, p. 69.

103. Woodward, *Fear*, p. 70.

104. Wolff, *Fire and Fury*, p. 38.

105. Wolff, *Fire and Fury*, p. 38.

Chapter 10

Flynn and the Russian Concussion

Obama was condemned for not having been more assertive in 'calling out' Russia's alleged interference. He made up for this in one of his last acts as president when on 29 December 2016 he sanctioned the GRU and the FSB, four senior officers in the GRU, and three companies that provided technical support for the GRU's cyber operations. In addition, the State Department expelled thirty-five Russian diplomats and closed two Russian-owned compounds, one in Maryland and the other in New York, which had allegedly been used for espionage. By then it was allegedly too late: 'A president beholden to Russia had been installed in the Oval Office: the most successful foreign espionage attempt against the United States in the nation's history'.[1] The gulf between the enormity of this claim and the weakness of the evidence is the core of the Russiagate problem. Omarosa notes how the Trump presidency became defined by what insiders called 'the Russian concussion'.[2]

FLYNN'S DOWNFALL

Michael Flynn was the controversial three-star general who as director of the DIA viewed Russia as a natural ally in what he considered a 'world war' against radical Islam, and to that end visited GRU headquarters in Moscow in June 2013.[3] In 2010, he co-authored a scathing analysis of U.S. intelligence failings in Afghanistan, which hardly enamoured him to the other security agencies.[4] As head of the DIA from July 2012, he provided a critical assessment of the Syrian Arab Army's fight against Al Qaeda and other jihadists, even though the CIA at the time was funding and training Syrian rebels. He was dismissed by Obama in August 2014 for alleged management failures, and possibly for his refusal to downplay the threat from anti-Damascus forces, earning him the enmity of Brennan and Clapper.[5] After retiring from the military, Flynn established a consulting agency advising foreign governments, a venture that would later cause him major headaches. In 2015, Flynn warned Trump that although Russia had updated its strategic forces and 'outsmarted us', 'You can't just have one view of Russia'.[6] In his book *The Field of Fight*, co-authored with the neoconservative hawk Michael Ledeen, Flynn called for the war against radical Islam to be ramped up, and for greater confrontation with Iran.[7] Flynn argued that Russia could be a potential ally against an 'enemy alliance' comprising such countries as Iran, Venezuela and North Korea.

In an interview with the *Washington Post*'s security analyst Dana Priest, he bragged about being the only U.S. officer allowed into the headquarters of the GRU.[8] Flynn was criticised for his paid visit to Moscow in December 2015 to celebrate RT's tenth anniversary. At the dinner he was placed next to Putin, although given the formal nature of the occasion, they hardly spoke.[9] In an interview there, he called for improved Russo-U.S. relations to defeat ISIS. Above all, despite those like Democratic senator Al Franken of Minnesota, who suggested that Flynn posed a 'danger to the republic', Flynn alerted his former employer, the DIA, about his visit, and later debriefed intelligence officials on what he had learnt during his trip. In short, 'Rather than a diplomatic embarrassment bordering on treason, Flynn's conduct at the RT event provided some modest benefit to the US intelligence community'.[10] Nevertheless, Obama's doubts about Flynn's judgement were confirmed when at the Republican National Convention on 18 July 2016 he led shouts of 'lock her up' against Clinton. A month later, on 16 August, the FBI started a counterintelligence probe against him called Crossfire Razor.[11] After the election, Obama warned Trump against employing Flynn, but the advice was ignored and on 18 November Flynn was designated national security advisor. There were always doubts about Flynn's suitability for the post, with Kissinger predicting that 'He'll be gone within a year'.[12] In fact, he lasted a mere twenty-four days in office.

Flynn and others in the Trump transition team swiftly became engaged in frantic diplomatic activity. Between election day and the inauguration, Kushner met with over a hundred people from more than twenty countries. On 1 December, Flynn and Kushner met the Russian ambassador Kislyak in Trump Tower where they discussed how to improve relations and the situation in Syria. Kushner advanced the surprising idea of establishing a private communication channel between the Trump team and the Kremlin, including possibly using encryption equipment in the Russian embassy, an idea rejected by Kislyak – not the action of a man engaged in collusion.[13] On 13 December, Kushner met Sergei Gorkov, a top executive at VEB (Vnesheconombank), to gauge how Putin viewed the new administration and how to work together.[14]

Then, in late December, Flynn held a series of conversations with Kislyak, which in the end precipitated his downfall.

In his press conference on 16 December, Obama lamented that the election had been 'dominated by a bunch of leaks', insisting that 'The Russians can't change us or significantly weaken us'. He revealed his condescending view: 'They are a smaller country. They are a weaker country. Their economy doesn't produce anything that anybody wants to buy, except oil and gas and arms'.[15] On 28 December, he signed Executive Order 13757 imposing exceptionally tough measures, to take effect the next day. It is not clear why Obama waited until just three weeks before the inauguration, with KT McFarland, Flynn's deputy, suspecting a trap to discredit the incoming administration.[16] On 28 December, Kislyak contacted Flynn about bilateral relations and the planned measures. Although Flynn is often represented as a maverick, in fact he coordinated his response with the White House in waiting. On 29 December, Flynn called senior Trump transition officials and after a twenty-minute discussion with McFarland the transition team at Mar-a-Lago 'hoped Russia would not ratchet up the aggression in responding to Obama's move'.[17] Flynn then asked Kislyak for Russia not to retaliate, to which Putin agreed on 30 December. On 31 December, Kislyak told Flynn that his request had shaped the response. Foreign minister Lavrov initially warned that Russia would respond reciprocally,[18] but later commented positively: Flynn 'urged us not to take the path of escalation and confrontation. Was that so bad? Was it against the interests of the American people or the American government that a potential member of the administration urged us not to harm the American diplomatic mission in the Russian Federation, not to take away property or expel diplomats?'.[19]

One of the first acts of the new DNI, John Ratcliffe, on 29 May 2020, was to declassify and release the record of the eight calls between Kislyak and Flynn between 22 December 2016 and 19 January 2017, five of which were initiated by Kislyak and three by Flynn (two of which were return calls requested by Kislyak).[20] The early calls dealt with an Egyptian UN Security Council resolution condemning Israeli settlements. In its final days, the Obama administration allowed the resolution condemning Israeli settlement-building in the West Bank to be placed on the UN Security Council's agenda, and then decided not to veto it. Obama had a testy relationship with the Israeli prime minister, Benjamin Netanyahu, but the timing of the contentious resolution, whether by chance or design (like the punitive measures against Russia), embarrassed the incoming administration. The Trump team sought to get Security Council members to delay or abstain, and Flynn specifically asked the Russians not to support the motion (he made similar calls to the other UNSC members). However, in the 23 December call Kislyak told Flynn that Russia would not vote against the resolution.[21] In response, Trump tweeted that the UN was 'just a club for people to get together, talk', and threatened that 'things will be different after January 20'.[22] Flynn's call to Kislyak on this issue and others was recorded by the NSA.

The crucial 29 December Flynn return call to Kislyak began with this topic. Kislyak reiterated that Russia would not support the U.S. position but stressed that Moscow was very interested in working with the new team on the peace process in Syria. The Kremlin sought a conversation on 21 January to congratulate Trump and discuss issues. The topic that would prove to be Flynn's downfall only came fourth, with Flynn telling Kislyak

> Do not allow this administration to box us in right now! ... depending on what actions the Obama Administration takes over this current issue of the cyber stuff ... they're gonna dismiss some number of Russians out of the country, I understand all that ... I know you have to have some sort of action, but to only make it reciprocal; don't go any further than you have to because I don't want us to get into something that have to escalate to tit-for-tat ... I really do not want us to get into the situation where we everybody goes back and forth and everybody had to be a tough guy here. We don't need that right now. We need cool heads to prevail. And we need to be very steady about what we are going to do because we have absolutely a common threat in the Middle East.

After some more discussion, Flynn repeats the request to reciprocate modestly, since if another sixty U.S. personnel were expelled 'you will shut down the embassy'. The most important thing was to 'keep this at even-kill level' to allow 'a better conversation where we are going to go regarding our relationship', above all to work together against common enemies, above all in the Middle East. The call ends with Flynn stressing 'Remember Ambassador, you are not talking to a diplomat; you are talking to a soldier. I am a very practical guy. It's all about solutions'. The transcript shows that Obama's sanctions were discussed, but only to the extent that they were an obstacle to rethinking the Russo-U.S. relationship and the ability to cooperate against common enemies.

Kislyak certainly considered Obama's measures a deliberate attempt to poison relations with the incoming administration. In his view, the allegations against Russia were sour grapes by the losers of the presidential election. In his 31 December call to Flynn, Kislyak says, 'And I just wanted to tell you that we found that these [Obama's] actions [were] targeted not only against Russia, but also against the president-elect ... and with all our rights to respond we have decided not to act now because, its because people are dissatisfied with the lost ... elections and, and its very deplorable'. Flynn responded, 'we are not going to agree on everything, you know that, but, but I think that we have a lot of things in common. A lot. And we have to figure out how, how to achieve those things . . . and be smart about it and keep the temperature down globally, as well as not just here in the United States and also over in Russia'. The final voicemail from Kislyak on 19 January enquired about scheduling the previously mentioned phone call between Trump and Putin after the inauguration on 21 January. Flynn did not return the call, which meant that Putin was not the first to congratulate Trump on his inauguration. By then, Flynn was engulfed in his own struggle for survival. On 28 January Trump told Comey 'that he has serious reservations about Mike Flynn's judgment'. He was furious about the missed call with Putin and blamed Flynn.[23] However, a fortnight later, on 14 February, he defended Flynn, stressing to Comey that his call with the Russians 'was not wrong in any way', but 'the leaks were terrible'.[24]

The Flynn probe launched in August had come up empty, and by 4 January the relevant case agent, Joe Pientka, prepared to close the Crossfire Razor file on the grounds that there was 'no derogatory evidence'. The Closing Communication was drafted, but at the last minute Strzok sent a text saying 'Hey, if you haven't closed [the Flynn case], don't do so yet'. He explained that the 'seventh floor involved', referring to Comey and McCabe. The reason for the change was the phone calls with Kislyak.[25] On the eve of the presentation of the ICA, at an Oval Office meeting on 5 January, Obama was briefed by intelligence leaders. In a follow-on meeting, attended *inter alia* by Comey, acting attorney general Sally Yates, vice president Joe Biden and national security advisor Susan Rice, Obama asked how much privileged information gathered by the NSC about Russia should be shared with the incoming Trump administration, and in particular Flynn. He insisted, curiously, that the FBI should do everything 'by the book', as if that would not be normal procedure in this case. A declassified email from Rice to herself dated 20 January notes that Comey affirmed that he was proceeding 'by the book', but he noted that Flynn was speaking frequently with Kislyak. Obama then asked directly whether 'the NSC should not pass sensitive information related to Russia to Flynn'. Comey answered 'potentially' but added that he so far had no indication that Flynn had passed classified information to Kislyak, but he noted that 'the level of communication is unusual'.[26] In June 2020, the DoJ made Strzok's notes on the meeting available to Flynn's new attorney, Sidney Powell, who had made her name years earlier in questioning the work of the Enron investigators.[27] There is some confusion over the date and precise attendance, and although Strzok is not listed as a participant, he must have been there to take notes.[28] The notes imply a top-level attempt to keep the Flynn case going, with Obama directing that 'the right people' investigate the case, even though up to then no wrongdoing had been discovered.[29] The controversial character of the discussion at the meeting has been used to justify Trump's claims that the outgoing administration was out to get him.[30]

This was the meeting when Yates learnt about the calls. In the next fortnight, she became increasingly concerned about the efforts to keep the Trump team in the dark about the Flynn probe, finding Comey's explanation of the investigation 'confusing and inconsistent'.[31] Yates believed that the White House should have been informed. At that meeting, Comey raised the idea that Flynn may have violated the Logan Act of 30 January 1799, which forbids negotiation by unauthorised persons with foreign powers with whom the United States is in conflict. In over 200 years, no one had ever been successfully prosecuted under this statute, and no one had even been charged with its violation since the Civil War. The Strzok notes reveal that Biden, who had earlier claimed no knowledge of the Flynn probe, endorsed the idea that Flynn had somehow violated the Act. Yates was sceptical, but deputy attorney general Rod Rosenstein's 'scope memo' of 2 August 2017 on the Mueller investigation authorised him to investigate whether Flynn had 'committed a crime or crimes by engaging in conversations with Russian government officials during the period of the Trump transition'.[32] As the incoming national security adviser, it would have been surprising if he had not. Instead, the FBI leadership investigated Flynn's conversation with Kislyak as some sort of criminal offence.

Pientka's memo moving to close the investigation, given to Flynn's counsel only in April 2020, revealed that one of the predicates to open the probe was the tip-off from a confidential human source (possibly Halper) about Flynn's contact with a person with links to the Russian state. The person in question is redacted but is most likely to be Svetlana Lokhova, who met Flynn and travelled in a car with him after a Cambridge University seminar in 2016. Far from Lokhova acting as some sort of honey trap on behalf of the Kremlin, the whole story smacks of a fabrication. This did not stop the FBI trawling the intelligence files to find something against Flynn, but after drawing a blank, the case was about to be closed. It was revived when David Ignatius, a reporter with 'long ties to the intelligence community',[33] published his column in the *Washington Post* on 12 January about the Kislyak calls and the sanctions issue.[34] The whole matter exploded into the public domain and set the wheels in motion that would crush Flynn. When Priebus, the incoming White House chief of staff and other officials questioned Flynn about the 12 January article, he insisted that he had not discussed sanctions. He repeated that claim to vice president Michael Pence and to press secretary Sean Spicer, and they in turn repeated this in press interviews.[35] When on 15 January Pence appeared on CBS's *Face the Nation,* he was asked about Ignatius's column, and Pence averred that Trump had won 'fair and square' and when asked about the Flynn calls declared 'I can confirm, having spoken to him about it', that Flynn's calls 'had nothing whatsoever to do with those sanctions'.[36] When it emerged that in fact sanctions (or more accurately, Obama's punitive measures) had been part of the conversations, Pence was furious.[37] At issue is the question of what precisely is meant by 'discussing' sanctions with Kislyak; does a request not to retaliate represent discussion? A genuine discussion would have entailed exploring how to get the painful sanctions lifted, and this was not discussed.

Telephone conversations of foreign officials are routinely recorded, but U.S. law stipulates that security agencies have to 'minimise' (i.e. keep secret) the names of any Americans caught up in such tapping. This was a legitimate transition call with the Russian ambassador, but in this case, the material was made available to Yates. She told the White House that Flynn's conversation with Kislyak had been recorded as part of the 'incidental collection' of authorised wiretaps, but the outgoing administration 'unmasked' Flynn's identity – which is illegal.[38] On 26 January, Yates told White House counsel Donald McGahn that intercepts showed that Flynn had not been truthful about his discussions with Kislyak, and she feared that Flynn could consequently become a target for Kremlin blackmail. This does not make sense, since even if he misrepresented the true character of his conversation to Pence about his conversations with Kislyak, this was hardly a blackmailing matter.[39] If the Kremlin did want to blackmail Flynn, they would have had no leverage, since Flynn had coordinated the Kislyak strategy with the Trump transition team.

Flynn repeatedly denied discussing sanctions, but the version of the recordings that made their way to the *Washington Post* in a further leak published on 9 February provided classified information revealing that the issue was at least implied.[40] The Obama punitive measures had been discussed, but not the broader issue of Ukraine-linked sanctions. Nevertheless, Flynn's position became untenable. McFarland believes that 'Flynn was targeted from the beginning by some highly placed intelligence community and Justice Department officials, as a way to get to Trump'.[41] Ultimately, the leaks created a media furore that reignited the Trump–Russia investigation and destroyed Flynn.[42]

This is the background to Flynn's fateful interview with the FBI on 24 January. The meeting was set up by McCabe, who called Flynn that day on other matters and casually suggested a talk with the agents.[43] McCabe told Flynn that he did not need a lawyer, and the FBI agents Brandon Van Grack and Peter Strzok did not warn him that he would be speaking under caution, allegedly because they wanted Flynn to be at ease.[44] Strzok and Pientka agreed not to show Flynn the transcript of the Kislyak call, inform him that he was the subject of a criminal or counterintelligence investigation or warn him that it was a crime to lie to the FBI. Bill Priestap, the FBI's counterintelligence head, was uncomfortable about not warning Flynn or informing the White House that Flynn was being interviewed, and he was not clear about the goal.[45] The chaotic character of the White House at the time allowed this to happen. Flynn believed the interview was purely informational, but as an intelligence professional, he was cautious and stressed that he could not recall precisely what was said or whether he asked Kislyak for Russia not to retaliate. The FBI's official record of the conversation (known as a 302 report) confirms that Flynn was non-committal, and that he did not directly deny talking about sanctions with Kislyak, and instead stated that he could not remember, was not sure and even conceded that it was possible.[46] The agents did not believe that Flynn sought to lie or cover anything up, but as Strzok put it, 'Flynn hadn't behaved as if he were lying. But what he had said wasn't true'.[47] It appeared that the recommendation once again would be to close the case. However, documents disclosed by the DoJ in May 2020 revealed that the draft 302 was prepared by Pientka, but it was then heavily edited by Strzok, who believed that Flynn had 'repeatedly and inexplicably lied'.[48] It was then revised further by FBI lawyer Lisa Page, who had not even attended the interview, and this version was never given to the court but instead a summary of the interview, a very unusual procedure.[49]

The agents did not believe that Flynn had knowingly lied to them, but the discrepancy between the transcript of his phone conversation and the interview apparently opened him up to blackmail (*kompromat*) by the Kremlin, and hence the case was kept open. The classified transcript of the conversation with Kislyak released in May 2020 showed that Flynn's behaviour was appropriate for an incoming national security advisor. The DoJ later argued that this was entirely consistent with U.S. national interests.[50] Pence also later reversed his position and on 11 May 2020 declared that he no longer believed that Flynn had lied to him and would welcome Flynn back to the White House.[51] Ultimately, as Glenn Greenwald argues, 'There was no valid reason for the FBI to have interrogated Flynn about his conversations with Kislyak in the first place. There is nothing remotely untoward or unusual – let alone criminal – about an incoming senior national security figure, three weeks away from taking over, reaching out to a counterpart in a foreign government to try to tamp down tensions'.[52] As a later report notes, 'If the goal was a legal trap, it worked'. The FBI agents had seen 'unmasked' transcripts of Flynn's calls with Kislyak but did not warn him that this was the case. Flynn was relaxed, especially since the counterintelligence probe into the Trump–Russia connection was secret, and he had done nothing wrong.[53] Nevertheless, the leaked transcripts allegedly showing discrepancies in his account made Flynn's position untenable. The official reason given for Flynn's resignation on 13 February was that he had lied to Pence, but Flynn continues to argue that he had been misrepresented. Nevertheless, his career as an administration official was over.

This was the beginning of intensifying difficulties for Flynn. He was investigated for failing to file income from Turkey or to report overseas contacts and his failure to register as a lobbyist before joining the Trump administration. In August 2016, Flynn accepted a contract with the Dutch firm Inovo BV to work on a project to investigate and defame Fetullah Gulen, an influential exiled Turkish cleric resident in Pennsylvania who had turned from ally to bitter enemy of Turkish president, Recep Tayyip Erdoğan. Flynn was threatened with criminal prosecution on the grounds that he had violated FARA. Flynn faced mounting legal fees, as did his son, also called Michael, who was also being investigated. On 1 December 2017, Flynn pleaded guilty to a single charge of lying to the FBI about the two conversations with Kislyak and promised to cooperate with the Russia investigation. As part of the plea deal, Mueller recommended no jail time. Pleading guilty to lying offered a lifeline out of what was becoming an escalating series of charges.

Flynn was under siege but so was the Trump administration. On 14 February, the *New York Times* ran a story stating, 'Phone records and intercepted calls show that members of Donald J. Trump's presidential campaign and other Trump associates had repeated contacts with senior Russian intelligence officials in the year before the elections, according to four current and former American officials'. In fact, there was no basis to the story. On 8 June, Comey testified under oath to the Senate intelligence committee that the *NYT* story 'In the main, it was not true'.[54] McCabe was more robust in his refutation, telling Priebus 'It's total bullshit . . . it's not true, and we want you to know that. It's grossly overstated'.[55] Nevertheless, the issue was turned to look as if the White House was trying to suppress the story. Communications 'between the Russian government and an incoming administration is a routine part of transition business'.[56] However, in the Trump era, nothing was routine as the Trump–Russia collusion charges rendered everything abnormal and destructive.

Flynn was replaced by H. R. McMaster who, interestingly in light of the deception examined in this book, in 1997 published *Dereliction of Duty*, an indictment of the Joint Chiefs of Staff and national leadership for the lies that led to the debacle in Vietnam. He concluded that more troops, more bombing and a land invasion of North Vietnam could have won the war.[57] McMaster was one of the 'adults in the room' who blocked some of Trump's worst instincts, but also blunted his attempts to end America's 'forever' wars. As for Flynn, a precedent was set for disrupting the peaceful transition of presidential power. The 'resistance' to Trump stressed the importance of institutions and due process, yet in this case, the new president's national security adviser was embroiled in a 'spurious investigation', and his career and reputation ruined, while the perpetrators went unpunished.[58]

Chapter 10

THE COMEY GYRATION

Comey is an old-style American public servant, with a strong sense of civic duty and commitment to American democratic institutions. This at least is how he presents himself in his memoirs. As deputy attorney general in 2004, he was prepared to resign in protest against the use of 'enhanced interrogation techniques' (aka torture) by the Bush administration.[59] He movingly describes the moment when Obama appointed him director of the FBI in summer 2013, recognising that an informal talk would no longer be possible once appointed: 'for over forty years [since the days of J. Edgar Hoover, who ran the FBI for 48 years from 1924 to 1972], the leaders of our government had understood that a president and an FBI director must be at arm's length'.[60] This is not the way that Trump understood matters. Comey describes the gruesome tête-à-tête dinner on 27 January 2017 in which Trump tried to impose a patronage relationship by asking whether he wanted to keep his job – although on more than one occasion Trump had confirmed that he wanted Comey to stay in post. Comey assured Trump that he could count on him to be 'reliable'. This was not enough, and Trump then expostulated: 'I need loyalty. I expect loyalty'.[61] Comey promised 'honesty', which Trump interpreted as 'honest loyalty'.[62] On escaping, Comey wrote up detailed notes on the conversation, which became his practice after all meetings with Trump.[63] Lewandowski and Bossie stress that Trump values loyalty above all else in employees.[64] Omarosa notes, 'His [Trump's] moblike loyalty requirements are exacting, imperishable, and sometimes unethical (as in James Comey's case')'.[65]

Trump soon became impatient with Comey, especially when the latter repeatedly refused to confirm publicly that he was not under investigation. Trump nevertheless may well owe the presidency to him. Comey made two decisive public statements about Clinton's emails: the 5 July 2016 announcement that on his own initiative he was dropping the email probe; and on 28 October that he was restarting it. Although the 5 July announcement condemned Clinton's conduct as 'extremely careless', his decision to drop the case pre-empted that of the DoJ.[66] Such matters are usually the prerogative of prosecutors attached to the DoJ and not the FBI (a department of the DoJ). However, DoJ head, attorney general Loretta Lynch, had been compromised by a chance encounter with Bill Clinton on the tarmac at Phoenix airport in Arizona on 27 June. Comey now took it upon himself to speak on behalf of the whole investigation, believing that it was a matter of ensuring that the 'reservoir of trust' in the independence of the FBI had to be maintained.[67] He used Russia to explain his odd behaviour, suggesting that classified information prompted him to act in this way. It is alleged that at some point in 2016, the FBI received unverified Russian intelligence about purported emails from Lynch to a member of the Clinton team in which she promised to go easy on Clinton. Although this information was almost certainly false, Comey allowed it to shape his action, fearing that should such exchanges become public the FBI would be discredited.[68] The tortuous logic is typical of Comey, whose 'loyalty was to his own conception of the truth' rather than to the law and institutions.[69] A later DoJ investigation found Comey's behaviour to be 'extraordinary and insubordinate' and his justifications unpersuasive.[70]

His revival of the email enquiry on 28 October is also closely bound up with Russia. Comey reopened the investigation 'to maintain the credibility of his original intervention', which was presented as part of a normal criminal enquiry and not a counterintelligence operation. But, 'Let's get to the bottom line. A handful of US intelligence officials, with Mr. Comey out front, meddled in the presidential race, potentially altering its outcome. They did so on grounds that they were somehow protecting America from Russia. This was their rationale for getting around the obvious and important inhibitions against such meddling'.[71] In other words, the substantive Russian influence on the contest was not what it did, but the response of others to what they imagined Russia may have done. Moreover, Comey's justification for his actions is illogical. He feared that false information could leak, and thus discredit Obama's DoJ by suggesting collusion between Clinton and Obama; but if the material did enter the public domain, they would still have to deal with the accusation, now compounded by Comey's action. There is therefore only one inescapable conclusion: Comey was 'trying to give the Obama administration a hand in clearing up the email problem of its anointed successor. Mr Comey himself has admitted that he might not have taken his second fateful intervention if he was not certain Mrs Clinton was going to win anyway'. Throughout, ostensible concerns about Russian intelligence activities were opportunistically entwined with anti-Trump motives.[72] The Clinton campaign has a justified grievance that reopening the email investigation just days before the election had a devastating effect on her campaign. However, by the same token, the Trump camp also has a legitimate claim that the collusion narrative undermined his support.

This leads us back to Comey's fateful decision to start the Crossfire Hurricane counterintelligence investigation on 31 July 2016. On the day that Comey dropped the probe into Clinton's emails, 5 July, Steele met FBI agent Gaeta and thereafter peddled his material to various other official contacts.[73] Bruce Ohr testified to Congress on 28 August 2018 that he met with Steele on 30 July and received information about his dossier, which he immediately took to the FBI's then-deputy director McCabe and Lisa Page, counsel to McCabe, and the investigation was started the following day. In August, he briefed Strzok and the DoJ's deputy assistant attorney Bruce Schwartz, lawyer Zainab Ahmad and Criminal Fraud section head Andrew Weissmann. With a reputation as an aggressive white-collar prosecutor, Weissmann in

June 2017 took on a managerial role in the Mueller investigation. He had been deputy and later director of the Enron task force, investigating the affairs of the Texas energy company in the early 2000s. In that capacity he doggedly investigated the failings of the illustrious accounting firm Arthur Andersen, leading to its closure with the worldwide loss of 85,000 jobs. Some years later, most of his convictions would be unanimously reversed by the Supreme Court.[74] Ohr made no bones about the fact that the material came from the Clinton camp, and told the others that Steele was 'desperate that Donald Trump not get elected', and that his wife Nellie Ohr, a former CIA analyst and expert on Russia, had been working for Fusion GPS since October 2015. Ohr sounded these warning before the FBI filed its first application for a surveillance warrant against Carter Page in October.

This is important, because the 'FBI and Justice Department have gone to extraordinary lengths to muddy these details'. Schiff, the HPSCI's top Democrat, incorrectly stated in January 2017 that the FBI probe team only received Steele's reporting in mid-September. This dating is designed to support the claim that the dossier played no part in the unprecedented decision to investigate a presidential campaign. The Papadopoulos material kick-started the probe, but it stretches credulity to believe that a stray conversation by a low-level campaign aide reported two months later by a foreign official could have sparked such a high-level response. The Ohr testimony also suggests that the FBI misled the FISA court in its warrant application. The FBI not only failed to inform the court that it knew that the dossier came from a rival campaign, but it also averred that Steele was 'reliable' and that his material was 'credible'.[75] The FBI effectively endorsed the 'uncorroborated narrative that Donald Trump and Russia were trying to hijack the presidential election'. Between July and October 2016, Clinton officials made over half a dozen attempts to get suspect evidence into the hands of FBI counterintelligence officials. It was a 'classic case of information saturation'; to inject political opposition research (known as 'oppo') into the FBI machinery. The FBI's counterintelligence apparatus was 'weaponized with political opposition research from one campaign against its rival'.[76] This was reason enough to dismiss Comey.

Comey's memoirs are remarkably unreflective about the Russiagate affair. Instead, he repeats three key points: that Russia 'sought to undermine confidence in the American democratic enterprise'; 'the Russians wanted to hurt Hillary Clinton'; and 'Putin wanted to help Donald Trump win'.[77] He notes that the FBI learnt in late July 2016 that Papadopoulos had earlier discussed obtaining damaging emails from the Russian government, and this is what prompted the FBI to open the investigation, although it was only made public in March 2017.[78] He thus discounts the Steele dossier, which he only mentions in the context of him making its contents known to Trump on 6

January 2017. On that day, as Comey puts it, 'We were sneaking in to tell him [Trump] what Russia had done to try to help elect him'.[79] Comey asserts that he was delegated by the other agencies to make the presentation, but Brennan suggests that Comey unilaterally decided to do this.[80] He briefed Trump on the existence of the Steele dossier, but failed to mention that it had been sponsored by the Clinton campaign and the Democratic Party. He also focused on the most 'salacious and unverified' parts of the dossier and avoided talking about the most controversial aspects suggesting that the Trump team was colluding with the Russians. McFarland provides a vivid eyewitness account of the dramatic events of these weeks and argues that the meeting was 'a blackmail attempt. Comey had information on Trump. It all turned out to be lies. Comey knew it was a lie'.[81]

By hiding its origins, Comey prevented Trump from defending himself adequately.[82] Comey told the president-elect that the FBI was not currently investigating him, although the broader question of possible collusion with Russia had been under investigation since the previous July. Comey describes the droll affair at a reception on 22 January for law enforcement agencies in the White House. Comey sought to blend in with the curtains to avoid being noticed, but Trump called him to the front and tried to hug him while whispering in his ear 'I'm really looking forward to working with you'. This looked to TV viewers like an embrace: 'The whole world "saw" Donald Trump kiss the man who some believed got him elected'.[83] The next meeting on 27 January was the one-on-one dinner. His next encounter with Trump was on 8 February, just after the notorious Bill O'Reilly interview on Fox News when Trump had been pressed whether he 'respected' Putin. 'I do respect him', Trump said. 'but I respect a lot of people. That doesn't mean that I'm going to get along with him'. 'But he's a killer', O'Reilly said. 'Putin's a killer'. Trump sensibly answered 'There are a lot of killers. We've got a lot of killers' ... 'What do you think? Our country's so innocent?'.[84] Trump asked what he was supposed to do: 'Say I don't respect the leader of a major country I'm trying to get along with?'.[85] The required response would have been ritual condemnation of Putin and his regime, something that Trump refused to do, reinforcing the suspicion that Moscow exercised some power over him.[86]

Their meeting on 14 February was devoted to the Flynn affair. The president insisted that Flynn 'is a good guy', and there was nothing wrong in talking with the Russians, but he had misled the vice president. He then said: 'I hope you can see your way clear to letting this go. . . . He is a good guy. I hope you can let this go'.[87] Comey certainly wasn't going to let the matter drop, and the rift between the two men widened. On 20 March, Comey dropped the bombshell to Nunes' HPSCI that the FBI was not only investigating Russian meddling in the election, but also 'the nature of any links between individuals associated with the Trump campaign and the Russian government and whether there was any coordination between the campaign and Russia's efforts'.[88] On 30 March, Trump called Comey at the FBI to ask him to 'lift the cloud of this Russia business', which made it difficult for him to do his job as president. He complained about the congressional hearing about Russia the previous week, in which Comey confirmed the FBI investigation into possible coordination between Trump and Russia. Comey once again stressed that 'we weren't investigating him', and Trump repeatedly asked Comey to make that public.[89] Trump was incensed by Comey's refusal to state publicly what he repeatedly told Trump in private – that he personally was not being investigated.

Trump came to regret not firing Comey at the beginning of his administration, and he felt that by holding the Steele dossier over him at the 6 January meeting, Comey was 'pulling a [J. Edgar] Hoover' to keep him in line (Hoover was famous for the pressure he exerted on politicians).[90] Bannon warned Trump against doing so: 'The day you fire him, he's the greatest martyr in American history. . . . They are going to name a special . . . counsel. You can fire Comey. You can't fire the FBI'.[91] Bannon argued 'This Russian story is a third-tier story, but you fire Comey and it'll be the biggest story in the world'.[92] Trump on 11 April again asked Comey to make public that he was not under investigation, but Comey was non-committal. Meantime, on 2 March 2017, attorney general Jeff Sessions recused himself from Russian matters. At his confirmation hearing on 11 January, Sessions asserted that 'I did not have communications with the Russians'.[93] The *Washington Post* publicised that in fact Sessions had on two occasions met with Kislyak, at Trump's Mayflower speech and then at the Republican National Convention in Cleveland, Ohio, from 18 to 21 July 2016.[94] These were cursory meetings (confirmed by the Mueller report), but Sessions felt that he was compromised and stood aside. Russian matters were now handled by Rod Rosenstein, who was confirmed as deputy attorney general on 26 April.

The end came in a typically Trumpian unceremonious manner. On 8 May, Trump requested that Rosenstein write a note describing Comey's performance as FBI director. Early on 9 May, Rosenstein delivered the three-page memorandum 'Restoring Public Confidence in the FBI' describing Comey's failings, in particular his pronouncements concerning Clinton's emails the previous July. He outlined the arguments in favour of sacking the erratic head of the FBI.[95] Later that day, Trump crudely announced Comey's dismissal in a tweet while the latter was in Los Angeles. This was only the second time in the FBI's eight-decade history that a director was fired before his ten-year tenure was over. Trump gave contradictory reasons for the sacking. At first he justified firing Comey because of his 'awful and unacceptable' behaviour in 2016 (meaning the Clinton emails), although Trump had said nothing about this earlier.[96] In his subsequent dismissal letter to Comey, Trump condemned him for mishandling the Clinton email affair and claimed that Comey had 'lost the confidence and respect of the FBI rank and file'. However, he added, 'While I greatly appreciate you informing me, on three separate occasions, that I am not under investigation, I nonetheless concur with the judgment of the Department of Justice that you are not able to effectively lead the bureau'.[97] In other words, he blamed Rosenstein, even though the memo had been drafted at Trump's request. Nevertheless, Rosenstein understood that Trump wanted to get rid of Comey, not the Russia investigation.[98]

Bannon believed that Comey had become a threat as the FBI was looking for Jared Kushner's tax records.[99] Trump's team at first tried to shift the blame onto Rosenstein, with Kellyanne Conway, Trump's spokesperson, arguing that 'This has nothing to do with Russia'. However, at the meeting with Lavrov and Kislyak in the White House on 10 May Trump told them: 'I just fired the head of the FBI. He was crazy, a real nut job. I faced great pressure because of Russia. That's taken off'.[100] In an interview on 11 May on NBC, Lester Holt suggested that Trump had accepted the DoJ's recommendation, but Trump would have none of it: 'But regardless of recommendation, I was going to fire Comey. In fact, when I decided to just do it, I said to myself, you know, this Russia thing with Trump and Russia is a made-up story, it's an excuse by the Democrats for having lost an election that they should have won'.[101] Comey fought back, releasing personal notes of his nine conversations with Trump (which itself could be considered an illegal leak of FBI documents). He let it be known that in the Oval Office meeting with Trump on 14 February about Flynn the president had asked him to 'let this go'.[102] As Trump stressed, Comey had assured 'on three separate occasions' that he was not under investigation but did not explain why he refused to make this public.[103]

McCabe argues that Comey's firing 'gave new urgency to the FBI's investigation of Russian interference in the 2016 elections – that interference was a fact, not a supposition – and into possible collusion by the Russians with the Trump campaign'.[104] This is odd because the top DoJ official overseeing the FBI's Russia investigation in early 2017, Dana J. Boente, was briefed as many as six times on its status and was told that there was no evidence of Trump campaign collusion.[105] Despite this, Comey ramped up the threat in his testimony to the HPSCI on 20 March, when he stated that the whole Trump campaign was being investigated for possible links with the Kremlin. McCabe now took this to a wholly new level. He was a lifelong Republican who took over as FBI acting director following Comey's dismissal. He enjoyed a successful career fighting organised crime and had strong views on Russia, considering it, as mentioned, 'a place where no distinction between crime and government exists'.[106] His dislike was only matched by the certainty of his belief that Russian interference in U.S. elections posed 'existential dangers to our life as a democratic nation' and the intensity of his detestation for the president. When Trump called the ICA a 'hoax', the FBI went into overdrive to investigate 'whether that man or his campaign solicited or cooperated with Russia's activities'.[107] McCabe believed that 'Russia is an existential threat to the United States'.[108] He feared that the Russian mafia and political interference, combined with Trump's disregard for democratic norms and civic virtues, represented a genuine threat to the American way of life. McCabe was later caught in the crosshairs of Horowitz's review of the release of information to the press about the FBI's investigation of the Clinton Foundation.[109] McCabe initially denied having authorised this, but a few days later conceded that he had in fact done so. This later provided a pretext for Sessions to dismiss McCabe on 16 March 2018, two days before his planned retirement, threatening his pension.

On 13 May, McCabe announced that the FBI had opened a formal criminal investigation into Trump.[110] At the same time, he sought to institutionalise the Russia investigation in the form of a special counsel investigation.[111] McCabe was not the only one looking for a scapegoat for America's domestic political crisis. Testifying before the HPSCI, Brennan on 23 May 2017 asserted that he was 'aware of information and intelligence that revealed contacts and interactions between Russian officials and US persons involved in the Trump campaign'.[112] He insisted, moreover, that he knew from past experience that 'the Russians try to suborn individuals, and they try to get them to act on their behalf either wittingly or unwittingly'. The 'witting or unwitting' phrase is straight out of the classic cold war playbook. In 1956, the chair of the House Un-American Activities Committee (HUAC), Francis E. Walter, declared that 'people who are not actually Communist Party members are witting or unwitting servants of the Communist cause'.[113] There is some justification for the view of Senate Judiciary Committee chair, Lindsey Graham, 'that Crossfire Hurricane was one of the most incompetent and corrupt investigations in the history of the FBI and DoJ'.[114] It was also one of the most politicised.

Lisa Page, counsel to McCabe, later testified that there had been 'indecision in the Bureau as to whether there was sufficient predication [evidence] to open [the investigation]'. However, within hours of Comey's dismissal, Strzok texted her: 'We need to open the case we've been waiting on now while Andy [McCabe] is acting [director]'.[115] They were keen to get McCabe's approval before someone perhaps less sympathetic to the idea was appointed permanent director. In the event, the *New York Times* on 11 January 2019 revealed that the FBI had earlier opened the counterintelligence investigation into Trump and that this morphed into the Mueller enquiry.[116] McCabe authorised both counterintelligence and criminal enquiries into Trump to give the cases solid footing.[117] A CNN article immediately after Comey's firing reported that Rosenstein and senior FBI officials 'viewed Trump as a leader who needed to be reined in, according to two sources describing the sentiment at the time'.[118] In a 13 May meeting with McCabe, Rosenstein even suggested wearing a bugging device to the Oval Office to entrap the president and mentioned invoking the 25th Amendment, which prescribes the action to be taken if the president is unable to fulfil his duties.[119] Rosenstein assumed that the Democrats would approve of the dismissal of Comey, the man who had done so much to undermine Clinton's campaign, but Comey was now useful to them as Trump's scourge.

On 16 May, Trump met Mueller to discuss the FBI directorship, although Mueller made clear that he was not a candidate. Then, on 17, May Rosenstein appointed Mueller special counsel to investigate 'any links and/or coordination between the Russian government and individuals associated with the campaign of President Donald Trump'.[120] Rosenstein had been considering this move for days and understood that the rules had changed since earlier broad investigations – Watergate in the early 1970s, Reagan's Iran-Contra in the 1980s and Clinton's Whitewater and Monica Lewinsky in the 1990s – and now investigations were more tightly controlled by the attorney general. With Sessions recused, it meant Mueller would report to him. Rosenstein maintained personal control over the whole Mueller enquiry, in large part to ensure that the FBI's over-heated suspicions that the U.S. government had been taken over by the Russians was contained.[121] Rosenstein was shocked to discover that on his own initiative, McCabe had made Trump a subject of an FBI investigation.[122] Rosenstein was trapped between Trump and the FBI and closely managed the process, hence it would not be inappropriate to call the whole business the 'Rosenstein investigation'.[123] When Sessions broke the news to Trump that a special counsel had been appointed, Trump was stunned: 'Oh my God. This is terrible. This is the end of my presidency . . . it takes years and years and I won't be able to do anything'.[124]

MICHAEL FLYNN ON TRIAL

One of the first victims of the Mueller investigation, not surprisingly, was Flynn, and the case demonstrates the dangers of coercive plea bargaining. Flynn is not a rich man, and he also apparently feared bankruptcy because of the Mueller probe. Flynn's son Michael worked in his father's consulting company, and his ties to foreign clients also exposed him to possible criminal charges.[125] In December 2017, Flynn pleaded guilty to the single charge of lying to the FBI about his contacts with Kislyak and agreed to cooperate with Mueller. He and his son were threatened with an unrelated FARA charge concerning lobbying work for Turkey. By the time of his sentencing in December 2018 the Mueller team had interviewed Flynn nineteen times and he had provided them with documents and communications about 'interactions between individuals in the presidential transition team and Russia'.[126] There was no evidence of collusion with Russia, so he was charged with lying; 'And it's not even clear he did that. The FBI officials who first interviewed Mr. Flynn [on 24 January 2017] didn't think he lied about his interactions with Russian ambassador Kislyak. More likely, Mr Flynn copped a plea to save his son from worse treatment at Mr Mueller's hands'.[127] As a CNN report in February 2017 put it, 'The FBI interviewers believed Flynn was cooperative and provided truthful answers. Although Flynn didn't remember all of what he talked about, they don't believe he was intentionally misleading them'.[128] Comey told HPSCI on 2 March that his agents 'concluded that Mr. Flynn hadn't lied but had forgotten what had been discussed'.[129] In new information, Flynn admitted failing to disclose a $530,000 lobbying contract with Turkey that he was fulfilling while advising Trump in 2016 and that he was being directed by Turkish government officials. Mueller recommended that Flynn should not receive a jail sentence after pleading guilty to lying to the FBI.[130]

The Flynn sentencing document outlined the 'serious' nature of his crimes and raised the question whether the Flynn–Kislyak conversation violated the Logan Act. As mentioned, this is the statute adopted in 1799 that criminalises negotiations by unauthorised persons with foreign governments that are in dispute with the United States. Only two people have ever been charged under this act, the last in 1852, and neither was convicted. Presidential transition teams routinely establish contact with their foreign counterparts, yet the moribund Logan Act was revived to send FBI agents to interview Flynn, who allegedly gave a false account of his discussions with Kislyak. At what was meant to be his sentencing on 18 December 2018, Judge Emmet Sullivan of the U.S. District Court in Washington launched an astonishing broadside: 'This is a very serious offence. . . . You were an unregistered agent of a foreign country [Turkey] while serving as the national security advisor to the president'. Referring to the secret payments from an agent of the Turkish government, he came close to calling Flynn's behaviour treasonous: 'Arguably, you sold your country out'.[131] It appears that Flynn ended his work for Turkey in November 2016, before taking up his official duties. Sentencing was postponed to allow Flynn to complete his collaboration with Mueller.

On 29 January 2020, Flynn petitioned the court to revoke his guilty plea, and on the eve of the scheduled 27 February 2020 sentencing hearing Flynn's new lawyer, Sidney Powell, filed for the case to be dismissed. The new legal team argued that the case against him was based on government misconduct, including withholding exonerative evidence, falsification of the 24 January 2017 interview, and political targeting against him as part of the plot to oust Trump. They called on Barr to probe FBI and DoJ abuses, which he did on 14

February when he appointed U.S. attorney for the Eastern District of Missouri Jeffrey Jensen to investigate the government's handling of the case. The remit covered such issues as whether the wiretap of his conversations was illicit and why he was 'unmasked'. On 7 May 2020, the DoJ on Jensen's recommendation filed a motion seeking to dismiss the prosecution of Flynn on the grounds that newly found documents revealed improper conduct by the FBI. Flynn had been cleared by FBI agents, and there appeared to have been no lawful reason to have interviewed Flynn. Barr stated the issue bluntly: 'They kept it [the case] open for the express purpose of trying to catch, to lay a perjury trap for General Flynn'.[132] Above all, 'there was no valid reason for the FBI to have interrogated Flynn in the first place', since it was entirely appropriate, and certainly not criminal, for an incoming national security adviser to communicate with an ambassador to reduce tensions.[133]

Nevertheless, Judge Sullivan opposed the recommendation and the case was sent into legal limbo amid attacks on the integrity of Barr himself.[134] Trump weighed in and on 7 May in the Oval Office warned that the officials involved in the Russia investigation and the Flynn case were guilty of 'treason' and would 'pay a big price'. The *New York Times* was right to warn that 'It is a small step from using the Justice Department to protect your friends to using it to go after your political enemies', but by insisting on Flynn's guilt and Barr's flaws, the paper added to the country's polarisation.[135] A three-person appeals court on 24 June ordered Sullivan immediately to dismiss Flynn's prior conviction for lying to the FBI.[136] Later the DoJ revealed a summary of its 17 September interview with William Barnett, the FBI's case agent on the Flynn investigation and later part of the Mueller enquiry, conducted as part of the Jensen review. The summary makes clear that Barnett believed that Flynn neither conspired nor colluded with Russia during the 2016 campaign, and above all believed that the Crossfire Hurricane investigation was 'opaque', with 'little detail concerning specific evidence of criminal events'. The predication to open the Crossfire Razor investigation into Flynn in his view was 'not great', and he considered the theory that there was something untoward in the changed wording of the Ukraine resolution at the RNC in July from the provision of 'lethal assistance' to 'appropriate assistance' was 'groping'. He believed the Flynn probe was an 'exercise in futility' and in December 2016 called for the case to be dropped. By 4 January, as we have seen, he was ready to close the case file, but this was blocked by Strzok. Barnett believes that this explains why he was excluded from the fateful 24 January interview with Flynn. He notes that by May, Crossfire Hurricane was winding down for lack of evidence but was revived by Mueller's appointment. In his view, the whole business was 'upside down', with investigators frantically looking for evidence of a crime. There was a 'get Trump' attitude by some in the special counsel office, with incidents involving Trump interpreted 'in the most negative manner'. For example, concerning Crossfire Razor he told Mueller attorney Jeannie Rhee that 'there was no evidence of a crime', but in his view 'Rhee was obsessed with Flynn and Russia and she had an agenda'. There appeared to be a competition between investigators to be the first to find 'something criminal there'. Investigators believed that interviewees were hiding information even when in Barnett's view they had no information. This explains the repeated and ultimately pointless but demeaning interviews of McFarland, which she describes in painful detail. In frustration, Barnett sought a transfer from the case.[137]

On 25 November 2020, Trump announced by tweet that he had granted Flynn a 'full pardon', provoking the now predictable partisan responses. Trump's allies welcomed the decision, but House speaker Nancy Pelosi called it an 'act of grave corruption and a brazen abuse of power'.[138] The Flynn charges always looked flimsy and politically motivated, but rather than exoneration by the courts, he was pardoned. The larger issue is well expressed by McFarland: 'The tragic irony not just for Flynn, but for the president and the country, is that the entire Russia investigation, the national hysteria, the collusion claims, and the obstruction of justice accusations all seemed to hinge on a supposed crime that had never been committed in the first place.'[139]

NOTES

1. Frum, *Trumpocracy*, p. 134.
2. Omarosa, *Unhinged*, p. 243.
3. Miller, *The Apprentice*, pp. 73–74.
4. Michael Flynn, Matt Pottinger and Paul D. Batchelor, *Fixing Intel: A Blueprint for Making Intelligence Relevant in Afghanistan* (Washington, DC, Center for a New American Security, January 2010), https://online.wsj.com/public/resources/documents/AfghanistanMGFlynn_Jan2010.pdf.
5. Larry C. Johnson, 'Michael Flynn Did Not Lie, He Was Framed by the FBI', *Sic Semper Tyrannis*, 6 May 2020, https://turcopolier.typepad.com/sic_semper_tyrannis/2020/05/01-december-2017-mueller-charges-against-flynn-exonerate-trump-of-russian-collusion-by-larry-johnson-the-news-of-mike-flynn.html#more.
6. Woodward, *Fear*, p. 61.
7. Michael T. Flynn and Michael Ledeen, *The Field of Fight: How We Can Win the Global War against Radical Islam and its Allies* (New York, St Martin's Griffin, 2017).
8. Nance, *The Plot to Hack America*, p. 55.
9. This comes from Putin: 'Putin's Dinner with Michael Flynn – "I Didn't Even Really Talk to Him"', Reuters, 4 June 2017, https://uk.reuters.com/article/uk-russia

-usa-putin/putins-dinner-with-michael-flynn-i-didnt-even-really-talk-to-him-idUK KBN18V0XX.

10. John Solomon, 'Exculpatory Russia Evidence about Mike Flynn that US Intel Kept Secret', *The Hill*, 2 January 2019, https://thehill.com/opinion/wh ite-house/423558-exculpatory-russia-evidence-about-mike-flynn-that-us-intel-kept -secret.

11. Eli Lake, 'The Railroading of Michael Flynn', *Commentary*, June 2020, https ://www.commentarymagazine.com/articles/eli-lake/michael-flynn-gets-railroaded-by -the-fbi/.

12. Bolton, *Room Where it Happened*, p. 7.

13. Miller, *The Apprentice*, pp. 209–10.

14. 'Statement of Jared Kushner to Congressional Committees', 24 July 2017, https://www.documentcloud.org/documents/3899497-Jared-Kushner-July-24-State ment-to-Congressional.html.

15. White House, 'Press Conference by the President', 16 December 2016, https ://obamawhitehouse.archives.gov/the-press-office/2016/12/16/press-conference-pre sident.

16. McFarland, *Revolution*, p. 178.

17. Rucker and Leonnig, *A Very Stable Genius*, p. 22.

18. 'Comment by Foreign Minister Sergey Lavrov on Recent US Sanctions and the Expulsion of Russian Diplomats', MFA, 30 December 2016, https://www.mid.ru /en_GB/foreign_policy/news/-/asset_publisher/cKNonkJE02Bw/content/id/2583996.

19. Embassy of the Russian Federation in the United States of America, *The Russiagate Hysteria: A Case of Severe Russophobia*, 18 April 2019, pp. 48–9, https:/ /washington.mid.ru/upload/iblock/3c3/3c3d1e3b69a4c228e99bfaeb5491ecd7.pdf.

20. ODNI, Flynn transcript of conversation with Sergei Kislyak, declassified 29 May 2020, https://assets.documentcloud.org/documents/6933340/Flynn-Transcripts .pdf. The release was prepared by the previous acting DNI, Richard Grennell. There are five summaries of conversations for 22, 23, 29 (twice) December and 5 January, and full transcripts of conversations on 23, 29, 31 December, 12 and 19 January. The transcripts can be found at https://www.foxnews.com/politics/read-flynn-kislya k-transcripts-of-conversations-during-trump-transition. For a good summary of the issues, see Larry C. Johnson, 'More Evidence of the Fraud against General Michael Flynn', *Sic Semper Tyrannis*, 31 May 2020, https://turcopolier.typepad.com/sic_semp er_tyrannis/2020/05/evidence-of-the-fraud-against-general-michael-flynn-by-larry-c -johnson.html.

21. For a full analysis of the incident, see Adam Entous, 'Donald Trump's New World Order', *New Yorker*, 18 June 2018, https://www.newyorker.com/magazine/ 2018/06/18/donald-trumps-new-world-order.

22. Natalie Samarasinghe, 'Can the UN Survive Trump?', *The World Today*, December 2018-January 2019, p. 34.

23. Bolton, *Room Where it Happened*, p. 417.

24. Comey, 'Ex-FBI Director James Comey's Memos'.

25. Kimberley A. Strassel, 'The FBI's Flynn Outrage', *Wall Street Journal*, 1 May 2020, https://www.wsj.com/articles/the-fbis-flynn-outrage-11588288438.

26. Susan Rice email available at https://www.foxnews.com/politics/susan-rice-email-declassified-release-is-imminent-source.

27. Weissmann, *Where Law Ends*, p. 66.

28. Andrew C. McCarthy, 'AG Barr Confirms: Strzok Notes are for January 5 White House Meeting', *National Review*, 25 June 2020, https://www.nationalreview.com/corner/ag-barr-confirms-strzok-notes-are-for-january-5-white-house-meeting/.

29. John Solomon, 'Strzok's Newly Discovered FBI Notes Deliver Jolt to "Obamagate" Evidence', *Just the News*, 24 June 2020, https://justthenews.com/accountability/russia-and-ukraine-scandals/strzoks-newly-discovered-fbi-notes-deliver-sensational. The link to the notes is: https://justthenews.com/sites/default/files/2020-06/231-1.pdf.

30. Christina Zhao, '"Trump was Right" About FBI Scramble to Assemble Evidence after 2016 Win, Texts Claim', *Newsweek*, 24 September 2020, https://www.newsweek.com/trump-was-right-about-fbi-scramble-assemble-russia-evidence-after-2016-win-texts-claim-1534191.

31. John Solomon, 'Obama DoJ Officials Privately Told Mueller they were Alarmed by FBI Treatment of Flynn', *Just the News*, 17 March 2020, https://justthenews.com/accountability/political-ethics/yates-other-obama-doj-officials-sounded-alarm-about-fbis-treatment; Lake, 'The Railroading of Michael Flynn'.

32. Lake, 'The Railroading of Michael Flynn'.

33. Toobin, *True Crimes*, p. 37.

34. David Ignatius, 'Why Did Obama Dawdle on Russian Hacking?', *Washington Post*, 12 January 2017, https://www.washingtonpost.com/opinions/why-did-obama-dawdle-on-russia-hacking/2017/01/12/75f87a0-d90c-He6-9a36-id296534b31e_story.html.

35. Mueller, *Report on the Investigation into Russian Interference*, Vol. 2, p. 29.

36. Lake, 'The Railroading of Michael Flynn'.

37. Mcabe, *The Threat*, p. 203.

38. Wolff, *Fire and Fury*, p. 95.

39. The argument is made by Jarrett, *The Russia Hoax*, p. 205.

40. Greg Miller, Adam Entous and Ellen Nakashima, 'National Security Advisor Flynn Discussed Sanctions with Russia Ambassador, Despite Denials, Officials Say', *Washington Post*, 9 February 2017, https://www.washingtonpost.com/world/national-security/national-security-adviser-flynn-discussed-sanctions-with-russian-ambassador-despite-denials-officials-say/2017/02/09/story.html.

41. McFarland, *Revolution*, p. 185. McFarland also became a victim of the investigation as she was questioned repeatedly by Van Grack (who had been recruited as one of the Mueller investigators) and other FBI agents, and thought that she was being punished for working in the Trump administration, *Revolution*, pp. 228–29.

42. Schrage, 'The Spies Who Hijacked America'.

43. Strzok, *Compromised*, p. 204.

44. Jarrett, *The Russia Hoax*, p. 192.

45. Lake, 'The Railroading of Michael Flynn'.

46. John Solomon, 'Dirty Dozen: The 12 Revelations that Sunk Mueller's Case against Flynn', *Just the News*, 9 May 2020, https://justthenews.com/accountability/russia-and-ukraine-scandals/dirty-dozen-12-revelations-sunk-muellers-case-against.

47. Strzok, *Compromised*, p. 204; for more details about the meeting, see pp. 205–13.

48. Strzok, *Compromised*, p. 209. The 2019 Horowitz review on FBI and DoJ misconduct in the handling of FISA Court applications found that on 10–11 February 2017 Strzok rewrote the FBI interview memo (the 302 Report) to suggest that Flynn had lied in the interview.

49. Solomon, 'Dirty Dozen'.

50. Eli Lake, 'Trump was Right to Pardon Michael Flynn', *Bloomberg*, 26 September 2020, https://www.bloomberg.com/opinion/articles/2020-11-26/trump-was-right-to-pardon-michael-flynn.

51. Lake, 'The Railroading of Michael Flynn'.

52. Glenn Greenwald, 'Obama Official Ben Rhodes Admits Biden Camp is Already Working with Foreign Leaders: Exactly what Flynn Did', 10 November 2020, https://greenwald.substack.com/p/obama-official-ben-rhodes-admits.

53. Editorial, 'The Flynn Entrapment', *Wall Street Journal*, 13 December 2018, https://www.wsj.com/articles/the-flynn-entrapment-11544658915.

54. 'Full Text: James Comey Testimony'; Woodward, *Fear*, p. 85.

55. Woodward, *Fear*, p. 84.

56. Schier and Eberly, *The Trump Presidency*, p. 130.

57. H. R. McMaster, *Dereliction of Duty: Johnson, McNamara, the Joints Chiefs of Staff, and the Lies that Led to Vietnam* (New York, Harper Perennial, 2017).

58. Lake, 'The Railroading of Michael Flynn'.

59. Comey, *Higher Loyalty*, pp. 100–15.

60. Comey, *Higher Loyalty*, p. 120.

61. Comey, *Higher Loyalty*, p. 237.

62. Comey, 'Ex-FBI Director James Comey's Memos'.

63. Comey, *Higher Loyalty*, p. 243.

64. Lewandowski and Bossie, *Let Trump be Trump*, pp. 43–44.

65. Omarosa, *Unhinged*, p. xxv.

66. For Comey's defence of his actions, see, *Higher Loyalty*, pp. 158–87, with the words 'extremely careless' at p. 175.

67. Comey, *A Higher Loyalty*, p. 180.

68. Comey, *A Higher Loyalty*, p. 178.

69. Toobin, *True Crimes*, p. 15.

70. Mayer, 'How Russia Helped Swing the Election for Trump'.

71. Holman W. Jenkins, Jr., 'Mueller's Report Will be a Bore', *Wall Street Journal*, 1 January 2019, https://www.wsj.com/articles/muellers-report-will-be-a-bore-11546298596.

72. Jenkins, 'Mueller's Report Will Be a Bore'.

73. John Solomon, 'How the Clinton Machine Flooded the FBI with Trump-Russia Dirt', *The Hill*, 22 January 2019, https://thehill.com/opinion/white-house/426464-how-the-clinton-machine-flooded-the-fbi-with-trump-russia-dirt-until.

74. Sidney Powell, 'Judging by Mueller's Staffing Choices, He May not be Very Interested in Justice', *The Hill*, 19 October 2017, https://thehill.com/opinion/white-house/356253-judging-by-muellers-staffing-choices-he-may-not-be-very-interested-in; for a full discussion, see Sidney Powell, *Licensed to Lie* (Sidney Powell self-publication, 2018). For commentary, see Wolff, *Siege*, pp. 63–94. For Weissmann's forceful defence of his actions, see his *Where Law Ends*, pp. 30–1.

75. Kimberley A. Strassel, 'What Bruce Ohr Told The FBI', *Wall Street Journal*, 17 January 2019, https://www.wsj.com/articles/what-bruce-ohr-told-the-fbi-11547770923.

76. Solomon, 'How the Clinton Machine Flooded the FBI'.

77. Comey, *Higher Loyalty*, pp. 188–9.

78. Comey, *Higher Loyalty*, p. 189.

79. Comey, *Higher Loyalty*, p. 212.

80. Andrew C. McCarthy, 'Was Brennan's "Intelligence Bombshell" the Steele Dossier', *National Review*, 31 May 2019, https://www.nationalreview.com/2019/05/john-brennan-steele-dossier-trump-russia-investigation/.

81. McFarland, *Revolution*, p. 274.

82. Holman W. Jenkins, 'Motive Matters in Trump Spygate', *Wall Street Journal*, 8 May 2019, https://www.wsj.com/articles/motive-matters-in-trump-spygate-11557268983.

83. Comey, *Higher Loyalty*, p. 232.

84. Comey, *Higher Loyalty*, p. 248. In some cases, such as the deaths of Badri Patarkatsishvili in 2008 and Alexander Perepilichny in 2012, Russia in the end was exonerated. See Paul Robinson, 'Death by Natural Causes', Irrussianality, 19 December 2018, https://irrussianality.wordpress.com/2018/12/19/death-by-natural-causes/.

85. Comey, *Higher Loyalty*, p. 249.

86. Contrast Biden's response to the same provocative question in an ABC interview on 17 March 2021, when he agreed that Putin was a killer, without asking for or providing context.

87. Comey 'Ex-FBI Director James Comey's Memos'; Comey, *Higher Loyalty*, p. 255; Woodward, *Fear*, p. 164.

88. Toobin, *True Crimes*, p. 46.

89. Comey 'Ex-FBI Director James Comey's Memos'; Miller, *The Apprentice*, p. 271; Comey, *Higher Loyalty*, p. 258.

90. Ray McGovern, 'Russia-gate Evidence, Please', *Consortium News*, 15 January 2019, https://consortiumnews.com/2019/01/15/russia-gate-evidence-please/.

91. Woodward, *Fear*, p. 162.

92. Wolff, *Fire and Fury*, p. 213; Toobin, *True Crimes*, p. 49.

93. Miller, *The Apprentice*, p. 266.

94. Wolff, *Fire and Fury*, p. 151.

95. McCabe, *The Threat*, p. 234; Woodward, *Rage*, pp. 44–54 describes the sequence of events.

96. Comey, *Higher Loyalty*, p. 264.

97. Woodward, *Fear*, p. 164; Omarosa, *Unhinged*, pp. 243, 244; McCabe, *The Threat*, pp. 10–11.
98. Woodward, *Rage*, p. 48.
99. Woodward, *Fear*, p. 163.
100. Matt Apuzzo, Maggie Haberman and Matthew Rosenberg, 'Trump Told Russians that Firing "Nut Job" Comey Eased Pressure from Investigation', *New York Times*, 19 May 2017, https://www.nytimes.com/2017/05/19/us/politics/trump-russia-comey.html.
101. Donald Trump, interviewed by Lester Holt, *NBC Nightly News*, NBC, 11 May 2017, https://www.nbcnews.com/news/us-news/trump-reveals-he-asked-comey-whether-he-was under-investigation-n757821.
102. Woodward, *Fear*, p. 164.
103. Weissmann, *Where Law Ends*, pp. 56–7.
104. McCabe, *The Threat*, p. 11.
105. Testimony given to Senate Judiciary Committee on 22 June 2020, and released by its chair, Lindsey Graham, on 15 January 2021. Rowan Scarborough, 'Justice Department Knew There was no Russia Collusion by Spring of 2017', *Washington Times*, 16 January 2021, https://m.washingtontimes.com/news/2021/jan/16/justice-department-knew-there-was-no-russia-collus/.
106. McCabe, *The Threat*, pp. x, 43.
107. McCabe, *The Threat*, p. 20.
108. Toobin, *True Crimes*, p. 78.
109. Strzok, *Compromised*, pp. 287, 308–9.
110. Toobin, *True Crimes*, p. 62.
111. McCabe, *The Threat*, p. 225; see also Woodward, *Rage*, pp. 52–54.
112. McGovern, 'Russia-gate Evidence, Please'.
113. Gareth Porter, 'The Real Motive behind the FBI Plan to Investigate Trump as a Russian Agent', *Consortium News*, 13 February 2019, https://consortiumnews.com/2019/02/13/the-real-motive-behind-the-fbi-plan-to-investigate-trump-as-a-russian-agent/.
114. Scarborough, 'Justice Department Knew'.
115. McGovern, 'Russia-gate Evidence, Please'.
116. Adam Goldman, Michael S. Schmidt and Nicholas Fandos, 'FBI Opened Enquiry into Whether Trump was Secretly Working on Behalf of Russia', *New York Times*, 11 January 2019, p. 1.
117. Sadie Gurman and Aruna Viswanatha, 'McCabe Approved Probe of Trump', *Wall Street Journal*, 15 February 2019, p. A4.
118. Cited by Porter, 'The Real Motive'.
119. Adam Goldman and Michael S. Schmidt, 'Rod Rosenstein Suggested Secretly Recording Trump and Discussed 25th Amendment', *New York Times*, 21 September 2018, https://www.nytimes.com/2018/09/21/us/politics/rod-rosenstein-wear-wire-25th-amendment.html; Toobin, *True Crimes*, pp. 66–67.
120. Toobin, *True Crimes*, p. 73.
121. Woodward, *Rage*, pp. 57–63.
122. Woodward, *Rage*, p. 59.

123. Woodward, *Rage*, p. 63.
124. Weissmann, *Where Law Ends*, p. 231; Toobin, *True Crimes*, p. 74.
125. Jarrett, *The Russia Hoax*, p. 197; Toobin, *True Crimes*, p. 130.
126. David Taylor, 'Trump Won't Speak to Mueller, Says Giuliani', *Guardian*, 17 December 2018, p. 35.
127. Strassel, 'Mueller's Gift to Obama'.
128. Reported by Glenn Greenwald, 'New Documents from the Sham Prosecution of Gen. Michael Flynn also Reveal Broad Corruption in the Russiagate Investigations', *The Intercept*, 14 May 2020, https://theintercept.com/2020/05/14/new-documents-from-the-sham-prosecution-of-gen-michael-flynn-also-reveal-broad-corruption-in-the-russiagate-investigations/.
129. Editorial, 'The Flynn Information', *Wall Street Journal*, 1 December 2017, https://www.wsj.com/articles/the-flynn-information-1512172863.
130. Jon Swaine, 'Tension for Trump as Ex-Aide Gives Inquiry "Substantial" Help', *Guardian*, 6 December 2018, p. 39.
131. Tom McCarthy and Stephanie Kirchgaessner, 'Michael Flynn: Former National Security Advisor Now Faces Jail', *Guardian*, 19 December 2018, p. 2.
132. John Solomon, 'Dirty Dozen: The 12 Revelations that Sunk Mueller's Case against Flynn', *Just the News*, 9 May 2020, https://justthenews.com/accountability/russia-and-ukraine-scandals/dirty-dozen-12-revelations-sunk-muellers-case-against.
133. Greenwald, 'New Documents'.
134. Kimberley A. Strassel, 'Barr vs. the Beltway: Swamp Creatures Heap Abuse on Him for Exposing Abuse at Justice Department', *Wall Street Journal*, 15 May 2020, https://www.wsj.com/articles/barr-vs-the-beltway-11589498654.
135. Editorial, 'Don't Forget, Michael Flynn Pleaded Guilty. Twice', *New York Times*, 8 May 2020, https://www.nytimes.com/2020/05/07/opinion/michael-flynn-charges-dropped.html.
136. 'Appeals Court Order Judge to Dismiss Charges in Flynn Case', *Just the News*, 24 June 2020, https://justthenews.com/government/white-house/appeals-court-orders-judge-dismiss-charges-flynn-case.
137. USA vs. Michael Flynn, 'Government's Supplemental Filing in Support of Motion to Dismiss', 24 September 2020, https://www.courtlistener.com/recap/gov.uscourts.dcd.191592/gov.uscourts.dcd.191592.249.0.pdf.
138. Katelyn Polantz, Laitlan Collins and Maegan Vazquez, 'Trump Announces Pardon for Michael Flynn in Tweet', *CNN*, 26 November 2020, https://edition.cnn.com/2020/11/25/politics/trump-pardon-michael-flynn/index.html.
139. McFarland, *Revolution*, p. 199.

Chapter 11

Suspicious Activity

There may have been no fire, but there was a lot of smoke. Even before Mueller published his report in March 2019, the investigation had resulted in over thirty indictments, six guilty pleas and two sentences. Although the Trump administration pressed for the enquiry to conclude before the November 2018 midterm elections, in fact it continued well after. What is striking about the mass of its activity is how tangential it was to the main charge – collusion between Trump and the Kremlin, as outlined in the Steele dossier and asserted by the Papadopoulos informants. Instead, collateral investigations resulted in trials and convictions, above all that of Trump's long-term lawyer and general fixer, Michael Cohen, who oversaw attempts to build Trump Tower Moscow. In the end, Trump's impeachment in late 2019 was provoked not by Russiagate but by 'Ukrainegate', his call with the new president of Ukraine, Volodymyr Zelensky, on 25 July 2019 and associated cold war and electoral matters. First, though, the investigation was gifted the extraordinary Trump Tower meeting, in which the Trump team appeared eager to solicit damaging information from a foreign power in the middle of an election campaign.

THE 9 JUNE 2016 TRUMP TOWER MEETING

The June 2016 Trump Tower meeting between Trump officials and a Russian lawyer came to light only after Mueller had been appointed, yet it became the cornerstone of collusion allegations. The story begins in May 2016 when the Russian lawyer Natalya Veselnitskaya met in Moscow with an old client, Aras Agalarov, and she told him about her work on the Magnitsky case. On 24 November 2008, the tax accountant Sergei Magnitsky was arrested and held in appalling conditions in pre-trial detention, and on 16 November 2009, aged only 37, he died in jail from pancreatitis aggravated by medical neglect. Magnitsky had worked for a decade for Bill Browder's Hermitage Capital Management, a joint venture registered in Guernsey with banking giant HSBC, which became the largest foreign-owned investment fund in Russia. Browder portrayed himself as an activist investor, who by pushing for improved governance increased the profitability of companies, and thus the value of his stake. Browder's company had long been accused of illegally exploiting various tax minimisation schemes, hence his offices in Moscow were raided by tax investigators on 2 June 2007. Soon after, a $230 million tax rebate was granted to some of his former companies in suspicious circumstances. According to Browder, Magnitsky exposed the subsequent abuse of office and wholesale fraud and corruption within the Russian investigative and executive establishment, although his account has been challenged.[1] After an indefatigable campaign by Browder, the U.S. Congress in December 2012 adopted the Magnitsky Act, against Obama's best instincts.[2] The Act sanctioned those allegedly involved in Magnitsky's death, although the factual basis may have been entirely false.[3] Not surprisingly, Moscow sought to lift the Magnitsky sanctions.

Veselnitskaya, a former prosecutor in the Moscow region and at the time head of a substantive law firm with some thirty employees, took up the case. The Mueller investigator Weissmann calls her a 'Russian operative', but the degree to which she was on a state-directed mission is unclear, although she was undoubtedly pursuing goals that aligned with those of the Kremlin – above all, to get the Magnitsky sanctions lifted.[4] The Human Rights Accountability Global Initiative Foundation (HRAGI) was created to pursue this goal, instructing the U.S. law firm Baker Hostetler, which in turn hired Fusion GPS – the very body that had hired Steele. Agalarov suggested that she meet with Don Jr, with whom he had worked during the 2013 Miss Universe competition.[5] Rob Goldstone had long been the main conduit between the Agalarovs and the Trumps, so it was natural to ask him to arrange the meeting. Emin Agalarov called Goldstone, and in turn Goldstone on 3 June emailed the young Donald:

> Emin just called and asked me to contact you with something very interesting. The Crown prosecutor of Russia met with [Emin's] father Aras this morning and in their meeting offered to provide the Trump campaign with some official documents and information that would incriminate Hillary and her dealings with Russia and would be very useful to your father.
>
> This is obviously very high level and sensitive information but is part of Russia and its government's support for Trump – helped along by Aras and Emin. What do you think is the best way to handle this information and would you be able to speak to Emin about it directly?[6]

Trump's response was famously enthusiastic: 'If it's what you say it is, I love it'. After several more email chains, the meeting took place on 9 June in Trump Tower. The repercussions resonate to this day. It was Goldstone and not the Russian government who offered 'dirt' on Clinton to entice Don Jr into the meeting, and no dirt was produced. However, the readiness to accept damaging information from foreigners was obviously inappropriate and evidence of 'collusion' between the Trump camp and Russia. Bannon considered the meeting 'treasonous' and 'unpatriotic'.[7] However, this view is shaped by his loathing for Don Jr., whom he referred to as Fredo, the gullible and weak son of mafia boss Vito Corleone in *The Godfather*.[8] Bannon was not the only one who had little respect for Don Jr; 'his father held him in extremely low esteem'.[9] For the Mueller investigators, 'There it was: The Russians made an offer. The campaign accepted'.[10]

The stage was set for the fateful meeting. Don Jr. was joined by Trump's campaign manager Paul Manafort and his son-in-law Jared Kushner.[11] Goldstone was present at the younger Trump's request. Four people attended from the Russian side: Veselnitskaya; her interpreter, Irakly Kaveladze, who held various positions in Agalarov's Crocus Group; Rinat Akhmetshin, a Washington lobbyist who had once served in Russian military intelligence and was now working for the Katsyv family in the Prevezon tax rebate case, but who appears to have turned up by accident (hence his sporty informal attire);[12] and Anatoly Samochornov, a New York state resident and a translator also working on the Prevezon and anti-Magnitsky Act cases. Veselnitskaya had defended Pyotr Katsyv, the former transport minister of the Moscow region (the territory surrounding Moscow city), who was also a wealthy and aggressive business entrepreneur. At the time of the Trump Tower meeting, Veselnitskyaya represented Katsyv's son, Denis, whose Cyprus-based company Prevezon Holdings had been charged by the U.S. attorney for the Southern District of New York (SDNY), Preet Bharara, of laundering the proceeds of the $230 million Russian tax fraud allegedly exposed by Magnitsky. Part of the money had been funnelled into the purchase of New York real estate.

Trump Jr. came to the meeting expecting to hear secrets about Clinton, and that is why he asked Kushner and Manafort to attend. Kushner turned up late and tried to leave early.[13] Veselnitskaya began by talking about Democratic abuses, but she soon turned to the Magnitsky Act and Russian countersanctions (the ban on Americans adopting Russian children). Veselnitskaya talked about the money that Browder had made for the Ziff Brothers (who had invested with Browder in Russia) that could have made its way to the DNC. Trump Jr. asked if she had any proof that the Clinton campaign or the DNC had received funds that could be traced back to Russia, and she answered negatively. At this point, Don Jr. texted Manafort to say that the meeting was a 'waste of time' and asked a subordinate to call him to provide an excuse to leave.[14] The meeting lasted no more than twenty minutes. There had been no discussion of the election and no cooperation.

The Trump Tower meeting is at the heart of the Russian collusion allegation. Goldstone was called to provide testimony to a special counsel grand jury, to both Senate and House committees, and nine hours of questioning to the Mueller investigation. His original email requesting the meeting has triggered a veritable avalanche of speculation, including a book (not surprisingly) by Goldstone himself.[15] Despite what the 3 June email said, there were no 'official documents' from 'the Crown Prosecutor of Russia', and nothing to 'incriminate Hillary', and it was not clear to what 'her dealings with Russia' referred. Trump, against all the odds, had just won the Republican primaries (although he was still to receive the official nomination), and thus a meeting with his team would be a premium event. Goldstone argues that he deployed exaggerated language to entice the junior Trump. He used the term 'crown prosecutor' which, since Russia is a republic, is nonsense, although a term familiar to Goldstone with his British background. Goldstone now argues that he was not entirely wrong in suggesting that the Russians wanted to help Trump, having witnessed the enthusiasm with which top Russian leaders sought to meet him during 2013 visit: 'Emin had spoken to me about how this woman was well protected, about money from Russians to the Democrats and that could mean Hillary Clinton, so surely that would have been useful to Trump'.[16] Goldstone admits that he 'puffed up' the language in his email, 'But I never thought in a million years that an email I wrote in about three minutes to Don Jr. would be examined by the world many times over. I just needed to get him to respond'.[17]

The matter is made murkier by the fact that Veselnitskaya had dinner with Simpson the night before, as well as after the Trump Tower meeting. She was a client of Fusion GPS, but Simpson plausibly denies discussing the Trump meeting on either occasion.[18] The relationship goes back to September 2013 when the U.S. Attorney's office in SDNY filed money-laundering charges against Prevezon Holdings, whose sole shareholder was the businessman Denis Katsyv. Browder initiated the case in December 2012 when he filed material alleging that Katsyv and Prevezon had been involved in laundering the illicit tax rebate associated with Browder companies. The defence against the charges, and against the Magnitsky Act as a whole, was led by Veselnitskaya, who had been the Katsyv family lawyer for a decade. She began to investigate Browder, and in spring 2014, Katsyv's defence team hired Simpson and Fusion GPS to find out more about his activities.[19] This was the beginning of a monumental feud between Simpson and Browder. They prepared a 600-page report, with some astonishing information about Browder's businesses. Links were suggested between Hermitage Capital's purchase of Gazprom shares and the New York investment firm Ziff Brothers, a long-standing Democratic donor for whom Browder had earlier made stock trades in Russia. Information about the Ziff Brothers appeared in Russian requests sent to the DoJ from the Prosecutor General's Office (PGO), headed by Yuri Chaika.

Although short, the meeting has generated a voluminous literature. The White House account of the meeting changed several times and involved 'deep layers of deception'.[20] The Trump team tried to obfuscate and deflect from the basic fact that it had been willing to accept assistance from a non-friendly foreign power during an election campaign. Trump later admitted that the meeting was indeed to 'seek political dirt', adding that this is 'totally legal', and this may be true. Trump later argued that he would listen if a foreign power had 'dirt' on an election rival – that was simply the way that politics, in his view, worked. This was at odds with the view of the new FBI director, Christopher Wray, who argued that the bureau would expect to be informed about any contact by a foreign power during an election.[21] Don Jr. may have violated federal statutes forbidding any foreign person to 'make a contribution or a donation of money or other thing of value, or expressly or implicitly promise to make a contribution or a donation, in connection with any Federal, State or local election; and for anyone to knowingly solicit, accept, or receive from a foreign national any contribution or donation prohibited [by this law]'.[22] Despite the comprehensive language, the law is vague, since it would make a foreigner writing a speech or providing information 'a thing of value'. It would be hard to put a value on Veselnitskaya's purported dirt.[23] The information provided by British intelligence and the Steele dossier was intended to affect the election, and thus would presumably fall foul of this statute. Equally, if Manafort, Don Jr. and Co. had met with Canadian agents in Trump Tower, no one would have batted an eyelid, or if Clinton had won, the meeting would have been irrelevant. However, the meeting became significant when Trump's victory became wrapped up in malfeasance allegations. When the meeting became public in July 2017, it encapsulated 'both the case against collusion with the Russians and the case for it. It was a case, or the lack of one, not of masterminds and subterfuge, but of senseless and benighted people so guileless and unconcerned that they enthusiastically colluded in plain sight'.[24]

Several complex stories intersect, and everyone appears to be deceiving everyone else. Veselnitskaya herself remains a controversial figure. It has been suggested that she indeed came to Trump Tower with material on Clinton that she anticipated would interest the Republican campaign, and that she had discussed the points to be raised with Chaika, covering Browder and the Ziff Brothers.[25] Goldstone recalls that these names were indeed mentioned, with Veselnitskaya bringing a memo that stated that Ziff

Brothers Investment, a U.S.-based firm, had made illegal share purchases in a Russian company (Gazprom) and evaded large sums in Russian taxes. Two of the three brothers were donors to Democratic campaigns, including Clinton's. Veselnitskaya also claimed that the Democrats benefitted from 'stolen money', material that the Republicans could have used against them. In April 2018, Veselnitskaya on NBC News declared that although she was privately employed, 'I am a lawyer and I am an informant . . . Since 2013, I have been actively communicating with the office of the Russian prosecutor-general'.[26] Goldstone, it appears, had been inadvertently correct in mentioning the involvement of the prosecutor-general (whom he called the Crown prosecutor). The meeting was also referenced by Putin at the Helsinki summit with Trump, when he talked about 'business associates of Mr Browder' who 'sent a huge amount of money' to Clinton.

When Browder was forced to provide a deposition in the Prevezon case on 15 April 2015, he was evasive and lacked a grasp of basic details about the Katsyv case and the Magnitsky affair in general.[27] A film by Andrei Nekrasov, *The Magnitsky Act: Behind the Scenes* provides a devastating examination of the inadequacies of the version advanced by Browder. The film portrays Browder as an entirely unconvincing witness.[28] A recent study, aptly titled *Grand Deception*, argues 'Rather than seeking justice for Sergei [Magnitsky], Browder gives the impression that he is cynically exploiting Sergei's death and his family's tragedy to vindicate himself and to inflict as much damage as he can on Russia and its legitimate leadership'.[29] The American Congress essentially adopted the Magnitsky Act in December 2012 on Browder's questionable version of events. The whole renewed cold war cycle of sanctions and countersanctions began with an act of deception.

Michael Cohen and Trump Tower Moscow

Cohen joined the Trump Organisation in 2006 as an all-round fixer and dealmaker, preparing property deals and silencing potentially hostile media stories.[30] Cohen progressed to become executive vice president of the Trump Organisation and acted as Trump's personal lawyer. At the heart of the Trump empire, he was uniquely placed to observe what was going on. In summer 2016, Cohen declared that 'he would take a bullet' for the president.[31] However, following the search of his premises by federal agents on 9 April 2018 and subsequent arrest, he 'put my family and country first'. Trump initially defended Cohen, arguing that the measures against Cohen were part of the 'witch hunt' and declared that 'I have your back', an implicit promise that as long as Cohen stayed loyal, Trump would stay loyal to him.[32] Trump condemned the investigation as 'an attack on our country', but thereafter relations broke down.[33] Cohen now believed that the president was 'unsuitable to hold the office', citing his refusal while standing next to Putin in Helsinki in July 2018 to accept the conclusion of U.S. intelligence agencies that Russia had disrupted the election.[34]

Threatened by a long prison sentence amid fears that his wife, Laura, would also be indicted, Cohen was induced to cooperate with the prosecutors – in other words, he 'flipped'. He makes some devastating comments about the American justice system, noting 'that if federal prosecutors want to get you, they will'.[35] Investigators looked into the limited liability company (LLC) he set up to manage cash flows for his work for Trump, and reached a plea deal with prosecutors. In the SDNY on 21 August 2018, Cohen pleaded guilty to eight felony charges, six of which involved bank fraud, tax fraud and campaign finance violations, and two implicated Trump in buying the silence of women with whom he had allegedly had affairs, and he later pleaded guilty of lying to Congress. Cohen is one of only two people to receive a substantial prison sentence (thirty-six months) as a result of the Mueller investigation. The SDNY continued to investigate the activities of the Trump Foundation, Trump University and the Trump Organisation as well as Giuliani and his two associates, the Soviet-born businessmen Lev Parnas and Igor Fruman, until the abrupt sacking of Geoffrey Berman, the U.S. attorney for the district, on 20 June 2020.[36]

The heart of the Cohen matter was cash payments in October 2016, just weeks before the ballot, to two women who claimed to have been paid hush money to keep quiet about their affairs with the future president. The payments were categorised as 'illegal campaign contributions' since the story would have embarrassed Trump in a tough election campaign. Stephanie Clifford, a pornography film actress who worked under the name of 'Stormy Daniels', was paid $130,000 to keep quiet about her affair with Trump. Karen McDougal, a former Playboy 'Playmate', was paid $150,000 in September 2016 by the *National Enquirer* scandal sheet for a story about her time with Trump, but then by arrangement with Cohen 'at the direction' of Trump did not publish.[37] This was a 'catch-and-kill' operation to silence McDougal, with the 'deception . . . designed to hide the true nature of Trump's character'.[38] Cohen claimed that Trump then repaid him the $130,000. Under oath, Cohen testified that Trump had directed him to commit a crime and encouraged him to file false invoices so that Trump could reimburse him. Trump insisted that the money did not come out of campaign finances but out of his own pocket. In a representative tweet of 10 December 2018, he insisted that the Democrats wrongly called 'a simple private transaction . . . a campaign contribution'. Once Trump was elected, the LLC was used to manage donations from companies seeking access to Trump, and its funds were used to pay for luxury items and the dues of private clubs. This was not the declared purpose of the LLC, which was real estate consultancy.[39] Cohen's lawyer, Lanny Davis, indicated that Cohen was ready to tell Mueller everything he knew 'about a conspiracy to corrupt American democracy by the Russians, and the failure to report that knowledge to the FBI', adding that 'If those payments were a crime for Michael Cohen, then why wouldn't they be a crime for Donald Trump'.[40]

Other matters were also investigated, including a $20m loan on a taxi business run by Cohen and his family. In an interview with CNN, Davis claimed that Trump knew in advance of the June 2016 Trump Tower meeting. By December 2018, federal prosecutors declared that Cohen acted at the direction of Trump when he committed the two election-related crimes in 2016. On 12 December, Cohen was sentenced to three years in jail for the crimes he had committed in Trump's employ. He also received a two-month jail term for lying to Congress when he stated that Trump Organisation efforts to build a tower in Moscow were terminated in January 2016, when in fact they continued to June. The charges focused on the hush-money payments to cover up the extra-marital affairs. Cohen insisted that Trump knew that he was doing wrong: 'He directed me to make the payments. He directed me to become involved in these matters'. He argued that he did as instructed out of 'blind loyalty' to Trump: 'I gave loyalty to someone who, truthfully, does not deserve loyalty'. Giuliani downplayed the charges, even though they were federal felonies: 'Nobody got killed, nobody got hurt . . . This was not a big crime'.[41] In the end, Mueller found nothing criminally of substance to connect the Trump Organisation's dodgy business practices and Moscow. The *Wall Street Journal* observed 'goodbye to Russia. You served your purpose. Vladimir Putin's effect on the 2016 election, we can now admit, was trivial – his real influence has come almost entirely through the willingness of US combatants to exploit Russia in pursuit of their own power ambitions and vendettas'.[42]

However, the story did not end there. Cohen was now cooperating with Mueller and in November 2018 headlines announced that Cohen admitted to lying over Trump's Moscow plans. The envisaged 100-storey Trump Tower would have been the tallest building in Europe, with Trump's name emblazoned in red at the top. In September 2015, Trump approved Cohen's plan to contact the Russian government about the project, and in December, Cohen began working with Felix Sater on the proposal. Cohen earlier claimed that such contacts ended in early 2016, before the crucial Iowa caucus vote that would set Trump on the road to the White House. In a letter to Congress on 28 August 2017, Cohen wrote that 'The proposal was under consideration at the Trump Organization from September 2015 until the end of January 2016. By the end of January 2016, I determined that the proposal was not feasible for a variety of business reasons and should not be pursued further', and insisted that he did not brief Trump or his family further on the project.[43]

In September 2017, in testimony before the Senate Intelligence Committee, Cohen stated that in January 2016 it was decided that the Moscow project 'was not feasible for a variety of business reasons and should not be pursued'. This allowed Trump to claim during the campaign that he did not have any business ties with Russia.

It was now revealed that the project continued until at least 14 June 2016, and there were even plans for Trump to travel to Moscow to discuss the proposal. Cohen admitted speaking to Kremlin officials in 2016 about securing Russian support for the project, even though earlier Trump had denied having any contact with them during his run for office. In his August 2017, submission Cohen admitted sending an email to Peskov, Putin's press secretary, about the project, but at the time said that he received no reply. Now Cohen admitted to Mueller that he did receive a reply from Peskov's office, and that in a phone call with Peskov on 20 January, he asked for help 'in moving the project forward'. Peskov later confirmed that his office had received two emails from Cohen in January 2016 requesting a meeting with Sergei Ivanov, then Putin's chief of staff, or with Peskov himself, to help establish the necessary business contacts.[44] Peskov stated that 'We called them back and asked what the Presidential Administration has to do with that and whether they are aware who they contacted'. Peskov showed the two emails, signed by Cohen, to reporters, and noted that in the twenty-minute conversation 'We told them that the Presidential Administration doesn't build houses, and if they want to invest in Russia then we will be happy to see them at the St Petersburg Economic Forum (SPIEF)'.[45] Cohen agreed to attend SPIEF, but on 14 June, two days before the event, he abruptly cancelled. As a result of the 9 June Trump Tower Veselnitskaya meeting, he had been shunning an increasingly desperate Sater.[46] Why Sater was so keen on pushing the Moscow project is itself a mystery. The cold call email to Peskov's team was clearly an act of desperation, described by Cohen himself as a Keystone Kop move.[47] Rather than showing high-level collusion, it revealed the amateurishness of Trump's associates. They lacked the high-powered real estate contacts required to build such an ambitious tower in Moscow.

The impression that they were out of their depth is reinforced by Cohen and Sater's suggestion that Putin would be offered a $50 million penthouse in the envisaged tower in the Moscow City business complex, and the rest of the units would be sold for $250 million each to the Russian elite.[48] By any standards, this was ludicrous – the 'Wild East' 1990s had long gone and Putin had no need for an apartment of this sort. In any case, such a development would have required the approval of Moscow's energetic mayor Sergei Sobyanin and collaboration with a top-notch development company. Instead, Trump's team worked with a second-tier company called I. C. Expert Investment with no experience of working in downtown Moscow, but with whom they signed a letter of intent in 2015.⁴⁹ There was little follow-up, but efforts to get the project off the ground apparently continued until June 2016, even though Mueller found emails showing that Cohen briefed Trump extensively even later. Emails with Sater moreover talked of a possible visit by Trump to Moscow once he had secured the nomination.⁵⁰ Peskov, as noted, suggested that Trump could be invited to SPIEF, where he would meet Putin and Medvedev.⁵¹ Trump was clearly keen on the project, but 'the campaign was far too chaotic and incompetent to actually conspire with the Russian government'. For Trump, 'politics was an opportunity to make money', and he was willing to bend U.S. foreign policy to that end.⁵²

Trump and his legal team submitted written answers in November 2018 and only then was Cohen's admission revealed. If the answers conflicted with Cohen's revised version of events, then the president would be open to charges of perjury. Trump apparently encouraged Cohen to travel to Moscow during the campaign to meet Putin and lock down the deal. 'Make it happen' is what Trump, according to *BuzzFeed* on 17 January 2019, told Cohen in one of at least ten meetings with him on the subject, and then characteristically denied having spoken to him at all on the topic.⁵³ The assumption, presumably, was that Trump expected to lose the election and sought to leverage his status as candidate while the going was good for a lucrative deal later.⁵⁴ The report alleged that Trump had personally directed Cohen to lie to Congress about the plans to build the tower. If true, Trump was now open to an obstruction of justice charge (the first article of the impeachment charge against Nixon), and something that Mueller appeared to have been angling for since the beginning. In the event, Mueller took the rare step to disavow the report as 'not accurate'. It was just one of over fifty Russiagate news stories that after a brief media feeding frenzy had to be retracted or seriously corrected.⁵⁵

As for Cohen, he served a year of his three-year sentence on federal charges of tax evasion, making false statements, lying to Congress and making illegal payments to women to silence allegations of past affairs with the president (which he denied). He was released in May 2020 because of fears of Covid-19 spreading in prisons. However, after tweeting about his forthcoming unflattering book about Trump, *Disloyal*, he was back in jail in July, although later once again allowed home. The book likens Trump to a Mafia boss and revealed all kinds of 'sins and crimes' in which Cohen got involved on behalf of his boss. This includes a discussion of Trump's rationale for approving the $130,000 payment to Stormy Daniels, fearing that exposure of the relationship would not play well with his supporters, although 'I bet they'd think it's cool that I slept with a porn star'. As for Trump's admiration of Putin, Cohen puts this down simply to Trump's love of money, believing that Putin was 'the richest man in the world by a multiple'. The book describes how bereft Cohen felt after his relationship with the president soured, since for years he had been 'Trump's first call every morning and his last call every night'. He knew Trump better than anyone, and he now described him as a con artist, a predator, a racist, a bully and a liar.[56]

PAUL MANAFORT AND UKRAINEGATE

In January 2016, the Obama White House convened a meeting of top Ukrainian corruption prosecutors and investigators, mostly from the National Anti-Corruption Bureau of Ukraine (NABU), with leading U.S. security officials to discuss anti-corruption efforts. By all accounts, the discussion quickly turned to two other politically sensitive investigations: Vice President Joe Biden's family involvement in Ukrainian business matters, and the participation of Paul Manafort's lobbying firm in Trump's campaign. On the former, Biden's son, Hunter, from April 2014 (two months after the regime change in Kiev) was on the board of the Burisma Holdings energy company owned by Mikola Zlochevsky, who under Viktor Yanukovych had been the minister for ecology and natural resources and who was under investigation in Ukraine and the UK for tax evasion, fraud and corruption allegedly committed while he was minister. The latter issue soon focused on reviving an investigation into payments to U.S. persons by the 'Russian-backed' Party of Regions. The 2014 FBI investigation focused on Manafort, whose company had long worked with Trump through his partner Roger Stone. The case was closed without prosecutions at the time, but it was not forgotten. Its revival is one of the earliest documented efforts to establish a Trump–Russia collusion narrative.[57]

Manafort was hired by the Ukrainian Party of Regions in 2004 and helped Yanukovych win the presidency in 2010. Between 2010 and 2015, Manafort worked for what the Western media invariably calls the 'pro-Kremlin' Yanukovych, although relations between Russia and Ukraine in this period were at best uneasy, and Putin is known to have loathed his Ukrainian counterpart. Luke Harding notes that Manafort was such an enthusiast for U.S. interests 'that the joke inside the Party of Regions was that he actually worked for the CIA'.[58] Typically, when Yanukovych in 2012 jailed his long-term rival, Yulia Tymoshenko, Manafort produced a 187-page report justifying her detention. Paradoxically, Manafort worked to turn Ukraine away from a pro-Moscow orientation by signing the Association Agreement with the EU. It is ironic that the main figure convicted in the Russiagate investigation into Russian collusion was in fact doing the opposite. By November 2013, he had convinced Yanukovych to sign the document, which would have marked the beginning of Ukraine's economic (and probably political) turn away from Russia. Manafort apparently also got the EU to agree to sign, even though

Tymoshenko remained incarcerated – earlier the EU position had been that there could be no deal while she remained in jail. In the event, at the last minute, on 21 November, Yanukovych decided to postpone signing, sparking protests that turned into an uprising, and ended in Yanukovych's flight from Kiev early on 22 February 2014. Manafort's former employee, Rick Gates, in his first trial in August 2018 claimed that Manafort received $42 million for his pro-EU lobbying from Sergei Lyovochkin, Yanukovych's chief of staff (although the latter denies this). Manafort's pro-EU work meant that he continued to play a role in Ukrainian politics even after the 'coup' against Yanukovych.

There are even suggestions (from cryptic exchanges between Manafort's daughters) that it was Manafort's idea to send militants to the Maidan on 29 November 2013 to provoke a reaction, which would force Yanukovych back to an EU-centred orientation. There is speculation that Lyovochkin deliberately used excessive force against the relatively small number of demonstrators that night to 'outrage the world'. The violence had the desired effect, and on 1 December up to half a million protestors came out on to the square. Arsen Avakov, Ukraine's interior minister between 2014 and 2021, is also of the view that the wanton and pointless violence of the riot police was a deliberate provocation, but events spiralled out of control. According to Gates, after Yanukovych's ouster, Manafort allegedly helped broker the deal on 25 March 2014 between Vitaly Klitschko and the oligarch Petro Poroshenko, whereby the former would stand for mayor of Kiev and the latter for the presidency. The deal was sealed in Vienna where the oligarch Dmytro Firtash was in exile fighting an extradition request to the United States. Lvyochkin was also there, and later we discover Manafort as well. Manafort remained a frequent visitor to Kiev, and he returned to participate in the regional elections of October 2015, where he supported Lvyochkin's new opposition party.[59] Just months later, he joined Trump's campaign. In sum, far from being 'pro-Russian', Manafort was playing a far more complex – and lucrative – game.

A secret 'black ledger' showing payments from the Party of Regions to Manafort had been known to the Ukrainian authorities since 2014, but on 29 May 2016, NABU announced its existence, just days after Manafort's appointment as Trump's campaign chair. Department of Justice documents, moreover, indicate once again the involvement of Bruce Ohr, his wife Nellie (who worked for Fusion GPS), and Steele. Nellie Ohr later admitted to Congress that she transferred Russian material on Trump from Fusion to the DoJ through her husband during the election. It was Nellie Ohr who on 30 May 2016 alerted her husband and other DoJ officials to the existence of the black ledger, which led to Manafort's downfall and subsequent prosecution.[60] Later, FBI documents, revealed by the conservative watchdog Judicial Watch, demonstrated just how central the opposition research firm Fusion

GPS was in driving forward the Russiagate narrative. Nellie Ohr compiled reams of research purporting to show connections between Trump, his associates and Russia. There are hundreds of emails between Bruce Ohr, Nellie Ohr and DoJ officials, with Bruce Ohr also acting as a conduit between Steele and the FBI after the former was cut off after speaking to the media.[61]

Fusion GPS throughout 2016 worked to encourage stories about the alleged corruption of Trump and his associates. One of these in late July discussed Manafort's activities in Ukraine.[62] In August 2016, the Ukrainian MP Serhiy Leshchenko published part of the ledger showing that Manafort received $12.7 million in undisclosed cash payments for his work in Ukraine between 2007 and 2012 on behalf of the Party of Regions and Yanukovych. Leshchenko reputedly was an associate of the Ukrainian oligarch Viktor Pinchuk, who donated millions to the Clinton Foundation. Leshchenko himself made no bones about his partisanship, telling the *Financial Times* that Trump was 'a pro-Russian candidate who can break the geopolitical balance in the world', hence most Ukrainian politicians were 'on Hillary Clinton's side'. This is what spurred Leshchenko and 'Kiev's wider political leadership to do something they would never have attempted before: intervene, however indirectly, in a US election'.[63] There were also investigations into various offshore accounts that helped fund Manafort's lavish lifestyle, as well as an $18 million deal to sell a cable TV station to a partnership put together by Manafort and the 'Russian oligarch' Oleg Deripaska, who the Western media invariably, although misleadingly, call 'a close of ally of President Vladimir V. Putin'.[64] Deripaska first hired Manafort in 2006 to help resolve his visa problems with the U.S. authorities, but the relationship later soured. Deripaska in 2014 launched a legal case in the Cayman Islands against Manafort for the recovery of $18.9 million he had invested in a cable-telecommunications deal and which had subsequently disappeared.[65] In September 2016, the FBI asked Deripaska to prove that Manafort was helping Trump collude with Russia, a notion that Deripaska dismissed as ludicrous. Steele and Bruce Ohr between December 2015 and February 2016 discussed securing evidence against Manafort.[66] Manafort's alleged Russia links ignited Russiagate concerns, even though the bulk of Manafort's work in Ukraine was directed against Russian strategic interests, above all by advancing Ukraine's closer association with the EU.

A Ukrainian court in December 2018 concluded that NABU's use of the ledger was an illegal attempt to influence the U.S. election. A NABU official is recorded as stating that the ledger had been released to help Clinton's campaign.[67] The judgement stated that Leshchenko had wrongly interfered in the 2016 election by releasing the documents about Manafort.[68] Leschenko admitted revealing the secret ledger payments to Manafort and conceded that he had been motivated by hostility to Trump. Later, there were allegations that the ledger had in part been forged or tampered with. Manafort insisted that its publication 'was a politically motivated false attack on me. My role as a paid consultant was public. There was nothing off the books, but the way that this was presented tried to make it look shady'. He was particularly upset that his work in Ukraine was presented as 'pro-Russian', when in fact 'all my efforts were focussed on helping Ukraine move into Europe and the West'.[69] As for Leshchenko, in evidence to Congress, it was later discovered that he was also a 'source' of Russian dirt on Trump that was fed to Clinton's opposition research firm Fusion GPS. Back in Ukraine, an investigation was opened into his purchase of a luxury apartment in mid-2016. Overall, this is another case of deceptive politics: 'a Ukrainian parliamentarian fed dirt to Clinton's team and leaked to the media information that harmed the Republican candidate's campaign? That seems like more collusion than was uncovered by special counsel Robert Mueller's investigation'.[70]

It is hardly surprising that the Ukrainian authorities favoured Clinton. She promised to supply offensive weapons to Kiev, a policy rejected by Obama fearing that it would exacerbate the new cold war. Trump's alleged pro-Russian sentiments prompted fears of a 'sell-out', above all by forcing Kiev to fulfil its commitments under the terms of the Minsk-2 agreement of February 2015. In March 2016, Trump stated that he did not want to 'go to World War 3 over Ukraine',[71] which seems an eminently sensible position. Nevertheless, his moderate stance on Ukraine 'boosted an inconvenient storyline for the campaign: that Trump was too cosy with Putin'.[72] The Democrats were certainly very cosy with the neo-nationalist regime that seized power in February 2014. Biden famously boasted at a meeting of the Council for Foreign Relations on 23 January 2018 that he had forced the Ukrainian president Petro Poroshenko to fire Ukraine's chief prosecutor, Viktor Shokin, by threatening to withhold a $1 billion U.S. loan. Shokin was conducting the Burisma investigation, and when he was sacked in March 2016, the probe transferred to NABU, and was promptly shut down – although it would be revived to haunt Biden's 2020 presidential bid and became part of the debates surrounding the impeachment attempt against Trump.[73] At issue is whether Biden sought Shokin's removal to protect his son Hunter from investigation for his work with Burisma, or whether Joe Biden's voice was just one of many calling for Shokin's dismissal because of his alleged failure to tackle corruption. Amid the welter of competing claims one thing is clear: the Burisma investigation was active at the time of Shokin's dismissal but became less so afterwards.

The Ukrainian embassy in Washington later admitted that DNC contractor Chalupa solicited dirt on Manafort, and even tried to enlist the Ukrainian president to help in the endeavour. Chalupa had earlier worked in the Clinton White House, and now worked as consultant for the DNC and prepared 'opposition research' on Trump. Chalupa's firm, Chalupa & Associates, was paid $72,000 by the DNC for its work in the 2016 election. She hoped to get information from the Ukrainian government about Manafort's dealings in the country and force the issue on to the congressional agenda. The Ukrainian ambassador to the United States, Valeriy Chaly, reported that the embassy considered her request to get Congress involved in investigating Manafort and rejected it 'as we were convinced that this is a strictly US domestic matter'. Chaly's written response nevertheless confirmed earlier stories that an American working for the DNC had tried to enlist Ukraine's help in the 2016 election. It appears that a senior embassy official, Andrii Telizhenko (who was later accused by the Democrats of being an agent of Russian disinformation), was instructed by the embassy to meet with Chalupa in March 2016 and to gather whatever dirt Ukraine had in its government records about Trump and Manafort. According to Telizhenko, Chalupa made no bones about what she was after: 'She said the DNC wanted to collect evidence that Trump, his organization and Manafort were Russian assets, working to hurt the US and working with Putin against the US interests'. Her ambition did not stop there: 'She indicated if we could find the evidence they would introduce it in Congress in September and try to build a case that Trump should be removed from the ballot, from the election'.[74] If this report is accurate, then this is incendiary material, exposing an attempt to enlist a foreign power in the attempt to remove an American presidential candidate from contesting an election. Telizhenko refused to take part in something that he considered illegal and unethical, but Chalupa kept up the work, attending an international symposium in April 2016 where she met sixty-eight Ukrainian investigative journalists to talk about Manafort, and in May the existence of the 'black ledger' was announced. Although the DNC has tried to portray Chalupa's work as that of a free-lancer, emails indicate that the DNC was fully informed of her activities.[75]

Chaly was at the Republican National Convention in Cleveland in July 2016 and met with members of Trump's foreign policy team. Despite his lobbying, an amendment to the Republican Party platform that promised to provide Ukraine with lethal weapons was watered down to keep it in conformity with what at the time was official U.S. policy.[76] Sanctions remained, but the only item that was rejected was the attempt to provide offensive weapons, a move that was also rejected by the Democratic Party platform adopted at this time.[77] Trump was sensitive to the issue, and on 25 July tweeted: 'Ukrainian efforts to sabotage Trump campaign – "quietly working to sabotage Trump campaign"'.[78] Trump was right, and the hostility of Ukrainians was evident in an op-ed written by Chaly in *The Hill* in August in which he condemned Trump's stance on Russia, arguing that it represented 'appeasement of an aggressor and supported the violation of a sovereign country's territorial integrity and another's breach of international law'.[79] The Ukrainians publicly questioned Trump's fitness for office and released materials that incriminated his campaign manager Manafort, forcing his resignation. This was a genuine case of meddling. Following Trump's victory, the Ukrainian authorities sought to make amends for their earlier support for Clinton until they were once again caught up in the impeachment scandal.

Before that, Manafort became one of the most high-profile victims of Russiagate. Manafort stood trial in Alexandria, Virginia, from July 2018 on charges of bank fraud and tax evasion and putatively in Washington in September on charges of making false statements about his foreign lobbying work and money laundering. Manafort had been part of Trump's campaign for only five months in 2016, working as campaign chair between June and August, but most of the charges predated this. His house in Virginia was raided by the FBI early in the morning of 27 July 2017, gathering much incriminating material. His Virginia trial ended on 21 August, and Manafort was convicted of eight federal felonies associated with financial crimes: five counts of tax fraud, two counts of bank fraud and one count of failure to report a foreign bank account, but there was a hung jury on the other ten charges. Manafort was accused of amassing $65m in foreign bank accounts between 2010 and 2014, while spending over $15m on luxury purchases. These offences had nothing to do with Trump, and even less with Russia, and were only prosecuted because they came into the crosshairs of the Mueller investigation. Manafort pleaded guilty to further charges to avoid the second trial in Washington, on FARA, money laundering, lying, tax conspiracy and witness tampering violations.[80]

By the time of the trial, Gates had been 'flipped' by the Mueller team, having cut a deal and now cooperated with the investigators in exchange for a reduced sentence.[81] Gates confessed to stealing money for and from Manafort, and confessed to a litany of offences, including falsified tax returns to setting up shell companies and misleading banks to gain loans, but claimed that he acted on Manafort's behalf. Gates along with Manafort was accused of working as 'unregistered agents of the government of Ukraine' and two Ukrainian political parties, that they had raised millions of dollars for Ukrainian entities, and laundered these funds through scores of 'corporations, partnerships and bank accounts', and drew on them without paying the required U.S. taxes.[82] Gates pleaded guilty in February 2018 to aiding Manafort in tax evasion, misleading accountants and deliberately misclassifying payments as loans.[83]

In a related case, on 20 February 2018, Alex van der Zwaan, a lawyer based in London who since 2012 had worked with Manafort on Ukrainian matters, pleaded guilty to lying to Mueller about his contacts with Gates and Manafort's associate Konstantin Kilimnik, and the part he had played in disseminating a report about Tymoshenko's trial.[84] He was sentenced to thirty days in prison and fined $20,000, but was pardoned by Trump in December 2020. There are many other incidents associated with Manafort. As we shall see, he was accused of passing on polling data to Kilimnik, who is alleged to have ties to Russian intelligence, who in turn passed on the information to two Ukrainian oligarchs (the initial story in the *New York Times* mistakenly named Deripaska).[85] Deripaska also figured in the rather strange story of the Belarusian model Anastasia Vashukevich (aka Nastya Rybka), who in early 2018 claimed to have sixteen hours of recordings made in August 2016 shedding light on the Trump campaign's ties with Russia.[86] In the tapes, Deripaska is allegedly heard discussing the election with other people, possibly Americans, leading to suggestions that Deripaska was the link between the Russian government and Manafort in the Kremlin's attempts to influence the election. In 2018, Deripaska won a court case against Vashukevich for having violated his privacy by publishing pictures of them together. The arrest and sentencing of the gun rights activist Maria Butina, and her fifteen months in an American jail before returning to Russia in October 2019, demonstrate the same new cold war presumptions and prejudices as Russiagate itself.[87] These stories, and there are many more, are part of the penumbra of Russiagate, intimating a web of conspiracy but dissolve on closer examination.

On 26 November 2018, Manafort's plea deal was rescinded by Mueller, on the grounds that he had repeatedly lied to the FBI despite agreeing to cooperate. According to Mueller, Manafort lied about five major issues after agreeing to cooperate with the prosecutors, including his 'contact with administration officials'.[88] The alleged lies constituted a new offence, and in March 2019, a Virginia court sentenced him to forty-seven months in jail, with nine months to be taken off for time already served, but a Washington court gave him three-and-a-half years in addition to the other sentence.[89] Manafort had been in jail since June 2018, largely in solitary confinement, when he was charged with witness tampering and had his bail revoked. It was at this time that it was alleged that Manafort had gone to see Assange in the Ecuadorian embassy in London in 2013, 2015 and March 2016, a few months before WikiLeaks published the Democrat emails. Assange denied that the two had met, and there was no record of his name in the visitors' log.[90] Craig Murray insisted that 'there were no exceptions' to the rule that visitors had to sign in, and he went further:

> I can also assure you that Luke Harding, the *Guardian*, *Washington Post* and *New York Times* have been publishing a stream of deliberate lies, in collusion with the security services. I am not a fan of Donald Trump. But to see the partisans of the defeated candidate (and a particularly obnoxious defeated candidate) manipulate the security services and the media to create an entirely false public

perception, in order to attempt to overturn the result of the US Presidential election, is the most astonishing thing I have witnessed in my lifetime.[91]

Greenwald commented on the allegation that Manafort had visited, and thus colluded, with Assange, with bitter humour: 'It is certainly possible that Paul Manafort, Roger Stone, and even Donald Trump himself "secretly" visited Julian Assange in the embassy. It's possible that Vladimir Putin and Kim Jong-un joined them'.[92] Possible, but unlikely.[93]

Campaign Financing and the November 2018 Midterms

The American public showed a healthy scepticism about the more exaggerated claims. A Gallup poll in August 2018 found that only 1 per cent considered Russia the top problem for the United States. The majority of Americans believed that it was important to continue efforts to improve relations between the two countries (58%), rather than taking strong diplomatic and economic steps (35%). In other words, the Trumpian line that it made sense to 'get on' with Russia was more popular than the Democrat line of piling on pressure.[94] The idea that a handful of GRU officers and hackers plus a bunch of people sitting in St Petersburg who spent about $100,000 on social media ads swayed the election result in 2016 was insulting and humiliating. The deregulation of campaign finances meant that Russian spending was a drop in the ocean. Expenditure on elections ballooned after the 2010 Citizens United case, which opened the floodgates on corporate and individual spending through so-called Super PACS (political action committees), allowing special interest lobbyists to spend millions on shaping voter preferences and getting the support of elected officials.[95] The decision allowed people like casino magnate Sheldon Adelson to spend his millions on elections, which in turn provoked the Cambridge Analytica scandal. Outside groups spent a record $6.8 billion in the 2016 presidential and congressional elections, some $300 million more than in 2012. Obama was right to argue that the Supreme Court decision 'strikes at democracy itself'.[96]

The midterm elections on 6 November 2018, with 35 Senate seats (26 Democratic and nine Republican) and all 435 House seats being contested, proved a testing ground for allegations of Russian interference. The midterms were widely seen as a referendum on Trump and his leadership. Trump once again proved himself a formidable campaigner, and although the Republicans lost control of the House, they consolidated their majority in the Senate. The Republicans won three seats to increase their majority to 53-47, but the Democrats won back control of the House of Representatives (235-199) by gaining 40 seats. The Republicans lost fewer seats (40) than the Democrats had in the 1994 and 2010 midterms (54 and 63, respectively). The structural imbalances of the U.S. electoral system were once again evident: the Democrats won 11 million more votes than the Republicans, yet proportionately the latter still came out ahead. The outcome was far from the anticipated drubbing, and it now looked possible for Trump to win a second term in 2020. His State of the Union 'unity' address on 5 February 2019 became his stump speech for the forthcoming campaign.

Although Russia had no particular dog in the midterms, it was once again accused of seeking to destabilise and subvert American democracy and to undermine trust in its institutions. In fact, the problem lay closer to home. Some $5.2 billion was spent on the election, a significant proportion of which came from America's leading 'oligarchs'. The three wealthiest families in the United States – the Waltons of Walmart, the Mars chocolate family, and the Koch brothers – enjoy a combined fortune of $350 billion, joined by the tech billionaires such as Amazon's Jeff Bezos, the owner of the *Washington Post*. The top three wealthiest billionaires – Jeff Bezos, Bill Gates and Warren Buffet – now enjoy as much wealth as the bottom half of the U.S. population combined. Adelson broke spending records on the election, donating $100 million to the campaign.[97] Not surprisingly, issues of social justice and inequality forced the Russiagate allegations near the bottom of voter concerns. The persistent problem of voting impediments once again came to the fore, with long queues, short voting hours, and various challenges to voter eligibility. The Economist Intelligence Unit assessed the United States to be a 'flawed' rather than a 'full' democracy.[98]

Democrats understood that other issues, notably health care and immigration, were more effective in challenging the Republicans than the Russia question. A Pew Research Centre poll at the time found that only 5 per cent of those who disapproved of Trump cited 'collusion with Russia' as the main reason.[99] The Mueller probe had lost potency and was regarded as biased. A CNN exit poll found that 54 per cent of respondents considered the Russia investigation 'politically motivated' and a 46 per cent plurality disapproved of the way that Mueller conducted it.[100] This also meant that a new wave of sanctions was unlikely, given that there was no evidence of Russian 'meddling' – Russiagate pressure appeared to be easing. Nevertheless, the collusion and interference charges remained the backbone of the attack against Trump, and with the Democrats back in control of the House, the charge was renewed.

Despite repeated warnings that Russia would attempt to 'meddle' in the midterms, there was no evidence of such activity. Shortly before the election, following a tip-off from the FBI, Facebook removed some 100 accounts allegedly linked to the IRA troll farm, but that was about it.[101] The U.S. Cyber Command, the military's cyber warfare division, launched a cyber-campaign against Russian operatives to 'curb misinformation' ahead of the 6 November vote.¹⁰² The IRA was taken off-line for the duration of the poll. Reflecting the military's dominance of the West Wing, in 2017 the Trump administration raised the status of the U.S. Cyber Command by placing it under the Department of Defence, and in August of the following year, it eased Obama-era rules governing the use of cyber weapons.¹⁰³ In the event, Russiagate was not salient, and Russia as a topic was well down the list of concerns. One study of the pre-election period found that only 0.1 per cent of ads aired in congressional races mentioned Russia. It was as if the whole vast furore over Russian interference had evaporated. The Russiagate affair had 'not gone as advertised'.¹⁰⁴ However, Bolton was right to note during an interview with the *Ekho Moskvy* radio station during his visit to Moscow on 22 October 2018 that Russian meddling in the U.S. election in 2016 did not affect the outcome but it did 'sow enormous mistrust of Russia'. He went on to warn that 'You shouldn't meddle in our elections because you are not advancing Russian interest', and he called meddling 'a major obstacle' to achieving agreement where the two countries had shared interests.¹⁰⁵ By this time, the Trump administration had come to view Chinese influence as rather more of a threat. Bolton notes that 'Viewed without partisan blinders, China could bring considerably greater resources to bear on this effort [election meddling] than Russia'.¹⁰⁶ This did not prevent Trump reportedly pleading with Xi to ensure that he would win in 2020 by increasing purchases of soybeans and wheat.¹⁰⁷

The Democrat take-over of the House gave it greater subpoena power. In the gleeful words of the *New Yorker,* 'the period of serious investigation of Donald Trump is about to begin'. The results certainly made it harder for Trump to terminate the special counsel's work. Half a dozen House committees enjoyed the power to investigate Trump, including Intelligence, Oversight, Judiciary and others, which issued subpoenas and compelled testimony.¹⁰⁸ The winners of the midterms were the Trumpist Republicans and radical Democrats, each offering voters 'an emotionally charged image of an enemy instead of a constructive image of the future', while the moderate Democrats and Republicans lost.¹⁰⁹ The House could now block Trump's legislative agenda, such as his wall with Mexico, and exert greater pressure for him to reveal his tax returns and private banking records, investigate possible conflicts of interest in his various businesses, and to reinvigorate the flagging investigation into his alleged collusion with Russia in 2016.

Schiff took over as chair of the HPSCI and made the Russia issue his top priority. His work enjoyed the support of the intelligence community, especially over the issue of whether Trump had tried to obstruct the FBI investigation into the president's dealing with Moscow when he fired Comey.¹¹⁰ Schiff examined whether Russia had financial leverage over the president through investments in Trump's business empire and whether Russians were laundering money through the Trump Organisation. Other questions included

Trump's financial relationship with Deutsche Bank, social media interference, the Republican Party's search for Clinton's emails and who Trump Jr. telephoned in between his calls setting up the meeting with Veselnitskaya.[111] Schiff tried to recall Bannon and Cohen 'to get answers that the GOP majority wouldn't or couldn't extract'. The Committee acted as 'Mueller's congressional backstop' and then its continuation.[112] The Committee effectively replicated the work of the Mueller investigation, hoping for a different outcome.

NOTES

1. For detailed investigation, see Lucy Komisar, 'The Man Behind the Magnitsky Act', *100Reporters*, 20 October 2017, https://100r.org/2017/10/magnitsky/ and her numerous other works on the subject. For a concise introduction to the case, see John Ryan, 'Bill Browder: A Billionaire Accused of Being a Fraud and a Liar', *The Unz Review*, 1 July 2020, https://www.unz.com/article/bill-browder-a-billionaire-accused-of-being-a-fraud-and-liar/.

2. For Browder's view and Obama's reservations, see Bill Browder, *Red Notice: How I became Putin's No. 1 Enemy* (London, Bantam Press, 2015).

3. Benjamin Bidder, 'Questions Cloud Story Behind US Sanctions', *Spiegel*, 26 November 2019, https://www.spiegel.de/international/world/the-case-of-sergei-magnitsky-anti-corruption-champion-or-corrupt-anti-hero-a-1297796.html.

4. Weissmann, *Where Law Ends*, covers the meeting pp. 78–99, and repeatedly calls Veselnitskaya a 'Russian Operative'.

5. Joshua Yaffa, 'How Bill Browder Became Russia's Most Wanted Man', *New Yorker*, 20 August 2018, https://www.newyorker.com/magazine/2018/08/20/how-bill-browder-became-russias-most-wanted-man.

6. Isikoff and Corn, *Russian Roulette*, pp. 117–18. Mueller exposed Don Jr.'s email chain about the meeting on 11 July 2017.

7. Weissmann, *Where Law Ends*, p. 95.

8. Hettena, *Trump/Russia*, p. 133.

9. Cohen, *Disloyal*, p. 37.

10. Weissmann, *Where Law Ends*, p. 83.

11. Andrew Roth, 'The Man Who Drives Trump's Russia Connection'' *Washington Post*, 22 July 2017; Ivan Watson, Barbara Arvanitidis and Darya Tarasova, 'Trump's Web of Russian Ties Grows with Miss Universe Links', *CNN*, 12 July 2017, http://www.cnn.com/2017/07/11/politics/trump-russia-lawyer-web/index.html.

12. Interesting material on Akhmetshin and Prevezon is in Meier, *Spooked*, pp. 77–83, 250–3.

13. Rucker and Leonnig, *A Very Stable Genius*, p. 116.

14. All sources are agreed on this, including Weissmann, *Where Law Ends*, p. 96.

15. Rob Goldstone, *Pop Stars, Pageants and Presidents: How an Email Changed my Life* (London, Oui2 Entertainment, 2018).

16. Sengupta, 'Trump Tried to Tempt Putin'.

17. Adam Birkan, 'The Magazine Interview: Rob Goldstone on Setting up Trump Jr and Russia', *The Sunday Times*, 19 November 2017, https://www.thetimes.co.uk/article/the-magazine-interview-rob-goldstone-on-setting-up-trump-jr-and-russia-hsl6jcn6g.
18. Simpson and Fritsch, *Crime in Progress*, pp. 71–72, 198–201.
19. Hettena, *Trump/Russia*, p. 171.
20. Weissmann, *Where Law Ends*, p. 99.
21. David Gardner, 'Trump I'd Want to Listen if Foreign Power had Dirt on Election Rival', *Evening Standard*, 13 June 2019, p. 18.
22. 52USC 30121, 36 UUSC 5210.
23. Weissmann, *Where Law Ends*, p. 97.
24. Wolff, *Fire and Fury*, p. 254.
25. Sharon LaFraniere and Andrew E. Kramer, 'Talking Points Brought to Trump Tower Meeting Were Shared with Kremlin', *New York Times*, 27 October 2017, p. A1, https://www.nytimes.com/2017/10/27/us/politics/trump-tower-veselnitskaya-russia.html.
26. Sengupta, 'Trump Tried to Tempt Putin'.
27. Yaffa, 'How Bill Browder Became Russia's Most Wanted Man'.
28. Andrei Nekrasov, *The Magnitsky Act: Behind the Scenes*, first released 25 June 2016, https://www.imdb.com/title/tt6028446/.
29. Alex Krainer, *Grand Deception: The Truth about Bill Browder and the Magnitsky Act and Anti-Russian Sanctions* (Otto, NC, Red Hill Press, 2018), p. 70.
30. For full details, see Jeffrey Toobin, 'Michael Cohen's Last Days of Freedom', *New Yorker*, 29 April 2019, https://www.newyorker.com/magazine/2019/05/06/michael-cohens-last-days-of-freedom.
31. Cohen, *Disloyal*, p. 328.
32. Cohen, *Disloyal*, p. 348.
33. Tom McCarthy, 'Blow to Trump as Former Lawyer Reaches Plea Deal', *Guardian*, 22 August 2018, p. 2.
34. David Smith and Erin Durkin, 'Trump: Aide "Made Up" Stories about Hush Money', *Guardian*, 23 August 2018, p. 9.
35. Cohen, *Disloyal*, p. 353.
36. Martin Pengelly, '"Base Motives": Attorney General Barr Challenged over Sacking of Prosecutor', *Guardian*, 22 June 2020, p. 21.
37. Cohen, *Disloyal*, pp. 284–306 for the sordid details.
38. Cohen, *Disloyal*, p. 291.
39. For Cohen's version and the context, see *Disloyal*, pp. 81–102, 137–44.
40. Smith and Durkin, 'Trump: Aide "Made Up" Stories about Hush Money', pp. 2; and Tom McCarthy, 'A Bad Day for the President, and it May Get Much Worse', *Guardian*, 23 August 2018, p. 9. For details of the later Stormy Daniels story, see Cohen, *Disloyal*, pp. 331-41.
41. Tom McCarthy, 'Trump Knew Hush Money was Wrong, Says Former Fixer', *Guardian*, 15 December 2018, p. 38.
42. Holman W. Jenkins, Jr., 'So Long, Russia. And thanks!', *Wall Street Journal*, 29 August 2018, https://www.wsj.com/articles/so-long-russia-and-thanks-1535495304.

43. Toobin, 'Michael Cohen's Last Days of Freedom'.
44. Cohen, *Disloyal*, p. 270.
45. Henry Foy, 'Putin Official Confirms Cohen Contacted Kremlin over Trump Tower Moscow', *Financial Times*, 1 December 2018, https://www.ft.com/content/fac2c9a8-f568-11e8-af46-2022a0b02a6c.
46. McCarthy, *Ball of Collusion*, p. 233.
47. Cohen, *Disloyal*, p. 17.
48. Anthony Cormier and Jason Leopold, 'Trump Moscow: The Definitive Story of How Trump's Team Worked the Russian Deal during the Campaign', *BuzzFeed*, 17 May 2018, https://www.buzzfeednews.com/article/anthonycormier/trump-moscow-micheal-cohen-felix-sater-campaign.
49. Fred Weir, 'Trump Tower Moscow: Doomed by Cultural Divides?', *Christian Science Monitor*, 6 December 2018, https://www.csmonitor.com/World/Europe/2018/1206/Trump-Tower-Moscow-doomed-by-cultural-divides. See also Cohen, *Disloyal*, pp. 253-60.
50. The whole business, including the close involvement of the Trump family, is described by Cohen, *Disloyal*, pp. 253–60.
51. Jon Swain and Victoria Bekiempis, 'Cohen Admits Lying over Trump's Russia Project', *Guardian*, 30 November 2018, pp. 1–2.
52. Cohen, *Disloyal*, p. 257.
53. Erin Durkin, 'Democrats Vow to Pursue Claims Trump Directed Cohen to Lie', *Guardian*, 19 January 2019, p. 26.
54. Trump made this point explicitly, Davis Richardson, 'Trump Responds to Cohen's Moscow Timeline: "Why Should I lose Lots of Opportunities?"', *Observer*, 29 November 2018, https://observer.com/2018/11/trump-cohen-moscow-timeline-lost-opportunities/.
55. Doug Johnson Hatlem lists them, 'Are we now Over 50 News Stories that have Had to be Retracted or Seriously Corrected, all in the Same Direction, with Russia since 2016?', Twitter, 18 January 2019, https://threadreaderapp.com/thread/1086424261709881344.html.
56. Cohen, *Disloyal*, p. 16 for the close relationship, and the text is littered with devastating comments on Trump's character.
57. John Solomon, 'How the Obama White House Engaged Ukraine to Give Russia Collusion Narrative an Early Boost', *The Hill*, 25 April 2019, https://thehill.com/opinion/white-house/440730-how-the-obama-white-house-engaged-ukraine-to-give-russia-collusion.
58. Harding, *Collusion*, p. 155.
59. Graham Stack, 'Everything You Know about Paul Manafort is Wrong', *Kyiv Post*, 17 September 2018, https://www.kyivpost.com/article/opinion/op-ed/graham-stack-everything-you-know-about-paul-manafort-is-wrong.html.
60. Solomon, 'How the Obama White House Engaged Ukraine'.
61. Jerry Dunleavy, 'Hundreds of Emails Show Nellie Ohr Researched Trump-Russia Connections', *Washington Examiner*, 25 August 2019, https://www.washingtonexaminer.com/news/hundreds-of-pages-of-emails-show-nellie-ohr-researched-trump-russia-connections.

62. Steven Lee Myers and Andrew E. Kramer, 'How Paul Manafort Wielded Power in Ukraine before Advising Donald Trump', *New York Times*, 31 July 2016; Simpson and Fritsch, *Crime in Progress*, p. 89.

63. Roman Olearchyk, 'Ukraine Leaders Campaign against "Pro-Putin" Trump', *Financial Times*, 28 August 2016, https://www.ft.com/content/c98078d0-6ae-11e6-aOb1-d87a9fea034f; McCarthy, *Ball of Collusion*, p. 119.

64. Andrew E. Kramer, Mike McIntire and Barry Meier, 'Secret Ledger in Ukraine Lists Cash for Donald Trump's Campaign Chief', *New York Times*, 14 August 2016, https://www.nytimes.com/2016/08/15/us/politics/paul-manafort-ukraine-donald-trump.html.

65. Simpson and Fritsch, *Crime in Progress*, pp. 50-53; Meier, *Spooked*, pp. 138-9.

66. John Solomon, 'As Russia Collusion Fades, Ukrainian Plot to Help Clinton Emerges', *The Hill*, 20 March 2019, https://www.realclearpolitics.com/video/2019/03/21/john_solomon_as_russia_collusion_fades_ukrainian_plot_to_help_clinton_emerges.html.

67. Solomon, 'How the Obama White House Engaged Ukraine'.

68. John Solomon, 'Ukrainian Embassy Confirms DNC Contractor Solicited Trump Dirt in 2016', *The Hill*, 5 February 2019, https://thehill.com/opinion/white-house/441892-ukrainian-embassy-confirms-dnc-contractor-solicited-trump-dirt-in-2016.

69. Kenneth P. Vogel and David Stern, 'Ukrainian Efforts to Sabotage Trump Backfire', *Politico*, 11 January 2017, https://www.politico.com/story/2017/01/ukraine-sabotage-trump-backfire-233446.

70. John Solomon, 'Ukrainian Who Meddled against Trump in 2016 is now under Russia-Corruption Cloud', *The Hill*, 16 May 2019, https://thehill.com/opinion/white-house/444167-ukrainian-who-meddled-against-trump-in-2016-is-now-under-russia.

71. Unger, *House of Trump*, p. 246.

72. Isikoff and Corn, *Russian Roulette*, p. 186.

73. For more details, see Leonid Bershidsky, 'Biden's Ukraine Problem has Nothing to do with his Son', *Bloomberg*, 8 May 2019, https://www.bloomberg.com/opinion/articles/2019-05-08/joe-biden-s-ukraine-scandal-is-his-policy-not-personal-interests.

74. Solomon, 'Ukrainian Embassy Confirms'.

75. Solomon, 'Ukrainian Embassy Confirms'.

76. Vogel and Stern, 'Ukrainian Efforts to Sabotage Trump Backfire'.

77. Weissman, *Where Law Ends*, p. 80 notes that this was one of the charges of collusion that proved false.

78. Woodward, *Fear*, p. 230.

79. Valeriy Chaly, 'Trump's Comments Send Wrong Message to the World', *The Hill*, 4 August 2016, https://thehill.com/blogs/pundits-blog/international/290411-ukraines-ambassador-trumps-comments-send-wrong-message-to.

80. Weissmann, *Where Law Ends*, p. 244.

81. Described in detail by Weissmann, *Where Law Ends*, pp. 188–210.

82. Robert Mueller, *Indictment of Paul Manafort and Richard Gates*, 27 October 2017, pp. 1–3.
83. Robert Mueller, *Statement of Offense of Richard Gates*, 23 February 2018, pp. 1–3.
84. McCarthy, *Ball of Collusion*, p, 52; Weissmann, *Where Law Ends*, p. 246.
85. Weissmann, *Where Law Ends*, p. 198.
86. Another of the false collusion leads identified by Weissman, *Where Law Ends*, p. 80.
87. James Bamford, 'The Spy Who Wasn't', *The New Republic*, 11 February 2019, https://newrepublic.com/article/153036/maria-butina-profile-wasnt-russian-spy. For her own account, see Mariya Butina, *Tyuremnyi dnevnik* (Moscow, AST, 2021).
88. Nathan Hodge, 'Trump Brand Now Toxic in Putin's Kremlin', CNN.com, 9 December 2018, https://edition.cnn.com/2018/12/08/europe/russia-putin-trump-bromance-intl/index.html.
89. David Smith, Manafort gets Second Jail Term as Judge Attacks "Lies and Fraud"', *Guardian*, 14 March 2019, p. 2.
90. Luke Harding, Dan Collyns and Fernando Villavicencio, 'Manafort "Held Secret Talks with Assange"', *Guardian*, 28 November 2018, pp. 1, 34–35.
91. Craig Murray, 'Assange Never Met Manafort', www.craigmurray.org.uk, 27 November 2018, https://www.craigmurray.org.uk/archives/2018/11/assange-never-met-manafort-luke-harding-and-the-guardian-publish-still-more-blatant-mi6-lies/.
92. *The Intercept*, 27 November 2018. For his coruscating critique of *The Guardian*'s neo-journalism, and its refusal to respond to the scandal, see Glenn Greenwald, 'Five Weeks after the Guardian's Viral Blockbuster Assange-Manafort Scoop, No Evidence has Emerged – Just Stonewalling', *The Intercept*, 2 January 2019, https://theintercept.com/2019/01/02/five-weeks-after-the-guardians-viral-blockbuster-assangemanafort-scoop-no-evidence-has-emerged-just-stonewalling/.
93. For detail on the three authors of *The Guardian* report, see Serge Halimi, 'The Guardian's Fake Scoop', *Le Monde diplomatique*, 24 December 2018, https://mondediplo.com/outsidein/guardian-fake-scoop.
94. Poll based on telephone interviews conducted between 1-12 August 2018 based on a random sample of 1,024 adults across the country, Jeffrey M. Jones, 'More in U.S. Favor Diplomacy over Sanctions for Russia', *Gallup*, 20 August 2018, https://news.gallup.com/poll/241124/favor-diplomacy-sanctions-russia.aspx.
95. Jane Mayer, *Dark Money: How a Secretive Group of Billionaires is Trying to Buy Political Control in the US* (London, Scribe, 2016).
96. Data from the Centre for Responsive Politics, Bronwen Maddox, 'Judgment on US Campaign Donations "Strikes at Democracy Itself"', *The Times*, 26 January 2010, https://www.thetimes.co.uk/article/judgment-on-us-campaign-donations-strikes-at-democracy-itself-m6glw7s9cs9.
97. Chuck Collins, 'The Wealth of America's Three Richest Families Grew by 6,000% since 1982', *Guardian*, 31 October 2018, https://www.theguardian.com/commentisfree/2018/oct/31/us-wealthiest-families-dynasties-governed-by-rich.

98. Paul R. Pillar, 'The Mueller Report Exposes US Election Weakness', *The National Interest*, 24 April 2019, https://nationalinterest.org/blog/paul-pillar/mueller-report-exposes-us-election-weaknesses-54052.

99. Paul J. Saunders, 'After US Midterms, Dialogue with Russia may become Easier, Not Harder', *Russia Matters*, 14 November 2018, https://www.russiamatters.org/analysis/after-us-midterms-dialogue-russia-may-become-easier-not-harder.

100. Kimberley A. Strassel, 'Doubling Down on Mueller', *Wall Street Journal*, 16 November 2018, https://www.wsj.com/articles/doubling-down-on-mueller-1542326829.

101. Dustin Volz and Robert McMillan, 'Russian Hackers Largely Skipped the Midterms, and No One Really Knows Why', *Wall Street Journal*, 13 November 2018, https://www.wsj.com/articles/russian-hackers-largely-skipped-the-midterms-and-no-one-really-knows-why-1542054493.

102. 'US Launches Cyber Operation against Russia Ahead of Elections, NYT Reports', *Moscow Times*, 23 October 2018, https://themoscowtimes.com/news/us-launches-cyber-operation-against-russia-ahead-of-election-nyt-reports-63278.

103. Dave Weinstein, 'America Goes on the Cyberoffensive', *Wall Street Journal*, 29 August 2018, https://www.wsj.com/articles/america-goes-on-the-cyberoffensive-1535495485.

104. Aaron Maté, 'With Just Days to go to the Midterms, Russiagate is MIA', *The Nation*, 29 October 2018, https://www.thenation.com/article/russiagate-2018-midterms-interference/.

105. 'Bolton Tells Kremlin: "Don't Mess with US Elections"', *Reuters*, 22 October 2018, https://www.reuters.com/article/us-usa-russia-elections/bolton-says-russian-meddling-in-us-elections-hardly-had-any-real-effect-idUSKCN1MW2K2.

106. Bolton, *Room Where It Happened*, p. 295.

107. Bolton, *Room Where It Happened*, p. 301.

108. Adam Davidson, 'The Investigations Trump will Face Now that Democrats Control the House', *New Yorker*, 7 November 2018, https://www.newyorker.com/news/swamp-chronicles/the-investigations-trump-will-face-now-that-democrats-control-the-house.

109. Ivan Danilov, 'Russian Comment Says Political System in US "Dysfunctional"', *RIA Novosti*, 8 November 2018.

110. Stephanie Kirchgaessner, 'Legal Firepower: Scrutiny of President to Intensify', *Guardian*, 8 November 2018, p. 7.

111. Jeremy Herb and Manu Raju, 'House Democrats Plan to Bring Russia Back to the Forefront', CNN.com, 7 November 2018, https://edition.cnn.com/2018/11/07/politics/russia-investigation-congress-midterm-results/index.html.

112. Susan B. Glasser, 'After the Midterms, Robert Mueller's Got a New Wingman on Capitol Hill', *New Yorker*, 15 November 2018, https://www.newyorker.com/news/letter-from-trumps-washington/after-the-midterms-robert-muellers-got-a-new-wingman-on-capitol-hill.

Chapter 12

Mueller Investigates

The first special prosecutor in U.S. history was dismissed by President Ulysses S. Grant in 1875, but when President Richard Nixon fired Watergate special prosecutor Archibald Cox on 20 October 1973 (the 'Saturday Night Massacre'), the public backlash was so intense that he was forced to appoint a replacement, who ultimately forced Nixon's resignation on 9 August 1974. President Bill Clinton was harried for over eight years (1994–2002) by the independent counsel investigation led by Kenneth Starr in the Whitewater investigation, and in December 1998, the House voted to impeach him over his affair with the White House intern Monica Lewinsky. In 1999, special counsel regulations were revised to stop such open-ended investigations, and thereafter probes were firmly subordinated to the DoJ. Trump no doubt looked to the Grant precedent, but times had changed, as demonstrated by the Watergate investigation. Mueller was director of the FBI for twelve years from 2001 to 2013 and became famous for his taciturn probity. Mueller now investigated a case in which domestic partisanship intersected with foreign policy and security concerns. McFarland notes that 'Trump was pummelled in the press every hour of every day for more than two years, with cable news pundits speculating on how the Mueller probe was going to find Trump guilty of some of the worst crimes in American history', while former Obama intelligence chiefs implied 'that they had inside information, suggested Trump was a Russian agent and would be charged with treason'.[1] In the event, the Mueller team found no smoking gun, but the investigation generated process crimes of obstruction of justice.

Chapter 12

THE SPECIAL COUNSEL GETS TO WORK

Trump developed an understandable loathing for attorney general Sessions. On election night, Trump praised him as 'a great man', but when Sessions in March 2017 recused himself from the Russia investigation, he rapidly fell from grace. Trump has a point in believing that 'The previous administration, its own candidate defeated, was not just disregarding the democratic custom of smoothing the way for the winner of the election; rather, in the White House view, Obama's people had plotted with the intelligence community to put land mines in the new administration's way'. Susan Rice had a spreadsheet listing all the contacts between Trump officials and Russians.[2] Perfectly legal conversations were 'unmasked', turning Russiagate into 'spygate', or as the scholar Stephen F. Cohen put it, 'intelgate'.[3]

Snowden revealed that since November 2010 the NSA was analysing domestic phone calls and emails to 'discover and track' connections, and this now turned into political espionage.[4] In a tweet of 4 March 2016 Trump exploded: 'Terrible! Just found out that Obama had my "wires tapped" in Trump Tower just before the victory. Nothing found. This is McCarthyism!' A few minutes later he added, 'How low has President Obama gone to tapp [sic] my phones during the very sacred election process. This is Nixon/Watergate. Bad (or sick) guy!'[5] Trump may have been 'half-right', since 'Trump Tower had been wiretapped, not to eavesdrop on his dealings, but to investigate one of the world's biggest illegal high-stakes gambling rings operating just below his own penthouse'.[6] His team was the subject of a counter-intelligence investigation, which may have included some monitoring of communications, but there is no evidence of systematic tapping.

Why did Rosenstein appoint a special counsel when there was little evidence that the president had committed a crime? Rosenstein was smarting from Trump's attempt to pin the blame for Comey's dismissal on him, while McCabe and his associates sought to institutionalise the Russia probe. Trump was clearly mystified about why meeting with Russians was wrong, an indication of how he failed 'to join the dots'. Trump's election was perceived not only to imperil America's democratic norms but also the country's national security. An influential analysis in the *New Yorker* remains one of the most unequivocal statements of the philosophy underlying the new cold war and the resistance to Trump.[7] The story connected 'the dots of Russia's geopolitical mortification, Putin's ambition, the country's cyber talents, Trump's own nascent authoritarianism, and the US intelligence community's suspicions about Putin and Russia – codified a narrative as coherent and as apocalyptic as the one in the original cold war'.[8]

Twelve days after Comey's dismissal and with Sessions recused, the way was open for his deputy, Rosenstein, on 17 May 2017 to appoint a special counsel. Mueller was commissioned to 'ensure a full and thorough investigation of the Russian government's efforts to interfere in the 2016 presidential election' and was 'authorised to conduct' the investigation that Comey had confirmed on 20 March. The brief was remarkably broad: to investigate (i) 'any links and/or coordination between the Russian government and individuals associated with the campaign of President Donald Trump, and (ii) any matters that arose or may arise directly from the investigation, and (iii) any other matters'. Mueller was authorised 'to prosecute federal crimes arising from the investigation of these matters'.[9] Trump was furious, tweeting that night 'This is the single greatest witch hunt of a politician in American history'.[10] He stressed that 'I am being investigated for firing the FBI Director by the man [Rosenstein] who told me to fire the FBI Director. Witch Hunt!'.[11] A special counsel has enormous powers to investigate any possible crime. Trump had cause to be alarmed: 'Now I have this person', he railed, 'who has no accountability who can look into anything, however unrelated it is? They're going to spend years digging through my whole life and finances'.[12]

Trump was right. The Mueller team investigated not only the extent and significance of contacts and possible collusion between members of the Trump campaign and representatives (real or claimed) of the Russian state but also campaign contributions and the failure to register work conducted on behalf of foreign powers, notably Ukraine and Turkey, by those associated with the Trump team. The investigation above all examined attempts by individuals and organisations linked to the Russian state to interfere in the 2016 presidential election. Members of Trump's family and associates who had dealing with Russia were now vulnerable. Bannon in this respect was beyond reproach: 'I've never been to Russia. I don't know anybody from Russia. I've never spoken to any Russians. And I'd just as well not speak to anyone who has'.[13] Trump denounced Mueller's 'team of partisans' as seventeen 'angry Democrats'.[14] In fact, thirteen of the seventeen were Democrats but Mueller and some others were lifelong Republicans, and most put professionalism above partisanship – but none could escape a political culture which demonised Russia and all its works. On 2 August 2017, Rosenstein's 'scope memo' broadened the investigation to cover collateral issues, including Trump campaign members Manafort and Page 'for a crime or crimes by colluding with Russian government officials', allegations that came from the discredited Steele dossier.[15] As noted, four warrants were issued against Page from October 2016, but the DoJ in early 2020 (following the Horowitz review) admitted to the FISA court that the last two of the three renewals should never have been filed.[16] We also noted earlier that the memo authorised Mueller to investigate the potential 'crime' of Flynn 'engaging in conversations with Russian government officials during the period of the Trump transition', a reference to the Logan Act.

Trump was advised to let the Russiagate investigation take its course, but that did not prevent him regularly railing against it. In conversation with his confidant Senator Lindsey Graham, Trump insisted that 'I didn't work with the Russians', to which Graham responded, 'I believe you . . . because you can't work with your own government. Why should you be working with the Russian government?'[17] Trump told John Dowd, the veteran seventy-six-year-old attorney who represented him, that the Mueller investigation 'was consuming him and his presidency', and he insisted that he had done nothing wrong: 'John, this thing is an enormous burden. It interferes particularly with foreign affairs'. Trump stressed that Russia was a nuclear armed state with over a thousand deployed weapons, which changed the strategic calculus of interactions.[18] Trump was outraged by the investigation, and he directed much of his anger at Sessions. In a rare interview with the *New York Times* on 19 July 2017, he launched a blistering attack, arguing that he would never have appointed him if he had known that he would refuse any involvement in Russian matters. Trump was also angry with Rosenstein, who had appointed Mueller without any consultation.[19] Worse, Rosenstein's 17 May order not only authorised 'a Russian investigation but it directed Mueller to investigate "any matters that arose or may arise directly from the [Russian] investigation". Dowd had never seen anyone in Justice with such broad authority'.[20] In practice, despite endless fulminations, Trump and his team cooperated with the investigation.

The collusion charge centred on Trump's visit to Moscow in 2013, what he knew about Manafort's dealings, what business his long-standing attorney Michael Cohen was doing with Russia during the campaign, and what he may have known about the involvement of his other associates, such as Roger Stone, with Clinton's hacked emails. The enduring fear was that Mueller would frame an obstruction of justice charge, including Trump's three attempts to get Comey to drop the Flynn investigation. Nevertheless, Dowd pursued a policy of cooperation, regularly meeting with James Quarles, adviser to Mueller's deputy Aaron Zebley. Dowd provided the requested materials, believing that the president had nothing to hide, and hoped thereby that the investigation would come to a speedy end. As a veteran of special investigations, he knew that 'The length of these investigations often became the abuse'.[21] As for Trump, he accused the investigation of provoking conflict: 'If it was the goal of Russia to create discord, disruption and chaos within the US then, with all the Committee Hearings, Investigations and Party hatred, they have succeeded beyond their wildest dreams. They are laughing their assess off in Moscow. Get smart America!'[22]

Dowd was particularly concerned about how the Veselnitskaya meeting had been blown totally out of proportion, and he told Trump so: 'Mr. President, it's horseshit'. 'And so what? Getting dirt on people was commonplace in campaigns and the nation's capital. It even had a name – "opposition research" or "investigative reporting". That's what half of Washington seemed to be paid for'. Dowd considered the media outrage 'disgusting'.[23] In his view, the stories were 'a big nothing burger'.[24] Nevertheless, as part of the cooperation strategy, he provided the Mueller enquiry with extensive materials, including the testimony of thirty-seven witnesses and 1,400,000 documents (with highlights of Trump's most intimate conversations), on the understanding that the enquiry would be expeditiously concluded, thus removing the shadow hanging over the administration.[25] This clearly was not enough, and on 20 July 2017, it was revealed that Mueller was investigating Trump's finances, an issue that was likely to be Trump's Achilles Heel. In the event, the financial aspect of the investigation stalled, and thus according to Weissmann, the question of financial support from Russia was never answered.[26] Russian purchases of Trump apartments, the 2013 Miss Universe tournament in Moscow, and Trump's sale of the Florida mansion to a Russian oligarch in 2008 were investigated. There was also the issue of continued attempts by Cohen and Sater to develop a Trump Tower in Moscow.

Dowd increasingly suspected that Mueller was dragging his feet, telling the latter on 21 December 2017:

> All the records have been produced.... All the witnesses have been interviewed except one or two. The entire inquiry appears to be the product of a conspiracy by the DNC, Fusion GPS – which oversaw the Steele dossier – and senior FBI intelligence officials to undermine the Trump presidency. The failure to investigate Comey's role precipitating the enquiry is a travesty. Comey's aberrant and dishonourable conduct demands scrutiny.

Woodward laconically notes, 'Mueller did not reply'.[27] Mueller and Quarles insisted that they wanted to interview the president, and on 8 January 2018, Mueller dictated a list of the sixteen topics they wanted to talk about, mostly dealing with Flynn, Comey and Sessions. Knowing Trump's prolixity and inability to focus for long on a particular issue, Dowd was adamant that Trump should never be allowed to testify on oath. In the course of a single answer, Trump would incriminate himself ten times. Dowd recalled the time when Trump gave a deposition to a lawyer in Florida: 'When the lawyer had asked him what he did for a living, it had taken Trump about 16 pages to answer the question'.[28] Dowd was shocked to discover at a meeting with Mueller on 5 March that the latter contemplated issuing a grand jury subpoena to force Trump to testify, despite Dowd having provided the enquiry with unprecedented access to White House files. A grand jury subpoena on a president, who ultimately was not the target of the investigation but a witness, had never been tried before.[29] Dowd was furious, telling Mueller:

'Talk about reciprocity. You guys tell me where the collusion is. And don't give me that chickenshit meeting in June [2016, with Veselnitskaya]. . . . That's a nothing. There's no collusion. And the obstruction? It's a joke'.

He went on to air the long-standing grievance that Flynn had spoken to the FBI not believing he was under jeopardy, since he had been told that the agents had closed his file.[30] As the conversation developed, according to Woodward, 'Dowd began to think that Mueller did not know the facts of the case'.[31] If true, this is an astonishing statement, but it could simply be a matter of Mueller playing his cards close to his chest.[32] Dowd believed that the Mueller investigation, lacking substantive evidence, repeatedly played the perjury trap to ensnare the president; so he told Mueller: 'You did it to Flynn, you did it to Gates, you did it to Papadopoulos. . . . you guys, that's the games you played'.[33] Reporting back to the president shortly afterwards Dowd said, 'You've never truly respected Mueller. You've got really good instincts, but I've never bought into it. But I've got to tell you, I think your instincts might be right. He really wasn't prepared. Why are we coming back here with nothing?'[34]

A week later, on 12 March, Mueller's team provided Dowd with what were now forty-nine questions, once again dealing with Trump's attitude to Flynn, Comey and Sessions, as well as the Trump Tower meeting and Trump's real estate development in Russia. Dowd knew that these questions had been repeatedly answered, but 'the broad range of issues suggested that Mueller had nothing and wanted to go on a giant fishing expedition. Setting a perjury trap for the volatile Trump would be child's play'.[35] Dowd now understood that the president had been right, telling him, 'I don't trust him [Mueller]'. Woodward goes on: 'The 49 questions troubled Dowd. Why not just five? Why no deference to the president of the United States', who daily had to deal with major global issues.[36] Nevertheless, the president's personal lawyer up to May 2018, Ty Cobb, recommended that Trump should take the witness stand, and Trump agreed – 'I'm a good witness. I'll be a real good witness'.[37] Woodward sums up:

> Dowd remained convinced that Mueller never had a Russian case or an obstruction case. He was looking for a perjury trap. And in a brutally honest self-evaluation, he believed that Mueller had played him, and the president, for suckers in order to get their cooperation on witnesses and documents. . . . Dowd believed that the president had not colluded with Russia or obstructed justice.[38]

Dowd resigned on 22 March when Trump refused to take his advice and continued to insist that he would make an excellent witness. The Mueller team received the president's written responses in late November, but already in

December the special counsel 'informed [Trump's] counsel of the insufficiency of those responses'.[39] The answers about Russian links to the campaign were apparently adequate, but not – hardly surprisingly – about the obstruction of justice issue.[40] There were also questions about what Trump knew about the June 2016 Trump Tower meeting, what he discussed with Stone and Manafort about Russia and WikiLeaks, and his ties to Russian oligarchs.[41]

Meanwhile, White House counsel Don McGahn spent thirty hours speaking with the Mueller team. The long-time Trump Organisation chief financial officer had been subpoenaed by Mueller. It was clear that while investigating Cohen the Mueller investigation learnt a lot about the inner workings of the Trump Organisation. McGahn cooperated fully with the Mueller investigation, to the point even that Trump's outside attorneys 'were all reportedly surprised by just how candid he was'.[42] This is why Trump in late August tweeted that McGahn would be leaving his post, which he did in October. There was some substance to Trump's claim that Mueller had been on a fishing expedition, since much of what he discovered had nothing substantively to do with Russia, the original purpose of the investigation.[43] As the investigation dragged on from months into years, the Mueller probe consumed 'too much of his [Trump's] emotional energy. It was a real distraction'.[44] Trump's fear that there had been wiretaps during the campaign induced in him 'a sense of sort of feeling violated . . . that there was someone that had some power over him where he wasn't the top dog'. Above all, Trump complained about Mueller because 'I can't be president', he said. 'It's like I have my hands tied behind my back because I can't do anything that looks like its favourable to Russia or to Putin because of Mueller'.[45] With the Mueller investigation hanging over him and the constant media coverage that Trump had colluded with the Russians or obstructed justice – 'a real feeding frenzy, vicious, uncivil' – undermined the capacity 'of the president to be president'.[46]

The White House was concerned that the investigation would move beyond Russian election interference into the Trump family finances. Instead, Mueller focused narrowly on his brief and did not examine Trump's history or personal finances or 'examine the roots of his [Trump's] special affinity for Putin's Russia'. Critics argue that this was the reason 'the Mueller investigation failed', although the criteria of success in this reading would not be establishing whether the Trump campaign had colluded with Russia but Trump's impeachment.[47] Trump in the end refused to engage in a face-to-face interview and Mueller did not issue a grand jury subpoena, and instead Trump repeatedly gave written answers about his campaign and possible collusion with Russia. Rudy Giuliani, Trump's new personal lawyer, noted that he was 'disgusted' with the conduct of the investigation, particularly the 'perjury trap' set for Flynn.[48]

MUELLER REPORTS

After twenty-two months of work (674 days), and at the cost of $34 million, on 22 March 2019, Mueller finally delivered his report to the Justice Department. Two days later, attorney general William Barr, in consultation with Rosenstein, sent a four-page letter to Congress highlighting the key findings.[49] Barr had been confirmed in post just weeks earlier, on 14 February, but he was a veteran of Washington politics, having first served as attorney general in the George H. W Bush administration between 1991 and 1993. On 8 June 2018, Barr submitted an unsolicited nineteen-page memo to the DoJ arguing that the chief magistrate (Trump) had the discretionary power to fire a person who was investigating him and supported Trump's refusal to submit to questioning by Mueller. He argued 'Mueller's core premise – that the President acts "corruptly" if he attempts to influence a proceeding in which his own conduct is being scrutinized – is untenable'.[50] In other words, Barr denounced Mueller's obstruction of justice enquiry as 'fatally misconceived'.[51]

Barr's letter was written in this spirit. He noted that the special counsel had 'thoroughly investigated allegations that members of the presidential campaign of Donald J. Trump, and others associated with it, conspired with the Russian government in its efforts to interfere in the 2016 presidential election, or sought to obstruct the related federal investigations'. In completing the investigation, Mueller

> employed 19 lawyers who were assisted by a team of approximately 40 FBI agents, intelligence analysts, forensic accountants, and other professional staff. The Special Counsel issued more than 2,800 subpoenas, executed nearly 500 search warrants, obtained more than 230 orders for communication records, issued almost 50 orders authorizing use of pen registers, made 13 requests to foreign governments for evidence, and interviewed approximately 500 witnesses.

The special counsel indicted thirty-four people – twenty-six Russian citizens, seven U.S. and one Dutch national. None of the Americans were accused of conspiracy with Russia. Barr stated that no conclusive proof of collusion had been found but failed to mention Mueller's argument that Russia and Trump were working towards similar goals. The potential incidents of obstruction of justice were noted but the eleven identified by Mueller were not enumerated. Neither were the 'multiple contacts . . . between Trump campaign officials and individuals with ties to the Russian government', as Mueller put it. It also failed to stress that the reason Mueller decided not to make a prosecutorial judgement was because of the DoJ's policy of not charging a sitting president with a federal crime.[52] Barr's handling of the report provoked intense controversy.[53] Mueller's report was released in redacted form to the public four weeks later, but by then public perceptions had been shaped.

Mueller clearly failed to answer some fundamental questions. He never found an inside witness to describe corrupt and illegal activity, whereas John Dean, Nixon's White House counsel, in 1973 testified to his own and Nixon's illegal activity. There was not even a Monica Lewinsky to demonstrate that the president lied in judicial and public statements.[54] We noted in chapter 1 Mueller's conclusion that 'The Russian government interfered in the 2016 election in sweeping and systematic fashion' but 'the investigation did not establish that members of the Trump campaign conspired or coordinated with the Russian government in its election interference activities'.[55] This was read by Trump as total exoneration and he tweeted endlessly about 'no collusion'. On the crucial issue of obstruction, Mueller writes

> Because we determined not to make a traditional prosecutorial judgment, we did not draw ultimate conclusions about the President's conduct. . . . if we had confidence after a thorough investigation of the facts that the President did not commit obstruction of justice, we would so state. Based on the facts and the applicable legal standards, we are unable to reach that judgment. Accordingly, while this report does not conclude that the President committed a crime, it also does not exonerate him.[56]

This was both inconclusive and confusing. Mueller believed that it was not at the special counsel's discretion to make a finding about obstruction, a view contested by other investigators.[57] It was not even clearly stated whether the facts justified an indictment, whether served immediately or later.[58]

It was left to the attorney general to determine whether the conduct analysed in the report constituted a crime. To help the dissemination of the findings while waiting for a review of grand jury material and other issues that should not be made public, the Mueller team had prepared a one-page introduction and a ten-page summary of each part highlighting the key conclusions and the evidence in both parts of the report. They expected that Barr would release these immediately, and his failure to do so was yet another matter for recrimination. Barr's letter was considered a tendentious interpretation, much to the fury of the investigators.[59] On Russia, Barr concluded that 'the evidence does not establish that the President was involved in an underlying crime related to Russian election interference', but he failed to quote Mueller's argument that the Russian government 'perceived that it would benefit from a Trump presidency and worked to secure that outcome'. Critics also condemned Barr for failing to stress adequately that the Trump campaign actively solicited Russian help in the 'hack and dump' operation and were willing to condone the crime as beneficiaries. More than that, Barr's interpretation apparently downplayed the degree to which the Trump campaign solicited support from Russia, notably in the June 2016 Trump Tower meeting, and attempted to coordinate the dissemination of the damaging emails against Clinton. The investigators also argued that Russian interference went far beyond being simply 'designed to sow social discord, eventually with the aim of interfering in the election', as Barr put it, but in fact sought to support Trump and undermine Clinton's campaign.

On obstruction, the presidential threat of dismissing the special counsel cast a dark shadow over the investigators' work, acting as a sword of Damocles over the whole process, while the possibility of pardons against potential malefactors inhibited them from 'flipping'. Despite Mueller's convoluted formulations, the president in the view of investigators had undoubtedly obstructed justice. However, Barr argued that 'while not determinative, the absence of such evidence bears upon the President's intent with respect to obstruction'. In short, 'the evidence developed during the Special Counsel's investigation is not sufficient to establish that the President committed an obstruction-of-justice offense', a decision made without regard to the constitutional considerations concerning the indictment or criminal prosecution of a sitting president. The reference here is to the DoJ's Office of Legal Counsel (OLC) ruling of 1973 and reaffirmed in 2000 barring the indictment of a sitting president.

The letter was not technically inaccurate, but Barr was accused of having distorted the essence of the report. His interpretation of Mueller's findings allowed Trump to declare that they represented a 'complete and total exoneration', and to argue, 'It's a shame that our country had to go through this. To be honest, it's a shame that your President had to go through this'.[60] Barr's summary, in Weissmann's view, amounted to 'deception' on a grand scale.[61] It represented 'a concerted refusal to deal with the fact that we were attacked by a foreign adversary and will continue to be unless we take decisive actions'.[62] Mueller communicated his unhappiness the following morning. On 27 March, he sent a private two-page letter of protest to Barr, which only became public a month later. Mueller wrote:

> The introductions and executive summaries of our two-volume report accurately summarize this Office's work and conclusions. The summary letter the Department sent to Congress and released to the public late in the afternoon of March 24 did not fully capture the context, nature, and substance of this Office's work and conclusions. We communicated that concern to the Department on the morning of March 25. There is now public confusion about critical aspects of the results of our investigation. This threatens to undermine a central purpose for which the Department appointed the Special Counsel: to assure full public confidence in the outcome of the investigations.[63]

The summaries were not published, with the DoJ arguing that it made sense to wait for the whole report to be cleared for public release. The confusion mentioned by Mueller was inherent in his ambiguous conclusion about obstruction. While the collusion allegation was largely put to rest, the obstruction of justice issue enjoyed a new lease of life. Mueller described plenty of unbecoming behaviour by the president and could not rule out that Trump had committed a crime but conceded that this did not add up to an actionable offence, and not just because of the OLC advice. The ambiguities in the Mueller report allowed Trump's opponents and supporters to interpret it in a manner that suited their purposes.

Part 1 of the Mueller Report

Some of these ambiguities apply to the substance of the report and some obvious investigatory lines appear not to have been pursued. When it comes to the section on hacking, it remains unclear how the various servers were attributed back to individuals in the GRU. The Netyshko indictment stated that the 'middle-servers' were overseas, so it was not clear what was the purpose of the U.S.-based server in Arizona. Mueller now stated that the GRU obtained the files from the DNC on 22 April (the Netyshko indictment states that the files were archived on that date), but this is earlier than the compile date of Fancy Bear malware reportedly discovered at the DNC on 25 April. On another issue, Assange announced on 12 June that WikiLeaks was working on the release of 'emails related to Hillary Clinton', two days before the DNC announcement that it had been hacked and three days before the appearance of Guccifer 2.0, and a month before Mueller reports Guccifer 2.0 sending anything to WikiLeaks. As noted, the Guccifer 2.0 persona made every effort to be perceived as Russian and claimed to have sent material to WikiLeaks before Mueller records any contact between the two parties. Mueller rejected the WikiLeaks version of the provenance of its posted DNC material, but the file transfer evidence does not conclusively prove that WikiLeaks published anything sent to it by Guccifer 2.0 or DCLeaks. They may have been controlled by the GRU, but Mueller does not reveal the evidence on which this judgement was based. The report also failed to address the question about the lack of independent access to the DNC network and reliance on CrowdStrike. Before joining CrowdStrike in 2012, Henry spent twenty-four years with the FBI, retiring as executive assistant director of its cyber-crime investigation unit. As for the alleged hack of state and local election networks, the DHS itself admitted that these attacks were 'only simple scanning ... which occurs all the time', and there was certainly no alteration of results, as admitted by Jeh Johnson on 21 June 2017.

In both the IRA and the cyber section, the view that the activities were ordered by Putin is asserted rather than demonstrated. Equally, the charges against the troll farm and hacking groups do not prove a conspiratorial link to the Trump campaign. They neither needed nor wanted American collaborators, some predated Trump's emergence as campaign favourite, and some of the material was even anti-Trump. Putin assumes a more active role in Section IV, which describes 'Russian government links to and contacts with the Trump campaign' and examines 'whether those contacts constituted a third avenue of attempted Russian interference'. The various attempts by the Trump team and the Kremlin to contact each other through various intermediaries are chronicled. The overall impression is that both sides were groping in the dark. Rather than there being a massive conspiracy to subvert American democracy, these efforts were haphazard and usually ended in failure. The section reprises what had already become public knowledge, including the attempts by Cohen and Sater to push ahead with the Trump Tower Moscow project, and the efforts of Trump campaign staffers Papadopoulos and Carter Page to establish back-channel links with the Kremlin.

In setting up the June 2016 Trump Tower meeting, Goldstone admits that he invented 'publicist puff' to get the Trump team interested, even though he admits that 'I had no idea what I was talking about'. Mueller is right when he notes that the younger Trump's response 'showed that the Campaign anticipated receiving information from Russia that could assist candidate Trump's electoral prospects, but the Russian lawyer's presentation did not provide such information'. Mueller recounts (as we have seen) that Kushner texted Manafort (at the time campaign chair) that it was a 'waste of time' and asked an assistant to 'call him to give him an excuse to leave'. Mueller notes that when 'Veselnitskaya made additional efforts to follow up on the meeting', after the election, 'the Trump Transition Team did not engage'.[64] As for Stone, who was charged in January 2019 for lying to Congress about his efforts to contact WikiLeaks, Mueller's indictment in fact showed that he had no contact with WikiLeaks before the election and no advance information about its releases. Mueller shows that Trump officials were trying to find out about the WikiLeaks releases through Stone, hence demonstrating that they had no privileged information. The report adds nothing to this, and although heavily redacted because of Stone's trial, appears only to confirm the earlier findings.

Equally, in January 2019, Manafort was accused of sharing polling data and discussing a peace plan with his Ukrainian-Russian business partner Konstantin Kilimnik, who allegedly had 'links to Russian intelligence services'.[65] Manafort hired Kilimnik in 2005 and relied on him for Ukrainian matters.[66] In July 2016, Manafort allegedly shared detailed local-level campaign polling data with Kilimnik, which would 'provide a boon to someone who wanted to know where key voting blocs were, where winning over voters would provide the strongest benefit in the race for Electoral College delegates'.[67] In fact, there is no evidence that polling data was given to Kilimnik.[68] Mueller, moreover, 'did not identify evidence of a connection between Manafort's sharing polling data and Russia's interference in the election'. His report agreed with Rick Gate's judgement that Manafort was trying to prove his financial value to future clients.[69] Mueller gave credence to FBI assertions that Kilimnik had 'ties to Russian intelligence' (the GRU),[70] but were unable to interview him and he denies association with Russian intelligence. In fact, Kilimnik may have been a 'sensitive' intelligence source for the State Department since at least 2013. He worked with the chief political officer at the U.S. embassy in Kiev, providing such detailed information about the Opposition Bloc (a movement critical of the neo-nationalist anti-Russian Ukrainian government after 2014) that it was immediately forwarded to Washington, something well-known to the FBI and Mueller. In August 2016, Kilimnik delivered a peace plan to Manafort for the Trump team, which Mueller portrayed as suspiciously pro-Russian, when in fact he had delivered a version of the plan to the Obama administration in May, with the explanation that Russia wanted 'a quick settlement' to get 'Ukraine out of the way and get rid of sanctions and move to economic stuff they are interested in'. The plan was reviewed by Nuland in the State Department. What Mueller portrayed as nefarious was in fact a serious attempt to bring peace to Europe, and by ignoring all the countervailing evidence, Mueller was guilty of 'deception by omission'. Not surprisingly, Kilimnik condemned the Mueller report's 'made-up narrative' about him, insisting 'I have no ties to Russian or, for that matter, any intelligence operations'.[71]

Mueller reports that the Kremlin 'appeared not to have pre-existing contacts . . . with senior officials around the President-Elect'. In addition, 'Putin spoke of the difficulty faced by the Russian government in getting in touch with the incoming Trump Administration . . . Putin indicated that he did not know with whom formally to speak and generally did not know the people around the President-Elect'.[72] The Kremlin also used another official, Kirill Dmitriev, the head of the Russian Direct Investment Fund, to connect with the incoming administration, especially Kushner and Don Jr., but repeatedly failed to do so. It was Dmitriev who in the end met the Trump transition team's informal envoy, Erik Prince, in the Seychelles to pass on Putin's plans for U.S.–Russian reconciliation. According to Mueller, Dmitriev was disappointed to be meeting such a junior figure, although the message was passed up to Bannon. There is nothing unusual in trying to establish such links, but the surprising thing is the absence of established channels. This was, after all, the job of the Russian ambassador. The report notes that 'while Kislyak was an important person, Kislak did not have a direct line to Putin', so other, more informal intermediaries were used.

One of these was Petr Aven, the head of Alfa Bank. In his testimony to the Mueller team, Aven revealed that Putin meets quarterly with some fifty top business executives in the Kremlin, with the meetings at the time prepared by Putin's chief of staff, Anton Vaino. In the meeting held in late 2016, Putin asked Aven to establish a line of communication with the incoming administration. Putin informed him that the United States planned to impose more sanctions on Aven personally and his bank. Russia feared the further deterioration of relations and now sought to improve matters. Aven told Mueller that Putin admitted having difficulty contacting the new administration and that he did not know the people around the president-elect. Aven took Putin's suggestion as an instruction, and shortly afterwards, following another 'all-hands' meeting between Putin and leading 'oligarchs' in December 2016, set out to fulfil Putin's commission. Aven requested Richard Burt, the U.S. ambassador to Germany in the Reagan era, to contact Trump's transition team. Burt in turn asked the president of the Center for the National Interest (CNI), Dmitry Simes, to set up a meeting with Jared Kushner to establish a 'high-level communications channel between Putin and the incoming administration'. Simes rejected the request since he did not want the CNI to be seen as an intermediary between Moscow and Washington. Aven dropped the matter after being told by Burt that it was 'too explosive to discuss'. When he told Vaino that he had been subpoenaed by the FBI about the request, Vaino 'showed no emotion in response to this report and did not appear to care'.[73] This is not the behaviour of someone with something to hide.

These incidents, and others in the report (including the use of Putin aide Yuri Ushakov and the head of VEB, Sergei Gorkov), reveals a rather less than omniscient operation in the Kremlin. Putin in the Mueller report comes over not as the fanatical KGB spy bent on revenge of Clintonian myth, but as someone intent on restoring relations with the other great nuclear superpower. The change of U.S. leader is always an opportunity to reset relations, and Putin sought to take advantage of this. It also reveals the way that Putin relies on informal mechanisms to complement official structures. This reflects both his natural proclivity to play his hand close to his chest, but it also explodes the myth of Putin the master strategist playing three-dimensional chess while his opponents play draughts (checkers). Like any leader in a fluid and unpredictable situation, he reacts to events while trying to exploit opportunities. Putin does have a grand vision of Russian foreign policy – to allow the country a breathing space for economic development while enhancing its status in international affairs – but in day-to-day affairs, this means managing dangerous situations, and there is none more dangerous than nuclear confrontation between the two great powers.

Part 1 of the report comes to two fundamental conclusions. First, the Russian government in 2016 tried to influence the election via social media and by obtaining and publishing Democratic Party emails. And second, no American colluded, cooperated or coordinated that effort. The Trump team's reaction and even anticipation of the release of materials was not criminal – this would have required coordinated actions, and there was no evidence of that. The report did not confirm the Steele dossier's central findings. Equally, the Trump Tower meeting, the Trump Tower Moscow project, the polling data, the Alfa Bank server, the changed Republican platform on arming Ukraine, Jeff Sessions' meeting with Kislyak, the meeting in the Seychelles, Cohen not visiting Prague, Manafort not meeting Assange, and Trump not ordering Cohen to lie to Congress, all turned out not to be smoking guns. Mueller did not consider them crimes, but this important conclusion (running against a mountain of media commentary) was overshadowed by the obstruction of justice issue.

Part 2 of the Mueller Report and Conclusions

The second part is devoted to obstruction. It deals at great length with events that happened because there was investigation into collusion and alleged crimes that did not happen. Obstruction is a process crime, and like perjury only exists because an investigation is underway. Mueller notes that after the election, the president 'expressed concerns to advisors that reports of Russia's election interference might lead the public to question the legitimacy of his election'.[74] This shaped Trump's response to the various investigations. The report examined eleven possible instances of obstruction, but they all ran into the inevitable wall. Trump's actions, and above all his statements, may have been provocative, but they were not illegal. The various Russian actions were not coordinated with Trump or his team, and thus there was no underlying crime whose investigation Trump tried to obstruct. He may have behaved badly, but his actions, the second part of the report concluded, were not intended to cover up an offence, since no crime had been committed. Nevertheless, Mueller found evidence of obstruction that was 'alarming and significant'. If there had been sufficient evidence for an obstruction case, he would have made it. Mueller dwelt at length on the instances of obstructed justice by Trump and hinted that some other body may wish to investigate them – but Mueller was not going to take them forward. Instead, Mueller concluded with the gnomic 'while this report does not conclude that the President committed a crime, it also does not exonerate him'.[75]

The major instance of potential obstruction was Comey's dismissal in May 2017. Although Trump muddied the waters, the report is clear that Comey was fired because of his mishandling of the Clinton emails. The report stresses that Trump was also angry at Comey for telling him privately that he was not under investigation but then refusing to say so publicly.[76] Comey's sacking was not a crime, but it was one of the many instances of actions by the president 'that were capable of exerting undue influence over law enforcement investigations, including the Russian-interference and obstruction investigations'.[77] The Mueller probe was locked in a logical trap: Trump could not take obstructive actions to cover up his Russian crimes, because they did not exist to be covered up. So, then, why did Trump behave as if he had something to hide? Mueller answers the question in this way:

> Evidence indicates that the President was angered by both the existence of the Russia investigation and the public reporting that he was under investigation, which he knew was not true based on Comey's representations. The President complained to advisers that if people thought Russia helped him with the election, it would detract from what he had accomplished. Other evidence indicates that the President was concerned about the impact of the Russia investigation on his ability to govern. The president complained that the perception that he was under investigation was hurting his ability to conduct foreign relations, particularly with Russia.[78]

Mueller was right in his analysis, but once again unwittingly undermined the rationale for his own investigation. All accounts agree that Trump was frustrated that the investigation impaired his ability to govern and reduced his foreign policy options. In the end, the Trump team allowed Mueller to complete an investigation. Trump was exonerated from the main charge of collusion, but he was potentially trapped in obstruction offences.

The report failed to establish evidence of a crime and confirmed the absence of any serious and sustained channels of communication between the Trump team and Moscow. The attempt by the Kremlin after the election to establish contact with senior members of the incoming Trump administration is farcical. Not only was there no collusion, neither side had the telephone numbers of the other. The email sent by Cohen to Peskov in January 2016 demonstrated not 'the most direct interaction yet of a top Trump aide and a senior member of Putin's government', as the *Washington Post* put it in one of its typically lurid accounts in March 2017, but precisely the absence of established communication channels.[79] The report failed to note that at this time Russian operatives sent emails to Hope Hicks, Trump's spokesperson, in an attempt to establish contact, about which the Russian embassy in Washington commented later as follows: 'the Russian outreach to Ms Hicks undercuts the idea that the Russian government had established deep ties to the Trump campaign before the election. If it had, Russian officials might have found a better entrée to the White House than unprompted emails to Ms Hicks'.[80] The report confirmed that the exchanges between Sessions and Kislyak at the Republican National Convention were 'brief, public and non-substantive'.[81] The report's effective dismissal of the Steele dossier put paid to the conspiracy narratives constructed on its basis.

In sum, Mueller demonstrated that every key plank in the collusion narrative was unfounded. Russiagate was promoted by the Democrats 'relentlessly and above all else', as Clinton campaign senior aide Jennifer Palmieri put it, and left them in a quandary. They could either accept the verdict and move on or double down and seek to continue the investigation by other means. The latter strategy was pursued by Schiff, but even his efforts were deflated by Mueller's findings. The Democrats had wasted enormous amount of effort on a futile quest and failed to address the domestic issues that had led to their defeat. Trump's repeated tweets about 'no collusion' had been proved right, and he was gifted a massive public relations prize as he prepared for re-election in 2020.

NOTES

1. McFarland, *Revolution*, p. 63.
2. Wolff, *Fire and Fury*, p. 153.
3. Cohen, *War With Russia*, pp. 152–7.
4. Justin Raimondo, 'Boomerang: Russiagate Turns into Spygate', Antiwar.com, 5 April 2017, https://original.antiwar.com/justin/2017/04/04/boomerang-russia-gate-turns-into-spy-gate/.
5. Omarosa, *Unhinged*, p. 227.
6. Hettena, *Trump/Russia*, p. 116.
7. Evan Osnos, David Remnick and Joshua Yaffe, 'Trump, Putin, and the New Cold War', *New Yorker*, 6 March 2017, https://www.newyorker.com/magazine/2017/03/06/trump-putin-and-the-new-cold-war.
8. Wolff, *Fire and Fury*, p. 154.
9. Rod Rosenstein, *Order Appointing Robert Mueller as Special Prosecutor*, 17 May 2017; also in Mueller, *Report*, Vol. 2, p. A-1.
10. Shane and Mazzetti, 'The Plot to Subvert an Election'.
11. Jarrett, *The Russia Hoax*, p. 273.
12. Woodward, *Fear*, p. 165.
13. Wolff, *Fire and Fury*, p. 239.
14. Jarrett, *The Russia Hoax*, pp. 275–80; Weissmann, *Where Law Ends*, p. 167.
15. US Department of Justice, Memo from Rod Rosenstein to Robert Mueller, 2 August 2017, https://assets.documentcloud.org/documents/4429623/Rosenstein-Aug-2-2017-Memo-on-Mueller-Authority.pdf.
16. Kimberley A. Strassel, 'The Mueller Coverup', *Wall Street Journal*, 8 May 2020, https://www.wsj.com/articles/the-mueller-coverup-11588892114.
17. Woodward, *Rage*, p. 101.
18. Woodward, *Rage*, p. 114.
19. Woodward, *Fear*, p. 168, McCarthy, *Ball of Collusion*, pp. 343–8.

20. Woodward, *Fear*, p. 169.
21. Woodward, *Fear*, p. 172.
22. Rucker and Leonnig, *A Very Stable Genius*, p. 205.
23. Woodward, *Fear*, p. 197.
24. Woodward, *Fear*, p. 198.
25. Woodward, *Fear*, pp. 325, 198.
26. Weissmann, *Where Law Ends*, p. 263.
27. Woodward, *Fear*, p. 327.
28. Woodward, *Fear*, p. 355.
29. Woodward, *Fear*, p. 344.
30. Woodward, *Fear*, p. 344–5.
31. Woodward, *Fear*, p. 347.
32. Toobin argues that the Trump team turned Mueller's probity against him, *True Crimes and Misdemeanors*.
33. Woodward, *Fear*, p. 348.
34. Woodward, *Fear*, p. 349.
35. Woodward, *Fear*, p. 350.
36. Woodward, *Fear*, p. 351.
37. Woodward, *Fear*, p. 355.
38. Woodward, *Fear*, p. 357.
39. Mueller, *Report*, Vol. 2, Appendix C provides the full list of questions. They are mainly focused on who knew what and when; for example, the 9 June Trump Tower meeting. With no underlying crime to investigate, the questions were inherently banal.
40. Weissmann, *Where Law Ends*, p. 274.
41. Weissmann, *Where Law Ends*, p. 279.
42. Bolton, *Room Where it Happened*, p. 227.
43. McCarthy, 'A Bad Day for the President', p. 9.
44. Woodward, *Fear*, p. 173.
45. Woodward, *Fear*, p. 174.
46. Woodward, *Fear*, p. 270.
47. Jeffrey Toobin, 'Why the Mueller Investigation Failed', *New Yorker*, 29 June 2020, https://www.newyorker.com/magazine/2020/07/06/why-the-mueller-investigation-failed.
48. Taylor, 'Trump Won't Speak to Mueller'.
49. 'Attorney General Barr's Letter Summarizing the Mueller Report's Findings', 24 March 2019, https://www.wbur.org/news/2019/03/24/read-attorney-general-barrs-letter-summarizing-the-mueller-reports-findings.
50. David Rohde, 'William Barr, Trump's Sword and Shield', *New Yorker*, 13 January 2020, https://www.newyorker.com/magazine/2020/01/20/william-barr-trumps-sword-and-shield.
51. Rucker and Leonnig, *A Very Stable Genius*, p. 330.
52. The Attorney General, Washington DC, 24 March 2019, https://judiciary.house.gov/sites/democrats.judiciary.house.gov/files/documents/AG%20March%2024%202019%20Letter%20to%20House%20and%20Senate%20Judiciary%20Committees.pdf; also in Mueller, *Report*, Vol. 1, p. 13.

53. Examined by Rucker and Leonnig, *A Very Stable Genius*.
54. Woodward, *Rage*, p. 160.
55. Mueller, *Report*, Vol. 1, pp. 5 and 173.
56. Mueller, *Report*, Vol. 2, pp. 8, 182.
57. Weissmann, *Where Law Ends*, p. 312.
58. Weissmann, *Where Law Ends*, p. 316.
59. Weissmann, *Where Law Ends*, pp. xiii, 352–7 and *passim*.
60. Toobin, 'Why the Mueller Investigation Failed'.
61. Weissmann, *Where Law Ends*, p. xvi.
62. Weissmann, *Where Law Ends*, p. xxiii.
63. The Special Counsel's Office, Washington, DC, 27 March 2019, https://int.nyt.com/data/documenthelper/796-mueller-letter-to-barr/02499959cbfa313c36d4/optimized/full.pdf. For discussion see 'Mueller's Letter to AG Barr Criticizing his Framing of the Russia Report's Findings', 1 May 2019, https://www.vox.com/2019/5/1/18525296/mueller-report-letter-william-barr-testimony.
64. Mueller, *Report*, Vol. 1, p. 110.
65. Strzok, *Compromised*, p. 128.
66. McCarthy, *Ball of Collusion*, pp. 50–1.
67. Strzok, *Compromised*, p. 128.
68. Aaron Maté, 'The Mueller Indictments Still Don't Add up to Collusion', *The Nation*, 13 June 2018, https://www.thenation.com/article/archive/mueller-indictments-still-dont-add-collusion/.
69. Mueller, *Report*, Vol. 1, p. 131.
70. Weissmann, *Where Law Ends*, p. 183.
71. John Solomon, 'Key Figure that Mueller Report Linked to Russia was a State Department Intel Source', *The Hill*, 6 June 2019, https://thehill.com/opinion/white-house/447394-key-figure-that-mueller-report-linked-to-russia-was-a-state-department.
72. Mueller, *Report*, Vol. 1, pp. 144, 146.
73. Mueller, *Report*, Vol. 1, p. 166.
74. Mueller, *Report*, Vol. 1, p. 3.
75. Mueller, *Report* Vol. 2, p. 182.
76. Mueller, *Report* Vol. 2, p. 75.
77. Mueller, *Report* Vol. 2, p. 157.
78. Mueller, *Report* Vol. 2, p. 61.
79. A point made by Matt Taibbi, 'The Press Will Learn Nothing from the Russiagate Fiasco', *Rolling Stone*, 23 April 2019, https://www.rollingstone.com/politics/politics-features/russiagate-fiasco-taibbi-news-media-826246/.
80. Embassy of the Russian Federation, *The Russiagate Hysteria*, p. 55.
81. Mueller, *Report*, p. 10.

Chapter 13

Russiagate Questioned

Mueller concluded that there was no conspiracy or coordination (he eschewed the term 'collusion') between Trump and the Russians. Glenn Greenwald, a former lawyer who worked on the first Snowden story for the *Guardian* and then established the Intercept website, stresses that 'Robert Mueller did not merely reject the Trump-Russia conspiracy. He obliterated it'.[1] Mueller's investigation led to thirty-four indictments, including Trump's personal attorney Michael Cohen, campaign chair Paul Manafort, deputy campaign chair and long-time Manafort associate Rick Gates, national security adviser Michael Flynn, public relations specialist Roger Stone and a clutch of Russians – but not any of Trump's family – Donald Trump Jr. or Jared Kushner. Neither did he charge anyone in the Trump team with conspiring with Russia to fix the 2016 election. Despite Trump's refusal to provide evidence in person, Mueller did not issue a subpoena against him. Mueller decided not to press charges against Trump for obstruction, a decision prompted not just by DoJ policy against indicting a sitting president but based on his own assessment of the evidence, although he left the door open for others to do so. On the other side, despite endless grumbles, Trump did not fire Mueller or covertly interfere in the investigation. Trump's fulminations against the special counsel were public and frequent. The Mueller report is as interesting for what it failed to cover as much as for what it did. Even as Mueller put to rest a number of myths, critics insisted that there were still questions to be answered.[2]

Chapter 13

AN INVESTIGATION IN SEARCH OF A CRIME

In his characteristically pithy way, Putin was scathing about the Mueller report. On 9 April 2019, he noted that it was

> total nonsense targeted exclusively to a domestic audience and used in internal political battles . . . a mountain gave birth to a mouse . . . It is evidence of a certain element of crisis in the American political system . . . mounting an offensive against the legitimately elected president and trying to annul the outcome . . . putting their party or group interests above the national interest.[3]

Later, in his meeting with secretary of state Mike Pompeo on 14 May in Sochi, Putin endorsed the sentiment expressed by Trump in a ninety-minute call (initiated by the American side) on 3 May about the restoration of relations and the resolution of issues of mutual interest. Putin declared that 'we also would like to rebuild fully fledged relations, and I hope that right now a conducive environment is being built for that'. He had in mind the Mueller report, which he lauded: 'For all special counsel Mueller's exotic work, he carried out an impartial investigation and confirmed the lack of any trace of any collusion between Russia and the acting administration – which we from the very beginning characterised as utter nonsense'.[4] The removal of the collusion allegations provided some space for manoeuvre, but as Putin noted shortly afterwards, U.S.–Russian relations were getting 'worse and worse', and he 'really hoped that common sense will prevail in the end'.[5] Trump once again asserted that he hoped the United States would have 'a great relationship with Russia', but pledged to deploy 1,000 U.S. troops in Poland and considered sanctions over the Nord Stream 2 natural gas pipeline project, warning Germany against becoming dependent on Russia for energy.[6] Conflict between the two countries long predated Russiagate, and the structural features of the antagonism would not be soon resolved. The interference question, moreover, did not disappear, and Pompeo warned that any action by the Russians in the 2020 election 'would put our relationship in an even worse place than it has been'.[7]

Papadopoulos claims to have known nothing about the DNC emails, and probably about any emails at all. Papadopoulos certainly made exaggerated claims about his status and magnified the significance of his putative Moscow connections. Above all, did Mifsud really tell him about Moscow having emails when they met in London on 26 April 2016? The Mueller report rather craftily implies that Mifsud was a Russian agent, but there is no evidence of this – and in fact, if Mifsud had any intelligence connections, they were with the British. Mueller phrases the issue in such a way as to obscure the weakness of his argument, and instead suggests that Papadopoulos had reason to believe that Mifsud was a Russian agent, not that he actually was. Mifsud was interviewed by the FBI on 10 February 2017 (an event not confirmed by the FBI) and denied knowing anything about or having said anything about Russia's possession of Clinton-related emails.[8] Mueller did not pursue or charge Mifsud, although his testimony is obviously crucial. The point is that before he was interviewed by the FBI in January 2017, Papadopoulos did not report anything about Russia having emails to Washington or to Downer – with the latter he at the most stated that the Russians had damaging information, but there was no mention of emails. It was only in his FBI interview that Papadopoulos claimed that Mifsud had told him that the Russians had 'thousands' of Clinton emails. The recording has not been made public, so the accuracy of the reports cannot be verified, and we cannot tell if Papadopoulos is telling the truth, or whether nine months after the events, his memory was distorted. As for the other half of the story, neither Mueller nor any other source suggests that Papadopoulos was ever told that Russia intended, either directly or through an intermediary, to disseminate damaging information about Clinton.

No less odd is the way that the Mueller remains studiously silent about the Papadopoulos–Downer meeting, and there is no statement from Downer. His position is stated obliquely, and Mueller quotes not what Papadopoulos said to Downer, but what Downer is said to have understood that Papadopoulos had 'suggested':

> Papadopoulos had suggested to a representative of that foreign government that the Trump Campaign had received indications from the Russian government that it could assist the Campaign through the anonymous release of information damaging to Democratic presidential candidate Hillary Clinton. That information prompted the FBI on July 31, 2016, to open an investigation into whether individuals associated with the Trump Campaign were coordinating with the Russian government in its interference activities.[9]

If we translate Mueller-speak, by the 'Trump Campaign' we mean Papadopoulos, and the 'Russian government' is represented by Mifsud. Mueller states that Papadopoulos was interviewed in late January 2017 because of his 'suggestion' to Downer that Russia sought to help Trump by releasing damaging information about Clinton.[10] Papadopoulos had 'suggested' no such thing, and instead Downer, and Mueller following his lead, read backwards to believe that the WikiLeaks material of 22 July 2016 was what Papadopoulos had been talking about, when in fact it could not have been. Downer, moreover, was not an impartial observer. In addition to his close links with the British security establishment, he had earlier supported Clinton's 2008 presidential bid.[11]

The Papadopoulos story offset the discredited Steele dossier as the *fons et origo* of Russiagate, yet there is an element of deception involved here. The first memo, it will be recalled, asserted that the Trump campaign was conspiring with the Kremlin to influence the 2016 election. Gaeta took the memo back to Nuland, who passed it on to the FBI, thus starting the Russiagate narrative. Steele shows no prescience about the DNC emails published by WikiLeaks, but once they emerged, he folded the story into his memos.[12] By then the information from British intelligence had already been fed to American agencies, and the highly political CIA director, Brennan, met with GCHQ head Hannigan at some unspecified time in the same month, July 2016. The Downer information only gave some sort of external legitimacy to an investigation that was already getting under way, but what Papadopoulos told Downer created a false connection between what Papadopoulos had told Downer and the publication of the hacked DNC emails.

Mueller's equivocations opened the door to political speculation. Nancy Pelosi, who following the November 2018 midterm elections had returned as speaker of the Democratic-majority House of Representatives, argued that the attorney general committed a 'crime' when he told a congressional hearing that he was unaware about Mueller's dissatisfaction with his portrayal of the report. Pelosi characterised Trump's obstructive actions as 'villainous to the constitution' but resisted calls for his impeachment (a two-thirds Senate majority was lacking), but asserted she would rather 'see him in jail'.[13] The chair of the House Judiciary Committee, Jerry Nadler, threatened to hold Barr in contempt of Congress if he failed to explain himself, although the underlying gripe was with his failure to provide them with the full unredacted version of the report and the underlying evidence, as demanded by the House.[14] Barr was accused of acting as 'Trump's human shield on capitol hill'.[15] At the same time, six separate committees in the House investigated Trump, Kushner, the Trump Tower Moscow project and much more. As for Nadler, his attempts to keep the Russiagate investigation going met understandable resistance, with former White House counsel McGahn in mid-May defying a subpoena to appear before Congress.[16] The investigative work by House Democrats indicated their refusal to accept that Mueller had provided the answers, and certainly not the answers that they wanted. This was accompanied by a public loss of faith in the investigation, with half believing Trump's contention that he was the victim of a 'witch-hunt'.[17]

Mueller himself kept the obstruction charge alive. In his second book on the Trump presidency, Michael Wolff added fuel to this by claiming that Mueller considered charging the president with three counts of obstruction: disrupting proceedings before a federal agency; tampering with witnesses, victim or informant; and retaliation against a witness, victim or informant. The indictment according to Wolff sat on Mueller's desk for a year before being rejected.[18] In the end, Mueller left it to the justice department to decide, but in his view, the over-riding theme of the Trump presidency was the 'extraordinary lengths' taken 'to protect himself from legal scrutiny and accountability'.[19] The published text was edited to remove references to information gained as a result of the grand jury process (in other words, to protect witnesses), and it is highly likely that unredacted copies provided to Congress (as demanded) would be leaked to the press. On 8 May, the HJC voted to hold Barr in contempt of Congress, to which Trump responded by invoking the principle of executive privilege, claiming the right to prevent members of Congress from reading the full report. Nadler declared that 'We are now in a constitutional crisis'.[20] In the event, the HJC was provided with the underlying evidence of the Mueller report.

The investigation came to focus on investigating obstruction to the investigation. Comey weighed in to argue that there was enough evidence in the Mueller report to prove that Trump had committed obstruction of justice, and only the fact that he was president prevented him being indicted. The key to any obstruction charge is criminal intent by the perpetrator, and Comey found this in at least two instances. The first was when Trump directed the former White House counsel McGahn to fire Mueller, and the second was when Trump tried to limit the scope of the special counsel's investigation.[21] The Mueller report appears to be less about colluding with Russia than about Trump obstructing an investigation into the collusion that did not exist. Trump presciently tweeted in June 2017: 'They made up a phony collusion with the Russians story, found zero proof, so now they go for obstruction of justice on the phony story. Nice'.[22] Mueller's failure to find evidence of collusion was proof of collusion: like Schrödinger's cat, it was both there and not there.

After keeping tight-lipped for the duration of his work, in his first press conference on 29 May 2019, Mueller reiterated the point that he had not exonerated Trump of obstruction charges, immediately prompting calls in Congress for Trump's impeachment. Breaking his two-year silence, Mueller stated, 'I have not exonerated Trump' and went on, 'If we had confidence that the president clearly did not commit a crime, we would have said that'. He noted, 'We did not, however, make a determination as to whether the president did commit a crime', but the decision not to proceed was based on the long-standing DoJ policy that 'A president cannot be charged with a federal crime while he is in office'. Trump tweeted in response: 'Nothing changes from the Mueller report. There was insufficient evidence and therefore, in our country, a person is innocent. The case is closed! Thank you'. However, Mueller's intervention was taken as a signal to Congress that they were not bound by the incumbency rule, and hence could proceed towards impeachment.[23] In the end they did, but not over Russiagate but its complement, 'Ukrainegate'.

The Mueller report implied that there was collusion while providing evidence that there was not. The fundamental premise appeared to be that the absence of evidence is not proof of the absence of evidence. Mueller reported Russian interference as something unprecedented and uniquely effective and which helped Trump gain the presidency. Congressional Democrats ignored the substantive findings of the report and argued that Barr should resign for 'misleading the American people about collusion between the Trump campaign and Russia'. In other words, the Mueller report failed to nail the charge, and partisans of Russiagate continued to issue warnings of further Russian interference as the 2020 presidential election approached.[24] Politicians and journalists who had invested in the collusion narrative advanced precisely the sort of conspiracy-laden alternative reality that they believed they were resisting.

CRIMES IN SEARCH OF INVESTIGATION

The report does not substantiate allegations of collusion let alone conspiracy (requiring substantial evidence), and its central claim that Russia interfered 'in sweeping and systematic fashion' is deceptive. This becomes clear when we look at what the report does not examine. It did not undertake a credible investigation of the source of the collusion allegations, or the central charge of the whole affair, that Russia not only hacked the DNC servers but passed the material to WikiLeaks. Mueller failed to call numerous relevant witnesses or to examine alternative narratives. He did not investigate the persistent claims, buttressed by considerable evidence, that in various ways the FBI, the CIA and British intelligence hyped up the various alleged 'links' between the Trump campaign and Russia, when in fact most of these links proved spurious. Russia ran various operations in the United States, but this is what intelligence agencies do. The Soviet Union created front companies and published and disseminated propaganda, just as the United States did in the USSR and continues to do in Russia today. In conditions of the new cold war, this is hardly surprising. What is new is that these so-called 'active measures' were turned against Russia by one of the candidates as a campaign weapon against the other, with the active support of parts of the intelligence establishment, the media and non-Russian foreign actors.

No compelling evidence to start the investigation into the Trump campaign has emerged. Instead, 'the FBI operated on the basis of an overheard conversation of third-tier campaign aide George Papadopoulos, as well a wild "dossier" financed by the rival presidential campaign'. Comey's gyrations have been described, but the question remains: 'How aware was the FBI that it was being gulled into a dirty-trick operation, and if so, how did it justify proceeding?'

> If Mr. Mueller [had] done his job properly... His team would have had to look into the sources of the allegations as part of determining the documents (lack of) veracity. A Mueller report that doesn't mention the dossier and its political provenance, or questionable news stories used to justify surveillance warrants, for instance, is a report that is playing politics.[25]

Mueller identified Mifsud as a 'London professor with ties to Russia'. This is accurate as far as it goes. I met Mifsud when he attended annual meetings of the Valdai Discussion Club and twice spoke at his London Academy of Diplomacy, with an extended lunch with him on one of these occasions. As befits a former diplomat, Mifsud was highly personable and knowledgeable, but his complex past may include, as alleged by WikiLeaks and Disobedient Media, that he had links with MI6 and the CIA. Given the resources at Mueller's disposal, the question should at least have been explored further, if nothing else to dispel the justified criticism that the special counsel investigators feared to go where uncomfortable truths could be found.

This applies above all to the provenance of the Steele dossier and its outlandish claims. The Steele dossier is barely mentioned, which is all the more surprising because of the central part that it pays in the whole Russiagate affair. Three of the Russiagate cast at one time or another were confidential human sources for the FBI: Felix Sater, since December 1998, and he was signed up by none other than Weissmann; Henry Greenberg, the mystery man who met Roger Stone in Miami six months before the 2016 election and tried to sell dirt on Clinton; and Steele himself. Greenberg (also known as Henry Oknyansky) was allegedly a long-term paid FBI informant.[26] Steele's status as a paid CHS was confirmed by a Judicial Watch Freedom of Information (FOIA) request in August 2018, showing that Steele received at least eleven payments during the nine-month period that he was signed up as a CHS between 2 February and 1 November 2016. Claims that Steele's relations with the FBI only began on 5 July 2016 have been disproved. Why did Mueller not report that Steele met the FBI's Strzok in July 2016? Mueller knew that Steele's dossier was possibly one of the predicates for opening Crossfire Hurricane and certainly for the FISA warrants against Carter Page. Steele was interviewed, but the failure to pursue obvious questions exposes the investigation to charges of bias and even deception.[27] Mueller notes that 'Trump would not pay for opposition research' but makes no comment on the Clinton campaign's enthusiastic search for 'dirt' on Trump.[28]

Mueller takes at face value the U.S. intelligence reports but fails to address the activities of people like Brennan at the head of the CIA in actively fostering the Russiagate narrative. He relies on contemporary media accounts and ignores the widespread evidence of journalistic malpractice throughput the whole affair, which some (e.g. Matt Taibbi) have likened to the distorted news reports in the run-up to the Iraq war in 2003. Above all, Mueller endorses the Clinton and Democratic version of the stolen emails – that Russia was responsible for their dissemination – and pays no attention to alternative accounts (for example, the VIPS reports) and did not conduct its own analysis. Why did Mueller not question Assange or Craig Murray, let alone look more deeply into the role of Mifsud?[29] Mueller accuses Assange of 'dissembling' by allegedly exploiting the murder of Seth Rich, yet he does not answer why Rich's computers were not subject to forensic examination. Murray could barely contain his rage, writing that 'Robert Mueller is either a fool, or deeply corrupt. I do not think he is a fool'. He noted that Mueller 'omitted key steps which any honest investigator would undertake', including commissioning a forensic examination of the DNC servers or interview Binney or Assange. 'His failure to do any of those obvious things renders his report worthless'.[30]

It may have been too much to expect the Mueller report to reflect on its findings, but some sort of assessment of how the thirteen persons and three organizations charged in February 2018 could have affected the electoral process in a nation of 323 million would have been useful. Instead, the report endeavoured to inflate its rather meagre findings of Russian interference. This obviously had enormous foreign policy implications, and the report's threat inflation can be categorised as an act of dangerous political irresponsibility. The indictment of the GRU officers allegedly responsible for the DNC hack on the eve of the first Putin–Trump summit in Helsinki sabotaged the meeting. Mueller's attempt to salvage the relevance of his investigation was prioritised over the stated goal of the Trump administration to improve relations with Russia. The same applies to the notion that 3,000 Russia-linked ads on Facebook costing about $100,000 could shape the preferences of the electorate. The report was prone to editorial comment, but most damaging was the implication that any contact between Trump campaign members and Russia was sinister or even criminal. This discredited what even Mueller admits was a desire for 'improved US–Russian relations', a 'new beginning with Russia', and attempts to bring about 'the end of the new cold war'. Mueller concedes that Putin sought 'reconciliation between the United States and Russia'.[31] The effect was to discredit advocates of détente, and those in favour were tainted as holding 'pro-Russian foreign policy positions'.[32]

Roger Stone in the Barrel

There was an air of inevitability about Stone's arrest by the FBI on 25 January 2019. His time 'in the barrel' had come.[33] Stone warned in August 2018 that

'Robert Mueller is coming for me'. He was charged with obstruction, lying to Congress and witness tampering. The essence of the charge was that Stone acted as a link between the Trump campaign and Assange, with WikiLeaks timing the disclosures to inflict maximum damage on Clinton. The twenty-four-page indictment filed the previous day alleged that Stone was asked by Trump's campaign to gain inside information about the Democrat emails that were passed to WikiLeaks. In June or July 2016, Stone is alleged to have told senior Trump campaign officials that he knew that WikiLeaks had damaging information about Clinton.[34] Assange first publicly stated on British TV on 12 June that he would be releasing information about Clinton, and two days later, it was reported that the DNC had been hacked. After WikiLeaks started publishing the material on 22 July, Stone repeatedly tried to contact WikiLeaks, then 'told the Trump campaign about potential future releases of damaging material'. He asked Jerome Corsi, a former contributor to the conspiracy website Infowars and who is best known for propagating the 'birther' falsehood that Obama was born outside the United States, to request that Ted Malloch, a London-based American academic, visit Assange in the Ecuadorian embassy. Then Stone contacted Randy Credico, a spirited radio show host with connections to WikiLeaks, and Credico on 1 October told Stone that there would be 'big news' that week. As we have seen, on 7 October, WikiLeaks began publishing the Podesta emails. Stone later took credit for passing on inside information to senior Trump staff.

The prosecutors wanted to know how Stone had correctly predicted that WikiLeaks would publish damaging emails about Clinton. To that end, they wanted Corsi to acknowledge that Stone had asked him during the campaign to contact Assange to find out what material they still had to release.[35] The idea that Corsi, who at the time was close on 80, had anything significant to do with Assange and the leaked emails is far-fetched. As for Malloch, in July 2016, he allegedly passed on a request from long-time Trump advisor Stone to Assange to provide advance copies of emails stolen from Trump's opponents and later published by WikiLeaks. Malloch was investigated by Mueller on the grounds that he may have linked the Trump campaign and the Brexit Leave campaign in the UK.[36] The charge for the first time linked the Trump campaign to the DNC emails, although White House press secretary Sarah Sanders insisted that the case had 'nothing to do with the president'.[37] To his chagrin, Stone held no official position in the Trump campaign, but he had been a long-standing informal political advisor and had been urging Trump to run for the presidency since the 1980s.

The Stone matter shared the prosecutorial bias of the other Russiagate cases. People were convicted not for Trump–Russia collusion but for financial improprieties and process crimes. Stone was charged with one count of obstructing a congressional investigation, five counts of lying to Congress and one count of witness tampering. They all concerned his alleged communications with WikiLeaks seeking information about its publication plans. Any advance knowledge that Stone may have had about WikiLeaks' publishing plans is not a crime. Trump officials may have asked for more information, which Stone does not appear to have had. WikiLeaks timed its publication on the eve of the Democratic convention to inflict maximum harm on Clinton, but there is no evidence that this was coordinated with the Trump campaign. As usual, the charges arise not from the original acts but the alleged lies about them. In this case, Stone testified to the HPSCI on 26 September 2017 that he had 'no emails, no texts, no documents whatsoever' concerning hacked documents or conversations about Assange. Stone mocked Mueller in an Instagram post a day after his arrest: 'Here's what Mueller has on me #nothingburger', with a picture of a platter and an empty bun, and he denounced the pre-dawn raid on his home as 'Gestapo tactics'.[38] Alarmingly, the *New Yorker* reported the arrest in Stalinist terms: 'Robert Mueller got Roger Stone'.[39]

He was charged with lying to and obstructing Congress about the WikiLeaks releases. At the time, there was intense speculation about when Assange would publish the next tranche, so Stone's interest was not surprising. There is no evidence that his communications with Credico, Corsi or Malloch established a secret 'back channel' to WikiLeaks, and the messages between Stone and the official WikiLeaks account (leaked to the press by the HPSCI) are far from incriminating. Stone was charged with witness tampering and intimidation, but in a letter to presiding judge Amy Berman, Jackson Credico stressed that 'I never in any way felt that Stone himself posed a direct physical threat to me or my dog [the latter had allegedly been threatened]', although he noted that Stone 'shamelessly invents and promotes outlandish and invidious conspiracy tales'.[40] The prosecutors recommended a sentence of between seven and nine years. Trump described the recommendation as 'horrible' and a 'miscarriage of justice', and the DoJ on 11 February revised the sentencing recommendation to no more than three or four years. All four federal prosecutors resigned from the case in protest.[41]

In November 2019, Stone was convicted on the charges arising from the Mueller investigation. Trial judge Jackson refused to allow Stone to call Binney and McGovern to testify. On 20 February, Stone was sentenced to forty months in jail. Jackson accused Stone of covering up for Trump and argued 'The truth still exists. The truth still matters'.[42] At sixty-eight and with serious medical conditions, Stone asked for the sentence to be deferred beyond the 14 July date when he was due to report since the designated correctional facility suffered an outbreak of Covid-19. Given the pandemic, he feared that his prison term would become a 'death sentence'. Jackson refused, contrary to the guidelines of the U.S. Bureau of Prisons, which advised that non-violent offenders were to be released into home confinement until the coronavirus pandemic was under control. However, on 10 July, Trump commuted the sentence, with the White House stating 'Roger Stone has already suffered greatly. He was treated very unfairly, as were many others in this case'.[43]

The decision prompted widespread outrage, with Mueller issuing a rare statement: 'I feel compelled to respond both to broad claims that our investigation was illegitimate and our motives were improper, and to specific claims that Roger Stone was a victim of our office'.[44] In an op-ed in the *Washington Post* on 11 July, Mueller asserted that Stone 'lied about the identity of his intermediary to WikiLeaks', as well as about the existence of written communications with his intermediary'.[45] However, his own investigation had failed to establish that Stone had an intermediary with WikiLeaks. Stone publicly claimed such links, but Mueller found that they were Credico and Corsi, and they never made contact with WikiLeaks. Credico did interview Assange on his radio show in August 2016, but there is no evidence of further contact. In fact, WikiLeaks sent Stone a Twitter message before the election asking him to cease making 'false claims of association', an exchange that for some reason was excluded from Stone's indictment and the Mueller report. Stone claimed that he had advance knowledge of WikiLeaks' publication of stolen DNC emails, but the Mueller report never argued that he had such knowledge. As demonstrated earlier, 'Stone's contact with Guccifer 2.0 was minimal and inconsequential'.[46] In late 2020, unredacted additional pages of the Mueller report finally revealed that investigators found 'insufficient evidence . . . to establish beyond reasonable doubt that Stone or any other persons associated with the Campaign coordinated with WikiLeaks on the release of the emails'.[47]

THE ACCUSED FIGHT BACK

Weissmann wanted to indict the president, but Mueller was more cautious. However, for lesser figures caught up in Russiagate, he was less merciful. Unreported lobbying by Flynn was leveraged to get him to plead guilty to lying to the FBI. Cohen was charged with numerous financial crimes, but his guilty plea was for campaign finance violations that could well be considered personal expenses. As for the Moscow Tower, while efforts did continue after January 2016, these were at the most desultory. It was a sign of desperation for Cohen to try to enlist Peskov to help. Papadopoulos was forced to plead guilty about lying about the timing of his contacts. The best-selling author Jerome Corsi was threatened about lying about his contacts with his friend Roger Stone, although there was nothing illegal about his activities. Roger Stone suggested in a tweet that the email of John Podesta would be the next to be revealed, and in an email to Corsi asked him to get the rest of the emails.

He appeared to want to know what was going on, and there was nothing illegal about what he did or that he was party to the deep secrets about Clinton team emails. Carter Page in November 2020 filed an eight-count complaint against the DoJ, the FBI and its former director Comey, seeking at least $75 million in damages over, among other things, obtaining what were claimed to be the four illegal FISA warrants against him.[48] Manafort's tax misdemeanours were levered to get him to work with Mueller, but he was one of the few to resist the pressure – and as a result was jailed (although he was released in May 2020 because of Covid-19). A special prosecutor vested with such wide powers as Mueller could not return empty-handed. Even more disturbing, the whole exercise appeared designed to undermine Trump and possibly even to destroy his presidency. America was at war with itself in a struggle in which there could be no winners.

Mueller anticipated the GRU hackers would accept trials in absentia, but he was shocked when in 2019 they commissioned representatives to fight the case on their behalf. Mueller was forced to backtrack and asked for an immediate adjournment when the case opened and fought to limit disclosure, individual by individual. A conviction was sought without the defendants seeing the evidence against them.[49] On the other side, the DNC brought a lawsuit against Russia, WikiLeaks, Assange and key members of Trump's team, including Trump himself, Kushner, Manafort, the Agalarovs, Roger Stone and Joseph Mifsud. The collusion charges would finally be tested in a court of law. In the event the judge, John Koeltl of the Federal District of New York, ruled that the Russiagate claims were insufficient even to merit a hearing. He argued that even if everything that the DNC alleged did indeed happen, there was no basis for a case. The Russian Federation cannot be sued in a U.S. court, and as for dissemination of the materials, the first amendment rights defended WikiLeaks as the publisher, as long as it was not directly involved in illegal activities to gain the material (a ruling with implications for the Assange extradition hearing in London).[50] Above all, he stated that the DNC offered no evidence of collusion between WikiLeaks and the other named parties to hack the DNC's computers or of a relationship between Russia and WikiLeaks. No evidence had been produced of collusion between WikiLeaks, the Trump campaign and Russia. Even if the facts at the heart of the Russiagate allegations were true, they did not add up to a plausible case in a court of law.[51]

Mueller charged thirteen IRA employees and three companies owned by Prigozhin with interfering in the 2016 election, but he was surprised that they turned up in court to fight their case. As the conservative commentator Rush Limbaugh put it, Mueller planned to use the indictments for public relations 'to convince people that the Russians did infiltrate and somehow meddle in the election'.[52] In May 2018, Concord Management and Concord Consulting pleaded not guilty and argued that special counsel Mueller was unlawfully appointed and lacked the legal authority to advance the case. Concord Management hired a leading U.S. legal company to defend itself against the allegations and called for the Mueller team to disclose how they obtained the detailed information about the Russian activities, including internal emails, travel itineraries, and personal details about the thirteen Russians. The defence team argued that it was impossible to charge Concord with interfering in U.S. elections, because there is no specific law against that. Not revealing identities at political rallies or on social media would confuse voters, but it is not evidence of intent to interfere with a U.S. government function. As so often, the Mueller team looked unprepared as they scrambled to find evidence of a crime, even though they had filed the indictment. The prosecutors also tried to limit Concord's access to the 3.2 million pieces of evidence on the grounds that they were too 'sensitive' for Russians to see. According to the federal judge in Washington presiding over the Concord Management case, Dabney Friedrich, the prosecution faced a 'heavy burden' in demonstrating that the trolls acted criminally and ordered Mueller's team to explain why they had indicted Concord for election meddling. The defence argued 'Mueller's office concocted a crime and that there's no law against interfering in elections'.[53]

There was no clear evidence that Concord sought to undermine Federal Election Commission (FEC) rules, hence the difficulty of proving the charge of a conspiracy to defraud the government. There are FEC rules prohibiting the use of foreign money to fund political candidates and restrictions on how foreigners can participate in elections, but it was a matter of free speech for someone to pretend to be someone else, and to say whatever they wanted within the law. While the indictment alleged that Concord defrauded the government by hiding the activity of trolls on a server within the United States and concealed that the trolls were operating from Russia, the defence asserted that was not illegal. They went further to argue that Mueller's 'prosecutorial adventure' was part of an Orwellian plot to use the Russian trolls as a way of constraining free speech on the internet. That was why the special counsel allegedly made up a crime to fit the facts: 'And that's the fundamental danger with the entire special counsel concept: that they operate outside the parameters of the Department of Justice in a way that is absolutely inconsistent with the behaviour of the Department of Justice in these cases for the past 30 years'.[54]

Mueller's claim of 'sweeping and systematic' Russian meddling was further challenged on 25 April 2019 when Concord filed an instant motion claiming that Mueller violated the law by releasing information to the public that was not contained in the original indictment. Concord argued that the special counsel's report 'improperly suggested a link between the defendants and the Russian government and expressed an opinion about the defendant's guilt and the evidence against them' and the Court ordered the government 'to refrain from making or authorising any public statement that links the alleged conspiracy in the indictment to the Russian government or its agencies'.[55] On 28 May, Friedrich famously ruled that Mueller's indictment of the 'troll farm' was not actually proof of it.[56] Mueller's implied link between the IRA and the Russian government was an assertion based on no stated evidence. A month before trial, on 16 March 2020, the Mueller charges against Concord were abruptly 'dismissed with prejudice' (meaning that it was permanently closed and could not be brought back to court). Prosecutors argued that the company had 'no exposure to meaningful punishment', and that the prosecution risked exposing investigative sources and methods. The next day, Prigozhin went on the offensive, arguing that the U.S. government 'feared publicity and just court proceedings', and claimed that it proved that charges of Russian interference were 'mendacious and false', and that he would sue the U.S. government for $50bn over 'wrongful persecution'.[57] The latter claim would go nowhere, but the case suggested that the indictment had been intended as a piece of political theatre rather than a serious criminal prosecution.

The only known individual to be charged with foreign interference in the November 2018 midterms is Elena Khusyainova, an employee of the IRA. A criminal complaint was filed against her by the DoJ on 19 October 2018. She was one of the thirteen previously indicted by Mueller for using fake accounts to spread divisive content on social media. She was charged with conspiring with others to 'spread misinformation about US political issues including immigration, gun control, the Confederate flag, and protests by NFL players. It [the IRA] also used events, including the Las Vegas mass shooting and the far-right rally in Charlottesville, to spread discord'. She had not personally engaged in such activity, but was the chief accountant overseeing Project Lakhta, responsible for 'meticulous record-keeping and management' of IRA accounts. She had apparently overseen the disbursement of $60,000 over the first six months of 2018 for advertisements on Facebook and $6,000 on Instagram, with both conservative and liberal messages. Most of the material was trivial, although some were racist and anti-Muslim. As Aaron Maté notes, 'All are so juvenile or inconsequential that it is difficult to see how they could have vastly greater influence than the millions of other pieces of political clickbait littering the Internet'. As with the rest of Russia's alleged misinformation, 'its most significant impact appears to be as fodder for ongoing efforts intent on convincing Americans that unsophisticated social-media trolling could somehow divide and weaken society'.[58] As for Khusyainova, she declared that 'my heart filled with pride' at the news that she had been accused of a covert media campaign in both the 2016 and 2018 elections. Speaking on Russian TV, she added, 'It turns out that a simple Russian woman could help the citizens of a superpower elect their president'.[59]

NOTES

1. Glenn Greenwald, 'Robert Mueller did not Merely Reject the Trump–Russia Conspiracy. He Obliterated it', 18 April 2019, https://theintercept.com/2019/04/18/robert-mueller-did-not-merely-reject-the-trumprussia-conspiracy-theories-he-obliterated-them/.
2. For example, Michael McFaul, 'Russia Attacked Us: The Mueller Report Still Doesn't Give us the Full Story', *Washington Post*, 21 April 2019, https://www.washingtonpost.com/opinions/2019/04/19/russia-attacked-us-mueller-report-still-doesnt-give-us-full-story/?utm_term=.b37520d82266.
3. 9 April 2019, Meeting of the Arctic Council, https://www.youtube.com/watch?v=q43_fS8rnfw.
4. Vladimir Putin, 'Meeting with US Secretary of State Mike Pompeo', 14 May 2019, http://en.kremlin.ru/events/president/news/60519.
5. 'Interv'yu Vladimira Putina Mezhgosudarstvennoi Teleradiokompanii "Mir"', 13 June 2019, http://kremlin.ru/events/president/news/60741.
6. Andrew Osborn, 'Putin Says US–Russia Relations are Getting "Worse and Worse"', Reuters, 13 June 2019, https://uk.reuters.com/article/uk-usa-russia-putin/putin-says-u-s-russia-relations-are-getting-worse-and-worse-idUKKCN1TE0LL?il=0%5D.
7. Darya Korsunskaya and Andrew Osborn, 'Pompeo Tells Russia: Don't Meddle in Next US Presidential Election', Reuter, 14 May 2019, https://uk.reuters.com/article/uk-russia-usa/pompeo-tells-russia-dont-meddle-in-next-u-s-presidential-election-idUKKCN1SK1GQ?il=0..
8. Mueller, *Report*, Vol. 1, p. 193.
9. Mueller, *Report*, Vol. 1, p. 1.
10. Mueller, *Report*, Vol. 1, p. 192.
11. Andrew C. McCarthy, 'The FBI's Trump-Russia Investigation was Formally Opened on False Pretenses, *National Review*, 6 May 2019, https://www.nationalreview.com/2019/05/fbi-trump-russia-investigation-george-papadopoulos/, from which the previous paragraphs draw.
12. McCarthy, 'The FBI's Trump-Russia Investigation'.
13. Sabrina Siddiqui, 'Speaker Pelosi Wants to see Trump "In Jail" Rather than Impeached', *Guardian*, 7 June 2019, p. 23.
14. Lauren Gambino, 'Pelosi says Barr Committed a Crime by Lying about Mueller Report', *Guardian*, 2 May 2019, https://www.theguardian.com/us-news/2019/may/02/pelosi-says-barr-committed-a-by-lying-about-mueller-report.
15. John Cassidy, 'Attorney General William Barr Acts as Donald Trump's Human Shield on Capitol Hill', *New Yorker*, 1 May 2019. https://www.newyorker.com/news/our-columnists/attorney-general-william-barr-acts-as-trumps-human-shield-on-capitol-hill.
16. Sabrina Siddiqui and David Smith, 'Democrats Thwarted: McGahn Defies Subpoena', *Guardian*, 22 May 2019, p. 24.
17. Poll conducted by *USA Today* and Suffolk University, Susan Page and Deborah Barfield Berry, 'Poll: Half of Americans say Trump is Victim of a "Witch Hunt" as Trust in Mueller Erodes', *USA Today*, 18 March 2019, https://eu.usatoday.

com/story/news/politics/2019/03/18/trust-mueller-investigation-falls-half-americans-say-trump-victim-witch-hunt/3194049002/.

18. Wolff, *Siege*, pp. 64, 312.

19. Edward Helmore, 'Mueller Drew up Trump Indictment, Book Claims', *Guardian*, 29 May 2019, p. 2.

20. David Smith, 'Will Trump Really Turn his Back on the Constitution', *Guardian*, 10 May 2019, p. 23.

21. Ed Pilkington, 'Comey Says Prosecutors Should Look at Charging Trump for Obstruction When He Leaves Office', *Guardian*, 11 May 2019, p. 26.

22. Cited by Stephen Kotkin, 'American Hustle: What Mueller Found – and Didn't Find – about Trump and Russia', *Foreign Affairs*, 21 May 2019, https://www.foreignaffairs.com/articles/2019-05-21/american-hustle.

23. David Smith, 'Mueller Breaks Two-Year Silence to Say: "I have not Exonerated Trump"', *Guardian*, 30 May 2019, pp. 1–2.

24. For example, Paul Waldman, 'Trump is Counting on Russian Help to get Re-elected', *Washington Post*, 7 May 2018, https://www.washingtonpost.com/opinions/2019/05/06/trump-is-counting-russian-help-get-reelected/?utm_term=.24ba824a12f9.

25. Kimberley A. Strassel, 'Mueller is Done: Now Probe the Real Scandal', *Wall Street Journal*, 25 March 2019, p. A19.

26. Larry C. Johnson, 'Glaring Omissions and Misrepresentations in Mueller's Report', Sic Semper Tyrannis, 9 May 2019, https://turcopolier.typepad.com/sic_semper_tyrannis/2019/05/the-mueller-report-cites-three-questionable-events-as-the-foundation-for-the-special-counsel-investigation-june-2016-the.html.

27. Larry C. Johnson, 'The Malevolent Farce that is Mueller and the Russia Hoax', *Sic Semper Tyrannis*, 5 May 2019, https://turcopolier.typepad.com/sic_semper_tyrannis/2019/05/the-mueller-dilemma.html. Johnson is a former CIA analyst.

28. Mueller, *Report*, Vol. 1, p. 61.

29. Many of these points are made by Stephen F. Cohen, 'Mueller's Own Mysteries', *The Nation*, 1 May 2019, https://www.thenation.com/article/muellers-own-mysteries/.

30. Murray, 'The Real Muellergate Scandal', www.craigmurray.org.uk, 9 May 2019, https://www.craigmurray.org.uk/archives/2019/05/the-real-muellergate-scandal/.

31. Mueller, *Report*, Vol. 1, pp. 5, 98, 105, 124, 157 and *passim*.

32. Mueller, *Report*, Vol. 1, p. 102.

33. For full, although biased, analysis, see Jeffrey Toobin, 'Roger Stone's and Jerome Corsi's Time in the Barrel', *New Yorker*, 18 & 25 February 2019, https://www.newyorker.com/magazine/2019/02/18/roger-stones-and-jerome-corsis-time-in-the-barrel.

34. *United States v. Roger Jason Stone, Jr.*, case 1: 18-cr-00215-ABJ, criminal indictment filed 24 January 2019, US District Court for the District of Columbia, https://www.lawfareblog.com/document-indictment-roger-stone.

35. Rucker and Leonnig, *A Very Stable Genius*, pp. 324–5.

36. Jon Swaine, 'Farage Ally Was Asked to Get Stolen Emails for Trump Team, Say Investigators', *Guardian*, 29 November 2018, p. 34.
37. Jon Swaine, Sabrina Siddiqui and Paul Owen, 'Key Trump Ally Charged in Mueller Investigation', *Guardian*, 26 January 2019, p. 2.
38. Tom McCarthy, '"Gestapo Tactics"', *Guardian*, 28 January 2019, p. 24.
39. Adam Davidson, 'Robert Mueller Got Roger Stone', *New Yorker*, 25 January 2019, https://www.newyorker.com/news/swamp-chronicles/robert-mueller-got-roger-stone.
40. Patrick Henningsen, 'Roger Stone's Conviction is the Last Hope to Save Russiagate', RT.com, 20 February 2020, https://www.rt.com/op-ed/481212-roger-stone-russiagate-trump/.
41. Michelle Goldberg, 'The Right's Big Lie about Roger Stone', *New York Times*, 16 February 2020, p. 3. She argues that Credico did in fact feel endangered when Stone warned Credico not to contradict him and warned that he would kidnap Credico's beloved dog.
42. Lauren Gambino, 'Trump Ally Roger Stone Sentenced to 40 Months in Prison', *Guardian*, 21 February 2020, p. 2.
43. Dareh Gregorian, Geoff Bennett, Pete Williams, Kristen Welker and Peter Alexander, 'Trump Commutes Roger Stone's Prison Sentence After he was Convicted of Covering up for the President', NBC News, 11 July 2020, https://www.nbcnews.com/politics/donald-trump/trump-commutes-roger-stone-s-prison-sentence-after-he-was-n1138981.
44. Joanna Walters and Mark Oliver, 'Mueller Joins Outcry over US President's Decision to Commute Stone Sentence', *Guardian*, 13 July 2020, p. 2.
45. Robert S. Mueller III, 'Robert Mueller: Roger Stone Remains a Convicted Felon, and Rightly So', *Washington Post*, 11 July 2020, https://www.washingtonpost.com/opinions/2020/07/11/mueller-stone-oped/?arc404=true.
46. Aaron Maté, 'Mueller and Weissman Op-Eds Greatly at Odds with their Report and Evidence', *RealClearInvestigations*, 16 July 2020, https://www.realclearinvestigations.com/articles/2020/07/16/mueller_and_weissmann_op-eds_greatly_at_odds_with_their_report_and_evidence_124483.html.
47. Aaron Maté, 'It's Trump's Last Chance to Declassify These Secrets of the Russia Collusion Dud', *Real Clear Investigations*, 10 January 2021, https://www.realclearinvestigations.com/articles/2021/01/10/its_trumps_last_chance_to_declassify_these_russia_non-collusion_mysteries_126696.html.
48. Sarah Elbeshbishi, 'Ex-Trump Campaign Adviser Carter Page Sues FBI, Comey, McCabe and Others for $75 Million over Russia Probe Surveillance, *USA Today*, 28 November 2020, https://eu.usatoday.com/story/news/politics/2020/11/28/carter-page-ex-trump-aide-sues-comey-fbi-over-russia-surveillance/6453096002/.
49. Craig Murray, 'The Real Muellergate Scandal', www.craigmurray.org.uk, 9 May 2019, https://www.craigmurray.org.uk/archives/2019/05/the-real-muellergate-scandal/.
50. 'DNC Lawsuit: Order Granting Motion to Dismiss', 30 July 2019, p. 3 and *passim*, https://www.scribd.com/document/420269577/DNC-lawsuit-ORDER-Granting-Motion-to-Dismiss-073019.

51. The case is summarised by Craig Murray, 'Russiagate is Dead, but for the Political Establishment, it is Still the New 42', *Consortium News*, 23 August 2019,

52. Cheryl K. Chumley, 'Robert Mueller's Sinking Russian Collusion Ship', *Washington Times*, 23 October 2018, https://www.washingtontimes.com/news/2018/oct/23/robert-muellers-sinking-russian-collusion-ship/.

53. Edvard Pettersson, 'Mueller Ordered to Clarify Claims against Putin Ally's Company', *Bloomberg*, 19 October 2018, https://www.bloomberg.com/news/articles/2018-10-19/mueller-ordered-to-clarify-claims-against-putin-ally-s-company.

54. 'Judge: Mueller Faces "Heavy Burden" to Prove Criminality of Russian Troll Farm', *Sputnik*, 30 October 2018, https://sputniknews.com/us/201810301069336594-judge-mueller-heavy-burden-criminal-troll-farm/.

55. Larry C. Johnson, 'A Cornerstone of Russia Hacked the 2016 Election Collapses', *Sic Semper Tyrannis*, 17 March 2020, https://turcopolier.typepad.com/sic_semper_tyrannis/2020/03/cornerstone-of-russia-hacked-the-2016-election-collapses-by-larry-c-johnson.html.

56. The ruling was issue in May but only unsealed on 1 July, 'Another Nail in the Russiagate Coffin?', RT.com, 11 July 2019, https://www.rt.com/usa/463880-judge-mueller-concord-russiagate/. See also Daniel Lazare, 'Concord Management and the End of Russiagate?', *Consortium News*, 12 July 2019, https://consortiumnews.com/2019/07/12/concord-management-and-the-end-of-russiagate/.

57. Andrew Roth, '"'Putin's Chef" Threatens to Sue US over Election Meddling Charges', *Guardian*, 18 March 2020, p. 36.

58. Maté, 'With Just Days to go to the Midterms, Russiagate is MIA'.

59. Angela Charlton, 'Why It's Still in Russia's Interest to Mess with US Politics', AP, 4 November 2018, https://apnews.com/877c37d98203426ea222ddf20071f92d.

Chapter 14

Fruit of a Poisoned Tree

Mueller's indictments focused less on the central charge of a Trump–Russia conspiracy than on process crimes. The Justice Department took the lead in examining the origins of Russiagate, which developed into a criminal investigation. Some fundamental questions were raised.[1] First, why did the FBI launch an investigation into Trump's presidential campaign based on tenuous and partisan predicates? How far did the FBI rely on the Steele dossier case to launch Crossfire Hurricane and, later, the FISA warrants against Carter Page? Second, Barr and Durham focused on the part played by the CIA in mobilising other security agencies in driving forward the Russia–Trump collusion narrative. The early FBI investigations had a political agenda, and then the same team was assigned to work with Mueller: 'And if Crossfire was politically motivated, then its culmination, the appointment of a special counsel, inherited the taint. All special counsel activities – investigations, plea deals, subpoenas, reports, indictments and convictions – are fruit of a poisonous tree, byproducts of a violation of due process'.[2] These conclusions flow inescapably from the Horowitz report. At the same time, the media was caught up in the frenzy. The evening newscasts on the main TV channels (ABC, CBS and NBC) between 21 January 2017 and 10 February 2019 devoted 2,202 minutes to the Trump–Russia collusion allegations but gave almost no coverage to their refutation.[3]

WHY IT ALL STARTED

In summer 2016, Brennan delivered a top-secret letter to the White House with the claim by a Russian mole that Putin had personally ordered an interference operation to install Trump. The 'mole' turned out to be a mid-level

Kremlin official named Oleg Smolenkov, well outside of Putin's inner circle and who had been fired some years earlier. He rebuffed early attempts by the CIA to exfiltrate him, but following American media reports, he finally defected during a trip to Montenegro in June 2017. Smolenkov was later found living under his own name in Stafford, a Virginia suburb. Brennan worked with the FBI to investigate and then took the lead in producing the inadequate ICA of 6 January 2017.[4] Despite the claims, Mueller did not find a single case where the Trump campaign team initiated contact with Russians to gain damaging information on his rival or to boost their campaign.

The Republican-controlled HPSCI in September 2018 voted unanimously to release the fifty-seven witness transcripts of its January 2017 to March 2018 Russiagate inquiry and sent them to the ODNI for declassification review. However, when Schiff took over as Democratic chair in January 2019, he ordered that the material be withheld from White House lawyers seeking to review them for executive privilege. It was only when acting ODNI director Richard Grenell in May 2020 threatened to release them himself that Schiff revealed the transcripts. In stark contrast to public assertions of confidence in the collusion allegations, many witnesses under oath were less sure. Former DNI Clapper testified on 17 July 2017 that 'I never saw any direct empirical evidence that the Trump campaign or someone in it was plotting/conspiring with the Russians to meddle with the elections'.[5] Other Obama administration officials, including Susan Rice, testified to the same effect.[6] This once again raises the question whether there was ever an adequate predicate to open a counterintelligence investigation into an opposition party's presidential campaign. Even more revealing, CrowdStrike, the company contracted to investigate the central Russiagate charge of hacking, admitted to Congress that it had no concrete evidence that Russian hackers stole the emails from the DNC server.

CrowdStrike president Shawn Henry, who personally led the forensic and remediation analysis, admitted that while material had been prepared, there was no confirmation that files had actually been exfiltrated. CrowdStrike installed its monitoring devices on 1 or 2 May, but when asked to specify the date when the Russian hackers stole the data from the DNC server, Henry responded that Crowdstrike was not sure whether the theft had taken place: 'We did not have concrete evidence that the data was exfiltrated from the DNC, but we have indicators that it was exfiltrated'. The material had been 'set up to be exfiltrated, but we just don't have the evidence that says it actually left'. Henry noted that 'There are other nation-states that collect this type of intelligence for sure, but the – what we would call the tactics and techniques were consistent with what we'd seen associated with the Russian state'.[7] Mueller's conclusion that Russian intelligence on or about 25 May and 1 June (over three weeks after CrowdStrike was monitoring the servers) 'appears to have compressed and exfiltrated over 70 gigabytes of data from the file server', unless he drew on another unknown analysis of the server (as noted, the grand jury material was redacted), becomes more questionable.[8] This does not mean that the GRU did not do so, but the uncertainty was hidden from the public. The result was intensified animosity towards Russia, amplifying the divisions of the new cold war.

These were among the issues examined by the various probes. Department of Justice inspector general Horowitz launched his investigation in March 2018 and on 19 December 2019 released his review of the four FISA applications and other aspects of the Crossfire Hurricane investigation. The report examined the FBI decision to start the investigation in July and to open cases on four current and former members of the campaign in August 2016: Papadopoulos, Page, Manafort and Flynn. It also examined the FBI's relationship with Steele; the use the FBI made of his memos, and its decision to close Steele as a confidential human source; the four FBI applications filed with FISC in 2016 and 2017 to conduct FISA surveillance of Page; the interactions of DoJ attorney Bruce Ohr with Steele; whether Nellie Ohr's work for Fusion GPS breached ethical rules applicable to her spouse; and whether any undercover operations were conducted against the Trump campaign.[9] The report is one of the most comprehensive analyses of the Russiagate affair. Its basic finding is that the FBI committed serious violations of its own procedures, with seventeen instances of improper behaviour identified, most associated with the investigative warrants issued against Page (above all withholding exculpatory evidence). However, the report concluded that the FBI had sufficient reason to open the investigation into purported links between the Trump campaign and Russia.

The immediate predicate was the receipt of information from what the report calls a Friendly Foreign Government (FFG), that is, Britain, as well as reasons to believe that WikiLeaks' publication of the DNC emails was coordinated with Russia.[10] Most controversially, the report argued that the FBI only became aware of Steele's memos weeks later, and therefore they played no part in triggering the investigation. The report also dismissed claims of political bias or improper motivation in opening the investigation, arguing that while both Lisa Page and Peter Strzok were part of the process, the decision after detailed consultation was ultimately taken by Bill Priestap, assistant director of the Counterintelligence Division. The use of CHS's against Page and Papadopoulos was criticised, but the operations were permitted under DoJ guidelines. The initial FISA surveillance application against Page in October 2016, a month after he had stepped down from the campaign, was approved at the highest levels, including deputy attorney general Sally Yates, but the Crossfire Hurricane team failed to inform the DoJ of significant information that was known at that time and the three subsequent renewals. When it comes to Steele, the report noted that as early as 2013 the FBI had completed the paperwork to appoint him a CHS, but the relationship was based on fundamentally different understandings of the role. The FBI considered Steele a former security agent with obligations to the FBI; whereas Steele considered the contractual ties were with his company and not himself, and that his obligations were to his paying clients, not the FBI. This misunderstanding 'affected the FBI's control over Steele during the Crossfire Hurricane investigation [and] led to divergent expectations about Steele's conduct in connection with his election reporting', provoking his termination as a CHS in November 2016, although the FBI continued its relationship with him through Ohr.[11]

Receipt of Steele's memos on 19 September prompted the FBI to seek the FISA application against Page.[12] The FBI is excoriated for failing to corroborate Steele's reports, although it did provide a gnomic footnote in its FISA application about the potential political bias of Steele's work. On this aspect, the report noted seven significant inaccuracies and omissions including that Page between 2008 and 2013 provided information to the CIA about his prior contacts with Russian officials (this came as a revelation), overstating the reliability of Steele's earlier reporting and relied on four dubious claims from the dossier, omitting Page's monitored statement that he had 'literally never met' Manafort and his denial that he had met Sechin or Diveykin.[13] The FISA renewals failed to mention negative assessments of Steele's work, above all that he was 'prone to rash judgments' and demonstrated a 'lack of self-awareness'.[14] More damningly, one of Steele's sources noted that they never expected Steele to present their material as 'facts' since there was 'no proof' but 'hearsay', the kind of 'conversation that [he/she] had with friends over beers'. The source stressed that Steele in any case 'misstated or exaggerated' statements and the source's access to Russian officials. The source noted that Trump's alleged romp in the Ritz-Carlton in 2013 was no more than 'rumor and speculation'.[15] The FISA applications also omitted Mifsud's denial to the FBI that he supplied Papadopoulos with the information that he allegedly passed on to Downer.[16] In short, the report listed seventeen errors or omissions in the Page FISA applications. It also concluded that Bruce Ohr had committed 'consequential errors' in failing to inform his superiors that he was communicating with Steele and Simpson or to pass on the information that Steele was 'desperate that Donald Trump not get elected and was passionate about him not being the US President'.[17]

The report basically confirmed the findings of Devin Nunes' 18 January 2018 memo and dismissed the rival summary by Schiff and the Democrats. The report was condemned by Barr for not going far enough, arguing that 'the FBI launched an intrusive investigation of a US presidential campaign on the thinnest of suspicions'. Horowitz conceded that the bar for opening an

Papadopoulos were pressured by Mueller to 'flip' and provide evidence against top Trump officials, but with no collusion, there was no incriminating evidence to give. If there was no crime, then what was the point of the investigation? The special counsel had had to find the evidence to justify the investigation.

Not surprisingly, there have been calls for the investigators to be investigated. On 13 May 2019, Barr opened an enquiry into whether the Trump–Russia investigation had been 'lawful and appropriate'. It was led by John Durham, the U.S. attorney in Connecticut, a respected career prosecutor nominated to his post by Trump and who had been unanimously confirmed by the Senate in February 2018. In one of his final acts before he resigned in December 2020, Barr on 19 October secretly appointed Durham a special counsel to ensure that the probe into the origins of Russiagate would continue after the end of the Trump administration. Biden confirmed the continuation of the investigation, although Durham along with fifty-five others resigned as U.S. attorney at his request in February 2021. The original appointment in 2019 came a month after Barr on 10 April informed Congress that he believed 'spying did occur' on the Trump campaign in 2016, finally turning attention on the FBI's behaviour. 'I think', he warned, 'spying on a political campaign is a big deal'.[27] Durham's enquiry focused on FBI surveillance of the Trump presidential campaign. The FISA warrants on Carter Page started in October 2016 and the last ninety-day one was issued in June 2017 – which Mueller did not renew when it ended in September. The FBI's use of informants when it was investigating Papadopoulos was also examined, as well as the provenance of the Steele dossier. In sum, Durham's enquiry focused on whether the methods used to gather intelligence on the Trump campaign were indeed 'lawful and appropriate'. The Durham investigation worked separately but in parallel with Horowitz's examination of political bias and the origins of the Russia probe. This investigated why the counterintelligence investigation was formally opened by the FBI on 31 July 2016, an issue also part of Durham's purview.

Durham examined the role of the FBI in Russiagate as well as the activities of other agencies. In particular, he explored whether Brennan's CIA withheld information from other agencies to steer the Russiagate investigation in a particular direction. He focused on the January 2017 ICA, which concluded that Putin ordered an influence campaign that 'aspired to help' Trump. It was now revealed that analysts working on the document disagreed over whether Putin really wanted to help Trump or just to 'sow chaos' and the weight to be attached to the Democrat-funded Steele dossier. As we have seen, the CIA and FBI reported 'high confidence' and the NSA, which conducts electronic intelligence, only a moderate degree of confidence in the assertion that Putin ordered intervention on Trump's behalf. Discussing Durham's work, Barr argued that 'The president bore the burden of probably one of the greatest conspiracy theories – baseless conspiracy theories – in American political history'. Durham examined the thinking that led to the inclusion of Steele's allegations as an appendix to the assessment.[28] Brennan denied that the CIA relied on the dossier in drafting the assessment, and Clapper made the same claim on behalf of the intelligence agencies more broadly. The FBI pushed hard for the unverified dossier to be included, and as Horowitz's report made clear, McCabe accused other intelligence chiefs of trying to minimise Steele's information. Comey insisted that Steele was reliable, but Clapper ignored Comey, according to Horowitz, while the CIA viewed the dossier as an 'internet rumor'.[29]

The list of investigations became absurdly long. Congressional Republicans also launched their own enquiry, focusing on whether there were any legal concerns.[30] Steele declared that he would not cooperate with the Durham enquiry but might work with Horowitz's. Steele had been interviewed twice by the Mueller team in September 2017 and gave written testimony to the Senate Intelligence Committee in August 2018.[31] Meanwhile, Sessions asked U.S. district attorney for Utah, John W. Huber, to investigate not only surveillance abuses by the DoJ and the FBI but also their handling of the probe into the Clinton Foundation and other matters. Even former NSA head, Michael Rogers, was reportedly cooperating with investigators.[32] The January 2017 ICA became the subject of an investigative referral in October 2020 when DNI Ratcliffe requested examination of potential wrongdoing.[33]

All investigations were prompted by a single glaring fact. If Mueller was right and there was no collusion or even substantive communication between the Trump campaign and Russia, then the behaviour of Obama administration officials and the mainstream media who insisted to the contrary is all the more disturbing. The Clinton campaign understandably sought to blame some outside force for its woes, but seasoned political and intelligence professionals were caught up in the scheme to blame Russia. They played up an alleged conspiracy that Mueller dismissed as a fiction. These officials 'collectively suffered from one of the most historically monumental cases of poor judgment in US intelligence history'.[34] The pressure was now on to declassify information about the origins of the Trump–Russia investigation. Not surprisingly, Brennan led the opposition to transparency on this issue: 'The concern is that very, very precious source and methods of the United States intelligence community as well as our partners and allies abroad – those who share this sensitive information with us'. Just as the Democrats called for the 'underlying evidence' of the Mueller report to be made public, so 'transparency has to cut all ways for this three-year national fiasco to be resolved in any way that makes sense'.[35]

The damaging Russiagate investigation and the failure of the Mueller report to answer the most pressing questions left many issues to be examined. The FBI counterintelligence investigation was opened by Strzok in July 2016, but in closed door congressional testimony, Lisa Page admitted that the FBI at that point 'knew so little' about whether the collusion allegation were 'true or not true'. She insisted that it was not unusual to start an investigation when there was just a 'small amount of evidence'.[36] The Trump investigation began with a false premise: that Trump must have known that Russia possessed emails concerning Clinton, and that Moscow planned to disseminate these emails, with the help of a third party, at a time that would do maximum damage to the Clinton campaign. The idea of some sort of link between Trump and the Kremlin was encouraged by the communication from Downer about his conversation with Papadapolous, which in turn was based on a conversation with Mifsud, who denied that he had ever said such a thing. Thrumming in the background were the explosive Steele dossier allegations, which purported to expose a conspiracy of mind-numbing proportions. The narrative was fed by contacts with British security officials, who remain typically tight-lipped about what they communicated. This is a remarkably thin thread on which to hang such weighty matters. Any investigation would have to examine the role of Britain and Australian officials in setting the Russiagate story going.

Democrats fought back against the various investigations by claiming that critics were essentially working on behalf of the Kremlin. Senate minority leader Chuck Schumer argued that Homeland Security chair Ron Johnson's investigation into the Biden family's dealings with Ukraine was a 'disgrace', claiming his committee was echoing 'Russian disinformation'. Democrats had long argued that foreign interference in elections was the greatest risk to American democracy, so Republicans argued that the links of the presidential nominee and his family with Ukraine should also be investigated.[37] Mueller's failure to provide clarity allowed these claims to fester and poison the American body politic. None of the eight cases of alleged Trump campaign interactions with Russian officials investigated by Mueller originated with Trump officials but came from FBI informants, MI6 assets or were paid for by Fusion GPS. Mueller provided no evidence that at any point the Trump team initiated contact with Moscow to gain derogatory information about Clinton or to boost Trump. This is why the Russiagate affair has been called a 'hoax', which the dictionary defines as 'an act intended to deceive or trick' or 'something that has been established or accepted by fraudulent means'.[38] Both definitions apply in this case. The Trump–Russia collusion allegation turned out to be false. Russia was at most a bit player in a drama that was played out elsewhere. We are left with a 'Russiagate without Russia'.[39]

Chapter 14

FURTHER INVESTIGATIONS

On 6 February 2020, the Senate Intelligence Committee released the third volume of its investigation into Russian election interference, focusing on the responses of the Obama administration. The report did not question the base assumptions of the ICA, and therefore had little meaningful to add to the Russiagate affair. Despite significant redactions, a footnote confirms that it was Brennan at the head of the CIA who first raised the alarm about 'Russian meddling' and that it was his briefings of the 'gang of eight' that set the Russiagate ball rolling.[40] The report notes that the Obama administration was torn between those officials who 'viewed WikiLeaks as a legitimate news outlet' and those who saw it 'as a hostile organization acting intentionally and deliberately to undermine US or allies' interests'.[41]

The fifth and final Senate Intelligence Committee report was published in August 2020 and focused on 'counterintelligence threats and vulnerabilities'.[42] Despite weighing in at nearly 1,000 pages, the report contained almost nothing new and was already outdated by the time it was published, with many of its assertions questioned (above all its treatment of the Steele dossier) or outright debunked (as in its endorsement of the FBI's decision to investigate Page). By then attention focused on Clinton's supporters' assumption that she would be the next president and hence did little to cover their tracks when they played fast and loose with the Constitution and the law, matters that were by then being investigated by Barr, Durham and others.[43] Yet, published just months ahead of the November presidential election, it revived the Russian interference allegations. The key finding was that Manafort had shared polling data with Russians who may have been intelligence officers – a rehash of the Kilimnik story. Nearly two years earlier, the *New York Times* had been forced to correct its coverage to explain that the data was intended not for Russian but Ukrainian oligarchs.[44] Manafort's work in Ukraine was once again examined to suggest that in fact Manafort had been working on behalf of the Russian state through 'pro-Russia' Ukrainian oligarchs as well as Deripaska, who all had agendas of their own and cannot be simply lumped together as 'pro-Russian' elements of 'Russia's own influence efforts'. As we have seen, Manafort took anything but a pro-Russian position and worked hard to get Ukraine to sign the Association Agreement with the EU, and a cache of emails released at this time demonstrates that Kilimnik also worked to achieve that goal.[45]

The Senate report alleges that Kilimnik was a Russian intelligence officer when in fact he worked closely with the U.S. embassy in Kiev and was an important source of information about Yanukovych.[46] Kilimnik had been a 'sensitive' intelligence source for the U.S. State Department since at least 2013 and as we have seen in May 2016 delivered a Russian peace plan to settle the Donbas conflict to the Obama administration, although the Mueller report omitted mention of that and instead focused on his delivery of the peace plan to the Trump team in August, an egregious case of 'deception by omission'.[47] Veselnitskaya and Akhmetshin were accused of having 'significant connections to the Russian government, including the Russian intelligence services', but no attempt was made to investigate whether the June 2016 Trump Tower meeting was part of a Russian intelligence operation (discounted by the Mueller report), and instead guilt by association and assertion remained the operative code. The obsession with RT continued, which can be traced back to Clinton's assertion in March 2011 that the United States was 'losing . . . the information war'. In short, the Senate report was egregiously wrong in its coverage of the story, avoiding known facts and relying on innuendo and assertion. Above all, the Senate report repeated discredited claims about WikiLeaks, and once again there had been no attempt to speak with Assange. It appears that the outgoing Intelligence Committee chair Richard Barr, who resigned in May 2020 but who had largely overseen work on the report, had been keen to establish its bipartisan character and had thus allowed the ranking Democrat Mark Warner to shape the narrative.[48]

The Senate Judiciary Committee conducted its own Russia investigation. Its chair, Lindsey Graham, noted that he had initially been in favour of Mueller's appointment but came to believe that the special counsel investigation was strewn with errors and driven by an anti-Trump animus. He warned, 'We're going to be talking about how it got off the rails, who's responsible for it getting off the rails, and making sure that they are punished'. One of the first witnesses on 3 June 2020 was Rod Rosenstein, who had left the DoJ in May 2019 and remained tight-lipped about his part in these historic events. In response to Graham's question whether he would agree that by August 2017 it was clear that there was 'no there there' to support the 'concept that the campaign was colluding with the Russians', Rosenstein offered a rather limp defence of the Mueller investigation and admitted that by then no evidence of collusion had emerged.[49] Nevertheless, he believed that it made sense to let the investigation be completed.[50] This does not explain why his 'scope memo' of 2 August broadened Mueller's remit, unless it was to ensure that the whole process did not come up empty. To find the answers, the Committee threatened to issue fifty-three subpoenas to relevant witnesses.

The question for the Judiciary Committee and other investigations was not so much to explain how contrary evidence was suppressed but why the Russiagate charges gained so much traction in the first place. The Steele dossier was clearly a deceptive foundation on which to build so much. On 17 July 2020, the Senate Judiciary Committee issued an annotated version of the *New York Times* article of 14 February 2017, published just hours after Flynn's ouster, claiming that 'Trump campaign aides had repeated contacts with Russian intelligence'.⁵¹ Strzok wrote an internal FBI analysis of the article highlighting the story's inaccuracies. The first comment was 'misleading and inaccurate . . . we are unaware of any Trump advisors engaging in conversations with Russian intelligence officials' and questioned the assertion that Manafort had contact with Russian security officers, noting 'We are unaware of any calls with any Russian govt officials in which Manafort was a party'. He dismissed the *NYT* assertion that Stone was part of the FBI's enquiry, curtly stating, 'We have not investigated Roger Stone'. Strzok also noted that 'recent interviews' reveal 'Steele may not be in a position to judge the reliability of his subsource network'.⁵² By this point, it was clear to the FBI that Steele was not a reliable source but failed to make this public and even continued to use him in the FISA warrants. As an editorial puts it, 'The more evidence that is made public, the clearer it becomes that the Steele dossier and collusion narrative were dirty political tricks that became abuses of power'.⁵³ The fundamental question is why the FBI continued to fan the flames of Russian collusion when it knew that the charges were 'unfounded, false and baseless'.⁵⁴ Trump was ridiculed for his response to the article when he said in a press conference, called to address the growing Russian collusion narrative on 16 February, that 'The leaks are real, the news is fake', but in fact leaks from anonymous intelligence officials and the faulty *NYT* story caused his administration real damage. McCabe privately told Priebus, according to reporting in Howard Kurtz's book *Media Madness*, that 'everything' in the story was 'bulls-t', but when Priebus asked him to state this publicly, he refused to do so.⁵⁵ Instead, the FBI leaked to CNN that the 'FBI refused White House request to knock down recent Trump–Russia stories', making it look as if the White House was trying to obstruct a legitimate investigation.⁵⁶ In June, Comey admitted under oath that the reporting was 'false', but by then, the narrative had become institutionalised in the form of the Mueller inquiry.

In August 2020, the Senate Homeland Security and Finance committees issued an eighty-seven-page joint report on Hunter Biden's business dealings with foreign nationals while his father served as vice president.⁵⁷ The committees reviewed over 45,000 pages of Obama administration material and most of the eight witnesses were current or former government officials. The report detailed transactions between Hunter Biden, his family and associates with Ukrainian, Russian, Kazakh and Chinese nationals, and noted 'these documents show that Hunter Biden received millions of dollars from foreign sources as a result of business relationships that he built during the period when his father was vice president of the United States and after'. Hunter apparently gained some $4 million in 'questionable financial transactions', partnering with Chinese businesspeople associated with the Communist Party of China and the People's Liberation Army, as well taking $3.5 million from Elena Baturina, the wife of the former Moscow mayor, Yuri Luzhkov.⁵⁸ The report detailed how Telizhenko had repeated contact with Obama administration officials in 2016, yet Democrats later claimed that he was involved in a Russian disinformation campaign.[59] The acting deputy head of mission at the U.S. embassy in Kiev, George Kent, repeatedly warned that Hunter's work with Burisma undermined the credibility of the administration's anti-corruption efforts, since the company's owner, Zlochevsky, in Kent's estimation was an 'odious oligarch'.[60] The report detailed how 'officials within the Obama administration ignored the glaring warning signs when the vice president's son joined the board of a company owned by a corrupt Ukrainian oligarch'.[61] Despite secretary of state John Kerry's later claim that he was not aware that Hunter served on the Burisma board, the report found evidence to the contrary.[62] Hunter's own account dismisses his place on the board as an 'epic banality' and a way of confronting Russia.[63] He was well-paid for his efforts, which appear to have consisted of attending two board meetings annually in such exotic locations as Monaco or a hunting lodge in northern Norway.

Continuing his series of exposures, on 7 October 2020, DNI Ratcliffe released more than 1,000 pages of documents to the DoJ concerning the origins of the Trump–Russia collusion allegations. A day earlier, he released a redacted hand-written note by then-CIA director Brennan shortly after he briefed Obama on Russian intelligence about Clinton. Trump asserted that he had authorised 'the total declassification of any and all documents' pertaining to what he called 'the single greatest political crime in American history, the Russia hoax', but his detractors argued that the 'selective declassification of information' was designed 'to advance Trump and Republicans aligned with him'.[64] One of the memos released by Ratcliffe made the explosive claim that Russian intelligence assessed that Clinton approved the campaign in July 2016 to link Trump to Russia's alleged hacking of the DNC to shift attention away from her own email scandal. We have noted that Mook at the time of the Democratic National Convention condemned Russia for the hacking, in part at least to divert attention from the scandalous revelations about DNC bias against Sanders. Brennan's note stated: 'We're getting additional insight into Russian activities from [redacted] . . . allegedly approved by Hillary Clinton a proposal from one of her foreign policy advisers to vilify Donald Trump by stirring up a scandal claiming interference by the Russian security service'.[65] According to Brennan's notes, Clinton approved the plan on 26 July, the day of her presidential nomination.[66] Brennan admitted that he briefed Obama and his national security team (with Comey possibly in attendance) 'about what the Russians were up to and I was giving examples of the type of access that the US intelligence community to Russian information and what the Russians were talking about and alleging'. Ratcliffe also declassified a secret CIA memo of 7 September 2016 'per FBI verbal request' addressed to Comey and Strzok, which also talked of 'Clinton's approval of a plan concerning US presidential candidate Donald Trump and Russian hackers hampering US elections as a means of distracting the public from her use of a private email server'. The case could hardly be less ambiguous. Wikileaks began publishing the DNC material on 22 July, Mook appeared on CNN on 24 July to make the first public claim that Russia hacked the DNC to support Trump, on 26 July Obama stated, 'What we do know is that the Russians hack our systems, not just government systems but private systems' and the Crossfire Hurricane investigation was opened on 31 July.[67]

NOTES

1. Maté provides a list of relevant questions, 'It's Trump's Last Chance to Declassify These Secrets'.
2. Rivkin and Foley, 'Mueller's Fruit of the Poisonous Tree'.
3. Christoforou, 'Corrupt Rosenstein'.
4. Aaron Maté, 'Uncovering Russiagate's Origins Could Prevent Future Scandals', *The Nation*, 28 October 2019, https://www.thenation.com/article/archive/russiagate-brennan/.
5. HPSCI, 'Interview Transcript of James Clapper', 17 July 2017, https://intelligence.house.gov/uploadedfiles/jc7.pdf.
6. HPSCI, 'Interview Transcript of Susan Rice', 8 September 2017, https://intelligence.house.gov/uploadedfiles/sr44.pdf.
7. HPSCI, 'Interview Transcript of Shawn Henry', 5 December 2017, https://intelligence.house.gov/uploadedfiles/sh21.pdf.
8. Mueller, *Report*, Vol. 1, p. 40.
9. Horowitz, *Review*, p. i.
10. Horowitz, *Review*, pp. ii–iii, 49–83.
11. Horowitz, *Review*, p. v.
12. Horowitz, *Review*, p. vi.
13. Horowitz, *Review*, pp. viii–ix, 121–171.
14. Horowitz, *Review*, pp. xi, 182, 258 and *passim*.
15. Horowitz, *Review*, p. 187.
16. Horowitz, *Review*, pp. xii, 229.
17. Horowitz, *Review*, pp. xv, 234, 369.
18. Charlie Savage, Adam Goldman and Katie Benner, 'Report on FBI Russia Inquiry Finds Serious Errors but Debunks Anti-Trump Plot', *New York Times*, 9 December 2019, https://www.nytimes.com/2019/12/09/us/politics/fbi-ig-report-russia-investigation.html.
19. Horowitz, *Review*, pp. xiii, 378.
20. Jordain Carney, 'Republicans Plow Ahead with Russia Origins Probe', *The Hill*, 18 April 2020, https://thehill.com/homenews/senate/493438-republicans-plow-ahead-with-russia-origins-probe.
21. Horowitz, *Review*, note 350.

22. John Solomon, 'Newly Declassified Evidence Casts Doubt on Obama Intel Assessment about Russia's Election Intentions', *Just the News*, 20 April 2020, https://justthenews.com/accountability/russia-and-ukraine-scandals/newly-declassified-evidence-casts-doubt-obama-intel.

23. Rich Lowry, 'It Looks Like Putin conned the FBI into the "Russiagate" Probe', *New York Post*, 13 April 2020, https://nypost.com/2020/04/13/it-looks-like-putin-conned-the-fbi-into-the-russiagate-probe/.

24. Kevin R. Brock, 'AG Barr Just Signalled that Things are About to Get Ugly for the Russia Collusion Team', *The Hill*, 13 April 2020, https://thehill.com/opinion/judiciary/492405-ag-barr-just-signaled-that-things-are-about-to-get-ugly-for-the-russia.

25. Andrew Coan, 'What Happens if Muller Comes up Empty', CNN.com, 4 January 2019, https://edition.cnn.com/2019/01/03/opinions/mueller-investigation-could-surprise-us-coan/index.html.

26. Lee Smith, 'System Fail: The Mueller Report is an Unmitigated Disaster for the American Press and the "Expert" Class that it Promotes', *Tablet*, 27 March 2019, https://www.tabletmag.com/jewish-news-and-politics/282448/system-fail.

27. Kimberley A. Strassel, 'Barr Brings Accountability', *Wall Street Journal*, 12 April 2019, https://www.wsj.com/articles/barr-brings-accountability-11555022792.

28. Katie Benner and Julian E. Barnes, 'Durham is Scrutinizing Ex-CIA Director's Role in Russian Interference Findings', *New York Times*, 19 December 2019, https://www.nytimes.com/2019/12/19/us/politics/durham-john-brennan-cia.html.

29. Horowitz, *Review*, pp. x, 384 n507.

30. 'Barr Appoints Prosecutor to Examine Russia Probe Origins', *Politico*, 14 May 2019, https://www.politico.com/story/2019/05/14/barr-prosecutor-russia-probe-origins-1319878.

31. Mark Hosenball, 'British Ex-Spy will not Talk to US Prosecutor Examining Trump Probe Origins: Source', *Reuters*, 28 May 2019, https://www.reuters.com/article/us-usa-trump-steele/british-ex-spy-will-not-talk-to-u-s-prosecutor-examining-trump-probe-origins-source-idUSKCN1SY20K.

32. Ray McGovern, 'Turn Out the Lights, Russiagate is Over', *Consortium News*, 19 May 2020, https://consortiumnews.com/2020/05/19/ray-mcgovern-turn-out-the-lights-russiagate-is-over/.

33. For a link to the 15 October letter, see Ivan Pentchoukov, 'US Intel Head Refers 2017 Russia Assessment to Inspector General', *Epoch Times*, 18 October 2020, https://www.theepochtimes.com/us-intel-head-refers-2017-russia-assessment-to-inspector-general_3542984.html.

34. Sharyl Attkisson, 'Two Scenarios on Trump-Russia Investigators – And Neither is Comforting', *The Hill*, 21 May 2019, https://thehill.com/opinion/white-house/444508-two-scenarios-on-trump-russia-investigators-and-neither-is-comforting.

35. Taibi, 'The Intelligence Community Needs a House-Cleaning'.

36. Singman, 'US Attorney John Durham has been Reviewing Origins of Russia Probe'.

37. Kimberley A. Strassel, 'From Russia (to Biden) With Love', *Wall Street Journal*, 18 September 2020, https://www.wsj.com/articles/from-russia-to-biden-with-love-11600383717.

38. Roger Kimball, 'Let's Call the Russian Collusion "Hoax" What it Really Is', *Spectator USA*, 27 May 2019, https://spectator.us/call-russian-collusion-hoax/.

39. It is not clear who coined the term, but *Nation* writer James Carden may have been the first, and it was used by Stephen F. Cohen, 'Media Malpractices is Criminalizing Better Relations with Russia', *The Nation*, 13 December 2017, https://www.thenation.com/article/archive/media-malpractice-is-criminalizing-better-relations-with-russia/.

40. Senate Committee on Intelligence, *Report*, Vol. 3, p. 11, n. 30, and p. 4.

41. Senate Committee on Intelligence, *Report*, Vol. 3, p. 23.

42. Senate Committee on Intelligence, *Report on Russian Active Measures Campaigns and Interference in the 2016 US Election*, Vol. 5, *Counterintelligence Threats and Vulnerabilities* (Washington, DC, US Senate, 5 August 2020), https://www.intelligence.senate.gov/sites/default/files/documents/report_volume5.pdf.

43. A point made by Ray McGovern, 'Catapulting Russian-Meddling Propaganda', *Consortium News*, 21 August 2020, https://consortiumnews.com/2020/08/21/ray-mcgovern-catapulting-russian-meddling-propaganda/.

44. The original story was Sharon LaFraniere, Kenneth P. Vogel and Maggie Haberman, 'Manafort Accused of Sharing Trump Polling Data with Russian Associate', *New York Times*, 8 January 2019, https://www.nytimes.com/2019/01/08/us/politics/manafort-trump-campaign-data-kilimnik.html. For analysis of the Kilimnik allegations, see Aaron Maté, 'The Manafort Revelation is Not a Smoking Gun', *The Nation*, 11 January 2019, https://www.thenation.com/article/archive/manafort-no-smoking-gun-collusion/.

45. Details are provided by Paul Robinson, 'Proof of Collusion at Last?', Irrussianality, 2 September 2020, https://irrussianality.wordpress.com/2020/09/02/proof-of-collusion-at-last/.

46. John Solomon, 'Ukrainian Flagged as Intel Danger had Extensive Contact with Obama Officials', *Just the News*, 25 August 2020, https://justthenews.com/accountability/russia-and-ukraine-scandals/ukrainian-flagged-spy-danger-trump-had-extensive-contact.

47. John Solomon, 'Key Figure that Mueller Report Linked to Russia was a State Department Intel Source', *The Hill*, 6 June 2020, https://thehill.com/opinion/white-house/447394-key-figure-that-mueller-report-linked-to-russia-was-a-state-department.

48. Editorial, 'The Russian Grassy Knoll', *Wall Street Journal*, 20 August 2020, https://www.wsj.com/articles/the-russian-grassy-knoll-11597879099.

49. Alex Christoforou, 'Corrupt Rosenstein Throws Mueller under the Bus (Video)', *The Duran*, 9 June 2020, https://theduran.com/corrupt-rosenstein-throws-corrupt-mueller-under-the-bus-video/.

50. Aruna Viswanatha and Sadie Gurman, 'Rod Rosenstein Offers Limited Defense of the Russian Probe', *Wall Street Journal*, 4 June 2020, https://www.wsj.com/articles/rod-rosenstein-testifies-before-senate-judiciary-committee-over-russia-investigation-11591193444.

51. Michael S. Schmidt, Mark Mazzetti and Matt Apuzzo, 'Trump Campaign Aides had Repeated Contacts with Russian Intelligence', *New York Times*, 14 February 2017, https://www.nytimes.com/2017/02/14/us/politics/russia-intelligence-communications-trump.html.

52. Declassified by the FBI on 16 July 2020, https://www.judiciary.senate.gov/imo/media/doc/Annotated%20New%20York%20Times%20Article.pdf.

53. Editorial, 'The FBI's Dossier Deceit', *Wall Street Journal*, 18 July 2020, https://www.wsj.com/articles/the-fbis-dossier-deceit-11595027626.

54. Holman W. Jenkins, Jr, 'The Unasked FBI Question: Why?', *Wall Street Journal*, 22 July 2020, https://www.wsj.com/articles/the-unasked-fbi-question-why-11595372128.

55. As he admitted in his book McCabe, *The Threat*, p. 204.

56. Mollie Hemingway, 'New FBI Notes Re-Debunk Major NYT Story, Highlight Media Collusion to Produce Russia Hoax', *The Federalist*, 23 July 2020, https://thefederalist.com/2020/07/23/new-fbi-notes-re-debunk-major-nyt-story-highlight-media-collusion-to-produce-russia-hoax/.

57. US Senate Committee on Homeland Security and Governmental Affairs and US Senate Committee on Finance, Majority Staff Report, *Hunter Biden, Burisma, and Corruption: The Impact on US Government Policy and Related Concerns*, 23 August 2020, https://www.hsgac.senate.gov/imo/media/doc/Ukraine%20Report_FINAL.pdf.

58. US Senate, *Hunter Biden*, p. 65.

59. US Senate, *Hunter Biden*, p. 53 and *passim*.

60. US Senate, *Hunter Biden*, pp. 5, 23.

61. US Senate, *Hunter Biden*, p. 4.

62. US Senate, *Hunter Biden*, pp. 4, 8.

63. Hunter Biden, *Beautiful Things: A Memoir* (London, Gallery, 2021).

64. Warren P. Strobel, 'Trump's Intelligence Chief Releases More than 1,000 Pages of Documents', *Wall Street Journal*, 8 October 2020, https://www.wsj.com/articles/trumps-intelligence-chief-releases-more-than-1-000-pages-of-documents-11602119001.

65. Brennan's notes are summarised in a letter from Ratcliffe to Lindsey Graham, chair of the Senate Judiciary Committee, of 29 September 2020, https://www.judiciary.senate.gov/imo/media/doc/09-29-20_Letter%20to%20Sen.%20Graham_Declassification%20of%20FBI's%20Crossfire%20Hurricane%20Investigations_20-00912_U_SIGNED-FINAL.pdf.

66. Staff writer, '"Stirring up a Russia Scandal to Vilify Trump": Declassified Brennan CIA Notes Prove Claims were Political Hoax', *The National Pulse*, 15 December 2020, https://thenationalpulse.com/breaking/stirring-up-a-russia-scandal-to-vilify-trump-declassified-brennan-cia-notes-prove-claims-were-political-hoax/.

67. Dave DeCamp, 'Former Intel Officials Try to Downplay Ratcliffe's Russiagate Releases', Antiwar.com, 8 October 2020, https://original.antiwar.com/dave_decamp/2020/10/07/former-intel-officials-try-to-downplay-ratcliffes-russiagate-releases/.

Chapter 15

Worse than Watergate

The Mueller investigation has been accused of 'antecedent political bias', in other words, partisanship. Carl Bernstein argues that 'This is worse than Watergate in the sense the system worked in Watergate and it's not apparent yet the system is working in the current situation'.[1] Bernstein is half of the legendary duo, who along with Bob Woodward doggedly investigated the break-in of the DNC in 1972, ultimately precipitating Richard Nixon's resignation. Woodward describes the chaotic decision-making and personnel choices in Trump's first eighteen months in power.[2] He explains that he chose the title *Fear* after an interview in which Trump remarked: 'Real power is through respect. I don't even want to use the word, fear'. Bernstein added that 'I think that this is a dangerous time for America, that we have a president with no regard for the rule of law or for the truth . . . I think that's what so extraordinary'.[3] No less extraordinary were the flaws in those who set themselves up as the 'resistance' to the administration. Neither accepted the legitimacy of the other, and both sought to exploit temporary control of institutions to press home their advantage. The 'norms of toleration and restraint [that] served as the soft guardrails of American democracy' were being eroded.[4]

RUSSIAGATE AND RESISTANCE

In 1964, Barry Goldwater had been perceived as a threat to the established conduct of U.S. politics, and he endured unprecedented vilification. This was accompanied by CIA surveillance ordered by President Lyndon Johnson led by none other than E. Howard Hunt, who later organised the notorious break-in to the DNC, at the time located in the Watergate building. In 2016, Trump was also considered an abnormal presidential candidate and elements of the establishment apparently conspired against him. The Horowitz report exonerated Comey of trying to influence the election, but the charge of making decisions based on political considerations remains. Comey told Horowitz that he decided to reopen the Clinton email investigation, because he wanted to protect the legitimacy of her assumed presidency. Crossfire broke with the long-standing convention not to investigate campaigns in an election year. Clinton's use of a private email server prompted a criminal investigation and began a year before the campaign, whereas Crossfire was not a criminal investigation (there was no crime to investigate), but a counterintelligence operation, governed by a very different investigative logic. It was prompted by fears of Trump–Russia collusion, although when Crossfire was launched, there was minimal evidence.

Despite straining mightily, Mueller was not able to find evidence of collusion. The hacking of the DNC and other Clinton team data breaches certainly deserved investigation, but Stone's queries are far from proving that Trump colluded with the perpetrators. The case then reverts to the generic assumption that Russia tried to help Trump get elected, and Trump reciprocated by embracing pro-Russian policies – but neither proposition has been proven. Hence, we come to the fundamental question: 'Given the paucity of evidence, it's staggering that the FBI would initiate a counterintelligence investigation, led by politically biased staff, amid a presidential campaign'.[5] In September 2020, it was revealed that only a small minority in U.S. intelligence considered that Russia had tried to influence the outcome of the 2016 election, with several senior analysts arguing that the Kremlin had in fact anticipated a Clinton victory and considered Trump a 'wild card'. However, CIA director Brennan moved aggressively to exclude dissenting voices from the ICA and to include the Steele dossier in the January 2017 Assessment. On his last morning in office, 20 January 2021, Trump ordered the declassification of a binder of material on the origins of the Crossfire Hurricane probe. The full 'FD-302' interview summary of Steele's meeting with the FBI in London's Grosvenor Hotel in September 2017 now demonstrated that Steele refused to name Danchenko as his main source, even though the FBI had interviewed him eight months earlier and had by then pieced together the provenance of the dossier. Danchenko by now had disappeared, not because he was scared (as suggested by Steele) but probably to avoid being drawn further into the web of deceit.[6] Steele doubled down on his assertion that Cohen visited Prague and other claims that have since been demonstrated to be false. He admitted that he leaked his dossier at the height of the 2016 campaign to divert attention from Clinton's renewed email scandal and to damage Trump, whose election he believed would be damaging for U.S.–U.K. relations.[7]

The progenitors of Russiagate went on to become the heart of the 'resistance' to the president. Brennan was unsparing in his attacks on Trump, accusing him of 'venality, moral turpitude and political corruption', and condemned Republican Party investigation of the FBI. He claimed on Twitter that Trump's performance at the July 2018 press conference in Helsinki 'rises to and exceeds the threshold of high crimes and misdemeanours. It was nothing short of treasonous. Not only were Trump's comments imbecilic, he is wholly in the pocket of Putin'.[8] His own behaviour, however, came under scrutiny. As a columnist with the *Wall Street Journal* put it,

> That's what Mr. Brennan is – a partisan – and it is why his role in the 2016 scandal is in some ways more concerning than the FBI's. Mr. Comey stands accused of flouting the rules, breaking the chain of command, abusing investigatory powers. Yet it seems far likelier that the FBI's Trump investigation was a function of arrogance and overconfidence than some partisan plot. No such case can be made for Mr. Brennan.

Brennan was a close Obama adviser, and he went on to use his position at the head of the world's most powerful spy agency to assist Clinton's campaign – and 'to keep his job'. According to the article, Brennan took credit for launching the Trump investigation. At the HPSCI hearing in May 2017, he explained how he became 'aware of intelligence and information about contacts between Russian officials and US persons'. Since the CIA is prohibited from investigating U.S. citizens, he shared 'every information and bit of intelligence' with the FBI. This information in turn 'served as the basis for the FBI investigation'. Brennan may well have been over-stating his early role, but he certainly played a key part in getting the investigation started. More importantly, Brennan helped shape 'the narrative that Russia was interfering in the election specifically to help Mr. Trump – which quickly evolved into the Trump-collusion narrative'. The Clinton team obviously supported the claim, especially in light of the embarrassing revelation of DNC bias against Sanders. There are solid reports that this was the line that Brennan aggressively pushed internally.[9] In other words, while there may have been no sustained 'conspiracy' to use Russiagate allegations to discredit the Trump and then to hobble his administration, there certainly was a disposition to deploy the new cold war to move in that direction.

Mueller's failure to investigate the Steele dossier opens yet another avenue for speculation. The dossier justified Page's wiretapping and influenced the decision to open a counterintelligence investigation into Trump himself, heralding the chain of events that led to Comey's dismissal, which in turn contributed to the establishment of a special counsel. The damaging consequences stimulated a major counter-conspiracy theory: the view that the devious Russians had started the whole thing. As a commentary in the *New York Times* puts it: 'Was any of the Steele dossier's bad intel deliberately drafted by the Russians'.[10] The question is logical, since why should the Kremlin provide damaging material against someone they ostensibly supported. The journalist David Satter has no doubts about it. In his view, the Mueller report 'shows that Donald Trump and his campaign did not collude with Russia but Russian intelligence used disinformation to create the impression that he did'. This is certainly a dastardly plan – to get the Americans to believe that Russia was meddling in the election with the connivance of the Trump team. The goal was not only to exacerbate partisan divisions in the country but also to paralyse the Trump presidency as it drowned in the subsequent investigation. From this perspective, Papadopoulos told Downer on 10 May 2016 that Moscow had compromising information on Clinton to set off a false lead that in the end helped trigger the destructive counterintelligence investigation into the Trump campaign. Equally, the June 2016 Trump Tower meeting 'was part of the effort to inflame US politics by creating the impression that candidate Trump was a Russian pawn'.[11] If Satter is right, then the Russians were playing a masterful hand of double-bluff – three-dimensional chess barely describes it. If he is mistaken, then his argument typifies everything that is wrong with neo-journalistic coverage of the Russiagate affair: distortion of the facts, fanciful and evidence-free assertions, and irresponsible speculation damaging to U.S. domestic and foreign policy.

The deception goes even deeper. Critics argue that the whole Mueller investigation was 'itself its own version of a hoax, precisely because there isn't a crime to investigate, and there never has been a crime to investigate'.[12] Stephen Cohen dismisses the exaggerated claims that 'Russia attacked American democracy during the 2016 presidential election', likened to Japan's nefarious attack on Pearl Harbour in December 1941. Instead, he argues, there was no 'attack' in 2016, only 'ritualistic "meddling" of the kind that both Russia and America have undertaken in the other's elections for decades'.[13] The Russiagate allegations became part of domestic political struggle. The heads of the intelligence agencies, notably Brennan and DNI Clapper, exaggerated the threat and played up charges of Trump's collusion, an operation that Cohen calls 'Intelgate'. The mainstream media also split along partisan lines, and not only failed to expose abuses of power but also amplified those abuses. Comey's FBI, wittingly or unwittingly, became a political player, leading to the appointment of the special counsel.

Here again comparisons are drawn with earlier cases of prosecutorial misconduct, arguably in the Enron case in which the Supreme Court overturned four of the five Anderson convictions. Weissmann himself was unrepentant, arguing in his memoir *Where Law Ends* that investigation of Russian election interference and links between Trump and Moscow did not go far enough and had been cowed by the power of the presidency, failing to go after the financial records or subpoena Trump family members, a charge rejected by

Mueller.[14] Corruption and security threats must be investigated, but Mueller's special counsel investigation, like the destabilising *mani pulite* (clean hands) anti-corruption campaign in Italy in the early 1990s and the equivalent *lava jato* (car wash) exposures in Brazil in the 2010s, damaged the American polity by deepening polarisation and the politicisation of the judiciary, the security services and the media. The enduring consequences were evident in the 2020 election.

RUSSIA AND THE 2020 ELECTION

After a lull following the publication of the Mueller report, the long shadow of Russiagate returned to cast a pall over the 2020 presidential election. When asked if Russian activity in 2016 was a one-off or a long-term proposition, Comey responded: 'Oh, it's a long-term practice of theirs. It's stepped up a notch in a significant way in '16. They'll be back', and later in his testimony he added, 'we remain that shining city on the hill. And they don't like it'.[15] DNI Coats was convinced that 'Putin had something on Trump. How else to explain the president's behaviour?'.[16] Mueller himself fed anxiety about continued Russian meddling when he testified to Congress on 24 July 2019: 'It wasn't a single attempt. They're doing it as we sit here. . . . And they expect to do it during the next campaign'.[17] In the 25 February 2020 Democratic primary debate, Biden said Russians are 'engaged now, as I speak, in interfering in our election', while former New York mayor Mike Bloomberg charged that Russia was backing Bernie Sanders to ensure a Trump victory – another example of dastardly double-bluff. The intelligence community at that time assessed that the Kremlin was backing Trump, while other reports suggested that Moscow backed Sanders. A major study in *The Atlantic* warned that 'Putin is well on his way to stealing the next election'.[18] Clinton for good measure added that 'Russians are back in our cyber systems' and that 'anyone who tries to deny it' is living in a 'sad dreamworld'.[19]

Democrats clearly thought that the American public still had the appetite for another bout of Russiagate. The logic of the new cold war generated the perception of heightened external threat to American values, democratic procedures and security, and domestic polarisation reinforced the search for external enemies. Russia inevitably re-emerged as the main adversary because in certain respects the original cold war had never ended. NATO expansion and the ideology of the 'end of history' precluded the possibility of a serious institutional or ideological alternative, and thus Russia's great power ambitions and normative challenge simply did not fit into the logic of cold war victory. Those who questioned the character of that victory, like Trump, were cast as sympathetic or even collusive with Russia. The mainstream media continued to feed the public with unproven stories of Russian election meddling and malign activity. The story was bigger than the facts, reproducing in new forms the 'red scare' practices of earlier years.

Five intelligence officials headed by Shelby Pierson (an aide to acting DNI Joseph Maguire) in a closed-door meeting on 13 February 2020 informed Schiff's HPSCI that Russia was trying to get Trump re-elected. This provoked the usual storm of outrage when the *New York Times* revealed the meeting.[20] Brennan tweeted to his 766,000 followers that 'we are now in a full-blown national security crisis' and 'Trump is abetting a Russian covert operation to keep him in office for Moscow's interests'.[21] However, a few days later, an official revealed that there was no evidence for the 'misleading' supposition that 'Russia's interference in this cycle is aimed at re-electing Trump . . . The intelligence doesn't say that'. At most, Russia may have preferred Trump as a 'deal-maker'.[22] Trump was furious that Maguire had allowed the briefing, and he was summarily replaced by the U.S. ambassador to Germany, Richard Grenell. The incident rekindled the struggle between the White House and the intelligence community. Schiff insisted that Russia had 'never really stopped being at it [interfering in elections], in terms of their social media campaign' and warned that 'the US intelligence community under Trump, cannot be relied upon to highlight and combat this threat'.[23] By now there was even less evidence than earlier that the Kremlin sought a Trump victory, hence the view that its goal was to 'sow chaos', a narrative based on little more than 'intuition than dispositive evidence'.[24] The weaponisation of an inflated Russian threat by Schiff and others damaged normal statecraft and pushed the United States towards actions (such as withdrawal from strategic arms control agreements) that may in the end cause the country incalculable damage. Long-term U.S. interests suffered as the 'Russia factor' was instrumentalised for partisan ends. The Democrats also prepared to fight the election on the grounds that Trump was 'soft on China' as he tried to get a trade deal, with the effect of toughening an already hard stance.

It is not clear why Moscow would prefer Trump in 2020. Some in Moscow had welcomed Trump's election in 2016 since it was thought that 'this very unusual guy might bring something completely new to the relationship. And he actually tried, but he failed'. Positive expectations about Trump soon waned, and by 2020 had largely evaporated.[25] Although Trump professed respect for Putin (as he did for Chinese leader Xi Jinping), his policies towards the respective countries were as hard, if not harder, than during the cold war. As his allies pointed out at the 13 February briefing, Trump had 'aggressively confronted Moscow' and strengthened 'the NATO alliance with new resources'.[26] Appeasement was an integral part of the Russia collusion narrative, with CNN insisting that Trump had been 'soft on Russia' no less than thirty-seven times.[27] In fact, Trump ended up 'embracing the worst features of liberal hegemony – overreliance on military force, disinterest in diplomacy, and a tendency towards unilateralism'.[28] This sentiment comes over strongly in Bolton's memoir of his time in Trump world: the slightest concession was taken as defeat, and in a hostile world only the complete and utter capitulation of adversaries enemies would do.[29] This gnostic hostility to diplomacy reinforced the mechanism whereby the Russia scandal 'swallowed' possible foreign policy initiatives vis-à-vis Moscow.[30] Trump's legitimacy was undermined by the allegations of collusion, and his presidency was swallowed as Trump himself put it by 'Russia, Russia, Russia'.

Trump's approach was significantly more uncompromising and confrontational than Obama's, especially when it came to Ukraine.[31] He not only maintained Obama-era sanctions but imposed a slew of new ones; his December 2017 National Security Strategy condemned Russia as an aggressive revisionist power; he repeatedly expelled Russian diplomats and closed diplomatic facilities; time and again he deployed the Magnitsky Act against Russian officials and businesspeople; sent lethal arms to Ukraine including Javelin man-portable anti-tank missiles; sold Patriot missiles to Poland; increased funds for the $4.5 billion European Deterrence Initiative and intensified military exercises on Russia's borders; doggedly imposed sanctions on companies building, insuring and regulating Nord Stream 2; undercut Russian gas sales to Europe by encouraging the building of LNG facilities; accelerated strategic nuclear modernisation, including the deployment of low-yield weapons that were explicitly directed against Moscow; withdrew from the Intermediate Nuclear Forces (INF) and the Open Skies treaties; refused to renew New Start; withdrew from the Iran nuclear deal (JCPOA), brokered with Russia's help; confronted Russia in Syria and Libya; and turned the Helsinki summit in June 2018 into a fiasco. Sanctions were no longer a discretionary instrument of statecraft but became a blunderbuss response for all occasions. Although Congress took the lead on Nord Stream 2, it suited Trump's mercantilist inclinations. The Democrats accused Trump of pandering to Putin in Afghanistan and Syria, but the planned U.S. pull-outs hardly benefited Russia.

Moscow looked for a U.S. president who could establish a new détente, and Trump did not deliver. Dmitry Medvedev, the former president and prime minister who in January 2020 was appointed deputy chair of the Russian Security Council, argued that in 2016 'it seemed that relations between the two countries could not be any worse' than under Obama, but 'the following years have dispelled this illusion. The Trump administration consistently strengthened the systemic confrontation between Washington and Moscow'.[32] There was certainly no reason for Putin to help Trump in 2020.[33] Polls showed that Russian citizens had also given up on Trump, with 37 per cent holding him responsible for the deterioration in relations, while 33 per cent conceded that he had avoided conflicts but failed to achieve the desired rapprochement.[34] Nevertheless, part of the Washington elite still considered Trump Putin's cat's-paw. Discussing his tumultuous eighteen months as national security adviser, Bolton argued that Putin learned that he could play Trump 'like a fiddle'. The report which quotes Bolton notes that while some in Putin's administration may have been disappointed,

> Yet consider the gifts Trump has given Putin in the past 3½ years. Trump has all but wrecked Putin's nemesis, the NATO alliance; this month [June 2020] he abruptly decided to withdraw more than a quarter of US troops from Germany. He opened the door for Russian meddling in the Middle East, and to greater influence over Turkey, Egypt and even Israel. He has poisoned the once-close relations between Washington and Ukraine; President Volodymyr Zelensky has still not been invited to Washington.[35]

Russian intervention in Syria was at the invitation of the constitutionally legitimate government in Damascus (however odious) to prevent Islamic State and other jihadist forces over-running a country with which it had long been allied, so why it should be considered 'meddling' is not clear. But the report was right to the degree that Trump lobbied for Russia's restored membership of the Group of Seven (G7) nations and that Trump was destructive of the U.S. system of multilateral security and other ties built up in the post-war years.

In 2020, the Democrats resurrected the Russiagate playbook, although Republicans did not shrink from using Russia when it suited their purposes. The Russian government as we have seen allegedly tried to help Sanders's campaign, and he was accused of being a 'Russian asset'.[36] Sanders was excoriated for visiting the Soviet Union in 1988, at a time when Gorbachev's reforms were gathering pace, and made some positive comments about universal health care and other social achievements.[37] It was thereby implied that Sanders was a closet communist, if not an outright traitor.[38] Reagan also visited Moscow that year and announced that he no longer considered the USSR an 'evil empire'. However, as Matlock (who was the U.S. ambassador at the time) stressed in a letter to the *New York Times*, the view of Sanders as some sort of fellow traveller was 'a distortion of history', since Sanders (who was then mayor of Burlington, Vermont) had established a sister-city relationship with Yaroslavl in 1988 'with the encouragement and strong support of the United States government'.[39] Now Sanders placed himself at the head of 'the resistance' and was sharply critical of Russia.[40] Just before the New Hampshire primary in February 2020, he accused Trump of 'cozying up to Putin', whatever that means, and in the Democratic primary debate in South Carolina on 25 February, instead of rebutting Bloomberg's assertion that Russia was helping get him elected, Sanders rather lamely addressed

Moscow: 'Mr Putin', he declared, 'if I'm president of the United States, trust me, you're not going to interfere in any more American elections'. Sanders fell into the 'absurd paradox where he was coerced into accepting the premise of an attack specially designed to destroy him'.[41] If he condemned Russiagate as a hoax, he would alienate Democrats who had made it an article of faith for years; but if he accepted it, he joined the camp of mainstream Russia-baiting cold war hawks. Tulsi Gabbard, a Representative from Hawaii and a Democratic candidate for president, faced a similar dilemma but handled it more adroitly. She warned that 'the Democrats' hyper-partisan impeachment process has increased the likelihood that he [Trump] will be re-elected'.[42] Gabbard was one of the few Democrats who challenged the normalisation of war as America's post-cold war default setting. In response, Clinton suggested that Gabbard was 'the favourite of the Russians', implying that she was a 'Russian asset'.[43] Gabbard responded by suing Clinton for defamation.

The 2016 DNC hack made its way back into the campaign. The secret U.S. indictment against Assange was revealed in November 2018, and on 11 April 2019 his asylum was revoked. Assange was unceremoniously dragged out of the Ecuadorian embassy and incarcerated in Belmarsh high security prison.[44] He was not released at the end of the custody period associated with absconding bail and instead remained in jail pending the U.S. extradition hearing. In May, the U.S. authorities revealed an expanded indictment in which all bar one of the eighteen counts were based on the 1917 Espionage Act. This treated him not as a publisher but as a 'hacker' and focused not on the 2016 election but the 2010 Pentagon disclosures.[45] Assange faced one charge of computer hacking and seventeen counts of espionage, threatening a 175-year prison sentence. The extradition hearing started in Westminster Magistrates Court in February 2020, and almost immediately was embroiled in controversy. Assange's lawyers talked of U.S. Congressman Dana Rohrabacher 'going to see Mr Assange and saying, on instructions from the president, he was offering a pardon or some other way out, if Mr Assange . . . said Russia had nothing to do with the DNC'. It was assumed that Trump was trying to deny or cover up what was assumed to be an established fact, that Russia had hacked the DNC and passed the material to WikiLeaks. Rohrbacher did visit Assange in the Ecuadorian embassy in London, who gave him 'definitive proof that Russia was not the source' for the DNC emails. However, when Rohrabacher tried to brief Trump about this, he was blocked on the grounds that with Mueller's investigation in full flood, such a meeting could put the president in legal jeopardy.[46] Trump's team feared that any discussion about Russia could be used by Mueller as evidence of collusion. In turn, as noted, Assange has not released the information so as not to compromise his source and methods.

The story does not make sense, since Assange had long proclaimed that Moscow was not the guilty party, so did not need the inducement of a pardon to say so. Assange in February 2017 tried to provide 'technical evidence ruling out certain parties [Russia]' in the handling of the DNC emails in 2016 but was blocked by Comey and Democratic Senator Mark Warner. The deal would have given Assange 'limited immunity' to allow him to leave the Ecuadorian embassy, and in exchange Assange would have redacted the published CIA materials.[47] When the deal was blocked, WikiLeaks launched a publication broadside, including the Vault 7 releases on 31 March, which included material on the Marble Framework tool that allows the CIA to mask its hacks. Marble had been deployed in 2016, and this may explain why Washington was so keen to keep Assange incommunicado in the embassy. It is not clear why Comey blocked the deal, although evidence demonstrating that Russia was not the WikiLeaks source would have embarrassed the FBI and its inept investigation (or more accurately, non-investigation, outsourcing the investigation to Crowdstrike). McGovern notes that if that was the reason, Comey and Warner 'put US intelligence agents and highly sophisticated cybertools at risk, rather than allow Assange to at least attempt to prove that Russia was not behind the DNC hack'.[48] Immediately prior to the extradition hearing in September 2020, the United States added a raft of new charges to the indictment. Assange was accused of recruiting hackers to steal military secrets, stealing data from banks, obtaining information on tracking police vehicles, and supposedly helping the whistleblower Edward Snowden in Hong Kong. Pleas by the defence team for time to review the new charges were denied by the Old Bailey judge. In January 2021, the U.S. extradition request was refused on the grounds that his life could be under threat in one of the American supermax prisons. However, he was considered a flight risk and so was refused bail and remained in jail, despite his poor health.

The coronavirus pandemic put the 2020 presidential campaign on hold, but politicking did not stop. In late June, the *New York Times* reported that 'Russia secretly offered Afghan militants bounties to kill US troops', based on anonymous intelligence sources.[49] Like so much in the Russiagate affair, the story lacked independent confirmation and was based on anonymous sources and was clearly designed to embarrass Trump. He had allegedly been briefed on the issue as early as February but had not responded. If true, the Russian actions would indeed represent an escalation of hostilities to the verge of war, and Trump's failure to react would represent an egregious failure to protect American lives. However, the claims were denied by a named Taliban spokesperson, and DNI Ratcliffe confirmed that neither the president nor the vice president had been briefed about the story. The *NYT* admitted that 'The intelligence assessment is said to be based at least in part on interrogations of captured Afghan militants and criminals'; in other words, it probably came from the Afghan government, keen to keep U.S. forces in the country, and by U.S. intelligence officials sympathetic to that view and opposed to Trump's attempts to normalise relations with Russia.⁵⁰ Worryingly, Trump's electoral rival Biden swallowed the story and demanded retribution:

> Not only has he [Trump] failed to sanction or impose any kind of consequences on Russia for this egregious violation of international law, Donald Trump has continued his embarrassing campaign of deference and debasing himself before Vladimir Putin . . . His entire presidency has been a gift to Putin, but this is beyond the pale. It's a betrayal of the most sacred duty we bear as a nation, to protect and equip our troops when we send them into harm's way.⁵¹

The problem is that none of it was true, but the new cold war had conditioned Biden to believe uncritically in Russia's malevolent hand. As Fred Weir, one of the most perceptive reporters in the field, noted, 'even the Kremlin's critics in the expert community now complain that US intelligence about Russia has become completely detached from reality'.⁵²

This was reflected in House Speaker Pelosi's argument that 'The American people need to know what the Russians are doing in this case and the American people believe that they should decide who the next president is, not Vladimir Putin'.⁵³ In early August, she complained about the lack of detail in intelligence briefings on 'Russia's continued interference in the 2020 election campaign'. This refers in particular to the ODNI official statement on election security, which allegedly 'played down the threat from Russia by listing it along with China and Iran, as well as other nation states and nonstate actors [who] could also do harm to our electoral process'.⁵⁴ This tempering of the Russian threat was also alleged to be at work in a National Intelligence Estimate, which asserted that Russia favoured Trump but was later (and correctly) modified. This was taken to signal continuing White House softness on Russia, making 'no distinction between Russia's sophisticated election-disrupting capabilities and the less insidious influence campaigns of the two supposedly anti-Trump countries'.⁵⁵ David Ignatius in the *Washington Post* once again weighed in, arguing that 'The United States is Putin's main target in this "anything goes" campaign to revive his country's reputation as a superpower'. He quoted William Evanina, director of the National Counterintelligence and Security Centre, who on 7 August stated 'We assess that Russia is using a range of measures to primarily denigrate former Vice President [Joe] Biden and what it sees as an anti-Russian "establishment"'.⁵⁶ He added that 'some Kremlin-linked actors are also seeking to boost Trump's candidacy'.⁵⁷ In fact, there was no consensus among the Russian elite about which of the candidates would suit Moscow's interests – neither was particularly appealing.⁵⁸ An open letter to Pelosi from VIPS tried to educate her by reprising their argument that the DNC emails were leaked and not hacked, a view reinforced by Shawn Henry's testimony of 5 December 2017, which was made public on 7 May 2020. They stated the obvious point that 'the lack of desired detail may simply betoken the absence of credible specifics on significant Russian interference, and the absence of Clapperesque officials to conjure it up. In a word, today's intelligence managers – unlike their predecessors – are not likely to find Russia-indicting evidence that "wasn't really there"'.[59]

Allegations of Russian meddling and attempts to 'manipulate public discourse' have become a tradition in American elections. However, 'A botched rollout [of meddling allegations] in the middle of the campaign season could become its own form of election interference'.[60] If in 2016 the emphasis was on hacking and social media disinformation, the concern focused now on attacks on election infrastructure and the hacking of voter databases. Russian reports revealed data on 7.6 million Michigan voters on the dark web Forum known as Gorka9, along with voter information from swing states like Florida and North Carolina. The allegation that the material was the result of a hack was rebutted by both the DHS and FBI, who stressed that most of the material was freely available.[61] Criminal hackers have long used more extensive versions of citizen data (with email addresses and other information, and not just names) from voter registration databases but also from driver licence, health care and other sources. Above all, it was not clear what benefit Russia would derive from hacking U.S. election data points, but speculation was assumed to become fact through endless repetition.[62] There were also claims the IRA sponsored a website called PeaceData (peacedata.net) that recruited left-wing American journalists to contribute, designed to depress the progressive vote, and thus help Trump.[63] The site ran articles critiquing Biden and other Democrats, but some also criticised Trump, both main parties and the flaws of American democracy. Following a tip-off by a software and analytical company called Graphika (with links to the U.S. government), the media and intelligence agencies became involved. Graphika accused PeaceData of 'information laundering', a rather chilling term to describe political debates.[64]

On 7 August, Evanina issued a carefully worded statement that Russia was once again meddling using a 'range of measures' to 'undermine former Vice President Biden's candidacy and the Democratic Party'. The failure to provide details elicited outrage in the *Washington Post* and *New York Times*, with Ratcliffe coming in for particular criticism because of his plan to curtail briefings in the run-up to the election.[65] Wray, eager to restore the FBI's reputation after Russiagate, briefed on 17 September that Russia had engaged in 'very active efforts' to interfere in the election by damaging Biden primarily though social media proxies.[66] In September, the CIA warned that Putin was probably still directing interference operations designed to improve Trump's chances of re-election, but the CIA itself had only 'moderate confidence' in its own analysis.⁶⁷ The CIA's *World Intelligence Review* of 31 August claimed that Andriy Derkach, who had provided information to the joint Senate report on Hunter Biden, was in fact working for the Russians as part of 'Russia's influence operations aimed at denigrating the former US vice president, supporting the US President, and fuelling public discord ahead of the US election in November'.⁶⁸ Given Trump's sensitivity over charges of Russian meddling, the CIA was accused of limiting the flow of Russian intelligence to the White House. When FBI director Wray testified to a Congressional hearing about Russia's attempts to undermine Biden, Trump launched a Twitter storm arguing that 'China is a FAR greater threat than Russia'.⁶⁹

Clinton failed to build bridges with the Sanders campaign in 2016 after her nomination, and as a result about a quarter of Sanders' primary supporters did not vote for her in the general election.⁷⁰ In 2020, Biden avoided making the same mistake and 'reached out' to the left wing of the Democratic Party, although his 'centrist' positions on fracking, health care, mass incarceration, policing and the environment alienated progressive voters.⁷¹ As for Trump, his cruel mishandling of Covid-19 and the accompanying economic crisis undermined the foundations of his appeal, namely his successful handling of the economy. On 15 July, Trump, smarting from the embarrassment of a poorly attended campaign rally in Tulsa on 20 June, ditched his long-time campaign manager Brad Parscale, demoting him to senior adviser (Parscale then quit following health issues). Trump played down the significance of the pandemic 'because I didn't want to create a panic', an approach that was of little comfort to the families of 300,000 Americans who had died of Covid-19 by the time of the ballot.⁷² The *New York Times* in late September published eighteen years of Trump's tax returns and exposed how in eleven of the eighteen years he paid no taxes at all, and in the campaign year of 2016, his tax bill came to just $750 and the same amount in his first year in office. Exposure of his chronic indebtedness undermined his credibility as a successful businessman and once again raised questions about who had lent him the money. Trump was 'more successful playing a business mogul than being one in real life'. His reputation and finances were salvaged by his role in *The Apprentice* and associated licensing and endorsement deals, which earned him $427.4 million. The *Times* noted that 'As president, he has received more money from foreign sources and US interest groups than previously known', but examination of Trump's assets and wealth did not 'reveal any previously unreported connections to Russia'.⁷³ He had over $300 million of debt due in the next four years, most of which was owed to Deutsche Bank, prompting concern that Russia may ultimately have been the guarantor. In fact, the collateral was on Trump's personal assets; hence, the loans were issued on normal commercial terms.⁷⁴

Trump's personal finances, his harsh and intolerant approach to Black Lives Matter protests following the police killing of George Floyd in Minnesota on 25 May 2020 and his mishandling of the coronavirus pandemic became key themes in the presidential debates. Soon after the ill-tempered first debate on 29 September, Trump contracted the disease himself, disrupting his campaign activities as polling suggested a widening lead in favour of Biden. Observers feared that Biden's victory and the Democratic takeover of the Senate would mean an end to the various investigations into the origins and conduct of Russiagate. The investigation conducted by the Senate Judiciary Committee under Lindsey Graham questioned Comey on 30 September about the FISA warrants taken out against Page. Comey claimed to have little memory of what was going on when, as in the words of one commentator, 'the FBI deceived the [FISA] Court into approving four warrants for surveillance of Trump campaign aide Carter Page'.[75] Ukraine also came back into the spotlight, with a *New York Post* report in October alleging that Hunter Biden traded access to his father with Ukrainian energy tycoons, sought deals for his family in China, and shared some of his foreign profits with his father. The newspaper had received a hard drive containing the emails from Trump's attorney, Giuliani, who in turn claimed that he was given the drive by a computer shop in Delaware, after a laptop was left there by Hunter in 2019. Although few disputed the authenticity of the emails, Schiff immediately claimed that the story was part of a 'Russian disinformation campaign', which DNI Ratcliffe immediately refuted, saying that there was no evidence to make such a claim.[76] Despite this, Twitter suspended the *New York Post*'s account on the grounds that it was spreading Russian disinformation by reporting on the laptop's contents. In the final presidential debate on 22 October, Biden dismissed the laptop scandal as a Russian plot to sabotage his campaign, and he referred to a letter to *Politico* signed by over fifty former intelligence officials asserting that the Hunter email scandal 'has all the classic earmarks of a Russian information operation', although they admitted that they had no evidence.[77] Biden once again condemned Trump for not taking action against Russia over the Afghanistan bounty scandal.[78] Ratcliffe at this time asserted that Russia and Iran had obtained U.S. voting registration data and were attempting to sow disinformation in the forthcoming election, a threat that FBI director Wray said would be met by imposing costs.[79] Putin noted that Hunter Biden had made 'good money' in Ukraine, but 'Russia saw nothing criminal in it', and in any case 'It doesn't concern us'.[80]

Putin repeated his offer of cyber security cooperation with the United States, but the proposal was ignored. Putin noted that 'there are ongoing complaints about Russia's hyperactivity, alleged hyperactivity, in the information sphere, interference in US elections, and other allegations, which are completely unfounded'. As for the election itself, in the first debate, Biden called Trump 'Putin's puppy'. Putin denied any Russian interference and noted that 'Everything that is happening in the United States is the result of the country's internal political processes and problems', although references to Russia's head of state in fact 'enhances our prestige, because they are talking about our incredible influence and power'. As for preferences, Putin observed that Trump had 'repeatedly expressed interest in the improvement of Russian-American relations. And we certainly appreciate that very much . . . we certainly heard him'. However, 'we must look objectively at what has been happening in recent years', and although there were some achievements, the aspirations had 'not been fully realised'. Putin attributed this to 'a certain bipartisan consensus on the need to contain Russia, to curb our country's development'. This represented containment 'on all tracks', with 'the greatest number of various kinds of restrictions and sanctions introduced during the Trump presidency. Decisions on imposing new sanctions or expanding previous ones were made 46 times'. Putin lamented the U.S. withdrawal from the INF treaty and announced Russia's withdrawal from the Open Skies Treaty. As for Biden, Putin noted that the Democrat came from the social-democrat tradition, from which the Communist Party, of whom Putin noted he had been a rank-and-file member for eighteen years, also came, so there was a certain ideological commonality – a rather far-fetched and mischievous argument, although technically correct.[81]

On an exceptionally high turnout of 66.7 per cent, Biden won by an impressive 7.1 million votes, the highest margin since 1908. Biden gained 81.3 million votes (51.4%), giving him 306 to Trump's 232 electoral college delegates (the same margin by which Trump beat Clinton in 2016), comfortably exceeding the 270 required for victory. However, Trump's vote also held up, and the 74.2 million ballots (46.9%) cast in his favour exceeded his 2016 tally. Trump increased his vote in Florida and Texas, and gained more white working-class support than in 2016, while also increasing his support among Latinos. This confirmed that his 2016 result was no mere fluke or the result of Putin's machinations, Comey's gyrations or Clinton's failings but represented a solid base of popular support. This helps explain why Trump obdurately refused to concede, making baseless claims about voter fraud. In part, this was revenge against those in the Democratic Party who never recognised the legitimacy of his earlier victory. As late as September 2019, nearly three years after her defeat, Clinton was still asserting that 'He [Trump] knows that he is an illegitimate president. I believe he understands that the many varying tactics they used, from voter suppression and voter purging to hacking to false stories, he knows that there were just a bunch of different reasons why the election turned out as it did'. Former President Jimmy Carter in June of that year went even further to argue 'There's no doubt that the Russians did interfere in the election. And I think the interference, although not yet quantified, if fully investigated would show that Trump didn't actually win the election in 2016. He lost the election and he was put into office because the Russians interfered on his behalf'.[82] Trump's refusal to concede prepared the ground for the Republicans to contest the legitimacy of Biden's election.[83] Trump sought to consolidate his base with an eye to a possible comeback in 2024, but his inflammatory appeals provoked the storming of the Capitol on 6 January, prompting his second impeachment on 13 January by a 232-197 vote on the charge of 'incitement of insurrection'.

The 2020 election was considered 'the most secure in history' by the administration's own officials. Christopher Krebs, the director of the Cybersecurity and Infrastructure Security Agency (CISA), the federal office responsible for election security, dismissed Trump's claims of widespread voter fraud but for his pains was sacked on 18 November.[84] This did not prevent a U.S. Intelligence Community Assessment prepared by seven of the seventeen agencies in March 2021 asserting 'with high confidence' that Putin authorised 'influence operations aimed at denigrating President Biden's candidacy and the Democratic Party, supporting former President Trump, undermining public confidence in the electoral process, and exacerbating sociopolitical divisions in the US'. This was to be achieved by proxies including 'Ukraine-linked individuals with ties to Russian intelligence and their networks' who would spread the narrative 'alleging corrupt ties between President Biden, his family, and other US officials and Ukraine'.[85] The Ukrainian legislator Andriy Derkach, one of Giuliani's prime sources, was accused of having ties with Russian intelligence. Above all, Kilimnik was once again accused of being a 'Russian influence agent' who meddled in the 2020 campaign to help Trump's re-election. A month earlier, the FBI offered a $250,000 reward for his arrest in connection with a 2018 witness tampering charge in Manafort's Ukraine lobbying case. No new evidence was revealed, and Kilimnik repeated that 'I have no relationship whatsoever to any intelligence services, be they Russian or Ukrainian or American, or anyone else'.[86] The substantive Russiagate charge of collusion by then had been discredited, but the Biden administration continued to investigate some of its many strands, including Devin Nunes' 2018 memo about FBI FISA surveillance abuses and Rudy Giuliani's actions in Ukraine. As for the 2020 election, Nakashima argues that Russia failed to mount any major hacking or disinformation operations because of the changed political environment, as well as the robust cyber-operations mounted by the U.S. Cyber Command, but above all because 'Americans themselves were the largest purveyors of disinformation, dwarfing Moscow's efforts to influence the campaign through social media and its propaganda channels'.[87] Claims of Russian interference suddenly disappeared, and one can assume the same would have happened if Clinton had won in 2016 – and the world would have been spared Russiagate.

NOTES

1. David Smith, 'Bernstein: This is Worse than Watergate, says Nixon Nemesis', *Guardian*, 13 August 2018, p. 21.
2. Woodward, *Fear*.
3. Smith, 'Bernstein'.
4. Levitsky and Ziblatt, *How Democracies Die*, p. 9.
5. Rivkin and Foley, 'Mueller's Fruit of the Poisonous Tree'.
6. Kit Klarenberg, 'Christopher Steele's Declassified FBI Interview', RT.com, 21 January 2021, https://www.rt.com/op-ed/513240-christopher-steele-declassified-fbi-interview/.
7. John Solomon, 'First Trump Declassified Document: Christopher Steele's 2017 Confession to the FBI', *Just the News*, 20 January 2021, https://justthenews.com/accountability/russia-and-ukraine-scandals/first-declassified-russia-document-steeles-confessional. The article includes links to the original document and a 4 October summary.
8. Peter Van Buren, 'John Brennan: Melting Down and Covering Up', *American Conservative*, 20 July 2018, https://www.theamericanconservative.com/articles/john-brennan-melting-down-and-covering-up/.
9. Kimberley A. Strassel, 'Brennan and the 2016 Spy Scandal: Obama's CIA Director Acknowledged Egging on the FBI's Probe of Trump and Russia', *Wall Street Journal*, 20 July 2018, https://www.wsj.com/articles/brennan-and-the-2016-spy-scandal-1532039346.
10. Douthat, 'A Spy by Any Name'.
11. David Satter, 'Collusion or Russian Disinformation?', *Wall Street Journal*, 1 May 2019, https://www.wsj.com/articles/collusion-or-russian-disinformation-11556663662.
12. Rush Limbaugh, 'The Mueller Clown Show Might as Well Indict Minnie Mouse', *Rush Limbaugh Show*, 28 November 2018, https://www.rushlimbaugh.com/daily/2018/11/28/this-mueller-clown-show-might-as-well-indict-minnie-mouse-2/.
13. Stephen F. Cohen, 'Inconvenient Truths', *The Nation*, 6 November 2019, https://www.thenation.com/article/archive/inconvenient-truths-2/.
14. Martin Pengelly, 'Mueller Rejects Prosecutor's Criticism of Trump-Russia Investigation', *Guardian*, 29 September 2020, https://www.theguardian.com/us-news/2020/sep/29/robert-mueller-prosecutor-criticism-trump-russia-investigation.
15. Full Text: James Comey Testimony, 8 June 2017.
16. Woodward, *Rage*, p. 152.
17. Julie Hirschfeld Davis and Mark Mazzetti, 'Highlights of Robert Mueller's Testimony to Congress', *New York Times*, 24 July 2019, https://www.nytimes.com/2019/07/24/us/politics/mueller-testimony.html.
18. Franklin Foer, 'Putin Is Well on His Way to Stealing the Next Election: RIP Democracy', *The Atlantic*, June 2020, https://www.theatlantic.com/magazine/archive/2020/06/putin-american-democracy/610570/. Foer is the original Russiagater, warning already in July 2016 about Putin's plan to destroy Europe and the US, Paul Robinson, '#DemocracyRIP and the Narcissism of Russiagate', *Irrussianality*, 12 May

2020, https://irrussianality.wordpress.com/2020/05/12/democracyrip-and-the-narcissism-of-russiagate/. The Foer article is 'Putin's Puppet', *The Slate*, 4 July 2016, http://www.slate.com/articles/news_and_politics/cover_story/2016/07/vladimir_putin_has_a_plan_for_destroying_the_west_and_it_looks_a_lot_like.html?via=gdpr-consent.

19. James S. Robbins. 'Maybe Our Social Media Obsession Is a Bigger Problem than Russian Election Interference', *USA Today*, 26 February 2000, https://eu.usatoday.com/story/opinion/2020/02/26/russia-election-interference-bernie-sanders-donald-trump-facebook-twitter-column/4879927002/.

20. Adam Goldman, Julian E. Barnes, Maggie Haberman and Nicholas Fandos, 'Lawmakers are Warned that Russia is Meddling to Re-Elect Trump', *New York Times*, 20 February 2020, https://www.nytimes.com/2020/02/20/us/politics/russian-interference-trump-democrats.html.

21. Jerry Dunleavy, 'Intelligence Community Disputes 2020 Trump-Russia Story Embraced by Democrats', *Washington Examiner*, 28 February 2020, https://www.washingtonexaminer.com/news/intelligence-community-disputes-2020-trump-russia-story-embraced-by-democrats.

22. Jeremy Diamond, Jake tapper and Zachary Cohen, 'US Intelligence Briefer Appears to Have Over-stated Assessment of 2020 Russian Interference', CNN.com, 23 February 2020, https://edition.cnn.com/2020/02/23/politics/intelligence-briefer-russian-interference-trump-sanders/index.html.

23. David Corn, 'Adam Schiff: Russia is Still Interfering with US Elections—And Trump is Covering it Up', *Mother Jones*, 15 April 2020, https://www.motherjones.com/politics/2020/04/adam-schiff-russia-is-still-interfering-with-us-elections-and-trump-is-covering-it-up/.

24. David B. Rivkin and George Beebe, 'Election Mirage: Why Claims of Russian Meddling Should be Questioned', *The National Interest*, 28 February 2020, https://nationalinterest.org/feature/election-mirage-why-claims-russian-meddling-should-be-questioned-127992.

25. Fyodor A. Lukyanov, 'US Election Seen From Russia: "No Rosy Expectations"', *Russia in Global Affairs*, 15 September 2020, https://eng.globalaffairs.ru/articles/us-election-seen-from-russia/.

26. Goldman et al, 'Lawmakers are Warned that Russia is Meddling', *New York Times*, 20 February 2020.

27. Marshall Cohen, '37 Times Trump Was Soft on Russia', *CNN*, 4 August 2020, https://edition.cnn.com/2019/11/17/politics/trump-soft-on-russia/index.html. This is an updated list of the 25 instances of 'softness' originally published on 17 November 2019.

28. Walt, *The Hell of Good Intentions*, p. 219.

29. Bolton, *Room Where It Happened*.

30. Micah Zenko, 'Trump's Russia Scandal is Already Swallowing his Foreign Policy', *Foreign Policy*, 6 June 2017, https://foreignpolicy.com/2017/06/06/trumps-russia-scandal-is-already-swallowing-his-foreign-policy/.

31. Ted Galen Carpenter, 'It's High Time to Reassess the United States' Relationship with Ukraine', *The Federalist*, 26 September 2019, https://www.cato.org/publications/commentary/its-high-time-reassess-united-states-relationship-ukraine.

32. Dmitry Medvedev, 'America 2.0: After the Election', *TASS*, 16 January 2021, https://tass.com/opinions/1245253.

33. A point made by Andrei Kortunov, 'Why Should Putin Help Trump?', *RIAC*, 25 February 2020, https://russiancouncil.ru/en/analytics-and-comments/analytics/why-should-putin-help-trump/.

34. 'Rossiyane razuverilis' v Trampe', VTsIOM, 11 February 2020, https://wciom.ru/index.php?id=236&uid=10155.

35. Jackson Diehl, 'In 2016, Putin Didn't Expect Trump to Win. Now, He Needs Him To', *Washington Post*, 22 June 2020, https://www.washingtonpost.com/gdpr-consent/?next_url=https%3a%2f%2fwww.washingtonpost.com%2fopinions%2fglobal-opinions%2fputin-is-having-a-bad-year-he-needs-the-reelection-of-president-trump%2f2020%2f06%2f21%2f4e7cdf62-b173-11ea-856d-5054296735e5_story.html

36. Christian Whitton, 'Democrats Have a Plan to Beat Bernie Sanders: Call him a Russian "Asset"', *The National Interest*, 23 February 2020, https://nationalinterest.org/blog/buzz/democrats-have-plan-beat-bernie-sanders-call-him-russian-asset-126436.

37. Yana Skorobogatov, Yakov Feygin and Artemy M. Kalinovsky, 'Critics of Bernie Sanders' Trip to the Soviet Union are Distorting It', *Washington Post*, 3 March 2020, https://www.washingtonpost.com/outlook/2020/03/03/critics-bernie-sanderss-trip-soviet-union-are-distorting-it/.

38. Anton Troianovski, 'As Bernie Sanders Pushed for Closer Ties, Soviet Union Spotted Opportunity', *New York Times*, 6 March 2020, p. 1.

39. Jack Matlock, 'Defending Bernie Sanders's Sister-City Efforts in the USSR', *New York Times*, 6 Match 2020, https://www.nytimes.com/2020/03/06/opinion/letters/bernie-sanders-soviet-union.html.

40. Bernie Sanders, *Where We Go From Here: Two Years in the Resistance* (London, Biteback Publishing, 2018).

41. Michael Tracy, 'How Sanders Was "Russia-gated" Out of the 2020 Race', *Real Clear Politics*, 19 April 2020, https://www.realclearpolitics.com/articles/2020/04/19/how_sanders_was_russia-gated_out_of_the_2020_race_142977.html.

42. Tulsi Gabbard, 'How Democrats' Impeachment Campaign Helped Trump', Fortune.com, 21 February 2020, https://fortune.com/2020/02/21/tulsi-gabbard-democrats-trump-impeachment/.

43. Dan Mangan, 'Rep. Tulsi Gabbard Sues Hillary Clinton for Alleged "Russian Aset" Smear in 2020 Democratic Presidential Contest, Claiming $50 million in Damages', CNBC.com, 22 January 2020, https://www.cnbc.com/2020/01/22/tulsi-gabbard-sues-hillary-clinton-for-alleged-russian-smear.html.

44. For context, see Max Blumenthal, '"The American Friends": New Court Files Expose Sheldon Adelson's Security Team in US Spy Operation against Julian Assange', *The Grayzone*, 14 May 2020, https://thegrayzone.com/2020/05/14/american-sheldon-adelsons-us-spy-julian-assange/

45. Patrick Cockburn, 'Julian Assange in Limbo', *London Review of Books*, 18 June 2020, pp. 29–30.

46. Ryan Grim, 'Congressman Says He Tried to Brief Trump on WikiLeaks after Meeting with Julian Assange, but John Kelly Blocked Him', *The Intercept*, 14 February 2018, https://theintercept.com/2018/02/14/dana-rohrabacher-trump-russia-wikileaks-julian-assange/.

47. John Solomon, 'How Comey Intervened to Kill WikiLeaks Immunity Deal', *The Hill*, 25 June 2018, https://thehill.com/opinion/white-house/394036-How-Comey-intervened-to-kill-Wikileaks-immunity-deal.

48. Ray McGovern, 'Did Sen. Warner and Comey "Collude" on Russia-Gate?', *Consortium News*, 27 June 2018, https://consortiumnews.com/2018/06/27/did-sen-warner-and-comey-collude-on-russia-gate/.

49. Charlie Savage, Eric Schmitt and Michael Schwirtz, 'Russia Secretly Offered Afghan Militants Bounties to Kill US Troops, Intelligence Says', *New York Times*, 26 June 2020, https://www.nytimes.com/2020/06/26/us/politics/russia-afghanistan-bounties.html.

50. The best analysis of the incident is by Scott Ritter, 'New York Times Takes Anti-Russian Hysteria to New Level with Report on Russian "Bounty" for US Troops in Afghanistan', RT.com, 28 June 2020, https://www.rt.com/op-ed/493174-nyt-report-russia-afghanistan/.

51. Eric Schmitt, Michael Schwirtz and Charlie Savage, 'Biden Criticizes Trump over Intelligence on Russian Bounties on US Troops', *New York Times*, 27 June 2020, https://www.nytimes.com/2020/06/27/us/politics/trump-russia-bounties-afghanistan.html.

52. Fred Weir, 'For Russian Experts, Taliban Bounty Report Just Doesn't Make Sense', *Christian Science Monitor*, 9 July 2020, https://www.csmonitor.com/World/Europe/2020/0709/For-Russian-experts-Taliban-bounty-report-just-doesn-t-make-sense.

53. William Cummings, '"They're Not Equivalent": Pelosi Says Russian Election Interference More Serious than that of China, Iran', *USA Today*, 9 August 2020, https://eu.usatoday.com/story/news/politics/elections/2020/08/09/pelosi-schumer-obrien-russia-election-interference/3331144001/.

54. Robert Draper, 'Unwanted Truths: Inside Trump's Battles with US Intelligence Agencies', *New York Times Magazine*, 10 August 2020, https://www.nytimes.com/2020/08/08/magazine/us-russia-intelligence.html.

55. Draper, 'Unwanted Truths'.

56. Press Release, ODNI, 7 August 2020, https://www.dni.gov/index.php/newsroom/press-releases/item/2139-statement-by-ncsc-director-william-evanina-election-threat-update-for-the-american-public.

57. David Ignatius, 'Putin is Reckless Because We Allow Him to Be', *Washington Post*, 12 August 2020, https://www.washingtonpost.com/opinions/putin-is-reckless-because-we-allow-him-to-be/2020/08/11/2e89b79c-dc17-11ea-b205-ff838e15a9a6_story.html.

58. Tatiana Stanovaya, 'A Farewell to Trump? Russia's Elite Braces for US Elections', *Carnegie Moscow Centre*, 21 October 2020, https://carnegie.ru/commentary/83007.

59. VIPS Memo, 'To Nancy Pelosi—Did Russia Hack the DNC Emails?', *Consortium News*, 3 August 2020, https://consortiumnews.com/2020/08/03/vips-memo-to-nancy-pelosi-did-russia-hack-the-dnc-emails/.

60. Jon Bateman, 'American Voters Deserve Facts on Outside influence on this Election', *Carnegie Endowment for International Peace*, 26 July 2020, https://ca

rnegieendowment.org/2020/07/26/american-voters-deserve-facts-on-outside-influenc e-on-this-election-pub-82455.

61. 'DHS, FBI Rebut Reports about Hacked Voter Data on Russian Forum', *Politico*, 1 September 2020, https://www.politico.com/news/2020/09/01/dhs-fbi-h acked-voter-data-reports-407212.

62. Gareth Porter, 'Dark Web Voter Database Report Casts New Doubts on Russian Election Hack Narrative', *The Gray Zone*, 13 September 2020, https://th egrayzone.com/2020/09/13/dark-web-voter-data-russian-election-hack-narrative/.

63. John Jiang, 'The Absurdity of the Latest "Russian Interference" Story', *American Spectator*, 2 September 2020, https://spectator.org/the-absurdity-of-the-la test-russian-interference-story/.

64. Joe Lauria, 'Russiagate: NYT, FB & FBI say Anti-Trump Site, Now Shutdown, Was Russian Effort to Help Trump Win', *Consortium News*, 6 September 2020, https ://consortiumnews.com/2020/09/06/russiagate-nyt-fb-fbi-say-anti-trump-site-now-s hutdown-was-russian-effort-to-help-trump-win/.

65. Editorial, 'The Director of National Intelligence is Providing Cover for Putin', *Washington Post*, 1 September 2020; Editorial 'American Intelligence Knows What Russia is Doing', *New York Times*, 1 September 2020, https://www.nytimes.com/2 020/08/31/opinion/john-ratcliffe-russia-election.html.

66. Hans Nichols, 'Biden's Hardline Russia Reset', Axios.com, 18 September 2020, https://www.axios.com/biden-russia-policy-putin-d8084624-ce24-425f-8718 -84c15cfb3bfd.html.

67. Julian E. Barnes and David E. Sanger, 'CIA Reasserts Putin is Likely Directing Election Influence Efforts to Aid Trump', *New York Times*, 22 September 2020, https://www.nytimes.com/2020/09/22/us/politics/cia-russian-election-interference .html.

68. Josh Rogin, 'Secret CIA Assessment: Putin "Probably Directing" Influence Operation to Denigrate Biden', *Washington Post*, 22 September 2020, https://www .washingtonpost.com/opinions/2020/09/22/secret-cia-assessment-putin-probably-di recting-influence-operation-denigrate-biden/. For commentary, see Scott Ritter, 'The American Deep State Revives its Tired Allegations of Russian Interference in November's Presidential Election', RT.com, 23 September 2020, https://qo she.com/rt-com/scott-ritter/the-american-deep-state-revives-its-tired-allegati/861 41166.

69. Natasha Bertrand and Daniel Lippman, 'CIA Clamps Down on Flow of Russia Intelligence to the White House', *Politico*, 23 September 2020, https://www.politico .com/news/2020/09/23/cia-russia-intelligence-white-house-420351.

70. Lauren Fedor, 'Sanders Supporters Make Peace with Biden Camp', *Financial Times*, 19 August 2020, p. 6.

71. Ankita Rao, 'The Leftwing Democrats who Reject both Biden and Trump', *Guardian*, 7 September 2020, p. 21.

72. Woodward, *Rage*, p. 286, and see also p. xxi.

73. Russ Buettner, Susanne Craig and Mike McIntire, 'The President's Taxes: Long-Concealed Records Show Trump's Chronic Losses and Years of Tax Avoidance', *New York Times*, 27 September 2020, https://www.nytimes.com/intera ctive/2020/09/27/us/donald-trump-taxes.html.

74. David Enrich, 'No, There Isn't Evidence that Trump Owes Money to Russia', *New York Times*, 13 October 2020, https://www.nytimes.com/2020/10/13/technology/no-there-isnt-evidence-that-trump-owes-money-to-russia.html.

75. Ray McGovern, 'Comey's Amnesia Makes Senate Session an Unforgettable Hop, Skip & Jump to Fraud', *Consortium News*, 5 October 2020, https://consortiumnews.com/2020/10/05/ray-mcgovern-comeys-amnesia-makes-senate-session-an-unforgettable-hop-skip-jump-to-fraud/.

76. Jake Gibson and Brooke Singman, 'FBI in Possession of Hunter Biden's Purported Laptop, Sources Say', Foxnews.com, 21 October 2020, https://www.foxnews.com/politics/fbi-purported-hunter-biden-laptop-sources.

77. Holman W. Jenkins, 'The US Has an "Intelligence" Problem', *Wall Street Journal*, 24 October 2020, https://www.wsj.com/articles/the-u-s-has-an-intelligence-problem-11603489696.

78. Mark Episkopos, 'Joe Biden Keeps the Fictions about Trump and Russia Alive', *The National Interest*, 24 October 2020, https://nationalinterest.org/blog/2020-election/joe-biden-keeps-fictions-about-trump-and-russia-alive-171366.

79. Maanvi Singh, 'Russia and Iran Obtained US Voter Data in Bid to Sow Unrest Before Election, Says FBI', *Guardian*, 23 October 2020, p. 33.

80. Vladimir Putin, interview with Rossiya-1, 25 October, RT.com, 'Putin Says Hunter Biden "Made Very Good Money" in Ukraine', 26 October 2020, https://www.rt.com/russia/504542-putin-hunter-biden-money-ukraine/.

81. Vladimir Putin, 'Interview with Rossiya TV Channel', 7 October 2020, http://en.kremlin.ru/events/president/news/64171.

82. Both quotations cited by William McGurn, 'Joe Biden's Bitter Harvest: Where Might Trump Voters Have Got the Idea that a President was Illegitimate?', *Wall Street Journal*, 10 November 2020, https://www.wsj.com/articles/joe-bidens-bitter-harvest-11604963930.

83. Joe Lauria, 'Election 2020: Payback for Russiagate', *Consortium News*, 12 November 2020, https://consortiumnews.com/2020/11/12/election-2020-payback-for-russiagate/.

84. Sam Levine and Joan E. Greve, 'Trump Lambasted as "Pathetic" for Sacking of Security Chief as Bid for Recount Fails', *Guardian*, 19 November 2020, p. 28.

85. ODNI, National Intelligence Council, *Intelligence Community Assessment on Foreign Threats to the 2020 US Federal Elections*, 15 March 2021, https://www.intelligence.gov/assets/documents/702%20Documents/declassified/ICA-declass-16MAR21.pdf.

86. For the full interview and details, see Aaron Maté, 'Accused Russiagate "Spy" Kilimnik Speaks: and Evidence Backs his "No Collusion" Account', *RealClearInvestigations*, 19 May 2021, https://www.realclearinvestigations.com/articles/2021/05/19/accused_russiagate_spy_kilimnik_speaks_-_and_evidence_backs_his_no_collusion_account_777328.html.

87. Ellen Nakashima, 'Fewer Opportunities and a Changed Political Environment in the US May Have Curbed Moscow's Election Interference this Year, Analysts Say', *Washington Post*, 17 November 2020, https://www.washingtonpost.com/national-security/russia-failed-to-mount-major-election-interference-operations-in-2020-analysts-say/2020/11/16/72c62b0c-1880-11eb-82db-60b15c874105_story.html.

Chapter 16

Deception and the New Cold War

Trump promised to be the great disruptor, and on this he delivered. However, when it came to fulfilling a positive agenda of economic transformation and the modernisation of strategic foreign policy thinking, his presidency turned into a grand deception. Trump's defenders point to the shadow cast by Russiagate to explain the failure to deliver on his promises, but the Trumpian deception is deeper than that. Nevertheless, the endless investigations and aspersions did constrain his presidency. In the end, though, despite the best endeavours of investigators, they were unable to locate a 'smoking gun', as Trump put it in a tweet on 10 December 2018: 'No collusion. That's because there was no collusion'. The U.S. intelligence agencies found that the Russian government ran a campaign to damage Hillary Clinton's presidential bid, to undermine the American democratic process and to sow discord in society. The two main strategies were the 'hack and leak' operation against the Democratic Party, and an online disinformation campaign. In turn, the Russiagate allegations became a way of pushing back against Trump, preventing the rapprochement with Russia that he had so loudly declared as his goal in 2016 while tying him down with endless investigations at home. Collusion charges became a routine part of American elections, accompanied by accusations of being 'soft' on Russia when the new orthodoxy was questioned. The Russiagate allegations prompted social media regulation that at times veered towards censorship, as well as hardening new cold war policies that further soured an already fractious relationship between Russia and America.

Chapter 16

CAUSES AND CONSEQUENCES

A report in the *New York Times* on 25 August 2018 suggested that the U.S. intelligence agencies had multiple 'informants close to . . . Putin in the Kremlin who provided crucial details' about Russiagate for two years.[1] Stephen Cohen noted that an earlier version of the sensational story appeared in the *Washington Post* on 15 December 2017, and he asks the fundamental question: If the U.S. intelligence community had such a priceless asset in the heart of Russian government, why reveal it in such an irresponsible way? The reason was the failure to find any real evidence to support the fundamental allegation that Putin ordered Russian operatives to put Trump in the White House. Instead, the Russiagate allegations delegitimized a presidential election and a presidency. The 'attack on American democracy' came not from Putin or Trump, but 'by whoever godfathered and repeatedly inflated Russiagate'. In Cohen's opinion, the intelligence agencies were the main sponsors of the narrative; less so the FBI, although Comey's antics pointed the finger of blame in that direction, than Brennan and Clapper. The intelligence agencies were central to the whole saga, suggesting that it could be better described as 'intelgate' rather than Russiagate. In Cohen's view, 'Russiagate has brought us to the worst American political crisis since the Civil War and the most dangerous relations with Russia in history'.[2]

Russia was involved in the 2016 election, with unwarranted social media activity and disputed claims about hacking the DNC and senior Democrat officials and coordinating release through WikiLeaks. However, the crucial charge of collusion between the Trump campaign and Moscow has been disproved. Russia was involved in a covert influence operation of the sort that was typical of the United States during and after the cold war, but there is no evidence of an actual attempt to rig the vote. Republicans naturally were sceptical of the Russiagate allegations from the start, and as the insubstantiality of some of the exaggerated charges were revealed, they hitched their wagons ever closer to Trump. This helps explain why the party failed to challenge Trump's repeated allegations of fraud in the November 2020 election, and then became mired in the fall-out of the attack on the Capitol of 6 January 2021. In the subsequent second attempt to impeach Trump, the Democratic House brought two charges against him: abuse of power and obstruction of Congress. Just one Republican, Mitt Romney, voted to support the first charge, and once again Trump escaped.

The Democrats, too, became tainted by the Russiagate saga. Their opposition to Trump became aligned with the Washington policy elite that was pushing for conflict with Russia, to the point that Schiff's dangerous claim that the Ukrainians 'are fighting our fight against Russia' went unchallenged. Democrats and liberals sought to build their opposition to Trump on the back of stoking a new cold war. Anti-Soviet sentiment from the 1950s rallied the right, and now anti-Russian sentiment mobilised the liberal left.[3] Democrats were guilty of condemning Trump for Russian connections without adequate evidence, and then pinning their hopes on the Mueller report exposing malfeasance and treachery on an epic scale. When that failed, they resorted to impeachment. The political mainstream and the two main parties were tainted by the whole story. Not surprisingly, the Democrats were only too pleased to put the whole ghastly episode behind them once Biden entered the White House. Russiagate had been the province of those seeking to explain Clinton's defeat and the meritocratic elite defending old-style globalism, groups that largely overlapped.[4] Biden had never personally invested much political capital in the story, so was ready to return to a more pragmatic realist relationship with Russia. However, the taint of Russiagate would not be expunged so easily.

The lessons of history are notoriously poorly learned but getting the history right is always important. History is always a matter of interpretation, but it is also about establishing the facts. In our case, some issues stand out. In the first place, Russiagate, the judgements of the security services were presented as canonical, with those questioning their assessments at risk of being investigated themselves. On 3 January 2017, Chuck Schumer, Senate minority leader, told MSNBC's Rachel Maddow, that Trump was 'being really dumb' by taking on the intelligence community and challenging its assessments on Russian cyber-activities: 'Let me tell you, [if] you take on the intelligence community, they have six ways from Sunday at getting at you'. In other words, the U.S. president should be intimidated by his intelligence officials.[5] Jared Kushner soon after was also warned by a senior Republican figure not to 'piss off the intel community', and he presciently outlined how things would develop: 'If you f*** with the intel community they will figure out a way to get back at you and you'll have two or three years of a Russian investigation, and every day something else will leak out'.[6] Trump condemned American intelligence failures on the eve of the Iraq war, as well as a 'litany of Obama Afghanistan-Iraq-Syria-Libya and other war-related intelligence failures', and now the 'intelligence leaks regarding his purported Russian relationships and subterfuges' appeared payback time.[7]

The concept of the deep state as an organised conspiracy by some sort of cabal is mistaken and misleading, but as a disposition and defined set of policy preferences, it helps explain the genesis of Russiagate. There was nothing 'deep' about the hostility of parts of the security apparatus to Trump and Russia. Brennan's characterisation of Trump's behaviour at the Helsinki press conference as 'nothing short of treasonous' implied that Trump's removal from office by any means would be justified. There was no organised 'deep state' collusion, let alone an organised resistance movement, but the myriad of uncoordinated actions, prompted mostly by genuine concerns about an external threat and the erosion of executive accountability, were rooted in the structural power of the Trumanite state and the ideological context of the new cold war. This explains why some marginal figures in Trump's entourage gained such exaggerated prominence and why Flynn's actions were seen in the worst possible light.[8] The foreign policy logic that underlay Trump rhetoric in favour of improved relations with Russia was not only suppressed but considered a 'highly suspicious' security threat.[9] He was suspected of being the Manchurian candidate propelled by Moscow to the White House.[10]

This in effect criminalised diplomacy and categorised challenges to the bipartisan new cold war consensus as appeasement if not treachery. This is not to suggest that there were no grounds for concern. Intelligence and security officers were genuinely worried that Trump acted criminally and that he represented a national security threat.[11] Americans, like Russians, abhor foreign interference in their domestic affairs. The 'resistance' came to see itself as 'guardian of the republic', one of the central features of the dual state model in which a force sets itself up to defend the constitution by flouting its principles. As McFarland puts it,

> there is some evidence that highly placed Hillary Clinton supporters in the intelligence community had an anti-Trump 'insurance plan' in place before the election. If Hillary won, no one would be any the wiser. But if the unthinkable happened and Trump won, they could activate the plan and claim he won unfairly with the help of America's arch enemy.[12]

She notes that American 'conservatives believe that there is a Deep State, a conspiracy within government that continues to rule, regardless of who's elected to office', and while there may not have been a 'Deep State plot against Trump', she certainly believes that there is a Democrat-leaning administrative state.[13] As for Russiagate, Russian interference became 'a mantra, accepted as fact by otherwise thoughtful Americans', and thus fed into 'conspiracism', the belief that major political and historical events are the result of manipulation and conspiracy between interested parties.[14]

A Yahoo analysis argues that the collusion investigation in 2017 was part of 'a broader effort by people within the national security bureaucracy to box Trump in on Ukraine'. Graham Fuller, a former Reagan official and a veteran CIA officer, argues that anti-Trump ex-intelligence officials like Clapper and Brennan were 'dismayed at any prospect that the official narrative against Russia could start falling apart under Trump, and want to maintain the image of a constant and dangerous Russian intervention into affairs of state'. Trump claimed as much in late 2017 when he argued, 'This artificial Democratic hit job gets in the way [of improved relations with Russia]', and warned 'people will die because of it'.[15] The Yahoo report also demonstrated one of Trump's persistent contradictions: while proclaiming his desire for improved relations, he gave the security agencies dangerous new powers, including in 2018 lifting previous restrictions on CIA cyber operations.[16] These were repeatedly used against 'adversary countries' such as Iran, China, North Korea and Russia. The Democratic narrative that Trump colluded with Russia encouraged demonstrative measures to prove that this was not the case, driving an escalation cycle that intensified the new cold war.[17] On the other side, Russia's neo-revisionist foreign policy stance after 2012 encouraged resistance to liberal hegemony and a more assertive stance all-round. 'Fortress Russia' felt itself under siege, accompanied by paranoia about the outside world'.[18] This encouraged a greater appetite for risk-taking, including arguably in U.S. elections.[19]

After the fall of communism in 1989–1991, the usual categories of 'left' and 'right' in domestic politics were inverted, and in Russiagate something similar occurred in foreign policy. The left, in the form of the Democratic Party and its allies, not only defended hawkish policies abroad (that was nothing new) but also high-handed and possibly abusive actions by the security state at home. Russiagate represented less a 'righteous campaign for truth and justice' than the unleashing of a security state accompanied by 'prosecutorial overreach, entrapment, and the criminalization of foreign policy dissent'.[20] The mainstream 'liberal establishment' was not only complicit but allied with the security services, raising the fundamental question: 'How could it be so blasé about what are clear abuses of power by law enforcement and intelligence officials in the now-infamous Russiagate collusion probe?'.[21] Glenn Greenwald argues that 'The ability to distinguish between *ideological* questions from *evidentiary* questions is vital for rational discourse to be possible, yet has been all but eliminated at the altar of tribal fealty' [italics in original]. Russiagate conspiracy theories became a matter of partisan affiliation for the left (broadly defined), even when evidence was lacking. Tribal loyalty substituted for 'substantive political debates', and as a result, 'US politics has been *depoliticized*, stripped of any meaningful ideological debates in lieu of mindless team loyalty oaths on non-ideological questions'.[22] Trump was entitled to seek a rapprochement with Russia, but this policy choice in the end became the subject of a criminal enquiry. The fundamental paradox is that 'The deep state, once an object of suspicion among liberal Americans, has turned into an object of longing under Trump'.[23]

This takes us to the fundamental question asked by Glennon: 'Why does national security policy remain constant even when one President is replaced by another [in this case Obama], who as a candidate repeatedly, forcefully, and eloquently promised fundamental changes in that policy?'[24]

The issue was posed by Trump, although less eloquently. The Trumanite security state naturally inflates threats,[25] but what remains a mystery is why defenders of Madisonian constitutionalism do so little to push back against ballooning military budgets and 'forever' wars. Interventionist Democrats if anything are more militaristic than traditional Republicans and in Russiagate allied with 'America's most powerful agencies' and 'weaponized against President Donald Trump'.[26] Brennan assisted by Clapper gathered foreign intelligence and fed it to the domestic intelligence community; the FBI handled Brennan's intelligence and conducted the requisite surveillance; the DoJ facilitated the FBI investigation while the State Department disseminated information through formal channels and leaks; Clinton's campaign and the DNC 'provided funding, support, and media collusion'; 'Obama officials were complicit, and engaged in unmasking and intelligence gathering and dissemination'; and 'the media was the most corrosive element in many respects. None of these events could have transpired without their willing participation. Stories were pushed, facts were ignored, and narratives were promoted'.[27] Brennan was instrumental in setting the ball rolling, and once the counter-intelligence investigation was launched in July 2016, he convinced the elite and the public of the gravity of the danger. First, in August and September, he briefed the 'Gang of Eight', the Congressional leaders, but did so separately and the transcripts have not yet been released. Second, he issued the 7 October joint statement from the ODNI and DHS, but notably not the NSA or FBI. Third, this culminated with the January 2017 ICA buttressing the Russiagate narrative. Selective leaking to a complaisant media 'weaponised' the media and exacerbated the problem of neo-journalism.[28] Many of the journalists who propagated the Trump–Russia theory were also responsible for the Iraq weapons of mass destruction fiasco.[29]

Russiagate achieved the 'magical transformation of intelligence agency heads into paragons of truth-telling'.[30] Anonymous intelligence officials fed information to the media, escalating to the point that unverified reports were taken as fact. This included the *New York Times* report during the 2020 presidential campaign that Russia paid the Taliban to kill American forces in Afghanistan, followed by an op-ed in the same paper by Obama's former national security advisor Susan Rice condemning Trump's failure to respond to 'Russian efforts to slaughter American troops in cold blood', confirming that the president was 'actively advancing our arch adversary's nefarious interests'. David Foglesong notes that

> Such reckless jingoism reflects the cumulative impact of a long campaign by American media. The demonization of Russia is driven by the desire to deflect attention from misconduct by the United States, to affirm American moral

superiority in contrast to Russian depravity, and to smear domestic political opponents' comments by associating them with Russia.

He notes that the executive editor Dean Baquet admitted that when the Mueller report failed to confirm the collusion story, the *New York Times* was left 'a little tiny bit flat footed'.[31] The response was as damaging as Russia's putative actions. Genuine concerns were amplified by the intelligence community, creating an echo chamber picked up by the media. The effect was rather like that of the former head of the CIA counter-intelligence (1954–1975), James Angleton, whose search for an imagined high-ranking mole destabilised the agency for decades. In this case, the entire American polity was destabilised. A parade of anonymous leaks endowed unverified information with the patina of credibility.

In a last gasp attempt to revive the fading Russiagate story, the *New York Times* magazine on 11 January 2021 published a major review of the Obama–Trump transition and the three major episodes – the DNC emails, the Steele dossier, and the fall of Michael Flynn – but added little critical analysis and even managed to mock the legitimate grievances of those who had fallen foul of the Russiagate juggernaut.[32] Adrian Chen, whom we have met before in relation to his work on the IRA, outlined the dilemma. After Mueller's February 2018 indictment of the trolls, he was called on to speak about the effect of social media campaigns on American public opinion, but he found himself on the horns of a dilemma. He could either stay silent and 'allow the conversation to be dominated by those pumping up the Russian threat, or I could risk giving fodder to Trump and his allies'. He cited the case of Facebook advertising executive Robert Goldman, who was forced to apologise to the entire company after having revealed that 'the majority of the [IRA's] Facebook ads were purchased after the election'. The choice was to join the 'resistance' to Trump or to be portrayed, as Chen puts, as a 'Trumpkin', which is no choice at all.[33]

The implications are disturbing. The Trumanite state appeared out of control, lending credence to Trump's claims that he was the target of a slow-motion coup. As Schuessler notes, 'Liberal institutionalists argue that democracy should serve as a deterrent to deception. This book makes the opposite case – that deception is a natural outgrowth of the democratic process'.[34] More than that, as Joshua Rovner notes, 'democracy actually promotes the politicisation of the intelligence services because elected leaders have strong incentives to use intelligence as a promotional vehicle for their policy decisions'.[35] The Trumanite national security state would not accept the Trumpian disruption without a fight and cloaked that struggle as a defence of the Madisonian state. Collusion charges provided 'cover for US intelligence and law enforcement bureaucracies to break the law, with what's left of the press gleefully going along for the ride'. Whereas Watergate defined an entire generation's opposition to politicians and the country's elite, Russiagate 'proved itself to be the reverse: It is a device that the American elite is using to define itself against its enemies – the rest of the country'.[36] And, we may add, major countries in the rest of the world.

Patterns of the New Cold War

The charges and counter-charges roiled the American elite, but poll after poll showed that Russiagate did not resonate as a major concern with the American people.[37] However, when it came to viewing Russia as an adversary, fear mongering and the associated intensification of cold war sentiments shifted views. If in 2004 only 18 per cent considered Russian military power a 'critical threat', by 2019, 52 per cent of those polled thought that it was, with the figure higher among Democrats (65%) than among Republicans (46%). By that time Russia had displaced North Korea as America's greatest adversary, while China now came in second.[38]

Kislyak returned to Russia in July 2017, and he shared the common Russian elite view that 'all the talk about us getting the president elected, that we helped him in the US, it's such nonsense that it's hard to take with a straight face'.[39] In his view, Russia was keeping the door open to normalisation, but relations were being destroyed because of 'political infighting inside the United States, where relations between Russia and the United States have become a bargaining chip, if not an instrument in the domestic political struggle'.[40] He forthrightly dismissed the idea of collusion, the knowing cooperation with an adversary, in 2016. By the time the next election came round in 2020, Russian deputy foreign minister Sergei Ryabkov condemned the 'media's mindless reiteration of allegations of Russia's purported meddling in US presidential elections'. He accepted 'that endless chatter about the meddling issue will rage on . . . and will be used as a tool in the political fight in the US'. There was no way out of the impasse, but 'the collateral damage is Russian-American relations plunging into this horrible trap, where those who speak in favour of improving ties are bound to be branded a Kremlin agent'.[41] He warned that 'we have no trust, no confidence whatsoever' in America.[42] Clinton's defeat turned Russia into a hostage of partisan domestic political conflicts.

On the other side, if Russia consciously and deliberately tried to shape the American political environment, then the endeavour backfired spectacularly. Russian meddling and its purported effects lowered trust, hardened American policy and reduced Washington's readiness to engage constructively with Moscow. Russo-American relations since the end of the cold war have been on a roller-coaster of ups and downs, but the overall downward trend was accelerated by Russiagate. This period of confrontation is one of the longest on record. Large majorities of Russians (85%) and Americans (78%) see the two countries as 'more rivals than partners'. Two-thirds of Americans believed that the Russian government tried to influence the 2016 election, but there was a strong partisan split to these sentiments. Some 90 per cent of Democrats but only 35 per cent of Republicans believed there was Russian interference. The deepening hostility with the United States shifted Russian perceptions of China. A Levada poll in 2016 found that 34 per cent of Russians viewed China favourably, but by 2019, 84 per cent viewed China as 'more a partner than a rival', while at the same time, 85 per cent viewed the United States as more a rival than a partner.[43] The escalating rivalry in conditions of the weakening of the nuclear arms control regime and numerous regional conflicts increased the danger of a slide into uncontrolled confrontation.

There is a deeper meaning to the idea of collusion, namely that Trump worked with Russia to undermine the U.S.-led liberal international order created at the end of World War II. Trump repeatedly criticised NATO, and he was no fan of the EU, a stance that aligned with Moscow's alleged ambitions to undermine both organisations. From this perspective, Trump's refusal to condemn Russia's interference was a symptom of his larger betrayal of traditionally defined U.S. interests. In this second sense, there is the suggestion that Putin and Trump in some way coordinated their policies, hence the febrile reaction every time they met. The three substantive meetings – Hamburg, Da Nang and Helsinki – repeated the deteriorating pattern of U.S.–Russian relations of the post-cold war years, to the point that both sides recognised the futility of summits. With the Mueller report published, Trump initiated a call to Putin on 3 May 2019 in which they discussed a wide range of pressing global and regional issues. They met at the Osaka G20 summit in June, but there was no talk of a broader summit. In spring 2020, there were numerous calls between the two men to discuss plunging oil prices, the Covid-19 pandemic and other issues. On 25 April, they issued the 'Elbe Declaration' to mark the 75th anniversary of the meeting of the two Allied armies towards the end of World War II, but even this symbolic gesture of reconciliation alarmed Russia's critics.[44] The United States announced that it would leave the 1992 Open Skies Treaty, allowing aerial inspections of military facilities of the thirty-four signatory states, and the chief arms control negotiator Marshall Billingsea warned that the United States knew how to send other countries 'into oblivion'.[45]

Trump and Putin were both critical of the post-war international order, and hence the coincidence of interests prompted the charge of collusion. However, although both Moscow and Trump's Washington disparaged the old order, this was for very different reasons. Trump came to the question from a narrow nationalist-mercantilist perspective, focused on whether America received its money's worth from the old alliance system – a view that he had held since at least the 1980s. Putin, however, as a conservative internationalist and realist, sought to enhance Russia's status in the international system while defending Russia's national interests as a great power. Both were aware that international politics were changing because of the West's relative decline, the shift of economic power to the Asia-Pacific region, and the re-emergence of China, but had very different responses. Moscow considered the changes an opportunity, but Washington increasingly perceived the shift in the correlation of forces as a threat. Divergent foreign policy orientations were exacerbated by domestic polarisation. Tsygankov argues that Russia became so prominent in domestic polarisation, because it reflected not only political partisanship but also the growing cultural divide between the values of Trump supporters and those of the liberal establishment.[46]

In an interview with the *Financial Times* in June 2019, Putin once again dismissed charges of Russian interference. He insisted that Trump won by his own efforts by tapping into the anti-establishment mood and the backlash against globalisation: 'Russia has been accused, and, strange as it may seem, it is still being accused . . . of alleged interference in the US election. What happened in reality? Mr Trump looked into his opponents' attitude to him and saw changes in American society'.[47] Moscow saw Trump's election as an opportunity genuinely to reset relations, but these expectations were not only disappointed, but relations deteriorated even further. As Putin's spokesperson Peskov lamented, 'The meaning of "getting along with Russia" has yet to be explained; we do not know what it stands for, considering that the reality of bilateral relations is in stark contrast with Trump's statements, to our deep regret'.[48] Russiagate prevented a new détente. Indeed, the authors of the Steele dossier took pride in what they had achieved:

> The dossier appears to have derailed a plan by the incoming Trump team to re-order the post-World War II Western alliance through a rapprochement with Russia that would transform US relationships with Europe, the Middle East, China and beyond. Domestically, it helped fuel an investigation that landed several of Trump's closest allies in jail and tied his administration in knots.[49]

There was to be no rapprochement, and instead Trump ramped up pressure. Lavrov lamented Washington's failure to take up Russia's repeated offer to discuss 'the absolutely baseless accusations' of U.S. election interference, including cybersecurity consultations and 'a bilateral political statement by Russia and the United States in which we both categorically undertake not to meddle in each other's domestic affairs', and he noted the law in support of Ukraine that allocated $200 million annually to the State Department to finance Russian NGOs and civil society. He noted a survey of U.S. politicians on whether Russia or China meddled most in U.S. elections, and he was disappointed to see that China had displaced Russia from the number one spot.[50]

This raises the fundamental question of how 'interference' should be defined. All great powers – the United States, Russia and China – routinely interfere in the internal affairs of other states. Sometimes this goes under the heading of 'democracy assistance', and at other times through support for foreign political parties, leaders and policies. Obama came perilously close to direct intervention when he made clear his support for the Remain camp in the U.K.'s Brexit vote. Earlier, the United States made no secret of its support for the insurgents who overthrew Yanukovych in Kiev and installed a neo-nationalist 'pro-Western' government. It was this geopolitical shock that provoked the Russian intervention in Crimea. Even earlier, U.S. advisors helped re-elect President Boris Yeltsin in 1996, and thus averted the threat of a Communist entering the Kremlin again. On the other side, Moscow supported sympathetic leaders from across the political spectrum in Europe and stood accused of having tilted the scales in the 2016 U.S. election. In this confused environment, there have been calls for some sort of international convention or conference, under the aegis of a leading international body such as the UN, to define the problem and to establish some ground rules. Putin himself returned to the idea of a non-interference pact on the eve of the 2020 presidential election.[51] Given the intensity of geopolitical contestation and ideational polarisation in the new cold war, the offer was ignored. By the time of the Geneva summit between Biden and Putin in June 2021, a leading Russian commentator notes that the relationship between Russia and the United States after 2016 'was not just bad. It was absolutely abnormal and irrational'. Russia became the subject of U.S. domestic politics as domestic and foreign affairs merged, and 'the specificity of the Trump administration contributed very much to make this relationship absolutely destructive'. Early expectations about Trump had turned into 'deep disappointment'.[52] Trump reversed virtually all of the Obama-era accommodations to Moscow, including sending lethal arms to Ukraine. The task of the Geneva summit was to find ways of managing confrontation to stop further decline, and this Biden achieved by establishing working parties with Russia on strategic stability and cyber conflict. The toxic atmosphere fostered by Russiagate had somewhat dissipated and U.S. elites were no longer so viscerally opposed to an improvement in U.S.–Russian relations – especially as China loomed ever-larger on the horizon.

The new cold war emerges out of the intersection of five processes. The first concerns Russia, whose motivations are often misunderstood. Russia is a conservative power, but since at least 2012, it has also become increasingly alienated from the practices of liberal hegemony. As far as Moscow is concerned, the 'rules-based order' stopped at its borders, turning Russia into an outsider. How else to understand the expansion of NATO without finding an adequate mode of integration for Russia in the changing European security order? The rules appeared to be suspended when it came to bombing Yugoslavia in 1999, invading Iraq in 2003, recognising Kosovo in 2008, overthrowing the Libyan regime in 2011 and trying to do the same in Syria from 2011, and above all, displacing a legitimate and democratically elected (although corrupt) president in Ukraine in February 2014. This is what turned Russia into a neo-revisionist power: opposed to the practices of the U.S.-led liberal power system but committed to the institutions of international society (the conservative institutionalist position). This does not mean that Russia is out to subvert Western democracy, a charge first formulated in the Steele dossier, repeated almost verbatim in the ICA of 6 January 2017, and then echoed *ad nauseam* in endless commentary thereafter. The charge simply does not make sense in any intelligible framework of Russian foreign policy. This is not to say that there are no 'active measures' by Russian agents, affiliated bodies and even civic activists. However, Russia is not the quasi-totalitarian authoritarian body portrayed by radical liberals, although it is far from the open and democratic society portrayed by much of the Russian mass media.

Second, domestic partisanship reinforced the deep cultural roots of the portrayal of Russia as America's 'dark double'. The renewed emergence of a challenger in the international system prompted the mobilisation of values as well as cultural stereotypes in the struggle.[53] As diplomacy and dialogue failed, sanctions become a permanent fixture in Russo-U.S. relations. The punitive actions against Russia far exceed anything imposed by Trump's predecessors even at the height of the cold war and are potentially comparable to the sanctions imposed on Japan in the months leading up to Tokyo's Pearl Harbour attack in December 1941. The Trump administration and Congress imposed no fewer than forty-six sanctions packages on Russia. The CAATSA measures adopted in August 2017 constrained Trump's room for manoeuvre and rendered it impossible for him to fulfil his ambition to 'get on' with Russia. The sanctions legislation is based on the view that they would split the Russian elite and encourage the 'oligarchs' to turn against Putin. Tony Wood rejects this premise, arguing that Russian political economy as it developed in the Yeltsin era simply does not work that way and intra-elite splits are unlikely to be provoked by external actions. In addition, when faced by outside pressure, the stoicism and powers of endurance inherited from the history of repeated invasions only tighten the bond between the elite and the people.[54] They also reinforce the alignment between Russia and China. A commentary in *China Daily* notes that 'When US political elites cannot solve the country's domestic problems, they tend to divert American's people's attention to external issues'.[55]

Third, the reaction to Russia's intervention in 2016 became part of the larger response to Trump's election. Gessen notes that 'Russia has served as a crutch for the American imagination. It is used to explain how Trump could have happened to us, and it is also called upon to give us hope. When the Russian conspiracy behind Trump is finally exposed, our national nightmare will be over'. She notes that the 'most troublesome aspect' of the Trump–Putin story was 'leaks from intelligence agencies': 'Virtually none of the information can be independently corroborated. The context, sequence, and timing of the leaks is determined by people unknown to the public, which is expected to accept anonymous stories on faith; nor have we yet been given any hard evidence of active collusion by Trump officials'.[56] The special counsel investigation became a weapon to devitalise incumbents, but it is pertinent to ask: 'Do we really want the special-counsel investigation to become a staple of presidential life?'.[57] The methods of the 'resistance' exacerbated the problems which they sought to address. Trump turned 'the country, and to some extent even the world, upside down', but his opponents, 'to get rid of their hated enemy, are ready to tear down their own house'.[58]

This brings us to the fourth point. This is where truth itself becomes the subject of contestation and subordinated to partisan goals. Gessen puts this well: 'The dream fuelling the Russia frenzy is that it will eventually create a dark enough cloud of suspicion around Trump that Congress will find the will and the grounds to impeach him. If that happens, it will have resulted largely from a media campaign orchestrated by members of the intelligence community – setting a dangerous political precedent that will have corrupted the public sphere and promoted paranoia'.[59] Trump is famous for his cavalier disregard for facts and the abusive use of the term 'fake news' to dismiss criticism, but there could be no automatic assumption that Trump's opponents, by mere dint of countering his falsehoods, were themselves the upholders of truth. Instead, too often the 'resistance' and others critical of Trump simply pursued axiological politics, only with an opposite polarity. This also applies to condemnation of Russian 'disinformation'. Russia's official agencies and media have a distinctive and often self-serving view of the world. There are well-documented cases when they have acted in concert to assert falsehoods or distorted material to fit the official narrative. Mostly, though, the Russian media advances positions that while often critical of the West are based on a legitimate different viewpoint, and thus add to the pluralism of information that is essential for healthy democratic societies. Attempts to muzzle the Russian international media undermine the principles that liberal democracies proclaim to uphold, while neo-containment policies against Russia destabilise global order.

The fifth point follows directly from this. Russia became the scapegoat not only for the failure of the Clinton campaign in 2016 but also for the larger crisis of the American polity. Russia was accused of exacerbating the polarisation of American politics by 'sowing discord'. However, the best way of dealing with domestic problems is to resolve them, rather than blaming some external force for talking about them. This also applies to Russia spreading 'fake news' and misinformation. As Trenin notes, 'The only meaningful way of dealing with adversarial (dis)information attacks is fixing the vulnerabilities of one's own system that invite such attacks'.[60] However, dealing with domestic problems, as the Black Lives Matter protests demonstrated, is much harder than simply blaming them on some external cause. Equally, in matters of international politics, it is too easy to dismiss Russian concerns as 'disinformation' when in fact they often represent policy differences that in the past were respected and addressed through diplomatic means. In the new cold war, the legitimacy of policy differences is rejected, and complex questions are presented in starkly binary moralistic and Manichaean terms.

Trump condemned America's crumbling infrastructure, as well as the marginalisation of communities by ill-managed globalisation and poorly considered military globalism, but he had no real solutions to offer. His advocacy of economic nationalism represented a beggar-my-neighbour approach to international affairs, in which America's global power dominance could be levered to its benefit. His liberal critics rightly stressed the importance of the rule of law and civility, but the norms of constitutionalism and impartial state institutions were undermined in the wake of the 2016 shock. Democrats believed that the election had been 'stolen', but it was lost in the most profound sense. The conditions that gave rise to Trump remain, and only when they are addressed will the crisis be resolved. Overcoming the Russiagate syndrome is no easy task, but the greater challenge is to address its causes. For that new politics is required that breaks out of cold war thinking at home and abroad. Trump is the destructive solution to the problem, while constructive ones await convincing articulation.

NOTES

1. Julian E. Barnes and Matthew Rosenberg, 'Kremlin Sources Go Quiet, Leaving the CIA in the Dark about Putin's Plans for the Midterms', *New York Times*, 24 August 2018, https://www.nytimes.com/2018/08/24/us/politics/cia-russia-midterm-elections.html.

2. Stephen F. Cohen, '"Vital" US Moles in the Kremlin Go Missing!', *The Nation*, 29 August 2018, https://www.thenation.com/article/vital-us-moles-in-the-kremlin-go-missing/; Cohen, *War with Russia*, pp. 204-206.

3. Joshua Zeitz, 'Can the Left Weaponize Russia?', *Politico*, 7 February 2017, https://www.politico.com/magazine/story/2017/02/can-the-left-weaponize-russia-214751/.

4. Ross Douthat, 'The Strange Death of Liberal Russophobia', *New York Times*, 20 June 2021, https://www.nytimes.com/2021/06/19/opinion/sunday/biden-putin-trump.html.

5. Ray McGovern, 'Justice Dept Likely to Slow-Walk Declassification', *Consortium News*, 18 September 2018, http://raymcgovern.com/2018/09/18/justice-dept-likely-to-slow-walk-declassification/.

6. Wolff, *Fire and Fury*, p. 41.

7. Wolff, *Fire and Fury*, p. 42.

8. To see this at work, see for example Strzok, *Compromised*, pp. 184–9, 314, 328.

9. Strzok, *Compromised*, p. 231.

10. For an example, see Strzok, *Compromised*, p. 200.

11. The argument is advanced eloquently by David Frum, 'Collusion Is Worse than a Crime', *The Atlantic*, 1 August 2018, https://www.theatlantic.com/ideas/archive/2018/08/collusion-is-a-question-of-loyalty-not-legality/566606/.

12. McFarland, *Revolution*, p. 258.

13. McFarland, *Revolution*, p. 275.

14. 'David C. Speedie and Krishan Mehta: Russiagate and the New "Conspiracism"', *ACEWA*, 19 August 2020, https://eastwestaccord.com/david-c-speedie-russiagate-and-the-new-conspiracism/.

15. Andrew Restuccia, 'Donald Trump Says "People Will Die" as a Result of Focus on Russia Allegations', *Politico*, 11 November 2017, https://www.politico.eu/article/donald-trump-says-people-will-die-as-a-result-of-focus-on-russia-allegations/.

16. Zach Dorfman, Kim Zetter, Jenna McLaughlin and Sean D. Naylor, 'Exclusive: Secret Trump Order Gives CIA More Powers to Launch Cyberattacks', *Yahoo News*, 15 July 2020, https://news.yahoo.com/secret-trump-order-gives-cia-more-powers-to-launch-cyberattacks-090015219.html.

17. Branko Marcetic, 'Trump the "Putin Puppet" Just Escalated the Undeclared War against Russia', *Jacobin*, 19 July 2020, https://www.jacobinmag.com/2020/07/donald-trump-putin-russiagate.

18. Ilya Yablokov, *Fortress Russia: Conspiracy Theories in Post-Soviet Russia* (Cambridge, Polity, 2018).

19. Kimberly Marten, 'Reckless Ambition: Moscow's Policy Toward the United States, 2016/17', *International Politics*, Vol. 56, 2019, pp. 743–61.

20. Branko Marcetic, 'Collusion is in the Eye of the Beholder', *Jacobin*, 15 May 2020, https://www.jacobinmag.com/2020/05/ignore-trumps-bluster-obamagate-is-a-serious-scandal.

21. Robert W. Merry, 'Remember When Liberals Despised the National Security State?', *American Conservative*, 25 May 2020, https://www.theamericanconservative.com/articles/remember-when-liberals-despised-the-national-security-state/.

22. Greenwald, 'New Documents'.

23. Adam Shatz, 'America Explodes', *London Review of Books*, 18 June 2020, at p. 7.

24. Glennon, *National Security and Double Government*, p. 3.

25. Glennon, *National Security and Double Government*, pp. 19–20.

26. Carlson, 'Spygate'.
27. Carlson, 'Spygate'.
28. McFarland, *Revolution*, pp. 277–91 describes the weaponised media.
29. Michael Tracey, 'How the US Media Failed in Russiagate', *The New Indian Express*, 15 April 2019, https://www.newindianexpress.com/opinions/2019/apr/15/how-the-us-media-failed-in-russiagate-1964457.html.
30. Jackson Lears, 'Russiagate Revisited', *London Review of Books Blog*, 22 February 2018, https://www.lrb.co.uk/blog/2018/02/22/jackson-lears/russiagate-revisited/.
31. David S. Foglesong, 'With Fear and Favor: The Russophobia of "The New York Times"', *The Nation*, 17 July 2020, https://www.thenation.com/article/world/new-york-times-russia/.
32. Mattathius Schwarz, 'The Last Standoff', *New York Times Magazine*, 11 January 2021, https://www.nytimes.com/interactive/2021/01/11/magazine/trump-obama-presidential-transition.html.
33. Chen, 'A So-Called Expert's Uneasy Dive into the Trump-Russia Frenzy'.
34. Schuessler, *Deceit on the Road to War*, p. 117.
35. Joshua Rovner, *Fixing the Facts: National Security and the Politics of Intelligence* (Ithaca, Cornell University Press, 2011), p. 198.
36. Lee Smith, 'Who Believes in Russiagate?', *Tablet*, 8 March 2018, https://www.tabletmag.com/jewish-news-and-politics/256899/left-right-russiagate.
37. Polling data in Gerald Sussman, 'The Russiagate Spectacle: Season 2?', *CounterPunch*, 13 July 2020, https://www.counterpunch.org/2020/07/13/the-russiagate-spectacle-season-2/.
38. Lydia Saad, 'Majority of Americans now Consider Russia a Critical Threat', 27 February 2019, https://news.gallup.com/poll/247100/majority-americans-consider-russia-critical-threat.aspx.
39. 'Legendary Russian Ambassador Kislyak Explains How he Personally Helped Steal the US Elections', Vesti.ru, 18 November 2017, https://www.vesti.ru/doc.html?id=2956309&cid=4441.
40. 'Sergei Kislyak on Russia-US Relations: It Takes Two to Tango', RIAC, 23 November 2017, http://russiancouncil.ru/en/analytics-and-comments/interview/sergei-kislyak-on-russia-u-s-relations-it-takes-two-to-tango/.
41. '"Horrible Trap": Diplomat Excoriates US Talking Heads who Parrot "Russian Meddling Claims"', *TASS*, 18 May 2020, https://tass.com/politics/1157639.
42. Jacob Heilbrunn interview, 'Russian Deputy Foreign Minister Sergei Ryabkov: "We Have no Trust, no Confidence Whatsoever" in America', *The National Interest*, 29 May 2020, https://nationalinterest.org/feature/russian-deputy-foreign-minister-sergei-ryabkov-%E2%80%9Cwe-have-no-trust-no-confidence-whatsoever%E2%80%9D.
43. Poll conducted by the Chicago Council on Global Affairs and the Levada Centre, reported by James Carden, 'How "Russiagate" has Reshaped American and Russian Public Opinion', *The Nation*, 11 April 2019, https://www.thenation.com/article/russiagate-bilateral-tensions-opinion-poll/.

44. Michael R. Gordon and Gordon Lubold, 'Trump, Putin Statement Stirs Concerns among Some', *Wall Street Journal*, 26 April 2020, https://www.wsj.com/articles/trump-putin-statement-stirs-concern-among-some-.

45. 'US Prepared to Spend Russia, China "Into Oblivion" to Win Nuclear Arms Race: US Envoy', *Reuters*, 21 May 2020, https://uk.reuters.com/article/uk-usa-armscontrol/u-s-prepared-to-spend-russia-china-into-oblivion-to-win-nuclear-arms-race-u-s-envoy-idUKKBN22X2LS.

46. Andrei P. Tsygankov, *The Dark Double: US Media, Russia, and the Politics of Values* (New York, Oxford University Press, 2019), p. zzz.

47. Lionel Barber and Henry Foy, 'Vladimir Putin: Exclusive Interview, *Financial Times*, 28 June 2019, pp. 1 and 9, at p. 9.

48. 'Russia-US Relations Far Cry From Trump's "Getting Along with Russia" – Peskov', Interfax, 8 October 2019, http://www.interfax.com/newsinf.asp?pg=6&id=930468.

49. Simpson and Fritsch, *Crime in Progress*, pp. 269–70.

50. 'Russia Ready for Honest Dialogue with US on Election Interference', TASS, 11 September 2020, https://tass.com/politics/1199783.

51. 'Statement by President of Russia Vladimir Putin on a Comprehensive Program of Measures for Restoring the Russia – US Cooperation in the Field of International Information Security', Kremlin.ru, 25 September 2020, http://en.kremlin.ru/events/president/news/64086.

52. Fyodor Lukyanov, 'The Putin-Biden Summit', *Russia in Global Affairs*, 11 June 2021, https://eng.globalaffairs.ru/articles/expect-putin-biden-summit/.

53. Tsygankov, *The Dark Double*.

54. Tony Wood, *Russia without Putin: Money, Power and the Myths of the New Cold War* (London, Verso, 2018).

55. Li Qingsi, 'US Wall Diverts Focus from Domestic Issues', *China Daily*, 21 January 2019, p. 9.

56. Masha Gessen, 'Russia: The Conspiracy Trap', *New York Review of Books*, 6 March 2017, https://www.nybooks.com/daily/2017/03/06/trump-russia-conspiracy-trap/.

57. T. A. Frank, 'Is This It? A Trump-Hater's Guide to Mueller Skepticism', *Vanity Fair*, 3 December 2018, https://www.vanityfair.com/news/2018/12/a-trump-haters-guide-to-mueller-skepticism.

58. Rein Müllerson, 'Donald Trump – Not an American Deng Xiaoping, Maybe its Gorbachev?', *Valdai Club*, 9 August 2018, http://valdaiclub.com/a/highlights/not-an-american-deng-xiaoping/.

59. Gessen, 'Russia: The Conspiracy Trap'.

60. Dmitri Trenin, 'How Russians are Reading Bolton and Trump', *Carnegie Moscow Centre*, 25 June 2020, https://carnegie.ru/commentary/82166.

Bibliography

Allen, Jonathan and Amie Parnes, *Shattered: Inside Hillary Clinton's Doomed Campaign* (New York, Broadway Books, 2017).
Alterman, Eric, *When Presidents Lie: A History of Official Deception and Its Consequences* (New York, Viking, 2004).
Arif, Ahmer, Leo G. Stewart and Kate Starbird, 'Acting the Part: Examining Information Operations Within #BlackLivesMatter Discourse', *Proceedings of the ACM on Human-Computer Interaction*, Vol. 2, CSCW, Article 20, November 2018, pp. 1–26.
Arutunyan, Anna, 'There is No Russian Plot against America: The Kremlin's Electoral Interference is all Madness and No Method', *Foreign Affairs*, 5 August 2020, https://www.foreignaffairs.com/articles/united-states/2020-08-05/there-no-russian-plot-against-america.
Bamford, James, 'The Spy Who Wasn't', *The New Republic*, 11 February 2019, https://newrepublic.com/article/153036/maria-butina-profile-wasnt-russian-spy
Barrett, Wayne, *Trump: The Greatest Show on Earth—The Deals, the Downfall, and the Reinvention* (New York, Regan Arts, 2016).
Bartlett, Jamie, *The People vs. Tech: How the Internet is Killing Democracy (and How We Can Save it)* (London, Ebury Press, 2018).
Beebe, George S., *The Russia Trap: How Our Shadow War With Russia Could Spiral Into Nuclear Catastrophe* (New York, Thomas Dunne Books, 2019).
Belton, Catherine, *Putin's People: How the KGB Took Back Russia and then Took on the West* (New York, Farrar, Straus and Giroux, 2020).
Benkler, Yochai, Rob Faris and Hal Roberts, *Network Propaganda: Manipulation, Disinformation, and Radicalization in American Politics* (New York, Oxford University Press, 2018).
Bidder, Benjamin, 'Questions Cloud Story Behind US Sanctions', *Spiegel*, 26 November 2019, https://www.spiegel.de/international/world/the-case-of-sergei-magnitsky-anti-corruption-champion-or-corrupt-anti-hero-a-1297796.html.
Biden, Hunter, *Beautiful Things: A Memoir* (London, Gallery, 2021).

Biden, Joseph R. Jr. and Michael Carpenter, 'How to Stand up to the Kremlin', *Foreign Affairs*, 2018, Vol. 97, No. 1, January-February 2018, pp. 44–57.

Birkan, Adam, 'The Magazine Interview: Rob Goldstone on Setting up Trump Jr and Russia', *The Sunday Times*, 19 November 2017, https://www.thetimes.co.uk/article/the-magazine-interview-rob-goldstone-on-setting-up-trump-jr-and-russia-hsl6jcn6g.

Bolton, John, *The Room Where it Happened* (New York, Simon & Schuster, 2020).

Bongino, Dan with D.C. McAllister and Matt Palumbo, *'Spygate': The Attempted Sabotage of Donald J. Trump* (New York, Post Hill Press, 2018).

Bongino, Dan, *Exonerated: The Failed Takedown of President Donald Trump by the Swamp* (New York, Post Hill Press, 2019).

Boyd-Barrett, Oliver, *RussiaGate and Propaganda: Disinformation in the Age of Social Media* (London, Routledge, 2020).

Browder, Bill, *Red Notice: How I became Putin's No. 1 Enemy* (London, Bantam Press, 2015).

Burgis, Tom, 'Trump's Tower of Secrets', *FT.com/magazine*, 14/15 July 2018, pp. 12–20.

Butina, Mariya, *Tyuremnyi dnevnik* (Moscow, AST, 2021).

Butler, Phil, *Putin's Praetorians: Confessions of the Top Kremlin Trolls* (Heraklion, Pamil Visions, 2017).

Campbell, Duncan, 'Briton Ran Pro-Kremlin Disinformation Campaign that Helped Trump Deny Russian Links', 31 July 2018, https://www.computerweekly.com/news/252445769/Briton-ran-pro-Kremlin-disinformation-campaign-that-helped-Trump-deny-Russian-links.

Carlson, Jeff, 'Spygate: The True Story Collusion (Infographic)', *The Epoch Times*, 12 October 2018, updated 25 March 2019, https://www.theepochtimes.com/spygate-the-true-story-of-collusion_2684629.html.

Cassidy, John, 'The FBI Needs to Explain its Reasons for Firing Peter Strzok', *New Yorker*, 13 August 2018, https://www.newyorker.com/news/our-columnists/the-fbi-needs-to-explain-its-reasons-for-firing-peter-strzok.

Cassidy, John, 'The Trump Family's Tax Dodging is Symptomatic of a Larger Problem', *New Yorker*, 3 October 2018, https://www.newyorker.com/news/our-columnists/the-trump-familys-tax-dodging-is-symptomatic-of-a-larger-problem.

Cassidy, John, 'Attorney General William Barr Acts as Donald Trump's Human Shield on Capitol Hill', *New Yorker*, 1 May 2019. https://www.newyorker.com/news/our-columnists/attorney-general-william-barr-acts-as-trumps-human-shield-on-capitol-hill.

Chait, Jonathan, 'Will Trump be Meeting with his Counterpart – or his Handler?', *New York Magazine*, 9 July 2018, http://nymag.com/daily/intelligencer/2018/07/trump-putin-russia-collusion.html.

Chen, Adrian, 'The Agency', *The New York Times Magazine*, 2 June 2015, https://www.nytimes.com/2015/06/07/magazine/the-agency.html.

Chen, Adrian, 'What Mueller's Indictment Reveals about Russia's Internet Research Agency', *New Yorker*, 16 February 2018, https://www.newyorker.com/news/news-desk/what-muellers-indictment-reveals-about-russias-internet-research-agency.

Chen, Adrian, 'A So-Called Expert's Uneasy Dive into the Trump-Russia Frenzy', *New Yorker*, 22 February 2018, https://www.newyorker.com/tech/annals-of-technology/a-so-called-experts-uneasy-dive-into-the-trump-russia-frenzy.

Clapper, James R. with Trey Brown, *Facts and Fears: Hard Truths from a Life in Intelligence* (New York, Viking, 2018).

Clinton, Hillary Rodham, *Hard Choices: A Memoir* (New York, Simon & Schuster, 2014).

Clinton, Hillary Rodham, *What Happened* (London, Simon & Schuster, 2017).

Cockburn, Patrick, 'Julian Assange in Limbo', *London Review of Books*, 18 June 2020, pp. 29–30.

Cohen, Michael, *Disloyal - A Memoir: The True Story of the Former Personal Attorney to President Donald J. Trump* (New York, Skyhorse Publishing, 2020).

Cohen, Stephen F., *War with Russia: From Putin and Ukraine to Trump and Russiagate* (New York, Hot Books, 2018).

Comey, James, *A Higher Loyalty: Truth, Lies, and Leadership* (London, Macmillan, 2018).

Comey, James, 'Ex-FBI Director James Comey's Memos', https://assets.documentcloud.org/documents/4442900/Ex-FBI-Director-James-Comey-s-memos.pdf.

Condon, Richard, *The Manchurian Candidate* (New York, McGraw Hill, 1959).

Cramer, Jane Kellett, 'Militarized Patriotism: Why the U.S. Marketplace of Ideas Failed before the Iraq War', *Security Studies*, Vol. 16, No. 3, 2007, pp. 489–524.

Cummings, Richard, 'Lockheed Stock and Two Smoking Barrels', *Corpwatch*, 16 January 2007, https://corpwatch.org/article/us-lockheed-stock-and-two-smoking-barrels.

Davidson, Adam, 'Where did Donald Trump get Two Hundred Million Dollars to buy his Money-Losing Scottish Golf Club?', *New Yorker*, 13 July 2018, https://www.newyorker.com/news/swamp-chronicles/where-did-donald-trump-get-200-million-dollars-to-buy-his-money-losing-scottish-golf-club.

Davidson, Adam, 'Is Fraud Part of the Trump Organization's Business Model?', *New Yorker*, 17 October 2018, https://www.newyorker.com/news/swamp-chronicles/is-fraud-part-of-the-trump-organizations-business-model.

Debord, Guy, *Society of the Spectacle* (London, Rebel Press, 1994).

Department of Justice, Office of the Inspector General, *Review of Various Actions by the Federal Bureau of Investigation and Department of Justice in Advance of the 2016 Election*, June 2018, https://www.justice.gov/file/1071991/download.

Department of Justice, Office of the Inspector General, *Report of Investigation: Recovery of Text Message from Certain FBI Mobile Devices*, December 2018, https://oig.justice.gov/reports/2018/i-2018-003523.pdf.

Department of Justice, Office of the Inspector General, *Review of Four FISA Applications and Other Aspects of the FBI's Crossfire Hurricane Investigation*, December 2019 (Horowitz Review), https://www.justice.gov/storage/120919-examination.pdf.

Department of State, *State Combined: Produced to HSGAC*, 13 October 2020, https://www.hsgac.senate.gov/imo/media/doc/STATE_combined.pdf.

Democratic National Committee, *Donald Trump Report*, Submitted 19 December 2015.

Draper, Robert, 'Unwanted Truths: Inside Trump's Battles with US Intelligence Agencies', *New York Times Magazine*, 10 August 2020, https://www.nytimes.com/2020/08/08/magazine/us-russia-intelligence.html.

Dueck, Colin, *Hard Line: The Republican Party and US Foreign Policy since World War II* (Princeton, NJ, Princeton University Press, 2010).

Embassy of the Russian Federation in the United States of America, *The Russiagate Hysteria: A Case of Severe Russophobia*, 18 April 2019, https://washington.mid.ru/upload/iblock/3c3/3c3d1e3b69a4c228e99bfaeb5491ecd7.pdf.

Entous, Adam, 'Donald Trump's New World Order', *New Yorker*, 18 June 2018, https://www.newyorker.com/magazine/2018/06/18/donald-trumps-new-world-order.

Federal Bureau of Investigation, *Interview of Primary Subsource*, Electronic Communication, 9 February 2017, https://www.judiciary.senate.gov/imo/media/doc/February%209,%202017%20Electronic%20Communication.pdf.

Filkins, Dexter, 'Was There a Connection between a Russian Bank and the Trump Campaign?', *New Yorker*, 15 October 2018, https://www.newyorker.com/magazine/2018/10/15/was-there-a-connection-between-a-russian-bank-and-the-trump-campaign.

Flynn, Michael, Matt Pottinger and Paul D. Batchelor, *Fixing Intel: A Blueprint for Making Intelligence Relevant in Afghanistan* (Washington, DC, Center for a New American Security, January 2010), https://online.wsj.com/public/resources/documents/AfghanistanMGFlynn_Jan2010.pdf.

Flynn, Michael T. and Michael Ledeen, *The Field of Fight: How we can Win the Global War against Radical Islam and its Allies* (New York, St Martin's Griffin, 2017).

Foer, Franklin, 'Putin is Well on His Way to Stealing the Next Election: RIP Democracy', *The Atlantic*, June 2020, https://www.theatlantic.com/magazine/archive/2020/06/putin-american-democracy/610570/.

Foglesong, David S., *The American Mission and the "Evil Empire": The Crusade for a "Free Russia" since 1881* (Cambridge, Cambridge University Press, 2007).

Foglesong, David S., 'Putin: From Soulmate to Archenemy', *Raritan*, Vol. 38, No. 1, Summer 2018), pp. 18–41.

Frank, T. A., 'Is This It? A Trump-Hater's Guide to Mueller Skepticism', *Vanity Fair*, 3 December 2018, https://www.vanityfair.com/news/2018/12/a-trump-haters-guide-to-mueller-skepticism.

Fridman, Ofer, *Russian Hybrid Warfare: Resurgence and Politicisation* (London, Hurst, 2018).

Free, Benjamin, *Hillary Clinton Shattered: How Donald Trump Shattered Hillary Clinton and the Democratic Party* (Google Books, June 2017).

Friedman, Robert, *Red Mafiya: How the Russian Mob has Invaded America* (Boston, Little, Brown and Company, 2000).

Frum, David, *Trumpocracy: The Corruption of the American Republic* (New York, Harper, 2018).

Frum, David, 'Collusion is Worse than a Crime', *The Atlantic*, 1 August 2018, https://www.theatlantic.com/ideas/archive/2018/08/collusion-is-a-question-of-loyalty-not-legality/566606/.

'Full Text: James Comey Testimony Transcript on Trump and Russia', *Politico*, 8 June 2017, https://www.politico.com/story/2017/06/08/full-text-james-comey-trump-russia-testimony-239295.

Geoghegan, Peter, *Democracy for Sale: Dark Money and Dirty Politics* (London, Apollo, 2020).

Gerasimov, Valerii, 'Tsennost' nauki i predvidenii', *Voenno-promyshlennyi kur'er*, No. 8, 27 February 2013, http://vpk-news.ru/articles/14632.

Gessen, Masha, 'Russia, Trump & Flawed Intelligence', *New York Review of Books*, 9 January 2017, https://www.nybooks.com/daily/2017/01/09/russia-trump-election-flawed-intelligence/.

Gessen, Masha, 'Russia: The Conspiracy Trap', *New York Review of Books*, 6 March 2017, https://www.nybooks.com/daily/2017/03/06/trump-russia-conspiracy-trap/.

Gittings, John, *The Glorious Art of Peace: Paths to Peace in the New Age of War* (Oxford, Oxford University Press, 2018).

Glasser, Susan B., 'After the Midterms, Robert Mueller's Got a New Wingman on Capitol Hill', *New Yorker*, 15 November 2018, https://www.newyorker.com/news/letter-from-trumps-washington/after-the-midterms-robert-muellers-got-a-new-wingman-on-capitol-hill.

Glennon, Michael J., *National Security and Double Government* (Oxford, Oxford University Press, 2015).

Goldstone, Rob, *Pop Stars, Pageants and Presidents: How an Email Changed my Life* (London, Oui2 Entertainment, 2018).

Green, Joshua, *Devil's Bargain: Steve Bannon, Donald Trump, and the Storming of the Presidency* (Melbourne/London, Scribe, 2017).

Greenwald, Glenn, 'New Documents from the Sham Prosecution of Gen. Michael Flynn also Reveal Broad Corruption in the Russiagate Investigations', *The Intercept*, 14 May 2020, https://theintercept.com/2020/05/14/new-documents-from-the-sham-prosecution-of-gen-michael-flynn-also-reveal-broad-corruption-in-the-russiagate-investigations/.

Gubarev et al v. Orbis Business Intelligence Ltd, and Christopher Steel, High Court of Justice, Queens Bench Division, Claim No. HQ17D00413, Defendant's Response to Claimants' Request for Further Information, 18 May 2017, https://www.scribd.com/document/368706403/Steele-Additional-Filing-in-London-Action.

Harding, Luke, *Collusion: How Russia Helped Trump Win the White House* (London, Guardian Faber Publishing, 2017).

Harding, Luke, 'How Putin Walked into Putin's Web', *The Guardian*, 15 November 2017, https://www.theguardian.com/news/2017/nov/15/how-trump-walked-into-putins-web-luke.

Haslam, Jonathan, *Russia's Cold War: From the October Revolution to the Fall of the Wall* (New Haven, CT, Yale University Press, 2012).

Hayden, Michael V., *The Assault on Intelligence: American National Security in an Age of Lies* (London, Penguin, 2018).

Hettena, Seth, *Trump/Russia: A Definitive History* (Brooklyn, Melville House, 2018).
Herbert, Jon, Trevor McCrisken and Andrew Wroe, *The Ordinary Presidency of Donald J. Trump* (London, Palgrave Macmillan, 2019).
Hill, William H., *No Place for Russia: European Security Institutions since 1989* (New York, Columbia University Press, 2018).
Hofstadter, Richard J., 'The Paranoid Style in American Politics', *Harper's Magazine*, November 1964, pp. 77–86.
House Permanent Select Committee on Intelligence (HPSCI), *Russia Investigation Transcripts and Documents: Materials from the Committee's Investigation into Russian Active Measures*, https://intelligence.house.gov/russiainvestigation/?fbclid=IwAR2_rtfHaNyIA1Q8bVhVjBlZOPPhJ31SvBjaYm3XCRTvQRw06g4zFJ6SFac.
House Judiciary Committee and House Oversight Committee, 'Full Transcript and Video of James Comey's Capitol Hill Testimony', 11 August 2018, https://www.zerohedge.com/news/2018-12-08/full-transcript-and-video-james-comeys-capitol-hill-testimony.
Howard, Philip N., Bharath Gnesh, Dimitra Liotsiou, John Kelly and Camille François, *The IRA, Social Media and Political Polarization in the United States, 2012-2018* (Oxford, Project on Computational Propaganda, Working Paper 2018).
Inglehart, Ronald F., *Cultural Evolution: People's Motivations are Changing, and Reshaping the World* (Cambridge, Cambridge University Press, 2018).
'Intel Vets Challenge "Russia Hack" Evidence', *Consortium News*, 24 July 2017, https://consortiumnews.com/2017/07/24/intel-vets-challenge-russia-hack-evidence/.
Isikoff, Michael and David Corn, *Hubris: The Inside Story of Spin, Scandal, and the Selling of the Iraq War* (New York, Crown Publishers, 2006).
Isikoff, Michael and David Corn, *Russian Roulette: The Inside Story of Putin's War on America and the Election of Donald Trump* (New York, Twelve, 2018).
Jacobson, Matthew Frye and Gaspar Gonzalez, *What Have they Built You To Do? The Manchurian Candidate and Cold War America* (Minneapolis, University of Minnesota Press, 2006).
Jamieson, Kathleen Hall, *Cyberwar: How Russian Hackers and Trolls Helped Elect a President—What We Don't, Can't and Do Know* (Oxford, Oxford University Press, 2018).
Jarrett, Gregg, *The Russia Hoax: The Illicit Scheme to Clear Hillary Clinton and Frame Donald Trump* (Northampton, MA, Broadside Books, 2018).
Johnston, David Cay, *The Making of Donald Trump* (London, Melville House Publishing, 2017).
Johnston, David Cay, *It's Even Worse than You Think: What the Trump Administration is Doing to America* (New York, Simon & Schuster, 2018).
Johnstone, Diana, 'The Real Russian Interference in US Politics', *Consortium News*, 29 August 2018, https://consortiumnews.com/2018/08/27/the-real-russian-interference-in-us-politics/.
Johnstone, Diana, *Circle in the Darkness: Memoir of a World Watcher* (Atlanta, GA, Clarity Press, 2020).

Jones, Seth, *Russian Meddling in the United States: The Historical Context of the Mueller Report* (Washington, DC, CSIS, 2019), https://csis-prod.s3.amazonaws.com/s3fs-public/publication/190328_RussianMeddlingintheUS_WEB_V.2.pdf.

Kaiser, Brittany, *Targeted: My Inside Story of Cambridge Analytica and how Trump, Brexit and Facebook Broke Democracy* (London, HarperCollins, 2019).

Kaufmann, Eric, *Whiteshift: Populism, Immigration and the Future of White Majorities* (London, Allen Lane, 2018).

Keefe, Patrick Radden, 'How Mark Burnett Resurrected Donald Trump as an Icon of American Success', *New Yorker*, 7 January 2019, https://www.newyorker.com/magazine/2019/01/07/how-mark-burnett-resurrected-donald-trump-as-an-icon-of-american-success.

Kengor, Paul, *Dupes: How America's Adversaries Have Manipulated Progressives for a Century* (Wilmington, DE, ISI Books, reprint 2018).

Khatchadourian, Raffi, 'Julian Assange, a Man without a Country', *New Yorker*, 21 August 2017, https://www.newyorker.com/magazine/2017/08/21/julian-assange-a-man-without-a-country.

Kimball, Roger, 'Let's Call the Russian Collusion "Hoax" What It Really Is', *Spectator USA*, 27 May 2019, https://spectator.us/call-russian-collusion-hoax/.

Kimmage, Michael, *The Abandonment of the West: The History of an Idea in American Foreign Policy* (New York, Basic Books, 2020).

Komisar, Lucy, 'The Man Behind the Magnitsky Act', *100Reporters*, 20 October 2017, https://100r.org/2017/10/magnitsky/.

Kotkin, Stephen, 'American Hustle: What Mueller Found—And Didn't Find—About Trump and Russia', *Foreign Affairs*, 21 May 2019, https://www.foreignaffairs.com/articles/2019-05-21/american-hustle.

Krainer, Alex, *Grand Deception: The Truth about Bill Browder and the Magnitsky Act and Anti-Russian Sanctions* (Otto, NC, Red Hill Press, 2018).

Kramer, Michael, 'Rescuing Boris: The Secret Story of How American Advisors Helped Yeltsin Win', *Time*, 15 July 1996, http://content.time.com/time/magazine/article/0,9171,984833,00.html.

Kribbe, Hans, *The Strongmen: European Encounters with Sovereign Power* (Newcastle, Agenda Publishing, 2020).

Lake, Eli, 'The Railroading of Michael Flynn', *Commentary*, June 2020, https://www.commentarymagazine.com/articles/eli-lake/michael-flynn-gets-railroaded-by-the-fbi/.

Lawrence, Patrick, 'Discerning Vladimir Putin', *Raritan*, Vol. 38, No. 1, Summer 2018, pp. 1–15.

Lears, Jackson, 'Russiagate Revisited', *London Review of Books Blog*, 22 February 2018, https://www.lrb.co.uk/blog/2018/02/22/jackson-lears/russiagate-revisited/.

Legvold, Robert, *Return to Cold War* (Cambridge, Polity, 2016).

Leonard, Tim, 'Guccifer 2.0's Hidden Agenda', *Consortium News*, 26 May 2020, https://consortiumnews.com/2020/05/21/guccifer-2-0s-hidden-agenda/.

Levine, Yasha, *Surveillance Valley: The Secret Military History of the Internet* (London, Icon, 2019).

Levitsky, Steven and Daniel Ziblatt, *How Democracies Die* (New York, Viking, 2018).

Lewandowski, Corey R. and David N. Bossie, *Let Trump be Trump: The Inside Story of his Rise to the Presidency* (New York and Nashville, Center Street, 2017).

Linvill, Darren L. and Patrick Warren, 'Troll Factories: The Internet Research Agency and State-Sponsored Agenda Building', unpublished paper, The Social Media Listen Center, Clemson University, http://pwarren.people.clemson.edu/Linvill_Warren_TrollFactory.pdf.

Lokhova, Svetlana, *The Spider: Stefan A. Halper and the Dark Web of a Coup* (New York, Post Hill Press, 2020).

Mahl, Thomas E., *Desperate Deception* (Lincoln, NE, Brassey's US, 2000).

Marantz, Andrew, 'The Man Behind Trump's Facebook Juggernaut: Brad Parscale used Social Media to Sway the 2016 Election. He's Poised To Do It Again', *New Yorker*, 2 March 2020, https://www.newyorker.com/magazine/2020/03/09/the-man-behind-trumps-facebook-juggernaut.

Marten, Kimberly, *Into Africa: Prigozhin, Wagner, and the Russian Military*, PONARS Eurasia Policy Memo No. 561, January 2019.

Marten, Kimberly, 'Russia's Use of Semi-State Security Forces: the Case of the Wagner Group', *Post-Soviet Affairs*, Vol. 35, No. 3, 2019, pp. 181–204.

Marten, Kimberly, 'Reckless Ambition: Moscow's Policy Toward the United States, 2016/17', *International Politics*, Vol. 56, 2019, pp. 743–61.

Maté, Aaron, 'New Studies Suggest Pundits are Wrong About Russian Social-Media Involvement in US Politics', *The Nation*, 28 December 2018, https://www.thenation.com/article/russiagate-elections-interference/.

Maté, Aaron, 'CrowdStrike Out: Mueller's Own Report Undercuts its Core Russia-Meddling Claims', Realclearinvestigations.com, 5 July 2019, https://www.realclearinvestigations.com/articles/2019/07/05/crowdstrikeout_muellers_own_report_undercuts_its_core_russia-meddling_claims.html.

Mayer, Jane, *Dark Money: How a Secretive Group of American Billionaires is Trying to Buy Political Control in the US* (London, Scribe, 2016).

Mayer, Jane, 'Christopher Steele: The Man behind the Steele Dossier', *New Yorker*, 12 March 2018, https://www.newyorker.com/magazine/2018/03/12/christopher-steele-the-man-behind-the-trump-dossier.

Mayer, Jane, 'How Russia Helped Swing the Election for Trump', *New Yorker*, 1 October 2018, https://www.newyorker.com/magazine/2018/10/01/how-russia-helped-to-swing-the-election-for-trump.

McCabe, Andrew, *The Threat: How the FBI Protects America in the Age of Terror and Trump* (New York, St Martin's Press, 2019).

McCarthy, Andrew C., *Ball of Collusion: The Plot to Rig an Election and Destroy a Presidency* (New York, Encounter Books, 2019).

McFarland, KT, *Revolution: Trump, Washington and 'We the People'* (New York, Post Hill Press, 2020).

McFaul, Michael, *From Cold War to Hot Peace: The Inside Story of Russia and America* (London, Allen Lane, 2018).

McFaul, Michael, 'Putin, Putinism, and the Domestic Determinants of Russian Foreign Policy', *International Security*, Vol. 45, No. 2, Fall 2020, pp. 95–139.

McGovern, Ray, 'FBI Never Saw CrowdStrike Unredacted or Final Report on Alleged Russian Hacking Because None was Produced', *Consortium News*, 17 June 2019, https://consortiumnews.com/2019/06/17/fbi-never-saw-crowdstrike-unredacted-or-final-report-on-alleged-russian-hacking-because-none-was-produced/.

McMaster, H. R., *Dereliction of Duty: Johnson, McNamara, the Joints Chiefs of Staff, and the Lies that Led to Vietnam* (New York, Harper Perennial, 2017).

Mearsheimer, John J., *Why Leaders Lie: The Truth about Lying in International Politics* (London, Duckworth Overlook, 2012).

Mearsheimer, John J., *The Great Delusion: Liberal Dreams and International Realities* (New Haven and London, Yale University Press, 2018).

Meier, Barry, *Spooked: The Trump Dossier, Black Cube, and the Rise of Private Spies* (New York, HarperCollins, 2021).

Miller, Greg, *The Apprentice: Trump, Russia and the Subversion of American Democracy* (New York, William Collins, 2018).

Mills, Daniel Quinn and Steven Rosefielde, *The Trump Phenomenon and the Future of US Foreign Policy* (London, World Scientific Publishing, 2017).

Monaghan, Andrew, *A 'New cold war'? Abusing History, Misunderstanding Russia* (London, Chatham House Research Paper, May 2015).

Mueller III, Robert S., *Report on the Investigation into Russian Interference in the 2016 Presidential Election* (Washington, DC, US Department of Justice, March 2019), https://www.justice.gov/storage/report.pdf. Published as *The Mueller Report: The Final Report of the Special Counsel into Donald Trump, Russia, and Collusion*, with an introduction by Alan Dershowitz (Washington, DC, Department of Justice, 2019). There is also a version edited by Rosalind S. Helderman and Matt Zapotsky, *The Mueller Report: Presented with Related Materials from the Washington Post* (New York, Simon & Schuster, 2019).

Müller, Jan-Werner, 'Capitalism in One Family', *London Review of Books*, 1 December 2016, pp. 10–14.

Müller, Jan-Werner, *What Is Populism?* (London, Penguin, 2017).

Nance, Malcolm, *The Plot to Hack America: How Putin's Cyberspies and WikiLeaks Tried to Steal the 2016 Election*, 2nd edn (New York, Skyhorse Publishing, 2016).

Nance, Malcolm, *The Plot to Destroy Democracy: How Putin and his Spies are Undermining America and Dismantling the West* (New York, Hachette Books, 2018).

Nelson, Michael, *Trump's First Year* (Charlottesville, University of Virginia Press, 2018).

New Knowledge, *The Tactics and Tropes of the Internet Research Agency*, 18 December 2018, https://www.hsdl.org/c/tactics-and-tropes-of-the-internet-research-agency/.

Newman, Omarosa Manigault, *Unhinged: An Insider's Account of the Trump White House* (London, Simon & Schuster, 2018).

Norris, Pippa and Ronald Inglehart, *Cultural Backlash: Trump, Brexit, and Authoritarian Populism* (Cambridge, Cambridge University Press, 2019).

O'Brien, Timothy L., *TrumpNation: The Art of Being the Donald* (New York, Grand Central Publishing, reprinted 2016).

Office of the Director of National Intelligence, *"Assessing Russian Activities and Intentions in Recent US Elections"*, Intelligence Community Assessment, ICA 2017-01D, 6 January 2017, https://www.dni.gov/files/documents/ICA_2017_01.pdf.

Office of the Director of National Intelligence, Letter from Richard Grennell to Senator Charles E, Grassley and Ron Jonson, DHS, 15 April 2020, https://www.grassley.senate.gov/sites/default/files/2020-04-15%20ODNI%20to%20CEG%20RHJ%20%28FISA%20Footnote%20Declassification%29.pdf, cited as Horowitz, *Review*, notes.

Office of the Director of National Intelligence, Flynn transcript of conversation with Sergei Kislyak, declassified 29 May 2020, https://assets.documentcloud.org/documents/6933340/Flynn-Transcripts.pdf.

Osnos, Evan, David Remnick and Joshua Yaffe, 'Trump, Putin, and the New Cold War', *New Yorker*, 6 March 2017, https://www.newyorker.com/magazine/2017/03/06/trump-putin-and-the-new-cold-war.

Office of the Director of National Intelligence, National Intelligence Council, *Intelligence Community Assessment on Foreign Threats to the 2020 US Federal Elections*, 15 March 2021, https://www.intelligence.gov/assets/documents/702%20Documents/declassified/ICA-declass-16MAR21.pdf.

Pabst, Adrian, *Liberal World Order and its Critics: Civilisational States and Cultural Commonwealths* (London, Routledge, 2018).

Papadopoulos, George, *Deep State Target: How I Got Caught in the Crosshairs of the Plot to Bring Down President Trump* (New York, Diversion Books, 2019).

Parker, Ian, 'Glen Greenwald, the Bane of Their Resistance', *New Yorker*, 3 September 2018, https://www.newyorker.com/magazine/2018/09/03/glenn-greenwald-the-bane-of-their-resistance.

Pernik, Piret, 'The Early Days of Cyberattacks: The Cases of Estonia, Georgia and Ukraine', in Nicu Popescu and Stanislav Secrieru (eds), *Hacks, Leaks and Disruptions: Russian Cyber Strategies*, Chaillot Papers No. 148 (Paris, European Union Institute for Security Studies, October 2018), pp. 53–64.

Phillips, Timothy, *The Secret Twenties: British Intelligence, the Russians and the Jazz Age* (Cambridge, Granta Books, 2017).

Plaskin, Glenn, 'The 1990 Interview with Donald Trump', *Playboy*, 1 March 1990, https://www.playboy.com/read/playboy-interview-donald-trump-1990.

Porter, Gareth, 'How the Department of Homeland Security Created a Deceptive Tale of Russia Hacking US Voter Sites', *Consortium News*, 28 August 2018, https://consortiumnews.com/2018/08/28/how-the-department-of-homeland-security-created-a-deceptive-tale-of-russia-hacking-u-s-voter-sites/.

Powell, Sidney, *Licensed to Lie* (Sidney Powell self-publication, 2018).

Rhodes, Ben, *The World As It Is: Inside the Obama White House* (New York, Vintage, 2019).

Rid, Thomas, *Active Measures: The Secret History of Disinformation and Political Warfare* (London, Profile Books, 2020).

Roh, Stephan C. and Thierry Pastor, *The Faking of Russia-gate: The Papadopoulos Case* (Zurich, ILS Publishing, 208).

Rohde, David, 'William Barr, Trump's Sword and Shield', *New Yorker*, 13 January 2020, https://www.newyorker.com/magazine/2020/01/20/william-barr-trumps-sword-and-shield.

Rosefielde, Steven, *Trump's Populist America* (London, World Scientific Publishing, 2017).

Rosenbaum, Ron, 'Trump's Nuclear Experience: In 1987 he Set out to Solve the World's Biggest Problem', *Slate*, 1 March 2016, http://www.slate.com/articles/news_and_politics/the_spectator/2016/03/trump_s_nuclear_experience_advice_for_reagan_in_1987.html?via=gdpr-consent.

Roth, Philip, *The Plot against America* (New York, Vintage, 2005).

Rovner, Joshua, *Fixing the Facts: National Security and the Politics of Intelligence* (Ithaca, Cornell University Press, 2011).

Rucker, Philip and Carol Leonnig, *A Very Stable Genius* (London, Bloomsbury, 2020).

Sabato, Larry J., Kyle Kondik and Geoffrey Skelley (eds), *Trumped: The 2016 Election that Broke all the Rules* (New York, Rowman &Littlefield, 2017)

Sakwa, Richard, *Putin* Redux*: Power and Contradiction in Contemporary Russia* (London & New York, Routledge, 2014).

Sakwa, Richard, *Putin and the Oligarch: The Khodorkovsky—Yukos Affair* (London, I. B. Tauris; New York, Palgrave Macmillan, 2014).

Sakwa, Richard, *Frontline Ukraine: Crisis in the Borderlands* (London and New York, I. B. Tauris, 2016).

Sakwa, Richard, *Russia against the Rest: The Post-Cold war Crisis of World Order* (Cambridge, Cambridge University Press, 2017).

Sakwa, Richard, 'Heterarchy: Russian Politics between Chaos and Control', *Post-Soviet Affairs*, Vol. 37, No. 3, 2021, pp. 222–241.

Sakwa, Richard, *The Lost Peace: How We Failed to Prevent a New Cold War* (Yale University Press, forthcoming 2022).

Samarasinghe, Natalie, 'Can the UN Survive Trump?', *The World Today*, December 2018–January 2019, pp. 34–36.

Sanders, Bernie, *Where We Go From Here: Two Years in the Resistance* (London, Biteback Publishing, 2018).

Schier, Steven E. and Todd E. Eberly, *Polarized: The Rise of Ideology in American Politics* (Lanham, MD, Rowman & Littlefield, 2016).

Schier, Steven E. and Todd E. Eberly, *The Trump Presidency: Outsider in the Oval Office* (Lanham, MD, Rowman & Littlefield, 2017).

Schrage, Steven P., 'The Spies who Hijacked America', 9 August 2020, https://taibbi.substack.com/p/the-spies-who-hijacked-america.

Schuessler, John M., *Deceit on the Road to War: Presidents, Politics and American Democracy* (Ithaca and London, Cornell University Press, 2015).

Schweizer, Peter, *Clinton Cash: The Untold Story of How and Why Foreign Governments and Businesses Helped Make Bill and Hillary Rich* (New York, Harper Paperbacks, 2014/2016).

Senate Committee on Intelligence, *Report on Russian Active Measures Campaigns and Interference in the 2016 US Election*, Vol. 1, *Russian Efforts against Election Infrastructure* (Washington, DC, US Senate, 25 July 2019), https://www.intelligence.senate.gov/sites/default/files/documents/Report_Volume1.pdf.

Senate Committee on Intelligence, *Report on Russian Active Measures Campaigns and Interference in the 2016 US Election*, Vol. 2, *Russia's Use of Social Media* (Washington, DC, US Senate, October 2019).

Senate Committee on Intelligence, *Report on Russian Active Measures Campaigns and Interference in the 2016 US Election*, Vol. 3, *Government Response to Russian Activities* (Washington, DC, US Senate, 6 February 2020).

Senate Committee on Intelligence, *Report on Russian Active Measures Campaigns and Interference in the 2016 US Election*, Vol. 4, *Review of the Intelligence Community Assessment with Additional Views* (Washington, DC, US Senate, 20 April 2020), https://www.intelligence.senate.gov/sites/default/files/documents/Report_Volume4.pdf.

Senate Committee on Intelligence, *Report on Russian Active Measures Campaigns and Interference in the 2016 US Election*, Vol. 5, *Counterintelligence Threats and Vulnerabilities* (Washington, DC, US Senate, 5 August 2020), https://www.intelligence.senate.gov/sites/default/files/documents/report_volume5.pdf.

Shaffer, Kris, *Data versus Democracy: How Big Data Algorithms Shape Opinions and Alter the Course of History* (New York, Apress, 2019).

Shane, Scott and Mark Mazzetti, 'The Plot to Subvert an Election: Unraveling the Russia Story So Far', *New York Times*, 20 September 2018, https://www.nytimes.com/interactive/2018/09/20/us/politics/russia-interference-election-trump-clinton.html

Shatz, Adam, 'America Explodes', *London Review of Books*, 18 June 2020, pp. 4–8.

Shekhovtsov, Anton, *Russia and the Western Far Right: Tango Noir* (London, Routledge, 2017).

Shimer, David, *Rigged: America, Russia, and One Hundred Years of Covert Electoral Interference* (London, William Collins, 2020).

Sides, John, Michel Tesler and Lynn Vavreck, *Identity Crisis: The 2016 Presidential Campaign and the Battle for the Meaning of America* (Princeton, NJ, Princeton University Press, 2018).

Simes, Dmitri K., 'The Case for Trump', *The National Interest*, 13 August 2020, https://nationalinterest.org/feature/case-trump-166808.

Simpson, Glenn and Peter Fritsch, *Crime in Progress: The Secret History of the Trump-Russia Investigation* (London, Allen Lane, 2019).

Smith, Lee, 'Who Believes in Russiagate?', *Tablet*, 8 March 2018, https://www.tabletmag.com/jewish-news-and-politics/256899/left-right-russiagate.

Smith, Lee, 'System Fail: The Mueller Report is an Unmitigated Disaster for the American Press and the "Expert" Class that it Promotes', *Tablet*, 27 March 2019, https://www.tabletmag.com/jewish-news-and-politics/282448/system-fail.

Snowden, Edward, *Permanent Record* (London, Macmillan, 2019).

Snyder, Timothy, *The Road to Unfreedom: Russia, Europe, America* (London, Bodley Head, 2018).

Stent, Angela, *Putin's World: Russia against The West and With the Rest* (New York, Twelve, 2019).
Strzok, Peter, *Compromised: Counterintelligence and the Threat of Donald J. Trump* (Boston, Houghton Mifflin Harcourt, 2020).
Taibbi, Matt, *Hate Inc.: Why Today's Media Makes us Despise One Another* (OR Books, 2019).
Talbott, Strobe, *The Russia Hand: A Memoir of Presidential Diplomacy* (New York, Random House, 2003).
Toobin, Jeffrey, 'Roger Stone's and Jerome Corsi's Time in the Barrel', *New Yorker*, 18 & 25 February 2019, https://www.newyorker.com/magazine/2019/02/18/roger-stones-and-jerome-corsis-time-in-the-barrel.
Toobin, Jeffrey, 'Michael Cohen's Last Days of Freedom', *New Yorker*, 29 April 2019, https://www.newyorker.com/magazine/2019/05/06/michael-cohens-last-days-of-freedom.
Toobin, Jeffrey, 'Why the Mueller Investigation Failed', *New Yorker*, 29 June 2020, https://www.newyorker.com/magazine/2020/07/06/why-the-mueller-investigation-failed.
Toobin, Jeffrey, *True Crimes and Misdemeanors: The Investigation of Donald Trump* (London, Bodley Head, 2020).
Trump, Donald J. with Tony Schwartz, *Trump: The Art of the Deal* (London, Arrow, 2016).
Tsygankov, Andrei P., *The Dark Double: US Media, Russia, and the Politics of Values* (New York, Oxford University Press, 2019).
Unger, Craig, *House of Trump, House of Putin: The Untold Story of Trump and the Russian Mafia* (London, Bantam Press, 2018).
Unger, Craig, 'When a Young Trump went to Russia', *The New Republic*, 15 August 2018, https://newrepublic.com/article/150646/young-trump-went-russia.
Unger, Craig, *American Kompromat: How the KGB Cultivated Donald Trump and Related Tales of Sex, Greed, Power, and Treachery* (London, Scribe, 2021).
US Department of Homeland Security, 'Joint Statement from the Department of Homeland Security and Office of the Director of National Intelligence on Election Security', 7 October 2016, https://www.dhs.gov/news/2016/10/07/joint-statement-department-homeland-security-and-office-director-national.
US Department of Justice, Memo from Rod Rosenstein to Robert Mueller, 2 August 2017, https://assets.documentcloud.org/documents/4429623/Rosenstein-Aug-2-2017-Memo-on-Mueller-Authority.pdf.
US Senate Committee on Homeland Security and Governmental Affairs and US Senate Committee on Finance, Majority Staff Report, *Hunter Biden, Burisma, and Corruption: The Impact on US Government Policy and Related Concerns*, 23 August 2020, https://www.hsgac.senate.gov/imo/media/doc/Ukraine%20Report_FINAL.pdf.
United States v. Internet Research Agency et al., No.-1:18-cr-00032-DLF (Washington, DC, filed 16 February 2018), https://www.justice.gov/file/1035477/download.

United States v. Netyshko et al., No. 1:18-cr-00215-ABJ, criminal indictment filed 13 July 2018, US District Court for the District of Columbia, https://www.justice.gov/file/1080281/download.

United States v. Roger Jason Stone, Jr., case 1: 18-cr-00215-ABJ, criminal indictment filed 24 January 2019, US District Court for the District of Columbia, https://www.lawfareblog.com/document-indictment-roger-stone.

Vogel, Kenneth P. and David Stern, 'Ukrainian Efforts to Sabotage Trump Backfire', *Politico*, 11 January 2017, https://www.politico.com/story/2017/01/ukraine-sabotage-trump-backfire-233446.

Walt, Stephen M., *The Hell of Good Intentions: America's Foreign Policy Elite and the Decline of US Primacy* (New York, Farrar, Straus, and Giroux, 2019).

Ward, Vicky, 'The Russian Expat Leading the Fight to Protect America', *Esquire*, 24 October 2016, https://www.esquire.com/news-politics/a49902/the-russian-emigre-leading-the-fight-to-protect-america/.

Watts, Clint, *Messing with the Enemy: Surviving in a Social Media World of Hackers, Terrorists, Russians, and Fake News* (New York, Harper, 2018).

Weissmann, Andrew, *Where Law Ends: Inside the Mueller Investigation* (New York, Random House, 2020).

Wertheim, Stephen, *Tomorrow, the World: The Birth of US Global Supremacy* (Cambridge, Belknap Press, 2020).

Wolff, Michael, *Fire and Fury: Inside the Trump White House* (London, Little, Brown, 2018).

Wolff, Michael, *Siege: Trump under Fire* (Boston, Little, Brown, 2019).

Wood, Tony, *Russia without Putin: Money, Power and the Myths of the New Cold War* (London, Verso, 2018).

Woodward, Bob, *Fear: Trump in the White House* (London & New York, Simon & Schuster, 2018).

Woodward, Bob, *Rage* (London and New York, Simon & Schuster, 2020).

Woodward, Bob and Carl Bernstein, *All the President's Men* (London, Simon & Schuster, 2012).

Wylie, Christopher, *Mindf*ck: Inside Cambridge Analytica's Plot to Break the World* (London, Profile Books, 2019).

Yablokov, Ilya, *Fortress Russia: Conspiracy Theories in Post-Soviet Russia* (Cambridge, Polity, 2018).

Yaffa, Joshua, 'How Bill Browder Became Russia's Most Wanted Man', *New Yorker*, 20 August 2018, https://www.newyorker.com/magazine/2018/08/20/how-bill-browder-became-russias-most-wanted-man.

Index

References to notes are indicated by n.

2016 election, 1, 2, 5, 6–8, 111; and IRA, 113–14, 115–19, 122–24; and Obama, 12–13; and presidential debates, 178–79; and Trump campaign, 24–29; and Ukraine, 237–38, 239. *See also* Russiagate
2020 election, 311–22

Abedin, Huma, 36
Access Hollywood (TV show), 95, 120, 178, 179
active measures (*aktivnye meropriyatiya*), 1, 9, 74–75, 276
Adelson, Sheldon, 242, 243
Afghanistan, 17, 39, 78, 313, 334; and Flynn, 199; and Russia, 316–17
African-Americans, 114, 118–19
Agalarov, Aras, 52–54, 225, 226
Agalarov, Emin, 53, 54, 226, 228
Ahmad, Zainab, 209
Ailes, Roger, 47
Akhmetshin, Rinat, 227, 299
Alabama (AL), 119–20
Alfa Bank, 153, 161–62, 176
Aliyev, Ilham, 53
Aliyeva, Leila, 53
Alliance for Germany (AfD), 76

Alperovitch, Dmitry, 90, 98; *Bears in the Midst*, 91
Al Qaeda, 199
America. *See* United States of America (USA)
'America first' policy, 16, 39, 67–68
analytics, 26
Angleton, James, 335
Anonymous International, 113
'anti-gay propaganda', 14
The Apprentice (TV show), 23, 24, 37, 53, 179
APT (Advanced Persistent Threat), 89–91
Arab Spring, 70, 75
Arif, Tevfik, 52, 56
The Art of the Deal (Trump), 37, 51
Al-Assad, Bashar, 17
Assange, Julian, 7, 10, 32, 35–36, 89; and DNC, 92–95; and imprisonment, 315–16; and Manafort, 241–42; and Mueller, 261, 278; and Senate Intelligence Committee, 299; and Stone, 279, 280, 281
Assessing Russian Activities and Intentions in Recent US Elections, 184

Atlantic Council, 32, 90
Atlantic system. *See* NATO
Australia, 134, 135, 139, 141, 297
Auten, Brian, 163
authoritarianism, 17
Avakov, Arsen, 236
Aven, Petr, 161–62, 264

Bagehot, Walter, 12
Baker, James, 156–57
banks, 55–56
Bannon, Steve, 26, 38, 39, 82, 179; and Comey, 212, 213; and Mueller, 253, 263; and Trump Tower meeting, 227
Baquet, Dean, 335
Barnett, William, 217–18
Barr, Richard, 299
Barr, William, 18, 216–17, 292, 294, 295–96; and Mueller, 258–60, 274, 275, 276
Baturina, Elena, 300
Bayrock Group, 52, 54, 56
Belton, Catherine, 55
Benghazi, 29, 31
Bensinger, Ken, 156
Berkman Klein Centre for Internet & Society, 124
Berlusconi, Silvio, 188
Berman, Geoffrey, 231
Bernstein, Carl, 11–12, 54–55, 307
Bezos, Jeff, 243
Bharara, Preet, 227
Biden, Hunter, 235, 238, 300–301, 319, 320
Biden, Joe, 28, 30, 190, 331; and 2020 election, 311, 317, 318, 319, 320–21, 322; and Flynn, 203, 204; and Russia, 79, 295, 339; and Ukraine, 235, 238, 297
big data, 26
Billingsea, Marshall, 337
Binney, William, 99–100, 101, 278, 280
Black Lives Matter movement, 119, 320, 342
black voters. *See* African-Americans

Blatter, Sepp, 150
Bloomberg, Mike, 311
Boente, Dana J., 213
Bogacheva, Anna, 113
Bolton, John, 8, 10, 80, 83, 244; and Trump, 313, 314
Bortnikov, Alexander, 174
Bossie, David N., 208
Bosworth, Andrew, 122
Boyd-Barrett, Oliver, 123–24, 130
Brazile, Donna, 28, 120, 178
Brennan, John, 102, 129–30, 131, 214, 334; and Comey, 211; and Durham, 296; and Flynn, 200; and Helsinki, 331; and ICA, 184; and Iraq, 190; and Mueller, 274, 277–78; and Ratcliffe, 301–2; and Smolenkov, 289–90; and Steele, 156; and Trump, 308–9, 332
Brexit, 24, 38, 339
Britain. *See* Great Britain
Broaddrick, Juanita, 179
Brookings Institution, 164, 165
Browder, Bill, 82, 83, 226, 227, 229, 230
Buffet, Warren, 243
Burisma Holdings, 235, 238, 301
Burnett, Mark, 53
Burns, William, 35
Burr, Richard, 33, 192
Burrows, Chris, 149
Burt, Richard, 264
Bush, Billy, 178
Bush, George H. W., 26, 51, 258
Bush, George W., 27, 28, 29–30, 72
Butina, Maria, 241
BuzzFeed, 150, 156, 161, 162–63

Cambridge Analytica, 122, 177, 242
Cambridge University, 136
Cameron, David, 134
campaign financing, 242, 243
Campbell, Duncan, 101
Cantor, Christian, 134, 139
Carter, Jimmy, 321–22

Chaika, Yuri, 229
Chait, Jonathan, 59
Chalupa, Alexandra, 91, 92, 238–39
Chaly, Valeriy, 239–40
Chazov, Yevgeny, 50
Chen, Adrian, 112–13, 114, 335
child sex ring, 7
China, 18, 25, 39, 51, 244, 300; and CIA, 333; and containment, 83; and hacking, 95; and interference, 339; and new cold war, 336; and Russia, 76, 79, 137, 337, 340; and Trump, 77, 151, 312
Christie, Chris, 130
Churkin, Vitaly, 49
CIA (Central Intelligence Agency), 14, 74, 90, 293–94, 333; and 2020 election, 318–19; and Durham, 295; and hacking, 173–74; and ICA, 186; and Page, 182; and Papadopoulos, 141; and Vault 7, 102. *See also* Brennan, John
Clapper, James, 102, 103, 173, 290, 332, 334; and CIA, 130, 131, 141; and Comey, 296; and Flynn, 200; and ICA, 184, 189, 190–91, 192; and joint statement, 177–78
Clifford, Stephanie 'Stormy Daniels', 231, 234
Clinesmith, Kevin, 130, 182
Clinton, Bill, 179, 208, 251
Clinton, Hillary Rodham, 5, 6, 7, 8, 18, 23, 297; and Brennan, 309; and campaign, 9, 28–29; and Comey, 208–9, 308; and defeat, 149, 180; and DNC, 92, 93–94, 96–97; and FSB, 151; and Gabbard, 315; and 'insurance' plan, 332; and Mifsud, 273; and Mueller, 267; and Obama, 13; and Papadopoulos, 133–35; and presidential debates, 179; and Putin, 14, 60, 71, 73, 177; and right-wing conspiracy, 38; and Russia, 29–37, 188, 301–2; and Steele dossier, 152–53, 156–57, 158–59, 162, 164–65; and Trump, 321; and Trump Tower meeting, 227, 228, 229–30; and Ukraine, 237, 238; and votes, 24, 120–21; and WikiLeaks, 279, 280
Clinton Foundation, 28, 237
Clovis, Sam, 131, 132
Coats, Dan, 97
Cohen, Laura, 231
Cohen, Michael, 24, 55, 59, 61, 230–32; and Mueller, 254, 255, 262, 266, 271, 281; and Steele, 152–53, 157, 163, 164; and Trump Tower Moscow, 225, 232–35
Cohen, Stephen, 310, 330
Cohn, Roy, 48
cold war, 2–3, 6, 68, 76–77. *See also* new cold war
collusion, 6–7, 8, 47, 74, 308, 329; and Mueller, 275–76; and Obama, 13; and Steele dossier, 151; and Trump, 337
Comey, James, 23, 24, 29, 95, 208–15; and 2020 election, 311; and Assange, 316; and Clinton, 36–37; and Crossfire Hurricane, 141–42; and DNC, 33; and email investigation, 31–32; and FISA, 181; and Flynn, 203, 204, 207, 216; and hacking, 173–74; and Horowitz, 308; and ICA, 192; and Mueller, 254, 255, 256, 265–66, 275; and Page, 320; and Senate Judiciary Committee, 300; and Steele, 157, 191, 296
communism, 48
Communist International (Comintern), 74
compromising material (*kompromat*), 1, 5, 6, 10, 48; and Flynn, 206; and Page, 181; and Putin, 173
Concord Management and Consulting, 112, 113, 115, 282–84
Condon, Richard: *The Manchurian Candidate*, 19n1
conservatism, 27
conspiracy theories, 7, 139–41, 295–96

Conway, Kellyanne, 26, 213
Corn, David, 155
Corsi, Jerome, 279, 280, 281–82
Covid-19 pandemic, 280–81, 316, 319, 320
Cox, Archibald, 251
Cozy Bear (APT29), 32, 89–91, 98
Credico, Randy, 279, 280, 281
Crimea, 71, 339
Crossfire Hurricane, 129, 139, 141–44, 173–74, 209–10, 308
Crossfire Razor, 200, 203, 217–18
CrowdStrike, 32, 33, 90–91, 92, 98–99; and testimony, 290; and Ukraine, 102–3
Cuba, 16
cyber-warfare, 9
Czechoslovakia, 48, 74

Danchenko, Igor, 163–65, 308
Daniels, Stormy. *See* Clifford, Stephanie 'Stormy Daniels'
Davis, Lanny, 157, 231–32
DCCC. *See* Democratic Campaign Congressional Committee
DCLeaks, 9, 89, 95
Dean, John, 259
Dearlove, Sir Richard, 136
deception, 16–17, 18, 229–30, 329
deep state, 12, 13, 331–32
Defence Intelligence Agency (DIA), 17, 90, 184, 199, 200
democracy, 3, 13, 14–15, 17, 30
Democracy Integrity Project, 177
Democratic Campaign Congressional Committee (DCCC), 7, 9, 96
Democratic National Committee (DNC), 7, 9–10, 282; and emails, 89–103; and hacking, 32–33; and ICA, 189–90; and Sanders, 34–35; and Steele dossier, 154; and Ukraine, 239
Democratic Party, 9, 13, 33–34, 174–75, 244, 330–31
Department of Homeland Security (DHS), 103–4, 105, 177, 179, 261, 318, 334

Department of Justice (DoJ), 18, 32, 95–96, 291–93, 334; and CIA, 130; and Comey, 208–9; and Flynn, 216–17; and Mueller, 258–61; and Steele, 156–57, 159, 161; and Ukraine, 236, 237
Deripaska, Oleg, 237, 241, 298
Derkach, Andriy, 319, 322
Deutsche Bank, 55, 56, 245, 319
DeVos, Betsy, 176
Dewey, Thomas, 24
DHS. *See* Department of Homeland Security
DIA. *See* Defence Intelligence Agency
Dibble, Elizabeth, 135
disinformation, 9, 12, 74–75, 119–20
Diveykin, Igor, 181, 292
Dmitriev, Kirill, 263
DNC. *See* Democratic National Committee
Dole, Robert, 26
Domain Name System (DNS), 176
Dowd, John, 183, 254–56
Downer, Alexander, 134–35, 138, 139, 143, 297; and Mueller, 273, 274; and Papadopoulos, 310
Dubinin, Yuri, 48–49
Dubinina, Natalia, 49
Durham, John, 293, 294, 295–96
Dvorkovich, Arkady, 180

economics, 25, 29, 38–39
Edgett, Sean, 118
Egypt, 201–2
elections, 2, 30, 73–74, 76, 242–44, 311–22. *See also* 2016 election
Elias, Marc, 154
Ellsberg, Daniel, 17
emails, 7, 9–10, 18, 178, 278; and Clinton, 24, 31–32, 36–37; and Corsi, 281–82; and DNC, 32–33, 89–103; and Lynch, 208–9; and Macron, 76; and Papadopoulos, 133–34
Enron, 203, 210, 310
Erdoğan, Recep Tayyip, 61, 207

espionage, 32, 187, 295. *See also* Steele, Christopher
Estonia, 90
European Union, 24, 68, 235–36, 237, 337
evangelicals, 27, 53
Evanina, William, 317, 318

Facebook, 9, 26, 121–22, 123, 335; and IRA, 116–17, 119
'fake news,' 3, 12, 14, 121
Fancy Bear (APT28), 32–33, 89–91, 98, 102–3
FARA (Foreign Agents Registration Act), 30, 142, 207, 215
FBI (Federal Bureau of Investigation), 8–10, 13, 297, 308, 334; and CIA, 130; and Clinton, 29, 31–32, 36–37; and Crossfire Hurricane, 129, 141–44; and DNC, 33, 90, 98; and DoJ, 291–92; and Durham, 295, 296; and Flynn, 200, 203, 204, 205–6, 216–17; and hacking, 173–74; and ICA, 186, 187, 189, 190; and Manafort, 26, 235, 236–37, 241; and Mifsud, 273; and Page, 180, 181–82; and Papadopoulos, 135, 136, 137, 138–41; and Senate Judiciary Committee, 300; and state hacking, 103, 104; and Steele, 150, 152, 154–60, 161, 163, 164–65, 182–83. *See also* Comey, James; Mueller, Robert S., III
Federal Election Commission (FEC), 283
Feinstein, Diane, 130, 175
FIFA, 150, 154
Firtash, Dmytro, 236
FISA. *See* Foreign Intelligence Surveillance Act
Fitton, Tom, 181
Five Eyes, 130–31, 134
Flynn, Michael, 17, 18, 130, 199–207, 332; and Comey, 211, 213; and Crossfire Hurricane, 142–43; and DoJ, 291; and Lokhova, 136; and Mueller, 253, 254, 255, 256, 257, 271, 281, 294–95; and Steele, 163, 164; and trial, 215–18
Foer, Franklin, 173, 176–77
Foglesong, David, 334–35
Folden, Skip, 99–100
Ford, Gerald, 26
'foreign agents law', 30–31
Foreign Intelligence Service (SVR), 89–90, 95
Foreign Intelligence Surveillance Act (FISA), 131, 135, 180–83, 291, 292
foreign policy, 12, 17, 29, 67–68, 333; and Trump, 6, 8, 10, 27–28, 39
Fox News, 47, 94, 95, 124
France, 76
Franken, Al, 200
Free, Benjamin, 29, 34
Fridman, Mikhail, 161–62
Friedrich, Dabney, 283, 284
Frum, David, 27, 37
Fruman, Igor, 231
FSB, 150–51
Fuller, Graham, 332
Fusion GPS, 152, 153, 154, 155, 160, 161–62; and hacking, 174–75; and Ukraine, 236–37

Gabbard, Tulsi, 315
Gaddy, Clifford, 164
Gaeta, Michael, 154, 155, 209
Galkina, Olga, 171n106
Gates, Bill, 243
Gates, Rick, 236, 240, 263, 271, 294
Georgia, 1
Gerasimov, Valerii, 75
Germany, 76, 90, 272
Gessen, Masha, 187–88, 189, 341
Gingrich, Newt, 25
Giuliani, Rudy, 74, 231, 232, 257, 320, 322
Glennon, Michael, 12, 333
globalism, 27, 28, 39
'golden showers' incident, 53, 151, 157, 164

Goldman, Rob, 116, 335
Goldstone, Rob, 54, 262; and Trump Tower meeting, 226, 227, 228, 229–30
Goldwater, Barry, 74, 307
Gorbachev, Mikhail, 48, 50, 51–52, 68
Gorkov, Sergei, 200, 264
Graham, Billy, 53
Graham, Lindsey, 214, 254, 299
Grant, Ulysses S., 251
Great Britain, 12, 16, 132, 291, 297; and GCHQ, 129–31; and Papadopoulos, 134, 136–37, 139, 141; and real estate, 58; and WikiLeaks, 35. *See also* Brexit; Steele, Christopher
Green, Joshua, 38
Greenberg, Henry, 277
Green Party, 176
Greenwald, Glenn, 206, 242, 271, 333
Grenell, Richard, 290, 293, 312
GRU (Russian military intelligence), 7, 8, 9, 95–97, 185; and Flynn, 199, 200; and hacking, 32–33, 89–91; and Mueller, 261, 263, 278, 282, 291
Gubarev, Alexei, 162, 163
Guccifer 2.0, 9, 89, 91–93, 95, 96–97; and Mueller, 261; and VIPS, 100–101
Gulen, Fetullah, 207
Gulf of Tonkin, 16

hacking, 7, 9, 18, 173–76; and 2020 election, 318; and DNC, 32–33, 90–95; and Mueller, 261–62; and state voters, 103–5
Hague, William, 35
Halper, Stefan, 136, 137, 138, 140
Hannigan, Robert, 130–31, 274
Harding, Luke, 150, 235
Hawkins, Adrian, 90
Hayden, Michael, 14
Helsinki Summit (2018), 80–83, 191, 313
Henry, Shawn, 98, 261, 290
Hermitage Capital Management, 226, 228–29

Hettena, Seth, 176
Hicks, Hope, 266
hoaxes, 112–13
Hoffman, Daniel, 293–94
Holt, Lester, 213
Hoover, J. Edgar, 208, 212
Horowitz, Michael, 132, 137, 214, 291–93, 296, 308; and Page, 182, 183; and Steele, 155, 157–59, 163, 181
House of Representatives, 274
House Permanent Select Committee on Intelligence (HPSCI), 33, 130, 139, 141, 153–56, 290; and 2020 election, 312; and Comey, 211, 213; and hacking, 174; and ICA, 189
House Un-American Activities Committee (HUAC), 214. *See also* McCarthy, Joseph
Huber, John W., 296
Human Rights Accountability Global Initiative Foundation (HRAGI), 226
human trafficking, 7
Humphrey, Hubert, 74
Hunt, E. Howard, 307
hybrid warfare (*gibridnaya voina*), 74–75

ICA. *See* Intelligence Community Assessment
I. C. Expert Investment, 233–34
identity theft, 113, 114
Idris, Naga Khalid, 132–33
Ignatius, David, 163, 204, 317
immigration, 25. *See also* Mexico
impeachment, 15, 331
independents, 176
Inglehart, Ronald, 25
intelligence, 80, 82, 132, 149–56, 331, 334–35. *See also* CIA; Defence Intelligence Agency; FBI; GRU; Intelligence Community Assessment
Intelligence Community Assessment (ICA), 173, 183–87, 188–92, 295
interference, 339
internationalism, 39

Internet Research Agency (IRA), 7–8, 9, 111–19, 120, 121, 122–24; and 2020 election, 318; and midterms, 243–44; and Mueller, 262, 282, 284
IRA. *See* Internet Research Agency
Iran, 17, 29, 200, 313, 320, 333
Iraq, 39, 331, 340; and War, 15, 16, 17, 35; and WMDs, 102, 131, 189, 190, 191
Isikoff, Michael, 155, 176
ISIS (Islamic State), 80, 188, 200
Islamic extremism, 17, 199, 200
Israel, 201–2
Italy, 74
Ivanov, Igor, 133
Ivanov, Sergei, 152–53

Jackson, Henry 'Scoop,' 74
Jamieson, Kathleen Hall, 111, 120
Japan, 50–51
Jarrett, Gregg, 13; *Witch Hunt*, 164
Jensen, Jeffrey, 217
Johnson, Gary, 176
Johnson, Jeh, 177–78, 261
Johnson, Larry, 98
Johnson, Lyndon, 307
Johnson, Ron, 297
Jones, Daniel, 177
Jones, Paula, 179
journalism. *See* media; neo-journalism

Kaine, Tim, 28
Katsyv, Denis, 227, 228, 230
Kavalec, Kathleen, 152
Kaveladze, Irakly, 227
Kelly, John, 10
Kennan, George F., 69
Kent, George, 301
Kerry, John, 301
KGB, 48, 51, 74
Khan, German, 161–62
Khodorkovsky, Mikhail, 57
Khusyainova, Elena, 284
Kiev. *See* Ukraine

Kilimnik, Konstantin, 240, 241, 262–63, 298–99, 322
Kim Jong-un, 61
Kisilëv, Dmitry, 115
Kislyak, Sergei, 7, 8, 72, 80, 212, 336; and Comey, 213; and Flynn, 200–6, 207, 215, 216; and Mueller, 263, 266–67
Kissinger, Henry, 79, 83, 200
Klitschko, Vitaly, 236
Knauss, Melania. *See* Trump, Melania
Koch brothers, 243
Koeltl, John, 282
Kogan, Alexander, 122
kompromat. See compromising material
Kosovo, 340
Kovalev, Anatoly, 96
Kramer, David, 156, 162–63, 167n50
Krebs, Christopher, 322
Kremlin. *See* Putin, Vladimir
Krugman, Paul, 34
Krylova, Aleksandra, 113
Kushner, Jared, 26, 39, 200, 331; and Mueller, 262, 263, 264, 271; and tax records, 213; and Trump Tower meeting, 227

Lauder, Leonard, 49
Lavrov, Sergei, 80, 201, 213, 338–39
League of Nations, 39
leaks, 7. *See also* WikiLeaks
Lehel, Marcel Lazar, 91
Le Pen, Marine, 76
Leshchenko, Serhiy, 237–38
Lewandowski, Corey, 25, 208
Lewinsky, Monica, 215, 251, 259
Liberal Democratic Party of Russia (LDPR), 188
liberalism, 27
Libya, 13, 29, 30, 70, 313; and NATO, 340; and WikiLeaks, 35
Limbaugh, Rush, 282
Linvill, Darren, 118
Litvinenko, Alexander, 149

Logan Act (1799), 204, 216, 253
Lokhova, Svetlana, 136, 204
London Centre for International Law Practice (LCILP), 132, 140
Lown, Bernard, 50
Lynch, Loretta, 208–9
Lyovochkin, Sergei, 236

Macron, Emmanuel, 76
Maddow, Rachel, 331
mafia, 52–53
Magnitsky, Sergei, 225–26, 227, 230
The Magnitsky Act: Behind the Scenes (film), 230
Maguire, Joseph, 312
Maine, USS, 16
Maison de l'Amitié (Florida), 57
Malkevich, Alexander, 115
Malloch, Ted, 279, 280
Manafort, Paul, 8, 25–26, 142, 300; and DoJ, 291, 292; and Mueller, 253, 254, 262–63, 271, 282, 294–95; and Steele, 151, 163, 164; and Trump Tower meeting, 227–28, 229; and Ukrainegate, 235–42, 298
Manning, Chelsea (Bradley), 35
Maples, Marla, 52
Marcos, Ferdinand, 26
Mars family, 243
Maté, Aaron, 122, 284
Matlock, Jack, 124, 189, 314
Mattis, Jim 'mad dog,' 10, 11
Mazzetti, Mark, 116–17
McCabe, Andrew, 32, 139, 213–15, 300; and Crossfire Hurricane, 142, 209; and Flynn, 203, 205; and Steele, 155, 159–60, 163, 296
McCain, John, 25, 27, 155–56
McCarthy, Andrew, 13
McCarthy, Joseph, 19, 48
McDougal, Karen, 231
McFarland, KT, 24, 25, 211, 332; and Flynn, 201, 205, 218
McFaul, Michael, 31, 72–73, 83
McGahn, Donald, 205, 257, 274, 275

McGovern, Ray, 100, 101, 280
McMaster, Gen H. R., 10, 207
Mearsheimer, John, 17
media, 2, 3, 12, 155–56, 192, 334–35. *See also* neo-journalism; social media
Medvedev, Dmitry, 30, 70, 152, 313
Meier, Barry, 154
Mercer, Robert, 28, 122
Mexico, 10, 23
MI6, 149–50
MIC (military–intelligence–cyber) complex, 90
Michigan (MI), 8, 29, 37, 111, 118, 122; and 2020 election, 318
middle classes, 25, 27
Mifsud, Joseph, 18, 129, 292, 297; and Mueller, 277, 278; and Papadopoulos, 132–34, 135, 138, 140, 272–73
Mikhailov, Andrei, 114–15
Millian, Sergei, 135–36, 137, 138, 140, 164
Mironyuk, Svetlana, 115
Miss Universe contest, 53–54, 226, 255
money laundering, 56, 57, 58, 227, 228, 240
Mook, Robby, 34, 180, 301
Moore, Roy, 119–20
Morell, Mike, 174
Moscow. *See* Russia
Moseri, Adam, 117
Mother Jones (magazine), 155, 162
Mueller, Robert S., III, 8–10, 33, 297, 308, 309, 310–11; and 2020 election, 311; and accused, 281–84, 294–95; and Cohen, 231, 232, 233, 234; and CrowdStrike, 290–91; and DNC, 98, 99; and Flynn, 207, 215–16, 217–18; and indictments, 80, 82, 86n61, 97; and investigation, 253–57, 272–76; and IRA, 113, 114, 115–16; and Manafort, 240, 241; and Papadopoulos, 131, 134, 135, 138–40; and real estate, 59; and report,

258–67, 271; and report failures, 276–78; and Senate Intelligence Committee, 299; and state hacking, 104; and Steele, 157; and Stone, 280, 281; and Ukraine, 299; and WikiLeaks, 92
Müllerson, Rein, 28
Murray, Craig, 101, 241–42, 278
Mutually Assured Destruction (MAD), 50

Nadler, Jerry, 274
Nakashima, Ellen, 32, 92, 98, 322
National Anti-Corruption Bureau of Ukraine (NABU), 235, 236, 237
nationalism, 25, 28
National Security Agency (NSA), 35, 97, 99, 102, 103–4; and CIA, 130, 131; and Flynn, 202; and ICA, 184, 186, 190
NATO (North Atlantic Treaty Organisation), 6, 12, 39, 68, 76; and Russia, 69, 70, 340; and Trump, 77–78, 337
Navalny, Alexei, 90
neo-journalism, 15, 59, 105, 117, 173, 310, 334
Netanyahu, Benjamin, 201
Netyshko, Viktor, 96, 97
new cold war, 2, 6, 11–16, 17, 69; and Democrats, 330–31; and patterns, 336–42
New Economic School (Moscow), 180–81
New Knowledge, 119–20, 123
Newman, Omarosa Manigault, 24, 37, 61, 199, 208
NGOs, 30–31
Nixon, Richard, 11–12, 25, 234, 251, 259, 307
Nord Stream 2 pipeline, 79, 272, 313
Norris, Pippa, 25
North Atlantic Treaty Organisation. *See* NATO
North Korea, 200, 333, 336

NSA. *See* National Security Agency
nuclear weapons, 49–50, 313
Nuland, Victoria, 154, 156
Nunes, Devin, 33, 141, 153–54, 182–83, 292, 322

Obama, Barack, 6, 10, 13, 68, 302; and black voters, 119; and Brexit, 339; and CIA, 130; and Clinton, 24, 29, 73; and Comey, 208, 209; and Flynn, 199–200, 203; and foreign policy, 67; and hacking, 33, 97; and ICA, 183–84, 190; and Putin, 175, 177, 179; and Russia, 14, 30, 70, 201, 202; and Syria, 17, 34; and Trump, 252; and Ukraine, 238
obstruction, 265–66, 271, 274–75
Ohr, Bruce, 150, 155, 159, 160, 291, 292; and Comey, 209, 210; and Ukraine, 236, 237
Ohr, Nellie, 160, 210, 236–37, 291
oil, 15, 50
oligarchs, 26, 49, 57–58
Olympic doping scandal, 185
Omarosa. *See* Newman, Omarosa Manigault
Open Skies Treaty, 313, 321, 337
Orbis Business Intelligence, 149, 154
O'Reilly, Bill, 211
Osadchuk, Alexander, 96
Oxford University, 119

Page, Carter, 8, 18, 131, 142, 180–83, 320; and CIA, 293; and DoJ, 291, 292; and Mueller, 253, 262, 282; and Papadopoulos, 133, 136, 139; and Steele, 151, 155, 157, 163, 164, 176
Page, Lisa, 155, 156, 158, 206, 297; and Comey, 209, 214
Palin, Sarah, 25
Palmieri, Jennifer, 100, 267
Panama Papers, 185
Papadopoulos, George, 8, 18, 129, 131–41, 157, 297; and Crossfire Hurricane, 142, 143; and DoJ, 291,

292; and Downer, 310; and FBI, 210; and Mueller, 262, 272–74, 281, 295
Parnas, Lev, 231
Parscale, Brad, 26, 123, 319
Party of Regions, 26, 235, 236, 237
Pelosi, Nancy, 218, 274, 317–18
Pence, Michael, 204–5, 206
Pennsylvania (PA), 8, 29, 37, 111, 118, 122
Pentagon Papers, 17
Perkins Coie, 98, 154, 161, 182
Perot, Ross, 176
Persian Gulf, 50–51
Peskov, Dmitry, 59, 151, 233, 234, 266, 338
Peston, Robert, 32
Philippines, the, 16
Phillips, Timothy, 79
Pientka, Joe, 130, 203, 204, 205, 206
Pierson, Shelby, 312
Pinchuk, Viktor, 237
Pizzagate, 7
pluralism, 3, 27
Podesta, John, 7, 9, 90, 98, 120, 281–82; and hacking, 95, 96; and WikiLeaks, 178, 179
Podobny, Viktor, 180
Poland, 272, 313
Political Action Committees (PACs), 9, 242
Polozov, Sergei, 115
Pompeo, Mike, 10, 101, 272
populism, 3, 24, 25, 27
Poroshenko, Petro, 236, 238
Porter, Gareth, 117, 118
Powell, Sidney, 203, 216
Prevezon Holdings, 227, 228
Priebus, Reince, 26, 204
Priest, Dana, 200
Priestap, Bill, 142, 205
Prigozhin, Yevgeny, 9, 112, 113, 114–15, 282, 284
Prince, Erik, 176, 263
propaganda, 112, 185–86, 188
property. *See* real estate

Pruitt, Bill, 179
Putin, Vladimir, 1, 2, 5, 9, 15, 53–54; and 2011 election, 13–14; and 2020 election, 320–21; and Clinton, 29–30, 31, 34, 177; and Flynn, 203; and hacking, 175; and Helsinki, 80–83; and ICA report, 184–85; and IRA, 112, 114, 116; and McFaul, 72–73; and Mueller, 262, 263–64, 272; and Steele, 159, 164, 293–94; and Tillerson, 10–11; and Trump, 59–61, 173, 187–88, 313–14, 337–38; and Trump Tower meeting, 230; and Trump Tower Moscow, 233; and Ukraine, 235; and the West, 70–71

Qaddafi, Col Muammar, 35
Quarles, James, 254, 255

radical Islam. *See* Islamic extremism
rallies, 114
Ratcliffe, John, 163, 186, 201, 296, 301–2; and 2020 election, 318, 320
Reagan, Ronald, 26, 74, 314
real estate, 52, 56–57, 58–59
Reid, Harry, 174, 176
remilitarisation, 1, 6
Republican National Committee (RNC), 26, 91
Republican Party, 24–25, 26–27
Rhee, Jeannie, 131, 218
Rhodes, Ben, 12, 179
Rice, Susan, 203, 252, 290, 334
Rich, Seth, 94–95, 278
Rid, Thomas, 116
right-wing groups, 76
Ritter, Scott, 97
Ritz-Carlton Hotel (Moscow), 53, 151, 164, 191, 292
Rogers, Mike, 131, 190, 296
Roh, Stephan, 132
Rohrabacher, Dana, 315
Romney, Mitt, 27, 68, 330
Roosevelt, Franklin, 16
Rosefielde, Steven, 27

Rosenbaum, Ron, 50
Rosenstein, Rod, 204, 212, 213, 214–15, 299; and Mueller, 252–53, 254, 258
Rosneft, 176, 181
Roth, Philip: *The Plot against America*, 5, 19n2
Rovner, Joshua, 335
RT (TV channel), 35, 115, 186, 200, 299
Rubio, Marco, 153
Russia, 25, 47, 68–70, 76, 78–79; and 2020 election, 311–22; and Clinton, 29–37; and finances, 55–56, 57–59; and 'hybrid warfare', 74–75; and motivation, 339–40; and real estate, 52, 54; and state hacking, 103–5; and Steele, 150–51; and Trump, 40, 71–72; and Trump Tower Moscow, 232–35. *See also* Putin, Vladimir; Russiagate; Soviet Union
Russiagate, 1–4, 5–11, 17–19, 187–90, 298–302; and Brennan, 129–30; and causes, 330–36, 341–42; and Comey, 209, 210–14; and Crossfire Hurricane, 141–44; and Flynn, 199, 200–7, 216, 217–18; and hacking, 89–103, 173–76; and Helsinki summit, 80–83; and ICA, 183–87, 190–91; and IRA, 111–19, 122–24; and joint statement, 177–78; and midterms, 243–44; and Mueller, 253–67, 271–76, 277–78, 282–84; and new cold war, 11–16, 336–37; and origins, 289–94, 297; and Page, 180–83; and Papadopoulos, 132–41; and presidential debates, 179; and resistance, 307–11; and Schiff, 244–45; and Steele, 152–53, 154, 155–65; and Trump server, 176–77; and Trump Tower meeting, 225–30
Ryabkov, Sergei, 336
Rybolovlev, Dmitry, 57

Saddam Hussein, 16, 189, 191
Samochornov, Anatoly, 227

sanctions, 11, 15, 112, 204–5, 313, 340
Sandberg, Sheryl, 121
Sanders, Bernie, 7, 28, 33–35, 175, 311, 314–15; and DNC, 92, 93, 94, 97, 100
Sanders, Sarah, 279
Sapir, Alex, 54
Sapir, Tamir, 56
Sater, Felix, 52, 56, 58–59, 262, 277; and Trump Tower Moscow, 232, 233, 234, 255
Satter, David, 310
Savimbi, Jonas, 26
Scarborough, Joe, 60–61
Schiff, Adam, 130, 244–45, 267, 290, 292; and Page, 183; and Steele, 210; and Ukraine, 330
Schrage, Stephen, 136
Schroeder, Gerhard, 188
Schuessler, John, 16, 335
Schumer, Chuck, 297, 331
Schwartz, Bruce, 209
Sechin, Igor, 176, 181, 293
security services, 2, 12
Senate Homeland Security and Finance committees, 300–301
Senate Intelligence Committee, 298–99
Senate Judiciary Committee, 299–300
Serbia, 70
Sessions, Jeff, 119, 133, 212, 215, 252, 296; and Mueller, 254, 255, 256, 266–67
Shane, Scott, 116–17
Shearer, Cody, 157, 164
Shelton, Kathy, 179
Shimer, David, 177
Shnaider, Alex, 55
Shokin, Viktor, 238
Shvets, Yuri, 48
Silver, Nate, 122
Simes, Dmitry, 264
Simpson, Glenn, 153, 154, 155, 160, 161, 228–29
Singer, Paul, 153
Skripal, Sergei and Yulia, 90

Smith, Claire, 132
Smolenkov, Oleg, 289–90
Snowden, Edward, 35, 99, 131, 252, 316
Snyder, Timothy, 111
Sobyanin, Sergei, 233
Sochi Winter Olympics, 14
socialism, 3, 33
social media, 7–8, 18, 111–19, 122–24. *See also* Facebook; Twitter
Solodukhin, Oleg, 152–53
Soviet Union, 48–50, 51–52, 73–74, 77, 314
special counsel. *See* Mueller, Robert S., III
Spectrum Health, 176
Spicer, Sean, 204
spies. *See* espionage
Starr, Kenneth, 251
Steele, Christopher, 53, 54, 156–65, 191–92; and Comey, 209, 210–11; and Danchenko, 308; and dossier, 149–56, 174, 175, 182–83, 297; and Durham, 296; and FBI, 291, 292; and Millian, 135–36, 137; and Mueller, 274, 277, 309–10; and Page, 176, 181; and Senate Judiciary Committee, 299–300; and Ukraine, 236, 237
Stein, Jill, 176
Stevens, Christopher, 29
Stone, Roger, 25, 95, 97, 300, 308; and arrest, 278–81; and Greenberg, 277; and Manafort, 235, 271; and Mueller, 254, 262
Stretch, Colin, 117, 122
Strzok, Peter, 10, 32, 130, 181, 214, 300; and Crossfire Hurricane, 142, 143, 209; and FBI, 297; and Flynn, 203, 204, 205, 206, 217; and Papadopoulos, 136, 138, 182; and Steele, 155, 156, 158–59
Sullivan, Emmet, 216, 217
Sun Tzu: *The Art of War*, 17
Surkov, Vladislav, 152

Sussmann, Michael, 33, 98, 156–57
SVR. *See* Foreign Intelligence Service
Syria, 17, 28, 34, 39, 112, 340; and Clinton, 71, 73; and Flynn, 199–200, 202; and Russia, 314; and Trump, 313

Taibbi, Matt, 15, 278
Talbott, Strobe, 164
Tawil, Charles, 138, 140
Tea Party, 25
Telizhenko, Andrii, 239, 301
terrorism, 17
Thiel, Peter, 27
Thompson, Erika, 134, 139
Tillerson, Rex, 10–11
Timofeev, Ivan, 133, 140
transparency, 3, 296
Treasury Department, 130
Trenin, Dmitri, 342
trolling, 112–13, 115
Trubnikov, Vyacheslav, 152
Truman, Harry, 24, 74
Trump, Donald J., 1–2, 3–4, 5, 6–7, 8–9, 23, 297; and 2016 campaign, 24–29; and 2020 election, 312–13, 318–22; and *Access Hollywood*, 178, 179; and Afghanistan, 316–17; and Brennan, 129–30, 308–9; and Clinton, 34; and Cohen, 230–32, 234–35; and collusion, 47, 74, 94; and Comey, 208, 210–15; and Crossfire Hurricane, 142, 143; and deception, 329; and finances, 55–57, 58–59; and Flynn, 203, 207, 217, 218; and foreign policy, 67–68; and governance, 10, 11, 12, 15–16; and hacking, 174; and Helsinki, 80–83; and ICA, 190–92; and IRA, 116, 119, 121; and midterms, 242–43; and Moscow visit, 53–54; and Mueller, 253, 254, 255, 256–57, 258–61, 265–66, 271; and nationalism, 50–51, 342; and NATO, 77–78; and Obama, 13; and obstruction, 274–75; and

Papadopoulos, 132, 133, 137, 139, 141; and presidency, 313–14; and Putin, 59–61, 173, 187–88, 337–38; and real estate, 52–53; and Russia, 14–15, 17, 18, 71–72, 79, 177; and Russiagate, 330–33; and sanctions, 340; and server, 176–77; and shock victory, 37–40; and Soviet Union, 48–50, 51–52; and special counsel, 252; and Steele dossier, 150–51, 158–59, 163–64; and Trump Tower meeting, 229; and Trump Tower Moscow, 232–33, 234; and Ukraine, 236–37, 238, 239–40; and UN, 201–2

Trump, Donald, Jr (son), 8, 52, 55–56, 263, 271; and Trump Tower meeting, 226–28, 229

Trump, Dr John, 50

Trump, Ivana (1st wife), 48, 49, 51

Trump, Ivanka (daughter), 39, 54

Trump, Melania (3rd wife), 48

Trump SoHo (NYC), 54, 56, 58

Trump Tower (NYC), 49, 56–57, 252; and June 2016 meeting, 129, 225–30, 299

Trump Tower (Toronto), 55

Trump Tower Moscow, 59, 179, 225, 232–35, 262, 281

Tsygankov, Andrei, 338

Turk, Azra, 137, 138

Turkey, 61, 131, 134, 137, 141, 142; and Flynn, 206, 207, 215, 216; and Mueller, 253

Twitter, 96, 116, 117–18

Tymoshenko, Yulia, 235, 236, 240

Ukraine, 1, 6, 10, 14, 91, 112; and 2020 election, 320, 322; and arms, 79; and Biden, 297; and Clinton, 71, 73; and Flynn, 217; and hacking, 102–3; and Kilimnik, 298–99; and Manafort, 26, 235–42; and Mueller, 253, 262–63; and NATO, 340; and Trump, 151, 313; and USA, 338, 339; and Zaporozhe steel mill, 55

Unger, Craig, 48, 51, 57

United Nations (UN), 201–2, 339

United States of America (USA), 2, 6, 12, 16–17, 73–74; and Putin, 10–11; and Russia, 69, 70–71, 78–79, 336–37, 339, 341–42; and state hacking, 103–5. *See also* 2016 election; 2020 election; Obama, Barack; Trump, Donald J.

Uranium One case, 28

Ushakov, Yuri, 264

USSR. *See* Soviet Union

Vaino, Anton, 264

Valdai International Discussion Club, 133–34, 188–89

Van der Zwaan, Alex, 240–41

Van Grack, Brandon, 205

Vashukevich, Anastasia, 241

Venezuela, 200

Veselnitskaya, Natalya, 225, 226, 227, 228, 229–30; and Mueller, 254, 262; and Senate Intelligence Committee, 299

veterans, 29

Vietnam War, 16, 17, 207

Vinogradova, Olga, 133

VIPS (Veteran Intelligence Professionals for Sanity), 99–102, 190, 317–18

virtual private networks (VPNs), 113

voters, 24, 26, 27, 29, 243; and 2020 election, 318; and African-American, 118–19; and Clinton, 120–21; and state hacking, 103–5

Voting Rights Act (1965), 119

Wagner Group, 112

Wallace, Henry, 74

Wallander, Celeste, 156

Walter, Francis E., 214

Walton family, 243

war, 16–17
Warner, Mark, 192, 316
Warren, Patrick, 118
Washington Free Beacon Foundation, 153
Wasserman Schultz, Debbie, 93–94, 97
Watergate, 11–12, 54–55, 251, 307
Watts, Clint: *Messing with the Enemy*, 118
Weinberger, Caspar, 50
Weiner, Anthony, 36
Weir, Fred, 317
Weissmann, Andrew, 32, 209–10, 226, 255; *Where Law Ends*, 310–11
West, Nigel, 151
Whitewater, 215, 251
WikiLeaks, 7, 9–10, 18, 35–36; and CIA, 102, 316; and Clinton, 32; and DNC, 92, 93, 94, 95, 99, 100, 282; and Macron, 76; and Mueller, 261, 262; and Podesta, 178, 179; and Senate Intelligence Committee, 299; and Steele, 151; and Stone, 279, 280, 281
Willey, Kathleen, 179
Wilson, Woodrow, 39
Winer, Jonathan, 154, 157
Wisconsin (WI), 8, 29, 37, 111, 118, 122

Wolff, Michael, 12–13, 39, 47, 192, 274–75
Wood, Sir Andrew, 167n50
Wood, Tony, 340
Woodward, Robert, 11–12, 54–55, 61, 192, 307; *Fear*, 78; and Mueller, 255, 256
working classes, 25, 27
World War II, 12, 16, 337
Wray, Christopher, 229, 293, 318, 319

Xi Jinping, 77, 244

Yanukovych, Viktor, 26, 235, 236, 237, 339
Yates, Sally, 203, 204, 205
Yeltsin, Boris, 68, 70, 339
Yermakov, Ivan, 96
Yohannes, Yared Tamene Wolde, 33
Yugoslavia, 340

Zakaria, Fareed, 61
Zebley, Aaron, 254
Zelensky, Volodymyr, 18, 225
Zelníčková, Ivana. *See* Trump, Ivana
Zhirinovsky, Vladimir, 188
Ziff Brothers, 227, 229–30
Zlochevsky, Mikola, 235, 301
Zuckerberg, Mark, 121

About the Author

Richard Sakwa is professor of Russian and European Politics at the University of Kent at Canterbury, UK, a senior research fellow at the National Research University-Higher School of Economics in Moscow and an honorary professor in the Faculty of Political Science at Moscow State University. After graduating in history from the London School of Economics, he took a PhD from the Centre for Russian and East European Studies at the University of Birmingham. He held lectureships at the Universities of Essex and California, Santa Cruz, before joining the University of Kent in 1987. He has published widely on Soviet, Russian, post-communist and international affairs. Recent books include *Putin* Redux*: Power and Contradiction in Contemporary Russia* (2014), *Frontline Ukraine: Crisis in the Borderlands* (2016), *Russia against the Rest: The Post-Cold War Crisis of World Order* (2017) and *Russia's Futures* (2019). His latest book is *The Putin Paradox*, published in 2020. He is currently working on *The Lost Peace: How We Failed to Prevent a Second Cold War.*

www.ingramcontent.com/pod-product-compliance
Lightning Source LLC
Chambersburg PA
CBHW021338300426
44114CB00012B/992